The Longshore Textbook

Seventh Edition

Editors

Steven M. Birnbaum, Esq.

Ralph R. Lorberbaum, Esq.

Contributors

Hon. Stephen R. Henley

David Barnett, Esq.
D.A. Bass-Frazier, Esq.
Alan G. Brackett, Esq.
Norman Cole, Esq.
Paul M. Doolittle, Esq.
Eric A. Dupree, Esq.
Kenneth G. Engerrand, Esq.
Thomas C. Fitzhugh III, Esq.
Lewis S. Fleishman, Esq.
Keith L. Flicker, Esq.
Jess Ghannam, Ph.D.
Joshua T. Gillelan II, Esq.
Howard S. Grossman, Esq.
Alexandra E. Grover, Esq.
Joseph B. Guilbeau, Esq.
Paul B. Howell, Esq.
Frank B. Hugg, Esq.
John F. Karpousis, Esq.
Robert Kessner, Esq.
Roger A. Levy, Esq.
Monica F. Markovich, Esq.
Kris R. Marotti, Esq.
Brian P. McElreath, Esq.
Robert A. McLaughlin, Esq.
Michael P. McQuinn, Esq.
Lara D. Merrigan, Esq.
Amie C. Peters, Esq.
Charles Robinowitz, Esq.
Bobbi N. Roquemore, Esq.
Collins C. Rossi, Esq.
John L. Schouest, Esq.
Scott L. Thaler, Esq.
Michael W. Thomas, Esq.
Ruth Bennett Whitfield, Esq.
Jeffrey Winter, Esq.

Lawyers & Judges Publishing Company, Inc.
Tucson, Arizona

Lawyers & Judges Publishing Company, Inc.
P.O. Box 30040 • Tucson, AZ 85751-0040
(520) 323-1500 • FAX (520) 323-0055
e-mail: sales@lawyersandjudges.com
www.lawyersandjudges.com

Library of Congress Cataloging-in-Publication Data

Names: Birnbaum, Steven M., editor. | Lorberbaum, Ralph R., editor.
Title: The longshore textbook / editors, Steven M. Birnbaum, Esq., Ralph R. Lorberbaum, Esq. ; contributors Hon. Stephen R. Henley [and 36 others].
Description: Seventh edition. | Tucson, Arizona : Lawyers & Judges Publishing Company, Inc., [2017] | Includes bibliographical references and index.
Identifiers: LCCN 2017021587| ISBN 9781936360864 (hardcover : alk. paper) | ISBN 1936360861 (hardcover : alk. paper)
Subjects: LCSH: Stevedores--Legal status, laws, etc.--United States. | Workers' compensation--Law and legislation--United States. | Employers' liability insurance--United States. | United States. Longshoremen's and Harbor Workers' Compensation Act.
Classification: LCC KF3628 .L66 2017 | DDC 344.7302/1--dc23
LC record available at https://lccn.loc.gov/2017021587

ISBN 13: 978-1-936360-86-4
ISBN 10: 1-936360-86-1

Printed in the United States of America
10 9 8 7 6 5 4 3 2 1

Contents

Part I: Defining Coverage and Its Issues

PART II: Medical Treatment

PART III: Compensation

Part IV: Process at the OWCP

Part VI: Appellate Practice

Part VII: Resources

Table of Cases

Part I

Defining Coverage and Its Issues

Chapter 1

Concurrent Jurisdiction

By Kenneth G. Engerrand, Esq.

Synopsis

1.1 Summary

There are numerous federal and state statutory and common-law remedies that are potentially applicable to maritime workers. The relationships between and among those remedies are addressed in this chapter, but there is one thread that binds the principles discussed in this chapter:

> "[T]he lines drawn are sometimes driven by the language of the . . . statutes, sometimes by the evidence, sometimes by the actual findings of fact or the lack thereof, sometimes by philosophy."[1]

1.2 Statutory Bases

Death on the High Seas Act, 46 U.S.C. §§ 30301–30308

Defense Base Act, 42 U.S.C. 1651–1655

Jones Act, 46 U.S.C. § 30104–30105

Longshore and Harbor Workers' Compensation Act, 33 U.S.C. §§ 901–950

Nonappropriated Fund Instrumentalities Act, 5 U.S.C. §§ 8171–8173

Outer Continental Shelf Lands Act, 43 U.S.C. §§ 1331–1356

State Workers' Compensation Laws

1.3 Introduction

The separation of powers between the state and federal governments and between the legislative and judicial branches of the federal government has resulted in shared responsibility over many fields in the law. However, in no area has there been a more difficult and confusing result from the shared authority than in the Maritime Law.[2] Congress has generally been content to allow the Supreme Court to declare the remedies available to maritime workers who are injured or killed in the course of their employment. However, when Congress has taken exception to a decision of the Supreme Court, it has reacted by legislating its own view on the subject.[3] The result has been a patchwork of state and federal statutory and common-law remedies whose relationships have troubled the courts for more than a century.

When there are two or more remedies that are potentially applicable to an injury, the remedies can be concurrent or mutually exclusive. This chapter addresses the relationships among the Longshore and Harbor Workers' Compensation Act (LHWCA)[4] and its extensions, state workers' compensation acts, the Jones Act,[5] and other potentially applicable remedies.

1. *CNA Ins. Co. v. Workers' Comp. Appeals Bd.*, 58 Cal. App. 4th 211, 68 Cal. Rptr. 2d 115 (Cal. App. 1997) (review denied).

2. *See generally* John R. Brown, *Admiralty Judges: Flotsam on the Sea of Maritime Law*, 24 J. Mar. L. & Com. 249 (1993).

3. See W. Eugene Davis, *Admiralty Law Symposium: A Sea Chest for Sea Lawyers, The Role of Federal Courts in Admiralty: The Challenges Facing the Admiralty Judges of the Lower Federal Courts*, 75 TUL. L. REV. 1355, 1361–68 (2001).

4. 33 U.S.C. §§ 901–950.

5. 46 U.S.C. § 30104–30105.

1.4 LHWCA and State Workers Compensation Acts

The LHWCA was enacted because the Supreme Court ruled in a series of cases that it is unconstitutional to apply state workers' compensation statutes to claims of maritime workers injured on navigable waters.[6] As initially enacted in 1927, the LHWCA covered injuries on navigable waters of the United States, including any dry dock, "if recovery . . . through workmen's compensation proceedings may not validly be provided by State law . . . ."[7] Despite the limiting language, the Supreme Court held that the LHWCA encompassed "all injuries sustained by employees on navigable waters," regardless of whether the claim fell within the scope of a state compensation scheme.[8] It was thus clear that the LHWCA provided a remedy for any injury in the course of a workers' employment on navigable waters as long as the location of the injury on navigable waters was not fortuitous or transitory.[9] However, the Court clouded the issue by ruling that some workers injured on navigable waters could bring a claim under the state workers' compensation statute because they fell into a maritime-but-local twilight zone where it was not unconstitutional to apply the state statute.[10] However, the shoreside boundary between the LHWCA and state compensation schemes was the fairly bright line of the water's edge, as the Supreme Court declined to extend the LHWCA landward in *Nacirema Co. v. Johnson*.[11] In summary, prior to 1972, there was a "shadowy"[12] zone of concurrent jurisdiction between the state and federal statutes for claims considered maritime-but-local that occurred on navigable waters.[13] Injuries on land fell solely under state compensation statutes.

When the 1972 Amendments to the LHWCA extended the coverage of the Act shoreside, Congress did not consider the relationship between the LHWCA and state statutes in the new area of overlapping jurisdiction. The effect of the Amendments on land-based injuries was addressed by the Supreme Court in *Sun Ship, Inc. v. Pennsylvania*.[14] In view of the fact that the Supreme Court had permitted some concurrent jurisdiction before the Amendments and the fact that Congress was silent as to the effect of the extended jurisdiction on state statutes, the Supreme Court held that there is concurrent jurisdiction between the state and federal statutes for injuries on the land.[15]

The concurrent authority of the two compensation schemes[16] does not require an election by the worker between the two statutes.[17] For example, a worker may collect state compensation and then seek LHWCA compensation thereafter.[18] The only relief to the employer and carrier is to assert a credit for the net recovery received by the em-

6. *E.g., S. Pac. Co. v. Jensen*, 244 U.S. 205 (1917); *Knickerbocker Ice Co. v. Stewart*, 253 U.S. 149 (1920); *Washington v. W.C. Dawson & Co.*, 264 U.S. 219 (1924).

7. 33 U.S.C. § 903(a).

8. *Calbeck v. Travelers Ins. Co.*, 370 U.S. 114, 124 (1962).

9. *Dir., OWCP v. Perini N. River Assocs.*, 459 U.S. 297, 324 n.34 (1983).

10. *Davis v. Dep't of Labor & Indus.*, 317 U.S. 249 (1942).

11. 396 U.S. 212 (1969).

12. *Id.* at 253.

13. The difficulty in determining whether the injury occurred within the twilight zone is exemplified by *Bourque v. Anco Insulations, Inc.*, 25 So.3d 1008 (La. App. 3 Cir. 2009) (declining to find concurrent jurisdiction for a worker exposed to asbestos on vessels on navigable waters).

14. 447 U.S. 715 (1980).

15. *Id.* at 722–26.

16. Deaths on the high seas have presented the question whether state compensation acts may afford a remedy or whether the Death on the High Seas Act, which provides that "the personal representative of the decedent may bring a civil action in admiralty against the person or vessel responsible" when the death was caused by a wrongful act on the high seas beyond three miles from the shore of the United States," 46 U.S.C. § 30302, is the exclusive remedy. In 1959, the Ninth Circuit held that the exclusive remedy for the death of a Flight Service Supervisor in an airplane crash on the high seas was pursuant to the California workers' compensation statute. *King v. Pan Am. World Airways*, 270 F.2d 355 (9th Cir. 1959). *See also Stoddard v. Ling-Temco-Vought, Inc.*, No. CV-72-1294-PGH, 1980 U.S. DIST. LEXIS 9649 (Apr. 14, 1980) (Texas workers' compensation law was the exclusive remedy against the employer for the wrongful death claims of those who died in an airplane crash on the high seas). However, after the Supreme Court held that DOHSA provided the exclusive remedy for wrongful deaths on the high seas, pre-empting state wrongful death statutes, in *Offshore Logistics, Inc. v. Tallentire*, 477 U.S. 207 (1986), some courts have reconsidered whether state compensation acts may afford a remedy for deaths on the high seas. Thus, in *Garofalo v. Princess Cruises, Inc.*, 85 Cal. App. 4th 1060, 102 Cal. Rptr. 2d 754 (Cal. App. 2000), the court held that DOHSA preempted the employer's claim for subrogation under the California workers' compensation statute when a fire on a cruise ship aggravated the injuries that were the basis of the claimant's state compensation claim. *See also Bernard v. World Learning, Inc.*, No. 09-20309-CIV-UNGARO, 2010 U.S. DIST. LEXIS 143538, at * 21, n.9 (S.D. Fla. June 4, 2010), in which the judge stated that if DOHSA were applicable, "it appears to the undersigned that the Death on the High Seas Act likely supersedes the Vermont Workers' Compensation Act" (citing *Tallentire*).

17. *Landry v. Carlson Mooring Serv.*, 643 F.2d 1080 (5th Cir.), *cert. denied*, 454 U.S. 1123 (1981).

18. *Calbeck*, 370 U.S. at 131. The Court noted that "no impermissible double recovery is possible." *Id.*

ployee.[19] This credit has been codified in the LHWCA.[20] When benefits are paid under the LHWCA and a credit is sought under the state workers' compensation act, the extent of the credit given under the state statute has differed according to state law.[21]

The fact that a claimant brings two claims does present a problem with the prospect of inconsistent results and doctrines such as collateral estoppel.[22] When the worker initially presented a state workers' compensation claim and the state workers' compensation commission ruled that the latest injury had "no lasting effect on [the claimant's] condition," the First Circuit ruled that the administrative law judge hearing the LHWCA claim for that injury was bound by the state commission's decision based on collateral estoppel.[23] The court reasoned that "the point of collateral estoppel is that the first determination is binding not because it is right but because it is first—and was reached after a full and fair opportunity between the parties to litigate the issue."[24]

While the states may provide concurrent jurisdiction for some injuries covered under the LHWCA, the states are not required to do so. Thus, the existence of concurrent state jurisdiction is decided by each state. For example, the revised Texas Workers' Compensation Act, effective in 1991, now provides that "a person covered by a method of compensation established under federal law" is "not subject to" coverage under the Texas Act.[25] Consequently, if a worker is covered under the LHWCA, he does not have a claim under a state act that does not afford concurrent coverage.[26]

Determining whether there is concurrent jurisdiction between the LHWCA and a state statute requires an interpretation of the state statute. For example, in *Morris v. Owensboro Grain Co.*,[27] Morris was injured after loading items onto a barge at his employer's soybean and grain processing refinery on the Ohio River while climbing from a dock onto a platform. After receiving benefits under the LHWCA, Morris filed a claim for benefits under the Kentucky Workers' Compensation Act. The Kentucky statute exempted from its coverage "[a]ny person for whom a rule of liability for injury or death is provided by the United States . . . ."[28] Morris argued that the LHWCA did not constitute a "rule of liability," as stated in the state act, because "the federal government never intended for the LHWCA to be the sole method for compensating injured maritime workers."[29] The court responded, however, that "we must deter-

19. *Landry*, 643 F.2d at 1088. Thus, there is no credit under the LHWCA for awards under the state statute for attorneys' fees. *See, e.g., Lustig v. U.S. Dept. of Labor*, 881 F.2d 593 (9th Cir. 1989). Similarly, penalties awarded under a state statute have not been credited against the compensation owed under the LHWCA. *See, e.g., Transbay Container Terminal v. U.S. Dep't of Labor Benefits Review Bd.*, 141 F.3d 907 (9th Cir. 1998).

20. 33 U.S.C. § 903(e).

21. For example, states such as California apply the same net-recovery credit as the LHWCA so that there is a dollar-for-dollar credit regardless of the category of benefits. *See Sea-Land Serv., Inc. v. Workers' Comp. Appeals Bd.*, 14 Cal. 4th 76, 58 Cal. Rptr. 2d 190, 925 P.2d 1309 (Cal. 1996). One Texas court indicated that the entire recovery should be credited. See *Johnson v. Tex. Employers Ins. Ass'n*, 558 S.W.2d 47, 52 (Tex. Civ. App–Beaumont 1997, writ ref'd, n.r.e.) ("should plaintiff below, Tom Johnson, recover any award under the Texas Act, the entire amount awarded under L.H.W.C.A. shall be deducted from that award"). Some states have denied a credit based on the nature of the payments made in that case. *See, e.g., Bouford v. Bath Iron Works Corp.*, 514 A.2d 470 (Me. 1986) (benefits for permanent partial disability to the claimant's back under the LHWCA, compensating him for loss of wage earning capacity, were not credited against the state disability benefits based on loss of function of a body part); *Cross v. Newport News Shipbuilding & Dry Dock Co.*, 21 Va. App. 530, 465 S.E.2d 598 (Va. App. 1996) (employer received credit for temporary total disability payments made under the LHWCA but not for permanent partial disability payments).

22. Concurrent jurisdiction may provide a choice of forum not just to the injured worker but also to his medical providers. Therefore, when a worker pursues a remedy under the LHWCA, his health care provider may pursue a remedy under the state workers' compensation act. *See St. Mary's Reg'l Med. Ctr. v. Bath Iron Works*, 2009 Me. 92, 977 A. 2d 431 (Me. 2009).

23. *Bath Iron Works Corp. v. Dir., OWCP*, 125 F.3d 18 (1st Cir. 1997).

24. *Id.* at 22; *see also Campbell Indus. v. U.S. Dep't of Labor Benefits Review Bd.*, 145 F.3d 1336 (9th Cir. 1998); *Valenzuela v. Dir., OWCP*, 142 F.3d 447 (9th Cir. 1998); *but cf. Garnett v. Ryan-Walsh, Inc.*, 151 F.3d 1029 (4th Cir. 1998) (estoppel arguments rejected with respect to prior determination of disability for pension from I.L.A. Pension & Welfare Fund).

25. Tex. Labor Code § 406.091(a)(2). Thus, the beneficiaries of a worker killed on navigable waters whose claim was covered by the LHWCA, were denied a gross negligence claim against the decedent's employer under Texas law by the exclusive remedy provision in the LHWCA. *See Anaya v. Traylor Bros., Inc.*, 478 F.3d 251, 255 (5th Cir. 2007) (the court "reject[ed] the Anayas' argument that Anaya was in a twilight zone" and held that "[a]n employee subject to Anaya's work conditions on navigable waters may only recover under the LHWCA").

26. Other states have declined to afford concurrent coverage. *See e.g.*, La. R.S. 23:1035.2 ("No compensation shall be payable in respect to the disability or death of any employee covered by the Federal Employer's Liability Act [sic], the Longshoremen's and Harbor Worker's Compensation Act, or any of its extensions, or the Jones Act").

27. 407 S.W.3d 559 (Kent. 2013).

28. Kent. Rev. Stat. § 342.650(4).

29. *Morris*, 407 S.W.3d at 562.

mine what the General Assembly intended for [the statute] to accomplish," and the court concluded that "the General Assembly intended to exempt any worker from Kentucky's Workers' Compensation Act where his injury is covered by a federal workers' compensation scheme . . . ."[30]

1.5 LHWCA[31] and Jones Act

The relationship between the LHWCA and Jones Act is different than the relationship between the LHWCA and state compensation statutes. The Jones Act provides a negligence remedy for "a seaman."[32] The LHWCA covers injuries on navigable waters but *excludes* "a master or member of a crew of any vessel."[33] The effect of the LHWCA exclusion "is to confine the benefits of the Jones Act to the members of a crew of a vessel plying in navigable waters."[34] "Thus, it is odd but true that the key requirement for Jones Act coverage now appears in another statute."[35] The provisions of the LHWCA and Jones Act are mutually exclusive.[36] There is no concurrent jurisdiction under the LHWCA and Jones Act, and a worker's injury is not compensable under both Acts.

While it is clear that the LHWCA and Jones Act do not overlap, the line between the Acts is not clear and the status of workers in many cases must be resolved by a fact finder.[37] Neither party is bound by the payment or acceptance of benefits under one scheme or the other.[38] The Supreme Court stated in *Southwest Marine, Inc. v. Gizoni*:

> It is by now "universally accepted" that an employee who receives voluntary payments under the LHWCA without a formal award is not barred from seeking relief under the Jones Act. This is so, quite obviously, because the question of coverage has never actually been litigated. Moreover, the LHWCA clearly does not comprehend such a preclusive effect, as it specifically provides that any amounts paid to an employee for the same injuries, disability, or death pursuant to the Jones Act shall be credited against any liability imposed by the LHWCA.[39]

The credit noted by the Supreme Court in *Gizoni* is applicable in both LHWCA and Jones Act claims.[40]

The preclusive effect may be different when a formal order[41] has been entered in either the LHWCA claim[42] or Jones Act suit.[43] In *Sharp v. Johnson Brothers*

30. *Id.* at 563 (footnote omitted).

31. Although the court in *CNA Ins. Co. v. Workers' Comp. Appeals Bd.*, 58 Cal. App. 4th 211, 68 Cal. Rptr. 2d 115 (Cal. App. 1997) (review denied), held that there could be concurrent jurisdiction between the Jones Act and the California workers' compensation statute, the court in *Ditmore v. Fairfield Indus.*, 855 F. Supp. 187, 191 (S.D. Tex. 1994) held that the claimant's mere "acceptance of Jones Act benefits was akin to accepting benefits under the law of 'another jurisdiction' as contemplated by the Texas Workers' Compensation Act, and as a consequence, he should no longer recover benefits under the Texas act."

32. 46 U.S.C. § 30104.

33. 33 U.S.C. § 902(3)(G).

34. *Swanson v. Marra Bros., Inc.*, 328 U.S. 1, 7 (1946).

35. *McDermott Int'l, Inc. v. Wilander*, 498 U.S. 337, 347 (1991).

36. *Id.*

37. The determination whether a worker is a seaman is "a mixed question of law and fact." *Id.* at 356. "When the underlying facts are established, and the rule of law is undisputed, the issue is whether the facts meet the statutory standard. 'Member of a crew' and 'seaman' are statutory terms; their interpretation is a question of law." *Id.* Therefore, "summary judgment or a directed verdict is mandatory where the facts and law will reasonably support only one conclusion." *Id.*

38. *E.g., Sw. Marine, Inc. v. Gizoni*, 502 U.S. 81 (1991); *Tipton v. Socony Mobil Oil Co.*, 375 U.S. 34 (1963); *Boatel, Inc. v. Delamore*, 379 F.2d 850, 856 (5th Cir. 1967).

39. *Gizoni*, 502 U.S. at 91–92 (citations omitted).

40. *See* 33 U.S.C. § 903(e); *Commercial Union Ins. Co. v. McKinnon*, 10 F.3d 1352, 1354 (8th Cir. 1993). *See also Ditmore v. Fairfield Indus.*, 855 F. Supp. 187 (S. D. Tex. 1994) (addressing credit and reimbursement when a claimant seeks benefits both under a state workers' compensation statute and as a seaman).

41. The decision by the ALJ that the claimant is not a seaman is sufficient to bar a Jones Act action even though the ALJ does not issue "a 'formal award' per se in the form of additional moneys" because he concludes that the claimant is not entitled to any further compensation. *Anders v. Ormet Corp.*, 874 F. Supp. 738, 741 (M.D. La. 1994).

42. In *Gros v. Fred Settoon, Inc.*, 855 So.2d 143 (La. App. 3 Cir. 2003), *writ denied*, 871 So.2d 352 La. 2004), the Louisiana court held that a formal award in an LHWCA proceeding, in which the dispute was whether the claimant was entitled to state or LHWCA benefits, did not preclude the pursuit of a Jones Act claim.

43. Awards and findings in claims involving a state workers' compensation statute have been held to have res judicata effect in a Jones Act suit. *E.g., Kalesnick v. Seacoast Ocean Servs.*, 866 F. Supp. 36, 39 (D. Me. 1994) (award of state compensation in contested case is an implicit conclusion that the worker was not a seaman so as to be eligible for state benefits and operates as res judicata in a federal Jones Act suit); *Polack v. Riverside Marine Constr., Inc.*, 22 F. Supp.3d 109, 118–20 (D. Mass. 2014) (consent decree in a proceeding for state compensation is an implicit conclusion that the worker was not a seaman and operates as res judicata in a federal Jones Act suit);

Corp.,[44] the worker was injured while performing bridge repair work. He reached a settlement with his employer's compensation carrier, and an ALJ entered an order approving the settlement. In the meantime, the worker brought a Jones Act suit. After the settlement of his LHWCA claim, the district court entered a summary judgment that the plaintiff had elected a remedy as a harbor worker under the LHWCA,[45] precluding a Jones Act suit. Although the issue of LHWCA coverage was not actually litigated in an adversarial proceeding, the Fifth Circuit affirmed the dismissal of the Jones Act claim:

> Having obtained the order of the ALJ and the aegis of the DOL to ratify and enforce his settlement, Sharp ensured that his rights were more secure under the agreement than they would have been if the settlement were considered merely a contract between the parties. It follows that where the ALJ issues a compensation order ratifying a settlement agreement, a "formal award" should be deemed to have been made . . . and the injured party no longer may bring a Jones Act suit for the same injuries.[46]

The Fifth Circuit has recognized "that there are differences between the fact-finding processes in the administrative forum and in the judicial forum, "but the court answered: "In enacting the LHWCA, Congress intended that it be the sole and exclusive remedy for workers within its scope, not a stepping stone on the way to a jury award."[47]

1.6 Other Remedies

The LHWCA interfaces with other remedies in situations where the LHWCA is adopted as the compensation remedy by other statutes. The Outer Continental Shelf Lands Act (OCSLA) provides that the workers' compensation remedy for an employee against his employer shall be pursuant to the provisions of the LHWCA in the case of disability or death resulting from an "injury occurring as the result of operations conducted on the outer Continental Shelf for the purpose of exploring for, developing, removing, or transporting by pipeline the natural resources, of the subsoil and seabed of the outer Continental Shelf;"[48] however, "the term 'employee' [as used in the OCSLA] does not include a mas-

Long v. Diamond Jo Casino, 2000 A.M.C. 2453, 2000 U.S. DIST. LEXIS 9204 (N.D. Ill. June 30, 2000) (finding of seaman status in state compensation proceeding collaterally estops employer from contesting seaman status in federal action).

44. 973 F.2d 423 (5th Cir. 1992), *cert. denied*, 508 U.S. 907 (1993). The Ninth Circuit reached a different result in *Figueroa v. Campbell Indus.*, 45 F.3d 331 (9th Cir. 1995), holding that a shipyard worker who had compromised and settled claims under both the California statute and LHWCA (resulting in the issuance of a Final Compensation Order by the Department of the Labor) did not bar him from bringing an action under the Jones Act. Instead of citing the later decision of the Fifth Circuit in *Sharp*, the Ninth Circuit quoted a district court in the Fifth Circuit in *Guidry v. Ocean Drilling & Exploration Co.*, 244 F. Supp. 691, 692 (W.D. La. 1965) (citations omitted):

> [W]here the Deputy Commissioner's finding and award do not disclose any facts upon which his jurisdiction existed, the rule should be and is that complainant's right to determine his status as a seaman under the Jones Act is not prejudiced thereby, and these questions are not subject to a plea of res adjudicata under the Longshoremen's and Harbor Workers' Compensation Act, 33 U.S.C.A. 921(a).

Figueroa, 45 F.3d at 316. Ninth Circuit added:

> Mr. Figueroa, an injured seaman, arguably acting as a person enumerated under the LHWCA at the time of his injury, is entitled to recover for his pain and suffering under the Jones Act, and additionally can recover for unpaid wages and medical expenses either by recovering workers' compensation benefits or by recovering those damage elements under the Jones Act, although not both. Clearly, Mr. Figueroa was entitled to bring an action for his pain and suffering under the Jones Act, having already recovered benefits for his unpaid wages and medical expenses from workers' compensation.

Id. Similarly, the California Court of Appeals has held that settlement of a worker's Jones Act and LHWCA claims did not preclude the California Workers' Compensation Appeals Board from asserting jurisdiction over the worker's claim under the California workers' compensation statute. *See CNA Ins. Co. v. Workers' Comp. Appeals Bd.*, 58 Cal. App. 4th 211, 68 Cal. Rptr. 2d 115 (Cal. App. 1997) (review denied).

45. The effect of LHWCA and Jones Act actions on claims brought by a longshoreman or harbor worker against his employer pursuant to 33 U.S.C. § 905(b) was addressed in *Cooper v. Int'l Offshore Servs., L.L.C.*, 390 Fed. Appx. 347 (5th Cir. 2010), and *Sharp v. Johnson Bros. Corp.*, 687 So.2d 568 (La. App. 4 Cir. 1997). In *Cooper*, the court held that the settlement of the claimant's LHWCA claim with a finding that the employer "was relieved from liability for 'any and all claims of whatsoever nature' arising out of the December 18, 2007 accident" would bar a section 905(b) action against the employer based on res judicata. *Cooper*, 390 Fed. Appx. at 351. However, the dismissal in *Sharp* of the claimant's federal Jones Act suit without litigating any section 905(b) issues did not operate as a res judicata bar to a suit in state court asserting a claim under Section 905(b). *Sharp*, 687 So.2d at 573.

46. *Sharp*, 973 F.2d at 426.

47. *Fontenot v. AWI, Inc.*, 923 F.2d 1127, 1133 (5th Cir. 1991).

48. 43 U.S.C. § 1333(b).

ter or member of a crew of any vessel."[49] "Consequently, there are two categories of workers with separate schemes in connection with OCSLA[50] operations: members of the crew (seamen) and workers who otherwise fail the seaman status [test] who are subject to the LHWCA."[51] While the LHWCA and state workers' compensation statutes may be concurrent for land-based accidents based on the decision of the Supreme Court in *Sun Ship*, the outer Continental Shelf is a federal enclave and the Fifth Circuit has held that the LHWCA provides the exclusive remedy for injuries covered by the OCSLA to the exclusion of state workers' compensation remedies.[52]

There are gaps in coverage of the federal statutory remedies for maritime workers (LHWCA and Jones Act) in which the general maritime law affords a negligence remedy for the worker against his employer.[53] Even though the workers who fall within these gaps may have been paid state compensation benefits, the exclusive liability provision of the state statute does not bar the worker from pursuing a maritime negligence remedy against his employer.[54]

The LHWCA has also been adopted as the compensation remedy by the Nonappropriated Fund Instrumentalities Act[55] and the Defense Base Act.[56] The exclusive remedy provisions of these statutes[57] are broader than the provision in the LHWCA,[58] and they have not been interpreted to afford concurrent jurisdiction with state statutes.[59]

---

49. *Id.* § 1333(b)(1).

50. Oilfield Workers who are not seamen and are injured on fixed platforms in state waters are generally subject to state workers' compensation remedies. *Herb's Welding, Inc. v. Gray*, 470 U.S. 414 (1985).

51. Kenneth G. Engerrand, *Primer of Remedies on the Outer Continental Shelf*, 4 Loy. Mar. L. J. 19, 42–43 (2005) (footnotes omitted).

52. *See, e.g., LeSassier v. Chevron USA, Inc.*, 776 F.2d 506 (5th Cir. 1985). However, before Louisiana eliminated its concurrent jurisdiction with the LHWCA, the Louisiana Supreme Court disagreed with the Fifth Circuit and held that there was concurrent jurisdiction of the Louisiana statute with respect to injuries on the outer Continental Shelf. *See Thompson v. Teledyne Movible Offshore, Inc.*, 419 So.2d 822 (La. 1982).

53. *E.g., Thibodaux v. Atl. Richfield Co.*, 580 F.2d 841 (5th Cir. 1978) (oilfield maintenance worker killed during transportation on a Louisiana canal); *Green v. Vermilion Corp.*, 144 F.3d 332 (5th Cir. 1998) (cook and watchman at duck camp injured on dock while mooring a vessel was excluded from the LHWCA by the club/camp exclusion in 33 U.S.C. § 902(3)(B)).

54. *See Thibodaux*, 580 F.2d at 847–48; *Green*, 144 F.3d at 338–42.

55. 5 U.S.C. §§ 8171–8173.

56. 42 U.S.C. § 1651–1654.

57. The Nonappropriated Fund Instrumentalities Act provides:

> The liability of the United States or of a nonappropriated fund instrumentality described by section 2105(c) of this title, with respect to the disability or death resulting from injury, as defined by section 2(2) of the Longshore and Harbor Workers' Compensation Act (33 U.S.C. 902(2)), of an employee referred to by sections 8171 and 8172 of this title, shall be determined as provided by this subchapter. This liability is exclusive and instead of all other liability of the United States or the instrumentality to the employee, his legal representative, spouse, dependents, next of kin, and any other person otherwise entitled to recover damages from the United States or the instrumentality because of the disability or death in a direct judicial proceeding, in a civil action, or in admiralty, or by an administrative or judicial proceeding under a workmen's compensation statute or under a Federal tort liability statute.

5 U.S.C. § 8173. The Defense Base Act provides:

> The liability of an employer, contractor (or any subcontractor or subordinate subcontractor with respect to the contract of such contractor) under this chapter shall be exclusive and in place of all other liability of such employer, contractor, subcontractor, or subordinate contractor to his employees (and their dependents) coming within the purview of this chapter, under the workmen's compensation law of any State, Territory, or other jurisdiction, irrespective of the place where the contract of hire of any such employee may have been made or entered into.

42 U.S.C. § 1651(c). Like the LHWCA and OCSLA, the Defense Base Act does not apply to "a master or member of a crew of any vessel." *Id.* § 1654.

58. The exclusive remedy provision of the LHWCA provides:

> The liability of an employer prescribed in section 904 of this title shall be exclusive and in place of all other liability of such employer to the employee, his legal representative, husband or wife, parents, dependents, next of kin, and anyone otherwise entitled to recover damages from such employer at law or in admiralty on account of such injury or death . . . .

33 U.S.C. § 905(a).

59. *See, e.g., Atkinson v. Gates, McDonald & Co.*, 838 F.2d 808 (5th Cir. 1988) (state-law bad-faith claims are preempted by the exclusive liability provision of the Nonappropriated Fund Instrumentalities Act); *Air Force Central Welfare Fund v. Henderson*, 1971 Ok. 46, 483 P.2d 1154 (Okla. 1971) (Oklahoma State Industrial Court lacks jurisdiction to hear case covered by Nonappropriated Fund Instrumentalities Act); *Flying Tiger Lines, Inc. v. Landry*, 370 F.2d 46, 52 (9th Cir. 1966) (beneficiaries of decedent, whose death was covered by the Defense Base Act, did not make a binding election of remedies when they sought and received benefits under the California

1.7 Conclusion

The relationships between and among state and federal remedies for maritime workers vary widely among the remedies and the courts addressing them. While states are permitted to extend concurrent jurisdiction of their workers' compensation remedies to land-based injuries that are also covered under the LHWCA, many states have elected not to do so. In contrast, the LHWCA and Jones Act do not afford concurrent jurisdiction as they are mutually exclusive. Despite the mutual exclusivity of the LHWCA and Jones Act, however, workers can collect benefits under one statute and then seek benefits under the other, as they can do under state compensation acts and then the LHWCA,[60] without fear of an election-of-remedies defense. However, proceeding with a claim to the point of the issuance of an order presents collateral estoppel issues that vary by remedy and circuit.

When workers are permitted to recover under more than one remedy, the benefits already paid pursuant to one remedy may be credited, in whole or in part, against the recovery in the subsequent forum. The extent of credit depends on the remedy as determined by the body authorized to adjudicate disputes for that remedy.

---

workers' compensation statute because the beneficiaries had no choice to make. "[T]he 'twilight zone' concept . . . has no application to the Defense Base Act."); *see also Vilanova v. United States*, 851 F.2d 1, 3, 6 (1st Cir. 1988), *cert. denied*, 488 U.S. 1016 (1989) (settlement of LHWCA claim against nonappropriated fund employer with administrative finding of LHWCA coverage bars subsequent suit against United States for malpractice of doctors at United States Naval Station Hospital based on the exclusive liability provision in Nonappropriated Fund Instrumentalities Act).

60. However, state statutes may contain election-of-remedies provisions that prevent recovery if the worker has collected benefits under another compensation scheme. *See, e.g., Ditmore v. Fairfield Indus.*, 855 F. Supp. 187, 191 (S.D. Tex. 1994) (accepting Jones Act benefits barred recovery under Texas act).

Chapter 2

Situs and Status Coverage and Jurisdiction Under the Longshore and Harborworkers' Compensation Act

John F. Karpousis, Esq.

Synopsis

The Longshore & Harborworkers' Compensation Act, 33 U.S.C. §901 et seq., (the "LHWCA") is a workers' compensation statute passed by Congress in 1927 for the purposes of providing compensation to injured longshoremen for injuries they suffer while in the course of their employment. The Act was amended many times during its existence, but most significantly in 1972[1], when Congress further defined the scope of jurisdiction of the Act, and then again in 1984, when it limited the coverage of employees not engaged in "Maritime Employment." This paper will provide an overview of coverage and jurisdictional issues under the Act, and provide some recent example of how courts are handling this issue. The article is by no means an exhaustive analysis of all of the cases decided by the courts over the last twenty years, but is meant instead to provide the practitioner and student with a perspective of the wide, varied, and somewhat inconsistent results achieved in this area of the law.

2.1 Background

The LHWCA provides disability dollar benefits for accidents arising out of the course of employment which results either in scheduled loss of use for certain body parts (enumerated in Section 908 of the Act), or for ⅔ of the worker's average weekly wage until he can earn wages. The concept of disability is contained in Section 908. In order to qualify as a longshoreman under the LHWCA, one must satisfy two tests: the status test and the situs test. Status refers to the nature of the work performed and situs refers to the place of that work's performance.

Section 902(3), as amended in 1972, provides the definition of status, but excludes certain types of employees from coverage. The most prominent of these would be individuals employed to perform office and clerical work or individuals employed by a club, camp, restaurant, etc. Members of a ship's crew are also excluded as they are covered by the Jones Act. With regard to situs, Section 903 provides the definition of covered places, implicitly excluding those locations not "adjoining" navigable waters.

A. Status

33 USC Sec. 902(3) states, in pertinent part, as follows:

> The term "employee" means any person engaged in maritime employment, including any longshoreman or other person engaged in longshoring operations, and any harbor-worker including a ship repairman, shipbuilder, and ship-breaker, but such term does not include—
> **(A)** individuals employed exclusively to perform office clerical, secretarial, security, or data processing work;
> **(B)** individuals employed by a club, camp, recreational operation, restaurant, museum, or retail outlet;
> **(C)** individuals employed by a marina and who are not engaged in construction, replacement, or

1. Prior to 1972, the Act applied only to injuries occurring on navigable waters. Longshoremen loading or unloading a ship were covered on the ship but not on the shore, even though they were performing the same functions whether on or off the ship. In 1972, Congress extended "situs" coverage to the area adjacent to the ship used for loading and unloading, but restricted the "status" test limiting coverage to those engaged in maritime employment.

expansion of such marina (except for routine maintenance);

(D) individuals who (i) are employed by suppliers, transporters, or vendors, (ii) are temporarily doing business on the premises of an employer described in paragraph (4), and (iii) are not engaged in work normally performed by employees of that employer under this chapter;

(E) aquaculture workers;

(F) individuals employed to build any recreational vessel under sixty-five feet in length, or individuals employed to repair any recreational vessel, or to dismantle any part of a recreational vessel in connection with the repair of such vessel;

(G) a master or member of a crew of any vessel; or

(H) any person engaged by a master to load or unload or repair any small vessel under eighteen tons net;

This list seems exhaustive and clear enough. Certainly, individuals who work loading and off loading containers in a marine terminal constitute maritime employees and are covered under the LHWCA. However, further inspection reveals that clarity, as is so often the case in statutory interpretation, is a lofty goal not always achievable. In this regard, it is useful to review a group of U.S. Supreme Court cases that have directly addressed the "status" issue.

1. The key Supreme Court cases on "status"

The United States Supreme Court, between the late 70s and mid 80s, issued several landmark "status" cases, which are critical to any analysis of the statute. These cases will be briefly discussed herein for their general principles; however, the practitioner is encouraged to review the nuances of these cases individually, as their factual twists and turns can easily affect any analysis of the status issue.

As stated in the statute, if the claimant's work at the moment of the injury involves loading, unloading or repair of a vessel, then he would be covered under the statute. However, in *Northeast Marine Terminal Co., Inc., v. Caputo*, 432 U.S. 249 (1977), the Supreme Court stated that a claimant need not be engaged in maritime employment at the time of the injury to be covered by the Act. Moreover, if an employee regularly performs duties relating to maritime employment and he is injured while temporarily performing some non maritime function, he will likely be covered.

The Supreme Court expanded on this theme, in *P.C. Pfeiffer v. Ford*, 444 U.S. 69 (1979), Ford was injured on a dock while securing military vehicles. Another claimant was injured while unloading a bale of cotton, from a wagon into a pier warehouse, for subsequent loading. Because these two claimants were engaged in the immediate steps of moving cargo between ship and land, and were not merely picking up the cargo for further land based trans-shipment, they were covered.

Director, OWCP v. Perini North River Associates, 459 US 297 (1983), held that regardless of status, if a claimant was covered under the LHWCA before the 1972 Amendments for injuries which occurred on navigable waters, he is covered for injuries on navigable waters after the 1972 Amendments. That is, when a worker is injured on actual navigable waters in the course of his employment on those waters, he likely satisfies the status requirement and is covered under the LHWCA.

Throwing a bit of a wrench into the *Perini* analysis, is *Herbs Welding, Inc. v. Gray*, 470 U.S. 414 (1985), when Justice White wrote that a welder injured while working on an oil platform offshore failed the status test. Although he was working on navigable waters, there was nothing inherently maritime about his tasks. The Court insisted that the work of the offshore platform was not a part of maritime commerce and that the 1972 Amendments to the Act refined the scope of coverage to those engaged involved in loading, unloading and vessel repair. Hence, the Supreme Court took a limiting, rather than an expansive view of the Amendments.

How does one then reconcile the Court's holding *Herb's Welding* with *Chesapeake & Ohio Railroad Co. v. Schwalb*, 493 U.S. 40 (1989), wherein Justice White, writing for a unanimous Court, held that a railroad employee injured while maintaining or repairing equipment essential to loading coal onto vessels was a covered employee because he was integral to the loading and unloading process? Justice White again wrote the opinion, stating that the status test is an "occupational test," which focuses in part on the job function of loading and unloading. The equipment being repaired and maintained by Schwalb was, in and of itself, integral to the loading and unloading process, seemingly making Schwalb and his co-workers integral to the loading and unloading process as well. The Court went so far as to say that the ship loading process had to be stopped when the equipment required repair—thereby evincing its level of importance to the ship loading process and placing squarely into the Act's coverage.

2. Recent cases regarding terminal workers and status

As discussed, anyone who is involved in the traditional longshoring operations of loading, unloading, stuffing, stripping containers, and checking containers, will be covered.

At what point in time do the traditional activities become too tangential and too far removed from longshoring operations to be covered? The answer is not so clear. For example, in *Maher Terminals, Inc. v. Dir., OWCP*, 330 F.3d 162 (3d Cir. 2003), Riggio worked at a marine terminal where he performed both clerical duties, as a delivery clerk, and longshoring duties, as a box checker. He performed clerical duties about half of the time and longshoring duties the other half. Riggio injured himself while performing his clerical duties, which are not covered under the LHWCA. His employer argued that Riggio did not satisfy the Act's status requirement. The Third Circuit disagreed! The Third Circuit relied on the Supreme Court's Caputo decision, which rejected the "moment of injury" principle. The Third Circuit found that coverage under the LHWCA does not depend on the task an employee performed at the time of the injury. Instead, the Third Circuit held that "when Congress said it wanted to cover 'longshoremen,' it had in mind persons whose employment is such that they spend at least some of their time in indisputably longshoring operations and who, without the 1972 amendments, would be covered for only part of their activity."

In comparison, the BRB denied a part time marine worker coverage under the LHWCA in *Eddie Gary v. The Bayou Companies LLC*, BRB No. 11-0600, 2012 WL 1391763 (DOL Ben. Rev. Bd. Mar. 5, 2012). Eddie Gray injured his back while working at a pipe coating plant in Louisiana as a yard foreman. The BRB noted that Gray's job duties consisted of loading trucks, building pipe racks, and cleaning the yard. On a few occasions, Gray also performed work on a barge when the crew was shorthanded. The parties disputed the amount of time Gray spent working on the barge. Regardless, the BRB found that because there was no dispute that working on the barge was not a part of Gray's regular job duties, such maritime employment was "sporadic" at best and "too brief and fortuitous to confer longshore jurisdiction."

Compare both the *Maher Terminals* and *Bayou Companies* cases to *Jacobs v. G&L Land and Marine Food Distributors*, 48 BRBS 9 (2014) and even less clarity exists. Jacob injured himself while carrying an ice chest from his truck to a grocery box, which would be loaded by other workers onto a supply boat for transport to an offshore rig. The BRB found that Jacob's job of transporting groceries to the port was not an intermediary step in maritime transportation, but instead the last step in land transportation. As a result, the BRB held that Jacob was not involved in maritime employment and was therefore not covered under the LHWCA.

These three cases show how courts can come to three different conclusions for three different reasons relying on the Supreme Court's interpretation of Congress' intent on the "status" requirement.

3. Harborworkers: a special analysis

What of the workers, commonly referred to as "harborworkers", who perform their jobs primarily over navigable waters but are *not* engaged in loading, unloading or ship repairs? For example, marine construction workers who are injured on structures adjoining navigable waters might also be engaged in maritime employment and covered under the LHWCA, depending on the circumstances. Harborworkers directly involved in the construction, repair, alteration, or maintenance of harbor facilities will be considered covered under the Act. While that does not mean any construction project near water is covered, under *Perini*, if a worker is injured over water and could recover under the Act's pre-1972 amendments, he will likely be covered. For example, in *Maclay v. M/V Sahara*, 926 F. Supp. 2d 1209 (W.D. Wash. 2013), plaintiff's daughter worked assisting in the process of converting a former research vessel into a luxury floating hotel. While throwing scrap metal over the side of the vessel, she fell overboard, hit her head, and drowned. As her injury occurred while repurposing a vessel on navigable waters, the court held that plaintiff's daughter was a marine worker under the LHWCA because she satisfied both the situs and status tests under *Perini*.

On the other hand, the LHWCA does not cover all employees who sustain injuries while employed over navigable waters. In *Peru v. Sharpshooter Spectrum Venture LLC*, 493 F.3d 1058 (9th Cir. 2007), Peru hit her head while working onboard an historic naval ship for a company that shot, processed, and sold photographs to tourists. The Ninth Circuit held that the Act's coverage inquiry required an examination of not only the employer's business, but also the claimant's workplace and duties. The court found that the employee fell within the retail sales exclusion of Section 902(3)(b) and was therefore not covered by the LHWCA, because her employment had little to nothing to do with traditional maritime work.

In this regard, the status test seems to turn on whether the harborworker's functions had furthered maritime commerce in some manner. *See also Sidwell v. Virginia International Terminals, Inc.*, 372 F.3d 238, 38 BRBS 19(CRT), (4th Cir. 2004) (holding that the essential inquiry for status was whether the worker had the "capacity to interrupt ongoing longshore activities," which could disrupt maritime commerce). Some examples may assist in explaining this standard.

A claimant who was a laborer in a storage yard, where materials were used by the employer in a variety of marine and non-marine construction projects, was not a harborworker. *Bazemore v. Hardwaway Constructions*, 20 BRBS 23 (1987). The reason that this worker failed the status test was because his job duties did not further maritime commerce in any way. *See also DeJesus v. Viking Yacht Company*, 2014 DOLBRB LEXIS 912 (the Board applies regulations excluding workers repairing recreational vessels from coverage under the LHWCA because such work does not further maritime commerce).

A pile driver, repairing a breakwater located off shore from a nuclear facility was covered because he was building a structure extending into navigable water to protect or form a harbor, and therefore furthering maritime commerce. *Olson v. Healy Tibbits Construction*, 22 BRBS 221 (1989). However, LHWCA coverage did not extend to a beach cleanup worker in *Smith v. Labor Finders and ACE American Insurance Co.*, BRB No. 12-0035, 2012 WL 5267628 (DOL Ben. Rev. Bd. Sept. 11, 2012). Smith injured himself while working as a temporary beach clean-up worker on an island in Mississippi following the oil spill from the Deepwater Horizon explosion. The BRB held that Smith's cleanup duties were environmental in nature and not related to navigation or maritime commerce. The BRB also found that his duties loading and unloading tools and supplies onto a transport vessel failed to constitute maritime employment. The BRB reasoned that *Herbs Welding* was dispositive as the Supreme Court in that case found the claimant's loading and unloading of tools from a vessel to be no more than incidental to non-maritime employment. Lastly, the BRB relied upon *Sea-Land Service, Inc. v. Rock*, 953 F.2d 56, 25 BRBS 112(CRT) (3d Cir. 1992), when rejecting Smith's contention that he was a covered maritime employee under the LHWCA because he periodically drove the "gator" to transport workers around the island. In *Sea-Land*, the BRB denied coverage under the LHWCA to a van driver who shuttled passengers to points within an employer's loading facility because while such work was "helpful," it was not "indispensable."

What of marine construction workers injured on land? *Perini* seems to leave open the question of whether an employee, building a pier or dock but *not* injured on navigable waters, is covered under the Act. In *Baker v. Gulf Island Marine Fabricators, LLC*, 48 BRBS 623(ALJ) (2014), Baker worked as a marine carpenter in the fabrication of the living quarters of the *Big Foot* – a tension leg platform. The Board found that the *Big Foot* was not a vessel, as defined by the LHWCA, because, pursuant to *Dutra*, it was not capable of marine transportation as it would be effectively immobile once towed to its final location. Because the *Big Foot* was not a vessel, Baker failed the status test as his work was not maritime in nature.

However, the Second Circuit extended LHWCA coverage to a marine construction worker in *Fleischmann v. Director*, OWCP, 137 F.3d 131 (2d Cir. 1998), *cert. denied*, 525 US 981 (1998). This case bears further analysis because it is an excellent example of the Gordian knot that the LHWCA practitioner faces in marine construction cases. Fleischmann suffered a right knee injury while in the scope of his employment with Sea Horse Coastal Assistance and Towing Co. Sea Horse paid him New York State Workers' Compensation Benefits, but Fleischmann filed a claim under the LHWCA. The only issue tried before the ALJ was the issue of whether claimant met the situs and status requirements of the LHWCA.

Seahorse was a contractor-employer hired to repair a retaining wall on private property. The retaining wall abutted a canal on Oyster Bay, Long Island, on Center Island, New York. The bulkhead acted as a retaining wall for the land. A portion of the retaining wall had collapsed forward into the water; the purpose of the bulkhead was to prevent the erosion of the land into the water. Fleischmann worked primarily on a floating dock that tied to a barge, and he was injured when he fell from the retaining wall. He was standing on the retaining wall and fell 12 to 15 feet into the water, about 15 feet from the private property line.

The ALJ found no jurisdiction, but the Second Circuit remanded this decision. Fleischmann's general employment of building piers and docks sufficed to "establish the requisite connection to ships," to confer him with the status of a harborworker. A certiorari petition was filed but denied. The Second Circuit's decision does not answer whether Fleischmann was truly engaged in a maritime employment under the *Perini* decision for a post-1972 injury.

Fleischmann was arguably injured on land, although he spent most of his time on a barge. If the BRB applied the same rationale it used in *Bazemore* or *Healy Tibbets* to *Fleischmann*, the case may have been resolved differently. Was the pier in *Fleischmann* inherently maritime in nature? Did it keep the canal clear from maritime commerce? Arguably, the "pier" was merely a retaining wall used to keep the property from collapsing into the canal. It was there to help the property, not the maritime commerce of the canal. The Second Circuit seemed to pay no mind to the BRB decisions in this regard.

The Ninth Circuit, in an opinion which was eventually withdrawn, inexplicably held that the construction of an oil discharge pier was not a maritime activity despite the pier itself satisfying the Act's situs requirement. *McGray Construction Co. v. Director, OWCP*, 181 F.3d 1008 (9th Cir. 1999). In comparison, the Ninth Circuit in *Healy Tibbitts*

Builders, Inc. v. Dir., 444 F.3d 1095 (9th Cir. 2006), found an employee who was killed near the water's edge while excavating a utility line trench, as part of a larger project renovating three submarine berths, to be a maritime employee. The Ninth Circuit relied on *Schwalb* when coming to its decision that a "harbor worker," under the LHWCA, includes any employee directly engaged in the construction of a maritime facility, even if his particular job duties are not maritime in nature. The Ninth Circuit believed that there should be no distinction between those who repair equipment used in the loading and unloading process, as in *Schwalb*, and those who build the facilities at which that same process takes place, as both are essential to the loading and unloading of vessels and, therefore, maritime commerce.

The "status" requirement is anything but clear except in the most obvious of longshoring employments. Certainly, in the "harborworker" arena (particularly in the case of marine construction workers), the waters are as muddy as these workers often ply their trade in.

B. Situs

In order to qualify for longshore benefits, a worker *must meet both* the status and the situs test; he cannot have one without the other. Unlike the status inquiry, the situs inquiry looks to the nature of the place of work at the moment of the injury. *Jacksonville Shipyards, Inc. v. Purdue*, 539 F.2d 533 (5th Cir. 1976) (subsequent history omitted). Section 903 of the Act enumerates the facilities which will give rise to situs coverage: adjoining piers, wharves, drydocks, terminals, building ways, railways, or other adjoining areas customarily used by an employer in loading, unloading, repairing or building a vessel.

33 USC Sec. 903 states, in pertinent, as follows:

> Except as otherwise provided in this section, compensation shall be payable under this chapter in respect of disability or death of an employee, but only if the disability or death results from an injury occurring upon the navigable waters of the United States (including any adjoining pier, wharf, dry dock, terminal, building way, marine railway, or other adjoining area customarily used by an employer in loading, unloading, repairing, dismantling, or building a vessel).[2]

As will be discussed herein, courts have developed their own particularly distinctive view on the "situs" test. For example, the Second Circuit follows four main factors in determining whether a site is an "adjoining area" covered under the LHWCA:

1. Suitability of the site for maritime LHWCA maritime purposes;
2. Whether the adjoining properties are devoted primarily to uses in maritime commerce;
3. Proximity to the waterway, and;
4. Given all circumstances whether the adjoining site is as close to the waterway as feasible.

Triguero v. Consolidated Rail Corp., 932 F. 2 d 95 (2nd Cir. 1991).

The *Fleischmann* case, supra, also invoked situs issues. The Second Circuit stated that the bulkhead at issue was built on pilings that extended into navigable waters and, therefore, constituted a pier within the meaning of Section 903(a). That the bulkhead was not called a pier did not affect their determination. *Fleischmann* exemplifies the concerns fueled by the 1972 Amendments; that is, if Fleischmann would have clearly been covered had he been injured while working on the work platform over navigable waters several feet away, where he spent a substantial portion of the work hours, then why would he not be covered on the breakwater? Arguably, Congress made it clear that it considered the

2. 903(d) contains the "small vessel" exemptions to cover, and states in pertinent part as follows:

> (1) No compensation shall be payable to an employee employed at a facility of an employer if, as certified by the Secretary, the facility is engaged in the business of building, repairing, or dismantling exclusively small vessels (as defined in paragraph (3) of this subsection), unless the injury occurs while upon the navigable waters of the United States or while upon any adjoining pier, wharf, dock, facility over land for launching vessels, or facility over land for hauling, lifting, or drydocking vessels.
> (2) Notwithstanding paragraph (1), compensation shall be payable to an employee—
> (A) who is employed at a facility which is used in the business of building, repairing, or dismantling small vessels if such facility receives Federal maritime subsidies; or
> (B) if the employee is not subject to coverage under a State workers' compensation law.
> (3) For purposes of this subsection, a small vessel means—
> (A) a commercial barge which is under 900 lightship displacement tons; or
> (B) a commercial tugboat, towboat, crew boat, supply boat, fishing vessel, or other work vessel which is under 1,600 tons gross as measured under section 14502 of title 46, or an alternate tonnage measured under section 14302 of that title as prescribed by the Secretary under section 14104 of that title.

An entire separate article can be devoted solely to this section, and thus will not be directly analyzed in this paper.

water's edge the jurisdictional line. Nevertheless, the bulkhead in *Fleischmann* prevented the erosion of the adjacent property into the water. Numerous docks existed within the water, including a dock belonging to the property owner to which a boat was tied. The fact that the area was residential did not affect the Second Circuit's analysis in finding situs.

The Second Circuit's decision raises several questions. It seems to adopt an "overall work duties" analysis rather than "a place of work at the moment of injury" type analysis. Courts sometimes look at the place of the work at the moment of injury when determining situs. *See, e.g., BPU Mgmt. v. Dir., OWCP, DOL*, 732 F.3d 457 (5th Cir. 2013) (holding dock worker failed to satisfy situs requirement because he happened not to be in an area customarily used for loading vessels when injured). In *Fleischmann*, the Second Circuit focused on Fleischmann's usual presence on the float stage, not his "moment of injury" presence on the bulkhead. Regardless, the Second Circuit draws the line when employees are injured too far from an "adjoining area." *See, e.g., Villaverde v. Dir., OWCP*, 335 F. App'x 79 (2d Cir. 2009) (distinguishing *Fleishmann* and denying LHWCA coverage where employee was not actually injured on the bulkhead, but 85–90 feet landward of the bulkhead towards the highway).

A certiorari petition was filed in *Fleischmann* because of a direct conflict with a case in the Eleventh Circuit, *Brooker v. Durocher Dock & Dredge*, 133 F.3d 1390 (11th Cir. 1998). *Brooker* held that a construction worker who was injured on a retaining wall did not satisfy the LHWCA situs requirement because the retaining wall was not a pier. Further complicating matters, in *Brooker*, the Eleventh Circuit held that whether a pier is a maritime site is a pure factual question because the LHWCA does not provide a clear definition. The Court found that the factual evidence in the record rendered the seawall in *Brooker* a non maritime site.

In *Fleischmann*, the Second Circuit relied on the Ninth Circuit's opinion in *Hurston v. Director, OWCP*, 989 F.2d 1547 (9th Cir. 1993), which used the expression "if it walks like a duck, if it sounds like a duck, it's a duck," to justify its holding that "if it is built like a pier and adjoins navigable waters, it's a pier." *Hurston* interpreted Congress' intent regarding adjoining piers and waterways as "unlimited," so long as they adjoin navigable waters of the United States. The Ninth Circuit found that unlike "other adjoining areas," which the LHWCA qualified as requiring a maritime nexus, the facilities explicitly enumerated in Section 903 were unqualified. Accordingly, *Hurston* could be read to mean that anytime one is on an enumerated Section 903 structure actually adjoining navigable waters, situs could exist, whether the site has something to do with maritime commerce or not. This arguably ignores one of the Second Circuit's *Triguero* factors.

Further complicating matters, in *Brooker*, the Eleventh Circuit held that whether a pier is a maritime site is a pure factual question, since the LHWCA does not provide a clear definition. The Court found that the factual evidence in the record rendered the seawall in *Brooker* a non maritime site. Before the certiorari petition could be determined by the United States Supreme Court could be decided, the *Brooker* case settled and the conflict between *Fleischmann* and *Brooker* was no more, leaving practitioners adrift to determine which of the two tests best describes the "situs" law.

Because Section 903 qualifies "other adjoining areas" as those sites "customarily used by an employer in loading, unloading, repairing or building a vessel," the Circuits establish situs for non-enumerated sites not only by analyzing its *geographic nexus*, but its *maritime nexus* as well. Historically, the Circuits have been split in how they determined whether "other adjoining areas" satisfied the geographic nexus test. *Compare Texas Stevedore Co. v. Winchester*, 632 F.2d 504 (5th Cir. 1980) *with Sidwell v. Express Container Services, Inc.*, 71 F.3d 1134 (4th Cir. 1995). In *Winchester*, the Fifth Circuit interpreted "adjoining" under Section 903(a) to mean "neighboring." Consequently, under *Winchester*, "other adjoining areas" did not actually have to be physically located next to navigable waters in order to have the requisite geographic nexus. On the other hand, in *Sidwell*, the Fourth Circuit held that geographic nexus required that the site actually adjoin the waterfront.

The Fifth Circuit recently abrogated *Winchester* in *New Orleans Depot Servs. v. Dir., Office of Worker's Comp. Programs*, 718 F.3d 384 (5th Cir. 2013), after adopting the Fourth Circuit's geographic nexus rule from *Sidwell.* As a result, the Fifth Circuit found that a claimant, who worked repairing containers in an industrial park yard 300 yards from the Intracoastal Canal, did not satisfy the situs requirement because the work site was separated from the waterfront by various non maritime businesses.

The Eleventh Circuit still interprets "other adjoining areas" to mean those sites "neighboring" navigable waters. Regardless, it reached the same conclusion as the Fifth Circuit in *New Orleans Depot*, in the factually similar *Ramos v. Dir., OWCP*, 486 F. App'x 775 (11th Cir. 2012). Ramos injured himself while working at a facility where shipping containers were stored and repaired. The facility was located about three miles from a deepwater port. The Eleventh Circuit found that the facility was not *actually* adjacent to, nor was it in the vicinity of, navigable waters as its location was chosen based on general business factors and the businesses surrounding the facility were non maritime.

The decision in *Ramos* illustrates the Eleventh Circuit's preference for a fact-intensive geographic nexus analysis when interpreting whether a site is *adjoining* under the LHWCA. This position directly conflicts with holdings such as the one in *New Orleans Depot*, which embodies the Fourth and Fifth Circuit's preference for using a bright-line test when determining a sites geographic nexus to navigable waters. Despite the two opposing methods, *Ramsos* and *New Orleans Depot* also show that the fact-intensive and bright-line tests do not always yield contrary results.

Unlike the geographic nexus test, the Circuits' application of the maritime nexus test is fairly consistent across the board. In *O'Donnel v. Nautilus Marine Protection*, 48 BRBS 67 (2014), O'Donnel worked entirely on land fabricating a trash collection boom to be used in navigable waters. The work site was located approximately two miles south of the West Pacific Coast Highway Bridge and about four miles from the mouth of the river at Long Beach Harbor. O'Donnel sought compensation under the LHWCA after being hit by a falling 30-foot container, which resulted in the loss of both of his legs and significant internal injuries. The Ninth Circuit held that because the primary purpose of the boom was environmental, the employer's temporary facility lacked the sufficient maritime nexus to be a covered situs under the LHWCA. Similarly, in *Bianco v. Ga. Pac. Corp.*, 304 F.3d 1053 (11th Cir. 2002), Bianco injured herself while working as a knife operator at a gypsum products plant. The Eleventh Circuit held that the gypsum plant failed the maritime nexus test as no maritime activity occurred there.

The site must satisfy the maritime nexus test even where it actually adjoins navigable waters. In *BPU Mgmt. v. Dir., OWCP, DOL*, 732 F.3d 457 (5th Cir. 2013), Martin injured himself while working as a dock worker at a waterside ore processing facility. The entire facility directly adjoined navigable waters, which satisfied the geographic nexus test. The Fifth Circuit held, however, that Martin failed to satisfy the maritime nexus test because a functional inquiry showed that Martin's employer did not customarily use the area where he was injured for the unloading of vessels.

Another Fifth Circuit example of this is *Glob. Mgmt. Enters., LLC v. Commerce & Indus. Ins. Co.*, 574 F. App'x 333 (5th Cir. 2014). De La Cruz worked as a temporary worker assisting with clean-up efforts in and around the Gulf of Mexico after the Deepwater Horizon explosion and subsequent oil spill. He injured himself while lifting a bag of oil-laden sand that would later be loaded onto a truck and transferred to a vessel for removal. De La Cruz spent up to two hours actively loading and unloading the vessel at the pier, and six or seven hours cleaning the beaches. Similar to the Ninth Circuit's holding in *O'Donnel*, the Fifth Circuit found that De La Cruz's cleanup efforts to be more environmental than maritime in nature. In other words, the Fifth Circuit's functional inquiry indicated that the beachfront lacked the sufficient maritime nexus to be covered under the LHWCA.

In *Coastal Prod. Servs. v. Hudson*, 555 F.3d 426 (5th Cir. 2009), the Fifth Circuit found that a fixed offshore platform satisfied the maritime nexus test. Hudson worked as a junior contract platform operator on a fixed platform that connected to several satellite wells and a sunken oil storage barge named *The Cherokee*. The platform facilities housed the workers and refined the oil, the latter of which was transferred for storage onto *The Cherokee* until loaded onto transport vessels for carriage to customers. Hudson performed several duties while working on the platform including servicing and maintaining the satellite wells, platform, and *The Cherokee*, as well as loading oil from *The Cherokee* to transport vessels when needed. He was injured while working on the platform when a pump next to him exploded. He sought compensation under the LWHCA.

The Fifth Circuit noted that the platform did not meet any of the enumerated locals defined in the statute. Therefore, the platform had to qualify as an "other adjoining area" in order for the situs requirement to be satisfied. The court found that the platform passed the geographical nexus test because it was *actually* located next to navigable waters. However, in order to determine if the platform passed the maritime nexus test the court first had to define the relevant area subject to the court's analysis. The court used a functional inquiry when determining that the platform and *The Cherokee* combined to constitute the same overall area. Accordingly, the court held that the entire platform was used for the loading of a vessel, which satisfied the maritime nexus test.

Scenarios exist where courts could deny marine employees coverage under the LHWCA even when the injury occurred on a site with the requisite geographic and maritime nexus. In *Ace USA/ESIS v. Joseph Tracy*, 696 F.3d 835, 2014 AMC 804 (9th Cir. 2012), Tracy performed land-based longshore work in the ports of Singapore and a shipyard in Indonesia, where he organized a yard and made major repairs and modifications to equipment. Tracy also helped to load and unload trucks, barges, and vessels. He suffered a heart attack, which ended his employment. Tracy argued that his assignment to the ports of Singapore and Indonesia satisfied the situs test. The Ninth Circuit found that claimant did not satisfy the LHWCA's situs requirements while working in Singapore and Indonesia because the LHWCA does not apply extraterritorially. The Ninth Circuit stated that there was no evidence that Congress meant "navigable waters of the United States" to include territorial waters of foreign sovereigns. Moreover, there was no hint that Congress intended the landward reach of the term "navigable waters" to include the "adjoining pier, wharf, dry dock, terminal, building way, marine railway, or other adjoining area" of a foreign nation.

C. A Word About Bridge Workers

Are bridge workers working over navigable waters covered under the LHWCA? The answer turns on whether the worker qualifies as a maritime employee, and whether the bridge aids highway or maritime navigation. Maritime employees who work on bridges used as an aid for navigation are covered. Workers on bridges used primarily for vehicular traffic are not.

For example, a bridge worker who was injured while painting a bridge that was permanently affixed to land was not covered because the base of the bridge connected to land and did not touch any water. The BRB found that the work was land based and was not actually performed upon navigable waters even though the bridge spanned water. *Johnsen v. Orfamos Contractors, Inc.*, 25 BRBS 329 (1992).

In a Fourth Circuit case, a concrete finisher, whose purpose was to assist in the demolition and replacement of an existing bridge, was covered under the Act. Both the existing bridge and the new bridge contained a stationary section and a draw section that could be raised to allow water traffic to pass through. Therefore, the proposed bridge was intended to provide additional horizontal clearance to allow more space for use by vessels passing each other beneath the bridge, and to reduce the chance of vessel collision with the bridge. The evidence established that the new lift span was designed to be an aid to marine navigation. Therefore, the worker was covered. *Lemelle v. B.F. Diamond Construction Co.*, 674 F.2d 296 (4th Cir. 1982), cert. den. 459 US 1177 (1983).

Similarly, in *Collado v. City of N.Y.*, 2009 NY Slip Op 30207(U) (Sup. Ct.), Collado worked on a barge as part of a gang of dock builders installing panels on a bridge fender system. The fender system protected the bridge against damage caused by collisions with ships. During the course of his work, Collado lost his footing, fell into the water, and drowned. The court stated that because the fenders are used to protect the bridge and are an aid in navigation, the situs test was satisfied because the fenders qualified as an area *adjoining* navigable waters. The court noted that although bridge construction is not classically maritime work "under ancient traditions of the sea," it has long been merged with such work given the realities of modern coastal land and sea traffic.

Bridge worker claimants without LHWCA status are unable to recover even where the bridge aids in maritime navigation. In *James D. Hough v. Vimas Painting Co., Inc.*, BRB No. 10-0534, 2011 WL 2174854 (DOL Ben. Rev. Bd. May 24, 2011), Hough worked cleaning a bridge. He used a vacuum to suck up and deposit debris onto a barge for collection and storage until the bridge cleanup project was completed. The BRB relied on *Munguia v. Chevron U.S.A., Inc.*, 999 F.2d 808, 27 BRBS 103(CRT), *reh'g en banc denied*, 8 F.3d 24 (5th Cir. 1993), *cert. denied*, 511 U.S. 1086 (1994) when finding that the storage of collected debris did not "enable" the barge to "engage in maritime commerce." The BRB further held that Hough's role in vacuuming the debris was not integral to any maritime purpose as he was merely employed to clean the bridge.

2.2 Conclusion

As can be seen from the above cited decisions, the question of which workers are subject to Longshore Act jurisdiction is less than settled. Practitioners in this area are encouraged to ensure themselves of the state of the law in their particular jurisdictions and the latest case law from the Benefits Review Board. But be wary—the more one reads, the less a definitive coverage answer appears!

Chapter 3

Unique Aspects of the Nonappropriated Fund Instrumentalities Act[1]

Ruth Bennett Whitfield, Esq.

Synopsis

The Nonappropriated Fund Instrumentalities Act (NFIA)[2] is an extension of the Longshore and Harbor Workers Compensation Act (LHWCA).[3] For the most part the two Acts are congruent. However, due to the status of Nonappropriated Fund Instrumentalities (NAFIs) as federal entities, and the dissimilar nature of the work involved, there are vast legal and practical differences in the application of the Longshore Act to NAFIs.

A Nonappropriated Fund Instrumentality is a unique legal entity. Nonappropriated funds (NAFs) are government monies derived from sources other than congressional appropriations. These revenues primarily come from the sale of goods and services to authorized patrons, including Department of Defense military and civilian personnel and their dependents. These funds are used to support or provide essential morale, welfare, recreational activities, lodging, post restaurants, and certain religious and educational programs.[4]

A NAF Instrumentality (NAFI) is a fiscal entity of the U.S. Government that is supported in whole or in part by NAFs. As an instrumentality of the U.S. Government, NAFIs have the same privileges and immunities of the federal government unless specifically waived.[5]

For the purposes of the NFIA, the primary NAFIs, in alphabetical order are:

- Army & Air Force Exchange Service (The Exchange) (https://www.shopmyexchange.com/);
- Army Morale, Welfare and Recreation (Army MWR): http://www.armymwr.com);
- Coast Guard Exchange System & MWR (CGX) (http://www.cg-exchange.com/);
- Marine Corps Community Services (http://www.usmc-mccs.org/):
- Navy Exchange Service Command (https://www.mynavyexchange.com/;
- Navy MWR (www.navymwr.org/); and
- USAF Services (http://www.usafservices.com/).

3.1 NAFI Employees

A. Diverse Workforce and Employment

The difference in the nature of the employment between a NAFI employee and a traditional Longshore employee is tremendous. As an example, the very types of employees that would be excluded from coverage under Section 2(3) of the Longshore Act—i.e., anyone who performs work that is exclusively ***clerical***, ***secretarial***, security, or ***data processing***, along with those who are employed by ***club***, ***camp***, ***recreational operation***, ***museum***, or ***retail outlet***—are by contrast, typical NAFI employees in both the U.S. and abroad.

Specifically, the NFIA extends the LHWCA to cover an employee of a Nonappropriated Fund Instrumentality, paid with NAF funds as described by 5 U.S.C. § 2105(c).[6] The names of various NAFIs include, but are not limited to the Army and Air Force Exchange Service, Navy exchanges, Marine Corp exchanges, and Coast Guard exchanges. Also included are "other instrumentalities of the United States under the jurisdiction of the armed forces conducted for the comfort, pleasure, contentment, and mental and physical improvement of personnel of the armed forces …."[7] Many of those NAFIs are traditionally referred to as Morale, Welfare and Recreation (MWR), services.

NAFI employees are so diverse their attorneys often mistake them for state act employees. NAFIs typically operate department stores, gas stations, convenience stores, military clothing sales, recreation centers, day cares, bowling alleys, golf courses, hotels, RV and campgrounds, enlisted and officer clubs, along with restaurants and literally dozens of different food chains. Some NAFIs have their own trucking fleets, distributions centers, credit cards, and call centers. This gives NAFIs the unique ability to bring many of their injured employees back to work at a much higher rate than in a traditional maritime setting.

B. Unique Job Retention and Leave Benefits

Another somewhat unique provision of NAFI employment is the governmental nature of its benefits. For instance, many employees retain employment rights for a set number of days after they go on Leave Without Pay (LWOP), typically for a very generous period and always set by regulation. Depending on how much leave an individual has accrued and whether the NAFI allows, whether the employee chooses to supplement workers' compensation with accrued leave, the time can also vary. It is not unheard of for an employee to have several hundred hours of accrued sick leave. While vacation leave is more limited, on average it is much higher than the private sector. Accordingly, an employee may receive full pay while on compensation and have protected rights to continued employment.

Some rights may generate from bargaining agreements, while others may be standard. One such policy is separation from leave without pay over a certain amount of time. The fact that an employee is separated for such a policy, as is every other employee out of leave, whether a workers' compensation claimant or not, is not discriminatory.[8]

C. Non-Citizen and Non-Resident Employees

Any NAFI employee, regardless of nationality, who is injured or killed while working within the continental U.S. (CONUS) is covered under the Act. However, if the employee is injured or killed outside the continental U.S. (OCONUS), which includes Hawaii, the employee ***must be either a citizen of the U.S. or a permanent resident of the U.S. or a territory or possession thereof***. If not, Section 8172 of the NFIA, provides that "compensation shall be provided in accordance with regulations prescribed by the Secretary of the military department concerned and approved by the Secretary of Defense or regulations prescribed by the Secretary of Transportation, as the case may be."[9] There is no jurisdiction under the Act for these employees.[10]

D. Volunteers

By special statute, NAFIs may accept volunteers who are providing services allowed under 10 U.S.C. § 1588. There are no reported cases calculating the average weekly wage of a NAFI volunteer. However, 10 U.S.C. § 1588(d)(4), provides for the calculation to be based on an average monthly wage, using the average monthly hours volunteered multiplied by the minimum wage according to the Fair Labor Standards Act of 1938.

E. Only Civilian Workers Covered

While volunteers may be covered, military members are not. The Act was written to provide coverage only for "civilian employees." It is not uncommon for military members to work at some NAFIs while off-duty. In *Hardgrove v. Coast Guard Exchange System*,[11] 37 BRBS 21 (2003), the Benefits Review Board held that military personnel in off-duty hours are excluded from the definition of employee. The Board reasoned that Congress did not mean to cover military members by changing the wording in the statute from "civilian employees" to "employees" as a part of the 1966 amendments.[12]

3.2 Course and Scope of Employment

A. Parking Lot Claims

Generally, when the injury occurs outside the time and space boundaries of employment, the claim is not compensable pursuant to the "coming and going rule."[13] While the "coming and going" rule is not unique to NFIA claims, the fact that there are so many cases that center on parking lots and sidewalks, makes it worth discussing. These so called "parking lot claims" are generally very fact specific. As NAFIs typically do not own the facilities in which they operate; there may be varying degrees, if any, of responsibility for the premises in or around the facility.

The U.S. Supreme Court has recognized exceptions to the "coming and going rule" where "the hazards of the journey may fairly be regarded as hazards of the service." *Cardillo v. Liberty Mutual Ins. Co.*[14] Under *Cardillo*,[15] there are recognized exceptions to the coming and going rule which include: a. Employer pays for the travel or furnishes the transportation; b. Employer controls the journey; c. Employee is on a special errand; and d. Employee is subject to emergency calls.[16]

In *Harris v. England Air Force Base Nonappropriated Fund Financial Management Branch*,[17] the employee slipped on a crack in the parking lot after leaving work, and severely injured herself. In *Cantrell v. Base Restaurant, Wright-Patterson Air Force Base*,[18] the employee slipped on a sidewalk on her way in to work, while about one half block away from the building.

Neither employer owned or controlled the premises where the respective claimants were injured. Neither employee was required to park in a specific area. Neither employee was on duty. No exception to the coming and going rule was found and benefits were denied.

Similarly, in *S.R. v. Air Force Insurance Fund*,[19] a daycare employee came to work, while on leave, to speak with a supervisor about light duty. She parked in an area reserved for parents and was asked to move. While doing so she slipped and fell, breaking her wrist. Employer did not own the lot. The ALJ granted summary judgment finding the claimant was on a personal errand. He specifically noted that Claimant was on leave and that moving her car was not a "special errand" for the employer so as to cause an exception to the coming and going rule.[20]

By contrast, exercising significant control over an area, even if it is not owned, can cause a court to find it to be part of one's premises for the purposes of coverage under the Act. In the case of *Shivers v. Navy Exchange*,[21] the employer did not own the area where the employee was injured. However, the Fourth Circuit distinguished the cases of *Harris*[22] and *Cantrell*[23] and noted that the level of control exercised by the Navy Exchange caused the parking lot to be its own premises.

The Court also noted that when an employee, with fixed hours, is on an employer's premises and is injured going to and from work, the injury is normally compensable and is not precluded by the "coming and going" rule.[24]

In determining that the employer controlled the lot to a degree that it became a part of its premises, the Court noted that the Navy Exchange: 1. Designated the lot as an employee only lot, including posing signs indicating the parking restrictions and warning of enforcement measures against violators; 2. Issued decals to its employees permitting them to park in the lot; 3. Employed persons to patrol the lot and to tow cars illegally parked there; 4. Prohibited its employees from parking in the customer lot unless the employee lot was full; 5. Mowed the grass on the median strip where the claimant slipped; 6. Removed trash from the parking lot and operated a street sweeper to clean both the employee and customer lots; and 7. Salted sidewalks leading to the employee parking lot when it snowed.[25]

Even in *Shivers*[26] though, the Court noted that not all such cases were properly compensable. Only those in which an employer took such control that the premises were its own. The Fourth Circuit cautioned that:

> Our holding is not sweeping. We do not suggest that LHWCA provides workers' compensation for all injuries suffered in parking lots used by employees. Navy Exchange's direction and control of its employee-designated parking lot, however, persuade us that the lot should be considered part of the employer's premises.[27]

In *Trimble v. Army and Air Force Exchange Service*,[28] a BRB case decided shortly after *Shivers*,[29] the Board reversed the ALJ's denial of benefits, and found an exception to the "coming and going" rule. The Board found that the employer controlled the journey when an employee was injured falling on an icy sidewalk, just adjacent to the employee-designated door, outside the building on her way into work. In reciting the evidence, the Board noted that along with the location of her fall, to reach the door she parked in the employee parking lot which she was instructed to do so by management. The employer maintained the sidewalk where she fell by salting it during icy conditions. The Board also noted patrons would not have entered the employee only entrance. All of this was enough to create control of the journey.[30]

In the 2012 case of *Sidney Webster v. Army Central Insurance Fund*,[31] ALJ Odegard found that the employer had not exercised such control to make the parking lot its own premises. While its employees, including the claimant, would pick up trash, sticks and rocks from the parking lot and common areas on a random basis, the parking lot was shared by others on base and was under the care and control of the U.S. Army. The claimant also admitted he was not forced to park in the lot and had no assigned spot. The judge found that the employer's control amounted to "nothing more than beautification on an occasional or incidental basis."[32]

3.3 Exclusive Remedy

Title 5 USC § 8173 is express in its limitation of liability in making this the exclusive remedy for disability or death.[33] This is another distinction due to the NAFI's federal status. NAFIs are recognized as government entities, entitled to sovereign immunity.[34] Courts have long held that immunity must be strictly construed in favor of the sovereign.[35] As such, while private employers may be subject to concurrent jurisdiction under the Longshore Act, that is not the case under the NFIA.[36] Likewise, in *Villanova v. United States*,[37] the claimant's medical malpractice suit against the military medical facility was barred because he had entered into a Section 8(i) settlement with his NAFI employer.

In 1997, in *Kinder v. Crawford & Co.*,[38] an employee of the Navy Exchange, tried unsuccessfully to bring a diversity action seeking bad faith damages through a Puerto Rico statute. The local tort law claim was dismissed.

Sovereign immunity extends to the issuances of subpoenas by state entities. It is also complicated by the fact that NAFIs and their employees are covered by the Privacy Act of 1974.[39]

A. NAFI Employees Not Covered by the DBA

Understandably, there may be confusion at times as to whether NAFI employees may be covered under the Defense Base Act (DBA).[40] The NFIA and the DBA are both extensions of the Longshore Act. Both Acts cover employees who work on military facilities and employers who have operations there. Both employers have civilian employees. However, claimants covered under the NFIA are not covered by the DBA.[41] Likewise, there is no "zone of special danger" doctrine recognized under the NFIA Act.[42]

Simply stated, NAFIs are instrumentalities of the government; an actual part of the Department of Defense, Homeland Security, or whatever the case may be. On the other hand, Defense Base Act employers are contractors with the government. The contractor may or may not be doing business with the government at any given time depending on the length and terms of a contract.

There are sometimes NFIA claims mistakenly categorized as DBA claims, and assigned "LDA" (a designation given to DBA cases) in its case number at the Office of Administrative Judges (OALJ) level. This can occur if Claimant's Counsel improperly designates the case from the beginning. In this writer's experience, these are easily corrected upon motion of the parties to the National Headquarters of the OALJ, or with the presiding ALJ if the case has already been referred to a district office.

3.4 Minimum Compensation Rate

Unlike traditional LHWCA, Outer Continental Shelf Lands Act (OCSLA) and DBA jobs, NAFI employment has a high percentage of service related, part-time and intermittent jobs. This often results in a lower average weekly wage and corresponding compensation rate. Not surprisingly, in 2015, the Benefits Review Board addressed the "newly awarded compensation" issue in the minimum compensation rate case of *Montoya v. Navy Exchange*,[43] the other end of spectrum from *Roberts v. Sea-Land Services, Inc.*,[44] a maximum compensation rate case.

In *Montoya*,[45] the claimant was injured in September of 2006, but was only partially disabled until November of 2006. The Board upheld the ALJ's finding that pursuant to *Roberts*,[46] Section 906(b)(2) provides for the minimum compensation rate at the time of temporary total disability, not at the time of injury and she was entitled to the rate increase in October 2006.

3.5 Anti-Alienation of Benefits

While it is too early to tell if the 1998 case of *Moyle v. Director, OWCP*[47] will be the eventual demise of the Anti-Alienation provisions of Section 16 with respect to garnishment for child and spousal support, it is clear times are changing. The language the Section 16 of the Longshore Act provides that benefits are free from "levy, execution, and attachment or other remedy for recovery or collection of a debt, which exemption may not be waived."[48] LHWCA employers operated with the clear understanding of a strict interpretation of the anti-alienation provision of the Act.[49] Even if the exemption cannot be waived, the courts seem to be slowly finding a way around the definitions.

In *Moyle v. Director, OWCP*[50] the Ninth Circuit upheld the summary judgment of the administrative law judge allowing garnishment of benefits being paid by the Special Fund of the U.S. Department of Labor.[51] The Court noted that the issue was whether the Social Security Administration (SSA) garnishment provisions of 42 U.S.C. § 659(a) had impliedly repealed the Anti-Alienation provision of Section 16 of the Longshore Act and found it had.

The Court found the SSA garnishment provisions allow for garnishment of "moneys (the entitlement to which is based upon remuneration for employment) due from, or payable by, the United States or the District of Columbia (including any agency, subdivision, or instrumentality thereof) (42 U.S.C. § 659(a);"[52] Likewise, the Office of Personnel Management promulgated 5 CFR § 581.103(c)(5) specifically to provide for garnishment of LHWCA benefits. The Court noted Special Fund payments, while financed by private employers, are "payable by the United States because the Treasurer is under an obligation to tender payments due…"[53]

What has now become significant is Moyle's then somewhat reaching language implying that LHWCA benefits, even from private sector employers, could be subject to garnishment as the LHWCA is a statute created by the federal government. To do so it had to rely on OPM's promulgated regulations.[54]

There are no reported NFIA decisions; however, the SSA provisions specifically list any "instrumentality" of the U.S., which would include NAFIs. This writer has dealt with garnishment issues in which OWCP Districts were most likely unaware of the legal status of NAFIs and thus did not initially apply *Moyle*.[55] However, that recommendation changed after an explanation of the circumstances, including the Garnishment section of the OWCP's own Policy Manual. Chapter 6-203 Subpart 11 of the Policy Manual allows garnishment of:

> "Notwithstanding any other provision of law... ***moneys*** (the entitlement to which is based upon remuneration for employment) ***due from, or payable by, the United States*** or the District of Columbia (including any agency, subdivision, ***or instrumentality thereof***) (42 U.S.C. § 659(a)." (emphasis added).

Courts in Florida, and now more recently Pennsylvania, have relied on longstanding definitions of child and spousal support to determine the definition of "debt" and "creditor" to determine if the anti-alienation provisions of Section 16 of the Longshore Act would apply.[56] Even more significant is the fact that, in the case 2014 case of *Uveges v Uveges*,[57] the court looked to *Moyle*[58] for the basis that private sector employees can be subject to garnishment.[59]

Given the public pressure against nonpayment of child support, there may eventually be less difference between government and private recipients of compensation benefits. There have now been two states to address the issue of garnishment of private sector benefits and both allowed it. The question becomes how soon will other state courts follow?

3.6 Appellate Jurisdiction

The very fact that the NFIA, like the DBA, covers employees beyond the U.S. is a distinction from the LHWCA. In addition, the plain language of 5 U.S.C. § 8171(d) provides for a different path for instituting judicial actions under Sections 18 and 21 if a claimant is injured or killed outside the continental United States (OCONUS), which would include Hawaii. Since instances under Section 18 are rare for NAFIs, this paper will focus on Section 21.

The DBA, enacted in 1941 and the NFIA, enacted in 1952, but amended several times since then, have very similar appeal provisions. The NFIA provides that an appeal shall be "instituted in the district court within the territorial jurisdiction of which is located the office of the deputy commissioner having jurisdiction with respect to the injury or death."[60]

Similarly, the DBA provides states that an appeal shall be "instituted in the United States district court of the judicial district wherein is located the office of the deputy commissioner whose compensation order is involved if his office is located in a judicial district, and if not so located, such judicial proceedings such judicial proceeding shall be instituted in the judicial district nearest the base at which the injury or death occurs."[61]

There are no reported NFIA cases. With respect to DBA cases, there is a split in the circuits on the issue as to whether appeal the "as amended" language in Section 1 of the DBA meant to include the amendments to Sections 18 and 21 of the LHWCA which occurred in 1972.

In its 2012 decision in *Truczinskas v. Director, OWCP*,[62] the First Circuit ruled on the side of direct appeal to the circuit court, as would be the case under Section 21 of the LHWCA. This places the Court in line with the Second,[63] Seventh and Ninth Circuits.[64]

The Court in Truczinskas noted,

> [t]he "as amended" language in section 1 of the DBA has been regularly read to mean that the DBA would incorporate "not only the version of the [Longshore Act] in force at the time the DBA was enacted, but all subsequent LHWCA amendments as well." ...Thus, presumptively a change Congress thinks suitable for the Longshore Act also applies to the DBA, unless otherwise provided in the new Longshore Act amendment. And Congress included no such provision precluding application to the DBA when, in 1972, it amended the Longshore Act to modernize the ordinary scheme for awarding compensation.[65]

The Court acknowledged the split in the circuits, namely the contrary rulings of the Fourth, Fifth, Sixth and Eleventh Circuits that hold the express language of the Act specifies judicial action to be instituted in the district court.[66] However, the Court's argument was that Congress seemingly overlooked the DBA and that the DBA could legitimately be read to confer such jurisdiction given Congress' overall intent in amending the LHWCA in 1972. Likewise, the Court made the assumption that the case would have ended up with them anyway and determined there would be efficiencies in bypassing the district courts.[67]

While like the DBA, the NFIA was enacted prior to the 1972 amendments to the LHWCA, unlike the DBA, Congress did amend the language of the NFIA in as recently as 1996 and addressed judicial proceedings.[68] Congress specifically removed the "as amended" language while keeping the distinction between cases arising OCONUS. Since Congress had the opportunity to, but did not, align the NFIA with the Longshore Act appeals process, this conceivably removes some argument for aligning the process. To do so would require the court to specifically determine it had the right to act even when Congress itself had done so. Accordingly, it could create a distinction between both DBA and LHWCA cases.

3.7 Representation

The Department of Justice, through the U.S. Attorney's Office represents the Federal Government in any matter in litigation. NAFIs have staff counsel, or retain defense counsel, to represent them in administrative proceedings before the Department of Labor through the Benefits Review Board level. If a claim is appealed to a district court, or a court of appeal, the Department of Justice, must represent the NAFI.[69] However, the NAFIs have also had their own staff counsel appointed as designated Special Assistant United States Attorney for the purpose of representing the NAFI on a case by case basis.

Endnotes

1. The opinions stated herein are solely those of Ms. Bennett Whitfield and not those of the Army and Air Force Exchange Service, any military departments, the Department of Defense, or the United States Government.
2. 5 U.S.C. § 8171 *et seq.*
3. 33 U.S.C. § 901 *et seq.*
4. DoD 7000.14-R, Volume 13, Chapter 1, 010213.
5. DoD 7000.14-R, Volume 13, Chapter 1, 010214.
6. 5 U.S.C. § 8172.
7. 5 U.S.C. § 2105(c).
8. *William Carson v. AAFES*, 25 BRBS 298 (ALJ) (1991).
9. 5 U.S.C. § 8172; See also *Army and Air Force Exchange Service v. Hanson*, 360 F. Supp 258 (D. Haw. 1970).
10. *Army and Air Force Exchange Service v. Hanson*, 360 F. Supp 258 (D. Haw. 1970).
11. *Hardgrove v. Coast Guard Exchange System*, 37 BRBS 21 (2003).
12. *Hardgrove v. Coast Guard Exchange System* at 24–25.
13. *Cardillo v. Liberty Mutual Ins. Co.*, 330 U.S. 469 (1947).
14. *Cardillo* at 479.
15. *Id.*
16. *Id.*
17. *Harris v. England Air Force Base Nonappropriated Fund Financial Management Branch*, 23 BRBS 175 (1990).
18. *Cantrell v. Base Restaurant, Wright-Patterson Air Force Base*, 22 BRBS 372 (1989).
19. *S.R. v. Air Force Insurance Fund*, 43 BRBS 120 (ALJ)(2009).
20. *S.R. v. Air Force Insurance Fund*, 43 BRBS 120, 123 (ALJ)(2009).
21. *Shivers v. Navy Exchange, Director, Office of Workers' Compensation Programs, United States Department of Labor*, 144 F.3d 322, 32 BRBS 99(CRT) (4th Cir. 1998).
22. *Harris v. England Air Force Base Nonappropriated Fund Financial Management Branch*, 23 BRBS 175 (1990).
23. *Cantrell v. Base Restaurant, Wright-Patterson Air Force Base*, 22 BRBS 372 (1989).
24. *Shivers*, at 324 citing 1 Arthur Larson & Lex K. Larson, *Larson's Workers' Compensation Law* § 15.00 (1997) and *Durrah v. Washington Metro. Area Transit Author*, 760 F.2d 322, 324 (D.C. Cir. 1985).
25. *Id.*
26. *Id.*
27. *Id.* at 325.
28. *Trimble v. Army and Air Force Exchange Service*, 32 BRBS 239 (1998).
29. *Shivers v. Navy Exchange, Director, Office of Workers' Compensation Programs, United States Department of Labor*, 144 F.3d 322, 32 BRBS 99(CRT) (4th Cir. 1998).
30. *Trimble*, at 239.

31. *Sidney Webster v. Army Central Insurance Fund*, 46 BRBS 331(ALJ) (2012).

32. *Id.* at 282.

33. *Atkinson v. Gates Mc Donald & Co.*, 838 F.2d 808 (5th Cir. Miss 1988).

34. *Standard Oil Company of California v. Johnson*, 316 U.S. 481 (1942).

35. *McMahon v. United States*, 342 U.S. 25, 27 (1951).

36. *Air Force Central Welfare Fund v. Henderson*, 1971 OK 46 (Okla. 1971).

37. *Villanova v. United States*, 851 F.2d 1 (1st Cir. 1988).

38. *Kinder v. Crawford & Co.*, 962 F. Supp. 10 (D.P.R. 1997).

39. 5 U.S.C. § 552a.

40. 42 U.S.C. § 1651 *et seq.*

41. *A.P. [Panaganiban] v. Navy Exchange Service Command*, 43 BRBS 123 (2009).

42. *Harris v. England Air Force Base Nonappropriated Fund Financial Management Branch*, 23 BRBS 175 (1990).

43. *Dolores Montoya v. Navy Exchange Service Command*, 49 BRBS 51 (2015).

44. *Roberts v. Sea-Land Services, Inc.*, 132 S.Ct. 1350, 46 BRBS 15 (CRT) (2012).

45. *Dolores Montoya v. Navy Exchange Service Command*, 49 BRBS 51 (2015).

46. *Roberts v. Sea-Land Services, Inc.*, 132 S.Ct. 1350, 46 BRBS 15 (CRT) (2012).

47. *Moyle v. Director, OWCP*, 147 F.3d 1116 (9th Cir. 1998), *cert. denied* 526 U.S. 1064 (1999).

48. 33 U.S.C. § 916.

49. *Thibodeaux v. Thibodeaux*, 454 So. 2d 813 (La. 1984).

50. *Moyle v. Director, OWCP*, 147 F.3d 1116 (9th Cir. 1998), *cert. denied* 526 U.S. 1064 (1999).

51. 33 U.S.C. § 944.

52. 42 U.S.C. § 659.

53. *Moyle v. Director, OWCP*, at 1121–1122.

54. *Cigna Prop. & Cas. v. Ruiz*, 834 So. 2d. 234 (Fla. Dist. Ct. App 3d Dist. 2002), *affirmed* 85 Fed. Appx. 726 (11 Cir. Fla. 2003), *cert. denied* 541 U.S. 937 (2004); *Uveges v. Uveges*, 103 A.3d 825 (Pa. Super. Ct. 251 2014), *denied* 114 A.3d 1041, 2015 Pa. LEXIS 901 (Pa., 2015), US Supreme Court *cert. denied* 193 L. Ed. 2d 427, 84 U.S.L.W. 3299 (U.S., Nov. 30, 2015); *Moyle v. Director, OWCP*, at 1121–1122.

55. *Moyle v. Director, OWCP*, 147 F.3d 1116 (9th Cir. 1998), *cert. denied* 526 U.S. 1064 (1999).

56. *Cigna Prop. & Cas. v. Ruiz*, 834 So. 2d. 234 (Fla. Dist. Ct. App 3d Dist. 2002), *affirmed* 85 Fed. Appx. 726 (11 Cir. Fla. 2003), *cert. denied* 541 U.S. 937 (2004); *Uveges v. Uveges*, 103 A.3d 825 (Pa. Super. Ct. 251 2014), *denied* 114 A.3d 1041, 2015 Pa. LEXIS 901 (Pa., 2015), US Supreme Court *cert. denied* 193 L. Ed. 2d 427, 84 U.S.L.W. 3299 (U.S., Nov. 30, 2015).

57. *Uveges v. Uveges*, 103 A.3d 825 (Pa. Super. Ct. 251 2014), *denied* 114 A.3d 1041, 2015 Pa. LEXIS 901 (Pa., 2015), US Supreme Court *certiorari denied* 193 L. Ed. 2d 427, 84 U.S.L.W. 3299 (U.S., Nov. 30, 2015).

58. *Moyle v. Director, OWCP*, 147 F.3d 1116 (9th Cir. 1998), *cert. denied* 526 U.S. 1064 (1999).

59. *Uveges v. Uveges*, at 829; *Moyle v. Director, OWCP*, at 1121–1122.

60. 5 U.S.C. § 8171(d).

61. 42 U.S.C. § 1653(b).

62. *Truczinskas v. Dir., OWCP*, 699 F.3d 672, (1st Cir. 2012).

63. *Serv. Emples. Int'l, Inc. v. Dir., OWCP*, 595 F.3d 447 (2d Cir. 2010).

64. *Pierce v. Director, OWCP*, 603 F.2d 763 (9th Cir. 1979), *transferred*, 647 F.2d 716 (7th Cir. 1981).

65. *Truczinskas*, at 674.

66. *Lee v. Boeing Co., Inc.*, 123 F.3d 801 (4th Cir. 1997); *AFIA/CIGNA Worldwide v. Felkner*, 930 F.2d 1111 (5th Cir. 1991), *cert. denied*, 502 U.S. 906 (1991) ; and Home *Indemnity Co. v. Stillwell*, 597 F.2d 87 (6th Cir. 1979), *cert. denied*, 444 U.S. 869 (1979); See also *HB Zachry v. Quinones*, 206 F.3d 474 (5th Cir. 2000).

67. *Truczinskas*, at 676.

68. National Defense Authorization Act for Fiscal Year1996, 1996 Enacted S. 1124, 104 Enacted S. 1124, 110 Stat. 186.

69. 28 U.S.C. § 516.

Chapter 4

The Defense Base Act and War Hazards Compensation Act

Roger A. Levy, Esq.

Synopsis

4.1 The Defense Base Act ("DBA")

For those who believe that the LHWCA serves only to cover workers engaged in maritime commerce on the coasts and other navigable waters of this great country, the past 20 years or so have been an eye-opener regarding the Act's Defense Base Act extension and have led to what this writer describes as a classic case of "the tail wagging the dog". Beginning with the war in Bosnia and Kosovo in the 1990s and continuing through today in the Middle East and Afghanistan, domestic and foreign workers covered by the DBA and WHCA extensions have far outstripped those employed under traditional coverage of the LHWCA. Predictably, this has led to a great administrative burden for the Office of Workers Compensation Programs ("OWCP") and Office of Administrative Law Judges ("OALJ").

While these developments have been the subject of much written material[1] and industry conference discussion during the past two decades, this chapter will attempt to summarize and highlight the coverage, interplays and differences between these acts.

The Defense Base Act ("DBA") (42 USC 1651 et seq) has been with us since 1941. Not surprisingly, with war clouds already darkening Europe and the Pacific with the United States' involvement a virtual certainty, Congress thought it best to have in place a comprehensive workers compensation scheme that would cover all civilian workers employed pursuant to government contracts regardless of their state of hire or duration of overseas employment. In short, they pre-empted and balanced the playing field for employers and workers alike. It is "...exclusive and in place of all other liability of such employer..." (42 USC 1651(c)). As we shall explore further on in this chapter, they added the War Hazards Compensation Act ("WHCA") a year later to complement the DBA and encourage employers to hire and insurers to underwrite in this risky business.

In the preamble to the Act congress provided that "*Except as herein modified*, the provisions of the LHWCA... as amended, shall apply in respect of to the injury or death of any employee...". (my emphasis).

A. Coverage

The DBA "...shall apply in respect to the injury or death of *any employee engaged in any employment—*" (my emphasis) at certain locations and under certain prescribed conditions which total: six. All are situs intensive. That is, the employment must, except in very limited circumstances, occur over seas. The six can be found in the DBA at 42 USC 1651(a)(1)-(6) and are summarized as follows:

1. At any military, air or naval base acquired after January 1, 1940 by the United Sates
2. Upon lands occupied or used by the United States for military or naval purposes
3. Upon any public work in any Territory or possession outside the continental United States under the contract of a contractor or subcontractor with the United States
4. Under a contract entered into with the United States where such contract is to be performed outside the continental United States and at places not within the areas described in 1, 2 or 3 above for the purpose of engaging in public work

1. For example, the *Defense Base Act and War Hazards Compensation Act Handbook*, 2013 edition, LexisNexis, Roger A. Levy editor-in-chief, is very comprehensive on a variety of DBA and WHCA subjects.

5. Under a contract approved and financed by the United States where such contract is to be performed outside the continental United States under the Mutual Security act of 1954
6. Outside the United States by an American employer providing welfare or similar services for the benefit of the Armed Forces

The full text of these subparagraphs are lengthy and would not be appropriate for this text. The author recommends reading them in their entirety if greater detail is required or reviewing the chapter on coverage in the aforementioned *Defense Base Act and War Hazards Compensation Act Handbook.*

B. LHWCA vs. DBA—Vive La Difference!

When it comes to compensation, medical care and death benefits afforded workers covered under the DBA, except for calculation of AWW and minimum compensation rates, the LHWCA and DBA are the same. However, there are differences, especially for foreign workers and their dependents, that separate the DBA from its senior cousin.

1. American and Canadian vs. other foreign residents—42 USC 1652(b)

American and Canadian workers are afforded some protection vs. other foreign workers by virtue of their nationality or residency. This subsection shields the worker from the potentially harsh result flowing from the carrier's right to seek a commutation and reduction of benefits it can utilize against non American and Canadian residents. The statutory language allows a carrier to reduce the amount of an LHWCA award of permanent and total disability, 33 USC 908(c)(21) permanent partial disability or death benefit award by a present value reduction utilizing a statutory present value rate and then further reduction of that product by 50%. A similar provision exists in the LHWCA at 33 USC 909(g). This seemingly "good neighbor policy" does not apply south of the border to Mexican nationals though.

Unfortunately, there is little or no guidance within the LHWCA or DBA to determine who is an alien, non-national or resident for the purposes of calculating the Sec. 1652(b) commutation. The word "resident" may take on a special legal meaning in some areas of the law such as in immigration where "resident alien" is defined but that is not the case when comes to Sec. 1652(b). In 2001 the Benefits Review Board decided a case under the aforementioned LHWCA section involving a Greek citizen who was a resident of the U.S. at the time of her husband's death as a covered LHWCA worker. About a year after the commencement of benefits the widow returned to Greece. Some twenty years later the carrier sought a commutation which was granted. The Board found that the relevant time was at the time the commutation was sought rather than the date of the event giving rise to liability. {*see Logara v. Jackson Engineering Co.* 35 BRBS 83(20010]. This infers that "resident" refers to physical status at the time commutation is sought as opposed to one where official action has taken place by the U.S. or Canadian governments. However, it is doubtful that if a widow or widower who is an American citizen moved permanently somewhere other than Canada, a commutation could be successfully procured.

2. Computation of benefits on account of injury or death

The aforementioned *Defense Base Act and War Hazards Compensation Act Handbook* contains an excellent and lengthy chapter on AWW in DBA cases authored by Richard Garelick. This is an attempt to summarize that material.

Section 1651(a)provides that there shall be no minimum for the purpose of calculating average weekly wages ("AWW") for compensation or death benefits as otherwise covered in the LHWCA. This provision seems straightforward, and in fact was applied in a straightforward way for decades. However, the rise in civilian support to do much of the work historically performed by the military following the invasions of Afghanistan and Iraq with concomitant increase in DBA claims, has led to much administrative and judicial strain to make sense of a complicated AWW situation. (See the chapter in this text book on calculating AWW for an overall discussion of the subject.)

LHWCA section 910 describes 3 methods for analyzing earnings for the purpose of computing average weekly wage. Subparagraph (a) prescribes the method for calculating AWW for 5 and 6 day a week earners who "... shall have worked in the employment in which he was working at the time of the injury, whether for the same or another employer, during substantially the whole of the year immediately preceding his injury..." (Sec. 910(a)).

Subparagraph (b) provides the method for calculating AWW for workers who "shall not have worked for substantially the whole of the year" preceding injury.

Subparagraph (c) says that if either (a) or (b) "...cannot fairly and reasonably be applied, such average annual earnings shall be such sum as, having regard to the previous earnings of the injured employee in the employment in which he was working at the time of he injury,...or other employment of such employee, including the reasonable value of the services of the employee engaged in self employment, shall reasonably represent the annual earning capacity of the injured employee".

Historically, LHWCA claims primarily involved workers in stevedoring, ship building and harbor work where wages were fairly steady with some gradual increases due to typical conditions in the work place such as newly negotiated contracts, acquisition of seniority and the typical ups and downs associated with the economy and the industry in general. For most workers employed under DBA covered employment prior to 2003, the circumstances were much the same. However the rule, as opposed to the exception, in DBA covered work during 2003 and forward commonly found workers employed under contracts which provided wages four and five times above the annual average of his/her previous life time annual average. In addition, these employments often required individuals to work 7 days a week. Not surprisingly, this attempt to "put a round peg into a square hole" led to a series of appellate level decisions dealing with the issue.

The reported cases have addressed primarily how to compute AWW for workers whose injuries or deaths occurred after being on the job less than an entire year of employment. It should be readily apparent that the quoted parts of LHWCA subparagraphs (a) and (b) don't fit. That leads us to the catch-all subparagraph (c) which directs us to determine what reasonably represents the annual earning capacity. Virtually all of employers' arguments have been based on the claimed unfairness resulting in the "spike in earnings" occasioned by the DBA covered employment contracts.

Chronologically, the first case of note and followed for several years was an administrative law judge decision adopted by the Benefits Review Board in an unpublished decision. (See *Zimmerman v. Service Employees International Inc.*, 39 BRBS 166 (ALJ) (2005), *aff'd*, BRB No. 05-580 (2006) (unpublished).) This decision employed the "contract wage approach" which took into account the prospective wages under the employee's contract when the injury occurred only 7 weeks into the contract and the substantial employment for the non-DBA covered work in the year before injury were dramatically lower. The requirements were threefold. First the employee shall have not worked in same or similar employment for the whole of the preceding year, and shall have worked in a war zone, and it was likely that the employee would have completed a year's work under the contract.

Next the Benefits Review Board took up the question of whether an administrative law judge had abused his broad discretion in refusing to use LHWCA Section 910(a) and used the Section 910(c) contract wage approach when the state-side job was similar to the DBA covered work but did not include managerial duties. (See *Proffitt v. Service Employees International, Inc.*, 40 BRBS 41 (2006). He found that it had not. The BRB affirmed.

Then came in *K.S. v. Service Employees International, Inc.* (41 BRBS 641 (ALJ) (2007). There, the employee worked only 6.7 weeks as a truck driver which was his job domestically but at much lower wages before suffering injury in Iraq. The employer urged the administrative law judge to utilize a blended approach taking into account earnings of the employee before deployment and coupling those with the higher wages enjoyed in the brief period of overseas work. The judge accepted employer's argument that the attrition rate for truck drivers in Iraq was so high that it would not be fair to use the contract wage approach as it was not reasonable to assume the worker would have worked an entire year. The Benefits Review Board reversed stating that the administrative law judge was wrong in taking this approach. While never taken up by the 5th Circuit Court of Appeals, the Benefits review Board decision was vacated by the Southern District Court of Texas (the proper 1st level of appeal after a Benefits Review Board decision in this circuit) stating that the Board's decision had deprived the administrative law judge of the "wide discretion" afforded him under LHWCA Section 910(c).

Now that more than a decade has passed since the onset of the wars in Afghanistan and Iraq, more workers have been at their jobs for more than a year triggering the traditional approaches under LHWCA Section 910 (a) and (b). However, the post KS, wide discretion blended approach is certainly argued in those cases where appropriate.

C. Zone of Special Danger

To this writer, no topic has presented a more controversial, historical and intellectual challenge than the Zone of Special Danger expansion of coverage. That is, a departure from the traditional requirement under workers compensation law that, except in certain narrow circumstances, an injury must arise out of and occur in the course of employment to be compensable. Numerous appellate courts, even the U.S. Supreme Court, have taken on the subject. The concept has evolved from one that took into account only the exacting or different circumstances of a foreign assignment to require such an expansion to what some urge as virtual "around the clock" coverage. This topic is so large a part of DBA jurisprudence that the editors of this textbook have deemed it worthy of its own separate chapter. Please see it for a thorough and worth while discussion.

4.2 The War Hazards Compensation Act ("WHCA")

Since its inception in 1942 and up to 2003, the WHCA had been a somewhat obscure and rarely called-upon, quasi-extension of the LHWCA. Enacted by Congress shortly after the United States' entry into World War II, its purpose is best summed up in the following from Senator Thomas of Utah during debates over passage [Congressional Record, June 18, 1942, page 5342]:

> I think this much should be said: When once total war, spherical war, global war or whatever one may choose to call it, is undertaken, the sooner we bring home to our people the fact that we are responsible for the war, all might suffer by the war, and therefore all should sustain the losses, the better off we will be in a social and governmental way.

This language reflects what Congress came to realize-that war is the business of government and its cost should be born by the citizenry as a whole rather than by the private sector. From a practical standpoint, recognizing that it would have to rely, to some degree, on private enterprise to prosecute the war, the legislators needed an inducement or safety net for employers and insurers if they were to accept the risks of war.

A. Coverage

The WHCA can be found at 42 USC 1701–1717. Regulations promulgated for its procedure can be found at 20 CFR 61.1 et seq. It is an act that imposes liability on the United States, not employers unless the worker was employed by the federal government. There is no provision for an appeal after final administrative ruling. Accordingly, there are no appellate court or BRB decisions to be found.

The act is administered by the Department of Federal Employees Compensation (DFEC). It addresses 3 circumstances for DFEC's liability to pay benefits:

1. For certain employees of the federal government for injuries or death the result of a hostile act of an enemy force. (Sec. 101 (a)) These benefits are identical to what is provided other government employees pursuant to the Federal Employees Compensation Act (FECA). These claims are made directly to DFEC who will administer and pay benefits as if the claim were made pursuant to FECA.
2. For detention when the employee of a contractor has been taken captive by an enemy force. There is no requirement that the detainee sustain an injury for benefits to be paid. (Sec. 101 (b)–(d)) These claims are also to be made directly to DFEC by the legal dependents of the detainee after first obtaining a negative finding by OWCP that there is no proof of injury compensable under the DBA.
3. For reimbursement to an employer or carrier for certain costs of claims if liability results pursuant to the DBA when injury or death is caused by a "war risk hazard." (Sec. 104(a)–(c)) It is this area where the vast majority of DFEC activity has occurred since 2003.

B. War Risk Hazard

42 USC 1701(b) describes the definition for a war risk hazard as contemplated by the WHCA. That is when the injury or death results from:

1. discharge of a missile
2. use of any weapon, explosive or other noxious thing by hostile forces
3. combating an attack or imagined attack
4. action of a hostile force or person without use of specified weapon discharge or explosion of munitions stored for use in a conflict
5. collisions of vessels in convoys or in the operation of aircraft in a zone of hostilities

C. Reimbursement

Not all injuries or deaths that occur in a war zone are eligible for reimbursement. As Senator Thomas said in 1942 in support of passage of the WHCA, they must result from the hostile act of an enemy force, including now, terrorist activity. A cynical observer might argue, with some credibility, that even those injuries not caused by the hostile act of an enemy force are circuitously covered by virtue of what goes into most government contracts.

Those costs of claims that are unallocated become eligible for a 15% add-on per 20 CFR 61.104(c) to compensate the employer or carrier for adjusting the matter. Unallocated expenses are those that are directly payable to the employee, his survivors, or on his or her behalf such as medical treatment for the DBA claim. Allocated expenses are such items as attorney fees and investigation services. While eligible for reimbursement, they are not subject to the 15% add-on.

Until recently, DFEC had been paying the 15% add-on for all unallocated costs incurred, even for, the entire amount of a LHWCA Sec. 8(i) settlement. However, now while the proceeds of settlement are subject to reimbursement, the employer or carrier is not entitled to add-on for those payments.

Generally speaking, cases must be final before the claim can be submitted to DFEC. Finality may occur in several ways; by findings and award after trial, by findings and award following stipulations and by LHWCA Sec. 908(i) settlement. However, in limited cases, DFEC will reimburse without finality if it can be shown that reasonable efforts have been made, without success, to obtain a final order. Sometimes there is no reason to settle or obtain a findings and award if, for example, all benefits have been properly paid. In these cases a memorandum from OWCP accepting such showing will suffice for DFEC to reimburse. This procedure has been especially prevalent in cases involving foreign workers where payments were made and medical treatment provided pursuant to the DBA and access to claimant has simply ceased. When this happens, DFEC will reimburse and pay the 15% add-on where applicable but will not accept the claim for future direct payment as discussed below.

D. Direct Payments by DFEC

The WHCA provides not only for reimbursement of what has been paid but for future direct payment of benefits pursuant to an OALJ findings and award or approved stipulations. In fact, in those cases DFEC will actually step into the shoes of the employer or carrier and handle the claim for the most part, pursuant to the LHWCA/DBA. That would include the furnishing of weekly compensation due, death benefits and adjusting the costs of appropriate medical treatment. However, early on the agency has made it clear via procedure bulletin, it will not assume this responsibility in cases involving foreign workers with or without finality and in those of American workers where there has been no finality.

As in any LHWCA/DBA case, issues may arise in the ongoing furnishing of benefits after award. This happens in cases accepted by DFEC for future direct payment as well. Because it is not accustomed to the administration of LHWCA cases, the question of whether they were to administer them as FECA as opposed to LHWCA claims has arisen. Fortunately, the issue has resolved by a "punt". Rather than subject DBA claimants to the sometimes different and onerous procedures under FECA, DFEC will send the matter back to OWCP who is charged with resolution of the question sometimes by calling the employer/carrier back into the dispute. This, for obvious reasons, will likely result in all kinds of consternation in the claims department which probably thought it had closed its claim for good.

It is hoped that the discussion herein has provided the reader with an overall taste of what the handful of practitioners face in submitting claims to DFEC for processing pursuant to the WHCA. For a fuller and more detailed over view, it is suggested that a reading of the act itself and its aforementioned regulations be undertaken as well as the agency policy statements found in FECA Bulletins 05-01 (October 18, 2005), 12-01 (October, 2011) and 13-01, January 29, 2013. These are too lengthy to be appended to this chapter but are readily available through a Google or other such search engine.

Chapter 5

The Zone of Special Danger

When a Claim Arises in the Course and Scope of Employment Under the Longshore Act and Its Extensions

Lewis S. Fleishman, Esq. and Lara D. Merrigan, Esq.

Synopsis

By its express terms, the Longshore and Harbor Workers' Compensation Act ("the Longshore Act") requires that injuries arise out of and in the course of employment. 33 USC § 902(2). In interpreting the boundaries of coverage, courts have applied the zone of special danger doctrine, primarily in Defense Base Act claims. The zone of special danger broadly defines what injuries arise in the course and scope of employment, encompassing any injuries that arise out of the obligations or conditions of the employment. This includes any injury that is not purely personal in nature and not unforeseeable to the employer, regardless of whether that injury occurs during work hours or in direct service to the employer. This chapter explains the origin of the zone of special danger and the boundaries of its applicability.

5.1 The Positional-Risk Doctrine and the Zone of Special Danger

More than forty years ago, Professor Arthur Larson wrote an article entitled "The Positional-Risk Doctrine in Workmen's Compensation." It appeared in the *Duke Law Journal*, Volume 1973, September, Number 4, p. 761–819. The article set forth a critical overview of the phrase "arising out of" employment. The purpose of the article was to show, by drawing on a wide assortment of apparently unrelated categories, that there can and should be recognized a universal and pervading causal principle—the positional-risk doctrine—and to demonstrate further that, once a jurisdiction has adopted the doctrine in one category, it should logically extrapolate it to every type of neutral-risk case presenting the question of causal relation between injury and employment.

Professor Larson describes the "positional-risk" doctrine as follows: An injury "arises out of" the employment if it would not have occurred but for the fact that the conditions or obligations of the employment placed claimant in the position where he was injured by a neutral force, meaning by "neutral" neither personal to the claimant nor distinctly associated with the employment. DUKE L.J. 761.

One of the earliest American statements of the positional risk principle occurred in the Colorado case *Aetna Life Ins. Co. v. Industrial Comm'n*, 81 Colo. 233, 254 P. 995 (1927). In that case, the Supreme Court of Colorado was presented with a classic positional-risk situation: A farm hand had been sent by his employer to work for a day at the neighbor's farm. He was killed by lightning while driving a team of horses, without a wagon, returning after his day of work. The effect of the decision was set forth in a concurring opinion:

> (W)hen one in the course of his employment is reasonably required to be at a particular place at a particular time and there meets with an accident, although one which any other person then and there present would have met with irrespective of his employment, that accident is one "arising out of" the employment of the person so injured.

Id. at 236, 254 P. at 996.

Justice Denison commented as follows regarding the court's opinion: "A majority of the court thinks that, since Oakley's employment required him to be in a position where the lightning struck him, there was a causal relation between employment and accident, so that the latter may be said to arise out of the former and therefore the judgment should be affirmed." *Id* at 234, 254 P. at 995.

Professor Larson acknowledged that even under the positional risk doctrine, there would be injuries in which the "origins of harm are so clearly personal" that "they could not possibly be attributed to the employment." One example given is if the employee had a mortal enemy who had sworn to seek him out and murder him wherever he may be, and he happens to find and kill him while at work. Another example is if the employee, for reasons entirely his own, decides to make and carry a bomb in his bosom, which accidentally detonates during business hours.[1] DUKE L.J. 764.

When passed in 1927, the Longshore Act was built upon the bones of the New York Workers' Compensation Act. Case law construing that Act has been held relevant to the Longshore Act because when Congress borrows from state statutes, settled state construction of the adopted provisions "will be deemed to have been adopted by Congress." *West Penn Sand & Gravel Co. v. Norton*, 95 F.2d 498 (3d Cir. 1938). Thus, the interpretation to the words "out of" in the Longshore Act has been augmented by New York Workers' Compensation cases, such as *Leonbruno v. Champlain Silk Mills*, 229 N.Y. 470, 471–72 (1920):

> The claimant's presence in a factory in association with other workmen involved exposure to the risk of injury from the careless acts of those about him. He was brought by the conditions of his work "within the zone of special danger" (*Thom v. Sinclair*, 1917 A. C. 127, 142). Whatever men and boys will do, when gathered together in such surroundings, at all events if it is something reasonably to be expected, was one of the perils of his service . . . . [It] was "but natural to expect them to deport themselves as young men and boys, replete with the activities of life and health. For workmen of that age or even of maturer years to indulge in a moment's diversion from work to joke with or play a prank upon a fellow workman, is a matter of common knowledge to every one who employs labor." The claimant was injured, not merely while he was in a factory, but because he was in a factory, in touch with associations and conditions inseparable from factory life. The risks of such associations and conditions were risks of the employment.

1. Though this latter example may seem particularly far-fetched, these are the facts underlying *Bogavich v. Westinghouse Elec. & Mfg. Co.*, 162 Pa. Super. 388, 57 A.2d 598 (1948). He was a flat-car loader, and his employer's plant used no explosives.

New York case law had acknowledged there are "general dangers" to all who walk upon sidewalks, such as some object falling from a building. *Connelly v. Samaritan Hospital*, 259 N.Y. 137 (1932). This "general danger" becomes a "special danger" when employment brings the employee to the location. Likewise, although a person might be "subject at all times and places to injury by a fall which might result in concussion, upon a hard surface," that general fall risk becomes a "special danger" when it occurs at the place of employment, even though the likelihood of the fall is no greater there than elsewhere. "Whenever conditions attached to the place of employment or otherwise incident to the employment are factors in the catastrophic combination, the consequent injury arises out of the employment." *Id.* at 144. As noted by Professor Larson in 1973, New York's test adds up to a positional risk theory, even if not expressly deemed to be one by its courts.[2] DUKE L.J. 777.

5.2 The Positional-Risk Doctrine Under the Defense Base Act: The Zone of Special Danger Outside of Working Hours

The but-for positional risk standard that conferred liability for a Colorado lightning strike has come to match the boundaries of what "arises out of" employment for Longshore Act purposes. This joined with the zone of special danger doctrine has resulted in an enhanced theory of coverage, which in all but the rarest of situations, confers 24-hour but-for coverage for Defense Base Act injuries even outside of the traditional course of employment. In the seminal Defense Base Act zone of special danger case, the Supreme Court of the United States extended the rescue doctrine to its ultimate limit in adopting the positional risk doctrine. The court held that the rescue of complete strangers was covered when the connection with employment was furnished, not by the nature of the employment, but solely by the fact that the employment brought the employee to the place where he observed the rescue attempt. *O'Leary v. Brown-Pacific-Maxon, Inc.*, 340 U.S. 504 (1951).

2. This characterization has been borne out by subsequent history. For example, after September 11, the vast majority of more-than-10,000 New York workers' compensation claims were accepted. "There could be no more stark example of a neutral or positional risk than the blind destruction wrought by an indiscriminate bombing or terrorist attack." Larson's Spotlight, "Larson's Spotlight: 9/11 – Terrorist Attacks as Positional Risks," available at https://www.lexisnexis.com/legalnewsroom/workers-compensation/b/workers-compensation-law-blog/archive/2009/09/11/larson_2700_s-spotlight_3a00_-9_2f00_11-_2d00_-terrorist-attacks-as-positional-risks.aspx?Redirected=true (last viewed 4/5/16).

The *Brown-Pacific-Maxon* case combines elements of third party rescue, reasonable recreation, and force of nature. The decedent worked in Guam. His employer maintained a recreation center near the shoreline, along a dangerous channel where swimming was forbidden. The decedent spent the afternoon at the center and was awaiting the employer's bus when he noticed two men on the reefs beyond the channel were signaling for help. He jumped into the water to rescue them, but drowned.

The United States Supreme Court established the zone of special danger test applies in Defense Base Act cases even outside of business hours:

> The test of recovery is not a causal relation between the nature of employment of the injured person and the accident. *Thom v. Sinclair*, (1917) A.C. 127, 142. Nor is it necessary that the employee be engaged at the time of the injury in activity of benefit to his employer. All that is required is that the "obligations or conditions" of employment create the "zone of special danger" out of which the injury arose.

Ibid. It held that as a matter of law, this employee's death was within the course and scope of his employment.

In *Brown-Pacific-Maxon*, the Court did not use the same "but for" language as seen in the Colorado Supreme Court's lightning strike case decided decades earlier. For practical purposes, though, that is the test applied. However, the Court did allow that an employee "might go so far from his employment and become so thoroughly disconnected from the service of his employer that it would be entirely unreasonable to say that injuries suffered by him arose out of and in the course of employment." *Brown-Pacific-Maxon*, 340 U.S. at 507, citing *Babington v. Yellow Taxi Corp.*, 250 N.Y. 14 (1928). The broad causation language used by the Supreme Court in this early rescue case has guided Defense Base Act course-and-scope litigation through the present.

In a subsequent case, the United States Supreme Court further defined the broad coverage provided under the Defense Base Act. In *O'Keeffe v. Smith, Hinchman & Grylls Associates*, 380 U.S. 359 (1965), the decedent drowned on a Saturday while boating on a South Korean lake. He was employed as an assistant administrative officer at a defense base in Seoul, South Korea. He was responsible for personnel in the stenographic and clerical departments. The employer did not provide housing, but paid his rent and provided him a per diem. He was on call at any time and usually worked 44 hours a week. He and the other employees were expected to seek recreation away from the jobsite on weekends and holidays. On the day of his death, he traveled to a lake 30 miles east of Seoul where a friend of his (not a co-worker) had a house. That afternoon, they decided to fill in the beach in front of the house with sand. In order to obtain the sand, they decided to cross the lake to a sandy beach, fill the boat with sand, and move it to the beach in front of the house. During that return trip, the sand-filled boat capsized and sank. The Court followed the rule set forth in *Brown-Pacific-Maxon*, holding that this injury was also covered. Here, as the dissent lamented:

> In no sense can it be said that [the decedent's] job created any "special" danger of his drowning in a lake, or more particularly, of his loading a small boat with sand and capsizing it. Nothing indicates that the lake was rougher, the boat tippier, or the sand heavier than their counterparts in the United States. If there were "exacting and unconventional conditions" in Korea, it did not appear that the lake, boat, or sand was one of them. There is nothing more than a 'but for' relationship between the accident and the employment.

Id. at 370.

In yet another United States Supreme Court case, we again see how far a claimant can stray and still stay within coverage of the Act. *Gondeck v. Pan American World Airways, Inc.*, 382 U.S. 25 (1965), involved the death of an employee as a result of a jeep accident on San Salvador Island outside a defense base at which the decedent was employed. The accident took place in the evening as Gondeck and four others were returning from a nearby town. In *Gondeck*, the Court noted that the decedent and three others had been sitting around the Reef Club drinking champagne from 4 P.M. to 7:30 P.M., when they took off for town in a jeep that they had been forbidden to use for personal missions. The employee's death in an automobile accident as he was returning to a defense base from a nearby town was noted to be related to "reasonable recreation." Therefore, the Court held that the obligations or conditions of employment created the zone of special danger out of which the injury or death arose.

While the three United States Supreme Court cases under discussion were decided under a 'zone of special danger' standard, the decisions are also consistent with Professor Larson's 'positional risk' analysis. In each case, but-for the employment, the employee would not have been injured by a "neutral" force. The risk itself is not necessarily increased; the danger is "special" only in that the employee's exposure to that particular injurious circumstance was due to employment.

The zone of special danger has since been likened to the notoriously broad seaman's test for maintenance and cure. In *O'Keeffe v. Pan American World Airways, Inc.*, 338 F.2d 319 (5th Cir. 1964), the Fifth Circuit Court of Appeals addressed a widow's claim concerning the death of her husband. The decedent was a recreation supervisor who died in a motor scooter accident on Grand Turk Island while he was returning home from a social visit after regular working hours. The court held that the death arose out of and in the course of employment and was compensable. In light of *Brown-Pacific-Maxon*, the court had little difficulty finding coverage "irrespective of the place where the injury or death occurs." *Id.* at 322. In comparing the seaman's right to maintenance and cure to the scope of coverage for contractor employees under the Defense Base Act, the court noted,

> [The] employer's responsibility for maintenance and cure extends beyond injuries sustained because of, or while engaged in, activities required by his employment. In this respect it is a broader liability than that imposed by modern workmen's compensation statutes. Appropriately it covers all injuries and ailments incurred without misconduct on the seaman's part amounting to ground for forfeiture, at least while he is on the ship, "subject to the call of duty as a seaman, and earning wages as such."

Id. at n.3. The Fifth Circuit explained, "We think that the principles governing shipboard injuries apply to the facts presented by these [Defense Base Act] cases. To relieve the shipowner of his obligation in the case of injuries incurred on shore leave would cast upon the seaman hazards encountered only by reason of the voyage . . . ." *Ibid.* Similar to this reasoning, while the Defense Base Act employee is on a metaphorical "voyage" for his employer, if that "voyage," including the attendant "shore leave," is a but-for cause of his injury, the injury is covered, so long as it is not so thoroughly disconnected from the service of his employer that it would be entirely unreasonable to say it arose outside of the course and scope of employment.

5.3 The Outer Limits of Defense Base Act Coverage: "Chutzpah Claims"

In the decades since the original *Brown-Pacific-Maxon* decision, the Benefits Review Board and reviewing circuit courts have clarified the outer limits of Defense Base Act coverage. Very few cases have avoided coverage. It is thus more straightforward to begin by focusing on the small number of cases that are not covered, rather than including a compendium of the many that are. There appear to be arguably four or five such appellate decisions under the Defense Base Act. These have all involved bizarre circumstances, unmitigated gall, or "chutzpah." They have not only involved purely personal circumstances, but were also entirely unforeseeable.

The first decision holding a factual scenario is outside of the zone of special danger is from 1973, and while it is a Benefits Review Board case, it predates the Benefits Review Board Service Longshore Reporter: *Trans-Asia Engineering Associates, Inc. v. Reichart*, BRBS No. 101-73 (June 25, 1973). This involved an employee in Vietnam who was living in Saigon in quarters furnished by the employer. He had a local mistress with whom he frequently fought. She was very jealous, and several weeks before his death, she threatened him with a pistol, telling him that if she was to die, she would take him with her. She ultimately made good on her threat. At 3 o'clock in the morning, their bodies were found: his with five gunshot wounds, and hers with one self-inflicted gunshot wound to the head. The Benefits Review Board held that this factual scenario is not "reasonably attributable to employment." It particularly relied upon the provision in the Longshore Act that limits coverage of "an injury caused by the willful act of a third person directed against an employee because of his employment," in holding that the mistress did not murder him because of his job, and thus the zone of special danger does not confer coverage. *See* 33 U.S.C. § 902(2).

The next decision took place fifteen years later. In *Gillespie v. General Electric*, 21 BRBS 56 (1988), *aff'd mem.*, 873 F.2d 1433 (Table) (1st Cir. 1989), the Benefits Review Board considered a widow's claim for death benefits. Her husband died while attempting to temporarily asphyxiate himself as part of an autoerotic activity. On December 6, 1962, while assigned to Ramstein Air Force Base in West Germany, Mr. Gillespie was found dead in the closet of his room on the base, having accidentally hanged himself. The administrative law judge in the *Gillespie* case found the widow's claim compensable. He concluded that the death arose from the 'zone of special danger,' which was created by the conditions of employment. The trier of fact concluded, "In this case the condition is the separation from his spouse and family with the attendant loneliness." On appeal, the Board decided that onanism taken to the extreme was not compensable. The death was held to be so thoroughly disconnected from the service of his employer that it would be entirely unreasonable to say that injuries suffered by him arose out of and in the course of his employment.

Two years later, the Board again considered another widow's claim for death benefits. Like *Reichart*, *Kirkland* involved a case of love gone bad. The claimant and the decedent met after the decedent's arrival in Vietiane, Laos. *See*

Kirkland v. Air America, Inc., 23 BRBS 348, 349 (1990), *aff'd. mem. sub. nom. Kirkland v. Director, OWCP*, 925 F.2d 489 (D.C. Cir. 1991). Less than a year after they married, the decedent was murdered during the burglary of his home. The widow-claimant was implicated in the crime by the men who confessed to actually killing her husband. The *Kirkland* case involved clear 'chutzpah.' For the uninitiated, the classic example of 'chutzpah' is as follows: A man, after killing both his parents, throws himself upon the mercy of the Court because he is an orphan. In *Kirkland*, the claimant created her status as a widow. Accordingly, the Board had no trouble in finding that the wrongdoer should not be allowed to benefit from her own foul conduct. Moreover, the court did not so-decide based upon the killing falling outside of the zone of special danger, but rather premised its holding upon the fact that she was a "knowing participant in the criminal activity which directly led to her husband's murder," and ineligible for recovery because "[n]othing is more deeply rooted in Anglo-American Jurisprudence than the notion that a wrongdoer should not be allowed to benefit from his or her own wrong." The Board thus held it "need not address" the claimant's argument that decedent was killed within the zone of special danger—her wrongdoing independently severed any causal nexus that might otherwise exist. *Id.* at n. 6.

The Board affirmed an administrative law judge's denial of benefits in *Fear v. CSA, Ltd.*, 43 BRBS 139 (2009). The claimant worked in Kuwait as a digital imaging specialist. He had a history of treatment for depression and anxiety and a history of undergoing cosmetic dermatological treatments and procedures. He sought treatment at a Kuwaiti clinic for facial skin care, including a chemical peel. He then began to believe that his face was "riddled with lines," and he "freaked out." When he perceived further dermatological treatment in Kuwait unhelpful, he returned to the United States to see his own dermatologists. *Id.* at 139. He alleged disability due to his skin disorder, anxiety, and stress condition (as aggravated by the skin disorder). The Benefits Review Board stated that "if an employee becomes so thoroughly disconnected from the service to the employer that it would be unreasonable to say that the injury occurred in the course of employment, the activity may not have occurred in the course of employment and his employer would not be held liable for any resulting injuries." *Id.* at 142. The claimant's chemical peel "was personal in nature and did not have its genesis in employment." *Ibid.* He had sought multiple skin treatments in Kuwait and had a long history of undergoing such treatments at home. He had been diagnosed as being obsessed with his skin. "Use of the chemical peel was not 'rooted in the conditions and obligations of his employment,' or in any way related to the fact that [he] was employed in Kuwait." *Id.* at 143. Because the chemical peel "is so thoroughly disconnected from his service to employer and did not have its genesis in employment," the perceived skin injury is not work-related under the zone of special danger

In 2012, the First Circuit actually had cause to revisit whether accidental death by autoerotic asphyxiation is covered by the zone of special danger.[3] *Truczinskas v. Dir., OWCP*, 699 F.3d 672 (1st Cir. 2012). It again held that it is not. The decedent was found in his villa in Saudi Arabia, hanging from the ceiling by a noose around his neck. A United States citizen, he worked as a military trainer. No suicide note was found. His feet were touching the ground. He was an occasional cross-dresser and was wearing make-up when found. His villa was on a protected compound controlled by his employer. His body was discovered by his mistress. His widow had a number of theories to explain how his death was related to his work as a military trainer. These included:

---

3. At least one administrative law judge has expressed skepticism regarding the continued viability of the *Gillespie* holding:

> It is difficult to square this with the Ninth Circuit's holding in [*Self v. C.F. Hanson*, 305 F.2d 699 (9th Cir. 1962)]. There, it was foreseeable that workers in a remote place, needing "recreation," would engage in romantic "parking," which brought them within the zone of special danger. The point in *Self*, as in [*Kalama Services, Inc., v. Dir., OWCP*, 354 F.3d 1085 (9th Cir. 2003)], is that employment at a distant military base that results in the worker's isolation makes foreseeable that the worker will require "recreation," and that this brings such "recreation" within the zone of special danger. Perhaps changing attitudes toward masturbation since the 1980's might lead the Board to affirm the administrative law judge in *Gillespie* today, and not inquire about a married worker's motivation when separated from his wife, he engaged in a sexual activity, which by being solo, allowed him to remain faithful to his wife.

Dill v. Service Employees International, Inc., 2008-LDA-00259 (Jan. 21, 2011), n.23. This multi-issue case has now been vacated twice by the Benefits Review Board, and as of this writing, it is pending on remand. *Dill v. Service Employees International, Inc.*, BRB No. 11-0395 (unpub.) (Feb. 28, 2012); *Dill v. Service Employees International, Inc.*, 48 BRBS 31 (2014). It is unknown where this decision will ultimately end, but in the original January 2011 decision, the administrative law judge held that the geographical separation between the decedent and his family was within the zone of special danger, and this led to him having "lost significant control of his wife's and daughter's actions and over the family finances" causing "a devastating devolution of conditions at home," which in turn led to him taking his own life. This same general reasoning led to the February 7, 2013, award of benefits.

(1) That he was killed by conservative Muslim vigilantes who were offended by his extramarital affair or alleged cross-dressing;
(2) That he had learned that one of his co-workers was involved in arms smuggling or selling military intelligence, and the co-worker may have killed him to silence him; or
(3) That he was investigating "a threat" to American's in the region and had "offended the Saudis" in the course of the investigation, leading to his murder.

The claimant presented an expert in Middle Eastern studies who opined these theories were "not far-fetched," but she failed to present any evidence in support of any of them other than testimony that the decedent had been wearing make-up when his body was found. The First Circuit held that "[g]iven the protected environs of the base and lack of evidence, the ALJ and [Benefits] Review Board could not easily have credited all or any of these theories," over the evidence that he caused his own death either by suicide or by auto-erotic asphyxiation. The First Circuit held that neither suicide in an ordinary case (per 33 U.S.C. § 903(c)) nor harm from unforeseeable or unreasonable recreation are within the zone of special danger. As such, the death was not a covered injury.

5.4 "Boys Will Be Boys" and "Girls Will Be Girls": Accepted Human Behavior Within the Zone

The small number of Defense Base Act cases in which the zone of special danger did not apply is no indication of the number of times this issue has been litigated and appealed. This resilient doctrine has been tested from many angles. The zone of special danger has encompassed a wide variety of fact patterns. *Self v. C.F. Hanson*, 305 F.2d 699 (9th Cir. 1962) involved what may well have been an after-work romantic liaison between a boss and his stenographer. In view of the employer's policy of providing vehicles and facilities for recreational purposes on Cabras Island, the after-work vehicular accident which occurred while the employees were "parking" and their car was struck by another vehicle, was held compensable. The stenographer's injuries which occurred outside the normal workday were held compensable whether the "parking" was due to a professed desire to view a vessel or to mutual attraction. Thus, a line exists between what was perceived as aberrant, unforeseeable sexual behavior in *Gillespie* and the more common sexual behavior approved as covered recreation in *Self*.

If an injury sustained during a probable romantic liaison is compensable under Ninth Circuit case law, then so is an injury occurring during horseplay in a bar. *Kalama Services, Inc., v. Dir., OWCP*, 354 F.3d 1085 (9th Cir. 2003), *cert. denied*, 543 U.S. 809 (2004).[4] In *Kalama Services*, claimant Ilaszczat sustained a hip injury at a bar after midnight during the early morning hours. The claimant had consumed several drinks at the Tiki Bar. He left the bar after midnight when it closed and proceeded to another bar. Several more alcoholic drinks were consumed. Then, the claimant, apparently on a bet, injured his hip when a soldier either "swept" claimant's foot out from under him, or kicked him, depending upon which version of events is believed. The Ninth Circuit Court of Appeals affirmed the Benefits Review Board in holding that injuries suffered by an off-duty employee during horseplay in a bar on Johnston Atoll were foreseeable and thus arose out of a zone of special danger created by the isolation of the island and the limited recreational opportunities available there.

In *N.R. [Rogers] v. Halliburton Svcs.*, 42 BRBS 56 (2008), an employee in Afghanistan took an unauthorized trip off-base in order to procure non-military transportation to the United States, as he alleged working conditions were unsafe. When he returned to the base, his employer and the military commander ordered he be detained and transported to Bagram Air Base to await a military flight to the United States. The claimant asserted that the trip to the base was unsafe and repeatedly refused to go. Military police tried to restrain him and put him into the transport vehicle. He sustained injuries when he resisted their efforts. The Board reversed the administrative law judge's denial of benefits, holding that although he was at fault for the altercation, fault is irrelevant to entitlement under the Longshore Act, and the dispute which led to his injuries "had its genesis in his em-

4. A recent administrative law judge decision denied benefits in a claim arising from a spat between a couple. *Munoz v. Black Veatch Special Projects Group*, 2013-LDA-00355 (ALJ) (July 31, 2015). As of this writing, the matter is on appeal to the Benefits Review Board, Case Number 15-0491. The claimant and his wife were coworkers in Afghanistan. On Thanksgiving Day, at the employer's compound, they were at the "pool bar" at the compound, where they drank alcohol. The claimant was ultimately involved in an altercation with a co-worker. He accused his co-worker of sleeping with his wife, and punched him in the eye. Thereafter, a different co-worker grabbed the claimant and threw him to the ground, causing the claimed injuries. The administrative law judge held that the causal events were so personal in nature that they were thoroughly disconnected from the service of his employer, and it would be entirely unreasonable to say his injuries arose out of and in the course of his employment. The administrative law judge distinguished this from *Kalama* in that it was a "domestic dispute" versus "horseplay" and not rooted in the conditions and obligations of employment or in any way related to the fact that the claimant was employed in Afghanistan, but rather rooted in the claimant's own personal problems.

ployment." *Id.* at 61. Accordingly, as a matter of law, his injuries fell within the zone of special danger.

The cases discussed so far in this chapter under the zone of special danger involve activity that would arguably be unforeseeable to the employer. But as this line of cases solidified, a sort of Goldilocks theory was formed: If an activity can be too unforeseeable and bizarre to be covered, can it also be too ubiquitous and routine, thus yielding only a middle swath of cases covered by the zone of special danger? Does the zone of "special" danger exclude everyday dangers? This "normalcy" argument has been repeatedly tested and has roundly failed.

In *Smith v. Board of Trustees, Southern Illinois University*, 8 BRBS 197 (1978), the decedent was working in Kathmandu, Nepal, as an educational advisor. He suffered a ruptured abdominal aortic aneurysm while golfing. He had suffered frequent dysentery while there, and it was unclear if the rupture was precipitated by that condition or by playing golf. The employer argued that it was caused by golf and that there was nothing more dangerous about playing golf in Kathmandu than in the United States. The Benefits Review Board held it unnecessary to determine the actual cause, as whether it was dysentery or golf, it was covered.

In *Ford Aerospace & Communications Corp. v. Boling*, 684 F.2d 640 (9th Cir. 1982), the decedent worked in a remote location of Thule, Greenland. His employer required that he stay in provided barracks. He suffered a myocardial infarction. The construction of the barracks prevented a stretcher from reaching his room. He was forced to walk twenty to forty feet to the stretcher, aggravating his injury and contributing to his death. The employer argued that the barracks were only one hundred yards from the hospital, resulting in faster treatment than he would have had at home, and that the standard of medical care provided was far above that available to most residents of the United States. The employer contended that to extend coverage would impose liability for any injury as long as the job location is less than the best place imaginable to survive a heart attack. The Ninth Circuit rejected this argument. It did not find it necessary to hypothesize about how the employee would have fared in the United States, only holding that because the architecture of the barracks was an identifiable causal factor in his death, it was covered.

In *Forlong v. American Security & Trust Co.*, 21 BRBS 155 (1988), a Peruvian, in Peru, in the middle of the night, in his brother-in-law's house, was covered by virtue of the zone of special danger. The claimant, a Peruvian native who worked as the Vice President of the bank's Latin American Division in Washington, D.C., was injured on a trip to Peru. His employer reimbursed him for his trip expenses as he was there to conduct business. One night, he hosted a cocktail party at his brother-in-law's house to meet with Peruvian Naval officials regarding their accounts with the bank. After the party, he spent the night at his brother-in-law's house. He got out of bed in the middle of the night to use the bathroom, opened the wrong door, and fell down a flight of stairs. The Board held that because such an injury was reasonably foreseeable and because he had not been in the house for purely personal reasons, he had not severed the employment nexus, and the resulting injuries were within the course and scope of his employment.

In *Urso v. MVM, Inc.*, 44 BRBS 53 (2010), the decedent was working in Beirut, Lebanon, living on the grounds of the United States Embassy. He decided to get an extensive six-hour back tattoo from a tattoo parlor nearby. He preemptively obtained painkillers to deal with the tattooing process. He overdosed on painkillers that night. The Benefits Review Board affirmed the administrative law judge's holding that the decedent's death is covered by the zone of special danger. In so-holding, it rejected the argument that this was excluded as a personal choice akin to the facial peel in *Fear*, because the administrative law judge had rationally held that it was reasonably foreseeable that someone in the paramilitary force would get a tattoo and that regardless of the tattoo, the self-administration of legally-obtained pain medications is a reasonably foreseeable activity. Thus, being personal in nature alone does not bring an activity outside of coverage—it must be both personal and unforeseeable.

The most recent circuit court opinion—and one of the clearest—to address this issue is *Battelle Memorial Institute v. DiCecca*, 792 F.3d 214 (1st Cir. 2015). It was written by retired Associate Justice of the Supreme Court, the Honorable David H. Souter, sitting by designation with the First Circuit. The decedent was a facility engineer in a Tbilisi, Georgia, laboratory, working for a contractor in assisting the United States Department of Defense on countering the threat of biological weapons. His formal hours were 8 A.M. to 5 P.M., but he could be called in at any time if needed in an emergency. The employer did not have housing accommodations nor a restaurant, and so it provided employees with a housing and utility allowance so that they could find their own place to live. It also provided taxi vouchers, payable to Lucky Cabs, which could be used for any purpose. There were two grocery stores that the claimant visited. The smaller one was a five-to-ten-minute walk from his apartment. His wife had visited him in Georgia and believed the food at that smaller store to be unsafe because she had seen flies on the meat. The larger one was like a Walmart and had a larger selection, but it was 12–14 km away from the claimant's apartment, so required a twenty-minute taxi ride.

The decedent was traveling to the larger grocery store in a Lucky Cabs taxi when it was hit head-on.

The employer argued that the zone of special danger can be satisfied only in two ways:

(1) The injury occurred during reasonable recreation in an isolated place with limited social opportunities; or
(2) Where the locale had an enhanced risk of injury beyond the domestic norm from which the injury arose.

The employer alleged that as neither test was met, the death was not covered. The First Circuit rejected this argument, explaining that in the phrase "zone of special danger," '[s]pecial' is best understood as 'particular' but not necessarily 'enhanced.' There is a pale of cognizability, however, which stops short of astonishing risks 'unreasonabl[y]' removed from employment." *Id.* at 220 (internal citations omitted). As it held: "Although the requisite 'special danger' covers risks peculiar to the foreign location or risks of greater magnitude than those encountered domestically, the zone also includes risks that might occur anywhere but in fact occur where the employee is injured." *Ibid.*

Although the original cases developing the zone of special danger doctrine under the Defense Base Act were recreation cases, *DiCecca* pointed out that the impetus of this reasoning is that recreation is a necessity. It thus stated that "because grocery shopping is a necessity, it too should be considered an incident to the employment." *Id.* at 223. The court went so far as to say that it would be "irrational" to adopt the employer's proposed distinction between technically optional and necessary activities—only covering activities that are optional. *Id.* at n.1. It pointed out the incongruity that would result from an opposite holding: "The short of it is that it is very hard, perhaps impossible, to distill a rule that injuries arising out of a night on the town are covered but not those incurred shopping for food." *Id.* at 223.

DiCecca approvingly cited the facial peel decision in *Fear* as an example of a "ubiquitous" activity that is not included because it was purely "personal in nature" and lacked a genesis in employment. It explained: "The question then is which 'ubiquitous' activities are covered. And the answer is a case-specific determination of foreseeable, reasonable incidence to foreign employment . . . ." *Id.* at n.2.

Shortly after *DiCecca*, the Benefits Review Board decided *Jetnil v. Chugach Management Services*, 49 BRBS 55 (2015).[5] The claimant was a citizen of the Republic of the Marshall Islands. He was a painter. He lived on Third Island. He usually worked on the island of Roi Namur, but was also assigned work each year on Gagan Island. All of these islands are within the Republic of the Marshall Islands. Gagan Island is an uninhabited island with no medical facilities. When the employer transports workers there, they remain at the island until the assignment is complete, staying in an employer-provided trailer (the only living quarters on the island), which is stocked with food provided by the employer—in this case, bread, hot dogs, bacon, chicken, and rice. One day, after work hours, the claimant went fishing on the reef. Reef fishing is common throughout the Marshall Islands, and he had been advised by his doctor to eat fish whenever possible because he was diabetic. He was wearing flip-flop sandals while fishing, and slipped and cut his right foot on the coral. He remained on the island, working there as scheduled through the next day. He did not seek medical care for several days. Ultimately, his foot became infected and his leg was amputated.

The employer argued that the zone of special danger does not apply to injuries that occur in one's home country. The administrative law judge reasoned that the risks the claimant faced on Gagan Island were unrelated to his citizenship and did not dissipate because he was born in the Marshall Islands. The Benefits Review Board agreed. It held that the zone of special danger doctrine may or may not be applicable to a local national working for a Defense Base Act employer in his home country, depending on the specific circumstances presented by the individual case. In this case:

> Where employer created employment obligations and conditions for claimant and his co-workers, requiring their restriction to an isolated location for the duration of a four-day period, the administrative law judge rationally found that those conditions gave rise to a zone of special danger notwithstanding claimant's status as a citizen and resident of the RMI.

Id. at 59. Further, the limited food selections offered by the employer did not satisfy the dietary restrictions caused by the claimant's pre-existing diabetes, leading to his reef-fishing for dinner. Accordingly, his reef fishing was foreseeable.

Similar to the argument rejected in *DiCecca*, the employer also argued that the zone of special danger only encompasses dangers unique to the foreign locale. It argued that fishing is common in the Marshall Islands, and the claimant probably would have been fishing for his dinner on a reef, regardless of which island in the atoll he was fishing

5. As of this writing, *Jetnil* is pending before the Ninth Circuit Court of Appeals, Case Number 15-72873.

from. The Benefits Review Board disagreed that the zone of special danger is limited to exclude risks that might be present elsewhere. The Board's opinion is a practical application of the positional risk doctrine as it did not require any increased threat or danger as a criteria of coverage.

Ritzhiemer v. Triple Canopy, 50 BRBS 1 (2016),[6] is a recent decision that the Benefits Review Board issued en banc following oral argument. In that matter, the claimant was injured in his apartment in Israel while stepping out of the shower. He was employed as a force protection officer. His apartment was selected and paid for by his employer. The room had come furnished and did not include a bath mat. The physical layout and condition of the bathroom were comparable to bathrooms in the United States. He was always on call and worked twelve or more hours a day, seven days a week. His job required him to maintain a good appearance and good hygiene. His job left him dusty and sweaty, and he showered after work. He also, however, showered on days off. While showering in his apartment on his date of injury, the shower curtain came out of the bathtub, and the floor became wet. He slipped on the floor and struck his right side against the tub, fracturing four ribs and puncturing a lung. All five members of the Benefits Review Board unanimously affirmed the administrative law judge's award of benefits. It rejected the employer's argument that showering was purely personal in nature, like the chemical peel in *Fear*. Further, it held there is no need for the bathroom to have presented unique risks in order for the zone of special danger to apply. It held that slipping in the shower was a foreseeable risk of the claimant's service.

The zone of special danger has also been held to encompass myriad other mundane scenarios, in which the link to employment is purely positional risk. A classic lightning-strike scenario was litigated under the Longshore Act in *J.W. [Wolford] v. Service Employees International, Inc.*, 41 BRBS 267 (ALJ) (April 30, 2007). The claimant, Jason Wolford, was in Iraq, walking to the DEFAC for a meal. He was on the job and on the employer's payroll. A bolt of lightning struck a nearby wall. He received an electrocution injury due to either step-voltage or a sideflash. The administrative law judge acknowledged that the lightning strike was a "neutral event and not peculiar to [the claimant's] employment." He held there was no necessity that the employment carry any "increased risk" and that under a positional risk or but-for causation theory, the lighting strike was in the course and scope of employment. "[H]ad [the claimant] not been about his job related duties at the time and place he was struck by lightning, he would not have been struck by lightning. It is as simple as that." *See also Bezuidenhout v. DynCorp Technical Services*, 47 BRBS 973 (ALJ) (August 15, 2013) (The zone of special danger covered the decedent choking to death while eating, even though there was no showing that he was any more likely to have choked to death than if eating at his own home.); *Troutman v. Kwajalein Range Services*, ALJ Case No. 2008-LHC-00605 (March 19, 2009) (A routine age-related colonoscopy that the employee elected to have performed on a remote island instead of while on leave and perforated his colon is within the zone of special danger.); and *Copeland v. DynCorp International*, ALJ Case No. 2013-LDA-00312 (May 19, 2015) (The decedent's use of "Ripped Fuel" supplement containing FDA-banned Ephedra is within the zone of special danger.).

Given the foregoing—which includes a mere sample of the cases found covered—if an injury occurs under the Defense Base Act while an employee is away from home for reasons of employment, it will almost always be held to have arisen in the course and scope of employment. The only cases found by appellate courts to not be covered are accidental death by autoerotic asphyxiation, murder of the decedent by his mistress followed by her own suicide, murder of the decedent by the claimant, and a facial peel gone wrong which had been obtained by a man diagnosed with being obsessed about his skin. Absent such a remarkably bizarre fact pattern that establishes the injury was both unforeseeable and purely personal in nature, appellate courts have consistently held the injury to have arisen out of and in the course of employment.

5.5 The Applicability of the Zone of Special Danger to Longshore Act Claims Beyond the Defense Base Act

The Benefits Review Board has declined to extend the zone of special danger doctrine to the Longshore Act itself, the Outer Continental Shelf Lands Act, or the Non-Appropriated Fund Instrumentalities Act. *Phillips v. PMB Safety & Regulatory, Inc.*, 44 BRBS 1 (2010).[7] "This test was for-

6. This case has been further appealed and as of this writing is pending at the Eleventh Circuit, Case Number 16-11584.

7. Note that even if the zone of special danger does not apply to these acts, the positional risk doctrine still governs when a claim arises out of employment, so long as the injury occurs during the *course of* employment. Classic workers' compensation principles can even extend coverage beyond business hours by virtue of rules like the bunkhouse rule and the coming-and-going rule. *See Vaught v. State of California*, 157 Cal. App.4th 1538 (2007); *Hinojosa v. WCAB*, 8 Cal.3d 150 (1972). For example, even though the Benefits Review Board declined to apply the zone of special danger doctrine in *Phillips*, 44 BRBS 1, it nevertheless held the claimant's injury—caused by a fellow employee hauling him out of bed and assaulting him—was covered by virtue of traditional workers' compensation principles. Thus, whether or not a claim benefits from

mulated in cases arising under the Defense Base Act and is well-suited to those cases since the conditions of the employment place the employee in a foreign setting where he is exposed to dangerous conditions." *Harris v. England Air Force Base*, 23 BRBS 175, 179 (1990).

However, the zone of special danger has been extended by the District of Columbia Court of Appeals to include cases brought under the District of Columbia workers' compensation extension to the Longshore Act. *See Hensley v. Washington Metropolitan Area Transit Authority*, 655 F.2d 264, 13 BRBS 182(CRT) (D.C. Cir. 1981), *cert. denied*, 456 U.S. 904; *Durrah v. Washington Metropolitan Area Transit Authority*, 760 F.2d 322 (D.C. Cir. 1985); *Phillips*, 44 BRBS 1. Workers in Washington, D.C., were covered by the Longshore Act until 1981 when Washington, D.C., passed the Workmens' Compensation Act. *See Dir. v. Newport News Shipbuilding & Dry Dock Co.*, 514 U.S. 122, 142 (1995).

The zone of special danger has long been applied to employees even when upon their own nation's soil. As noted above, *Forlong v. American Security & Trust Co.*, 21 BRBS 155 (1988), applied the zone of special danger to find coverage for a Peruvian in Peru, in the middle of the night, at his brother-in-law's house. That claim was a Washington, D.C. workers' compensation claim. Obviously, other cases under that extension apply to United States citizens in the United States. *See Hensley*, 655 F.2d 264. Since its inception, the Defense Base Act has applied the zone of special danger to United States territories without question. *O'Leary v. Brown-Pacific-Maxon, Inc.*, 340 U.S. 504 (1951) (Guam); *Hastorff-Nettles, Inc. v. Pillsbury*, 203 F.2d 641 (9th Cir. 1953) (Alaska). Further, *Jetnil v. Chugach Management Services*, 49 BRBS 55 (2015), applied the zone of special danger in a Defense Base Act case to a Marshallese citizen in the Marshall Islands.

Given the foregoing, the decision in *Phillips* declining to apply the zone of special danger to an Outer Continental Shelf Lands Act case is questionable. Platforms—particularly, fixed platforms—on the Outer Continental Shelf have been legally treated as artificial islands. *See Rodrigue v. Aetna Casualty & Surety Co.*, 395 U.S. 352 (1969); *Herb's Welding v. Gray*, 470 U.S. 414, 421 (1985). Why would a United States citizen be denied benefits when forced to live on a remote "island" because it does not invoke the zone of special danger, when a Marshallese citizen like Jetnil injured on an island in his home island's chain is covered? The Longshore Act surely does not endeavor to provide greater solicitude to foreign nationals than United States citizens. Further, a drilling platform is presumably at least as remote and dangerous as Guam, Korea, or a golf course in Kathmandu. It is thus difficult to justify a continued denial of the zone of special danger on platforms.

In an unpublished decision, the Fifth Circuit Court of Appeals held that the zone of special danger applied in an Outer Continental Shelf Lands Act matter. *Hotard v. Devon Energy Corp., L.P.*, 308 Fed.Appx. 739 (5th Cir. Jan. 23, 2009). There, the plaintiff-claimant had been bitten by a dangerous, venomous spider while sleeping aboard the platform. Likewise, the zone of special danger was applied in an Outer Continental Shelf Lands Act case in *Latimer v. Chet Morrison Constr.*, Case No. 11-CV-806, 2013 U.S.Dist. LEXIS 147037 (W. Dist. LA. Oct. 9, 2013).

One district court applied the zone of special danger to a Longshore Act claim where the employee was injured aboard the employer's vessel, upon which the employer had provided him living quarters. *James v. Wards Cove Packing Co.*, 409 F. Supp. 2d 1252 (W.D. Wash. 2005). This matter was appealed to the Ninth Circuit Court of Appeals, which issued an unpublished decision vacating the finding on summary decision that the plaintiff is not a crewmember, and otherwise upholding the findings under the Longshore Act, without specifically addressing this aspect of the holding. *James v. Wards Cove Packing Co.*, 209 Fed. Appx. 648 (9th Cir. Oct. 20, 2006). Therefore, the zone of special danger may have wider-spread applicability than just the Defense Base Act and pre-1981 Washington, D.C. workers' compensation cases.

5.6 Conclusion

Even before the Longshore Act was passed, the concept of positional risk recognized that if someone is walking down a public sidewalk when randomly struck by an object falling from an adjacent building, that is considered a "general danger" of life, unless that walk was in the course of employment, in which case it is a "special danger" covered by workers' compensation. The consistency of this doctrine over the past century has been admirable. If but-for the obligations and conditions of employment, the claimant would not have been in the position in which the injury occurred, then that injury arose in the course and scope of employment. There is no need to show an increased risk under the Longshore Act. When applied to Defense Base Act claims, employees are generally living away from their homes as a job requirement, and the employment places the claimant in a different geographic position even when not actively working. Thus, a claimed Defense Base Act injury that meets the but-for causation test will evade coverage in only rare cases. These exempt cases are marked by chutzpah, involving fact patterns that are purely personal and so unforeseeable that they sound fictitious.

eligibility for "zone of special danger" application may often be a purely academic debate.

As the zone of special danger persists, there may be some changes on the horizon. As noted, recent federal cases have applied it to both the Longshore Act and the Outer Continental Shelf Lands Act where the claimant is living away from home due to the employment. It may be that if the Department of Labor has occasion to reconsider *Phillips v. PMB Safety & Regulatory, Inc.*, 44 BRBS 1 (2010), it would agree that the zone of special danger can apply in such situations. There are also active Defense Base Act appeals in the Ninth and Eleventh Circuits, both challenging the inclusion of common dangers.[8] If either is successful, it would likely yield a circuit split of authorities given *Battelle Memorial Institute v. DiCecca*, 792 F.3d 214 (1st Cir. 2015). In the meantime, little if anything about the zone of special danger doctrine in Defense Base Act cases has changed since its adoption in *O'Leary v. Brown-Pacific-Maxon, Inc.*, 340 U.S. 504 (1951). It has so far remained stalwart in the face of the appellate onslaught, a rarity among legal doctrines in providing claimants and carriers alike with the ability to assess a case's outcome with good predictability.

8. *Jetnil v. Chugach Management Services*, 49 BRBS 55 (2015), Ninth Circuit Case Number 15-72873; *Ritzhiemer v. Triple Canopy*, 50 BRBS 1 (2016), Eleventh Circuit Case Number 16-11584.

Chapter 6

Price and the Bright, Fuzzy Line of Traumatic Two-Injury and Cumulative Orthopedic Claims

Frank B. Hugg, Esq.

Synopsis

In the six years since the Ninth Circuit decided *Metropolitan Stevedore Co. v. Crescent Wharf and Warehouse Co. (Price),* 339 F.3d 1102 (9th Cir. 2003) *cert denied* 543 U.S. 940 (2004), its "bright line" has become fuzzy. The last responsible employer in a traumatic, two-injury case is not always the last chronological employer.

Price still remains, however, a seminal decision which established a powerfully new and adroit variation of an old rule of occupational disease law. In traumatic two-employer and cumulative orthopedic injury claims, liability shall be assigned to the "last responsible employer" where the ultimate disability is "at least partially the result of a subsequent injury *aggravating, accelerating or combining with a prior injury...*" 339 F.3d 1107.

This chapter will discuss the *Price* decision in detail and review the origins of the two-employer rule with a focus on and citation to post-*Price* opinions. The chapter will also examine the burdens of proof that the two-employer rule imposes in the trial of Longshore cases.

Finally, confession being good for the soul, the author will admit and explain that his dire predictions about the *Price* doctrine from the 2005 edition of *The Longshore Textbook* have not come true. That is because the current variation of the *Price* rule is another variation on even older theme. The best medical evidence at the trial usually determines the last responsible employer.

6.1 The *Price* Rule Restated: The Last Employer Buys the Farm?

Price involved a common pattern of waterfront employment and injury. Namely, the claimant had a 30-year history of arduous employment on the waterfront as a mechanic and forklift driver. By early 1990, claimant Price tried to obtain work only as a forklift driver and would occasionally refuse work that he thought was harmful to his knees.

In 1992, he first sought medical care for his knees. By September 1993, a physician had diagnosed a joint line collapse that required bilateral total knee replacements. Treatment continued and x-rays showed "bone on bone" joint spaces with no remaining cartilage. The employer before that study was Crescent City Marine.

Nonetheless, Price continued working. In December 1994, he asked his physician to schedule the surgery. The last employer before that visit was Crescent Wharf. After surgery was scheduled and the claimant had a pre-operative evaluation, he worked the final shift of his waterfront career for Metropolitan Stevedore on April 22, 1995.

Two days later, the claimant had surgery. Thereafter, Price brought a claim against Metropolitan, which was consolidated with his claims against Crescent City, Crescent Wharf, two other employers, and their respective carriers: a veritable free-for-all with one claimant and five employers.

Administrative Law Judge Paul Mapes found that the claimant sustained an injury from his one day of employment with Metropolitan on April 22, 1995, and that injury caused "some minor but permanent increase in the extent of his disability and increased his need even though the surgery had already been scheduled." The Judge relied upon the testimony of physicians that there was a gradual loss of bone and cartilage, even on the day before surgery, and ruled that Metropolitan Stevedore was the responsible employer.

The Benefits Review Board affirmed and found that the Judge's decision was rational in relying upon the physicians who described the bone loss and that Metropolitan's employment aggravated the claimant's condition. The Board rejected the contention that the decision was not based on substantial evidence.

In upholding the Board and ALJ decisions, the Ninth Circuit acknowledged that its version of the last responsible employer rule "might seem harsh" but reasoned that ultimately every employer under the Longshore Act will sooner or later be a last employer a "proportionate share of the time." *Price,* 339 F.3d 1107, citing *Foundation Constructors v. Director,* 950 F.2d 621, 622 (9th Cir. 1991). The Court concluded that, "Having a bright line rule eliminates the need for costly litigation and helps ensure that workers receive timely and adequate compensation for their injuries under the LHWCA." *Id.*

The *Price* court rejected the arguments by Metropolitan and the Director that disability in two-injury cases should be synonymous with diminished earning capacity rather than physical harm. Instead the Ninth Circuit essentially promoted the notion that any physical harm will be sufficient to assign liability, so long as supported by expert medical opinion that there was some physical injury, change for the worse, or contribution to pathology.

6.2 The Origins and Development of the Two-Employer Rule

The rationale of the *Price* decision is also based upon its analysis of the two-employer rule as a "branch" of the last employer rule for occupational diseases, which is traced to the seminal decision of *Travelers Insurance Co. v. Cardillo,* 225 F.2d 137 *cert. denied* 350 U.S. 913 (1955). In the context of hearing loss claims against numerous employers, the *Cardillo* rule assigns liability on claims against multiple employer in the following manner:

> "[T]he employer during the last employment in which the Claimant was exposed to injurious stimuli, prior to the date upon which the Claimant became aware of the fact that he was suffering from an occupational disease arising naturally out of his employment, should be liable for the full amount of the award."

The Ninth Circuit adopted the rule in *Cordero v. Triple A Machine Shop*, 580 F.2d 1331 (9th Cir. 1978) *cert denied* 440 U.S. 911 (1979) and has followed it on many later occasions.

The Ninth Circuit did not formally explain, however, that the last employer rule had "spouted a branch" of the two-employer rule until *Foundation Constructors, Inc. v. Director, OWCP,* 950 F. 2d 621, 623 (9th Cir. 1991). The rule was formulated as follows:

> If the disability resulted from the natural progression of a prior injury and would have occurred notwithstanding the subsequent injury, then the prior injury is the compensable and accordingly, the prior employer is responsible. If, on the other hand the subsequent injury aggravated, accelerated or combined with claimant's prior injury, thus resulting in claimant's disability, then the subsequent employer is responsible." citing *Kelaita,* 799 F.2d at 1211.

The citations to authority by the Ninth Circuit in *Kelaita* are, however, entirely to cases from the Benefits Review Board.

Indeed, after the work product of the Ninth Circuit in *Kelaita* and *Foundation Constructors,* the Benefits Review Board has carried the banner of the two-employer rule. See, *Buchanan v. International Transportation Services, Inc.*, 33 BRBS 32 (1999) *aff'd mem. sub nom, Int'l Transp. Services v. Kaiser Permanente Hospital, Inc.*, 7 Fed. Appx 547 (9th Cir. 2001) (unpublished). The Board's decision in *Buchanan* is also good review of the evolution of the two-employer rule and precursor of the presumptions and burdens of proof that *Price* now makes final in the Ninth Circuit.

First, the presumption of Section 20 plays no role in a two-employer claim. *Buchanan,* 33 BRBS at 35. Next, each employer has a burden of persuasion of proving by a preponderance of the evidence that a claimant's disability is due to the injury with the other employer. Thus, the first employer need not prove that the injury with the second employer played no role in the ultimate disability, but only that the second incident aggravated, accelerated, or combined with the prior injury to produce the overall disability.

Finally, in the unlikely event that neither employer is able to persuade the ALJ that its evidence is entitled to greater weight, "the purposes of the Act would be best served by assigning liability to the later employer, consistent with the case law defining responsible employer in an occupational disease context. *Buchanan,* 33 BRBS at 36.

6.3 *Price* Two-Employer Rule Applied

While the *Price* decision does not address evidentiary burdens and presumptions that were discussed by the Board in *Buchanan, Price* leaves little room for doubt. If an injured worker experiences pain, discomfort, symptoms, or any other complaints, however seemingly trivial, which a physician characterizes as injurious, harmful, or in some way contributing to the overall disability or need for treatment, then in the Ninth Circuit there *may be* a presumption that the second employer is the last responsible employer.

Indeed in the Ninth the cases that have held the second employer liable on the basis of very slight symptoms are always buttressed by medical opinion of contribution. In *Price,* the knee condition had not progressed to the point of maximum disability because the claimant was still able use his legs, and did so one last day that caused a "marginal increase in the need for surgery." In *Buchanan,* the claimant felt "twinges" in his back that were characterized by a physician as the harmful loosening of an already damaged disc fragment, thus one day of employment was an injury to the spine.

In *Foundation Constructors,* the last six months of jackhammering and pile driving were "cumulative trauma," which in a physician's opinion was "harmful" to the claimant's back condition. In *Kelaita*, the claimant had painful flare ups that "could have aggravated and contributed" to an attritional rotator cuff tear. The last employer was liable.

As a practical matter, these cases well illustrate the fluid boundaries of two-employer claims. One day is enough, but in some instances the injury may occur over a period of months or even years, all without history of a specific injury. The litmus test for shifting liability to the second employer is, however, the best medical opinion.

Does a physician explain in credible, succinct medical terms the role of the last incident or period of employment? Is there medical opinion sufficient to constitute substantial evidence that a claimant's complaints, flare-ups, and pain were harmful and injurious? Even if a claimant returned to work one last day for the purpose of shifting liability to another employer, do the medical opinions of harm and injury still determine the liable *Price* employer?

6.4 Post-*Price*: The Ninth, Other Circuits, and the Board

Thus, the post-*Price* results in the Ninth Circuit depend entirely upon the answers to these and similar medical questions at the ALJ level, but with a touch of timidity of the Court in publishing opinions that are of similar landmark status or for further guidance. For example, in *Stevedoring Services of American v. (Arel) Price*, 38 BRBS 34 (9th Cir. 2004) (unpublished), the Ninth Circuit affirmed an award against the last chronological employer on the grounds that the ALJ had made sufficient determinations of "significant probative [medical] evidence" without necessarily addressing "*all* probative contrary evidence." 38 BRBS 36.

Likewise it was within the "ALJ prerogative" to give greater weight to the opinion of one physician over another in that the ALJ, as finder of fact, may "credit the testimony of one witness over another." *Id.* Further, in light of the ALJ findings, the Court found no error by the Board in placing the burden of persuasion on the last chronological employer under *Buchanan* principles.

By the exact same logic, however, the Board affirmed an ALJ award against the first employer, where the ALJ rejected the testimony of one physician over that of another. *Avant v. National Steel & Shipbuilding Co.,* 37 BRBS 142 (2003); *aff'd* BRB No. 03-414, 414A, (Dec. 18, 2003)(unpublished); *aff'd sub nom National Steel & Shipbuilding Co. v. Avant*, No. 04-72223 (May 31, 2006)(unpublished). Strangely enough this also involved a knee injury, where the first injury was found responsible for the permanent disability!

The Fifth Circuit has also demonstrated some ambivalence towards the *Price* doctrine, at least when the Fifth Circuit sticks it to the first employer. For example, while citing *Price*, in an unpublished decision, the Fifth Circuit goes to great length to discuss aggravation principles in upholding an ALJ award against the first employer. *Operating & Consulting Services, Inc. v. Director, OWCP (Morrison)*, 170 Fed.Appx. 931 (5th Cir. 2006) *cert. denied* 127 S.Ct. 1038 (2007).

The Fifth Circuit also well describes in *Morrison* the role of an appellate court in the evaluation of medical evidence when it stated as follows:

> We are neither doctors nor the original fact finders in this matter, and so, under the appropriate standard of review, we need not assess the plausibility of these medical accounts, nor do we assess the weight they should be accorded relative to other evidence in the record. See *Pool Co. v. Cooper*, 274 F.3d 173, 178 (5th Cir. 2001) (stating that like the BRB, "we may not substitute our judgment for that of the ALJ, nor reweigh or reappraise the evidence, but may only determine whether evidence exists to support the ALJ's findings") (quoting *New Thoughts Finishing Co. v. Chilton*, 118 F.3d 1028, 1030–31 (5th Cir. 1997)). Our task is more limited: we ask only whether this evidence was relevant to the ALJ's decision, and whether the ALJ's decision was reasonable based on this evidence. *Ceres Marine Terminal v. Dir., OWCP*, 118 F.3d 387, 391 (5th Cir. 1997) 170 Fed.Appx. 936.

See also, *Berry Brothers General Contractors, Inc., v. Director, OWCP (Taylor)*, No. 07-060370, 2008 WL 59523, Jan. 3, 2008 (Unpublished) (Reliance by ALJ upon opinion of physician that subsequent work "would likely" aggravate a knee injury was improper where nothing indicates that it "actually did.").

The Seventh Circuit, like the Ninth, has no hesitation in publishing its opinions to affirm liability on the second or last chronological employer liable. See, *Marinette Marine Corp. v. OWCP (Baumler)*, 431 F.3d 1032 (7th Cir. 2005) (In a two-injury case also involving differences of opinion between orthopedic experts, the Court noted that "we are not equipped to decide" whether a temporary back spasm contributed to a worsening of symptoms because "that was the ALJ's call").

While pre-dating *Price*, the published approach of the Third Circuit is ominously similar to the BRB *Buchanan* approach. In *Delaware River Stevedores, Inc., v. Director, OWCP (Loftus)*, 279 F.3d 233 (3rd Cir. 2002), the Court upheld the Board's reversal of the ALJ where the later work "aggravated" the original injury and the Judge had used the incorrect legal standard of a "precipitant injury." 279 F.3d at 243.

Finally, in spite of *Buchanan* the Board has actually affirmed at least one award against a middle employer. *Reposky v. International Transportation Services, Inc.*, 40 BRBS 65 (2006). The Board found substantial evidence supporting the finding of further injury after the first injury, but no further injury from later employment after a spinal fusion.

6.5 Conclusion: *Price*—The New is Old Rule For Evidence

The discussion and prediction of *Price* issues may still hold true from this chapter as it appears in the Fifth Edition (2005) of this book. Namely, the last employer rule now evolves with at least three branches, maybe even a small shrub. Indeed, the author submits that in the Ninth Circuit there are three distinct last employer rules, the application of which depends upon the type of alleged injury and exposure.

In hearing loss claims, there may now be two or more last responsible employers under the mandate of *Stevedoring Services v. Director, OWCP (Benjamin)* 297 F.3d 797 (9th Cir. 2002), so long as a determinative audiogram establishes a ratable impairment and separate injury with different employers. In accordance with the decision of the United States Supreme Court in *Bath Iron Works v. Director, OWCP*, 506 U.S. 153 (1993), *Benjamin* rejects the merger of separate hearing loss claims into a single injury.

The conclusion in *Benjamin* is as follows:

> In hearing loss cases, a claimant may continue working despite being considered disabled in the eyes of the law. Therefore, he may be exposed to additional injury over time. This should not mean that an employer who is liable under the application of the "last employer doctrine" should be able to escape liability just because a second employer can also be assigned liability under the same doctrine." 297 F.3d at 805.

Yet, under *Price* the first employer will almost always escape liability precisely because the traumatic, orthopedic claims are considered merged into a single injury and the second employer can be assigned liability.

Even more ironic is the *Price* conclusion that "having a bright line" will eliminate litigation and provide for prompt payment of benefits. The very facts of *Price* and later cases illustrate the attendant delays and denials that will inevitably arise as employers and carriers seek to shift the paddle of liability ever downstream upon the slightest additional cumulative contribution to an orthopedic condition.

Thus, *Price* establishes a second last employer rule that is remarkably different than the last employer rule in hearing loss claims. That rule, most certainly endorsed by the Board, is that all two-employer orthopedic claims, specific and cumulative, are deemed merged into a single condition. The Board's rule and published rule of the Ninth, is that all else being equal, the last day of employment and aggravation, however slight, shall be deemed as a matter of law the basis to assign liability to the last chronological employer.

Third, there still remains a last employer rule for occupational diseases that involve latent conditions that develop over many years (i.e., asbestos-related conditions, silicosis, etc.). Only this branch of the last employer rule remains true to its *Cardillo* origins.

Namely, upon the convergence of a claimant's awareness of the industrial origins of his condition and disability (i.e., earnings impairment), the last employer shall be liable. *Todd Shipyards Corp. v. Black*, 717 F.2d 1280 (9th Cir. 1983). On the other hand, there must be some rational link between the alleged exposure and the employment. *Todd Shipyards Corp. v. Director (Picinich)* 914 F.2d 1317 (9th Cir. 1990). Thus, for occupational disease, the third branch of the last employer rule is that the last means last.

The author submits that the last employer rules for hearing loss and latent manifestation disease are rational and well rooted in the *Cardillo* doctrine. In contrast, the *Price* decision seems untrue to its roots and likely to continue in the future to foist uncertainty, delays, and denials of benefits to an ever greater number of injured workers covered under the Longshore Act.

In preparing to go forward with or defend against a *Price* claim in light of the ever-emerging case law, the author suggests that the old has become new. The outcome of all *Price* proceedings depends on the evidence upon which the ALJ chooses to rely.

That quantum of *Price* evidence must only be "*more than a mere scintilla*" and sufficiently reasonable to support the ultimate findings of fact and conclusion of law. *Wendler v. American National Red Cross*, 23 BRBS 408, 412 (1990)

(ALJ vested with sole authority to evaluate claimant's credibility about when she became aware of injury), as quoting *Universal Camera Corp. v. NLRB,* 340 U.S. 474, 477 (1951).

Likewise, the Courts of Appeals are unanimous in following the axiom that the evidence upon which the ALJ chooses to rely must be "more than a mere scintilla" on a wide variety of issues. *Lockheed Shipbuilding v. Director, OWCP*, 951 F.2d 1143, 1145, 25 BRBS 85, 87 (CRT) (9th Cir. 1991) (Substantial evidence supported ALJ finding that claimant had not recovered from a prior injury); *Newport News Shipbuilding & Dry Dock Co. v. Faulk*, 228 F.3d 378 , 380-81 (4th Cir. 2000) (In a last employer occupational disease case, the evidence of asbestos exposure upon which the ALJ relied "must still be sufficient- more than a *scintilla* but less than a preponderance"). *New Thoughts Finishing Co. v. Chilton*, 118 F.3d 1028, 1030-31 (5th Cir. 1997) (Insufficient findings to support AWW).

Price disputes may now be added to the list of issues that must be decided by this standard. In all *Price* cases, make sure you have at least a scintilla of evidence, but hopefully the preponderance of evidence. In either event, expect a long haul.

Part II
Medical Treatment

Chapter 7

The Health Insurance Portability and Accountability Act of 1996 & The Longshore and Harbor Workers' Compensation Act

Robert Kessner, Esq. & Robert A. McLaughlin, Esq.

Synopsis

7.1 Background

The Health Insurance Portability and Accountability Act (HIPAA), Public Law 104-191, was enacted by Congress to improve the efficiency and effectiveness of the healthcare system and was signed into law on August 21, 1996. HIPAA added a new part C, Administrative Simplification, to chapter 7, 42 U.S.C. § 1320d which directed, *inter alia*, the Secretary of the Department of Health and Human Services (HHS) to adopt national standards for electronic healthcare[1] transactions, making it easier for health plans, doctors, hospitals and other healthcare providers to process claims and other transactions electronically and to incorporate provisions mandating the adoption of federal security and privacy standards to protect individually identifiable health information, 42 U.S.C. § 1320d-2, and providing penalties for the wrongful disclosure of individually identifiable health information, 42 U.S.C. § 1320d-6.

The primary objectives of the HIPAA legislation were to

- assure health insurance portability by eliminating job-lock due to pre-existing medical conditions,
- reduce healthcare fraud and abuse,
- enforce standards for health information, and
- guarantee security and privacy of health information.

In enacting HIPAA, Congress authorized HHS to promulgate standards governing disclosures of an individual's health information to be submitted to Congress for consideration in enacting privacy legislation. HIPAA further provided that if Congress did not pass privacy standards legislation by August 21, 1999, HHS was to promulgate final regulations containing such standards by February 21, 2000. Since Congress did not enact legislation for a privacy standard, HHS proposed and later adopted the Privacy Rule, the Standards for Privacy of Individually Identifiable Health Information (the "Privacy Rule"), 45 CFR parts 160 and 164, on December 28, 2000. In March 2002, specific changes were made to ensure that the Privacy Rule protected privacy without interfering with access to care or quality of care and to improve workability. On August 14, 2002, the final modifications to the Privacy Rule were adopted and the compliance date for implementation of the requisite standards to protect and guard against the misuse of individually identifiable health information was set for April 14, 2003 (April 14, 2004 for small health plans) with civil or criminal penalties triggered under certain circumstances for failure to timely implement standards.

This article provides an overview of sections of the Privacy Rule that affect the handling of workers' compensation claims, including those subject to the LHWCA and other federal law.

7.2 The Privacy Rule

The Privacy Rule establishes national standards for the protection of health information created or maintained by 'covered entities.' Covered entities include health plans, healthcare clearinghouses and healthcare providers who conduct certain healthcare transactions electronically. It limits the use and release of 'protected health information.' Protected health information is defined as individually identifiable health information that has been transmitted or maintained as electronic media whether transmitted or maintained in any other form or medium such as paper or oral. The Privacy Rule gives patients the right to access their medical records; restricts most disclosure[2] of protected health information to the minimum needed for the intended purpose; and establishes safeguards and restrictions regarding the disclosure of records for certain public responsibilities. In addition, HIPAA delineates the criminal and civil sanctions to which a covered entity may be subject for improper uses or disclosures. The Privacy Rule, however, does not apply to workers' compensation insurers, workers' compensation administrative agencies, or employers, except to the extent they are also covered entities.[3]

The primary purpose of the Privacy Rule is to require covered entities to maintain administrative and physical safeguards to protect the confidentiality of health information and against unauthorized access. See U.S. Department of Labor, Office of Administrative Law Judges website, www.oalj.dol.gov. While the Privacy Rule establishes a foundation of federal protections for the privacy of protected health information, it does not replace federal, state, or other law that grants individuals greater privacy protections. Moreover, covered entities are permitted to retain or adopt more protective policies or practices.

The following discussion focuses on the sections of the Privacy Rule with the most impact on workers' compensation processes: 45 CFR § 164.502 which provides the general rules for the uses and disclosures of protected health information, 45 CFR § 164.508 which governs the uses and disclosures for which an authorization is required, and 45 CFR § 164.512 which specifies the uses and disclosures for which an authorization or opportunity to agree or object is not required.

A. General Rules for Use and Disclosure of Protected Health Information— 45 CFR § 164.502 General rule. 45 CFR § 164.502(a)

The general rule is that a covered entity may not use or disclose protected health information except as permitted or required by the Privacy Rule. 45 CFR § 164.502(a). The Privacy Rule mandates disclosure in only two instances: (1) when the disclosure is requested by the individual and required to be disclosed to the individual by the Privacy Rule, and (2) when it is required by HHS to investigate or determine if the covered entity has complied with the Privacy Rule. 45 CFR § 164.502(a)(2). All other disclosures by the covered entity are permissive. 45 CFR § 164.502.

B. Minimum Necessary—45 CFR § 164.502(b)

The Privacy Rule mandates that the covered entity make reasonable efforts to limit the use or disclosure of protected health information to the 'minimum necessary' to accomplish the intended purposes of such use or disclosure. 45 CFR § 164.502(b)(1). However, the minimum necessary standard does not apply to certain disclosures permitted by the Privacy Rule. 45 CFR § 164.502(b)(2). In particular, with respect to workers' compensation issues, the minimum necessary standard does not apply to uses or disclosures that are required by law pursuant to 45 CFR §164.512(a), nor to uses or disclosures made pursuant to a valid authorization under 45 CFR §164.508. 45 CFR § 164.502(b)(2) at (ii), (v). The minimum necessary standard is significant when considering other permitted uses and disclosures applicable to LHWCA. Thus, further exploration of the HHS meaning and intent of this standard is warranted.

HHS's responses to comments on the proposed rule provide insight as to how the 'minimum necessary' language should be interpreted. HHS's comment responses indicate that a covered entity is presumptively in violation of the minimum necessary standard if it releases an entire medical file of an individual in response to a request for disclosure that fails to articulate why release of the entire file is justified.[4] HHS recommends that for common, routine disclosure requests, the covered entity implement standard policies and procedures that permit only the disclosures of protected health information reasonably necessary to achieve the purpose of the disclosure.[5] These procedures must identify the types of protected health information to be disclosed, the types of persons who would receive the protected health information, and the conditions that would apply for such access.[6] For non-routine disclosures, HHS places the burden on covered entities to develop reasonable criteria for determining and limiting disclosure to the minimum necessary to accomplish the purpose of the disclosure.[7] In addition, covered entities must establish and implement procedures that are tailored to review such requests on an individual basis in accordance with these criteria.[8]

The final version of the minimum necessary standard also requires that the covered entity make 'reasonable efforts' to comply with the standard.[9] This was a change from the initial proposed rule, which used the term 'all reasonable efforts,' indicating that HHS did not intend to apply a 'good faith' standard.[10] HHS made clear that the standard also applies to covered entities requesting protected health information from other covered entities in regard to non-treatment matters.[11] Therefore, a 'good faith' error in a disclosure will not excuse the covered entity from its duties under the Privacy Rule if the error is unreasonable, where there are no reasonable policies and procedures in place for the type of disclosure requested that caused the error, or where the disclosure is made in violation of the reasonable policies and procedures in place for the type of disclosure requested. HHS has imposed extensive burdens on covered entities to protect the medical privacy of individuals and such precautions should not be taken lightly.

Thus, there is a strong indication that the minimum necessary standard should be applied broadly in light of the surrounding facts of a situation.

7.3 Uses and Disclosures Permitted by the Privacy Rule—45 CFR §§ 164.512 & 164.508

Section 164.512 explains the circumstances in which a CE may use or disclose PHI without written authority. 45 CFR §164.512(a), 45 CFR §164.502(b)(2) & 65 Fed. Reg. 82525. The requirements for the application of each section permitting disclosure or use are set forth in that section. The individual requirements range from: providing the individual an opportunity to agree or object, to no notice in particular situations. However, the sections are not mutually exclusive and may overlap. These provisions of the Privacy Rule are permissive and do not mandate that the CE disclose the information.

The are several disclosures permitted to the Privacy Rule but the disclosures that most impact practice under the LHWCA are: (A) Disclosures required by law 45 CFR § 164.512(a), (B) Disclosures for workers' compensation 45 CFR § 164.512(l), (C) Disclosures for judicial and administrative proceedings 45 CFR § 164.512(e), and (D) Disclosures in which an authorization has been provided 45 CFR § 164.508.

A. Uses and Disclosures Required by Law—45 CFR § 164.512(a)

A covered entity may only disclose protected health information to the extent required by law. 45 CFR § 164.512(a). What is required by law is defined in 45 CFR §164.103, which provides: "required by law means a mandate *contained* in a law that compels a covered entity to make a use or disclosure of protected health information *and* that *is enforceable* in a court of law." 45 CFR § 164.103. The section then provides some examples, which are not all inclusive. Examples include: court orders, subpoenas or summons issued by a court or an administrative body authorized to require the production of the information, and statutes or regulations that require the production of information. 45 CFR § 164.512(e). Because this paragraph applies to laws mandating disclosure of PHI and the paragraph limits the disclosure to the requirements of such law, the minimum necessary standard does not apply to this paragraph. 45 CFR 164.512(a) & 45 CFR § 164.502(b)(2).

Of interest is that this paragraph is explicitly referenced in the response to comments made in the proposed final rule contained in 65 Federal Register and 67 Federal Register to the workers' compensation disclosure provisions contained in paragraph §164.512(l).[12] The response demonstrates how the provisions of §164.512(a) and §164.512(l) interrelate with respect to the LHWCA and other workers' compensation laws.

In reviewing various workers' compensation laws, HHS discussed Texas laws that provide two different scenarios. In one, Texas law requires the covered entities to provide records related to treatment to the carrier. In the other, Texas law provides, according to HHS, that a covered entity is permitted, but not required, to disclose to the carrier records relating to diagnosis and treatment of the injured employee without his/her authorization to determine the amount of payment or entitlement to payment.

In discussing the first scenario, HHS noted, "[s]ince such disclosure is required by law, it also is permissible under the Privacy Rule at §164.512(a) and exempt from the minimum necessary standard." When addressing the second scenario of permissive disclosure under the Texas workers' compensation laws, HHS stated:

> [s]ince the disclosure only is permitted and not required by Texas law, the provisions at §164.512(l) would govern to permit such disclosure. In this case, the minimum necessary standard would apply to the disclosure but would allow for information to be disclosed as authorized by the statute, that is, as necessary to 'determine the amount of payment or the entitlement to payment.[13]

Thus, if a statute, regulation, or case law comprising the LHWCA states that a covered entity shall provide the protected health information of a claimant to the carrier and that statute, regulation, or case law is enforceable either by the District Director's Office, Office of Administrative Law Judges, Benefits Review Board, or the appellate courts, the covered entity is permitted to disclose the protected health information to the carrier. With one caveat, if the PHI is required by law pursuant to the provisions of §164.512(e), the CE must still comply with provisions of paragraph (e) in order to disclose the PHI to the carrier. 45 CFR § 164.512(a)(2). The provisions of 45 CFR §164.512(e) will be discussed in further detail below.

What protected health information under the LHWCA may be required by law to be disclosed? The answer may be protected health information indicating the type of treatment to be furnished to the claimant that is necessary given the claimant's injury, and other similar treatment recommendations.

Finally, if a covered entity may provide the protected health information by statute, regulation, or case law comprising the LHWCA, the provisions at §164.512(l) could apply, but the provisions of §164.512(a) do not apply. Whether the CE must disclose the PHI to the carrier will depend on the law in question. On certain issues all parties will agree that the law requires disclosure, while litigation may be necessary on other issues.

B. Disclosures for Workers' Compensation—45 CFR § 164.512(l)

As specifically related to workers' compensation matters, the Privacy Rule was adopted with the intent of keeping the existing processes intact as evinced in 45 CFR § 164.512(l) which states:

> A covered entity may disclose protected health information as authorized by and to the extent necessary to comply with laws relating to workers' compensation or other similar programs, established by law, that provide benefits for work-related injuries or illness without regard to fault.

This paragraph allows a covered entity to disclose protected health information as "authorized by and to the extent necessary" to comply with laws related to workers' compensation which includes the LHWCA. However, what does "authorized by and to the extent necessary" to comply with workers' compensation laws mean? In its initial comments, HHS indicated the difficulty in dealing with the Privacy Rule and its interrelation with workers' compensation systems. HHS apparently struggled with this authorization paragraph in part because of the many varied workers' compensation systems versus the different privacy issues each system causes. One factor relevant in interpreting this phrase is that the minimum necessary standard applies to disclosures under this paragraph. 45 CFR § 164.502(b).

Another factor relevant to interpreting the phrase, "authorized by and to the extent necessary" is that HHS made clear that the Privacy Rule permits disclosures necessary for the administration of workers' compensation systems. This includes the sharing of information without consent between providers and workers' compensation carriers.[14] HHS stated that the Privacy Rule was not intended to impede the flow of protected health information that is needed by workers' compensation carriers in order to "process or adjudicate claims and/or coordinate care" under the workers' compensation system.[15] What protected health information would constitute to the extent necessary to process or adjudicate claims under the LHWCA?

As indicated above, if the law requires disclosure of protected health information, it comes under the provisions of §164.512(a). If the disclosure comes under the heading of discovery, or it is not covered by any other provision, it is covered by the provisions of §164.512(e). Therefore, we can discern that "authorized by and to the extent necessary" is something less than the 'required by law' provision but something more than searching for admissible evidence. While courts will need to clarify this point in the future, there is a certain amount of protected health information that likely falls under this definition.

First, in order for the treating physician and other health care providers to be compensated for their services, reports and test results generally need to be provided to the carrier. However, reports with protected health information not relevant to the adjudication or coordination of care should not be provided to the carrier under the minimum necessary standard. For example, an individual's treatment for HIV, medications taken for psychological conditions, or an individual's history of sexual abuse or marriage problems are unrelated to a covered entity's request to obtain payment for the lower back treatment provided to a claimant. But certain comorbid conditions may need to be provided. If the patient has a diabetic comorbid condition it will not be discoverable, however if the patient needs an industrial surgery for which the diabetes needs to be treated to allow the surgery to go forward, the diabetes diagnosis and proposed treatment for it are now relevant to the adjudication of the claim. On the other hand, the patient's prior medical history records regarding his or her diabetes would not be relevant and should not be provided. Some practitioners believe that the protected health information for billing purposes is limited only to routine coded descriptions.[16]

Second, protected health information contained in the attending physician's first report, LS-1a, and any supplemental reports the Secretary through the District Director's office may request on the claimant's status such as reporting indicating continued temporary total disability status, temporary partial disability status, or the maximum medical improvement status of the claimant should be permitted to be disclosed under this provision.

Third are medical reports indicating the existence and extent of permanent partial or permanent total disability, as well as reporting indicating the need for review by a vocational advisor are examples of protected health information that may be disclosed under this provision.

Some of the above noted reports may on occasion be required by law and thus permitted under 45 CFR §164.512(a). However, discovery of protected health information for purposes of 8(f), to find another responsible carrier or to determine apportionment in state workers' compensation cases, cannot be disclosed under this provision.

C. Uses and Disclosures for Judicial and Administrative Proceedings—45 CFR § 164.512(e)

Under §164.512(e), a covered entity is permitted to disclose protected health information during the course of judicial or administrative proceedings. The paragraph addresses two different situations in which disclosure is permitted: (1) in response to an order of a court or administrative tribunal, and (2) in response to a subpoena, discovery request or other lawful process. 45 CFR § 164.512(e)(1)(i) & (ii). Although the minimum necessary standard applies to both situations, the standard is ineffective when applied to the first situation as discussed below. 45 CFR § 164.502(b).

1. In response to an order of a court or administrative tribunal—45 CFR § 164.512(e)(1)(i)

The first situation is disclosure in response to a court order or administrative tribunal. 45 CFR § 164.512(e)(1)(i). In this situation, the covered entity is limited to disclosing only PHI that is expressly authorized by such order. Disclosure of protected health information expressly authorized by the order constitutes *per se* compliance with the minimum necessary standard.[17] In responding to comments on the regulation, HHS stated that notice to the individual is not necessary in these instances because a court or administrative tribunal is in the best position to evaluate the merits of the arguments of the party seeking disclosure and the party who seeks to block such disclosure before it issues the order.[18] This being so, HHS acknowledged that an order from a court or an administrative body should provide a degree of protection for individuals from unnecessary disclosure.[19] Therefore, HHS concluded that imposing further procedural obstacles was unnecessary and a covered entity may honor the order and disclose the requested protected health information.[20] In fact, HHS specifically refused to include language that the protected health information had to be relevant and material, specific and narrowly drawn as reasonably practicable, and only disclosed if de-identified information could not reasonably be used.[21] HHS believed it should not impose such requirements on courts and administrative tribunals and furthermore, HHS's authority is limited to control of covered entities only.[22] Thus, it is up to the individual court or administrative tribunal and the parties involved to address what protected health information can be requested and disclosed.

The comments also clarify that the order is in response to or obtained as a result of some discovery motion or dispute that was resolved by the court or administrative tribunal in which all parties to the issue participated or were given the opportunity to participate.[23] Thus, if after a discovery motion and hearing, a court or administrative tribunal issues an order for production of protected health information, the covered entity is permitted to disclose the protected health information expressly authorized by the order under either §164.512(e) or the required by law provision set forth in §164.512(a). This also includes psychotherapy notes as defined in §164.501 because once the order is issued and final, it also complies with the required by law provision under §164.512(a)(2).

Unfortunately, these sections do not address what is to occur if the order is appealed. Is the covered entity nonetheless permitted to disclose the protected health information? Also not discussed is what the covered entity is to do if the order is ambiguous. Since the covered entity is only permitted, yet not required, to disclose upon a receipt of an order, counsel opposing or appealing the order would be best served by notifying the covered entity of the appeal or the ambiguity that counsel believes exists. Hopefully the covered entity will take this into consideration when deciding whether to disclose the protected health information in response to the order, which, from the covered entity's perspective, is permitted but not mandated.[24]

In addition, it would be wise for counsel to ensure that any court order express the protected health information to be disclosed in clear language and unambiguously set forth the rules governing how parties should obtain and dispose of the protected health information after completion of the litigation.

2. In response to a subpoena, discovery request or other lawful process—45 CFR § 164.512(e)(1)(ii)

This situation contemplates the covered entity providing disclosure in response to some type of formal or informal discovery request. 45 CFR § 164.512(e)(1)(ii). In this situation the covered entity must notify or attempt to notify the individual before it may disclose the protected health information in response to the discovery request. T he covered entity may satisfy this requirement in several different ways.

The first way is to provide the covered entity with 'satisfactory assurances' that the requesting party has made reasonable efforts to notify the individual who is the subject of the protected health information. 45 CFR § 164.512(e)(1)(ii)(A). 'Satisfactory assurance' is any written statement and accompanying documentation demonstrating the following: (1) the party requesting the protected health information has made a good faith attempt to provide written notice to the individual including mailing a notice to the individual's last known address if the individual's location is unknown; (2) the notice included sufficient information about the litigation or proceeding in which the protected health information is requested to permit the individual to raise an objection to the court or administrative tribunal; (3) the time for the individual to raise objections to the court or administrative tribunal has elapsed and either no objection has been filed or all objections filed by the individual have been resolved by the court or administrative tribunal and the disclosures sought are consistent with such resolution. 45 CFR § 164.512(e)(1)(iii)(B).

The second method for complying with the precondition is providing the CE with 'satisfactory assurances' from the party seeking the protected health information that reasonable efforts have been made by such party to secure a 'qualified protective order' that meets the requirement set out below. 45 CFR § 164.512(e)(1)(iv)(A), (B). As used in this method, 'satisfactory assurances' to the covered entity means the covered entity receives from such a party a written statement and accompanying documentation demonstrating either of the following. One, that the parties to the dispute giving rise to the request for the protected health information have agreed to a 'qualified protective order' and have presented it to the court or administrative tribunal with jurisdiction over the dispute. Two, that the party seeking the protected health information has requested a 'qualified protective order' from such court or tribunal. A 'qualified protective order' means an order of a court or administrative tribunal or a stipulation by the parties to the litigation or administrative proceeding that complies with the following. First, it prohibits the parties from using or disclosing the protected health information for any purpose other than the litigation or proceeding for which such information was requested. Second, it requires that the protected health information (including all copies made) be destroyed or returned to the covered entity at the end of the litigation or proceeding. 45 CFR § 164.512(e)(v).

Lastly, the covered entity may comply with the precondition by disclosing the protected health information in a formal or informal discovery request without any 'satisfactory assurances' if the covered entity makes reasonable efforts to provide notice to the individual sufficient to meet the requirements of method one outlined above or to seek a 'qualified protective order' sufficient to meet the requirements of method two outlined above.

HHS makes a point of stating that the provisions of this paragraph do not supersede other provisions of the Privacy Rule that otherwise permit or restrict uses or disclosures of protected health information. 45 CFR § 164.512(e)(2). This provision is in addition to other provisions, but may overlap with, for example, §164.512(a). This permitted disclosure applies to discovery of protected health information that a party requests as part of a judicial or administrative proceeding under the LHWCA. This intent is made apparent by HHS's response to a comment specifically expressing a concern that this proposed paragraph would adversely affect the informal administrative process usually followed in processing workers' compensation claims.[25] The commenter urged that less formal means of obtaining relevant medical evidence be allowed while the matter is pending before an agency. The comment sought to revise the rule to allow disclosure of protected health information without authorization for purposes of federal or state benefit determinations at all levels of processing.

The HHS response discusses how the three main disclosure paragraphs interplay with one another with respect to discoverable protected health information and is provided here in its entirety:

> *Response:* If the disclosure is required by a law relating to workers' compensation, a covered entity may disclose the protected health information as authorized by and to the extent necessary to comply with that law under §164.512(l). If the request for protected health information in connection with a workers' compensation claim is part of an administrative proceeding a covered entity must meet the requirements set forth in §164.512(e), and discussed above, before disclosing the information. As noted, one permissible manner by which a covered entity may disclose protected health information under §164.512(e) is if the party seeking the disclosure makes reasonable efforts to provide notice to the individual as required by this provision. Under this method, the less formal process noted by the commenter would not be disturbed. Covered entity may disclose protected health information in response to other types of requests *only* as permitted by this regulation.[26] (Emphasis added.)

This statement strongly suggests that if none of the other provisions of the Privacy Rule allow the disclosure of the protected health information sought by the defendant, this is the provision of last resort and the defendant must comply with its requirements to obtain the protected health information.

This approach also makes sense from an evidentiary perspective. What is relevant for purposes of discovery is broader than what is relevant for purposes of admissibility at trial. The standard for what is discoverable in most jurisdictions is any matter relevant to the subject matter of the litigation or that is reasonable calculated to lead to the discovery of admissible evidence. On December 1, 2015, Federal Rule 26(b) was amended to limit discovery to that regarding any non-privileged matter that is relevant to any party's claim or defense and proportional to the needs of the case but the information discoverable need not be admissible in evidence. It is unclear if this will make any substantial change to what information can be produced during discovery. In either situation, when a party requests medical discovery, the requester usually lacks the medical expertise to determine what information is medically relevant to the condition or injury at issue. Thus, protected health information may be disclosed during the course of discovery, which may not be discoverable, admissible, nor relevant to the underlying medical condition placed in issue once reviewed by the medical expert. Or, the covered entity may have obtained information that is not relevant to the medical condition that the party has placed in issue but is relevant for purposes of the covered entity's treatment of the party. For example, a covered entity may obtain information during the course of treatment of the individual regarding psychological conditions of the individual as well as psychological medications the individual is currently taking. This information may be pertinent to allowing the covered entity to effectively treat the individual, as the covered entity may need to ensure the psychological medications will not adversely interact with the medications the covered entity prescribes, or confirm that the individual has the capacity to be compliant with the treatment recommendations made by the covered entity. However, a determination as to whether those psychological conditions that constitute protected health information, as noted in the covered entity's records, are admissible or discoverable requires review by a court or administrative tribunal.[27] The individual may have shared information regarding abortions, cosmetic surgeries, a history of sexually transmitted diseases, or alcohol or drug addiction counseling about themselves or other individuals such as family members. Certainly, the individual should be notified of the request for disclosure and provided the opportunity to obtain limitations on the discovery or a qualified protective order pursuant to §164.512(e). The fact that the minimum necessary standard applies to this paragraph further confirms this approach. The covered entity would be compelled to disclose only the protected health information minimally necessary to comply with the disclosure request contained in the formal or informal discovery request. As stated by HHS, "under the statutory framework adopted by Congress in HIPAA, there is a presumption that the information in an individual's medical record belongs to the individual and must be protected from disclosure to third parties."[28]

Thus, even in situations where the individual has placed their medical condition(s) in issue, the balance between the individual's right to privacy and the agency or carrier's right to obtain discovery of protected health information not otherwise allowable compels the use of paragraph §164.512(e) and the protections it provides. This would also hold true for discovery of protected health information under the LHWCA, such as discovery for determining or proving an 8(f) claim or other medical discovery.

D. Disclosures in Which an Authorization Has Been Provided—45 CFR § 164.508

The Privacy Rule differentiates between consent and authorizations. 45 CFR §§ 164.506 & 164.508. The Privacy Rule requires an 'authorization' for uses and disclosures of protected health information not otherwise allowed by the Rule in which case, a voluntary consent is insufficient to permit a use or disclosure unless it satisfies the requirements of a valid authorization. When a state law does not expressly authorize disclosure, then, an individual authorization for the disclosure of protected health information by a covered entity is required. In addition, pursuant to 45 CFR § 164.508(a), an authorization is required for any use or disclosure of psychotherapy notes except for treatment, payment or healthcare operations and other conditions delineated in 45 CFR § (2)(I) and (ii).

A valid authorization is a detailed document, *written in plain language*, giving a covered entity permission to use protected health information for specified purposes and meeting the following requirements: (1) a description of the information to be used or disclosed, (2) the person or class of persons authorized to make the requested use or disclosure, (3) the person or class of persons to whom the covered entity may make the requested use or disclosure, (4) a description of each purpose of the requested use or disclosure, (5) an expiration date or an expiration event relating to the individual or the purpose of the use or disclosure, and (6) the signature of the individual and date. 45 CFR § 164.508(b)(1)(I), (c)(1) and c(3).

In addition, the authorization must include statements to notify the individual of (1) the individual's right to revoke the authorization in writing, how to revoke said authorization and a reference to the covered entity's privacy notice, (2) the covered entity's ability or inability to condition treatment, payment, enrollment or eligibility for benefits including specific statements delineated in 45 CFR § 164.508(c)(2)(ii)(A), (B), and (3) the potential for information disclosed to be subject to redisclosure by the recipient and no longer protected by the Privacy Rule. 45 CFR § 164.508(c)(2).

The covered entity must provide the individual with a copy of the signed authorization. 45 CFR § 164.508(c)(3).

A covered entity is permitted to disclose protected health information described in the authorization to a workers' compensation insurer and others involved in workers' compensation systems when the insurer has obtained the individual's authorization and said authorization contains the elements and meets the requirements specified at 45 CFR § 164.508.

If a claimant's medical record includes portions of a medical record created by another provider, said records may be disclosed provided that the disclosure is permitted by the Privacy Rule (e.g., for treatment).

7.4 Ex Parte Communication Between Representatives of the Carrier and Claimant's Treating Physician

Many state and federal courts have addressed whether HIPAA allows ex parte communications at all.[29] The majority of courts have stated that such ex parte communications under HIPAA and the Privacy Rule are permissible if allowable under applicable state laws.[30] Courts that prohibit ex parte communications have concluded that HIPAA preempts the state laws and HIPAA does not allow ex parte communications.[31] This is incorrect because HIPAA anticipates oral communications of protected health information and oral disclosure of protected health information.[32]

With respect to the LHWCA, neither the Federal Rules of Evidence nor the Federal Rules of Civil Procedure preclude ex parte communications. Using the analysis on permitted disclosures of protected health information, ex parte communications are not required by the LHWCA. In addition, ex parte communications are not authorized by and to the extent necessary to comply with the LHWCA. Hence, the disclosure of protected health information permitted when disclosure is required by law or to comply with laws related to workers' compensation do not apply. Thus ex parte communications generally occur during discovery or in preparation for trial and will generally fall under 45 CFR §164.512(e). Section 164.512(e)(1)(i) provides that a CE may disclose PHI "in response to an order of a court or administrative tribunal." If a requesting party obtains a court order the claimant will have an opportunity to address his or her concerns with the Administrative Law Judge.

A requesting party may also obtain protected health information under 164.512(e)(1)(ii), "in response to a subpoena, discovery request, *or other lawful process*." (Emphasis added.) According to (e)(1)(ii) there is no prohibition under federal law nor the LHWCA that bars a representative of a carrier from communicating orally with a CE on medical discovery issues. In this context an ex parte communication constitutes "[an]other lawful process" permitted under the Privacy Rule.[33] Thus, ex parte communications with a claimant's treating physician is allowed when a party requests protected health information. However, because (e)(1)(ii) governs the ex parte communication, the carrier must comply with subsection (e)(1)(ii)(A) or (B), which requires the carrier to provide satisfactory assurances to the covered entity before disclosure. This provides the claimant the opportunity to object and obtain a qualified protective order. As courts have stated, HIPAA does not preclude ex parte communications, but only establishes the procedures by which these communications may be obtained.[34] These procedures indicate that there is a concern that unfettered ex parte communications could violate a claimant's medical privacy rights protected by HIPAA. For example, the covered entity could make an improper disclosure of the claimant's protected health information or even another individual's protected health information. There is also a risk of disclosing information that may be irrelevant to the litigation, but ultimately prejudicial to the claimant such as the covered entity's attorney work-product.[35]

For these reasons, while ex parte communications are permissible under the LHWCA and the Privacy Rule, HIPAA and the Rule superimpose the procedural protections and requirements of 45 CFR §164.512(e) onto ex parte communications under the LHWCA.

7.5 Implications of the Privacy Rule on the Handling of Workers' Compensation Claims

The Privacy Rule will affect practice under the LHWCA. However, there are several exceptions that will allow an employer or carrier to obtain the necessary protected health information it needs to effectively handle claims and yet still protect the claimant's medical privacy. At times, this will require the carrier to obtain a detailed authorization or a qualified protective order for the medical discovery, including informal medical discovery such as ex parte communications between defense counsel and claimant's treating physician.

From the perspective of counsel for the claimant or injured worker, upon representation of the claimant it would be advisable for counsel to issue a revocation of all prior authorizations signed by claimant prior to representation. This will avoid employer and carriers obtaining medical records of the injured worker without the knowledge of counsel. Also, it will make sure that any authorizations executed by claimant comply with the authorization requirements set out in the Privacy Rule. In addition, all authorizations signed by claimant should be closely reviewed by counsel or the authorizations should be drafted by counsel for the injured worker. If counsel drafts their own template authorization it will guarantee that the authorization will comply with the requirements of the Privacy Rule. Moreover, counsel can add provisions to the authorizations that qualifies with the provisions for a 'qualified protective order,' i.e., prohibits the employer from using or disclosing the protected health information for any purpose other than the litigation for which such information is requested and requires that the protected health information be destroyed at the end of the litigation process.

In the final analysis, the carrier can obtain most, if not all of the claimant's relevant PHI just as it could prior to the implementation of the Privacy Rule. Furthermore, the employer is not precluded from obtaining ex parte discovery with claimant's treating physician under the Privacy Rule. However, the Privacy Rule does superimpose procedural protections and requirements on the employer that must be satisfied in order to obtain the relevant PHI of a claimant or to obtain ex parte discovery from the claimant's treating physician.

Endnotes

1. Health care means care, services or supplies related to the health of an individual. Health care includes the following: (1) preventive, diagnostic, therapeutic, rehabilitative, maintenance, or palliative care, and counseling, service, assessment, or procedure with respect to the physical or mental condition, or functional status, of an individual or that affects the structure or function of the body; (2) sale or dispensing of a drug, device, equipment, or other item in accordance with a prescription 45 CFR §§ 160.103.

2. Disclosure means the release, transfer, provision of access to, or divulging in any other manner of information outside the entity holding the information. 45 CFR 164 § 501.

3. The Privacy Rule considers that certain employers are also covered entities such as pharmacies. The Privacy Rule defines these entities as a "Hybrid entity." In the setting of LHWCA some employers also provide onsite clinics, nursing services and medical services. To the extent that the employer does, those employers may fall under the Hybrid entity rules and employers should be aware of such and comply with the appropriate provisions of the Privacy Rule. Also employers have been sued under such a Hybrid entity theory. *See Doe v. Walgreens Company*, 2010 WL 4823212.

4. Standards for Privacy of Individually Identifiable Health Info., 65 Fed. Reg. at 82,544, 82,714.

5. *Id.*

6. *Id.*

7. Standards for Privacy of Individually Identifiable Health Info., 65 Fed. Reg. at 82,545.

8. *Id.*

9. Standards for Privacy of Individually Identifiable Health Info., 65 Fed. Reg. at 82,714.

10. *Id.* The HHS also rejected using a "good faith" standard for compliance by the covered entities.

11. *See* Standards for Privacy of Individually Identifiable Health Info., 65 Fed. Reg. at 82,544, 82,545.

12. Standards for Privacy of Individually Identifiable Health Info., 65 Fed. Reg. at 82,708 ; Standards for Privacy of Individually Identifiable Health Info., 67 Fed. Reg. at 53,198.

13. *Id.* As a further comment on this issue of the minimum necessary standard applying to the workers' compensation disclosure section, the HHS noted that it was aware that it may have a chilling effect on the workers' compensation system and thus the HHS would actively monitor the effects of the PR on the industry and if deemed appropriate proposing modifications to the minimum necessary standard for disclosures for workers' compensation purposes. In the latest proposed amendments to the PR which became effective on March 26, 2013, no such changes have been proposed.

14. Standards for Privacy of Individually Identifiable Health Info., 65 Fed. Reg. at 82,707.

15. *Id.*

16. Under 45 CFR §164.501 the definition of psychotherapy notes may provide us some guidance. The definitions specifically excludes medication prescriptions, monitoring, counseling sessions start and stop times, the modalities and frequency of treatment furnished, results of clinical tests, and summaries of diagnosis, functional status, treatment plan, symptoms, prognosis and progress to date. It appears that the exception is in place for billing purposes so that the payor can confirm the services provided and the accuracy of the billing submitted. Thus, this may have some probative value in determining what protected health information may be provided to a LHWCA carrier for payment or billing for treatment provided to a claimant by a covered entity.

17. Standards for Privacy of Individually Identifiable Health Info., 65 Fed. Reg. at 82,676.

18. *Id.*

19. *Id.*

20. *Id.*

21. *Id.*

22. Standards for Privacy of Individually Identifiable Health Info., 65 Fed. Reg. at 82,676.

23. Id.

24. This does present what could be an interesting dilemma for the covered entity. If the covered entity does believe that the order is ambiguous or defective on its face, failure to comply with the order could lead to contempt proceedings against the covered entity despite the fact that the covered entity is permitted under the Privacy Rule not to comply in such a situation. What action the covered entity should take in such a situation should be discussed by the covered entity with its counsel.

25. Standards for Privacy of Individually Identifiable Health Info., 65 Fed. Reg. at 82678.

26. *Id.*

27. On the federal level there is no recognition of a physician-patient privilege. However, there is a federal psychotherapist-patient privilege. *See Jaffee v. Redmond*, 116 S. Ct. 1923 (1996). Thus, an individual placing their orthopedic condition into issue under the LHWCA would not constitute an automatic waiver of any psychotherapist-patient privilege. Also, the psychotherapist privilege has been extended to cover EAPs in the Ninth Circuit. *See Oleszko v. State Comp. Ins. Fund*, 243 F.3d 1154, 2001 WL 267027 (9th Cir. 2001). In addition, the Southern District of Indiana has extended the privilege to medical doctors who are not mental health professionals because the doctor's notes at a clinic the individual went to included notes of psychological symptoms and conditions. The court concluded that these notes were protected by the psychotherapist-patient privilege. *See Finley v. Johnson Oil Co.*, 199 F.R.D. 30, 2001 WL 125294 (S.D. Ind. Jan. 18, 2001).

28. Standards for Privacy of Individually Identifiable Health Info., 65 Fed. Reg. at 82,677.

29. District of Columbia, Georgia, Michigan, Mississippi, Missouri, New Jersey, New York, Ohio, Oklahoma, federal district courts of California, Connecticut, Florida, Illinois, Kansas, Maryland, Pennsylvania.

30. *Id.*

31. *Proctor v. Messina*, 320 S.W.3d 145 (Mo. 2010) (en banc).

32. 42 U.S.C. §1320d(4) (2006); 45 CFR §160.103 (2013).

33. *See* 45 U.S.C. §164.512(e)(1)(ii) (2013).

34. *Law v. Zuckerman*, 307 F. Supp. 2d 705 (S. Div. D. Md. 2004); *Crenshaw v. Mony Life Ins. Co.* 318 F. Supp. 2d 1015 (S.D. Cal. 2004); *Keshecki v. St. Vincent's Med. Ctr.*, 785 N.Y.S.2d 300 (N.Y. Sup. Ct. 2004); *Bayne v. Provost*, 359 F. Supp. 2d 234 (N.D.N.Y. 2005); *Holmes v. Nightingale*, 158 P.3d 1039 (Okla. 2007); *Moreland v. Austin*, 670 S.E.2d 68 (Ga. 2008); *Block v. Del Campo*, 2010 WL 2698295 (N.D. Ill. 2010); *Holman v. Rasak*, 785 N.W.2d 98 (Mich. 2010); *Baker v. Wellstar Health Sys.*, 703 S.E.2d 601 (Ga. 2010); *Lowen v. Via Christi Hosps. Wichita, Inc.*, 2010 WL 4739431 (D. Kan. 2010); *Tender Loving Health Care Servs. of Ga., LLC v. Ehrlich*, 734 S.E.2d 276, 283 (Ga. Ct. App. 2012).

35. *Tender Loving Health Care Servs. of Ga., LLC*, 734 S.E.2d at 283; *Browne v. Horbar*, 792 N.Y.S.2d 314 (N.Y. Sup. Ct. 2004).

Chapter 8

Medical Treatment

Ralph R. Lorberbaum, Esq.

Medical treatment for injuries under the Longshore and Harbor Workers' Compensation Act and its extensions is covered under Section 7 of the Act, 33 U.S.C. §907. It must be remembered that claims for medical treatment are never time barred.[1] Therefore, even if a timely claim for income benefits has not been made, an injured worker can always file for medical benefits. An injured worker need not be disabled in order to be eligible for medical services under Section 7.[2] Since medical benefits are not considered "compensation", the payment of medical expenses will not toll the Section 12 statute of limitations requirement for income benefits.

Medical care must be furnished as long as the nature of the injury requires. Medical expenses must be reasonable and necessary.[3] An administrative law judge has the authority to reject the payment for unnecessary medical treatment.[4] A claimant establishes a prima facie case for compensable medical treatment when a qualified physician indicates treatment is necessary for a work-related injury.[5] An administrative law judge is required to make specific findings of fact regarding an employer's contention that any medical expenses which are the "natural and unavoidable result of the work-related injury" are not due to any intervening cause.[6] An employer is not liable for medical expenses that arise solely from the degenerative aging process.[7] However, medical benefits are allowed even if the treatment is due only in part because of the work-related condition.[8] Therefore, an employer would be liable for all medical expenses which are the natural and unavoidable result of a work-related injury.[9] If an injured worker suffers an aggravation or new injury with a second covered employer, then the second covered employer becomes liable for the ongoing medical treatment.[10]

If an injured worker suffers an additional injury during a medical examination, the resulting medical expenses are covered under the Act.[11] In addition, an employer may be liable for additional medical expenses caused by errors of the treating physician.[12]

The Benefits Review Board has awarded medical expenses for corrective lens,[13] modification to a claimant's house necessitated by his injury,[14] biofeedback treatment,[15] chiropractic treatment,[16] medical travel expenses[17] and attendant care.[18] Medical care also includes technical services such as lab tests, x-rays and other diagnostic tests, as well as the travel necessary to have the tests performed.[19]

It must be remembered that an injured worker has the right to choose an attending physician under Section 7(a) of the Act. Once this free choice is made, an injured worker may not later change his primary physician without prior approval from the employer or the Department of Labor.[20] An authorized treating physician is allowed to make referrals to a specialist without first getting written approval.[21] Once an employer refuses to provide further medical treatment, the workers is free to select any physician without getting the employer's permission, and the worker will only have to show the treatment was necessary to win the payment of the expenses.[22]

If an injured worker unreasonably refuses to submit to medical or surgical treatment or to an examination set up by the employer, then the District Director Secretary of Labor or administrative law judge may suspend all further compensation during the period of unreasonable refusal.[23] The Board has held that a two-part test must be satisfied before benefits may be suspended. First, the refusal must be "unreasonable" and second, it must not be "justified." However, even if the worker fails one or both parts of the test, there is no automatic right to have income benefits suspended.[24]

When medical questions arise, the Secretary of Labor or District Director may select a physician to examine the claimant, with the examination to be paid for by the employer.[25] Unfortunately, the results of these examinations are not binding on the parties.[26] If there is a question as to the reasonableness or appropriateness of the treatment, and the employee is faced with two or more valid medical options, it is the employee's right to choose his course of treatment. Thus, an administrative law judge may not find that the course chosen by the injured worker is unreasonable or unnecessary if there is no medical evidence in opposition to the course chosen by the worker. Additionally, the treating physician's opinion is usually given more weight than an employer's examining physician.[27] Additionally, the Act does not prevent an injured worker from relying on treatment solely from prayer or spiritual means by an accredited practitioner of a recognized church or religious denomination without suffering a loss of income benefits. Thus an injured worker who refuses medical services solely because he relies on prayer or spiritual means cannot be said to have "unreasonably refused" medical care.[28]

Medical fees are generally limited to the prevailing charges in the community for such treatment.[29] If the jurisdiction has official state medical fees, then they may be used as guidelines.[30] If an injured worker has to go to a hearing over medical expenses and is successful, then the employer may be liable to the injured worker's attorney for his attorney fees.[31] This raises an interesting point in light of the decision of many circuits that there must be a favorable recommendation at the informal conference level before assessed attorney fees may be awarded.

Endnotes

1. *Ryan v. Alaska Constructors, Inc.*, 24 BRBS 65 (1990).
2. *Winston v. Ingalls Shipbuilding, Inc.*, 16 BRBS 168, 174 (1984).
3. *Pernell v. Capitol Hill Masonry*, 11 BRBS 532, 539 (1979).
4. *Scott v. C&C Lumber Co.*, 9 BRBS 815 (1978).
5. *Turner v. Chesapeake & Potomac Telephone Co.*, 16 BRBS 225 (1984).
6. *Atlantic Marine v. Bruce*, 661 F.2d 898, 14 BRBS 63 (5th Cir. 1981), *aff'd* 12 BRBS 65 (1980).
7. *Haynes v. Rederi A/S Aladdin*, 362 F.2d 345, *cert. denied* 385 U.S. 1020 (1967).
8. *Bruce, supra* note 6.
9. *Bruce, supra* note 6.
10. *Abbott v. Gillingham Marine & Manufacturing Co.*, 14 BRBS 453 (1981), *aff'd mem. sub nom. Willemette Iron & Steel Co. v. Director*, OWCP, 698 F.2d 1235 (9th Cir. 1982).
11. *Weber v. Seattle Crescent Container Corp.*, 19 BRBS 146, 148 (1986).
12. *Lindsay v. George Washington University*, 279 F.2d 819 (D.C. Cir. 1960).
13. *Fraley v. Todd Shipyards*, 4 BRBS 252 (1976), *vacated and remanded in part and rev'd in part on other grounds*, 592 F.2d 805, 10 BRBS 9 (5th Cir. 1979).
14. *Dupre v. Cape Remain Contractors*, 23 BRBS 86, 94 (1989).
15. *Barbour v. Woodward & Lothrop, Inc.*, 16 BRBS 300 (1984).
16. *Blanchard v. General Dynamics Corp.*, 10 BRBS 69 (1979).
17. *Day v. Ship Shape Maintenance Co.*, 16 BRBS 38 (1983).
18. *Falcone v. General Dynamics Corp.*, 21 BRBS 145, 147 (1988).
19. 20 C.F.R. §702.401.
20. 33 U.S.C. §907(c)(2); 20 C.F.R. §702.406.
21. 33 U.S.C. §907(b); 20 C.F.R. §702.406(a); *Senegal v. Strachan Shipping*, 21 BRBS 8 (1988); *Rogers Terminal and Shipping Corp. v. Director, OWCP*, 784 F.2d 687, 12 BRBS 79, 86 (1986).
22. *Betz v. Arthur Snowden Co.*, 14 BRBS 805, 809 (1981); *Rieche v. Tracer Marine, Inc.*, 16 BRBS 272, 225 (1984).
23. 33 U.S.C. §907(d)(4).
24. *Pettus v. American Airlines, Inc.*, 6 BRBS 461 (1977).
25. 20 C.F.R. §702.408; 409, 412(a).
26. *Shell v. Teledyne Marble Offshore, Inc.*, 14 BRBS 585, 589 (1981).
27. *Amos v. Director, OWCP*, 153 F3d 1051 (1998), *amended* 164 F3d 480, 32 BRBS 144 (CRT)(9th Cir. 1999), *cert. denied* 120 S.Ct. 40 (1999).
28. 33 U.S.C. §907(k).

29. 33 U.S.C. §907(g).

30. 20 C.F.R. §702.413.

31. *Geisler v. Continental Grain Co.*, 20 BRBS 35 (1987); *Gardner v. Railco Multi Construction Co.*, 19 BRBS 238 (1987), *vacated on other grounds*, 902 F2d 71, 23 BRBS 69 (CRT)(D.C. Cir. 1990).

Chapter 9

New Frontiers in Industrial Psychiatric Injuries

Jess Ghannam, Ph.D.

Psychiatric claims of industrial injury are often a challenge. Determining the compensability of psychiatric or psychological claims are complex as these injuries may or may not involve concomitant physical, orthopedic, or muscular components. The adjudication of these claims are often very difficult and are frequently denied or aggressively litigated.

Under state Worker's Compensation standards, which are widely disparate, predominant industrial causation is typically required where 51% or greater industrial causation is needed before a psychiatric claim can be deemed compensable. However, under the Longshore and Harbor Workers' Compensation Act/Defense Base Act ("The Act"), the threshold for presumption is much lower. The determination is based on the present condition of the applicant, or working conditions, and whether or not it combined, contributed to or aggravated a psychiatric condition or a pre-existing psychiatric condition. (n 1,2)

Traditionally, under "The Act", psychiatric industrial injuries have been recognized as a compensable condition and, especially since the Afghanistan and Iraq Wars, we have seen an increase in claims for these types of injuries. However, the majority of these claims are the result of physical injuries or physical trauma which occurs within the usual and customary course of employment. The nature of these wars has resulted in the production of more complex and nuanced psychiatric and neuropsychiatric injuries. These injuries are often subtle and can be overlooked. Despite being subtle, they can result in significant disability.

There is, however, an emerging body of research and clinical evidence that suggests that psychiatric or psychological industrial injuries may be compensable under "The Act", even in the absence of overt physical injury or trauma. In fact, according to "The Act", specifically 33 U.S.C. 920, any claim for compensation under "The Act" shall be presumed in the absence of substantial evidence to the contrary and then (n 1,2):

a. The claim comes within the provisions of the act
b. The sufficient notice of such claim has been given
c. The injury was not occasioned solely by the intoxication of the injured employee
d. That the injury was not occasioned by the willful intention of the injured employee to injure or kill himself or another

Accordingly, in order to invoke this low threshold presumption, the injured worker must establish (n 1,2):

1. That he or she has suffered a psychological psychiatric impairment
2. That this occurred during or while working
3. The conditions existed which could have caused, aggravated or accelerated the allegation of the psychological condition.

In the absence of obvious physical injury, a more nuanced and complicated analysis must be undertaken and there must be a determination of whether or not the conditions of the injured worker's job created, produced, accelerated or caused psychological or psychiatric injury. There must be a determination made as to whether or not the conditions of employment aggravated, or accelerated a psychiatric or psychological condition which ended up being work-impairing or work-disabling. (n 1,2)

According to "The Act," an injured worker is not necessarily required to show that the conditions are stressful and given the low threshold condition, the stress may prima-facie appear to be relatively mild and non-traumatic. Even under these conditions, psychological and psychiatric injury may be possible and disabling. In addition, cumulative stress under certain conditions of employment do not necessarily have to be extraordinary events. (Well-established legitimate personnel actions of any nature, including those of termination, are generally not considered a compensable under "The Act". (n 1,2)

In light of the large number of individuals returning from Iraq and Afghanistan—including contractors, cultural advisers, linguists, and translators—there are multiple reasons why psychiatric claims may be considered. And, as noted above, psychiatric injury may or may not occur within the context of an observable orthopedic or physical injury nor have to dramatic. The following conditions may actually contribute to a psychiatric or psychological claim not being made:

1. The injured worker, for multiple reasons, may not even notice, and be in denial about, the nature of the conditions of employment or the nature of the traumatic exposure and its subsequent development while at work and subsequent to work.
2. Physicians filling out the Doctor's First Report of Occupational Injury or Illness may also not be aware of the wide range of psychiatric, psychological, and neurological sequelae of injuries and symptoms. Especially in the acute and subacute phases, the symptoms are often subtle, nuanced and need careful exploration and may not even develop for months afterwards. Frequently physicians filling out the Doctor's First Report of Occupational Injury or Illness are not trained specifically in ascertaining the nature of psychiatric and neurological injury, especially as it relates to traumatic exposure including post concussive events and post-traumatic stress disorders.
3. Lastly, applicant and defense attorneys may be unaware of the complex and nuanced nature of psychiatric and psychological symptoms, injuries and their subsequent manifestation as work disabling. Frequently, there is an emphasis on what is observable and seen. In the absence of observable physical or orthopedic injury causing impairment and disability, many attorneys, both defense and applicant, may not be aware of the full impact of psychiatric and neurologic impairment that cause disabling symptoms, thereby reducing the possibility of claims being made.

9.1 Posttraumatic Stress Disorder, Complex Posttraumatic Stress Disorder, Traumatic Brain Injury, and Post Concussive Syndrome

Since 2002, the wars in Afghanistan and Iraq, there has been a dramatic increase in psychiatric and neuropsychiatric injuries. The nature of warfare has changed and the individuals sent to war are no longer solely from the military. Additionally, rocket attacks and improvised explosive devices (IEDs) are so common that very few individuals deployed to these theatres are spared exposure. Traditional diagnoses may no longer fit with this new reality. The nature of warfare in these theatres has resulted in large numbers of contract employees sent to support traditional armed forces. These people include translators, cultural advisors, security support staff, and a wide range of other personnel who are sent to active theatres to support combat operations. The number of non-military individuals sent to active combat theatres is staggering. This increases the number of individuals who may be exposed to traumatic and concussive events.

Because of these new realities, the traditional diagnosis of Post-traumatic Stress Disorder (PTSD), which is a disorder that develops in some people who have seen or have lived through a shocking, scary or life-threatening event, may not be recognized. We now observe the emergence of more complex conditions referred to as Complex Posttraumatic Stress Disorder (C-PTSD) and Mild Traumatic Brain Injury (mTBI). (n 3,4,5)

With respect to traditional PTSD Diagnoses, according to the DSM-V and ICD-10 an adult must have all the following for a diagnosis: At least one re-experiencing symptom, at least one avoidant symptom, at least two arousal and reactivity symptoms, and at least two cognition and mood symptoms. Re-experiencing symptoms include flashbacks, bad dreams and frightening thoughts. Avoidant symptoms include staying away from places, events or objects that are reminders of the traumatic experience, feeling emotionally numb, feeling strong guilt, depression or worry and losing interest in activities that were enjoyable in the past. Additional avoidant symptoms include having trouble remembering things including events around the events causing the symptom itself. Arousal and reactivity symptoms include being easily startled, feeling tense or on edge, having difficulty sleeping and having angry outbursts. The cognitive and mood symptoms include trouble remembering key features of the traumatic events, negative thoughts about oneself or the world, distorted feelings like guilt or blame and loss of interest in enjoyable activities. These signs and symptoms are based on information obtained from the National Institute on Health and National Institute of Mental Health. (n 3).

More recently, however, a new diagnosis—Complex PTSD—has been observed in many people returning from active war theatres. Traditional PTSD involves traumatic events like car accidents and natural disasters and are of a time-limited duration. Typically Complex PTSD occurs in situations where people experience chronic traumatic exposure that continues or repeats itself for many months or years. The current diagnosis of Posttraumatic Stress Disorder does not fully capture events that are chronic in nature and occur over the span of many months and in some cases, even years.

It is certainly possible that an individual would not meet criteria for PTSD, but at the same time be exposed to a chronic traumatic situation that, over the course of many months and sometimes years, who could develop severe psychiatrically-disabling symptoms. In fact, according to a recent field study, 92% of individuals with Complex PTSD (sometimes referred to of disorders of extreme stress Not Otherwise Specified) did not meet diagnostic criteria for PTSD. (n 5)

The symptoms of Complex Posttraumatic Stress Disorder (C-PTSD) include: problems with emotional regulation or dysregulation, persistent sadness, suicidal thoughts, explosive anger or inhibited anger, difficulties with consciousness—including forgetting traumatic events, reliving traumatic events—episodes in which one feels detached from ones self or body or mental processes, difficulties with self perception which may include helplessness, shame, guilt, stigma and a sense of being completely different, distorted perceptions, difficulties with relationships with others including extreme isolation, distress, repeated difficulties in maintaining relationships and dysregulation of relationships and, finally, often times Complex PTSD includes a sense of deep despair. (n 5).

In addition to PTSD and Complex PTSD phenomenon, numerous individuals in these theatres are often exposed to IEDs and other explosive and concussive events, thereby resulting in Traumatic Brain Injury (TBI), sometimes referred to as Post Concussive Disorder or Syndrome. According to the NIH and NIMH, Traumatic Brain Injury (TBI) is a form of acquired brain injury which occurs when a sudden trauma causes damage to the brain. TBI can result when the head suddenly and violently hits an object or when an object pierces the skull and enters the brain, or when concussive forces move through the brain and central nervous system.

There are many kinds of concussive events—IEDs, rockets that explode, or other explosive events. These events can produce concussive events to the brain and result in Traumatic Brain Injury. More importantly, it is now being well established that loss of consciousness is no longer a necessary requirement to have a diagnosis of Traumatic Brain Injury. (n 4).

In the past, emergency room physicians, attorneys and even patients themselves will frequently say that because they didn't lose consciousness a diagnosis of TBI could not be made. Nothing could be further from the truth. Traumatic Brain Injury is not only possible, but oftentimes can result in severe impairment without loss of consciousness. In general, a person with TBI may have the following symptoms: headaches, confusion, light-headedness, dizziness, blurred vision or tired eye, ringing in the ears or tinnitus, bad taste in the mouth, fatigue or lethargy which easily comes on, change in sleeping patterns, behavioral or mood changes, and trouble with memory, concentration and attention There may also be experiences of nausea, repeated vomiting and ongoing difficulty with cognitive functioning. (n 4).

Recently, results from a study of individuals returning from war theatres, including contractors and military personnel from Afghanistan and Iraq, suggest that 50% or more of these individuals do experience concussive events while on deployment that go undiagnosed and untreated. The comorbidity between post concussive events, TBI and Complex Post Traumatic Stress Disorder are, in my opinion, significant and often are overlooked in assessing the potential for psychiatric or psychological injury, despite causing severe disabling symptoms. Given that large number of people deployed to Iraq and Afghanistan, the possibility of being exposed to traumatic psychiatric and concussive events is high. (n 4) As a result, large numbers of returning workers often go without treatment and end up with severe life-long disability.

9.2 Cultural Factors, Reflections, and Recommendations

Because psychiatric and neurologic injuries often do not have visible manifestations, they are easy to miss and ignore. There is another factor that causes injured workers, attorneys, and physicians to miss these kinds of injuries—denial. There is a general cultural bias against having psychiatric problems. There is an even greater cultural bias in the military and among contractors to having psychiatric problems. Despite reaching an epidemic level (every 30 minutes a veteran from Iraq and Afghanistan attempts suicide), very few returning contractors ever notice these symptoms nor receive treatment. As a result, a very small number of individuals receive psychiatric help despite having severe symptoms and an even smaller number of individuals may make claims of psychiatric industrial injury.

Individuals with these symptoms may be so incapacitated that they are unable to work, unable to function socially, and may be unable to perform basic activities of daily living. It is not unusual for individuals with these diagnoses to have life-long disability, even with treatment. When mTBI, PTSD, or C-PTSD are co-morbidly associated in one person, the disabilities are not only life-long, but frequently require a higher level of care than outpatient treatment. Residential care and intensive day-treatment are frequently necessary. Treatment approaches must be multi-disciplinary and involve providers from medicine, neurology, rehabilitation medicine, psychiatry and behavioral medicine. Because the diagnosis of these disabling conditions is sometimes subtle, neuropsychological testing or assessment is required together with MRI, fMRI, and qEEG analyses. It is very easy to miss these diagnoses and careful diagnostic work-ups are essential.

Without a careful and deliberate assessment and comprehensive treatment, these individuals are at risk for life-long disability, homelessness, and even suicide and homicide. Despite the large prevalence and significant morbidity and mortality consequences, there continues to be a culture of missing and denying these diagnoses. With more awareness these consequences can be mitigated with a possibility of a restored life and a return to the workforce.

9.3 Checklist

Finally, I would like to offer a checklist that may be useful in determining whether or not an individual may have a diagnosis of PTSD, Complex PTSD or Traumatic Brain Injury. The following checklist may be helpful when reviewing history of injury:

1. Headaches
2. Confusion
3. Light-headedness
4. Dizziness
5. Blurred vision or tired eyes
6. Ringing in the ears or tinnitus
7. Bad taste in the mouth
8. Fatigue or lethargy which easily comes on
9. Change in sleeping patterns or poor sleep
10. Behavioral or mood changes
11. Trouble with memory, concentration and attention
12. Nausea and vomiting
13. Difficulty with attention and concentration
14. Nightmares
15. Hopelessness
16. Crying easily
17. Increased isolation from friends and family
18. Noise and light sensitivity
19. Relationship problems, fighting and arguing
20. Increased alcohol or drug use
21. Despair, Shame, and Guilt

If five or more of these are present, a more careful psychiatric or neurologic examination may be indicated.

References

1. Psychiatric Claims Under the Longshore and Harbor Workers' Compensation Act. David C. Barnett. Copyright (c) 2012 Loyola University College of Law *Loyola Maritime Law Journal*, 22nd Annual Longshore Conference.

2. Division of Longshore and Harbor Workers' Compensation (DLHWC), LHWCA, Title 33 Navigation and Navigable Waters, Chapter 18, Longshore and Harbor Workers' Compensation Act. http://www.dol.gov/owcp/dlhwc/lhwca.htm#901

3. Post-Traumatic Stress Disorder, https://www.nimh.nih.gov/health/topics/post-traumatic-stress-disorder-ptsd/index.shtml

4. NINDS Traumatic Brain Injury, http://www.ninds.nih.gov/disorders/tbi/tbi.htm

5. Complex PTSD, http://www.ptsd.va.gov/professional/PTSD-overview/complex-ptsd.asp

Part III
Compensation

Chapter 10

Compensation Rates and Cost of Living Adjustments Under the LHWCA

Joseph B. Guilbeau, Esq.

Synopsis

10.1 Overview

Determining the "compensation rate" in a claim is generally straightforward and normally does not require much more than reviewing the appropriate provision, if not remembered outright, once the average weekly wage (AWW) is determined. The determination of the AWW can be a challenge and is covered elsewhere in this Edition. Once the AWW is determined, the corresponding compensation rate changes only in special instances under the LHWCA. The more common Section 10(f) cost of living adjustments (COLA) is applicable only to permanent total disability and death benefits, but applies regardless of the amount of the current compensation rate. Less encountered by most practitioners is the *effect* of the §906(c) increases to each fiscal year's maximum rate. This applies to the lesser subset of claimants who not only are currently receiving compensation for permanent total disability or death benefits, but are relatively high wage earners such that two-thirds of the average weekly wage determined under §10 initially exceeds and perhaps continues to exceed 200 per centum of the National Average Weekly Wage as determined by the Secretary for each fiscal year beginning October 1 (the fiscal year maximum rate). As discussed in detail below, §6(b)(3) provides the methodology for determining the numerical increase (recalculation of the national average weekly wage each October 1 ending with September 30 for the next year) which methodology is expressly incorporated by §10(f) for COLA, whereas §6(c) purports to tell us who is entitled to the increases brought about by annual adjustments to the maximum rate. For simplicity sake, this Chapter will refer to the increases brought about by operation of §6(b)(3) and §6(c) as "§6(c)" escalations or increases. That some confusion resulted in determining how the two independent provisions of §6 and §10(f) operate should not be surprising since both are based on the change, usually an increase, in the newly calculated national average weekly wage. As a result, the increases under each will often be the same numerical percentage, although the §10(f) COLA are fixed at the nearest dollar, §10(g), and the COLA are capped at the lesser of the NAWW increase, or 5 per centum, §10(f)(2).

This is nothing more than a hunch based on the observations of many years of practice, but it seems that 95% of the jurisprudence in this area concerns itself with the application of §6(c) escalations, its coordination with §10(f) COLA to qualifying claimants or beneficiaries, and the interpretation of the language ambiguities of §6(c). However, the two provisions unquestionably operate independently and for different purposes. Fortunately, at this point, this relatively rarely traveled trail, which probably represents less than 5% of the cases experienced by most practitioners, is rather well marked, as most of the primary arguments and questions have been answered by the jurisprudence. In the vast majority of cases handled by practitioners, once the AWW is determined and the corresponding total disability compensation rate is known, that rate does not change. Jurisprudential enlightenment regarding the application of §6(c) escalations and their coordination with §10(f) COLA was mandated because, as we shall see, the "text of §906(c), in isolation, is indeterminate."[1] Moreover, "Although §6(d) and §10(f) "overlap substantially" they are "not entirely duplicative."[2]

10.2 Primary Statutory Provisions

33 U.S.C. §§906; 909; 910(f)

10.3 Discussion of Compensation Rates Including Maximum and Minimum Rates

Regarding compensation rates, once the AWW is determined, permanent total disability benefits, §8(a), temporary total disability benefits, §8(b), and scheduled permanent partial disability benefits, §8(c)(1)–(13), are paid at the rate of two-thirds (66⅔%) of the average weekly wage. Non-scheduled permanent partial disability benefits are payable at two-thirds of the difference between the average weekly wage and the employee's post-accident wage earning capacity, §8(c)(21). Temporary partial disability benefits are paid at the rate of two-thirds of the difference between the employee's average weekly wage and post-accident wage earning capacity, for no greater than five years, §8(e). Scheduled permanent partial disability benefits are payable at two-thirds of the average weekly wage for the period determined under §8(c) for the particular anatomical injury by multiplying the maximum weeks assigned by the impairment rating.

Since the 1984 Amendments, death benefits are payable at the rates established in §9, recapped as follows:

a. Widow or widower with no child of the deceased—50 per centum of the AWW of the deceased (with two years compensation in one sum upon remarriage). §9(b)
b. For each surviving child of the deceased, the additional amount of 16⅔ per centum for each such child, but in the case of death or remarriage of widow or widower, or in the case of no surviving spouse, if there be one surviving child of decedent, such child shall receive 50% of the average weekly wage or if there be more than one such surviving child, they each receive in equal parts 66⅔ per centum of the decedent's average weekly wage. §9(b), 9(c)
c. When there are two or more children AND a surviving spouse, such children split the 16⅔ per centum of the average weekly wage evenly. §9(b)
d. If there is no surviving wife or husband or child; parents and grandparents may receive 25% of the decedent's average weekly wage. §9(d)
e. If there is no surviving spouse; brothers and sisters, grandchildren, and other dependents may receive 20% of the decedent's average weekly wage. §9(d)

The aggregate payment by employer/carrier for death benefits is "capped" by 66⅔ per centum of the average weekly wage of the decedent subject to the annual §10(f) COLA, but the payments can increase annually by §10(f) COLA or §6(c) escalations. The average weekly wage of a decedent has an applicable minimum under §9(e) such that it cannot be less than the national average weekly wage as prescribed in §6(b). However, the total weekly benefits shall not exceed the lesser of the average weekly wage of the decedent or the benefit rate which the deceased employee would have been eligible to receive under §6(b)(1). In the case of a claim based upon death due to occupational disease for which the "time of injury" (as determined under §10(i) occurs after the employee has retired), the total weekly benefits shall not exceed one fifty-second part of the employee's average annual earnings during the 52-week period preceding retirement (§9(e)).

The §6(b)(1) maximum for compensation rates applies to both disability and death benefits (other than compensation for death required to be paid by lump sum—remarriage of widower) and shall not exceed an amount equal to 200 per centum of the applicable National Average Weekly Wage as determined each fiscal year by the Secretary.

Section 6 of the LHWCA provides for the maximum and minimum compensation rates and, potentially, for the annual upward adjustment of the compensation rate of certain claimants. To qualify for the §6(c) increase, claimant must be: (1) an employee or survivor who is entitled to compensation for permanent total disability or death benefits, the threshold for consideration, *and* (2) the AWW calculated under §10 for such claimant is so high that two-thirds of it is initially above and remains above the applicable fiscal maximum rate for one or more years.

The compensation rate applicable to workers entitled to permanent total disability, temporary total disability, and scheduled permanent partial disability benefits are subject to the statutory maximum and minimum compensation rates of §6(b)(1) and (2). The establishment of the annual maximum and minimum rates as well as the §6(c) increases to the maximum rate and the §10(f) COLA are all set by the National Average Weekly Wage as determined annually by the Secretary of Labor by no later than October 1 of each year. Applying the maximum and minimum rates is easy. The application of the §6(c) rate increases to qualifying claimants independent of the §10(f) cost of living adjustments, to those relatively rare claimants/beneficiaries who are entitled to such increases in benefit rates, has prompted a good bit of tedious complication in the caselaw, which this section of the Textbook will attempt to explore and succinctly explain to a practitioner in hopefully a single reading. Fortunately, jurisprudence has ultimately provided a well-marked trail through this somewhat obscure and less traveled area of the LHWCA.

10.4 §906 Max/Min Rates and AWW Adjustments

Section 6(a) provides that no weekly compensation shall be paid for the first three days of the disability unless the injury results in disability of more than 14 days, in which case weekly compensation shall be paid from the date of disability.

Section 6(b) provides the minimum and maximum rates for compensation benefits. Prior to the 1972 Amendments, the maximum rate for disability benefits was $70.00 a week and the minimum rate was the lesser of $18.00 or the employee's actual AWW. The 1972 Amendments changed §6(b)(1) by setting the maximum rate for disability benefits at 200% of the National Average Weekly Wage (NAWW) beginning October 1, 1975. The 1972 Amendments also provided for a series of phased-in maximums to be applied during the years between 1972 and 1975 for injuries after the effective date. A complementary provision, §10(h), applicable to permanent total disability and death benefits which commenced prior to the effective date of the 1972 Amendments provided for a similar adjustment in those benefits. These increases were payable from the Special Fund and appropriations. The 1984 Amendments continued the 200% NAWW maximum and subsection 6(b)(1) now provides as follows:

> Compensation for disability or death (other than compensation for death required by this Act to be paid in a lump sum) shall not exceed an amount equal to 200 per centum of the applicable national average weekly wage, as determined by the Secretary under paragraph (3).

Prior to 1972, §9(e) provided a maximum rate for death benefits stating that in computing death benefits the average weekly wages of the deceased shall not be considered to be greater than $105.00 or less than $27.00, but regardless, could not exceed the decedent's actual average weekly wage. The 1972 Amendments changed that provision to state that the AWW of the decedent could not be less than the NAWW of §6(b), and that the *total weekly benefits* could not exceed the AWW of the decedent, but Congress neglected to include a reference to death benefits in the §6(b)(1) maximum provision. In *Director, OWCP v. Rasmussen*[3], the Supreme Court therefore held that death benefits were not subject to the §6(b) maximum. The 1984 Amendments righted the error by expressly applying the maximum limit to both "disability and death benefits" and consistent language was adopted in the amended §9(e), such that as of 1984, the maximum limit of 200 per centum of the NAWW, adjusted annually each October 1, applies to both disability and death benefits.

Section 6(b)(2) sets the minimum level of benefits for total disability at 50 per centum of the NAWW. The minimum applies only to total disability benefits of §§8(a) and (b) and not the partial disability benefits of §§8(c) and (e). There is one exception, §6(b)(2), which provides that if the employee's AWW as computed under §10 are less than 50 per centum of such NAWW (the applicable minimum rate) then the worker's AWW shall be his compensation rate for total disability.

Section 6(b)(3) provides that prior to October 1 each year, the Secretary shall determine the NAWW for purposes of determining the maximum and minimum rates on benefits for the following year.

So how exactly does §6 fit in the overall statutory scheme? This was explained thoroughly in the United States Supreme Court decision of *Roberts v. Sea-Land Services, Inc.*[4] Generally, as has been covered, §8 establishes the rate at which weekly disability benefits are paid and §9 establishes the rate for death benefits. The 1984 Amendments straightened things out regarding the application of the maximum rate to appropriate disability and death benefits. Section 6(c) provides for recalculation of the compensation rate for certain qualifying (very high wage-earning) claimants, who were "currently receiving compensation for permanent and total disability or death benefits" and those "newly awarded compensation" during such period resulting from the new maximum rate determined each fiscal year. §10(f) provides for annual cost of living adjustments to the compensation rate of qualifying claimants thereunder, specifically, anyone receiving permanent total disability or death benefits. To appreciate (if not merely follow) jurisprudence interpreting §6(c) and determining its placement in the overall statutory scheme, it helps to view the provision itself, set forth below:

> (c) *Applicability of determinations.* Determinations under subsection (b)(3) with respect to a period shall apply to employees or survivors *currently receiving compensation for permanent and total disability or death* benefits during such period, as well as those *newly awarded compensation* during such period. (emphasis added)

The Ninth Circuit Court of Appeals decision in *Roberts*, 625 F.3d 1204, 44 BRBS 73 (CRT) addressed two questions regarding the interpretation of §6(c). The first issue involved the "newly awarded" clause of §6(c) and pertained to the maximum rate applicable to the claimant's temporary, total, and permanent partial disability benefits. The second issue considered by the Ninth Circuit in *Roberts* involved the "currently receiving compensation for permanent total disability" clause of §6(c). The United States Supreme Court granted review only with respect to the first issue, regarding the interpretation of the "newly awarded" clause, ultimately upholding the Ninth Circuit's interpretation of that clause to the effect that an employee is considered "newly awarded compensation" when he or she first becomes disabled and thereby becomes statutorily entitled to benefits, no matter whether, or when, the compensation order is issued. The second issue was addressed by the Benefits Review Board (BRB) one year later in *Lake v. L-3 Communications.*[5]

Dana Roberts' accident occurred in fiscal year 2002 and he received voluntary compensation benefits until 2005 when benefits were discontinued. Roberts then filed a claim under the LHWCA which Sea-Land controverted. After a formal hearing in 2007, the ALJ awarded Roberts benefits at the statutory maximum rate of $966.08 a week, which was the maximum rate for fiscal year 2002, the year Roberts became disabled. The issue Roberts brought before the Supreme Court did not directly involve adjustments of the compensation rate under §6(c) or §10(f) COLA, but more simply, which maximum rate applied, that of fiscal year 2002 (the year of disability—$966.08) or that of fiscal year 2007 (when the formal Order awarding benefits was issued by the ALJ—$1,160.36). The Supreme Court first determined that the term "award" could mean something other than a grant of benefits in a formal compensation order and ultimately decided that "newly awarded" meant the point at which a person first becomes statutorily entitled to benefits regardless of whether or when a favorable compensation award is entered. Accordingly, the maximum compensation rate that applies to the claim is that maximum rate in effect for the fiscal year when the claimant first became disabled regardless of "whether, or when, a compensation order issues on his behalf."[6] The *Roberts* court specifically rejected the argument that "newly awarded" referred only to those claimants who are receiving compensation pursuant to a formal order. To do otherwise, the court felt, would thwart the manner in which Congress intended the LHWCA to work. It would also render §6(c) superfluous in all but those relatively rare instances in which benefits are being paid specifically pursuant to the issuance of a compensation order. To do otherwise would also arbitrarily treat similarly situated employees differently because, as the court noted, "two employees who earn the same salary and suffer the same injury on the same day could be entitled to different rates of compensation based on the happenstance of their obtaining orders in different fiscal years."[7] The court specifically expressed its intent to avoid gamesmanship by either side and declined to "reward employees with windfalls for initiating unnecessary administrative proceedings, while simultaneously punishing employers who have complied fully with their statutory obligations."[8] Recognizing that the vast majority of claims are paid and resolved voluntarily without formal hearing and orders awarding benefits, the court characterized Roberts' proposal that orders issue in every case such that employers could lock in the caps in effect at the time their employees became disabled, as "a solution in search of a problem."[9]

Since the Supreme Court left unanswered the meaning of §6(c)'s "currently receiving compensation for permanent total disability or death benefits" clause, which was the second issue considered by the Ninth Circuit in *Roberts*, the BRB took the opportunity to answer it in *Lake v. L-3 Communications.*[10]

Charles Lake was a DBA claimant whose AWW at the time of injury on December 6, 2005 was a huge $2,865.33. In the Decision and Order of November 1, 2012, the ALJ found Lake entitled to temporary total disability benefits from March 21, 2006 through December 9, 2008 and to permanent total disability benefits from December 10, 2008 and continuing. Lake argued that he became entitled to the fiscal year 2009 statutory maximum rate of $1,200.62 as of December 10, 2008 when the entitlement to permanent total disability benefits commenced. The ALJ had rejected Lake's position, relying on the BRB decision in *Reposky*, discussed below, and applied the 2006 fiscal year maximum rate of $1,073.64 (for an accident on December 6, 2005) (effective October 1, 2005). The BRB reversed the ALJ on that issue and determined that the claimant was entitled to the fiscal year 2009 maximum compensation rate as of December 10, 2008, the date his entitlement to permanent total disability benefits commenced, and for each October 1 thereafter he would be entitled to the new fiscal year's statutory maximum (as long as two-thirds of the §10-determined AWW still exceeded the then current maximum rate).

In doing so, the BRB in *Lake* overruled its previous decision in *Reposky v. International Transportation Service*[11] such that if a worker's disability changes from temporary total to permanent total in the middle of a given year, as did Lake's, the compensation rate payable for permanent total disability for the remainder of that fiscal year immediately increases to the current fiscal year's maximum rate. In *Reposky*, the BRB had held that the rate increase would be delayed until the next October 1, when the compensation rate would be increased in accordance with the new maximum rate. The BRB's rationale in *Lake* was that upon obtaining permanency, such a claimant is considered to be "currently receiving" permanent total disability benefits thereby entitling him immediately to that fiscal year's maximum rate subject to future increases under §10(f) (or perhaps by continuing application of §6(c)).

The BRB in *Lake* flatly rejected the employer's argument that once a claimant attains permanent total disability status, the compensation rate can only increase through the yearly §10(f) adjustments, having previously considered and rejected that very argument in *Marko v Morris Boney Co.*[12] In *Marko*, the BRB held, and in *Lake* reconfirmed, that "pursuant to the plain language of §6, as long as two-thirds of claimant's average weekly wage remains higher than 200% of the current NAWW, the claimant 'currently receiving' permanent total disability or death benefits is entitled to receive the new maximum compensation rate each year.[13] Consequently, the BRB also recognized that once two-thirds of the claimant's actual AWW is less than 200% of the applicable NAWW, the claimant's actual AWW becomes the basis for his permanent total disability compensation rate, and he is then entitled to annual §10(f) adjustments in the amount of the lesser of the percentage increase in the NAWW as determined under §6(b)(3) (which, at the great risk of confusing rather than clarifying—is the basis for the §10(f)(1) calculation) or the §10(f)(2) five per centum cap.[14]

10.5 §10(f) COLA and §6(c) Increases Overlap but Operate Independently

Initially it should be noted that §6(c) and §10(f) were both added by the 1972 amendments. Both reference the NAWW in determining the applicable increases in compensation rates, but the purposes of the two independent provisions are not identical. The purpose of permanent total disability compensation to which §6 applies is to fully replace two-thirds of an injured worker's loss in wage earning capacity caused by injury.[15] The purpose of §10(f) is to ensure that the value of the compensation benefits is not eroded over time by inflation.[16] The COLA increase of §10(f) has a cap on the increase though, that being by 5% under §10(f)(2).

It is important to remember that the escalations of a benefit rate under §6(c), as it has become known, apply only to those relatively high wage earners whose average weekly wage is so high that two-thirds of it (i.e., the compensation rate) continues to exceed twice the annually determined NAWW. At some point in the future, two-thirds of such a worker's AWW will no longer exceed twice the NAWW, at which point the §6(c) escalations cease for that claimant. However, that same individual would continue to receive the annual COLA under §10(f). This is so because the §10(f) COLA has nothing to do with whether a beneficiary is subject to §6(c) as a maximum benefit rate cap. The Supreme Court in *Rasmussen* dismissed the argument that the §6(c) escalations could somehow be avoided by jurisprudence regarding the application of the §10(f) annual increases. Section 10(f) applies only when permanent total disability or death benefits extend across two consecutive fiscal years. As the BRB succinctly stated in *Lake*:

> in a permanent total disability case in which two-thirds of the claimant's actual average weekly wage exceeds the Section 6(b)(3) statutory maximum rate, he is entitled to the benefit of the new maximum rate each fiscal year. *Marko*, 23 BRBS at 361-62. Such a claimant is entitled to receive the new Section 6(b)(3) maximum rate each fiscal year until such time as two-thirds of his actual average weekly wage falls below 200 percent of the applicable NAWW, and then annual adjustments under §10(f) apply.[17]

Under this scenario, the fortunate claimant whose AWW is so high that he has the benefit of one or more §6(c) escalations until such time as those escalations cease will have a much higher compensation rate starting point to which the subsequent §10(f) escalations thereafter apply. This benefit path, not often encountered, has been jurisprudentially paved for those few who might venture upon it in their Longshore travels.

Endnotes

1. *Roberts v. Sea-Land Services, Inc.*, 132 S.Ct. 1350, 1357; 566 U.S. 93, 182 L.Ed. 2d 341, 46 BRBS 15 (CRT)(2012)
2. *Director, OWCP v. Rasmussen*, 99 S.Ct. 903, 912, 440 U.S. 29, 43-44, n.16, 59 L.Ed. 2d 122, 99 S.Ct. 903, 9 BRBS 954 (1979). Note: The 1972 version of §6(d) was replaced by §6(c) as supplemented and redesignated by the 1984 Amendments.
3. *Id.*
4. *Roberts v. Sea-Land Services, Inc.*, 132 S.Ct. 1350, 566 U.S. 93, 182 L.Ed. 2d 341, 46 BRBS 15 (CRT) (2012)
5. *Lake v. L-3 Communications*, 47 BRBS 45 (2013).
6. *Roberts, supra,* 132 S.Ct. at 1354.
7. *Id.*, 132 S.Ct. at 1359.
8. *Id.*, 132 S.Ct. at 1360.

9. *Id.*, 132 S.Ct. at 1358.

10. *Lake v. L-3 Communications*, 47 BRBS 45 (2013).

11. *Reposky v. International Transportation Service*, 40 BRBS 65 (2006).

12. *Marko v. Morris Boney Co.*, 23 BRBS 353 (1990).

13. Lake, *supra*, 47 BRBS at 49, *Marko*, 23 BRBS at 361-362.

14. *Id.*, citing *Marko*, et al., 23 BRBS at 361 n.6.

15. *Metropolitan Stevedore Co. v. Rambo [Rambo 1]*, 515 U.S. 291, 298, 115 S.Ct 2144, 2148, 132 L.Ed. 2d 226, 30 BRBS 1, 3-4 (CRT) (1995).

16. *Roberts, supra,* 132 S.Ct. at 1359, 46 BRBS at 19 (CRT).

17. *Lake*, 47 BRBS at 50, citing *Marko*, 23 BRBS at 361 n.6.

Chapter 11

Average Weekly Wage Calculations & *Per Diem* Considerations

Brian P. McElreath, Esq.

Synopsis

11.1 Introduction

Section 10 of the Longshore and Harbor Workers' Compensation Act (LHWCA) specifies that the average weekly wage of an injured employee at the time of the injury is the basis upon which compensation is awarded. Because a claimant's average weekly wage is what compensation awards are based upon, increasing average weekly wage is the most efficient method by which to increase the of a claimant's claim for compensation. Likewise, reducing average weekly wage is the most effective means of decreasing exposure from the employer and carrier's prospective. Given the potential increase or decrease in exposure through increasing or decreasing average weekly wage, average weekly wage continues to be a consistent source of litigation under the LHWCA and its extensions.

11.2 Basic AWW Considerations

Any discussion of earnings and average weekly wage must begin with the question what constitutes wages? Section 2(13) of the LHWCA provides a three prong test for defining wages: the money rate provided (1) for the employee's services (2) by an employer (3) under the contract of hiring in force at the time of the injury.[1,2] Section 2(13) notes that wages include the reasonable of any advantage received from the employer and included for purposes of any withholding of tax under subtitle C of the Internal Revenue Code of 1954.[3,4] Wages include overtime pay if overtime is a regular and normal part of claimant's employment.[5] This is all helpful, but not determinative as to what falls under the umbrella of wages. What is not include in wages? Wages do not include unemployment compensation.[6] Wages do not include fringe benefits, including, but not limited to, employer contributions to retirement, pension, health, and welfare, insurance, training, social security or other employee or dependent benefit plans.[7] The word including does not connote an all-inclusive list as it has been held to be illustrative of the general principle.[8] The LHWCA defines wages as the money rate at which services rendered are compensated. Accordingly, nonmonetary compensation must be converted to a monetary equivalent.[9] The Fifth Circuit concluded that wages are monetary compensation plus taxable advantages.[10] The Ninth Circuit has held that nonmonetary advantages are included in wages only when they are subject to tax withholding.[11] The Ninth Circuit subsequently held that monetary advantages must also be subject to tax withholding to be considered wages under Section 2(13).[12] The Supreme Court affirmed the BRB's finding that the value of nonmonetary compensation received by a claimant that are readily identifiable and calculable should be included as wages.[13] The D.C. Circuit held that the value of employer-provided meals are included as wages.[14] The Supreme Court held that benefits received from employer-funded trust funds for health and welfare, pensions, and training are not similar advantages to board, rent, housing, and lodging.[15] The Court reasoned that board, rent, housing, and lodging are "benefits with a present value that can be readily converted into a case equivalent on the basis of their market values."[16] However, the value of benefits a claimant receives from trust funds are not "so easily converted" and, therefore, they were not found to be similar advantages whose value is included in wages.[17] When a claimant's right to a tangible benefit does not depend on contingent factors, the value of the benefit is not too speculative to be readily converted into a case equivalent under the LHWCA.[18]

Vacation, holiday, and container royalty payments are wages as long as they are earned with actual work.[19] Vacation, holiday, and container royalty payments are compensation for services only when they are earned with actual work.[20] A claimant that uses disability credits to obtain vacation, holiday, and container royalty payments is not being compensated for services but because disability prevents him/her from doing so.[21] Consequently, vacation, holiday, and container royalty payments earned only because of disability credit are not paid for services and are not included in wages.[22] Finally, a claimant's average weekly wage should include all of his or her earnings at the time of injury to include any earnings from additional part-time jobs.[23] Average weekly wage is calculated on gross wages, and the Board has confirmed that wages should not be reduced by the effective tax rate.[24] The Board also held that overseas post allowances, completion awards, and cost of living adjustments are properly included in wages as they are readily calculable.[25]

Section 10 of the LHWCA sets three methods for determining a claimant's annual earnings.[26] Once a claimant's annual earnings are determined, the annual earnings are divided by 52 to calculate the employee's average weekly wage.[27] A claimant's compensation rate is based on a percentage of the employee's average weekly wage, subject to Section 6 of the LHWCA.[28] Subject to the limitations of Sections 906(b)(1)–(2) and 909(b)–(d), compensation benefits are paid at 66⅔ percent of the average weekly wage.[29] If an injury causes death, compensation benefits shall be known as death benefits and shall be payable as outlined in Section 909(a)–(e).

Prior to October 1 each year the Secretary determines the national average weekly wage (NAWW) to determine the maximum and minimum limitations on benefits for the following year.[30] A claimant's maximum compensation rate for disability or death shall not exceed twice the applicable national average weekly wage.[31] A claimant's minimum compensation rate shall not be less than half the applicable national average weekly wage.[32] However, if a claimant's average weekly wage is less than half the national average weekly wage, the employee's shall receive his/her average weekly wage as compensation for total disability payments.[33] The plain language of § 906(b)(2) does not mention a minimum compensation rate of payment of partial disability payments. The Benefits Review Board (BRB) has confirmed that the minimum compensation rate applies to both permanent and temporary total disability.[34] The BRB has also affirmed that the minimum compensation rate does not apply to partial disability benefits.[35]

In the case of hearing loss claims, a claimant is limited to the maximum compensation rate in effect when disability commences.[36] Hearing loss disability is complete as of the date of the last exposure to injurious noise and, therefore, a claimant is limited to the maximum compensation rate in effect at the time of the last injurious exposure.[37] In regard to lost time claims, the Supreme Court held that a claimant is "newly awarded compensation" when the employee first becomes disabled and becomes statutorily entitled to benefits regardless when, or if, a compensation order is issued.[38] However, the Court did note if the "time of injury" and the "time of onset of disability" differ, the applicable national average weekly wage is that in effect at the latter date.[39]

It is never too late to raise an average weekly wage issue.[40] The BRB has held a stipulation is not a waiver of compensation under Section 915(b).[41] The Fourth Circuit held a deputy commissioner erred in awarding compensation based on an average weekly wage set in an agreement between the union and the employer's association rather than relying on the claimant's actual wages.[42] Likewise, the Ninth Circuit affirmed a deputy commissioner that disregarded a stipulation as to average weekly wage which was not properly computed under Section 910.[43]

11.3 Section 10(a) & (b) AWW Calculations

To borrow a phrase from a longshore legend, Section 10(a) and (b) calculations work well in a factory or shipyard with a hierarchical structure, but they are not particularly well suited for the seven-day work week that we often see in Defense Base Act (DBA) claims or for the casual and varying work schedule that is often necessary in waterfront employment. However, Section 10(a) and (b) calculations continue to be used particularly on the west coast.

Section 10(a) is applicable for a claimant that has worked in the employment in which he/she was working at the time of injury during the substantial whole of the year immediately preceding the injury.[44] The employee's average annual earnings are calculated by multiplying the average daily wage or salary for a six-day worker by 300 and the average daily wage or salary for a five-day worker by 260.[45,46] The employee's average daily wage is determined by dividing the gross earnings of the employee by the actual number of days worked by the employee in the fifty-two week period prior to the injury.[47] Once the actual annual earnings have been calculated, it is divided by 52 to calculate the employee's average weekly wage.

Usage of the Section 10(a) calculation is premised on the employee's having worked for "substantially" the entire year prior to the injury in the same employment.[48] "Substantially the whole of the year" refers to the nature of the claimant's employment, not the availability of wage records.[49] The Board has held 42 weeks to be substantially the whole of the year.[50] The Board has ruled 33 weeks is not a substantial part of the previous year.[51] The Board has found 34.5 weeks satisfies the substantial part of the previous year requirement.[52] The Board affirmed a finding that 34.8 weeks satisfied the substantial whole of the year.[53] The Ninth Circuit adopted a bright line rule that a claimant is entitled to a Section 10(a) average weekly wage calculation as a 5-day worker, if he or she actually worked at last 75% of the 260 days presumptively available to a 5-day worker.[54] The Fifth Circuit considered *Matulic*, but did not adopt a bright line rule.[55] The Fifth Circuit held Section 10(a) applied when a claimant worked 91% of available days.[56] The Ninth Circuit affirmed the bright line rule in *Matulic* when it found a Section 10(a) calculation proper when the claimant worked 75.77% of available days.[57] Where a claimant worked 77.4% of available workdays, a Section 10(a) calculation was found proper in spite of producing wages of more than $12,000.00 more than the claimant's actual annual earnings.[58] The board held that overcompensation alone is an insufficient basis for rejecting the use of Section 10(a).[59] The Board held that the record lacked the necessary evidence to apply a Section 10(a) calculation where the claimant's W-2 statements and payroll records failed to indicate the actual number of days worked.[60]

Section 10(b) is applicable when a claimant has not worked in his or her employment for the substantial whole of the year, but there is wage information available for the same class worker that has worked the substantial whole of the year in the same or similar employment in the same or neighboring location.[61,62] If Section 10(b) applies, the calculation is then the same as Section 10(a) it just uses like kind employee wages. The employee's average annual earnings are calculated by multiplying the average daily wage or salary for a six-day worker by 300 and the average daily wage or salary for a five-day worker by 260.[63] Section 10(b) is applicable for recent hires or those promoted from lower paying positions.[64,65] The Board affirmed a finding that Section 10(b) should not apply in view of claimant's frequent job changes, frequent firings, prior convictions, brief length of employment with the employer, lack of seniority, misrepresentations on his employment application, and his routine lay-off shortly after the injury.[66] If an employee or employer wishes to use a Section 10(b) calculation presentation of evidence of wages of co-workers who worked substantially the whole year in the same or similar employment is mandatory.[67]

11.4 Section 10(c) AWW Calculation

Section 10(c) is the catch all provision for average weekly wage calculations and is applicable when Sections 10(a) and (b) cannot be reasonably and fairly applied.[68] Section 10(c) is typically applied when a claimant's work is seasonal, intermittent, discontinuous, and provides less than a year of wages.[69] Under Section 10(c), average annual earnings the earnings of the claimant in the employment in which he/she was injured at the time of injury, and of other employees of the same or most similar class working in the same or similar locality, including the reasonable vale of the service of the employee engaged in self-employment.[70] Average annual earnings are divided by 52 to calculate the claimant's average weekly wage.[71] However, a divisor of fewer than 52 weeks may be affirmed where it achieves the same result as extrapolating wages earned in fewer than 52 weeks over an entire year and then dividing by 52.[72] Section 10(c) has no requirement that the previous earnings considered be within the year immediately preceding the injury.[73] An administrative law judge may compute average annual earnings under Section 10(c) based on a claimant's earning pattern over a period of years.[74]

The determination as to whether the claimant's employment is casual, irregular, seasonal, intermittent, and discontinuous is based on the nature of the employment and of the industry itself, not merely on the prior work history of the particular claimant.[75] The purpose of Section 10(c) is to determine a fair and reasonable approximation of the claimant's earning capacity at the time of injury.[76] Earning capacity is defined as the "ability, willingness, and opportunity to work," or "the amount of earnings the claimant would have the potential and opportunity to earn absent injury."[77] A Section 10(c) calculation should include a pay raise received shortly before the injury.[78] Section 10(c) calculations also include promotions received shortly before the injury.[79] The Board has affirmed the use of actual wages where a claimant shows an unwillingness to work at higher wages by rejecting work opportunities and has earnings lower than his earning capacity.[80] When a claimant is self-employed, the Board held Section 10(c) applicable and reversed an annual earning capacity determination based on claimant's gross earnings.[81] The Board found the more appropriate calculation is based on the cost of hiring another welder of equivalent skill and experience to perform the same work but excluding profits or goodwill.[82] The Board has affirmed a Section 10(c) calculation based on claimant's net earnings in self-employment.[83] The Board noted that *Roundtree* did not hold that the cost of hiring a similar employee was the only method of calculating average annual earnings in self-employment and any reasonable method may be used.[84] The Board found no authorization in the LHWCA for reducing the compensation base because of criminal or other socially undesirable activity that may have affected the claimant's earning history.[85]

The administrative law judge has broad discretion in determining annual earning capacity under Section 10(c).[86] If Section 10(a) is not applicable, the parties may move directly to a Section 10(c) calculation without attempting a calculation under Section 10(b).[87] The Ninth Circuit has held that a claimant may choose to calculate his or her average weekly wage pursuant to Section 10(c) even if the claimant could have proceeded under Section 10(b). Section 10(c) calculations will be affirmed if the reflect a reasonable approximation of earning capacity and the claimant fails to establish a basis for a higher award.[88]

11.5 DBA AWW Calculations

Claims arising under the Defense Base Act present unique complications in calculating average annual earnings and, therefore, average weekly wage. Defense Base Act employees are typically employed overseas and oftentimes in a war zone. The employment is typically for a limited term and the pay is at a substantial higher rate than the same employment stateside. The Board has held that work in a combat zone is inherently different as it involves dangerous working conditions.[89] The dangerous working conditions and substantially higher wages lead to unique considerations in the calculation of average weekly wage for claims falling under Defense Base Act jurisdiction. The three methods for calculating average weekly wage set forth in Section 10(a)–(c) can be used to calculate a claimant's average weekly wage under the Defense Base Act, but Section 10(c) is typically used in the vast majority of cases since DBA contractors are typically 7 day workers. The computation methods set forth in Section 10 are used to establish a claimant's earning power at the time of injury.[90] Section 10(c) seeks to determine a fair and reasonable approximation of a claimant's wage earning capacity at the time of injury.[91] If the calculation of average weekly wage falls into the Section 10(c) category, the Administrative Law Judge has broad discretion in determining annual earning capacity.[92]

Relative to longshore claims, DBA claims are relatively new and average weekly wage jurisprudence is still being cultivated. The main focus of average weekly wage in DBA claims is usage of a blended rate to calculate a claimant's average weekly wage. DBA litigation is attempting to create a bright line rule as to if, and when, a blended rate is applicable in the calculation of average annual earnings. The Fifth Circuit has noted that wages earned at the time of injury best reflect a claimant's earning capacity and it would be an "exceedingly rare case" for a claimant's earnings at the time of injury to be wholly disregarded.[93] In *Lopez v. Dynacorp Int'l*, the Administrative Law Judge used a blended rate of the average of the claimant's average annual earnings from the four years of prior work history, which was then averaged with the claimant's average weekly wage from the seven months of employment as a DBA contractor in Afghanistan.[94]

In using the blended rate in *Lopez* the ALJ relied upon *Service Employees Int'l, Inc. v. Dir., OWCP*, in which the Southern District of Texas overturned the Board's holding in *Simmons*. *Simmons* worked two months as a DBA contractor and the Board held that the administrative law judge had to rely solely on the two months of DBA contractor earnings to reflect the claimant's higher wages under at least a one-year contract in exchange for work in a dangerous environment.[95] The board opined that overseas "earnings under this contract thus provide the best evidence of claimant's capacity to earn absent injury" which is the focus of Section 10(c).[96] The Southern District of Texas vacated the Board's decision that *Proffitt*[97] was controlling authority on the issue of average weekly wage calculation.[98] The Southern District of Texas held that the Board failed to adhere to its substantial evidence standard of review and provided no support for requiring all cases with similar facts to have similar outcomes, which deprives the administrative law judge of the discretion to calculate average weekly and relegates the judge "to simply playing the role of calculator."[99] Prior to the Southern District of Texas vacating Simmons the only exception that allowed for the use of a blended rate, post *Proffitt*, was producing credible evidence that a claimant's employment overseas was in fact, or was intended to be, short-term, for less than a one-year contractual term, in which the use of solely overseas earnings would not necessarily control.[100] In *Jasmine* the claimant's employment contract was short-term (six months) and the Board affirmed the ALJ's usage of a blended rate.[101] The Board also noted that *Jasmine* did not establish "a long-term commitment to overseas employment."[102] The application of a blended rate typical benefits the employer; however, there are exceptions to every rule. In *Luttrell* the Board did not include *Luttrell's* higher wages from an earlier job on the premise that the prior job was performed in a hostile environment.[103] *Luttrell* voluntarily left a higher-paying job in the Middle East for lower-paying jobs in the Bahamas and the South Pacific.[104] At the time of injury *Luttrell* was working in the lower paying job and was not receiving any hazard pay and the Board found it appropriate to calculate *Luttrell's* average weekly wage using only the lower paying wages.[105]

DBA average weekly wage jurisprudence seems to trending toward the usage of blended rate in contracts of less than one year and contracts for greater than one year in which the claimant is injured prior to one year of service. The on-going question, much like a Section 10(a) calculation is where is the bright line as when an overseas contractor has crossed over to the substantial whole of the year and a blended rate is no longer the appropriate calculation? That bright line is still being developed, but *Lopez* gives us some guidance that a blended rate is still appropriate at seven months. Absent statutory certainty average weekly wage in DBA claims will likely continue to be a source of litigation for some time.

11.6 *Per Diem* Considerations

The final area of discussion in any average annual earnings and average weekly wage discussion is the inclusion of *per diem*. The Ninth Circuit held that the definition of wages is controlled by the Internal Revenue Code's criteria.[106] The *Wausau* court noted under 26 U.S.C. Section 119(a), meals and lodging were not income, because they were provided for the convenience of the employer and were furnished on the employer's business premises and should not be considered in the calculation of wages.[107] The Board declined to follow *Wausau* outside the Ninth Circuit and noted that the plain language of Section 2(13) is not consistent with the restrictions that *Wausau* placed on wages.[108] The Fifth Circuit held that Section 2(13) excludes from the definition of wages the value of meals and lodging that are exempt from federal income taxation by Section 119 of the Internal Revenue Code.[109] The Fifth Circuit held that wages equals monetary compensation plus taxable advantages.[110] In keeping with *Wausau*, the Ninth Circuit held while *per diem* received in order to pay for room and board while working abroad was an advantage, it was not a wage because it was not subject to withholding under the Internal Revenue Code.[111]

Cash *per diem* payments have been includable in wages but the value of meals and lodging have been excluded when not subject to withholding.[112] However, the plain language of Section 2(13) does not mandate that a benefit not subject to withholding is not a wage.[113] Where subsistence and quarters were provided to a claimant by an employer under the employment contact and the value of same were calculable, the room and board cannot be deemed a fringe benefit.[114] The Board was subsequent overturned, but the takeaway is in the discussion noting that the fact that funds were not subject to withholding is not dispositive of the issue as the funds were wages within the meaning of the LHWCA and the Board modified the ALJ's award to include the funds in the average weekly wage calculation.[115] The Fourth Circuit found *per diem* included in wages where the employer provided the claimant with a *per diem* for food and lodging in addition to free room and board.[116] The Fourth Circuit held the *per diem* was a disguised wage and rejected the argument that *per diem* was a nontaxable payment intended to reimburse the claimant for meal and lodging expenses as the employer provided free room and board.[117] The Fifth Circuit affirmed the inclusion of *per diem* benefits as wages and rejected the carrier's nontaxable argument.[118] The Fifth Circuit restated it's holding in *Quinones* that wages are the money rate at which the employee is compensated plus any taxable advantages.[119] The Fifth Circuit noted that the money rate prong does not require taxability.[120] *Pearley* put forth the closest thing we have to a test and included *per diem* in the wage calculation on the following grounds: (1) *Per diem* that is calculated based on the number of hours worked points to disguised wages; (2) *Per diem* paid in the same paycheck as claimant's normal wages points to disguised wages; (3) *Per diem* that is an unrestricted payment that is unrelated to actual cost of meals, lodging, or travel points to disguised wages; (4) Payment of the same *per diem* to all employees regardless of where they live points to disguised wages; and (5) *Per diem* that constitutes almost half of the claimant's gross pay points to disguised wages. The Fifth Circuit provided an additional prong to the test above in noting that per diem payments intended, at least in part, to make the job more attractive to potential employees are "more akin to wages" than compensation of expenses.[121]

The Ninth Circuit follows the bright line rule that any advantage that is not subject to withholding under the Internal Revenue Code is not a wage.[122] So, if *per diem* in the Ninth Circuit is not subject to withholding under the Internal Revenue Code it is not included as wages. The other circuits take a more case by case fact specific analysis to determine if the employer is using *per diem* as a way to pay its employees disguised wages. The general rules is that *per diem* payments must be tied to the area in which the employee is working, must be related to the actual cost of meals, lodging, or travel, and must not play the role of money wages.[123] However, this is not dispositive and *per diem* payments may still be included as wages depending upon the facts of the case.

11.7 Acknowledgements

The author gratefully acknowledges the following folks for their assistance in providing local knowledge on the west coast application of Section 10(a) & (b) AWW Calculations section of this chapter: Skip Jones & Matt Francis from Ports Insurance Company, Tom Scherting & Stan Henslee from Homeport Insurance Company, Steve Wiper from Enstar, Erik Lassow from Signal Mutual Indemnity Association, Ltd., and John Dudrey from Williams Fredrickson, LLC. Additionally, thank you to Ralph R. Lorberbaum for allowing me to contribute to this project.

Endnotes

1. 33 U.S.C. § 902(13).

2. *Universal Mar. Serv. Corp. v. Wright*, 155 F.3d 311, 318 (4th Cir. 1998).

3. 33 U.S.C. § 902(13).

4. *Wright*, 155 F.3d at 318 n.8 ("Under subtitle C of the Internal Revenue Code, 26 U.S.C. §§ 3101-3510, Federal Insurance Contributions Act (FICA) taxes, *see id.* at § 3202(a), and income taxes, see id. § 3402(a)(1), are withheld from an employee's paycheck. Cf. 26 U.S.C. §§ 3101, 3201 (defining FICA and railroad retirement taxes). Withholding is calculated from the employee's "wages" and "compensation" which are defined by 26 U.S.C. §§ 3121(a), 3231(e), and 3401(a) respectively.").

5. *Brown v. Newport News Shipbuilding & Dry Dock Co.*, 23 BRBS 110 (1989).

6. *Strand v. Hansen Seaway Serv., Ltd.*, 614 F.2d 572 (7th Cir. 1980); *Blakney v. Delaware Operating Co.*, 25 BRBS 273 (1992).

7. *Id.*

8. *Fed. Land Bank v. Bismark Lumbar Co.*, 314 U.S. 95, 100 (1941).

9. *Wright*, 155 F.3d at 319 n.9.

10. *H.B. Zachery Co. v. Quinones*, 206 F.3d 474 (5th Cir. 2000).

11. *Wausau Ins. Co. v. Dir., Office of Workers Comp. Programs*, 114 F.3d 120, 121 n.2 (9th Cir. 1997).

12. *McNutt v. Benefits Rev. Bd.*, 140 F.3d 1247, 1248 (9th Cir. 1998).

13. *Morrison-Knudsen Constr. Co. v. Dir., Office of Workers Comp. Programs*, 461 U.S. 624 (1983).

14. *Harris v. Lambros*, 56 F.2d 488, 489 (D.C. Cir. 1932).

15. *Morrison-Knudsen Construction Co. v. Director, OWCP*, 461 U.S. 624, 630 (1983).

16. *Id.*

17. *Id.*

18. *Parks v. John T. Clark & Son of Maryland, Inc.*, 9 BRBS 462, 465-66 (1978).

19. *Universal Maritime Service Corp. v. Wright*, 155 F.3d 311, 325 (4th Cir. 1998).

20. *Id.* at 326.

21. *SEACO v. Richardson*, 136 F.3d 1290, 1293 (11th Cir. 1998).

22. *Wright* at 326.

23. *Lawson v. Atlantic & Gulf Grain Stevedores Co.*, 6 BRBS 770 (1977); *Stutz v. Independent Stevedore Co.*, 3 BRBS 72 (1975).

24. *Denton v. Northrop Corp.*, 21 BRBS 37 (1988).

25. *Id.*

26. 33 U.S.C. 910(a), (b), & (c).

27. 33 U.S.C. 910(d).

28. *Duncanson-Harrelson Co. v. Dir., OWCP*, 686 F.2d 1336 (9th Cir. 1982), *vacated in part on other grounds*, 462 U.S. 1101 (1983), *decision on remand*, 713 F.2d 462 (9th Cir. 1983); *National Steel & Shipbuilding Co. v. Bonner*, 600 F.2d 1288 (9th Cir. 1979); *Turney v. Bethlehem Steel Corp.*, 17 BRBS 232 (1985); *Strand v. Hansen Seaway Service, Ltd.*, 9 BRBS 847 (1979), *aff'd in part and rev'd in part*, 614 F.2d 572, 11 BRBS 732 (7th Cir. 1980); *Duzant v. General Dynamics Corp.*, 8 BRBS 670 (1978).

29. 33 U.S.C. 908(a)-(c).

30. 33 U.S.C. 906(b)(3).

31. 33 U.S.C. 906(b)(1).

32. 33 U.S.C. 906(b)(2).

33. *Id.*

34. *Brandt v. Stidham Tire Co.*, 16 BRBS 277 (1984), *rev'd on other grounds*, 785 F.2d 329 (D.C. Cir. 1986).

35. *Smith v. Paul Bros. Oldsmobile Co.*, 16 BRBS 57 (1983): *Stutz v. Independent Stevedore Co.*, 3 BRBS 72 (1975).

36. *Tracy v. Global Int'l Offshore, Ltd.*, 43 BRBS 92 (2009).

37. *Bath Iron Works v. Dir., OWCP*, 506 U.S. 153 (1993).

38. *Roberts v. Sea-Land Services, Inc.*, 566 U.S. 93 (2012).

39. *Id.*

40. 33 U.S.C. 915(b).

41. *Fox v. Melville Shoe Corp., Inc.*, 17 BRBS 71 (1985).

42. *Belton v. Traynor*, 381 F.2d 82 (4th Cir. 1967).

43. *California Ship Service Co. v. Pillsbury*, 175 F.2d 873 (9th Cir. 1949).

44. 33 U.S.C. 910(a).

45. *Id.*

46. *Universal Maritime Corp. v. Moore*, 126 F.3d 256 (4th Cir. 1997).

47. *Ingalls Shipbuilding, Inc. v. Wooley*, 204 F.3d 616 (5th Cir. 2000); *Universal Maritime Corp. v. Moore*, 126 F.3d 256 (4th Cir. 1997).

48. *Duncanson-Harrelson Co. v. Dir., OWCP*, 686 F.2d 1336 (9th Cir. 1982).

49. *Eleazer v. General Dynamics Corp.*, 7 BRBS 75 (1977).

50. *Hole v. Miami Shipyards Corp.*, 12 BRBS 38 (1980), *rev'd and remanded on other grounds*, 640 F.2d 769 (5th Cir. 1981).

51. *Lozupone v. Stephano Lozupone and Sons*, 12 BRBS 148 (1979).

52. *Duncan v. Wash. Metro Area Transit Auth.*, 24 BRBS 133 (1990).

53. *Ezell v. Direct Labor, Inc.*, 33 BRBS 19 (1999).

54. *Matulic v. Dir., OWCP*, 154 F.3d 1052 (9th Cir. 1998).

55. *Gulf Best Electric, Inc. v. Methe*, 396 F.3d 601 (5th Cir. 2004).

56. *Id.*

57. *Stevedoring Services of America v. Price*, 328 F.3d 878 (9th Cir. 2004).

58. *Castro v. General Constr. Co.*, 37 BRBS 65 (2003), *aff'd* 401 F.3d 963 (9th Cir. 2005).

59. *Id.*

60. *Proffitt v. Serv. Employers Int'l, Inc.*, 40 BRBS 41 (2006).

61. 33 U.S.C. 910(b).

62. *McKee v. D.E. Foster Co.*, 14 BRBS 513 (1981); *Holmes v. Tampa Ship Repair & Dry Dock Co.*, 8 BRBS 455 (1978).

63. *Id.*

64. *Duncanson-Harrelson Co. v. Director, OWCP*, 686 F.2d 1336 (9th Cir. 1982), *vacated and remanded*, 462 U.S. 1101 (1983), *decision on remand*, 713 F.2d 462 (9th Cir. 1983).

65. *O'Hearne v. Maryland Casualty Co.*, 177 F.2d 979 (4th Cir. 1949).

66. *Harrison v. Todd Pacific Shipyards Corp.*, 21 BRBS 339 (1988).

67. *Hall v. Consolidated Employment Systems, Inc.*, 139 F.3d 1025 (5th Cir. 1998); *Proffitt v. Serv. Employers Int'l, Inc.*, 40 BRBS 41 (2006).

68. 33 U.S.C. 910(c).

69. *Palacios v. Campbell Industries*, 633 F.2d 840 (9th Cir. 1980); *Strand v. Hansen Seaway Service, Ltd.*, 614 F.2d 572 (7th Cir. 1979); *Walker v. Washington Metropolitan Area Transit Authority*, 793 F.2d 319 (D.C. Cir. 1986).

70. 33 U.S.C. 910(c).

71. 33 U.S.C. 910(d).

72. *Staftex Staffing v. Dir., OWCP*, 237 F.3d 409 (5th Cir. 2000); *James J. Flanagan Stevedores, Inc. v. Gallagher*, 219 F.3d 426 (5th Cir. 2000).

73. *Anderson v. Todd Shipyards*, 13 BRBS 593, 596 (1981).

74. *Cummins v. Todd Shipyards Corp.*, 12 BRBS 283 (1981).

75. *Stevedoring Services of America v. Price*, 382 F.3d 878 (9th Cir. 2004), *cert. denied* 544 U.S. 960 (2005).

76. *Barber v. Tri-State Terminals, Inc.*, 3 BRBS 244 (1976), *decision after remand*, 8 BRBS 411 (1978), *aff'd sub nom.*

77. *Jackson v. Potomac Temporaries Inc.*, 12 BRBS 410, 413 (1980); *Tri-State Terminals*, 596 F.2d at 757; *Marshall v. Andrew F. Mahony Co.*, 56 F.2d 74 (9th Cir. 1932).

78. *Le v. Sioux City & New Orleans Terminal Corp.*, 18 BRBS 175 (1986); *Miranda v. Excavation Constr., Inc.*, 13 BRBS 882 (1981); *Eckstein v. General Dynamics Corp.*, 11 BRBS 781 (1980); *Feagin v. General Dynamics Corp.*, 10 BRBS 664 (1979); *Sobolewski v. General Dynamics Corp.*, 5 BRBS 474 (1977), *aff'd on other grounds sub nom. General Dynamics Corp. v. Benefits Review Board*, 565 F.2d 208, 7 BRBS 831 (2d Cir. 1977).

79. *Feagin v. General Dynamics Corp.*, 10 BRBS 664 (1979).

80. *Conatser v. Pittsburgh Testing Laboratory*, 9 BRBS 541 (1978).

81. *Roundtree v. Newpark Shipbuilding & Repair, Inc.*, 13 BRBS 62 (1987), *rev'd on other grounds*, 698 F.2d 743 (5th Cir. 1983), *vacated on reh'g en banc*, 723 F.2d 399 (5th Cir. 1984), *cert. denied*, 469 U.S. 818 (1984).

82. *Id.*

83. *Wayland v. Moore Dry Dock*, 25 BRBS 53 (1991).

84. *Id.*

85. *Daugherty v. Los Angeles Container Terminals, Inc.*, 8 BRBS 363 (1978) (rejecting employer's argument that Section 10(c) was not available due to claimant's criminal activity and incarcerations in years prior to his employment, or that a calculation should include those years).

86. *Hicks v. Pacific Marine & Supply Co., Ltd.*, 14 BRBS 549 (1981); *Anderson v. Todd Shipyards, Inc.*, 13 BRBS 593 (1981); *Matthews v. Mid-States Stevedoring Corp.*, 11 BRBS 509 (1979); *Bonner v. National Steel & Shipbuilding Co.*, 5 BRBS 290(1977), *aff'd in pert. part*, 600 F2.d1288 (9th Cir. 1979).

87. *Proffitt v. Serv. Employers Int'l, Inc.*, 40 BRBS 41 (2006).

88. *Richardson v. Safeway Stores, Inc.*, 14 BRBS 855 (1982).

89. *Proffitt v. Serv. Employers Int'l, Inc.*, 40 BRBS 41 (2006).

90. *SGS Control Services v. Director, OWCP*, 86 F.3d 438, 441 (5th Cir. 1996); *Johnson v. Newport News Shipbuilding & Dry Dock Co.*, 25 BRBS 340 (1992); *Lobus v. I.T.O. Corp.*, 24 BRBS 137 (1990); *Barber v. Tri-State Terminals, Inc.*, 3 BRBS 244 (1976); *aff'd sum nom. Tri-State Terminals, Inc. v. Jesse*, 596 F.2d 752 (7th Cir 1979).

91. *Barber v. Tri-State Terminals, Inc.*, 3 BRBS 244 (1976).

92. *Hayes v. P & M Crane Co.*, 930 F.2d 424, 431 (1991); *Hicks v. Pacific Marine & Supply Co., Ltd.*, 14 BRBS 549 (1981).

93. *Hall v. Consolidated Employment Systems, Inc.*, 139 F.3d 1025, 1031 (5th Cir. 1998).

94. *Lopez v. Dynacorp Int'l*, 2012-LDA-00613 (ALJ Romero, 02/27/2014).

95. *Simmons v. Service Employees Int'l, Inc.*, 43 BRBS 18 (2009), *aff'd on recon. en banc*, 43 BRBS 136 (2009).

96. 33 U.S.C. § 910(c).

97. *Proffitt v. Service Employers Int'l, Inc.*, 40 BRBS 41 (2006).

98. *Service Employees Int'l, Inc. v. Dir., OWCP*, 2013 U.S. Dist. LEXIS 32887 (S.D. Tex. Mar. 11, 2013).

99. *Id.*

100. *Jasmin v. Can-Am Protection Grp.*, BRB No. 11-0610 (Apr. 19, 2012).

101. *Id.*

102. *Id.*

103. *Luttrell v. Alutiiq Global Solutions*, BRB No. 10-0555 (2011).

104. Id.

105. *Id.*

106. *Wausau Ins. Companies v. Dir., OWCP*, 114 F.3d 120 (9th Cir. 1997).

107. *Id.*

108. *Quinones v. H.B. Zachery, Inc.*, 32 BRBS 6 (1998), *rev'd in pert. part*, 206 F.3d 474, (5th Cir. 2000).

109. *Id.*

110. *Id.*

111. *McNutt v. Benefits Review Board*, 140 F.3d 1247 (9th Cir. 1998).

112. *Compare B & D Contracting v. Pearley*, 548 F.3d 338 (5th Cir. 2008), *and Custom Ship Interiors v. Roberts*, 300 F.3d 510 (4th Cir. 2002), *cert. denied*, 537 U.S. 1188 (2003), *with H.B. Zachery Co. v. Quinones*, 206 F.3d 474 (5th Cir. 2000), *and Wausau Ins. Companies v. Dir.*, OWCP, 114 F.3d 120 (9th Cir. 1997). *Cf. McNutt v. Benefits Review Board*, 140 F.3d 1247 (9th Cir. 1998) (cash per diem to pay for meals and lodging treated as an advantage and excluded from "wages").

113. 33 U.S.C. 902(13).

114. *Guthrie v. Holmes & Narver, Inc.*, 30 BRBS 48 (1996), *rev'd sub nom. Wausau Ins. Companies v. Director, OWCP*, 114 F.3d 120, 31 BRBS 41(CRT) (9th Cir. 1997).

115. *Id.*

116. *Roberts v. Custom Ship Interiors*, 300 F.3d 510 (4th Cir. 2002).

117. *Id.*

118. *B & D Contracting v. Pearley*, 548 F.3d 338 (5th Cir. 2008).

119. *Id.*

120. *Id.*

121. *Gonzales Electrical Systems v. Dir., OWCP*, 496 Fed. Appx. 378 (5th Cir. 2012).

122. *McNutt v. Benefits Review Board*, 140 F.3d 1247 (9th Cir. 1998).

123. *B & D Contracting v. Pearley*, 548 F.3d 338 (5th Cir. 2008).

Chapter 12

Calculation of the Average Weekly Wage Under the Defense Base Act

Monica F. Markovich, Esq.

The Defense Base Act (DBA) incorporates the provisions of the Section 10 Longshore and Harbor Workers' Compensation Act (LHWCA) for the calculation of the average weekly wage ("AWW").[1] Section 10 establishes three alternative methods for determining a claimant's AWW based on the date of injury; the appropriate method depends on claimant's work history as well as on the extent of available evidence. Section 10(i) defines the "time of injury" where disability does not immediately occur.[2] There can only be one AWW calculation per claim regardless of whether the claim facts might support a different AWW for temporary disability than for permanent disability.[3] While Sections 910(a) and (b) are more frequently applied in LHWCA claims, in the DBA realm the AWW calculation more often falls under Section 10(c).

12.1 Wages

The LHWCA defines "wages" as "the money rate at which the service rendered by an employee is compensated by an employer under the contract of hiring in force at the time of the injury, including the reasonable value of any advantage which is received from the employer and included for purposes of any withholding of tax under subtitle C of the Internal Revenue Code of 1954 [26 U.S.C. 3101 et seq.](relating to employment taxes)."[4]

In the Defense Base Act context, "wages" are not limited to the base salary earned. DBA "wages" are often defined as a base salary plus salary multipliers for area differentials and hazard pay. As these salary factors are generally reflected on the claimant's W-2 as earnings, they are included as "wages" for average weekly wage. The wages may also include quantifiable "advantages" if they are taxable to the employee.[5] An "advantage" like a per diem is typically included as "wages" if taxes are withheld for that advantage; otherwise further scrutiny is required before determining if the advantage is excluded from the average weekly wage.[6]

12.2 Section 10(a)

Section 10(a) focuses on the actual wages earned; this Section is applicable when the claimant worked in the same or similar employment for substantially the whole of the year prior to the injury. In order for Section 10(a) to apply, the parties to the claim must have evidence to show an adequate length of employment as well as evidence upon which a daily wage can be calculated.[7] Substantially the whole of the year refers to the nature of the claimant's employment rather than to the identity of the employer. Thus, as long as the skills used are highly comparable, the claimant may work for several employers during the substantial part of the year.[8] The Benefits Review Board has determined that

1. *See* 42 U.S.C. § 1651(a) ("Except as herein modified, the provisions of the Longshore and Harbor Workers' Compensation Act, approved March 4, 1927, as amended, shall apply in respect to the injury or death of any employee. . . .,"); 33 U.S.C. §910.

2. 33 U.S.C. § 910(i).

3. *Raymond v. Blackwater Security Consulting, LLC.*, 45 Ben. Rev. Bd. Serv. (MB). 5 (2011); *aff'd, Blackwater Sec, Consulting, LLC v. Dir., OWCP*, 503 Fed. Appx. 498 (9th Cir. 2012).

4. 33 U.S.C. 902(13).

5. *Custom Ship Interiors v. Roberts*, 300 F.3d 510, 515 (4th Cir. 2002); *H.B. Zachry Co. v. Quinones*, 206 F. 3d 474, 479 (5th Cir. 2000).

6. *Colbert v. CDI Aircraft Maintenance*, 31 BRBS 344 (ALJ 1997) citing *Cretan v. Bethlehem Steel Corp.*, 24 BRBS 35, 43 (1990).

7. *See eg. Adams v. Trapac, Inc.*, BRB No. 12-0671 (June 24, 2013) (unpublished).

8. *Mulcare v. E.C. Ernst, Inc.*, 18 Ben. Rev. Bd. Serv. (MB) 158, 160-61 (1986); *Bolton v. Service Employers Int'l, Inc.*,

thirty-four and a half weeks of full-time, steady, or regular employment would satisfy the "substantially the whole of the year" requirement.[9]

The actual earnings for that "year" are determined by reviewing the claimant's wages for the time period in question. The actual earnings of the claimant are divided by the actual number of days worked by the claimant in that fifty-two week period prior to the injury to produce the average daily wage ("ADW"). Then, the ADW is multiplied by either two hundred and sixty if the claimant was a five-days-per-week worker or three hundred if the claimant was a six-days-per-week worker to produce the average annual earnings ("AAE"). The AAE is then divided by fifty-two to produce the average weekly wage.

As Section 10(a) does not contain a geographic requirement, the focus for whether prior employment is similar to employment at the time of injury depends on the skills, knowledge and expertise required of each position.[10] Consideration should be given to whether the employment is intermittent or permanent. Section 10(a) may not be used for seven-days-per week workers.[11]

While some Administrative Law Judges and the Benefits Review Board have applied Section 10(a) in the DBA context,[12] Section 10(a) is more often rejected due to characteristics of the overseas employment.[13] Section 10(a) fails where there is inadequate evidence upon which to calculate the average daily wage. Section 10(a) is also inapplicable to a DBA claimant who generally worked seven days per week while overseas.

12.3 Section 10(b)

Section 10(b) calculates the claimant's AAE by using the wages earned by an employee of the same or similar class who has worked substantially the whole of the year in the same or similar place. Once the AAE is determined, the figure is divided by the total number of days worked by the comparable employee to produce the ADW, which is then used in an identical fashion to the Section 10(a) calculation, depending upon whether the claimant is a five-days-per-week worker or a six-days-per-week worker. If a claimant's work is intermittent or discontinuous, or if its use would result in an unfair result, Section 10(b) should not be applied.[14]

Section 10(b) should be considered when Section 10(a) cannot be used due to the fact that the claimant has not worked in the same or similar employment for the fifty-two weeks prior to the injury.[15] However, Section 10(b) only applies where the claimant's specific employer employed workers in the same or similar class as the claimant in the neighborhood of the claimant's injury for substantially the whole of the year prior to the claimant's injury. Section 10(b) may not be used for seven-days-per-week workers.[16] A Section 10(b) calculation may not take into account the post-injury wages earned by the comparable employees.[17]

Section 10(b) has received limited application in the DBA context. Several categories of cases have developed with respect to the reasons why Section 10(b) has not been widely used in the DBA context. Administrative Law Judges relying on Section 10(a) never reached Section 10(b) as the claimant worked substantially the whole of the year in the same or similar employment.[18] Administrative Law Judges have skipped over Section 10(b) to 10(c) where the claimant had worked substantially the whole of the year in the same or similar employment prior to the injury, but the Administrative Law Judge determined that application of Section 10(a) was unfair.[19] In these situations, the claimant's work history prevented the application of Section 10(b). Another

---

2002-LHC-00804 (ALJ) (May 30, 2003) (unpublished).

9. *Duncan v. Wash. Metro Area Transit Auth.*, 24 Ben. Rev. Bd. Serv. (MB) 133, 135 (1990) (per curiam).

10. *Mulcare v. E.C. Ernst, Inc.*, 18 Ben. Rev. Bd. Serv. (MB) 158, 160-61 (1986); *Bolton v. Service Employers Int'l, Inc.*, 2002-LHC-00804 (ALJ) (May 30, 2003) (unpublished).

11. *See eg.,J.T. v. Am. Logistics Services*, 40 Ben. Rev. Bd. Serv. (MB) 731, 742 (ALJ) (2006).

12. *See eg.,Bills v. Sci. Applications Int'l. Corp.*, 39 Ben. Rev. Bd. Serv. (MB) 304 (ALJ) (2005), vacated and remanded on other grounds by BRB No. 04-0107, at 3-4 (Sept. 28, 2004) (per curiam) (unpublished); *Bolton v. Service Employers Int'l.*, Inc., 2002-LHC-00804 (ALJ) (May 30, 2003) (unpublished); *V.S. v. USA Environmental, Inc.*, 2007-LDA-00042 (ALJ) (Aug. 21, 2007) (unpublished).

13. *Patton v. Brown & Root Services*, 40 Ben. Rev. Bd. Serv. (MB) 32 (ALJ) (2006), *aff'd,*, BRB No. 06-0401 (Nov. 28, 2006) (unpublished).

14. *See Empire United Stevedores v. Gatlin*, 936 F.2d 819, 822 (5th Cir.1991).

15. *See Goldbach v. Service Employers Int'l., Inc.*, 38 Ben. Rev. Bd. Serv. (MB) 595 (ALJ) (2004).

16. *See eg. Patton v. Brown & Root Services*, 40 Ben. Rev. Bd. Serv. (MB) 32, 41 (ALJ) (2006), *aff'd*, BRB No. 06-0401 (Nov. 28, 2006) (unpublished).

17. *Walker v. Wash. Metro Area Transit Auth.*, 793 F.2d 319, 322-23 (D.C. Cir. 1986).

18. *See eg.,Bills v. Science Applications Int'l. Corp.*, 39 Ben. Rev. Bd. Serv. (MB) 304 (ALJ) (2005), *Bills v. Sci. Applications Int'l. Corp.*, BRB No. 04-0107, at 3-4 (Sept. 28, 2004) (per curiam) (unpublished); *Bolton v. Service Employers Int'l. Inc.*, 2002-LHC-00804 (ALJ) (May 30, 2003) (unpublished), *V.S. v. USA Environmental, Inc.*, 2007-LDA-00042 (ALJ) (Aug. 21, 2007) (unpublished).

19. *See Goldbach*, 38 Ben. Rev. Bd. Serv. (MB) at 609-610; *see also Meyer v. Service Employers Int'l., Inc.*, 40 Ben. Rev. Bd. Serv. (MB) 44, 53 (ALJ) (2006).

explanation for the non-use of Section 10(b) is a lack of comparable workers in neighboring areas for the year prior to the injury.[20] Finally, Section 10(b) has been held inapplicable where the claimant works seven days per week rather than five days or six days per week.[21]

12.4 Section 10(c)

Section 10(c) serves as the catch-all provision of the act, and is used when both Sections 10(a) and 10(b) cannot be reasonably and fairly applied. The Fifth Circuit has recognized that the prime objective of Section 10(c) is to "arrive at a sum that reasonably represents a claimant's annual earning capacity at the time of injury."[22] This may be done by using any method of combining the wages earned or the contract rate to achieve rate commensurate with the claimant's AAE at the time of the injury. Under Section 10(c), the finder of fact has broad discretion in the calculation of the AAE and average weekly wage.

Numerous methods of calculating an average weekly wage under Section 10(c) have been recognized as appropriately capturing the annual earning capacity discussed by Section 10(c). For example, some judges have multiplied the claimant's hourly rate at the time of the injury by a variable representative of the number of hours worked in an average week. Other judges have used more than one year of the wage earning history of the claimant to determine the average weekly wage. Section 10(c) has been construed in a non-DBA context to permit the evaluation of post-injury wage fluctuations. The Seventh Circuit has allowed the finder of fact to calculate the average annual earning capacity that a claimant would have "the potential and opportunity to earn absent injury."[23] As the goal of Section 10(c) is to define the claimant's annual earning capacity, consideration can be given to the expected duration and temporary versus permanent nature of employment.

The decisions best illustrate the complexity of the average weekly wage calculation. The Administrative Law Judges have created a variety of fact specific equations for addressing average weekly wage in the Defense Base Act context.

20. *See Stoessel v Brown & Root, Inc.*, 2002-LHC-649 p. 21 (ALJ) (Feb. 20, 2003) (unpublished); *Kaylani v. AITECH USA, Inc.*, 2005-LDA-5, p. 11 (ALJ) (Dec. 29, 2005) (unpublished).

21. *Patton v. Brown & Root Services*, 40 Ben. Rev. Bd. Serv. (MB) 32, 41 (ALJ) (2006), *aff'd*, BRB No. 06-0401 (Nov. 28, 2006) (unpublished).

22. *Catlin*, 936 F.2d at 823, quoting *Cummins v. Todd Shipyards Corp.*, 12 Ben. Rev. Bd. Serv. (MB) 283, 285 (1980).

23. *Tri-State Terminals, Inc. v. Jesse*, 596 F.2d 752, 757 (7th Cir. 1979).

Goldbach v. Service Employers International, Inc. involved an electrician who injured his back almost immediately upon arriving at his overseas employment.[24] The claimant was an experienced electrician who worked in similar employment domestically prior to his acceptance of a three month contract for overseas employment in Croatia. The claimant requested that Section 10(b) be used, while the employer and carrier argued that claimant's work history from the previous year met the definition of Section 10(a). The Administrative Law Judge acknowledged that the claimant's work history was continuous for the twelve months prior to his injury, but took issue with the fact that the use of Section 10(a) would result in no appreciation for the claimant's increased wage earning capacity as a result of his recent employment overseas. The Administrative Law Judge also noted that the claimant was not entitled to a Section 10(b) calculation, as he "did work the majority of that year as an electrician ... using the same skills and training that he was expected to use overseas while working for Employer."

The Administrative Law Judge in *Goldbach* calculated the claimant's average weekly wage from the three month overseas contract (thus including expected post-injury earnings) in combination with nine months of domestic earnings prior to the injury. The Administrative Law Judge reasoned that the only equitable way to calculate the average weekly wage was to consider the wages that claimant was capable of earning under the contract with the employer as well as the wages earned domestically in the year prior to his injury. The Administrative Law Judge analogized the claimant's situation with that of a worker who had received a raise or promotion immediately prior to his injury, and stated that in those circumstances, Section 10(c) was the most appropriate method to calculate the average weekly wage. Rather than extrapolating the claimant's actual earnings over the remainder of the contract period, the Administrative Law Judge included the base salary plus foreign incentives, but not expected overtime pay.

In *Jasmine v. Can-Am Protection Group, Inc.*, the Benefits Review Board affirmed a blend of domestic and overseas earnings where the claimant was working overseas on a six month contract.[25] While the claimant had testified to an intent to work overseas for a longer term than specified in his contract, the Benefits Review Board found that there was also substantial evidence to support the Administrative Law Judge's interpretation of the claimant's actual employment history. Like in *Goldbach*, the Administrative Law Judge ultimately determined that a blend of the overseas and

24. 38 Ben. Rev. Bd. Serv. (MB) 595 (ALJ) (2004).

25. 46 Ben. Rev. Bd. Serv. (MB) 17 (2012).

prior domestic earnings constituted a reasonable estimate of claimant's average weekly wage at the time of injury; however, the *Jasmine* formula differs from the *Goldbach* formula as each calculation was performed to reflect the unique facts of the claim.

In *Meyer v. Service Employers International, Inc.* the claimant was a truck driver who worked nineteen weeks and six days overseas before sustaining a back injury on July 19, 2004.[26] The claimant worked as a truck driver domestically in the fifty-two weeks prior to his incident. The claimant advocated that his average weekly wage should be calculated using solely his overseas earnings. Employer and carrier argued for a Section 10(a) calculation using both the domestic earnings and overseas earnings from the fifty-two week period prior to claimant's injury. The Administrative Law Judge calculated the average weekly wage under Section 10(c) using the claimant's domestic and overseas earnings from the fifty-two weeks prior to the incident but dividing them by the actual number of weeks worked. The Administrative Law Judge noted that the calculation "allows Claimant to benefit from the higher wages of Iraq while recognizing the fact that employment in Iraq was for no set period of time under an at will employment contract but with an understanding that it would last twelve months." The Administrative Law Judge stated that the claimant's "true earning capacity is a compromise between what claimant made in Iraq and what he earned in the U.S."

The case of *Kaylani v. Aitech USA, Inc.* provides another example of an Administrative Law Judge compromising between the overseas wages and the domestic wages earned by an employee working in similar employment for the year prior to his injury.[27] In that case, the claimant was a pipeline inspector originally employed in Houston, Texas who was offered the opportunity to work overseas in Iraq in the same capacity. The claimant worked for approximately two and a half months overseas until he developed a severe case of dehydration, diarrhea, and eventually a pulmonary embolism. After finding that the pulmonary embolism was causally related to the claimant's employment overseas, the Administrative Law Judge turned to the issue of calculating the claimant's average weekly wage. The claimant advocated a Section 10(c) calculation using solely his overseas earnings. While the Administrative Law Judge found it inappropriate to use a strict Section 10(a) calculation, he divided claimant's total wages by the total number of weeks actually worked in the year prior to claimant's injury to determine the average weekly wage. The Administrative Law Judge noted that this lower average weekly wage "is more appropriate than just using his wages in Iraq since that job was admittedly of limited duration."

The decision in *Zimmerman v. Service Employers International, Inc.* contains a different analytical method from the cases previously discussed. The Administrative Law Judge reasoned that a calculation based on the increase in wages realized by the claimant from working in Iraq was the fairest method of resolving the average weekly wage issue.[28] Accordingly, he based claimant's average weekly on only his overseas contract wages. The *Zimmerman* decision was upheld on appeal by the Benefits Review Board. The Benefits Review Board affirmed, but did so because as claimant was a seven-day worker rather than either a five-day-week or a six-day-week worker, Section 10(a) could not be used to determine his average weekly wage. The Benefits Review Board specifically noted that their rationale avoided the issue of whether the skills inherent in a truck driver overseas in a war zone were the same skills as a truck driver in the United States. The Benefits Review Board affirmed the use of and method of calculation under Section 10(c) by the Administrative Law Judge, and determined that the use of the total overseas earnings divided by the days worked overseas was a fair and reasonable method of determining the claimant's average daily wage. The Benefits Review Board further stated that since the parties stipulated that the Claimant worked seven days a week, it was appropriate to multiply the average daily wage by seven to produce the average weekly wage under Section 10(c).[29]

While several Administrative Law Judges have referenced the *Zimmerman* decision in conjunction with their choice to apply Section 10(c),[30] the Benefits Review Board's decision is unpublished and thus has "questionable precedential value."[31] In electing to not apply *Zimmerman* to another injured truck driver in *R.L. v. Service Employers International, Inc.*, the Administrative Law Judge noted that the *Zimmerman* approach "provides a windfall to Defense Base Act claimants" as the high overseas wages fail to account for the "temporary duration of these high-paying, war-

26. 40 Ben. Rev. Bd. Serv. (MB) 44 (ALJ) (2006).

27. 39 Ben. Rev. Bd. Serv. (MB) 854 (ALJ) (2005).

28. 39 Ben. Rev. Bd. Serv. (MB) 166 (ALJ) (2005), *aff'd*, BRB No. 05-0580, (Feb. 22, 2006) (unpublished) (per curiam) (remanding for entry of a formal order), *remanded to* No. 2004-LHC-927, (ALJ) (May 16, 2006) (unpublished) (entering the formal order), *aff'd*, BRB No. 06-0663 (June 28, 2006) (unpublished).

29. *Zimmerman v. Service Employers Int'l, Inc.*, BRB No. 05-0580 (Feb. 22, 2006) (unpublished) (per curiam).

30. *See eg. J.S. v. Service Employees Int'l, Inc.*, 41 Ben. Rev. Bd. Serv. (MB) 164, 173 (ALJ) (2007); *A.K. v. L-3 Communications-Titan Corp.*, 41 Ben. Rev. Bd. Serv. (MB) 115 (ALJ) (2007).

31. *R.L. v. Service Employers Int'l, Inc.*, 41 BRBS (MB) 1279 (ALJ) (2007).

time jobs" and creates an "artificially high" compensation rate.[32] The Administrative Law Judge found that the blended rate approach in the *Goldbach* and Meyer line of cases more properly compensates claimants for their higher overseas earnings while also referencing their longer term domestic earning potential. In order to include both the "fleeting" higher overseas earnings and the more permanent domestic earning potential, the Administrative Law Judge based the average weekly wage on the total earnings for the 52 weeks prior to the injury divided by the number of weeks actually worked.

In *Fern v. Service Employers International, Inc.*, the claimant was a forty-five year old truck driver who re-injured a pre-existing back condition while overseas.[33] The claimant began working for employer on November 29, 2004, and was injured on February 1, 2005. While the claimant had worked domestically as a truck driver for many years, he had not worked immediately prior to his overseas employment due to the prior back injury. The employer argued for a 10(c) calculation using an average of all of the claimant's domestic earnings and a full year's wages in Iraq, while the claimant requested a Section 10(c) calculation using solely his overseas earnings. The Administrative Law Judge found merit in the employer's position that the use of only overseas earnings would amount to a "spike" in wage earning capacity due to temporary employment. The Administrative Law Judge compromised by basing the average weekly wage on an average of the last full domestic year of the claimant's wages and a full year of overseas wages.[34]

The decision regarding a claimant who was injured and then returned to overseas work after receiving treatment highlights the fact specific nature of the average weekly wage issue. In *Collins v. Service Employers International, Inc.*, the claimant was a sixty-six year old truck driver who originally was injured when a brick came through the windshield of his vehicle, damaging his left eye.[35] The claimant returned to his regular job duties in Iraq until he sustained an unrelated injury. The claimant advocated a Section 10(b) calculation, but provided no evidence of similar employees in the same or neighboring region that had worked for substantially the whole of the year prior to his injury. The claimant testified that he intended to stay overseas in Iraq for two or three years, and that he was promised a salary of $8,000.00 monthly. The employer advocated inclusion of claimant's domestic salary prior to his overseas employment in a Section 10(c) calculation. The Administrative Law Judge stated that in deciding several claims involving the average weekly wage issue "I have ruled differently in each depending on the circumstances." The Administrative Law Judge then used solely the claimant's overseas earnings to calculate the average weekly wage under Section 10(c), noting that he was impressed with the claimant's willingness to return to work after being injured, and felt that the claimant "had a real willingness to stay and earn as much as he could while the opportunity existed." The Administrative Law Judge therefore found that "in this instance the use of his prior earnings would be unfair and unreasonable given his newly discovered earning power and his obvious effort to take advantage of those earnings." When the Administrative Law Judge ruled on the average weekly wage with respect to the second injury, he repeated his rationale and the evidence of the claimant's proven desire to work overseas when basing the claimant's earnings on his overseas earnings only under Section 10(c).[36]

In *Patterson v. Omniplex World Services*, the claimant had overseas experience as a security guard when he started working in a similar position in July of 1997 with the employer in Moscow.[37] The Benefits Review Board noted that "claimant's employment as a security guard was neither regular nor continuous…as claimant was unemployed for over eight months in the year preceding his injury." The Claimant injured his back in the course and scope of his employment with the employer on August 10, 1997. The Administrative Law Judge multiplied the claimant's hourly rate by forty hours to arrive at the average weekly wage. The Administrative Law Judge indicated that this calculation was performed under Section 10(a). While the Benefits Review Board agreed with the ultimate average weekly wage, the Benefits Review Board re-classified the method as falling under Section 10(c). The Benefits Review Board reasoned that Section 10(a) was inappropriate in light of the fact that the claimant had not worked substantially the whole of the year in the same or similar employment prior to his injury.

The unpublished decision in *S.T. v. Titan Corporation* reinforces the requirement that the average weekly wage reflect the earning capacity at the time of injury rather than subsequent to the time of injury.[38] The claimant was an Iraqi national injured in Iraq while performing similar work to expatriate translators from the United States. While the claim-

32. *Id.*

33. 39 Ben. Rev. Bd. Serv. (MB) 820 (ALJ) (2005).

34. *See also Dalton v. Maritime Services Corp.*, BRB No. 11-0868 (February 27, 2013) (unpublished) (AWW may be based on a two year period including the depressed year prior to the injury even though the wages in the year prior to injury were relatively low).

35. 40 Ben. Rev. Bd. Serv. (MB) 1 (ALJ) (2006).

36. *Id.* at 4.

37. 36 Ben. Rev. Bd. Serv. (MB) 149 (2003) (per curiam).

38. No. 2005-LDA-00069, (ALJ) (Mar. 10, 2006).

ant was paid $10.00 per day, United States citizens were paid $80,000.00 per year for the same job in Iraq. After his injury, the claimant and his family moved to the United States. The claimant argued that as his work was similar to that of the American translators, their pay should be considered in the calculation of his average weekly wage pursuant to Section 10(c). The Administrative Law Judge did not agree that the claimant was of the "same or most similar class" as the American translators as the claimant's "nationality and nation of residence distinguish him from the other translators." The Administrative Law Judge based the claimant's average weekly wage on his daily rate at the time of the injury, but the Administrative Law Judge agreed with the employer that the claimant would work for 360 days in a year. While the Administrative Law Judge expressed sympathy for the inadequacy of the claimant's average weekly wage in his new homeland, she noted that "a claimant's average weekly wage is determined at the time of injury, and any change in circumstance occurring subsequent to the injury is not relevant to the calculation of the average weekly wage."

The decision in *Patton v. Brown & Root Services* serves as another example of an Administrative Law Judge using Section 10(c) instead of Section 10(a) to determine a claimant's average weekly wage.[39] The claimant in this case was a truck driver involved in a motor vehicle accident while driving in a convoy in Iraq. The claimant had worked 15.5 weeks overseas as a heavy truck driver prior to his injury, and had worked 36.5 weeks prior to his deployment overseas as a self-employed truck driver in the United States. The Court determined that Section 10(a) could not reasonably and fairly be applied to the claimant's situation because the heavy truck driving position maintained by the claimant for three months in Iraq was found to not be similar employment to a self-employed truck driver in the United States. The Court specifically determined that Section 10(a)'s provisions for five-day and six-day workers did not apply to seven-day workers. The Court also determined that Section 10(b) could not be applied, again because the mechanism in that section did not provide for a seven-day-a-week calculation. The Court then held that the best reflection of the claimant's earning capacity at the time of his injury was his actual earnings, relying upon *Miranda v. Excavation Construction, Inc.*[40] to support its reasoning. The Court determined that the claimant had a long-term prospect for employment overseas based upon the claimant's testimony that other workers renewed their contracts and that he desired to work overseas for five years. The Court also noted that Section 10(c) required that the finder of fact determine the claimant's average weekly wage under Section 10(c) based upon the claimant's potential earning capacity at the time of the injury. On appeal, the Benefits Review Board adopted the rationale of the Administrative Law Judge when it affirmed his average weekly wage calculation.

In *A.K. v. L-3 Communications-Titan Corporation*, the claimant worked for an entire year overseas for the employer in a translator position.[41] The Administrative Law Judge eliminated Sections 10(a) and 10(b) due to the seven day workweek and due to the dramatic difference between claimant's work as a translator and his prior domestic employment in a hotel. The Administrative Law Judge cited the original opinions in *Zimmerman* and *Patton* in support of his determination to base the claimant's average weekly wage on only the 52 weeks of overseas earnings. The Benefits Review Board affirmed the average weekly wage determination, but vacated a determination on a disability issue and remanded the case for further consideration.

The case of *Purcella v. Service Employers International, Inc.* provides an evaluation of a claimant alleging both physical and mental trauma as a result of driving trucks in convoys.[42] The claimant was allegedly attacked on several occasions while driving trucks in convoys, sustaining injuries to multiple parts of his body as well as contracting post-traumatic stress disorder while working in Iraq. The claimant also had a prior history of mental illness, which Employer and Carrier contended would have required rejection of his application for overseas employment had that information been properly disclosed. The Court determined that these injuries were compensable, then turned to the determination of the claimant's average weekly wage. The claimant requested that the Court follow *Zimmerman v. Service Employers International, Inc.* by calculating his average weekly wage under Section 10(c) using solely his overseas earnings. The Court acknowledged that Section 10(a) appeared to be inapplicable because of the claimant's status as a seven-day-worker. The Court then turned to Section 10(b), but disregarded the application of that section due to a lack of information regarding comparable workers. Applying Section 10(c), the Court conducted a combined calculation of the claimant's domestic wages as a truck driver with his overseas wages to produce an average weekly wage that had a corresponding compensation rate less than the maximum compensation rate. The ALJ noted that this combined calculation was appropriate due to the fact that if the claimant had

39. 40 Ben Rev. Bd. Serv. (MB) 32 (ALJ) (2006), *aff'd*, BRB No. 06-0401 (Nov. 28, 2006) (unpublished).

40. 13 Ben. Rev. Bd. Serv. (MB) 882, 886 (1981).

41. 41 Ben. Rev. Bd. Serv. (MB) 115 (ALJ) (2007).

42. 40 Ben. Rev. Bd. Serv. (MB) 160 (ALJ) (2006) [hereinafter *Purcella I*]. This case was reconsidered as *Purcella v. Service Employers Int'l, Inc.*, 40 Ben. Rev. Bd. Serv. (MB) 506 (ALJ) (2006) [hereinafter *Purcella II*].

disclosed his prior history of mental illness, he likely would not have been hired.

The Court reconsidered its analysis and holdings regarding the claimant's average weekly wage in *Purcella II*. In an order issued on May 24, 2006, the ALJ again rejected application of the unpublished Benefits Review Board decision on the *Zimmerman* case, and instead used actual payroll records from the claimant's time in the Middle East to slightly reduce the claimant's average weekly wage. The Court maintained a combined calculation of the average weekly wage using both domestic and overseas earnings.

Efforts by the Benefits Review Board to limit the discretion of the Judges have been chastised on appeal. In the "K.S." line of cases, the United States District Court for the Southern District of Texas declared "While the BRB may not agree with the ALJ's factual findings, 'the Board does not have the authority to engage in a *de novo* review of the evidence or to substantiate its views for those of the ALJ.'"[43] In the underlying claims, the Benefits Review Board had addressed the question of the appropriate Section 10(c) method for employees working under one-year contracts in dangerous locales. The Benefits Review Board rejected the Administrative Law Judges' unique blended average weekly wages so that the cases would be consistent with the Benefits Review Board's prior decisions to base average weekly wage only on overseas earnings for one-year contract claimants. On appeal the sole issue was whether the Benefit Review Board's decisions impermissibly restricted the discretion of the Administrative Law Judges to determine each claimant's average weekly wage under Section 10(c). The Court borrowed from the 5th Circuit's decision in *Bay, Ltd. V. Dir., Office of Workers' Comp. Programs* by providing that an Administrative Law Judge should consider three factors for the Section 10(c) calculation: "(1) past earnings of the employee in which he was working at the time of injury; (2) the earning history of employees of the same or most similar class working in the same or most similar employment; and (3) the employment history of the injured employee."[44] The Court provided that an Administrative Law Judge has wide discretion in determining what calculation would be fair and reasonable under Section 10(c). The Court determined that the Benefit Review Board had usurped the role of the Administrative Law Judges, because "to require all cases with facts similar to those [in other cases] to have similar outcomes would relegate the ALJ to simply playing the role of calculator."[45] In vacating the Benefits Review Board decisions and remanding the cases, the Court noted that by attempting to hold an Administrative Law Judge to a prior Section 10(c) calculation in a similar case, the Benefits Review Board "essentially deprived the ALJ of the 'wide discretion' mandated by the statute."[46]

The case examples illustrate the broad discretion of Administrative Law Judges to generate an average weekly wage formula to suit the specific facts of a claim. The established precedent has expanded, rather than limited, the power of the Judges to generate the most appropriate average weekly wage on a case by case basis.

12.5 Section 10(i)

In 1984 the LHWCA was amended to incorporate a later average weekly wage calculation where a claimant did not become immediately disabled.[47] The new subsection, Section 10(i), provides that "For purposes of this section with respect to a claim for compensation for death or disability due to an occupational disease which does not immediately result in death or disability, the time of the injury shall be deemed to be the date on which the employee or claimant becomes aware, or in the exercise of reasonable diligence or by reason of medical advice should have been aware, of the relationship between the employment, the disease, and the death or disability."

Section 10(i) historically has benefitted the claimant as it has resulted in a higher average weekly wage than would have applied on the date of last injurious exposure.[48] In the Defense Base Act context the application of Section 10(i) may drastically reduce the effective average weekly wage. As can be seen by the case examples applying Section 10(c), most DBA claimants argue for an AWW based solely on their overseas earnings as those overseas earnings are usually significantly higher than the pre-injury domestic earnings. Where a claimant files an occupational disease claim years after returning to domestic employment, his resulting average weekly wage may be much lower if it is based on the more recent domestic earnings.

While Section 10(i) arose from case precedent on the appropriate "time of injury" for later-filed claims, this Section has been far less litigated that Sections 10(a), 10(b) and 10(c) since its enactment.

43. *Service Employees Int;l, Inc.v. Director, OWCP*, 2013 U.S. Dist. LEXIS 32887 (S.D. Tex. March 11, 2013) (unpublished), *citing Mijangos v. Avondale Shipyards, Inc.*, 948 F. 2d 941, 944 (5th Cir. 1991).

44. *Service Employees Int'l, Inc.*, 2013 U.S. Dist. LEXIS 32887 at 6, citing *Bay, Ltd.*, 300 F. App'x 282, 285

45. *Service Employees Int'l, Inc.*, 2013 U.S. Dist. LEXIS 32887 at 7.

46. *Id.* at 5.

47. 33 U.S.C. 910(i).

48. *See eg. Johnson v. Director,* OWCP, 911 F.2d 247 (9th Cir. 1990).

12.6 DBA Indemnity Benefits: Trends But Still No Consensus

Despite extensive litigation at the Office of Administrative Law Judges over average weekly wage, the methods for determining average weekly wage under Section 10(c) are continuing to evolve without the development of any absolute rules. The more recent appellate decisions confirm that the Administrative Law Judge bears broad discretion to determine the most appropriate average weekly wage where neither Section 10(a) nor 10(b) apply. While substantial evidence must support a determination under Section 10(c), as long as the Judge has relied upon facts in evidence his calculation should stand. Unique factors in calculating a claimant's average weekly wage under the DBA include whether the overseas job is temporary or permanent, whether the overseas employee is exposed to extra workplace hazards or war hazards, and the higher wages earned by civilian workers in overseas employment as compared to the wages available in the United States for similar positions of employment. The Administrative Law Judges have endorsed multiple methods in their effort to identify a rate that suits the characteristics of each claimant. As the decision in *K.S.* effectively overturned the Board's prior standard for similarly situated claimants, a general consensus still does not exist with respect to the appropriate method of calculating a DBA claimant's average weekly wage. Where the evidence cannot support a calculation under Section 10(a) or 10(b), the calculation of average weekly wage in Defense Base Act claims will depend primarily on the facts of each claim.

Acknowledgements

The author gratefully acknowledges the attorneys of Brown Sims, P.C. for their assistance in developing commentary on average weekly wage topics upon which the chapter was based.

Chapter 13

Scheduled Injuries Versus Unscheduled Injuries Under the Act

Paul B. Howell, Esq.

The Longshore and Harbor Workers' Compensation Act provides for four different general types of disability. 33 U.S.C. § 908. A claimant may be deemed temporarily and totally disabled or temporarily partially disabled prior to the date that the claimant achieves the maximum benefit of treatment, or reaches maximum medical improvement. 33 U.S.C. § 908(b); 33 U.S.C. § 908(e); *Trask v. Lockheed Shipbuilding & Construction Co.*, 17 BRBS 56 (1980); *Luce vs. Bath Iron Works Corp.*, 12 BRBS 162 (1979). After a claimant reaches maximum medical improvement, any continuing disability is considered permanent and he may be either permanently and totally disabled or permanently partially disabled. 33 U.S.C. § 908(a) and 33 U.S.C. § 908(c). There are two specific types of permanent partial disability. Permanent partial disability to the whole man (unscheduled disability), encompasses injuries to the head, neck, back, etc., and are compensated based upon two-thirds of the difference between the claimant's average weekly wage and the claimant's post-injury wage-earning capacity. 33 U.S.C. § 908(c)(21); *Devillier v. National Steel & Shipbuilding Co.*, 14 BRBS 598 (1981). Permanent partial disability to scheduled members such as the arm, leg, hand, foot, eye, fingers, and toes are payable under a statutory schedule for loss of use of the member which allows payment of a claimant's compensation rate for a set number of weeks for total loss of the member, or a proportionate number of weeks based upon the claimant's disability rating. 33 U.S.C. § 908(c)(1-12)(19). For example, a claimant with a 7% disability to the leg would be entitled to two thirds of his average weekly wage (his compensation rate) for 7% of 288 weeks (which is the maximum number of weeks available for total loss of a leg), or 20.16 weeks. *Boone v. Newport News Shipbuilding & Dry Dock Co.*, 37 BRBS 1 (2003). In determining the percentage of disability, the administrative law judge is technically not limited to awarding disability based upon the impairment rating assigned by the physician. *Pimpinella v. Universal Maritime Service, Inc.*, 27 BRBS 15 (1993); *Bachich v. Seatrain Terminals of California*, 9 BRBS 184 (1978); *Mazze v. Frank J. Holleran, Inc.*, 9 BRBS 1053 (1978).[1] However, the general rule of practice is that the judges assign a disability rating commensurate with the impairment rating assigned by the most credible physician. *Nash v. Strachan Shipping Co.*, 782 F.2d 513 (5th Cir. 1986); *Brown v. National Steel and Shipbuilding Co.*, 34 BRBS 195 (2001); *DeNoble v. Maritime Transportation Management, Inc.*, 12 BRBS 29 (1980).

It cannot be emphasized enough that the schedule is limited to permanent *partial* disabilities. An injury to a scheduled member which renders the claimant permanently and totally disabled is not limited to the schedule and therefore the claimant may recover permanent and total disability under 33 U.S.C. § 908(a). *Carter v. Merritt Ship Repair*, 19 BRBS 94 (1986); *Jacksonville Shipyards Inc. v. Dugger*, 587 F.2d 197 (5th Cir. 1979); *Picoriello v. Caddell Dry Dock Co.*, 12 BRBS 84 (1980). Accordingly, the same burdens are on the parties in a case involving an injury to a scheduled member as there are in a case which does not involve a scheduled member. Claimant may make out a *prima facie* case for permanent and total disability by proving that he is restricted from performing his regular duties, at which time the burden shifts to the employer to establish the availability of suitable alternative employment, after which the burden returns to the claimant to prove that he diligently sought such work without success. *New Orleans (Gulfwide) Stevedores v. Turner*, 661 F.2d 1031 (5th Cir. 1981); *P & M Crane Co. v. Hayes*, 930 F.2d 424 (5th Cir. 1991).

The schedule does not become applicable until the employer establishes that the claimant is not permanently and totally disabled even if that is well after the date of maximum medical improvement. *R.V. v. Friede Goldman Halter*, 43 BRBS 22 (2009); *Seguro v. Universal Maritime Service Corp.*, 36 BRBS 28 (2002); *Director, OWCP v. Bethlehem Steel Corp.*, 949 F.2d 185 (5th Cir. 1991); *Rinaldi v. General Dynamics Corp.*, 25 BRBS 128 (1991).

1. Hearing loss and retiree benefits are required to be based upon the AMA impairment ratings. *Pimpinella*, 27 BRBS at 159 n.4.

The good news for employers with regard to scheduled injuries is that if the claimant is rendered permanently partially disabled due to an injury to a scheduled member, he may not elect to receive permanent partial disability based upon a loss of wage-earning capacity, even if that loss would be much greater than the recovery allowed under the schedule. *Potomac Electric Power Co. v. Director, OWCP*, 449 U.S. 268 (1980). The good news for claimants is that disability under the schedule is payable for a proportionate loss of use of the member, even though the claimant has no loss of wage-earning capacity. *Henry v. George Hyman Construction Co.*, 749 F.2d 65 (D. C. Cir. 1984).

Unlike scheduled injuries, unscheduled injuries are compensated based upon a loss of wage-earning capacity rather than loss of use or physical impairment. *Freiwillig v. Triple A South*, 23 BRBS 371 (1990). Accordingly, a claimant with a 10% disability of the back is not entitled to any compensation where his impairment does not prevent him from performing his regular job and earning his regular wage. *Jennings v. Sea-Land Serv., Inc.*, 23 BRBS 312 (1990). In effect, the impairment rating is virtually irrelevant to determining unscheduled disability which instead is driven by restrictions and their effect on claimant's capacity to earn wages. *Carroll v. Hanover Bridge Marina*, 17 BRBS 176 (1985). Actual post-injury earnings create a presumption that they are commensurate with claimant's post-injury wage-earning capacity. *Burch v. Superior Oil Co.*, 15 BRBS 423 (1983). The party contending that the employee's actual earnings are not representative of his wage-earning capacity therefore has the burden of establishing an alternative, reasonable, wage-earning capacity. *Avondale Shipyards, Inc. v. Guidry*, 967 F.2d 1039 (5th Cir. 1992). A party may rebut this presumption by proving that the post-injury earnings do not fairly and reasonably represent his wage-earning capacity. 33 U.S.C. § 908(h). Accordingly, a claimant may prove entitlement to disability, despite equivalent post-injury earnings, in the following ways:

1. He may prove that the job he is performing is incompatible with his medical restrictions. *Newport News Shipbuilding & Dry Dock Co. v. Riley*, 262 F.3d 227 (4th Cir. 2001).
2. He can prove that he is only able to receive these earnings based upon extraordinary effort and in spite of excruciating pain. *CNA Ins. Co. v. LaGrow, 935 F.2d 430* (1st Cir. 1991); *Argonaut Ins. Co. v. Patterson*, 846 F.2d 715 (11th Cir. 1988).
3. He could assert that he is receiving the earnings in sheltered employment. *Patterson v. Savannah Shipyard & Machine*, 15 BRBS 38 (1982), *aff'd sub nom*; *Argonaut Ins. Co. v. Patterson*, 846 F.2d 715 (11th Cir. 1988).
4. He may prove entitlement to a *de minimus* award where he has a reasonable expectation of a future loss of wage-earning capacity, even though he has no present loss of wage-earning capacity. *Metropolitan Stevedore Co. v. Rambo*, 521 U.S. 121 (1997).

Likewise, an employer may prove that claimant's post-injury wage-earning capacity is greater than his actual post-injury earnings by proving that the claimant is underemployed compared to what he could reasonably earn in the open labor market. *Penrod Drilling Co. v. Johnson*, 905 F.2d 84 (5th Cir. 1990).

Where a claimant has no post-injury earnings, or his post-injury earnings do not fairly and reasonably represent his wage-earning capacity, the judge must determine a specific wage-earning capacity with due regard to the nature of his injury, the degree of physical impairment, his usual employment, and any other factors or circumstances in the case which may effect his capacity to earn wages in his condition now and into the future. 33 U.S.C. § 908(h). Generally, an administrative law judge will determine claimant's post-injury wage-earning capacity from an average of the suitable alternative employment established by the employer through vocational evidence or otherwise. *Shell Offshore v. Director, OWCP*, 122 F.3d 312 (5th Cir. 1997), *cert denied* 523 U.S. 1095 (1998); *Southern v. Farmers Export Co.*, 17 BRBS 64 (1985); *B. H. v. Northrup Grumman Ship Systems, Inc.*, 43 BRBS 129 (2009). However, where there is a substantial period between the date the suitable alternative jobs are identified and the date of claimant's injury, the administrative law judge must adjust the pay scale of the post-injury jobs back to what they would have paid at the time of the injury so that it could be compared to the claimant's average weekly wage at the time of the injury (comparing apples to apples). *Richardson v. General Dynamics Corp.*, 19 BRBS 48 (1986). An administrative law judge has some discretion in calculating the post-injury wage-earning capacity. *Neff v. Foss Maritime Co.*, 41 BRBS 46 (2007).

Due to the inherent differences between scheduled and unscheduled permanent disability, the parties often are at odds as to whether a claim comes within the schedule. Claimants, on rare occasions, will assert that permanent disability falls within the schedule in the following scenarios:

1. Where the claimant has no loss of wage-earning capacity and would recover nothing, but for the schedule. *Greto v. Blakesley, Arpaia & Chapman*, 10 BRBS 1000 (1979).

2. Where the permanent disability arises after the claimant's voluntary retirement since a claimant can recover for a loss of use after he no longer has any wage-earning capacity to lose due to his voluntary retirement. *Hoffman v. Newport News Shipbuilding and Dry Dock Co.*, 35 BRBS 148 (2001); *Burson v. T. Smith & Sons, Inc.*, 22 BRBS 124 (1989).
3. The claimant's survivors are entitled to the balance of his scheduled award. 33 U.S.C. § 908(d)(2).

Claimants usually assert that injuries fall outside the schedule where greater benefits may be recovered over the claimant's lifetime. Claimants assert entitlement to unscheduled permanent disability for injuries to scheduled members in the following situations:

1. Where the scheduled disability renders the claimant permanently and totally disabled. *Potomac Electric Power Co. v. Director, OWCP*, 449 U.S. 268, 277 n. 17 (1980).
2. Injuries to the shoulder are considered unscheduled disabilities since shoulders are not specifically mentioned in the list of scheduled members, even though the AMA Guides consider shoulders as part of the arm. *McDevitt v. George Hyman Construction Co.*, 14 BRBS 677 (1982); *Grimes v. Exxon Co.*, U.S.A., 14 BRBS 573 (1981); *Andrews v. Jeffboat, Inc.*, 23 BRBS 169 (1990); *Keenan v. Director for Benefits Review Board*, 392 F.3d 1041 (9th Cir. 2004).
3. Injuries to scheduled members can result in unscheduled disability in other parts of the body for which a claimant may be entitled to combined scheduled and unscheduled disability. *Thompson v. Lockheed Shipbuilding & Construction Co.*, 21 BRBS 94 (1988); *Bass v. Broadway Maintenance*, 28 BRBS 11 (1994).
4. A claimant with both a scheduled injury and a non-scheduled injury arising out of the same accident may recover for both injuries subject to the maximum compensation rate. *Green v. ITO Corp. of Baltimore*, 185 F.3d 239 (4th Cir. 1999).

In conclusion, there are inherent differences between scheduled and unscheduled permanent disabilities. Scheduled disabilities involve permanent partial disability to statutory scheduled members and are driven by medical impairment ratings. However, unscheduled disabilities involve permanent disability to the head, neck, back, etc., and recoveries are based upon loss of wage-earning capacity or economic factors. A good practitioner should be able to immediately recognize the differences and when it is advantageous to argue one over the other.

Chapter 14

The Difference Between Temporary Total, Temporary Partial, Permanent Partial, and Permanent Total Disability

Alan G. Brackett, Esq.

The World Health Organization has stated that "disability" is an "umbrella term," covering impairments, activity limitations, and participation restrictions. An impairment is a problem in body function or structure; an activity limitation is a difficulty encountered by an individual in executing a task or action; while a participation restriction is a problem experienced by an individual in involvement in life situations. Thus, disability is a complex phenomenon, reflecting an interaction between features of a person's body and features of the society in which he or she lives. Under the Longshore and Harbor Workers' Compensation Act[1] disability can be no less complex, but it is both a description of physical limitation and an economic concept based upon impairment of earning capacity. It is decidedly not purely an evaluation of physical impairment. An injured worker is entitled to compensation under the Act to the extent his or her ability to earn wages following a compensable accident has been diminished. Congress has, in some instances, presumed that certain injuries adversely affect earning capacity.[2] Under certain circumstances, benefits are payable even if no immediate effect on earnings results.

The use of the term "disability" under the LHWCA is, therefore, a misnomer in the sense of how the term is generally understood. The Act does not evaluate physical impairment to an injured worker in a true sense and attempt to compensate the worker for that loss. Rather, the Act is designed to compensate the injured worker for a real or presumed impairment of wage earning capacity arising from a physical or mental injury.

Disability itself is defined in section 2(10) of the Act[3] as follows:

> "Disability" means incapacity because of injury to earn the wages which the employee was receiving at the time of injury in the same or any other employment; but such term shall mean permanent impairment, determined (to the extent covered thereby) under the guides to the evaluation of permanent impairment promulgated and modified from time to time by the American Medical Association, in the case of an individual whose claim is described in section 10 (d)(2).

Compensation for disability is provided for in section 8 of the Act[4] and is classified as either *temporary total*, *temporary partial*, *permanent partial*, or *permanent total disability*.

Temporary total disability results when a worker is unable to earn any wages following an injury, but the nature of the condition is temporary.[5] This type of disability is common to most every injury where a worker loses time from his or her duties as a result of an accident. The worker is unable to perform any duties for a certain period of time while recovering from the immediate results of the physical harm sustained. During this period of disability, the worker is entitled to the receipt of 66⅔% of his or her average weekly wage, subject to the statutory maximum and minimum compensation rates. There is an exception to this under the Defense Base Act, which is limited by the maximum compensation rate, but not the minimum compensation rate that applies under the LHWCA. It is important to note that although this type of disability is described as temporary, these benefits can continue indefinitely, until the worker's treating physician (or an Administrative Law Judge, if the claim is litigated) declares the worker to have reached maximum medical improvement from the injury sustained. The Act does not place any statutory limitation on the duration of temporary total disability benefits.

As a practical matter, an injury should eventually "plateau," such that a condition is no longer temporary, but permanent, but this is not a legal determination. Rather, it is and should be a medical one.

Temporary partial disability is provided for section 8 (e) of the Act.[6] This type of disability occurs where an injury temporarily prevents a worker from earning his or her pre-injury wages, but the worker is nevertheless able to earn wages in some amount. There are two common scenarios where this applies. If a worker can still work after the accident, but is limited to working fewer hours than he or she worked prior to the injury, such as being limited to an eight-hour shift where previously overtime could be worked, the worker would be entitled to benefits. Likewise, if an injured worker returns to work in a light or modified duty capacity which either pays lower wages or provides fewer hours of available work, the worker is entitled to benefits.

Temporary partial disability benefits are payable based on two-thirds of the difference between the worker's pre-accident average weekly wage and the worker's post-accident earnings. Unlike temporary total disability benefits, temporary partial disability benefits are payable for a maximum period of five years.[7] Presumably, if a "temporary" condition exceeds five years in duration, it was Congress' intent that the condition be deemed permanent, and benefits converted to permanent partial disability. Despite this intent, the Act does not place a limit on temporary total benefits, as stated above.

Permanent partial disability is intended to compensate an injured worker for a condition which is both permanent in nature and which adversely affects his or her earning capacity. This type of disability, however, does not necessarily require any limitation of wage earning capacity in fact. Under numerous scenarios, as with most other statutory compensation schemes, an adverse effect on wage earning capacity is presumed.

Section 8 (c) of the Act[8] sets forth a list of anatomical losses for which the Act mandates benefits be paid, without regard to whether the worker has sustained any measurable loss in earning capacity. These are commonly referred to as "scheduled" losses, and the specific compensation due for such losses is set forth in section 8 (c)(1) through (13). This class of disability applies primarily to a worker's extremities, hearing, and vision. Congress assigned a set number of weeks of compensation for such injuries in an attempt to value the economic loss that the loss of certain body parts brings about. The schedule is as follows:

(1) Arm lost, three hundred and twelve weeks' compensation.
(2) Leg lost, two hundred and eighty-eight weeks' compensation.
(3) Hand lost, two hundred and forty-four weeks' compensation.
(4) Foot lost, two hundred and five weeks' compensation.
(5) Eye lost, one hundred and sixty weeks' compensation.
(6) Thumb lost, seventy-five weeks' compensation.
(7) First finger lost, forty-six weeks' compensation.
(8) Great toe lost, thirty-eight weeks' compensation.
(9) Second finger lost, thirty weeks' compensation.
(10) Third finger lost, twenty-five weeks' compensation.
(11) Toe other than great toe lost, sixteen weeks' compensation.
(12) Fourth finger lost, fifteen weeks' compensation.
(13) Loss of hearing:
    (A) Compensation for loss of hearing in one ear, fifty-two weeks.
    (B) Compensation for loss of hearing in both ears, two-hundred weeks.
(14) Phalanges: Compensation for loss of more than one phalange of a digit shall be the same as for loss of the entire digit. Compensation for loss of the first phalange shall be one-half of the compensation for loss of the entire digit.
(15) Amputated arm or leg: Compensation for an arm or a leg, if amputated at or above the elbow or the knee, shall be the same as for a loss of the arm or leg; but, if amputated between the elbow and the wrist or the knee and the ankle, shall be the same as for loss of a hand or foot.
(16) Binocular vision or per centum of vision: Compensation for loss of binocular vision or for 80 per centum or more of the vision of an eye shall be the same as for loss of the eye.
(17) Two or more digits: Compensation for loss of two or more digits, or one or more phalanges of two or more digits, of a hand or foot may be proportioned to the loss of use of the hand or foot occasioned thereby, but shall not exceed the compensation for loss of a hand or foot.
(18) Total loss of use: Compensation for permanent total loss of use of a member shall be the same as for loss of the member.
(19) Partial loss or partial loss of use: Compensation for permanent partial loss or loss of use of a member may be for proportionate loss or loss of use of the member.
(20) Disfigurement: Proper and equitable compensation not to exceed $ 7,500 shall be awarded for serious disfigurement of the face, head, or neck or of other normally exposed areas likely to handicap the employee in securing or maintaining employment.

In the event a worker loses the function of a scheduled member, but not the member itself, the worker is compensated as if the worker lost the member.[9] A percentage of loss of use less than total loss will entitle the worker to a proportionate percentage of the schedule of benefits.[10] For example, a loss of use of 20% of the arm entitles a worker to 62.4 weeks of benefits (312 weeks × 20% = 62.4 weeks of benefits).

The Act provides for the loss of portions of scheduled members. For example, loss of one phalange of a digit (finger or toe) is treated as a 50% loss of that digit, and loss of more than one phalange of a digit is treated as a total loss of the digit.[11] However, the combined loss of digits or phalanges may not exceed compensation for the loss of the whole member.[12] The loss of an arm or leg below the elbow or knee is treated as the loss of a hand or foot, respectively. If an amputation is above the elbow or knee, the loss is treated as a loss of the entire limb.[13]

If the worker has a pre-existing loss to a scheduled member, but was not compensated under the Act for that loss (meaning that the loss could be congenital or the result of a non-work related event), the worker is entitled to be compensated for the entire loss sustained. In this respect, the employer takes the worker "as he finds him," and bears responsibility for the full measure of the worker's disability.[14]

An injured worker may also be compensated for "disfigurement" as a permanent partial disability. Compensation not to exceed $7,500 may be awarded for serious disfigurement of the face, head, neck, or other normally exposed area of the body, which disfigurement would be likely to impede the worker's ability in securing or maintaining employment.[15] Unlike any other form of compensation, benefits for disfigurement run concurrently with an award for a non-scheduled permanent partial disability.[16]

Where multiple scheduled members are injured, awards of permanent partial disability benefits run consecutively, with the only exception being when, as discussed above, multiple phalanges or digits are involved.[17] Scheduled benefits must be paid in full, without regard to whether the worker dies prior to payment in full of the schedule of benefits (of unrelated causes) prior to the benefits being paid.[18] Of course, if death results from causes related to the original work injury, death benefits are triggered as of the date of death, but the schedule must still be paid, as the right to those benefits accrued prior to death.[19]

Permanent partial disabilities other than those covered by the schedule include any disabilities which are permanent in nature, but which do not totally foreclose wage earning capacity, and are not specifically included in the statutory schedule. For those conditions, benefits are paid based on 66⅔ of the difference between the worker's pre-accident average weekly wage and the worker's post-accident wage earning capacity.[20] Benefits are by their nature payable for the duration of the disability, which is typically for the worker's lifetime, subject to modification under the Act.[21]

Permanent Partial disability can give rise to permanent total disability benefits under the Act. If a partial disability or a combination of partial disabilities prevent a worker from returning to his or her prior employment, it is presumed that the worker is totally disabled and the employer or its carrier has the burden of establishing the worker's wage earning capacity.[22] In the event of a scheduled injury, if the worker has any wage earning capacity at all, the worker is limited to the statutory schedule of benefits.[23] For a non-scheduled injury, benefits are determined by the worker's post-accident wage earning capacity.

The last statutorily described class of disability is **permanent total** disability.[24] In the case of such disability, where a worker is found to be unable to engage in any form of gainful employment, benefits are payable based on 66⅔ of the worker's average weekly wage at the time of injury, subject to annual escalations to reflect percentage changes in the national average weekly wage or, in other words, inflation. This takes place at the beginning of the federal government's fiscal year, each October 1st.[25] As with the case of permanent partial disability, Congress has presumed that certain injuries give rise to permanent total disability, without regard to whether such conditions are totally disabling in fact. In the case of a permanent total disability, the conditions giving rise to the presumption are much more serious in nature. A worker who loses both arms, both feet, both legs, both eyes, or any combination of the two is presumed to be permanently and totally disabled. This presumption can only be overcome by conclusive proof of wage earning capacity.[26] This is an extremely high burden of proof for an employer and carrier to meet.

Workers can sustain a permanent partial and permanent total disability, or a combination of a permanent total orthopedic injury and a later developed occupational disease. The case law interpreting the Act makes clear that a worker subject to the Act cannot be more than totally and permanently disabled. If a worker is receiving benefits for a permanent total disability, that same worker cannot obtain additional benefits for any other condition.[27]

There is a fifth classification of disability that does not appear in the Act, but was judicially created by the United States Supreme Court in what is commonly referred to as the "*Rambo II*" decision.[28] In that case, a worker had been injured in longshore employment and had, following his recovery, returned to work in a job paying wages three times higher than he earned prior to his accident. Under the provisions of the Act, the worker would not be entitled to the payment of any compensation benefits, because he had not sustained any loss in his wage earning capacity. His wage earning capacity had in fact increased post-accident.

The Supreme Court authorized the concept of awarding nominal compensation to an injured worker who would otherwise not be entitled to any benefits, when there is evidence that, although the worker does not currently suffer any loss, there is a significant potential that the injury will cause diminished wage earning capacity in the future. The Supreme Court's rationale in granting these benefits was that although an injury may not immediately affect wage earning capacity, if economic or physical circumstances change as a result of the injury later than one year following the last payment of compensation, the worker would be precluded from seeking modification of the award of benefits, as such review is barred following the initial one year period.

Under this ruling, an employer or carrier may find itself paying so-called "de minimus" benefits to a worker with no actual loss in wage earning capacity, to facilitate the worker reasserting his or her claim at some later date and seek an increase in benefits. The Supreme Court did not define how "nominal" these benefits should be, but in reported decisions applying *Rambo II*, the payment of nominal benefits has not been governed by the statutory minimum compensation rate provided for in the Act. The typical award appears to be $1.00.[29]

The Act attempts to make workers within its coverage economically whole following an injury by directing the payment of benefits for the real or presumed effect a physical injury has on the worker's wage earning capacity. Whether a "disability" exists begins as a medical concept, but then becomes an economic analysis. Whether an injury is total or partial can be difficult to discern and is often litigated, being a fact dependent inquiry.

Endnotes

1. 33 U.S.C. §901, *et seq., as amended.*
2. 33. U.S.C. §908(c)(1-20).
3. 33 U.S.C. §902(10).
4. 33 U.S.C. §908.
5. 33 U.S.C. §908(b).
6. 33 U.S.C. §908(e).
7. *Id.*
8. 33 U.S.C. §908(c).
9. 33 U.S.C. §908(c)(18).
10. 33 U.S.C. §908(c)(19).
11. 33 U.S.C. §908(c)(14).
12. 33 U.S.C. §908(c)(17).
13. 33 U.S.C. §908(c)(15).
14. *Strachan Shipping Co. v. Nash*, 782 F.2d 513, 18 B.R.B.S. 45 (CRT) (*en banc*)(1986).
15. 33 U.S.C. §908(c)(20).
16. *Fuduli v. Maresca Boat Yard, Inc.*, 7 B.R.B.S. 982 (1978).
17. 33 U.S.C. §908(c)(22).
18. 33 U.S.C. §908(d)(1).
19. 33 U.S.C. §909.
20. 33 U.S.C. §908(c)(21).
21. 33 U.S.C. §922.
22. *Norfolk Shipbuilding & Drydock Corp. v. Hord*, 193 F.3d 797 (4th Cir. 1999).
23. *Potomac Electric Power Co. v. Director, OWCP*, 449 U.S. 268, 14 B.R.B.S. 363 (CRT) (1980).
24. 33 U.S.C. §908(a).
25. 33 U.S.C. §910(f).
26. 33 U.S.C. §908(a).
27. *Korineck v. General Dynamics Corp.*, 835 F.2d 42 (2d Cir. 1987).
28. *Metropolitan Stevedore Co. v. Rambo*, 117 S.Ct. 1953 (1997) (*Rambo II*).
29. *See e.g. Deweert v. Stevedoring Services of America*, 272 F.3d 1241 (9th Cir. 2001).

Chapter 15

Limiting Employers' Liability

Michael W. Thomas, Esq. and Michael P. McQuinn, Esq.

Synopsis

15.1 Introduction

A compensable injury to an employee covered under the Longshore and Harbor Workers' Compensation Act ("the Act") can amount to a major expense to the employer. Sometimes, the application of the Act can result in liability to the employer that is not commensurate with the liable employer's relationship with the injured worker. The Act itself does not provide for apportionment to prior injuries, nor does it provide for contribution among multiple employers whose employment of claimant may have partially caused or contributed to the disability. Accordingly, employers and their insurers are forever searching for ways to limit their liability and costs associated with industrial injuries. The Act does provide for some relief in the form of credits against certain types of alternate compensation received by the claimant as well as relief from the Special Fund when a prior injury has at least partially contributed to the claimant's overall disability. This chapter will focus on the employers' and carriers' ability to limit their liability under the Act.

15.2 Credit for Payments Received by Claimant from Prior Awards, Alternate Sources, and Advance Payment Under the Act

It is well understood that the intent of the Act is to fully compensate injured Longshore and Harbor employees for their industrial injuries. However, there is a longstanding policy against double recovery for injuries occurring under the Act. *E.P. Paup Co. v. Director, OWCP* 999 F.2d 1341 (9th Cir. 1993). As a result, under certain circumstances, employers and carriers are entitled to credits for benefits received by the claimant.

15.3 Credit for Workers' Compensation and Jones Act Benefits

The 1984 amendments to the Act created section 3(e) which provides employers and carriers paying benefits under the Act a credit for "any amounts paid to an employee for the same injury, disability or death . . . pursuant to any other workers' compensation law" or the Jones Act.

In 1980, the United States Supreme Court ruled that coverage under the Act does not preclude an injured employee from pursuing benefits under a concurrent state workers' compensation law, but the employer would be entitled to credit for payments received in the state forum. *Sun Ship v. Pennsylvania* 447 U.S. 715 (1980). The 1984 amendment to the Act codified this credit and included credit for Jones Act payments as well. Such credit entitles the employer to full economic credit for all state workers' compensation payments arising out of the same injury, regardless of whether or not such payments were made for different categories of benefits. *D'Errico v. General Dynamics Corp.*, 996 F.2d 503, 505 (1st Cir. 1993).

When the claimant has been compensated under a state workers' compensation act, the employer is entitled to credit for all state workers' compensation payments applicable to an injury for which benefits are sought under the Act, regardless of the type of disability involved. *Loe v. General*

Dynamics, 26 B.R.B.S. 633 (ALJ) (1993), *citing Garcia v. National Steel & Shipbuilding Co.*, 21 B.R.B.S. 314 (1986). Thus, for example, all temporary and permanent disability payments made under a state workers' compensation statute for the same injury will be credited against an award made under the Act. This is so even if the payments are not made by the Longshore and Harbor employer, as section 3(e) specifies credit for payments made "to the employee" and not "by the employer." *Lustig v. Todd Shipyards Corp.* 881 F.2d 593, 595 (1989). The rule in *Lustig* is the general guiding principle. However, the situation found in the *Alexander* case, addressed below, produces an exception.

Given the U.S. Supreme Court's finding in *Sun Ship* that the Act is meant to supplement, not supplant, state workers' compensation laws, it follows that any payments made under the Act would be entitled to full credit in the state forum. In states in which permanent disability is calculated by different means than under the Act, a claimant may not have rights to Longshore and Harbor permanent disability, but may be entitled to permanent disability in the state forum. This typically occurs in unscheduled injury cases in which the claimant returns to full duty without wage loss, but has rateable factors of permanent disability for the purposes of a state act. Of course, in most cases, temporary disability under the Act is in excess of that available under a state workers' compensation law. This will raise the question in the state forum as to the employers' right to credit for Longshore and Harbor temporary disability against state permanent disability. Employers will claim "full economic credit" in the state forum for the full amount of temporary disability payments claimed under the state act. The injured employee will argue that the credit should only extend to the particular category of benefit provided (temporary disability). The California Supreme Court wrote a detailed analysis and opinion on this issue and, relying on the rationale in *Sun Ship* that double recovery should not be permitted, found that the employer was entitled to a "dollar for dollar" credit for Longshore and Harbor payments for an injury also covered under the California workers' compensation act. *Sea-Land Service, Inc. v. WCAB and Chris Lopez*, 14 Cal.4th 76 (1996). However, each state workers' compensation act is unique, and determination of credits for Longshore and Harbor payments under a state act should be determined on a state by state basis.

Despite the straightforward wording of section 3(e) there has been much litigation surrounding its application. First, payments must be made to the employee. Payments made under a claim to persons or entities who are not the employee are not entitled to credit against benefits due an employee under the Act. Thus, payments under a state act to a medical lien claimant will not be considered as credit for payments made to the claimant under the Act. *Lustig*, 881 F.2d 593 (1989).

Second, the payments must be for the same injury, disability or death. This has presented a dilemma regarding injuries when there is a dispute as to the last responsible employer. In such cases, the employer and carrier who are ultimately found to be the liable Longshore and Harbor employer under the last responsible employer rule may not take credit for settlements received by the claimant from other defendants in a long-term exposure claim. *Alexander v. Director, OWCP*, 273 F.3d 1267 (9th Cir. 2001). The *Alexander* court reasoned that the settlements received from the prior employers were "alternative awards" to an entire award against any of the defendants and that applying the credit to such alternative settlements would extend the credit beyond its intended purpose and discourage settlement. In essence, the *Alexander* court disallowed such credit because the settlements were not received for the *same injury*, but rather for other hypothetical injuries.[1]

Third, the payments must be made pursuant to any other workers' compensation law or the Jones Act. All state workers' compensation laws and the Federal Employees' Compensation Act have been held to meet the test of other workers' compensation laws. However, what otherwise is, or isn't, a "workers' compensation law" is open to interpretation.

Saudi Arabian social insurance received for the same injury claimed under the Act has been determined to be workers' compensation law for the purpose of section 3(e) credit. *Lee v. Boeing Co., Inc.*, 7 F.Supp. 2d 617 (D. Md. 1988). U.S. Department of Veterans Affairs benefits are not eligible for credit against a Longshore and Harbor award. *Todd Shipyards Corp. v. Director, OWCP*, 848 F.2d 125 (9th Cir. 1988).

State disability insurance benefits paid to a claimant have been found by several courts not to constitute other workers' compensation and are generally not creditable against a Longshore and Harbor award. In *Manen v. Exxon Corp.*, 36 B.R.B.S. 331 (ALJ) (2002), the ALJ undertook a detailed analysis of the California state disability insurance system and its application to section 3(e). Relying primarily on the fact that the California state disability system is funded, at least in part, through employee payroll deductions, the ALJ found that such payments were not "other workers' compensation" under the Act, and no credit was allowed. *Manen, supra.* The reasoning of the court in *Manen* was recently applied by another ALJ in *Dodd v. Science Applications International Corp.*, 46 B.R.B.S. 205 (ALJ) (2012). The court in *Dodd* likewise concluded that employers may not credit state disability payments against a Longshore and Harbor award pursuant to section 3(e).

Similarly, an employer's reimbursement of a state disability insurance fund for short-term disability benefits paid to a claimant also does not constitute other workers' compensation and is thus not creditable against a Longshore and Harbor award. In *Cutietta v. National Steel and Shipbuilding Company*, 49 B.R.B.S. 37 (2015), the Benefits Review Board considered whether a section 3(e) credit is available to an employer that reimbursed California's state disability insurance fund for short term disability payments that the fund made to the claimant. The Board held that the claimant's employer was not entitled to take a credit for such reimbursements. The Board relied on the Ninth Circuit's analysis of Congress' enactment of section 3(e) in *Todd Shipyards Corp.* in concluding that only payments made under "other worker's compensation laws" (i.e. state worker's compensation laws and the Federal Employees' Compensation Act) or the Jones Act should be creditable against a Longshore and Harbor award, to the exclusion of *"other forms of state or federal benefits,"* such as disabled veteran benefits. *Cutietta, supra*, at 42 (emphasis added) citing *Todd Shipyards Corp., supra*. The Board rejected the trial court ALJ's characterization of the employer's reimbursement payments as constituting an indirect payment of worker's compensation to the claimant under California's worker's compensation laws, even though California's state disability fund is lawfully entitled to obtain reimbursement for payments that are made on disability claims later determined to be work-related. The fact that the claimant never filed a state claim for worker's compensation appears to have been the determinative factor in the Board's conclusion that the employer's reimbursement under these circumstances did not constitute a payment to claimant, indirect or otherwise, of worker's compensation that would otherwise come within the ambit of section 3(e). Moreover, the Board also rejected the employer's argument that California's payment of short-term disability benefits to the claimant should be creditable under section 3(e). The Board's determination here is in accord with *Manen, supra*.

The holdings in *Manen*, *Dodd*, and *Cutietta* were reached even though the injuries for which each claimant sought state disability benefits had an industrial basis and were the subject of the claimant's claim for benefits under the Act. In denying the employers in those cases a credit for payments of state disability insurance benefits (or, alternatively, for the employer's reimbursement of the state disability insurance fund for those payments), the ALJs in *Manen* and *Dodd* and the Board in *Cutietta* have applied the law in a way that effectively permits claimants to recover twice for the same injury.[2]

When seeking section 3(e) credit against any other type of benefit received by the claimant, it is necessary to determine the exact nature of such payments. If those payments may fairly be characterized as "other workers' compensation," credit will be allowed. For a detailed discussion of what constitutes a workers' compensation law for the purposes of section 3(e) credit, see *Lee v. Boeing, supra*, at 622.

15.4 Credit for Advance Payments of Compensation

Unlike section 3(e) which allows credit for payments made to the employee, for the same injury, under other workers' compensation laws, section 14(j) allows credit to an employer for advance payments of compensation made under the Act against any unpaid installments or installments of compensation due. Section 14(j) allows employers to recover payments made to, and received by, the claimant under the Act to which it is later found that the claimant is not entitled. Such policy ensures prompt payment of benefits and prevents double recovery, two primary goals of the Act. See *Phillips v. Maine Concrete Structures*, 877 F.2d 1231 (5th Cir. 1989); *Flynn v. John T. Clark & Sons*, 30 B.R.B.S. 73 (1996).

Case law also generally establishes that the payments be compensation (not other types of benefits such as medical benefits, interest, or attorney fees), be made voluntarily, and be made under the Act (as opposed to non-occupational disability payments or salary continuation that were not intended as advance payments on compensation). Such advance compensation payments do not need to be made intentionally. Credit can be taken for temporary disability overpayments, including miscalculation of average weekly wage to the employee's benefit and temporary disability paid after the employee reaches maximum medical improvement. The employer may claim credit under section 14(j) by filing an LS-208 with an explanation of the credit and its duration.

15.5 Independent Credit Doctrine

There is also a judicially-created "independent credit doctrine" which allows employers, under certain circumstances, to take credit for prior disability payments to avoid double recovery. For example, the **aggravation rule** exists under the Act and provides that, when an industrial injury worsens or combines with a preexisting impairment to produce a greater disability than that which would have been produced by the industrial injury alone, the entire disability is compensable by the employer. *Strachan Shipping Co. v. Nash*, 782 F.2d 513, 18 B.R.B.S. 45 (CRT) (5th Cir. 1986) (*en banc*). In cases in which there is a prior award to the same body part there is a potential for double recovery which is disfavored under the Act. Case law has established the **credit doctrine** to avoid such double recovery. When there is a prior scheduled injury to the same body part involved in the new injury, the subsequent employer may limit its liability to the increase in permanent disability over the prior injury. However, credit will only be allowed for compensation *actually received* by the employee. *Strachan, supra.*

The credit doctrine does not, however, apply to successive injuries to different body parts or against prior unscheduled awards, as a claimant's disability rate at the time of the subsequent injury will necessarily already have accounted for the lost earning capacity. Even when the current injury involved an unscheduled body part, no credit will be allowed for a prior unscheduled award for the same body part. Additionally, no credit is generally provided to an employer for prior settlements made under section 8(i) of the Act.

15.6 Credit for Third-Party Lawsuit Recoveries

Section 33(f) of the Act Provides the employer with credit for third-party recoveries under certain circumstances. This topic is covered in detail in another chapter.

15.7 Section 8(f)—Limitation of Liability

It has long been held that Congress' purpose in creating section 8(f) was to alleviate potential employment discrimination against disabled employees. *Lawson v. Suwannee Fruit & S.S. Co.*, 336 U.S. 198 (1949). Section 8(f) encourages employers to hire and retain disabled workers by shifting some of the increased compensation liability for combined injuries from the employer to the Special Fund. *Director, OWCP v. Campbell Industries*, 678 F.2d 836, 839, 14 B.R.B.S. 974 (CRT) (9th Cir. 1982). The Special Fund is created under section 44 of the Act and is established in the Treasury of the United States and maintained by the Department of Labor. When 8(f) applies, the "encouragement" comes from a 104-week limitation on a permanent disability award. However, as will be discussed at the end of this chapter, there is one big catch.

Despite the noble intent of 8(f), relief under the section is not easily attained. To prove entitlement to 8(f) relief, the employer must show all of the following.

- There is a new injury.
- The claimant had pre-existing permanent partial disability.
- The pre-existing disability was manifest to the employer prior to the new injury.
- The disability subject to the compensation claim is not due solely to the new injury.
- In cases of permanent partial disability, the disability is materially and substantially greater than that which would have resulting from the new injury alone.

15.8 New Injury

Obviously, if there is no new injury the subsequent employer cannot be held liable. The natural of a pre-existing injury or disability will not constitute a new injury. However, an aggravation of a pre-existing injury or disability can satisfy the new injury requirement. The pre-existing disability and new injury or aggravation may develop from the same employment, promoting the goal of encouraging the employer to retain a disabled employee. Whether or not an "aggravation" is considered a new injury or a natural progression of the pre-existing injury is a factual question that should be cautiously evaluated and adequately developed by the employer.

15.9 Pre-Existing Permanent Partial Disability

The employer applying for 8(f) relief does not meet this requirement simply by showing a previous injury. The pre-existing injury must produce a serious and lasting disability. *Lockheed Shipbuilding v. Director, OWCP*, 951 F.2d 1143 (9th Cir. 1991); *Director, OWCP v. Belcher Erectors*, 770 F.2d 1220 (D.C. Cir. 1985). Although one means of showing pre-existing permanent partial disability is to establish a reduced wage-earning capacity, or economic impairment, it is not necessary. If a non-economic disability existed which would have motivated a cautious employer to terminate an employee because of an increased risk of industrial accident and compensation liability, the test is also met. *Director, OWCP v. Campbell Industries*, 678 F.2d 836 (9th Cir. 1982). It is this "cautious employer" test that determines whether or not pre-existing permanent partial disability is met.

15.10 Manifest to the Employer Before the New Injury

In order to satisfy the purpose of encouraging employers to hire and retain disabled workers, the courts have established a requirement that the pre-existing disability was known, or manifested itself to the employer. Naturally, actual knowledge of the pre-existing disability will meet this requirement. Actual knowledge generally exists when the prior disability arose out of prior employment with the employer, or when the worker told his employer of the disability voluntarily.

As the employer is forbidden from inquiring into disabilities at the time of hire by the Americans with Disabilities Act (ADA), the employer often does not have actual knowledge of the pre-existing disability. However, constructive knowledge of the pre-existing disability will satisfy the requirement and is typically how manifestation is shown.

Constructive knowledge may be proven from medical records that existed at the time of the new injury from which the pre-existing disability was objectively determinable. *Director, OWCP v. Universal Terminal & Stevedoring (De Nichilo)*, 575 F.2d 452 (3rd Cir. 1978). The medical records do not need to establish the severity or nature of the pre-existing disability to establish manifestation, so long as a cautious employer viewing such records might consider terminating or not hiring an employee based on the information in the medical records. The condition established by the records need not be disabling at the time of hire, so long as it became so at the time of injury. *Director, OWCP v. General Dynamics Corp.*, 26 B.R.B.S. 116 (CRT) (1st Cir. 1992).

15.11 Disability Not Due Solely to the New Injury

Previous to the 1972 Amendments, 8(f) relief was available if two injuries "combined" to create permanent total disability. However, the 1972 Amendments extended 8(f) to cases of permanent partial disability, and the language of the Act changed. The current version of 8(f) requires that the employer to show that the current injury *by itself* would not have led to the ultimate level of permanent disability.[3] If the new injury would have caused permanent total disability, absent any pre-existing injury or condition, 8(f) relief is not available. It is insufficient that the evidence indicates that the two injuries create a greater disability than would the new injury alone. The employer must show, by medical or other evidence, that the new injury would not have independently caused the claimant to be 100 percent permanently disabled. See *E.P. Paup Co. v. Director, OWCP*, 999 F.2d 1341 (9th Cir. 1993); *Director, OWCP v. Lucitelli*, 964 F.2d 1303 (2nd Cir. 1992). For instance, if an employee had a prior back injury that was partially disabling and then has a new industrial injury from which he or she is totally blinded, 8(f) will not be available just because there was prior disability. It is immaterial that he or she is now blind with a bad back. The employee would have been 100 percent disabled from the new injury causing blindness, and 8(f) will not apply.

Section 8(f) can also be a source of relief to the employer in death cases. When industrial liability for death is created by a work injury in combination with a pre-existing condition, 8(f) is applicable. Typically, this arises in situations of occupational disease, such as asbestos-related diseases in combination with emphysema or heart disease. To succeed in establishing 8(f) relief, the employer must show that the pre-existing disability hastened the employee's death. Expert testimony must be carefully developed, and the expert should give an opinion that the decedent would have lived longer (and preferably, how much longer) were it not for the pre-existing condition. At the very least, the expert will need to state that the decedent would not have died when he did, but for the pre-existing condition. See *Stilley v. Newport News Shipbuilding & Dry Dock Co.*, 33 B.R.B.S. 224 (2000).

15.12 Disability is Materially and Substantially Greater: The Contribution Element

When the issue is permanent partial disability there is an added requirement under section 8(f) that the employer must show that the ultimate combined permanent partial disability is "materially and substantially greater than that which would have resulted" from the new injury alone, absent the pre-existing condition. See *Sproull v. Director, OWCP*, 86 F.3d 895 (9th Cir. 1996).

A review of the case law on this requirement will show that there is no uniform interpretation of this requirement, or how it is established by the employer. However, recent case law out of the Fourth Circuit has applied a stringent standard for employers to establish the material and substantial requirement, commonly referred to as the "contribution" element. In four cases dealing with the issue, all issued at the same time (*Newport News Shipbuilding & Dry Dock v. Winn*, 326 F.3d 427 (4th Cir. 2003); *Newport News Shipbuilding & Dry Dock v. Ward*, 326 F.3d 434 (4th Cir. 2003); *Newport News Shipbuilding & Dry Dock v. Cherry*, 326 F.3d 449 (4th Cir. 2003); *Newport News Shipbuilding & Dry Dock v. Pounders*, 326 F.3d 455 (4th Cir. 2003)), the Fourth Circuit ruled that to prove the contribution element the employer must quantify the type and extent of the disability the claimant would have suffered without the pre-existing disability. In each of the four cases, the court rejected the methods of the employers and their experts in proving contribution. In *Winn*, *Ward* and *Pounders*, the court rejected the method of the employers because they did not produce evidence specifically quantifying the level of disability the claimant would have had absent the pre-existing condition. In *Cherry*, the court found that such analysis was made, but that the doctor's opinion was conjecture on the basis that claimant was working without restriction after the previous injuries and therefore had no permanent disability.

To succeed on the contribution element under the Fourth Circuit's guidelines will be difficult. Apparently, the employer will first need to establish the impact of the new injury standing alone. This will supply the ALJ with a foundation on which to judge whether any increase in disability due to the pre-existing condition is material and substantial. To accomplish this, the evidence relied on will necessarily be well-supported factually in order to satisfy the requirement of substantial evidence. This will be difficult because it will require the employer to provide evidence of a factual scenario that never really existed: that is, how can one first accurately determine what would have been the impact of the new injury on a nondisabled body in a case in which the new injury indeed affected a disabled body? Such proof almost requires conjecture. Presumably, experts will need to testify that "on a reasonable medical basis" the claimant would have a disability of a certain level, given all circumstances of the new industrial injury, absent the pre-existing disability. Pursuant to the new standards articulated by the Fourth Circuit, the contribution element *will not be established* by an expert opinion that assesses the total disability and then subtracts the pre-existing disability to derive the disability attributable to the new injury.

15.13 Procedural Pitfalls and the Catch

The time for filing a formal petition for 8(f) relief and the information necessary is set forth in 20 C.F.R. § 702.321. Generally speaking, the petition must be filed (not mailed) as soon as the permanency of the claimant's condition is known or in dispute. If notice is given that permanency will be an issue at informal conference, the application must be filed at or before the conference. The application must be made to the district director and must be fully documented. A fully documented application will include a statement of the grounds for 8(f) relief and must be supported by medical evidence. Failure to adhere to any of these requirements can be, and usually is, fatal to the request for 8(f) relief. There has been much litigation surrounding timeliness and completeness of 8(f) petitions. The district director is charged with guarding the integrity of the Special Fund and carefully reviews all petitions for such relief. If 8(f) relief is sought, it is best to file a fully documented application with the district director as soon as possible or risk absolute bar to the relief.

If the employer wishes to pursue 8(f) relief, settlement becomes difficult. Section-8(f) relief is not allowed in cases settled pursuant to section 8(i) of the Act. Any attempt in the 8(i) application to reserve jurisdiction for 8(f) relief or to impose liability on the Special Fund will be void. See *Cochran v. Matson Terminals, Inc.*, 33 B.R.B.S. 187 (1999). Likewise, stipulations between the parties will not be binding on the district director, except in some circumstances in which the district director has proper notice and the opportunity to be heard on the issue. *Director, OWCP v. Coos Head Lumber & Plywood Co. (Ibarra)*, 194 F.3d 1032, 33 B.R.B.S. 131 (CRT) (9th Cir. 1998).

When the requirements for relief under 8(f) are met, and all procedural hurdles have been cleared, 8(f) relief appears too good to be true. Indeed, it is. The Special Fund is funded pursuant to section 44 of the Act, in large part, by assessments against the self-insured employers and insurers covered by the Act. Although all carriers and self-insured employers pay into the fund, the assessment is calculated primarily on a formula based largely on each entity's use of the fund. Consider it a user tax. The more you use it, the more you pay. On the bright side, there is likely a 20–30 percent savings over making direct payments to the claimant.

Endnotes

1. The rationale applies in the context of section 3(e) because the settlements received by claimant in *Alexander* were received from other defendants in the state workers' compensation forum. The employer also asserted credit under section 14(j) of the Act, but such argument was rejected by the court on the basis that section 14(j) applies only to advance payment made by the liable employer, not plural employers. The court similarly rejected the employer's claim to credit pursuant to the independent credit doctrine on the basis that the aggravation rule was not in issue. Section 14(j) and the independent credit doctrine are addressed below.

2. Although the U.S. Supreme Court has stated that the Act *generally* reflects a policy of avoiding double recoveries by claimants, the Court will permit a double recovery under the Act that is in accord with the Act's plain statutory language and is not so "absurd or glaringly unjust" to warrant a departure from the statutory text. *Ingalls Shipbuilding, Inc. v. Director, OWCP (Yates)*, 519 U.S. 248, 261 (1997). A claimant's recovery of both state short term disability benefits and the benefits available under the Act does not, at least from the perspective of the OALJ and BRB, appear to qualify as an absurd or glaringly unjust result.

3. The requirement that the injury be "due solely to" the new injury technically applies to both permanent total and permanent partial disability cases. However, due to the contribution element at play in permanent partial disability cases, discussions involving disability "due solely to" the new injury generally refer to cases of permanent total disability.

Chapter 16

Death Benefits Under the Longshore & Harbor Worker's Act

Howard S. Grossman, Esq. and Scott L. Thaler, Esq.

Synopsis

16.1 Introduction

In this chapter, we explore the filing of a death benefits claim with the United States Department of Labor; the beneficiaries entitled to recover death benefits; the computation of benefits due various beneficiaries and the presumption of causation under the Longshore Act, as well as the Defense Base Act.

16.2 Providing Timely Notice of Death §12

§12(a) of the Act requires that a claimant give written notice within 30 days of death or 30 days after the claimant is aware, or in the exercise of reasonable diligence should have been aware, of the relationship between the death and employment.[1] For claims involving occupational diseases, which do not immediately result in death, the claimant must give written notice within one year of the date the claimant "becomes aware, or in the exercise of reasonable diligence, or by reason of medical advice, should have become aware, of the relationship between the employment, disease and death or disability."[2] Notice should be provided to the employer, and to the District Director. The minimal contents for a notice sufficient to satisfy §12(b) are such that it shall contain the name and address of the employee and a statement of the time, place, nature and cause of death, and shall be signed by any person claiming to be entitled to compensation for such death, or by a person on his behalf.[3]

The failure to give notice to the employer and the District Director shall not act as a bar to the claim if the employer, or its designated agent, has knowledge of the death, if the Deputy Commissioner [now District Director] determines that the employer or carrier has not been prejudiced by the failure to give such notice, or if the District Director determines that notice was given to an official of the employer or the employer's insurance carrier and that neither were prejudiced due to the failure to provide the notice.[4]

16.3 Initiating the Process to Obtain Death Benefits With the Office of Workers' Compensation Programs

To initiate a claim for death benefits under the Longshore Act, it must be in writing and filed with the District Director's office in the compensation district in which the death occurred.[5] While preferably, an LS-262 should be completed, there is no requirement that the claim be filed on any particular form.[6] Any written document will suffice so long as it evinces an intention to assert a right to compensation.

A. Timeliness of Filing a Claim for Death Benefits Under §13(A) of the Act

Even though the decedent may have timely filed a claim for *inter vivos* compensation benefits, in order to timely obtain death benefits, a separate claim must be filed within the applicable timeframe. The right to compensation for disability of death shall be barred unless a claim is filed within one year after the death has occurred. If payment of compensation has been made without an award on account of death, a claim will be timely filed within one year after the date of the last payment of compensation.[7] The time for filing a claim does not begin to run until the beneficiary is aware, or by the exercise of reasonable diligence should have been aware, the relationship between the death and the employment.[8]

For occupational diseases, a claim for compensation for death which does not immediately result in such death is timely if filed within two years after the claimant becomes aware, or in the exercise of reasonable diligence, or by reason of medical advice should have been aware, of the relationship between the employment, the disease, and death.[9]

An occupational disease consists of three elements: (1) a disease, which is expansively defined to include "any serious derangement of health;" (2) caused by hazardous conditions of employment; (3) which are "peculiar to" the employee's employment as opposed to other employment generally.[10] The hazardous activity need not be exclusive to a particular employment, but it must be sufficiently distinct from hazardous conditions associated with other types of employment.[11]

If the potential beneficiary is incompetent, or a minor, the one year provision under §13(a) shall not be applicable so long as such person has not had a guardian or other authorized representative. If no guardian is appointed of a minor, then the statute runs from the date the minor becomes of age.[12]

"Minor" and the phrase "becomes of age" are not defined in the Act, and thus, state law is "appropriate to determine when an individual is entitled to file a claim under the Act in her own right."[13]

Where a suit is brought on behalf of a person at law or in admiralty to recover damages for death, and such recovery is denied on the ground that the decedent was an employee; that the defendant was an employer within the meaning of the Act; and that the employer had secured coverage [and or was properly self-insured] under the Act, the one year statute of limitations within which to file a claim begins to run from the date of termination of the lawsuit.[14]

B. §20(b) Presumption

Both the timeliness of notice and the timeliness of filing a claim must be considered in light of §20(b) which provides in the absence of substantial evidence to the contrary, it is presumed that sufficient notice of the claim has been given.[15]

The employer's burden is to show by substantial evidence that it was unable to effectively investigate some aspect of the claim due to claimant's failure to provide adequate notice.[16]

C. What Constitutes Prejudice?

In a situation where an employee dies from an occupationally related disease, both §12 and §13 time limitations do not begin to run against a previous employer where the claim is timely filed against the later employer, until such time that the claimant is aware that liability could have been asserted against the earlier employer under the last employer doctrine.[17]

16.4 Who is Entitled to Receive Death Benefits?

While it would seem straightforward who the eligible beneficiaries are entitled to receive death benefits under the definition section of the Act, §§(14-17), scores of decisions of administrative law judges and appellate decisions have been dedicated to interpreting who is:

i. a "widow" or "widower;"[18]
ii. a child;[19]
iii. "adopted" or "adoption;"[20]
iv. a stepchild or acknowledged illegitimate child dependent upon the deceased;[21]
v. a grandchild;[22]
vi. a "brother" and "sister;"[23] and
vii. a parent.[24]

A. Status as "Widow" or "Widower"

A widow or widower under the Act includes only the decedent's wife or husband living with or dependent for support upon the spouse at the time of his/her death; or who are living apart for justifiable cause or, by reason of his/her desertion at such time.[25] Thus, a marriage certificate, cohabitation and the absence of a divorce decree in the vast majority of death benefits claims by a widow or widower, assuming compensability, is relatively straightforward.

Whether a claimant is a "widow" or "widower" is determined by applying the law of the forum to resolve the marital status of the couple.[26] A person who is legally married to the decedent, and living together at the time of death, need not show any dependency.[27]

The Act does not define "marriage," and thus state law controls in determining whether a marriage has been created.[28] In order for a "widow" or "widower" to be married, it cannot be "similar to" marriage—it must be marriage."[29]

A 'commitment ceremony' in Mexico was "similar to a wedding ceremony" except that it lacked a license or Civil Registry filing. Despite exchanging rings and vows before a Christian minister, and 50 guests; representing themselves to the world as "husband and wife;" the claimant having legally changed her name, and conceiving children with the decedent; jointly owning bank accounts and real estate; providing life insurance on their own lives naming each other beneficiaries, the Benefits Review Board determined that concubinage was not equivalent to common law marriage, concubinage was not therefore equivalent to marriage; and that the intent to contract to marry is an essential element of marriage. Since the decedent and the widow specifically intended not to marry, they could not have been held to have married.[30]

B. What Constitutes Living Apart for Justifiable Cause or by Reason of Desertion

If the married couple is not living together at the time of the employee's death, then the spouse must be "dependent upon" the decedent or be living apart from the decedent for "justifiable cause" (e.g. employee's excessive drinking)[31] or by reason of the decedent's desertion. If the separation was for justifiable cause, the Supreme Court has stated that the essential requirement for demonstrating 'widow' or 'widower' status under the Act is the maintenance of a 'conjugal nexus' between the decedent and the claimant.[32] A "conjugal nexus" depends on the "behavior" of the claimant and not necessarily that of the decedent.[33]

1. Living apart: test is partial dependency

In determining whether a widow who is living apart from the deceased employee is entitled to death benefits, the test is not the Internal Revenue Code §152(a) definition of "dependent," (i.e., "an individual that receives *over half of his or her support from the decedent*") but rather §9(b) which requires only that the decedent's wife, who is not living with him, be "dependent for support upon him" at the time of his death.[34] Partial dependency is sufficient in determining "dependence" in cases in which Internal Revenue Code §152 is not applicable.[35]

Section 9(f) provides that all questions of dependency are determined as of the "time of injury," and in *Henderson* the Board held that an individual must establish his dependency on the decedent at the time of the work-related death.[36] Where the claimant established that she was dependent upon decedent at the time of his death by presenting evidence that they: "pooled their income, mutually owned property, filed joint tax returns, held joint checking and savings accounts from which their household expenses were paid, and the decedent regularly contributed his disability benefits amounting to more than two-thirds of the couple's total income that constituted substantial evidence that the claimant, at the time of decedent's death was, at least in part, dependent upon him for maintenance of her "accustomed standard of living."[37]

It is the latter part of §2(16) that is the source of extensive litigation: [O]r living apart for justifiable cause or by reason of his desertion at such time. Usually this separate but married position advanced by the claimant, leads to the inevitable defense by the carrier that while still perhaps legally married, the conjugal nexus was broken; or the claimant was not financially dependent upon the decedent at the time of his/her death.

Even where a spouse has filed for separation, "justifiable cause" was found where a wife who had been separated from the decedent for sixteen years, and had established a relationship with another man having a child with that second man, but having had continued sexual relationship with the decedent throughout the sixteen years and caring for him in his final days, was determined to be the legal wife and statutorily entitled to benefits under the Act.[38]

However, where the decedent lived separate and apart from the claimant for five years prior to his death; there was never any reconciliation in the form of living together and the decedent had obtained a legal separation shortly after their actual separation and filed for divorce more than three months prior to his death while living with his "fiancé" for several years prior to his death; having changed his will to name his fiancé as the executor; named her as his personal representative on his union health plan; gave her power of attorney over his medical treatment and looked after the decedent through his terminal illness, the ALJ concluded that there had been a lack of conjugal nexus severing the relationship between the decedent and his still legally married spouse disqualifying her as a surviving spouse under the Act and disentitling her to death benefits.[39]

C. Children Under §2(14)

"Child" includes a posthumous child, a child legally adopted prior to the injury of the employee, a child in relation to whom the deceased employee stood *in loco parentis*, for at least one year prior to the time of injury, and a stepchild or acknowledged illegitimate child dependent upon the deceased.[40] While a birth certificate evidencing paternity of the decedent is direct proof of being a "child;" and likewise documents confirming adoption, it is in the areas of "an acknowledged illegitimate child" dependent upon the deceased that is the subject of much litigation under this subsection. A "child" is a person who is under 18 years of age, or who is over 18 years of age, and is: (1) wholly dependent on the employee and incapable of self-support by reason of mental or physical disability, or (2) a student as defined in paragraph 19.[41] However, a "child" does not include married children unless wholly dependent on the decedent.[42]

A "student" is a person regularly pursuing a full-time course of study or training at a school, college, or university that is: (a) operated or directly supported by the United States, or by any state or local government political subdivision; (b) a school or college or university which has been accredited by a State, or by a State nationally recognized accrediting agency or body; (c) a non-accredited school, college, or university but whose credits will be accepted, on transfer, by not less than three accredited institutions who will accept credits; or other educational or training institutions as defined by the Secretary of Labor[43]. A student who meets the requirement of pursuing a full-time course of study or training at any of those institutions and who is between the ages of 18 through 23 is entitled to death benefits if they are a child, grandchild, or brother or sister who are not married brothers or married sisters unless wholly dependent on the decedent.

Alternatively, a "child" has been defined by the Board for death benefits claims under the laws of the pertinent state as a person standing *in loco parentis* to a child—under Mississippi law—"one who has assumed a status and obligations of a parent without a formal adoption."[44]

Any person who takes a child of another into his home and treats it as a member of his family, providing parental supervision, support and education as if it were his own child, is said to stand *in loco parentis*. A person stands *in loco parentis* to a child only when the person intends to assume toward the child the status of a parent.[45] As there is no dependency requirement for a child under 18, unless, he or she is a stepchild or an acknowledged illegitimate child, a child *in loco parentis* must also show the intent of the adult, as revealed by his actions or his intent to provide for that child as a parent would.

1. Dependent children of the decedent at the time of death

While a legitimate, adopted child or a child to whom the deceased employee stood *in loco parentis* does not require proof of dependency in order to be eligible for death benefits, a stepchild or "acknowledged illegitimate child" must prove dependence upon the deceased.[46]

An adult child who is not included within the definition of a 'student' must prove that she is wholly dependent upon the employee and incapable of self-support by reason of mental or physical disability."[47] In *DiCecca*, the employer did not challenge the administrative law judge's finding that the claimant was incapable of self-support due to her mental disability.[48] The sole issue thus was whether the claimant was "wholly dependent" upon decedent at the time of his death. There, the 24 year old daughter of the decedent moved in with her father and stepmother after she had quit her job more than a year prior to her father's death. The decedent had bought the claimant a car, allowed her to live rent-free at their home, paid for claimant's health insurance and provided her with money. The claimant testified that she had never lived independently and was unable to care for herself, or the home for extended periods of time. While there was no physical documentary evidence of the payments made to support the claimant, the the Benefits Review Board affirmed the administrative law judge's finding of dependency and held that documentary evidence was not required to support claimant's claim that she was wholly dependent upon decedent.[49]

D. Grandchild

Grandchild means a child of a child as defined by statute.[50] A grandchild includes only a person who is under 18 years of age.[51] "It is well settled that under the Act, partial dependency is sufficient to support an award of death benefits to a minor child or a grandchild.[52] Contributions to the family grocery bill and joint bank account "may be miniscule and minute support in terms of dollars and cents" but is sufficient to establish dependency.[53]

E. Brothers and Sisters

"Brother" and "sister" include: (1) step-brothers and sisters; (2) half-brothers and sisters; and (3) brothers and sisters by adoption. Married brothers or sisters are excluded unless wholly dependent upon the deceased employee.[54] The United States Court of Appeals for the Fifth Circuit has defined "dependency" within the meaning of the Act by looking to its common meaning, e.g., "not self-sustaining," "relying on for support," "helping to maintain the dependent on his customary standard of living."[55]

F. Parent

"Parent" includes stepparents and parents by adoption, parents-in-law, and any person who for more than three years prior to the death of the deceased employee stood in the place of a parent to him, if dependent on the injured employee.[56] Under §9(d), if there is no surviving spouse or child, then benefits may be paid to other familial dependents. Parents are entitled to death benefits if they establish that, at the time of decedent's death, they were dependent at least in part upon the decedent for the maintenance of their accustomed standard of living.[57] In determining dependency under §9(d), in *Urso v. MVM, Inc.*, the administrative law judge incorrectly analyzed the issue of dependency pursuant to §152(d) of the Internal Revenue Code.[58] "Partial dependency is sufficient, and the test is whether the contributions were needed and relied upon to maintain the alleged dependent in the position in life to which she or he was accustomed."[59] The Ursos, while having at least $3,791 per month in income from their social security benefits, food stamps, rental income from their own property and from their son's property, as well as money from the decedent's aunt, were determined to be partially dependent upon decedent to maintain their standard of living. The administrative law judge found that the decedent provided his parents money ranging from $200 to $1,000 per month to pay for their food, repair and maintenance of their home, pay for his parents' dental needs, a computer, multiple appliances for their new home, a new roof, and their cell phones. The employer's contention that these were gifts and should not be applicable to the dependency consideration was rejected as it is appropriate to consider gifts in determining dependency.[60] The key factor is consistent, substantial contributions to parents made during the decedent's lifetime.

G. Alien Non-Residents of the United States or Canada

Dependents of the decedent residing in foreign countries are limited to surviving wife and children. If there is no surviving wife or children, then benefits are payable to the surviving father or mother whom the employee has supported, either wholly or in part, for the period of one year prior to the date of death.[61]

16.5 Computation of Death Benefits Award

A surviving widow or widower without any children of the deceased is entitled during widowhood to benefits equaling 50 percent of the employee's average weekly wage,[62] subject to the maximum compensation rate then in effect at the time of death, adjusted annually in accordance with §10(f).[63] These benefits continue for the rest of the surviving spouse's life or until remarriage. Upon remarriage, the surviving spouse is entitled to two years' compensation in a lump sum.[64]

A surviving widow with a child or children is entitled to benefits equaling 50 percent of the employee's average weekly wage, plus an additional 16⅔ percent of such wages for each surviving child, provided that the total does not exceed 66⅔ percent of the employee's average weekly wage (subject to the maximum compensation rate cap and §10(f) annual increases).[65] If there is more than one surviving child of the deceased employee, they will receive 50 percent of the average weekly wage increased by 16⅔ percent for each child, not to exceed 66⅔ percent.[66] Where the decedent's wife dies or remarries and there is only one surviving child, the child receives 50 percent of such wages.[67]

If the employee is survived by only one child and no surviving widow or widower, the surviving child is entitled to receive 50 percent of the average weekly wage of the deceased employee.[68] If there is more than one child, but no surviving spouse, an additional 16⅔ percent will be added to the 50 percent, to be divided equally among the surviving children.[69]

If there is no widow or widower, or child, or if the amount payable to a surviving widow or widower and to children is less than 66⅔ percent of the average weekly wage; then dependent grandchildren or brothers and sisters, or other qualified dependents [as defined by 26 U.S.C. §152] are entitled to receive 20 percent of the deceased employee's average weekly wage.[70]

Additionally, each dependent parent or grandparent can receive 25 percent of the deceased employee's average weekly wage. However, the total amount shall not exceed 66⅔ percent of the deceased employee's average weekly wage.[71]

Computation of the average weekly wage is determined by §9(e).[72] The benefits cannot exceed either 200% of the national average or the deceased worker's average weekly wage, whichever is the lower figure;[73] except in claims under the Defense Base Act, where there is no minimum average weekly wage.[74]

16.6 Commutation of Death Benefits

As previously discussed Section 9(g) provides benefits to survivors of decedents who reside in foreign countries.[75] However, 9(g) provides that either the Secretary or the carrier, can apply to commute all future installments of compensation to be paid by paying to the survivors one half of the commuted amount of future installments of benefits. Of note, this only applies to future installments of compensation of benefits, and not benefits that have already accrued. Additionally, the payment must be made within ten days of filing the Commutation Order. The benefit recipients do not have the option to reject a commuted sum in lieu of a continuing award.

To commute a beneficiary's claim, one must first determine the beneficiary's life expectancy. In the event the beneficiary is a minor, determine the number of years until the beneficiary turns eighteen years of age. To determine the present value discount rate: 1) use the United States Treasury one year constant maturity rate; 2) ascertain the current percentage of increase of the National Average Weekly

Wage used to calculate § 10(f) adjustments; 3) subtract this rate from the Treasury one year constant maturity rate to arrive at the commutation interest rate. Determine the future value of compensation using a spreadsheet that calculates the cumulative annual increase or decrease in weekly benefit rate. Divide the sum of future value by two to arrive at the commuted payment. In the event there are multiple beneficiaries, the commuted payment must be separately calculated for each beneficiary.

16.7 There is Only One Death Benefit Even if there are Multiple Surviving Beneficiaries

Under Section 9 of the Act, there is but one death benefit paid, despite two children settling their claims where a third surviving child did not. That child is only entitled to her statutorily computed portion of the death benefit and not an increased amount due to the other sibling's settlement.[76]

16.8 Compensability of Death

Section 9 provides for death benefits to certain survivors "if the injury causes death."[77] In order to establish an entitlement to benefits, the claimant is aided by Section 20(a) of the Act, which presumes, in the absence of substantial evidence to the contrary, that the claim for death benefits comes within the provisions of the Act, *i.e.*, that the death was work-related.[78] In order to establish a *prima facie* case, and thus entitlement to invocation of the Section 20(a) presumption, the claimant is not required to introduce affirmative medical evidence that the working conditions in fact caused decedent's death; rather, claimant must only show the existence of working conditions which *could have* caused decedent's death.[79] In a case involving death benefits, the presumption applies where death occurs in the course of claimant's employment.[80] It is also well established where the immediate cause of death is not work related, the Board has applied the maxim that "to hasten death is to cause it."[81] Once the Section 20(a) presumption is invoked, the burden then shifts to the employer to provide substantial evidence that the employee's death was not caused, contributed to or hastened by his employment.[82] An unequivocal opinion, given to a reasonable degree of medical certainty, that the employee's injury is not work-related is sufficient to rebut the Section 20(a) presumption.[83] If the administrative law judge finds that the Section 20(a) presumption is rebutted, the administrative law judge must weigh all of the relevant evidence and resolve the causation issue based on the record as a whole, and the claimant bears the burden of persuasion.[84]

In claims arising under the Defense Base Act, the claimant is aided by the "Zone of Special Danger" doctrine which expanded the test of recovery such that there need not be proof of a direct causal connection between the nature of the decedent's employment and the death. Nor is it necessary that the employee be engaged at the time of injury [or death] in an activity related to his employer. "All that is required is that the obligations or conditions of employment create the Zone of Special Danger out of which the injury arose. They must simply fall within foreseeable risks occurred by or associated with the employment abroad."[85] "They must simply fall within foreseeable risks occasioned by, or associated with, the employment abroad."[86]

A. What Constitutes a Causal Connection Between the Work Injury/Occupational Illness?

A claimant must only establish only the existence of working conditions which *could have* caused the harm.[87] In order to prove a claimant's *prima facie* case, the administrative law judge must determine whether the alleged employment events in fact occurred.[88]

B. Suicide—Is it a Bar to Recovery of Death Benefits?

Section 3(c) precludes recovery of death benefits by the employee if he commits suicide.[89] Section 20(d) provides the presumption that "the injury was not occasioned by the willful intention of the injured employee to injure or kill himself or another."[90] To rebut the presumption, an employer must present "substantial evidence to the contrary."[91] If an employer does so, the presumption falls from the case. Generally, the analysis courts undertake when an injured employee committed suicide was whether the employee had the "willful intention" to commit suicide.[92] If the decedent's death was caused by an "irresistible suicidal impulse" resulting from an employment-related condition, Section 3(c) will not bar compensation.[93]

In *Gillespie*, the Benefits Review Board reversed the administrative law judge's award of benefits when the Claimant died accidently while attempting to temporarily asphyxiate himself as part of an autoerotic activity.[94] The Board relied on the dicta in *O'Leary*, when the Supreme Court stated:

> This is not to say that there are not cases 'where an employee ... might go so far from his employment and become so thoroughly disconnected from the service of his employer that it would be entirely unreasonable to say that injuries suffered by him arose out of and in the course of his employment.'[95]

The Board affirmed since there was no evidence the Claimant's death was work related and could not find the administrative law judge's ruling unreasonable.

Recently, the Ninth Circuit Court of Appeals held the proper analysis in a suicide case is whether there is an "unbroken chain of causation from the injury to the suicide."[96]

16.9 Alcohol Intoxication

Section 3(c) of the Act states: "No compensation shall be payable if the injury [death] was occasioned solely by the intoxication of the employee."[97] Pursuant to Section 20(c) of the Act, it is presumed, in the absence of substantial evidence to the contrary, "that the injury was not occasioned solely by the intoxication of the injured employee."[98] The employer bears the burden of producing substantial evidence that claimant's intoxication was the sole cause of injury.[99] The employer must proffer substantial evidence that intoxication was the **sole** cause of the claimant's injury, then the presumption falls from the case.[100] The administrative law judge must then weigh the evidence to determine whether intoxication was the sole cause of injury.[101]

In *Birdwell*,[102] the employee was found dead the morning after he had been drinking while performing his duties. The ALJ determined that the medical opinion addressing the effect of claimant's intoxication was based on speculation and was therefore less than credible. The Board affirmed the administrative law judge's determination that the Section 20(c) presumption was not rebutted, as the relevant medical opinion stating that intoxication was the *primary* cause of death did not establish intoxication as the *sole* cause of death.[103]

Endnotes

1. 33 U.S.C. §912(a).
2. *Id.*
3. 33 U.S.C. §912(b).
4. 33 U.S.C. §912(d).
5. 33 U.S.C. §913(a); 20 C.F.R. §702.221.
6. Form LS-262 is included at the end of this chapter.
7. 33 U.S.C. §913(a).
8. *Id.*
9. 33 U.S.C. §913(b)(2).
10. *Gencerelle v. General Dynamics Corp.*, 892 F.2d 173, 23 BRBS 13 (CRT) (2d Cir. 1989).
11. *Bunge Corp. v. Carlisle*, 227 F.3d 934, 34 BRBS 79 (CRT) (7th Cir. 2000).
12. 33 U.S.C. §913(c).
13. *Charlita Smith v. Shell Offshore, Inc.*, 1999 WL 35135294, *at* *3 (DOL Ben. Rev. Bd.).
14. 33 U.S.C. §912 (d).
15. *Sheller v. Cramp Shipbuilding & Drydock Co.*, 23 BRBS 140 (1989).
16. *Jones Stevedoring Co. v. Director, OWCP [Taylor]*, 133 F.3d 683, 31 BRBS 178 (CRT) (9th Cir. 1997).
17. *Smith v. Aerojet General Shipyards, Inc.*, 647 F.2d 518, 13 BRBS 391 (5th Cir. 1981).
18. 33 U.S.C. §902(16).
19. 33 U.S.C. §902(14).
20. 33 U.S.C. §902(17).
21. 3 U.S.C. §902(14).
22. *Id.*
23. *Id.*
24. 33 U.S.C. §902(15).
25. 33 U.S.C. §902(16).
26. *Johnston v. Haywood Baker*, 2014 WL 5795792 (DOL Ben. Rev. Bd.).
27. *Griffin v. Bath Iron Works, Corp.*, 25 BRBS 26 (1991).
28. *Powell v. Rogers*, 496 F.2d 1248 (9th Cir.) *cert. denied*, 419 U.S. 1032 (1974).
29. *A.S. v. Advanced American Diving*, 2009 WL 1161358, at *4 (DOL Ben. Rev. Bd.).
30. *Id.*
31. *Matthews v. Walter*, 512 F.2d 941 (D.C. Cir. 1975).

32. *Thompson v. Lawson*, 347 U.S. 334 (1954); *Logan v. IAP Worldwide Services*, BRB No. 16-0162 (DOL Ben. Rev. Bd.).

33. *Omar v. Al Masar Transp. Co.*, 46 BRBS 21 (2012).

34. 33 U.S.C. §902(16).

35. *Id.* see *Urso v. MVM, Inc.*, 44 BRBS 53, 56-57 (2010).

36. *Henderson v. Kiewit Shea*, 39 BRBS 119 (2006).

37. *Id.*

38. *Matthews v. Walter*, 512 F.2d 941 (D.C. Cir. 1975); *see also Leete v. Dir.*, OWCP, 790 F.2d 418 (5th Cir. 1986).

39. *Johnston v. Haywood Baker*, 2014 WL 5795792 at *29 (DOL Ben Rev. Bd.).

40. 33 U.S.C. §902(14).

41. *Id.*

42. *Id.*

43. 33 U.S.C. §902(18).

44. *Brooks v. General Dynamics Corp.*, 1998 WL 377766 at *3 citing *Worley v. Jackson*, 595 So.2d 853, 855 (Miss. 1992).

45. 59 Am. Jur. 2d, Parent and Child, §88; *Worley*, at 855.

46. 33 U.S.C. §902(14).

47. 33 U.S.C. §902(14).

48. *DiCecca v. Battelle Memorial Institute*, BRB No. 15-0504 (unpublished June 6, 2016).

49. *Id.*

50. 33 U.S.C. §902(14).

51. *Id.*

52. See *Myers v. Bethlehem Steel Co.*, 250 F.2d 615 (4th Cir. 1957).

53. *Texas Employers' Ins. Ass'n v. Shae*, 410 F.2d 56 (5th Cir. 1969); *A'sha Bonds v. Ceres Marine Terminals*, 2002 WL 34716096 at *4 (DOL Ben. Rev. Bd.).

54. 33 U.SC. §902(14).

55. *St. John Stevedoring Co., Inc. v. Wilfred*, 818 F.2d 397 (5th Cir. 1987).

56. 33 U.S.C. §902(15).

57. *Urso v. MVM, Inc.*, 2010 WL 3204569 *4 (DOL Ben. Rev. Bd.).

58. 26 U.S.C. §152(c)(1). "(D) who has not provided over one-half of such individuals own support for the calendar year in which the taxable year of the taxpayer begins…"

59. *Texas Employer's Ins. Ass'n v. Sheppeard*, 62 F.2d 122 (5th Cir. 1932); *Urso*, at *5.

60. *Id.*; *St. John Stevedoring Co., Inc. v. Wilfred*, 818 F.2d at 399-400 (5th Cir. 1987).

61. 33 U.S.C. §909(g).

62. 33 U.S.C. §909(b).

63. 33 U.S.C. §910(f).

64. 33 U.S.C. §909(b).

65. *Id.*

66. *Id.*

67. *Id.*

68. 33 U.S.C. §909(c).

69. *Id.*

70. 33 U.S.C. §909(d).

71. *Id.*

72. 33 U.S.C. §909(e) In computing death benefits, the average weekly wages of the deceased shall not be less than the national average weekly wage as prescribed in section 906(b) of this title, but—

    (1) the total weekly benefits shall not exceed the lesser of the average weekly wages of the deceased or the benefit which the deceased employee would have been eligible to receive under section 906(b)(1) of this title; and (2) in the case of a claim based on death due to

an occupational disease for which the time of injury (as determined under section 910(i) of this title) occurs after the employee has retired, the total weekly benefits shall not exceed one fifty-second part of the employee's average annual earnings during the 52-week period preceding retirement.

73. 33 U.S.C. §§909(e)(1); 906(b)(1).

74. 42 U.S.C. §1642 Sec.2.

75. 33 U.S.C. 909(g).

76. *Welch v. Fugro Geosciences, Inc.*, 44 BRBS 89 (2010).

77. 33 U.S.C. §909.

78. *See, e.g., American Grain Trimmers v. Director, OWCP*, 181 F.3d 810, 33 BRBS 71 (CRT)(7th Cir. 1999), cert. *denied*, 120 S.Ct. 1239 (2000).

79. *Sinclair v. United Food & Commercial Workers*, 23 BRBS 148 (1989); *U.S. Industries/Federal Sheet Metal, Inc. v. Director, OWCP*, 455 U.S. 608, 14 BRBS 631 (1982).

80. *Bell Helicopter Int'l, Inc. v. Jacobs*, 746 F.2d 1342, 17 BRBS 13(CRT) (8th Cir. 1984).

81. *Fineman v. Newport News Shipbuilding & Drydock, Co.*, 27 BRBS 104 (1993).

82. *American Grain Trimmers, Inc. v. OWCP*, 181 F.3d 810 (7th Cir. 1999), 33 BRBS 71(CRT).

83. *O'Kelley v. Dep't of the Army/NAF*, 34 BRBS 39 (2000).

84. *Universal Maritime Corp. v. Moore*, 126 F.3d 256, 31 BRBS 119(CRT) (4th Cir. 1997).

85. *Batelle Memorial Institute v. DiCecca*, 792 F.3d 214 (1st Cir. 2015).

86. *Id.*

87. *Port Cooper*, 227 F.3d 285, 34 BRBS 96(CRT); *Brown v. I.T.T./Continental Baking Co.*, 901 F.2d 289, 24 BRBS 75(CRT) (D.C. Cir. 1990); *Stevens v. Tacoma Boatbuilding Co.*, 23 BRBS 191 (1993).

88. *See Noble Drilling Co. v. Drake*, 795 F.2d 478, 19 BRBS 6(CRT) (5th Cir. 1986); *Frederick v. M-I Drilling Fluids Co.*, 2011 WL 4455004, (DOL Ben. Rev. Bd. Aug. 25, 2011) (decedent exposed to lime dust and diesel fumes was casually related to the decedent's death).

89. 33 U.S.C. §903(c). "No compensation shall be payable if the injury was occasioned … by the willful intention of the employee to injure or kill himself or another."

90. 33 U.S.C. §920(d).

91. *Del Vecchio v. Bowers*, 296 U.S. 280 (1935).

92. *Konno v. Young Bros., Ltd.*, 28 BRBS 57 (1994).

93. *Cooper v. Cooper Associates, Inc.*, 7 BRBS 853 (1978), *aff'd in pert. part sub nom. Director, OWCP v. Cooper Associates, Inc.*, 607 F.2d 1385, 10 BRBS 1058 (D.C. Cir. 1979) (death due to suicidal impulse related to stress of work); *see also Voris v. Texas Employers Ins. Ass'n*, 190 F.2d 929 (5th Cir. 1951) (work injury resulted in manic-depressive insanity and suicide that was not voluntary and willful).

94. *Gillespie v. General Electric Co.*, 21 BRBS 56 (DOL Ben.Rev.Bd.)(1988).

95. *Id.* at 3, *citing O'Leary v. Brown-Pacific-Maxon, Inc*, 340 U.S. 504, 71 S.Ct. 470, 472 (1951).

96. *Kealoha v. Director*, OWCP, 713 F.3d 521, 47 BRBS 1(CRT) (9th Cir. 2013).

97. 33 U.S.C. §903(c).

98. 33 U.S.C. §920(c).

99. *G.S. v. Marine Terminals Corp.*, 42 BRBS 100, *modified on recon.* 43 BRBS 108 (2009).

100. *Walker v. Universal Terminal & Stevedoring Corp.*, 645 F.2d 170, 13 BRBS 257 (3d Cir. 1981).

101. *Del Vecchio v. Bowers*, 296 U.S. 280 (1935).

102. *Birdwell v. Western Tug & Barge*, 16 BRBS 321 (1984).

103. *Id.* at 323–324.

Claim for Death Benefits

U.S. Department of Labor
Office of Workers' Compensation Programs

1. Name of deceased employee (First, middle Initial, last)	For Office Use Only	OWCP Number / Carrier's Number	OMB No. 1240-0014
a. Social Security Number (Required by Law)			
2. Last address of last deceased (Number, street, city, state, ZIP)	8. Place of Death		9. Date of Death
3. Name and address of employer (Number, street, city, state, ZIP)	10. Place where injury occurred		11. Date of Injury
4. Name and address of undertaker	12. Nature of injury or occupational Illness and cause of death (Give parts of body affected if Injured)		
5. Amount of undertaker's bill / 6. Amount Paid	13. Name and address of last attending physician (or hospital)		
7. Name of person paying undertaker's bill			

14. Widow or Widower

a. Full name and address	b. Social Security Number	c. Date of birth	d. Nationality
	Telephone Number		
e. Date married to deceased	f. Place of marriage (City, State, Country) United States	g. Signature of widow, widower, and/or guardian of children	Date

15. Children of deceased (see page 2 for qualification)

a. Full name	b. Address	c. Social Security Number (Required by Law)	d. Date of birth	e. Nationality

16. All other persons partially or wholly dependent on deceased support (See page 2 for instructions)	b. income for one year preceding death: Source	Amount	c. Relationship	d. Age	e. Dependent: Wholly	Partially
a. Full name and address Signature Date (mm/dd/yyyy) Guardian? ○					○	○
f. Full name and address Signature Date (mm/dd/yyyy) Guardian? ○					○	○

Important Notice

Section 31 (a)(1) of the Longshore Act, 33 U.S.C. 931 (a)(1), provides, as follows: Any claimant or representative of a claimant who knowingly and willfully makes a false statement or representation for the purpose of obtaining a benefit or payment under this Act shall be guilty of a felony, and on conviction thereof shall be punished by a fine not to exceed $10,000, by imprisonment not to exceed five years, or by both.

This Form Replaces Form LS-263 Which Is Obsolete

Form LS-262
Rev. April 2012

Instructions:

1. Use this form to claim death benefits under the Longshore and Harbor Workers' Compensation Act, Defense Base Act, Outer Continental Shelf Lands Act, or Nonappropriated Fund Instrumentalities Act. The information provided will be used to determine entitlement to benefits.

2. Submit claim in duplicate to a district office of the Office of Workers' Compensation Programs (OWCP).

3. individual claims must be filed by or in behalf of each person eligible for benefits [33 U.S.C. 913(a)]. (included are grandchildren, brothers and sisters under 18 years, parents, step-parents, parents by adoption, parents-in-laws, and any person who for more than one year prior to the employee's death stood in place of a parent to him/her.)

4. Under item 16(b), state all your income for the year preceding death by source (Social Security pension, bonds, etc.) and amount. List separately support deceased furnished you, including the value of any shelter, food, clothing, or other supplies. Use space below or additional sheets if needed.

5. A person other than the claimant may complete claim for the beneficiary.

6. Persons are not required to respond to this collection of information unless it displays a currently valid OMB number.

Conditions of Eligibility

Coverage for Death Benefit

A death benefit is payable under the Longshore Act, or related law, if a covered employee dies as a result of work-related injury or occupational disease.

Who is eligible for a Death Benefit?

1. The deceased worker's widow or widower living with or dependent for support at the time of death; or widow or widower living apart for good cause or because of desertion by worker.

2. Unmarried child(ren) under age 18, or if over 18: (a) was (were) wholly dependent on deceased worker and unable to support self(ves) because of mental or physical disability, or (b) student(s) up to age 23 (must meet certain requirements). Includes a posthumous child, legally adopted child, child to whom deceased acted as parent for one year before injury, stepchild, or acknowledged illegitimate child.

3. If the combined amount due a surviving widow or widower and child or children is not greater than two-thirds (66 and 2/3 percent) of the worker's average weekly wages subject to a maximum benefit of 200 percent of the national average weekly wage, a benefit is payable for any one of the following: Grandchildren, brothers or sisters (if dependent at time of injury), parents, grandparents, or others satisfying legal requirements of dependency. (Consult the Office of Workers' Compensation Programs for more information.)

What terminates widow's or widower's benefits?

1. Death

2. Remarriage, in which case the widow or widower receives a lump sum payment of two year's compensation.

What evidence is needed to support a claim?

1. Widow or widower. Proof of marriage to deceased worker. If either party was married before, proof that earlier marriage was legally ended. A certified copy of the final divorce decree, or proof of death of a previous marriage partner may be required before benefits are paid. Certified copy of the death certificate of the deceased worker.

2. Children - Certified copy of birth certificate or Order of Adoption. If a legal guardian has been appointed, a certified copy of the Letters of Guardianship.

Time requirement of filing claim

Within one year of employee's death. The time may not begin to run, however, until the person claiming the benefit would reasonably have related the employee's death to his or her employment. In case of death due to an occupational disease, a claim may be filed within two years after the claimant becomes aware, or in the exercise of reasonable diligence or by reason of medical advice should have been aware, of the relationship between the employment, the disease and the death.

Use the space below or a separate sheet of paper to continue answers. Please number each answer to correspond to the number of the item being continued.

Privacy Act Notice

In accordance with the Privacy Act of 1974, as amended (5 U.S.C. 552a) you are hereby notified that (1) the Longshore and Harbor Workers' Compensation Act, as amended and extended (33 U.S.C. 901 et seq.) (LHWCA) is administered by the Office of Workers' Compensation Programs of the U.S. Department of Labor, which receives and maintains personal information on claimants and their immediate families. (2) Information which the Office has will be used to determine eligibility for and the amount of benefits payable under the LHWCA. (3) Information may be given to the employer which employed the claimant at the time of injury, or to the insurance carrier or other entity which secured the employer's compensation liability. (4) Information may be given to physicians and other medical service providers for use in providing treatment or medical/vocational rehabilitation, making evaluations and for other purposes relating to the medical management of the claim. (5) Information may be given to the Department of Labor's Office of Administrative Law Judges (OALJ), or other person, board or organization, which is authorized or required to render decisions with respect to the claim or other matter arising in connection with the claim. (6) Information may be given to Federal, state and local agencies for law enforcement purposes, to obtain information relevant to a decision under the LHWCA, to determine whether benefits are being or have been paid properly, and, where appropriate, to persue salary/administrative offset and debt collection actions required or permitted by law. Disclosure of the claimant's Social Security Number (SSN) or tax identifying number (TIN) on this form is mandatory. The SSN and/or TIN and other information maintained by the Office may be used for identification, and for other purposes authorized by law. (8) Failure to disclose all requested Information may delay the processing of the claim, the payment of benefits, or may result in an unfavorable decision or reduced level of benefits.

Note: The notice applies to all forms requesting information that you might receive from the Office in connection with the processing and/or adjudication of the claim you filed under the LHWCA and related statutes.

Public Burden Statement

We estimate that it will take an average of 15 minutes to complete this collection of information, including time for reviewing instructions, searching existing data sources, gathering and maintaining the data needed, and completing and reviewing the collection of information. If you have any comments regarding these estimates or any other aspect of this collection of information, including suggestions for reducing this burden, send them to the U.S. Department of Labor, Division of Longshore and Harbor Workers' Compensation, Room C4315, 200 Constitution Avenue, N.W., Washington, DC 20210.

DO NOT SEND THE COMPLETED FORM TO THIS OFFICE

Part IV
Process at the OWCP

Chapter 17

Administrative Claims Handling at the District Director's Office

Thomas C. Fitzhugh III, Esq.

SUMMARY: This chapter explains the responsibilities of the District Director's office and the wide range of activities supervised and facilitated by it. A short explanation of the function of this office since the LHWCA originated is also included.
STATUTORY BASIS: 33 U.S.C. §§ 907(c), 914(h), and 919; 20 C.F.R. §§ 702.102-.331; 702.401-.422; 702.501-.508

Since 1972 their title has changed: deputy commissioners are now district directors who supervise the daily administration of longshore claims, and even though their adjudicative powers have sharply curtailed, these individuals and their staffs are the most important connections any longshore practitioner can have. With their assistance, handling claims and claimants from either side of the docket becomes a manageable task; without it, a nightmare. The unique role of the district office in the longshore system is unlike that of any other compensation commission or staff, and professionals involved in longshore claims need to understand the many responsibilities of the district staff.

Prior to 1972 deputy commissioners wielded enormous powers. Not only did they supervise administrative aspects of the claims but also they sat as trial judges for disputed claims. The trial authority was shifted to administrative law judges in the 1972 Amendments to the Act. Now the district directors must use their finesse and knowledge of the Act to facilitate claims. One should not automatically assume that the shift of adjudicatory power from district directors emasculated that office; quite the contrary. Only now the district directors must use their finesse and knowledge of the Act to facilitate claims. This chapter will explain the various duties of the district director's office.

A predicate to action by the district office is the filing of a claim. Significant changes to that process have occurred since the last edition of this book. The OWCP has changed initial reporting and communication with district offices to increase efficiency and to expedite crucial documents reaching the OWCP file expeditiously.

ALL new files are to be reported to the New York District Office for file creation:

201 Varick Street, Room 750
Post Office Box 249
New York, NY 10014-0249
646-264-3011 (phone)
646-264-3002 (fax)

There is no electronic reporting for initial injuries or claims. The OWCP office in New York will assign an OWCP number and thereafter, any claim will be transferred to the district office nearest the claimant's residence for administrative handling, regardless of where the insurance company or employer are located or supervise the claim. Each claim will be assigned to a claims examiner or perhaps even to the district director. That individual will have primary responsibility for the claim until the claim is resolved or transferred for trial. There is one case in which an attorney requested the file transferred to the OWCP nearest him (San Francisco) though the claimant lived in Oklahoma and ordinarily the claim would have been handled by the Houston office. The New York office transferred the case to San Francisco, even though that violated internal operating procedures of the OWCP. The Benefits Review Board affirmed this irregular action in *McDonald v. Aecom Technology Corp.*, 45 BRBS 45 (2011).

ELECTRONIC FILING: The OWCP now has a quick was to get documents and correspondence to the proper office and claims examiner through the Secure Electronic Access Portal (SEAPortal), located at https://seaportal.dol-esa.gov/portal/,

- No need to register or enroll to use.
- You need: the OWCP case number and the injured worker's last name, date of birth and date of injury.

> Any document, including forms (after the claim has been created in New York), correspondence, settlements, and other documents can be submitted via SEA Portal. All correspondence on ALL files, regardless of district office handling, to be sent to Jacksonville office for transmittal to district offices unless you use the SEA Portal. This includes 8(i) settlements. Send certified mail, return receipt requested, to Jacksonville, 400 W. Bay Street, Room 63A, Jacksonville, FL 32202, Phone: (904) 357-4788 Fax: (904) 357-4787.

Claims management—The claims examiner will monitor medical reports and see that all appropriate forms are filed. If benefits are paid and no dispute arises, the OWCP involvement will be minimal. At any time, however, any party may request OWCP intervention. This normally occurs when benefits are terminated or treatment is denied. Employers contesting jurisdiction may want to accelerate the trial dates so the parameters of their liability can be established quickly. When either party reports an impasse or requests an informal conference, the claims examiner will schedule an informal conference. Regulations now permit these to occur by conference call, and this method saves a tremendous amount of travel time and money. Face-to-face meetings may be useful to nudge the parties toward a resolution; however, the OWCP will work with the parties to schedule hearings at times that permit participation of all parties and their counsel.

Regulations require a ten day notice to all parties for an informal conference, but this period can be waived. Regulations now permit these conferences to be conducted via phone. Once the conference convenes, the claims examiner will ask the party who requested the informal to state its position, and then the other side will be given opportunity to respond. After all discussion is concluded, the conference adjourns, and the claims examiner issues a Memorandum of Informal Conference summarizing the proceedings and recommending a course of action. This recommendation is *not binding*, and the OWCP has no power to enforce it. The recommendation cannot even be introduced as evidence at the formal hearing.

If the dispute is not resolved between the parties, either party can request referral of the claim for trial (formal hearing). Regulations contemplate a separate informal conference, called a Pre-Hearing Conference, so the OWCP can narrow the issues in dispute and frame the case for trial; however, if it is clear that no progress is possible, the claims examiner can waive a Pre-Hearing Conference and simply request LS-18's (Pre-Hearing Statements) from each party. The parties have 21 days to complete the form and return it; once that time limit has run, if the OWCP has at least one LS-18, it will refer the case to the Office of Administrative Law Judges for trial.

This is *not* the end of the OWCP's district office's activity. Medical reports must still be filed with the district office, and all compensation payments must be reported on the proper form. If only a portion of the claim is referred for formal hearing, all other issues remain under management of the district director. After the formal hearing, the ALJ's decision is sent to the district director for filing and service on all parties along with the record of the hearing. If an appeal is filed, the district office forwards the record to the Benefits Review Board.

Medical management—One of the most important statutory duties given to district directors is the obligation to supervise medical care and treatment. This involves reviewing necessity of medical treatment, and verifying that charges are reasonable and in line with customary charges in the area. If a medical dispute arises, the district director has authority to order an independent medical examination, and this is usually paid for by the employer/carrier. Once a claimant has selected a treating physician, the district director has authority to change medical management on request of the claimant. Even the employer can request the district office direct a change in physicians if the claimant's doctor does not file written reports or respond to queries from the employer or carrier. Because the district offices handle thousands of open claims at a time, the claims examiners and district director are very familiar with doctors in the area. This is especially useful when an IME is needed in an obscure location where few longshore claims are handled. If a dispute arises between a health care provider and the carrier or employee, the OWCP will advise the provider of the Act's requirements. If the dispute persists, the only recourse for the provider is to file a claim for reimbursement of medical expenses with the OWCP.

Settlements—Another major responsibility of district directors is the consideration of settlement proposals. If both parties are represented by attorneys, a settlement will be automatically approved 30 days after submission unless it is specifically rejected by the OWCP via certified letter with a detailed explanation of why the settlement is either inadequate or procured by duress. No other basis for disapproving a settlement submitted by attorneys is allowed. If the claimant is unrepresented, there is no time limit for consideration of a proposed settlement, but the claims examiners will customarily look very closely at such agreements to insure the adequacy of the settlement. Once approved, settlements are final within 30 days and virtually impossible to overturn or review.

Attorneys fees—Successful claimants are entitled to a reasonable attorneys fee, and if the parties do not agree on a fee, the district director must set the fee. The fee is based on a detailed description of the work done backed by daily time records broken down by minimum increments (.1 in some jurisdictions; .125 in others). The hourly rate must reflect the experience of the attorney, geographic location, results obtained, complexity of the issues, etc.

Penalties—The district office assesses penalties for late payments of benefits and failure to file forms timely. The office will also calculate interest due on awards or late payments of compensation. These calculations can be complicated, but the OWCP has computer programs to calculate such figures precisely. When an employer does not pay an order within the specified time, the OWCP will, on request of the claimant, institute default proceedings.

Special Fund (8(f))—Applications for Section 8(f) relief ***must*** be filed with the district office as soon as permanency becomes an issue in a claim. Deadline for filing the application will be set by the district director who can, under certain circumstances, extend the deadline until medical records can be obtained. The district director will review all applications and forward them to the National Office with a recommendation for approval or rejection. Should 8(f) relief be granted, the district office will monitor payments and calculate reimbursement to the employer. Some district directors will assist employers gather information for the 8(f) application by issuing OWCP Subpoenas. These forms are not expressly mentioned in the statute or regulations and are not enforceable in court; however, they usually succeed in prying medical records from custodians looking for anything appearing to be from the government as justification to release information.

Rehabilitation—Every district office has a rehabilitation advisor who will offer retraining and rehabilitation assistance to qualified claimants. These advisors have funds to pay tuition, buy books, tools, and meet other retraining expenses, but they do not personally handle the individual claimants. Instead they commission private rehabilitation counselors to evaluate claimants and design a tailored vocational program. Participation in these programs is entirely voluntary, and the claimant cannot be penalized for refusing to cooperate. The OWCP pays for training and pays the private consultants to monitor and assist in it. The money for this program comes from the Special Fund.

Death claims—The district director will conduct a beneficiary investigation if aware of a compensable death. If no beneficiaries are found, he can order payment of $5,000 to the Special Fund and close the file.

Clerical—The district office provides information to claimants and carriers, provides guidance to the longshore community, disseminates national policy, and assists claimants receive medical care and compensation to which they are entitled. The director also insures that orders are promptly and correctly served on parties obligated to pay benefits and maintains voluminous records on each file, including medical and compensation payment information.

The law and its interpretations grow more complex, and the OWCP district staffs continue to shrink. Whenever possible, offer to help: make copies of medical records, schedule appointments, insure filings are correct, and promptly respond to correspondence and queries. You can build a good reputation with the OWCP even without agreeing with every recommendation it makes. You can disagree without being disagreeable. Integrity and consistency in action build trust, and solid professional relationships founded on these values can lead to more orderly administration of the Act.

Chapter 18

Discrimination

Norman Cole, Esq.

§48 a prohibits a employer from discriminating against an employee because the employee has claimed or attempted to claim compensation or testified or is about to testify in a proceeding under the LHWCA. If proven, the employee can receive lost wages and reinstatement and the employer can be ordered to pay a penalty to the Special Fund plus the employee's attorney fees. Administrative rules describe in greater detail the procedure the Congress contemplated when discrimination is claimed. Caselaw has defined the limited scope of the statute, the burden of proof, and when lost wages and reinstatement may be awarded.

18.1 Statute and Administrative Rule

33 USC §948a (§48a) states:

> It shall be unlawful for any employer or his duly authorized agent to discharge or in any other manner discriminate against an employee as to his employment because such employee has claimed or attempted to claim compensation from such employer, or because he has testified or is about to testify in a proceeding under this chapter. The discharge or refusal to employ a person who has been adjudicated to have filed a fraudulent claim for compensation is not a violation of this section. Any employer who violates this section shall be liable to a penalty of not less than $1,000 or more than $5,000, as may be determined by the deputy commissioner. All such penalties shall be paid to the deputy commissioner for deposit in the special fund as described in section 944 of this title, and if not paid may be recovered in a civil action brought in the appropriate United States district court. Any employee so discriminated against shall be restored to his employment and shall be compensated by his employer for any loss of wages arising out of such discrimination: *Provided*, That if such employee shall cease to be qualified to perform the duties of his employment, he shall not be entitled to such restoration and compensation. The employer alone and not his carrier shall be liable for such penalties and payments. Any provision in an insurance policy undertaking to relieve the employer from the liability for such penalties and payments shall be void.

The statute was previously known as §49, and some litigants and judges still refer to §49 claims instead of the correct reference, §48a. 1984 amendments added: "The discharge or refusal to employ a person who has been adjudicated to have filed a fraudulent claim for compensation is not a violation of this section," and increased the penalty from $100 to $1,000 to $1,000 to $5,000. (Amended Sept. 28, 1984, Pub. L. 98-426, § 26, 98 Stat. 1654.)

20 CFR §702.271(a) generally copies the language in the statute:

> (1) No employer or its duly authorized agent may discharge or in any manner discriminate against an employee as to his/her employment because that employee: (i) Has claimed or attempted to claim compensation under this Act; or (ii) has testified or is about to testify in a proceeding under this Act. To discharge or refuse to employ a person who has been adjudicated to have filed a fraudulent claim for compensation or otherwise made a false statement or misrepresentation under section 31(a)(1) of the Act, *33 U.S.C. 931(a)(1)* is not a violation of this section.

(2) Any employer who violates this section shall be liable to a penalty of not less than $1,000.00 or more than $5,000.00 to be paid (by the employer alone, and not by a carrier) to the district director for deposit in the special fund described in section 44 of the Act, *33 U.S.C. 944*; and shall restore the employee to his or her employment along with all wages lost due to the discrimination unless that employee has ceased to be qualified to perform the duties of employment. *Provided however*, that for any violation occurring on or after November 17, 1997 the employer shall be liable to a penalty of not less than $1,100.00 or more than $5,500.00.

The penalty was increased from not less than $1,000.00 or more than $5,000.00 to not less than $2,259.00 or more than $11,293.00 as a result of the Federal Civil Penalties Inflation Adjustment Act Improvements Act of 2015 and 20 CFR §702.271(a)(2) (effective August 1, 2016).

The remaining sections of 20 CFR §702.271 outline a procedure for raising a discrimination claim:

1. The employee notifies the district director;
2. Within five days the district director notifies the employer and initiates an investigation, which can include an interview of or written communication with the employee, employer representatives, and other parties;
3. The district director can convene an informal conference.

If it is determined the employee has been discriminated against, the district director shall determine if the employee is qualified to perform the duties of employment. To do so, the district director can consider medical evidence and schedule an independent medical examination, at the Special Fund's expense.

(b) When a district director receives a complaint from an employee alleging discrimination as defined under section 49, he or she shall notify the employer, and within five working days, initiate specific inquiry to determine all the facts and circumstances pertaining thereto. This may be accomplished by interviewing the employee, employer representatives and other parties who may have information about the matter. Interviews may be conducted by written correspondence, telephone or personal interview.

(c) If circumstances warrant, the district director may also conduct an informal conference on the issue as described in Secs. 702.312 through 702.314.

(d) Any employee discriminated against is entitled to be restored to his employment and to be compensated by the employer for any loss of wages arising out of such discrimination provided that the employee is qualified to perform the duties of the employment. If it is determined that the employee has been discriminated against, the district director shall also determine whether the employee is qualified to perform the duties of the employment. The district director may use medical evidence submitted by the parties or he may arrange to have the employee examined by a physician selected by the district director. The cost of the medical examination arranged for by the district director may be charged to the special fund established by section 44, 33 U.S.C. 944.

20 CRF §702.272 states the district director's conclusions should be incorporated in a recommendation. If the employer and employee accept the recommendation, it will be incorporated in an order mailed to each party within ten days. If they do not agree, the district director prepares and distributes another memorandum summarizing the disagreement and within fourteen days refers the case to the Office of Administrative Law Judges.

(a) If the district director determines that the employee has been discharged or suffered discrimination and is able to resume his or her duties, the district director will recommend that the employer reinstate the employee and/or make such restitution as is indicated by the circumstances of the case, including compensation for any wage loss suffered as the result of the discharge or discrimination. The district director may also assess the employer an appropriate penalty, as determined under authority vested in the district director by the Act. If the district director determines that no violation occurred he shall notify the partries of his findings and the reasons for recommending that the complaint be denied. If the employer and employee accept the district director's recommendation, it will be incorporated in an order and mailed to each party within 10 days.

(b) If the parties do not agree to the recommendation, the district director shall, within 10 days

> after receipt of the rejection, prepare a memorandum summarizing the disagreement, mail a copy to all interested parties, and shall within 14 days thereafter refer the case to the Office of the Chief Administrative Law Judge for hearing pursuant to Sec. 702.317.

20 CFR §702.273 states an Administrative Law Judge is responsible for final determinations regarding a discrimination complaint:

> The Office of Administrative Law Judges is responsible for final determinations of all disputed issues connected with the discrimination complaint, including the amount of penalty to be assessed, and shall proceed with a formal hearing as described in Secs. 702.331 to 702.394.

If a penalty is assessed and employer refuses to pay, the matter is referred to the Associate Solicitor for Employee Benefits for appropriate legal action, per 20 CRF 702.274:

> In the event the employer refuses to pay the penalty assessed, the district director shall refer the complete administrative file to the Associate Director, Division of Longshore and Harbor Workers' Compensation, for subsequent transmittal to the Associate Solicitor for Employee Benefits, with the request that appropriate legal action be taken to recover the penalty.

18.2 Scope of §48a Discrimination

§48a does not apply if the employee has not filed a claim, attempted to file a claim, testified in a LHWCA claim, or is about to testify in a LHWCA claim. It prohibits employers from treating an employee who has filed a claim, attempted to file a claim, testified in a LHWCA claim, or is about to testify in a LHWCA claim different from workers not in those categories. For example, it does not prohibit an employer from administering illegal or unfair treatment to an employee as long as all employees are subject to the same illegal or unfair treatment. §48a it does not prohibit an employer from refusing to provide reasonable accommodations to an employee who filed an LHWCA claim if the employer also refuses reasonable accommodations to other workers even though refusal to provide reasonable accommodations could be a violation of the Americans with Disabilities Act (42 USC §12101–12213). The ADA and a LHWCA discrimination claim are two distinct causes of action involving different standards. The issues presented by a LHWCA discrimination claim cannot be litigated in an ADA action, so a decision in an ADA action does not collaterally estop the worker from pursuing a LHWCA discrimination claim. *Dunn v. Lockheed Martin Corp.*, 33 BRBS 204 (1999).

The issue under §48(a) is not whether an employer may discipline its employee for the occurrence of work accidents or whether such discipline is objectively reasonable. The issue is whether the discipline imposed was due to the employee's filing of a compensation claim. *Babick v. Todd Pacific Shipyards Corporation*, 2015 WL 1510753 (BRB 14-0177, 2015). The ALJ does not have authority to adjudicate whether an employee was terminated for justifiable cause according to the terms of an employment contract or collective bargaining agreement. *Winburn v. Jeffboat, Inc.*, 9 BRBS 363 (BRB 1978).

§48a does not prohibit an employer from discriminating against an employee because the employee filed a claim against a former employer. In *Buchanan v. Boh Bros. Constr. Co. Inc.*, 741 F.2d 750 (5th Cir. 1984), the employer discharged a current employee after learning the employee had filed a Jones Act claim against a former employer. The discharge did not violate §49 (as the statute was then numbered).

To the extent prohibited conduct under §48a overlaps with conduct prohibited by other statutes, the worker must exhaust administrative remedies under the LHWCA before seeking relief in other forums. In *Brink v. Continental Ins. Co.*, 787 3d 1120 (DC Cir. 2015), civilian government contractor employees, or their survivors, brought a class action suit against government contractors and their insurance carriers alleging violations of the LHWCA, RICO, and ADA and several tort claims based on defendants' handling of their claims for medical benefits under the Defense Base Act (DBA). The court held plaintiffs must first exhaust their administrative remedies under the DBA, which incorporated administrative procedures under the LHWCA for filing, adjudication, and payment of workers' compensation claims. Plaintiffs did not file a complaint with district director of applicable compensation district, the district director did not conduct investigation of the complaint, determine discrimination occurred, or recommend reinstatement, restitution, or compensation for lost wages.

Likewise, in *Sickle v. Torres Advanced Enterprise Solutions, LLC*, 17 F.Supp 3d (D.D.C., 2013), former subcontractors for a military defense contractor could not bring claims for retaliatory termination under the DBA in district court without first exhausting administrative remedies under the LHWCA, as incorporated into DBA. The court referenced the comprehensive administrative procedure for

DBA/LHWCA discrimination and retaliation claims that enabled the agency to exercise its expertise and discretion in resolving such claims, while allowing for eventual federal court review. No reason existed to allow former subcontractors to sidestep that process, particularly given the Department of Labor's power to require reinstatement, back pay, and restitution. Plaintiffs could not bring a §48a claim in federal district court without following the prescribed administrative procedures, and they could not bring a common law retaliation claim arising out of facts and circumstances the DBA/LHWCA scheme arguably covers.

18.3 Burden of Proof

§20(a) (33 USC 520(a)) states "it shall be presumed, in the absence of substantial evidence to the contrary – that the claim comes within the provisions of this chapter." This section has been interpreted to require the claimant to produce evidence of an injury that could have been caused by a work injury. Then, to rebut the presumption, the employer must produce substantial evidence there was no injury, or the injury was not related to employment. If employer produces such evidence, the presumption vanishes, and the claimant must *prove*, by a preponderance of the evidence, the injury was work related. *Ceres Gulf, Inc. v. Director, OWCP*, 683 F.3d 225 (5th Cir. 2012).

The Board, in *Babick v. Todd Pacific Shipyards Corporation*, 2015 WL 1802689 (BRB 14-0177, 2015), adopted a similar concept in discrimination claims. Claimant must first *produce* evidence to permit a trier to infer: (1) The employer committed a discriminatory act; (2) motivated by discriminatory animus or intent. Once done, the burden shifts to the employer to *produce* substantial evidence it acted for non discriminatory reasons. If employer produces this evidence the presumption falls from the case, and the claimant must prove by a preponderance of the evidence the employer committed a discriminatory act motivated by his claim for compensation, i.e. that the action was taken because of the claimant's protected activity. In so doing the Board overruled a prior standard, based on *Geddes v. Benefits Review Board [Geddes I]*, 735 F.2d 1418 (D.C. Cir. 1984), which held after the claimant established a *prima facie* case of discrimination, the burden shifted to the employer to *prove* its *animus* was not even partially motivated by the claimant's exercise of his rights under the LHWCA. *Geddes I* was contrary to *Director, OWCP v. Greenwich Colleries*, 512 US 276 (1994), which held the "true doubt" rule violated §7(c) of the APA because it improperly shifted the burden to the party opposing the claim. To comply with *Greenwich Colleries* the claimant has the ultimate burden of proof if the employer produces evidence to rebut the presumption.

18.4 Discriminatory Act

To justify relief the employer must commit a discriminatory act. In *Geddes v. Director, OWCP*, 851 F.2d 440 (D.C. Cir. 1988), claimant contended employer would not let him return to work after his injury because he had criticized the employer at a public hearing that predated the compensation claim. Claimant, however, resigned rather than accept employer's offer to return to work upon presentation of required medical clearance and passing a driving test. Even though there was no question employer evidenced ill-will toward claimant and it may be employer intended to prevent him from returning to work, employer did not, in fact, prevent claimant from returning to work. "It is not murder to intend to kill someone if the potential victim commits suicide before the would be murderer ever has the chance to act on that intent." 851 F.2d at 188.

In *Nooner v. National Steel & Shipbuilding Co.*, 1986 WL 66391,10 BRBS 43 (BRB 1986), employer would not rehire claimant in December 1972 and in March 1973 for medical reasons. The ALJ concluded claimant was medically unable to work from July 14, 1972 to February 28, 1974. Therefore, there was no discrimination cognizable under §49.

In *Brooks v. Newport News Shipbuilding & Dry Dock Co.*, 2 F.3d 64 (4th Cir .1993), *Hunt v. Newport News Shipbuilding & Dry Dock Co.*, 61 F.3d 900 (4th Cir. 1995) (unpublished), *Jaros v. National Steel & Shipbuilding Co.*, 21 BRBS 26 (1988), *Leon v. Todd Shipyards*, 21 BRBS 190, 1988 WL 232747 (BRB 1988), and *Williams v. Newport News Shipbuilding & Drydock Co.*, 14 BRBS 300 (BRB 1981), claimants were discharged after employer discovered pre-employment medical forms or employment applications that failed to disclose prior injuries or medical conditions or contained false information. Each claimant failed to prove his discharge was a discriminatory act. Evidence indicated each claimant was not treated differently than any other employee who provided incomplete or false information on an employment application. In *Ventura v. Marisco, Ltd.*, 2012 WL 423904 (BRB 11-0376, 2012) (unpublished), however, the employer terminated claimant for failure to comply with its policy to call in daily when sick. The policy was not consistently applied, and the ALJ concluded it was a pretext to terminate the claimant, constituting a violation of §49.

In, *Holliman v. Newport News Shipbuilding & Dry Dock Co.*, 852 F.2d 759 (4th Cir. 1988) all employees were required to call employer if absent for five workdays, regardless of the nature of the absence. Because the rule was customarily enforced against employees absent due to personal or occupational injuries, claimant did not prove his discharge was due to a discriminatory act. In *Ledet v. Phillips Petroleum*

Co., 163 F.3d 901 (5th Cir. 1998), a supervisor contacted claimant several times in December 1989 and January 1990 advising him he should provide medical evidence from the attending physician showing he could not return to work. He was cautioned failure to do so would result in termination. On February 8, 1990 he was terminated retroactive to November 30, 1989 for abandonment of job. The ALJ concluded this was not a discriminatory act.

In *Dickens v. Tidewater Stevedoring Corp.*, 656 F.2d 74 (4th Cir. 1981), employee guaranteed annual income was reduced eight hours for every day absent, even if absent for a compensable LHWCA injury. There was no discriminatory act because injured and uninjured employees experienced deductions in amounts equal to the number of hours for which they received compensation and employees who were absent due to illness were subject to identical deductions.

In *Manship v. Norfolk & Western Ry. Co.*, 30 BRBS 175 (BRB 1996), the employer suspected claimant filed a fraudulent claim. It controverted the claim, terminated the claimant, and convened a hearing to investigate the claim pursuant to the Railway Labor Act and collective bargaining agreement. The ALJ concluded the claim was compensable but denied claimant's §49 claim because there was no evidence claimant was treated differently than other employees and no evidence of discriminatory animus.

In contrast, in *Strickland v. Newport News Shipbuilding & Dry Dock Co.*, 34 BRBS 604 (ALJ 2000), the employer discriminated against the claimant when it routinely denied leave of absence to workers with controverted compensation claims.

18.5 Animus—A Discriminatory Intent

An employer who discriminates against an employee must be motivated to do so because the employee filed a claim, attempted to file a claim, testified in a LHWCA claim, or is about to testify in a LHWCA claim. It is no defense if employer's actions were based on other reasons in addition to a desire to retaliate because the claimant filed a claim. *Machado v. National Steel & Shipbuilding co.*, 9 BRBS 803 (BRB 1978). "An employer who discriminates against an employee both because the employee filed a compensation claim and because of other, independent reasons nonetheless violates §49." *Geddes. v. Benefits Review Board*, 735 F.2d 1418 (D.C. Cir. 1984).

Animus may be inferred from the surrounding circumstances when determining if the employer's reasons for taking the discriminatory action were credible or merely pretext. *Ledet v. Phillips Petroleum Co.*, 163 F.3d 901 (5th Cir. 1998). In *Powell v. Nacirema Operating Co., Inc.*, 1986 WL 66434, 19 BRBS 124 (BRB 1986), employer had paid claimant to settle his compensation claim, only to have client return to full time work for five months before being fired, with no complaints from employer about his performance. The ALJ inferred animus from Captain Chamber's testimony he was irate and indignant at being required to employ a totally disabled person.

In *Gondolfi v. Mid-Gulf Stevedores*, 621 F.2d 695 (5th Cir. 1980), claimant settled a 1974 claim for $500 and returned to work In 1975 he reported late to work. This delayed the start of loading and resulted in a financial loss to the employer. Employer summarily discharged him. Claimant filed a claim alleging his discharge was in retaliation for the prior claim. The ALJ acknowledged the discharge may have been harsh, but the prior claim played no part in the discharge. Similarly, in *Miller v. Prolerized New England Co.*, 14 BRBS 811, 819 (1981), *aff'd on other grounds*, 691 F.2d 45 (1st Cir. 1982), claimant was terminated due to his union activity and not because he filed a workers' compensation claim.

In *Tibbs v. Washington Metro. Area Transit Auth.*, 17 BRBS 92 (BRB 1985), 1985 WL 55374, *aff'd mem.*, 784 F.2d 1132 (D.C. Cir. 1986), the evidence indicated employer's decision to fire and not reinstate the claimant was justified by claimant's overall record of absenteeism, following a progressive system of discipline involving cautions, reprimands, various degrees of suspension, and finally dismissal.

In contrast, in *Dill v. Sun Shipbuilding & Dry Dock Co.*, 6 BRBS 738 (BRB 1978), employer's real reason to termination claimant was to avoid a future compensation liability. In *Norfolk Shipbuilding & Drydock Corp, v. Nance*, 858 F.2d 182 (4th Cir. 1988), *cert. den.*, 492 US 911 (1989), employer discharged the claimant after the parties entered in an agreement to settle the claims for disability, age discrimination, discrimination under §49, and a grievance to his union. The agreement did not state claimant would be discharged after the agreement was approved, but after the agreement was approved claimant was terminated. Employer contended claimant had verbally agreed to termination. Claimant contended otherwise, and the ALJ refused to receive evidence of the oral agreement. Employer's representative testified that employer wanted a "clean slate" after claimant had filed his compensation claim. The Board ruled employer's general policy of conditioning settlements on termination violated §49. There was substantial evidence of discriminatory intent on part of the employer to warrant finding employer violated §48a.

18.6 Discrimination is an Uninsured Liability

§48a prohibits the employer from securing insurance to pay for penalties and other payments owed. When discrimination is claimed employers should consider hiring independent counsel.

18.7 Remedies

§48a entitles the discriminated worker to restoration of employment, compensation for lost wages, and attorney fees. Additionally, the employer will be ordered to pay a penalty of not less than $1,100.00 or more than $5,500.00 to the Special Fund.

The employer's right to restoration should be evaluated as of the date of maximum medical improvement. *Monta v. Navy Exchange Service Command*, 39 BRBS 104 (BRB 2005); *Ventura v. Marisco, Ltd.*, 2012 WL 423904 (BRB 11-0376, 2012) (unpublished).

§48a states "if such employee shall cease to be qualified to perform the duties of his employment, he shall not be entitled to such restoration and compensation." Therefore, the employee is entitled to compensation for lost wages only if the worker could have performed the former job. Additionally, the ALJ cannot order the employer to provide short term or long term disability payments in lieu of lost wages. *G.M.[Golet Mann] v. P&O Ports Louisiana, Inc.*, 2009 WL 1615789 (BRB 08-0780, 2009).

The amount a longshoreman receives as Guaranteed Annual Income, holiday, and vacation payments during periods when entitled to lost wages should offset the amount due under §48a. These payments are traceable to the employer, not administered as a social program by the state, and do not constitute a collateral benefit. If not offset, the employee would be made more than whole at employer's expense. *Raynor v. Maritime Terminals, Inc.*, 1998 WL 232815, 22 BRBS 5 (BRB 1988).

In general, §28 allows attorneys to receive a fee when successful obtaining compensation for the claimant. "Compensation" is defined in §2(12) as "the money allowance payable to an employee or to his dependents as provided for in this Act." Lost wages may be awarded under §48(a), but the penalty is not "payable to an employee or his dependents" and is not within the definition of compensation. Nevertheless, it generally has been assumed an attorney who prevails on a discrimination claim is entitled to fees payable by the employer.

When an attorney pursues a claim for compensation and a discrimination claim on behalf of the worker, the fee petition should itemize the work performed on the separate disability and discrimination claims because an insurer is not responsible for paying fees associated with a discrimination claim. *R.S. v. National Rural Electric Cooperative Assn.*, 20078 WL 7629708 (BRB 07-0209) (unpublished). If an attorney is unsuccessful in pursuit of the discrimination claim but successful in obtaining disability, the attorney can still receive a fee. *Battle v. A.J. Ellis Construction Co.* 16 BRBS 329 (1984).

18.8 Limitations

Although §13 of the LHWCA limits the time within which a worker can file a claim for disability or death, the LHWCA does not identify a time limit for filing a claim for discrimination. When a federal statute does not establish a statute of limitations, the Supreme Court "has repeatedly 'borrowed' the state law of limitations governing an analogous cause of action." *Board of Regents v. Tomanio*, 446 US 478, 100 S.Ct. 1790 ,1795 (1980). "When Congress has not established a time limitation for a federal cause of action, the settled practice has been to adopt a local time limitation as federal law if it is not inconsistent with federal law or policy to do so." *Wilson v. Garcia*, 471 US 478, 105 S.Ct. 1938, 1941 (1985).

Chapter 19

Uses and Abuses of the Section 20 Presumptions

John L. Schouest, Esq., Bobbi N. Roquemore, Esq., and D. A. Bass-Frazier, Esq.

Synopsis

19.1 The Employer's Point of View

A. Introduction

Section 20 of the Longshore and Harbor Workers' Compensation Act creates a broad presumption of compensability designed to tilt the scales of justice in favor of injured workers. Its structure is consistent with advancing the "grand bargain" between employers and employees and facilitating compensation to injured workers regardless of fault.

The four presumptions in Section 20 assist claimants in meeting the standard of proof for their claims and relieve claimants, at least initially, of having to prove certain elements of their claims.

Section 20 provides that, "[i]n any proceeding for the enforcement of a claim for compensation under this Act it shall be presumed, in the absence of substantial evidence to the contrary—

(a) That the claim comes within the provisions of this Act.

(b) That sufficient notice of such claim has been given.

(c) That the injury was not occasioned solely by the intoxication of the injured employee.

(d) That the injury was not occasioned by the willful intention of the injured employee to injure or kill himself or another."

What results is a burden-shifting scheme for proof of liability determinations. The Act provides a presumption in favor of the claimant for the areas covered; however, Section 20(a) is unique in that a claimant must first show that an injury or death arose in the course of his employment before the presumption is invoked. The burden of proof then shifts to the employer to rebut the presumption with substantial evidence. Generally, once the presumption is rebutted, it falls out of the case, and the claimant must prove his case to the trier of fact by a preponderance of the evidence.

The text of Section 20 has remained intact since the passage of the Act on March 4, 1927.

Yet the presumptions afforded by Section 20, particularly Section 20(a), have been both used in a way that is true to the Act's intent and abused in such a way that they are far removed from the context in which they were enacted.

Recent trends have resulted in situations where an injury—no matter how minor—with a connection to the employment—no matter how tenuous—along with medical report associating the two—no matter how exaggerated—results in a prima facie case and, for the claimant, the benefit of the Section 20(a) presumption that the claim comes within the provisions of the Act.

In effect, what once was a tilt in favor of the claimant has sometimes turned into a mountain for an employer to climb on rebuttal.

This chapter will largely focus on Section 20(a), which addresses causation, i.e. whether the injury or death is causally related to the employment. The chapter concludes with a brief discussion of the presumptions afforded by Section 20(b) (timely notice of injury and filing of a claim), 20(c) (intoxication), and 20(d) (willful intent to injure oneself or another).

B. How the Section 20(a) Presumption is Used

On its face, Section 20(a) states that the claim comes within the provisions of the Act. This presumption is most frequently applied to aid a claimant in proving that his injury arises out of and in the course of his employment under Section 2(2).

To invoke the Section 20(a) presumption, a claimant must first make out a *prima facie* case of causation. In doing so, he must establish 1) that he suffered some harm or pain and 2) that an accident occurred or work conditions could have caused a harm. *U. S. Industries/Federal Sheet Metal, Inc. v. Director, OWCP*, 455 U.S. 608, 14 BRBS 631 (1982), *rev'g* 627 F.2d 455, 12 BRBS 237 (D.C. Cir. 1980); *Kelaita v. Triple A Machine Shop*, 13 BRBS 326 (1981). In establishing a causal connection between the injury and claimant's work, the Act should be liberally applied in favor of the injured worker in accordance with its remedial purpose. *Stafftex Staffing v. Director*, OWCP, 237 F.3d 404, 406 (5th Cir. 2000), *on reh'g*, 237 F.3d 409 (5th Cir. 2000).

An injury cannot be found absent some work-related accident, exposure, event or episode; while a claimant's injury need not be caused by an external force, something still must go wrong within the human frame. *Adkins v. Safeway Stores, Inc.*, 6 BRBS 513, 517 (1978). Yet the mere existence of a physical impairment is insufficient to shift the burden of proof to the employer. *U.S. Industries/Federal Sheet Metal Inc.*, 455 U.S. at 616, 14 BRBS at 633; *Bludworth Shipyard Inc., v. Lira*, 700 F.2d 1046, 1049 (5th Cir. 1983).

In establishing that working conditions could have caused the harm, the claimant is not required to show unusually stressful working conditions, *Cairns v. Matson Terminals, Inc.*, 21 BRBS 252 (1988), but the claimant's theory as to how the injury occurred must go beyond "mere fancy." *Stevens v. Tacoma Boatbuilding Co.*, 23 BRBS 191 (1990).

In addition, cases arising under the Defense Base Act, an extension of the LHWCA, courts have held that a claimant need not establish a causal relationship between his employment and the accident that occasioned his injury; the Supreme Court has allowed benefits where the injury did not occur within the space and time boundaries of work. *O'Leary v. Brown-Pacific-Maxon*, 340 U.S. 504, 506-507 (1951). Rather, all a claimant must prove is that the "obligations or conditions" of his employment created a "zone of special danger" out of which the injury or death arose. *Id.* at 507.

The Section 20(a) presumption applies to whether an injury is caused directly by the employment or is the result of the aggravation of a pre-existing injury or condition. *Bath Iron Works Corp. v. Preston*, 380 F.3d 597, 38 BRBS 60(CRT) (1st Cir. 2004); *Kubin v. Pro-Football, Inc.*, 29 BRBS 117 (1995).

Section 20(a) applies in death benefits cases in helping establish whether the death arose out of employment. *Bell Helicopter Int'l, Inc. v. Jacobs*, 746 F.2d 1342, 17 BRBS 13(CRT) (8th Cir. 1984), *aff'g Darnell v. Bell Helicopter Int'l, Inc.*, 16 BRBS 98 (1984).

The Section 20(a) presumption is applicable in psychological injury cases. *Konno v. Young Bros., Ltd.*, 28 BRBS 57 (1994). A claimant is not required to be diagnosed pursuant to the DSM-IV in order to prove the existence of psychological injury. *S.K. [Kamal] v. ITT Industries, Inc.*, 43 BRBS 78 (2009), *aff'd in part and rev'd in part mem.*, No. 4:09-MC-348, 2011 WL 798464 (S.D. Tex. Mar. 1, 2011).

The section 20(a) presumption can aid claimants in occupational disease cases, specifically in cases involving asbestos exposure.

In *Ramsay Scarlett & Co. v. Director, OWCP*, 806 F.3d 327, __ BRBS __(CRT) (5th Cir. 2015), the administrative law judge relied on the claimant's diagnosis of asbestosis; the claimant's testimony that he changed brakes and clutches on a variety of equipment that he believed had asbestos in them while working for employer; and the report issued by the industrial hygienist who reviewed the claimant's work history and stated it was well documented that brakes and clutches, the components that the claimant handled, exposed workers to "significant concentrations of asbestos," in invoking the Section 20(a) presumption. The Fifth Circuit found that the ALJ was entitled to credit the evidence, which was "more than a scintilla," and the Section 20(a) presumption was properly invoked.

The Ninth Circuit has developed a test for using the Section 20(a) presumption in a multi-employer, occupational disease case: 1) the presumption must be invoked (by "some" evidence) against each employer and if not invoked against a particular employer, that employer may not be held liable; 2) each employer may rebut the presumption with substantial evidence that it is not the last employer to expose the employee to injurious stimuli; 3) once the employer rebuts the presumption, it may only be held liable if the claimant has shown that the employer is responsible by a preponderance of the evidence supporting a finding that it is responsible; and 4) the analysis with respect to each employer is to be applied sequentially beginning with the (last) most recent employer and working backwards. *Albina Engine & Machine v. Director, OWCP*, 627 F.3d 1293, 44 BRBS 89(CRT) (9th Cir. 2010). If a more recent employer is found to be responsible, then the administrative law judge need not address the liability of earlier employers. (*Id*).

The Section 20(a) presumption is also applicable in hearing loss cases. A claimant's testimony of exposure to injurious noise has been held sufficient to invoke the Section 20(a) presumption that working conditions existed at the last employer which could have caused his hearing loss. *Ramey v. Stevedoring Services of America*, 134 F.3d 954, 31 BRBS 206(CRT) (9th Cir. 1998).

The Section 20(a) presumption is not considered evidence for the claimant, but is merely a procedural mechanism which shifts the burden of proof to the employer one the claimant establishes a prima facie case. *Sprague v. Director, OWCP*, 688 F.2d 862, 15 BRBS 11 (CRT) (1st Cir 1982), *aff'g* 13 BRBS 1083 (1981) (Miller, dissenting). The employer must then go forward with substantial countervailing evidence to rebut the presumption that the injury was caused by the claimant's employment.

Employer's burden is one of production, as it must show "through facts—not mere speculation—that the harm was not work-related." *Ceres Gulf, Inc. v. Director, OWCP*, 683 F.3d 225, 228 (5th Cir. 2012).

Once the employer produces substantial evidence of the absence of a causal relationship—not just "any" evidence — the Section 20(a) presumption is rebutted. Substantial evidence is such evidence is more than a scintilla but less than a preponderance of the evidence, such that a reasonable mind might accept as adequate to support a conclusion." *Ramsay Scarlett*, 806 F.3d at 330; *Ingalls Shipbuilding, Inc. v. Dir., Office of Workers' Comp. Programs*, 991 F.2d 163, 165 (5th Cir.1993).

Once the Section 20(a) presumption is rebutted, it falls from the case, and the administrative law judge must then weigh all the evidence and resolve the case based on the record as a whole. *Universal Maritime Corp. v. Moore*, 126 F.3d 256, 31 BRBS 119(CRT) (4th Cir. 1997); *Swinton*, 554 F.2d 1075, 4 BRBS 466.

The Supreme Court has determined that the "true-doubt" rule, which resolves factual doubt in favor of the claimant when the evidence is evenly balanced, violates Section 7(c) of the Administrative Procedure Act, 5 U.S.C. Section 556(d), which specifies that the proponent of a rule or position has the burden of proof and, thus, the burden of persuasion. *Director, OWCP v. Greenwich Collieries*, 512 U.S. 267, 28 BRBS 43(CRT) (1994). Thus, once Section 20(a) drops out of the case, the claimant bears the burden of persuasion and must prove his claim by a preponderance of the evidence. If after evaluating all of the evidence, the fact-finder feels the evidence is equal, i.e. in equipoise, then the claimant must lose. *Santoro v. Maher Terminals, Inc.*, 30 BRBS 171 (1996).

C. How the Section 20(a) Presumption Cannot be Used

Use of the Section 20(a) presumption does have its limits.

The presumption that a claim comes within the provisions of the Act does not apply to the threshold question of coverage. Specifically, the presumption does not apply to whether a claimant has satisfied the status and situs requirements under Sections (2)(3) and 3(a) of the Act. *Cunningham v. Director, OWCP*, 377 F.3d 98, 38 BRBS 42(CRT) (1st Cir. 2004), *aff'g Cunningham v. Bath Iron Works Corp.*, 37 BRBS 76 (2003) (Hall, J., concurring and dissenting). Situs and status questions typically involve a legal interpretation of otherwise undisputed facts.

The Section 20(a) presumption cannot aid a claimant in establishing the existence of an employer-employee relationship, as this is a question of fact to be determined by the administrative law judge after evaluating evidence and applying the relevant legal tests. *Holmes v. Seafood Specialist Boat Works*, 14 BRBS 141 (1981) (Miller, J., dissenting).

A claimant in a survivor's claim cannot use the Section 20(a) presumption to establish her status as a beneficiary under Section 9. *Meister v. Ranch Restaurant*, 8 BRBS 185 (1978), *aff'd mem.*, 600 F.2d 280 (D.C. Cir. 1979).

The Act does not support putting the cart before the horse, as the Section 20(a) presumption cannot be used by a claimant to establish his prima facie case; it can only be invoked afterward. A claimant cannot use the presumption where there the fact of injury is disputed, as there must be proof of injury, i.e. harm or pain, before a presumption can arise. *Murphy v. SCA/Shayne Brothers*, 7 BRBS 309 (1977) (Miller, dissenting), *aff'd mem.*, 600 F.2d 280 (D.C. Cir. 1979). Similarly, a claimant cannot use the presumption to prove that an accident occurred or working conditions existed which could have caused a harm. *Mock v. Newport News Shipbuilding & Dry Dock Co.*, 14 BRBS 275 (1981); *Jones v. J. F. Shea Co.*, 14 BRBS 207 (1981);

While the Section 20(a) presumption applies to the issue of whether the claimant's disability is work-related, it does not apply to issues regarding the nature (temporary or permanent) and extent (partial or total) of disability. *Jones v. Genco, Inc.*, 21 BRBS 12 (1988); *Carlisle v. Bunge Corp.*, 33 BRBS 133 (1999), aff'd, 227 F.3d 934, 34 BRBS 79(CRT) (7th Cir. 2000).

Regarding Section 7 medical benefits, the presumption applies to whether the condition that treatment is sought for is work-related. However, the presumption cannot aid a claimant in establishing that the medical treatment under Section 7 is reasonable and necessary for the work injury, and that other requirements for employer-paid benefits have been met. *Maryland Shipbuilding & Drydock Co. v. Jenkins*, 594 F.2d 404, 10 BRBS 1 (4th Cir. 1979), *rev'g* 6 BRBS 550 (1977). *Shahady v. Atlas Tile & Marble Co.*, 13 BRBS 1007 (1981) (Miller, J. dissenting), *rev'd on other grounds*, 682 F.2d 968 (D.C. Cir. 1982), *cert. denied*, 459 U.S. 1146 (1983).

Courts are divided on whether the Section 20(a) presumption attaches to any secondary injuries that may have been caused by the work-related injury. In *Amerada Hess Corp. v. Director, OWCP*, 543 F. 3d 755, 42 BRBS 41(CRT) (5th Cir. 2008), the Fifth Circuit found that the Section 20(a) presumption applied only to the claim for back and groin injuries, pursuant to the Supreme Court's decision in *U.S. Industries*, 455 U.S. 608. And because the claim did not reference a work-related heart injury, the Section 20(a) presumption did not apply to the claimant's heart condition. Thus, the compensability of a claimant's secondary injury should be assessed by determining whether it was the natural or unavoidable result of the first injury pursuant to Section 2(2) and without reference to the Section 20(a) presumption. *Ins. Co. of the State of Pennsylvania v. Director, OWCP [Vickers]*, 713 F.3d 779, 47 BRBS 19(CRT) (5th Cir. 2013).

The Fourth Circuit parted ways with the Fifth Circuit in *Metro Mach. Corp. v. Director, OWCP*, 846 F.3d 680, 690-691 (4th Cir. 2017). The Fourth Circuit held that the Section 20(a) presumption "does not distinguish between claims concerning primary injuries and those concerning secondary injuries, and in fact Section 20(a) makes no reference to injuries at all." *Metro Mach. Corp*, 846 F.3d at 690. The Section 20(a) presumption, the court continued, "unambiguously applies to all types of claims," whether the injuries involved are primary, secondary or both. *Id.*

Courts have also taken up the issue of how to use the Section 20(a) presumption in determining the responsible employer on a claim. The Benefits Review Board ("the Board") and the Seventh Circuit have held that the presumption does not apply in determining the identity of the responsible employer. *Marinette Marine Corp. v. Director, OWCP*, 431 F.3d 1032, 39 BRBS 82(CRT) (7th Cir. 2005); *McAllister v. Lockheed Shipbuilding*, 39 BRBS 35 (2005) and 41 BRBS 28 (2007). As discussed earlier in this chapter, the Ninth Circuit moved away from *McAllister* and its progeny in *Albina Engine*. It held that Board erred in stating that the Section 20(a) presumption applies to "the claim" instead of against each individual employer or to the responsible employer issue, and thus its four-step analysis is the proper application for a multi-employer, occupational disease case.

Nonetheless, employers cannot use the Section 20(a) presumption against each other. *Lins v. Ingalls Shipbuilding, Inc.*, 26 BRBS 62 (1992).

D. How the Section 20(a) Presumption is Abused

Under the Act, an injury occurs within the scope of employment if it occurs within the time and space boundaries of employment and in the course of an activity whose purpose is related to the employment.

Again, the administrative law judge ("the ALJ") invokes Section 20(a) in favor of a claimant once the claimant establishes a *prima facie* case, which is consistent with the remedial nature of the Act. However, the case law is riddled with instances where the Section 20(a) presumption was successfully invoked, even with tenuous, questionable evidence of the work-relatedness.

For instance, the Board affirmed that ALJ's finding that an employee who injured his left knee while playing ping-pong on the employer's premises during his lunch break had established the work-relatedness of his injury, and thus the Section 20(a) presumption could be applied. *Sheerer v. Bath Iron Works Corp.*, 35 BRBS 45 (2001). The ALJ found that employees regularly engaged in ping pong on the employer's premises within the period of employment, with the employer's acquiescence. Since the employer provided the equipment and the site, it was "sufficient to establish the employer's knowledge and acquiescence in this activity if not its outright sanctioning." *Sheerer*, 35 BRBS 45.

A claimant who was injured during altercation with another employee and who had no private or personal relations with the assailant was granted the benefit of Section 20(a) even though, at time of altercation, the claimant had merely entered place of employment preparatory to actually beginning work. *Twyman v Colorado Security*, 14 BRBS 829 (1982).

Where the claimant had an on-the-job seizure causing him to fall and sustain an injury to his head and hands, the Board held that the judge properly found that the claimant's injury was work-related pursuant to Section 20(a), even though the seizure was not induced by a condition of his employment. *Perry v. Carolina Shipping Co.*, 20 BRBS 90 (1987). The medical expert stated he could not rule out the possibility that the claimant's fall at work caused his condition. Moreover, a compensable injury need not involve unusually dangerous employment conditions, and employers have been held liable where a claimant is injured in a fall even though the fall was due to an idiopathic condition. (*Id*).

Nonetheless, courts have drawn a line at criminal activity. In *Compton v. Avondale Industries, Inc.*, 33 BRBS 174 (1999), a claimant detoured from his job to a remote area of the ship to smoke marijuana. When the claimant attempted to climb out of the ballast tank, he lost his footing and suffered injuries to his right ankle and hip. The ALJ found that this was a personal frolic which served no purpose related to his employment and was sufficient to sever the employment nexus, and it was illegal. Thus, the Section 20(a) presumption was rebutted by circumstantial evidence, and the presumption fell out of the case. The ALJ found, on the record as a whole, that the claimant's version of the incident was not persuasive and that the claimant did not fulfill his burden of proof. The Board upheld the ALJ's denial of benefits. *Compton*, 33 BRBS 174.

While so-called "company doctors" have historically been cast in a negative light, "plaintiff's doctors" who see claimants on referral from their attorneys can cast just as big a shadow on a case, especially in terms of the Section 20(a) presumption. All that is needed for the Section 20(a) presumption are and injury and the magic words from a physician reporting the possibility that the injury is work-related.

The Board affirmed the ALJ's finding that the employer failed to rebut presumption of causation where, despite the contention that medical test results suggested that the claimant's back injury resulted from fights and other active conduct subsequent to work-related accident and two doctors opined against causation, a finding of causation was supported by the claimant's subjective complaints and by opinions of his two doctors. *Sam v Loffland Bros. Co. & Travelers Inc. Co.*, 19 BRBS 228 (1987).

Nonetheless, the case law is also riddled with cases where employers failed to offer rebuttal evidence once the claimant had made out a prima facie case. By failing to do so, no matter how much of a stretch the case appears to be down the line, there is no "abuse"—the claimant rightfully seizes entitlement to the Section 20(a) presumption.

Where employer did not offer direct evidence to rebut the Section 20(a) presumption but only relied on the speculative testimony of a medical witness, the Board held that the ALJ erred in finding the presumption was rebutted. *Dixon v. John J. McMullen & Associates, Inc.*, 13 BRBS 707 (1981).

Cases arising under the Defense Base Act and its zone of special danger test have been especially problematic in abuse of the Section 20(a) presumption. While the Supreme Court recognized in *O'Leary* that "an employee might go so far from his employment and become so thoroughly disconnected from the service of his employer that it would be entirely unreasonable to say that injuries suffered by him arose out of and in the course of his employment," pretty much every case, other than a claimant whose husband accidentally died from autoerotic asphyxiation (*Gillespie v. General Electric Co.*, 21 BRBS 56 (1988), *aff'd mem.*, 873 F.2d 1433 (1st Cir. 1989), and a claimant who was injured psychologically by personal use of a cosmetic peel, *R.F. [Fear] v. CSA, Ltd.*, 43 BRBS 139 (2009), has survived Section 20(a) and has been deemed compensable.)

E. Additional Presumptions under Section 20, and Their Uses and Abuses

1. Section 20(b): Notice

The Section 20(b) presumption is related to the claimant's responsibilities to notify his employer of an injury and to file a timely claim for benefits under Sections 12 and 13 of the Act, respectively, as well as the employer's responsibility to report a work-related injury under Section 30 of the Act.

Section 20(b) provides, in the absence of substantial evidence to the contrary, that an employer has been given sufficient notice of an injury from the claimant pursuant to Section 12. Section 20(b) also provides, in the absence of substantial evidence to the contrary, that a claimant timely filed his claim for compensation pursuant to Section 13.

To overcome the Section 20(b) presumption, the employer must first establish that it complied with Section 30(a)'s reporting requirements. Under Section 30(a), the employer must file a "first report of injury" with the Department of Labor, usually through DOL Form LS-202, within 10 days from the date any injury causes a claimant to miss work or causes his death, or the date employer has knowledge of a "disease or infection of such injury." *Blanding v. Director, OWCP*, 186 F.3d 232, 33 BRBS 114(CRT) (2d Cir. 1999), *rev'g in pert. part* 32 BRBS 174 (1998). If the employer has been given notice or has knowledge of an injury but does not timely file the Section 30(a) report, the statute of limitations provided in Section 13(a) does not begin to run until such report has been filed. 33 U.S.C. §930(f); *see Nelson v. Stevens Shipping & Terminal Co.*, 25 BRBS 277 (1992); *Ryan v. Alaska Constructors, Inc.*, 24 BRBS 65 (1990).

Ultimately, the employer may overcome the Section 20(b) presumption with substantial evidence that it never gained knowledge or received notice of the injury for Section 30 purposes. *See Steed v. Container Stevedoring Co.*, 25 BRBS 210 (1991); *see also Stark v. Washington Star Co.*, 833 F.2d 1025, 20 BRBS 40(CRT) (D.C. Cir. 1987). Thus, the time for filing a claim would not be tolled by operation of Section 30(f), and the claimant's claim, if not timely filed, would be barred under Section 13(a). *Stark*, 833 F.2d 1025, 20 BRBS 40(CRT); *Wendler v. American Red Cross*, 23 BRBS 408 (1990) (McGranery, J., dissenting).

In *Bath Iron Works Corp. v. U.S. Dept. of Labor [Knight]*, 336 F.3d 51, 37 BRBS 67(CRT) (1st Cir. 2003), the First Circuit held that the Section 20(b) presumption applies to occupational disease cases.

A claimant's contact with an employer's agent can be sufficient to impute the employer's knowledge of a work injury. *Steed v. Container Stevedoring Co.*, 25 BRBS 210 (1991). Since the agent had knowledge of the work injury and the employer failed to file a Section 30(a) report, the statute of limitations was tolled pursuant to Section 30(f), and the employer failed to overcome the Section 20(b) presumption. (*Id.*).

2. Section 20(c): Intoxication

Section 20(c) provides a presumption that the claimant's injury was not occasioned solely by his intoxication. It is applied in conjunction with Section 3(c), which bars compensation for injuries due solely to intoxication.

Like the other presumptions in this chapter, it can only be overcome by substantial evidence to the contrary. Specifically, the employer must show that the claimant was intoxicated and the injury was caused solely by the intoxication. *Walker v. Universal Terminal & Stevedoring Corp.*, 7 BRBS 1019 (1978), *rev'd*, 645 F.2d 170, 13 BRBS 257 (3d Cir. 1981). Proof of intoxication alone cannot rebut the presumption. *Sheridon v. Petro-Drive, Inc.*, 18 BRBS 57 (1986). Even if drunkenness is the primary cause of injury, the employer must proffer evidence such that there is no other rational conclusion but that the claimant's intoxication was the sole cause of injury. (*Id*).

In a case where the employer presented expert opinion that the claimant's fall was due solely to his intoxication, hospital records, and site reports; and where claimant testified that he was too drunk to recall the event, the Board reversed the ALJ's finding and held that the employer had rebutted the Section 20(c) presumption. *G.S. [Schwirse] v. Marine Terminals Corp.*, 42 BRBS 100 (2008), *modified in part on recon.*, 43 BRBS 108 (2009).

3. Section 20(d): Willful Intent to Injure Self

Section 20(d) provides a presumption that the injury or death was not caused by the claimant's willful intent. Like Section 20(c), this provision is applied in conjunction with Section 3(c), which bars compensation for injuries due solely to the willful intention to kill oneself or another.

The most common use of the 20(d) presumption involves cases where the claimant has committed suicide.

In *Del Vecchio v. Bowers*, 296 U.S. 280 (1935), the seminal case on the Section 20(d) presumption (and essentially all Section 20 presumptions), the Supreme Court held that the presumption did not have the quality of affirmative evidence as to whether the claimant shot himself by accident or as the result of a suicide. After the employer has carried its burden of proof by offering testimony sufficient to justify a finding of suicide, the presumption falls out of the case. Even if the evidence is as consistent with an accident as it is with a suicide, the presumption does not require a finding for the claimant and cannot be used as evidence in favor of a claimant. The deputy commissioner held that the claimant, Bowers' widow, had failed to establish that Bowers' duties required the use of a weapon, and therefore there was no showing that his injury arose out of his employment. Since the finding was supported by substantial evidence, it should not have been set aside by the Court of Appeals.

If it is undisputed that the claimant committed suicide, then the Section 20(d) presumption is effectively rebutted and it falls out of the case. *Cooper v. Cooper Associates, Inc.*, 7 BRBS 853 (1978), *rev'd on other grounds sub nom. Director, OWCP v. Cooper Associates, Inc.*, 607 F.2d 1385, 10 BRBS 1058 (D.C. Cir. 1979). The issue then becomes whether the employee had a willful intention to do so or whether there was an irresistible suicidal impulse resulting from an employment-related condition. *Id.*; *see also Voris v. Texas Employers Ins. Ass'n*, 190 F.2d 929 (5th Cir. 1951).

The Section 20(d) presumption is rebutted and coverage is denied if there are two obvious possibilities of death—suicide and misadventure—none of which are covered under the Act, and the claimant has failed to establish a likely cause of death that would be covered under the Act. *Truczinskas v. Director, OWCP*, 699 F.3d 672, 46 BRBS 85(CRT) (1 st Cir. 2012).

F. Conclusion

Oftentimes, application of the Section 20 presumptions, specifically causation under Section 20(a), can defy logic and be a source of frustration for employers. Nonetheless, that is exactly how the drafters of the Act designed the presumptions to operate. Unless a groundswell of case law swings away from the liberal construction of the Act or legislation implements fundamental changes, relief for employers under Section 20 is a way's away.

References

Paul H. Felser, *Presumptions*, Ch. 24, The Longshore Textbook, Steven M. Birnbaum, Stephen C. Embry, Ralph R. Lorberbaum, eds., 5th ed., 2005.

Longshore Deskbook, U.S. Department of Labor, Benefits Review Board, *available at*: http://www.dol.gov/brb/References/Reference_works/lhca/lsdesk/main.htm.

Thomas A. Robinson, *The Role of Presumptions Within the Workers' Compensation Arena*, Lexis Nexis Legal Newsroom – Workers' Compensation Law, Jan. 21, 2014, *available at*: http://www.lexisnexis.com/legalnewsroom/workers-compensation/b/recent-cases-news-trends-developments/archive/2014/01/21/the-role-of-presumptions-within-the-workers-compensation-arena.aspx#sthash.1ev727Yx.dpuf.

19.2 The Claimant's Point of View

In 1927, Congress passed the "Longshoremen's and Harbor Workers' Compensation Act" (LHWCA) in order to "provide compensation for disability or death resulting from injury to employees in certain maritime employments, and for other purposes."[1]

Section 20 of the Act provides for presumptions in favor of finding the injured workers' claim compensable. It states:

> In any proceeding for the enforcement of a claim for compensation under this chapter it shall be presumed, in the absence of substantial evidence to the contrary –
> (a) That the claim comes within the provisions of this chapter.
> (b) That sufficient notice of such claim has been given.
> (c) That the injury was not occasioned solely by the intoxication of the injured employee.
> (d) That the injury was not occasioned by the willful intention of the injured employee to injure or kill himself or another.

However, before the presumption can be considered, the injured worker bears the initial burden of proof to prove a *prima facie* case by meeting the two foundational elements. First, the Claimant must prove that an injury was suffered or that "something unexpectedly [went] wrong within the human frame."[2] Rather than limiting claims to specific traumas or accidents, this definition is much broader in scope. Even so, the "mere existence of a physical impairment is plainly insufficient to shift the burden of proof to the employer."[3]

Second, the Claimant must at least allege "that conditions existed at work, or an accident occurred at work, that *could* have caused, aggravated, or accelerated the condition."[4] The Supreme court identified arising "out of" and "in the course of" employment as two separate factors. "Out of" employment addresses the cause of the injury or harm and "in the course of" refers "to the time, place, and circumstances of the injury."[5] A work-related aggravation or an aggravation of symptoms is sufficient for a claim—even where the underlying disease or condition is not work-related.[6] Once the injured worker proves these two threshold elements, the *prima facie* claim has been proven and the claim is then presumed compensable. While not often plainly stated, a primary part of the injured worker establishing a *prima facie* claim is the ALJ's findings on the credibility of both the injured worker and other testimony or documents that were offered as part of the claim. In contrast, when offering evidence to rebut the presumption of compensability, the employer is exempt from credibility considerations or the weighing of any evidence.

Even though courts like to claim that the injured worker benefits from a relatively easy or low burden of proof to establish the elements of a *prima facie* claim, the claimant nevertheless carries the burden of persuasion throughout the process.[7]

It is critical to be aware that courts have held that the "presumption applies only to the claim." Therefore, if an illness or condition is not specifically alleged, it shall not be considered as part of the claim and, in turn, be completely excluded from the presumption of compensability.[8] If this occurs, the injured worker must prove by substantial evidence that any other conditions are causally related to the qualified work-related injury. This happens more frequently when a "secondary" condition is claimed as the result of the initial injury and/or its treatment.

If an injured worker can establish a *prima facie* claim for compensability, inevitably the employer wants to offer rebuttal evidence to disprove the claim and avoid liability. This requires an employer to offer substantial evidence that there is no causal relationship between the alleged injury or condition and work. This determination is treated as a finding of law by the ALJ. Substantial evidence "means such relevant evidence as a reasonable mind might accept as adequate to support a conclusion."[9] Substantial evidence was recently defined by the Fifth Circuit as "that relevant evidence — more than a scintilla but less than a preponderance — that would cause a reasonable person to accept the fact finding."[10] As the ultimate finder of fact, the ALJ can make reasonable inferences from the evidence. A mere fancy, wisp, or a scrap of evidence is insufficient to rebut the presumption of compensability. However, not only positive evidence that the injury or accident did not happen or that there was no connection between the alleged injury and any work conditions can rebut a claim; the employer's negative evidence can also meet its burden of proof.

An employer is not required to disprove or rule out every other possible cause of the alleged injury or event. However, once the presumption applies, employers are required to prove that there is at least some "factual doubt" or that there is "substantial evidence to the contrary" to rebut the claim.[11] The production of substantial evidence sufficient to deny a claim includes not only submitting factual evidence, but includes introducing alternate causes that *could* support an inference of a fact.[12] It is important to note that the rebuttal evidence need only be adequate for a reasonable mind to find there is no causal relationship between the claimed harm and work. Unlike the injured worker's responsibility in establishing a *prima facie* claim, the credibility of the employers evidence does not play a role in determining if the claim was successfully rebutted.

Once an employer offers substantial evidence to dispute the claim, the presumption of compensability vanishes. As such, the burden of proof returns to the injured worker to establish, by a preponderance of the evidence, that there is a disability and it was causally related to work. If the court finds that the facts or inferences drawn from the evidence are equally balanced, the injured worker's claim must be denied.[13]

In the ideal world, the LHWCA provides a no-fault system for the prompt provision of monetary and medical benefits when an employee is injured at work. In exchange for giving up common law negligence defenses, the LHWCA provides a scheme that dramatically limits an employer's potential damages.

Historically, claims were determined with consideration of the underlying humanitarian purpose of the LHWCA to promptly provide benefits for work-related injuries. Simply put, if the injured worker could show that a harm or injury happened and that an accident or working conditions *could have* caused the harm, this was sufficient to establish that the condition was work-related and thus, compensable in accordance with the LHWCA. If the trial court found the injured workers and employers evidence to be equally balanced, the injured worker was given the benefit of the doubt and the claim would be found compensable. Thus, the "true doubt" rule was developed to benefit injured workers. Sadly, the longstanding concept that the LHWCA is based upon a public-spirited and humanitarian purpose is fast becoming a blur in the rearview mirror. Lip service is still given to the assertion that there is an easy or light burden of proof for a claimant to establish the two elements of a *prima facie* claim for compensability. In practice, this appears to be less and less the case.

In 1994, the Supreme Court dealt sounded the death blow to the decades old "true doubt" rule in *Greenwich Collieries*. After vigorously stirring together the legal concepts of the burden of proof, the burden of production, and the burden of persuasion, the Court held that the 1946 Administrative Procedure Act applied to the 1927 Longshore Act. In light of this, if the evidence between the parties is found to be equally balanced, the injured worker loses.[14] On paper, substantial evidence is defined as "such relevant evidence as a reasonable mind might accept as adequate to support a conclusion."[15] The present challenge is to predict what subjective views might be incorporated into the "reasonable mind" standard when deciding LHWCA claims. Ultimately, no matter how much courts have struggled to explain this standard, determining what a reasonable mind could think and rule what the outcome would be when applied to a particular fact situation is an attempt to project the outcome of a future factual analysis.

The courts are now suggesting, yea encouraging, that injured workers must first be subjected to a strict credibility evaluation before moving to the two-step *prima facie* claim analysis.[16] Too often, the simple days of finding that if an injury happened within the course and scope of employment, it was presumed as compensable are no more. If the claimant does not consistently remember each minute detail of how the injury happened and have a precise recollection of every medical encounter, the quick and easy conclusion is that the injured workers testimony is "inconsistent" and thereby worthless.[17]

Many well-heeled law firms provide promptly-paid defense services for LHWCA employers. This is not the same situation for injured LHWCA workers searching for counsel that are willing to undertake representation. The growing hostile nature of litigation of LHWCA claims, combined with the willingness of courts to drastically reduce hourly fee rates and then further limit the number of approved hours that are submitted based on claimed non-success on every possible issue, does not make beginning the type of work appealing. But, there is much to be said for the professional and personal gratification that comes from obtaining compensation benefits for injured workers.

It comes as no surprise that factual and legal issues abound when unsophisticated workers are caught between moneyed employers and the law. Unlike insurance companies, injured workers seldom have the ability to withstand years of being financially and medically stonewalled—even if there may be the ultimate vindication of an award of benefits. The frequent series of appeals also adds years until there is a final enforceable order. Unlike death or taxes, a LHWCA order for ongoing monetary benefits is never final. § 22 permits the modification of an order within a year of the last payment. Therefore, if there is an ongoing compensation order, the claim could end with the death of the injured worker. Further, awards of permanent and total disability can be accompanied by the trial court's all but engraved invitation to the employer urging it to never drop the pursuit of allegations of suitable alternative employment. This same invitation places a neverending obligation for the injured worker to document a potentially lifelong diligent search for suitable alternative post-injury work. In light of the growing use of computers and other technology in even the most basic of entry-level jobs, this demand is particularly onerous for the aging injured shipyard worker that has no marketable computer skills.

Since its 1927 inception, the courts' views on what is required to prove a LHWCA claim have changed. For many decades, the consistent focus was on the liberal construction of the Act in favor of injured workers as part of its inherent humanitarian purpose. If there were doubts about questions of fact, the "true doubt" rule gave the injured worker the legal benefit of the doubt. Therefore, if the evidence submitted by the claimant and the employer were of equal weight, the claim was ruled compensable.[18] In practice, if there was any room for doubt in the evidence offered in the battle between the lowly individual workers and the large and powerful employers, the injured worker prevailed.

In 1994, sixty-seven years after the LHWCA became law, the "true doubt" rule came to a screeching halt. In *Greenwich Collieries*, the Supreme Court decided that the 1946 Administrative Procedure Act (APA) prohibited the application of the true doubt rule in cases under the 1927 Longshore Act. Accordingly, the Court held that § 7 (c) of the APA requires that when the evidence offered by claimant and the employer is "evenly balanced, the benefits claimant must lose."[19]

Greenwich Collieries was an appeal of two Third Circuit cases. The first was a Black Lung case where the Circuit Court held that the true doubt rule was inconsistent with the Black Lung Benefits Act. The second case was a LHWCA claim where the Third Circuit held that the "true doubt" rule could not be applied because of the APA. Prior to *Greenwich Collieries* but after the 1946 APA, every appellate circuit with the exception of the Third Circuit had applied the "true doubt" rule in evaluating claims. Prior to the APA, the Third Circuit had explicitly noted that a Longshore claimant "was entitled to a liberal construction of the Act and that doubts would be resolved in [the claimant's] favor.[20]

In *Greenwich Collieries*, the Supreme Court determined that the claimant's evidentiary burden of proof is one and the same as the burden of persuasion. Claimants must now establish a *prima facie* claim by the preponderance of the evidence before the presumption of compensability is invoked. The Court acknowledged that a proving a case by the preponderance of the evidence was less than the clear and convincing standard.[21] Although proving the two elements of a *prima facie* claim was historically claimed to be a "light" burden of proof, it is clear that this is no longer the situation. It is painfully evident that after *Greenwich Collieries*, if the ALJ finds the evidence between the injured worker and employer to be equally balanced, the injured worker loses.

Now, for the practicable: gird your loins for the lions are coming.

A. If the ALJ Totally Discredits the Claimant's Testimony, then Objective Medical Testimony Based Upon the Claimant's Subjective Complaints Can Not Meet the *Prima Facie* Standard

On his first hitch as a sandblaster on a rig that was 150 miles offshore. *Meeks* was being transferred from the rig to a boat in a personnel basket when rough seas caused the basket to hit the boat causing the basket to flip over. *Meeks* claimed back, neck and dental injuries from this accident.[22] In finding that a work-related accident occurred, the ALJ relied upon the *Bis Salimis* supervisor's testimony where he stated,

> the seas were rough but the boat captain thought they could safely transfer [the workers] and the [sic] decided to go ahead. After they started, he heard the boat captain say on the radio that the first load had taken a spill and [the *Bis Salimis* workers] were spooked, so maybe they should wait. He asked if the four people in the spill were OK, and they said they were. They waited 15 or 20 minutes

> and the boat captain said it would be safe to start again. They started up again and after the second or third man made it across, [the supervisor] saw a large swell pick up the boat and drop it on the landing.[23]

In light of the supervisor's testimony, the ALJ managed to acknowledge that there was "little doubt" that something happened when the Claimant and other employees "were tossed about" in a personnel basket when being moved from a rig to a vessel.[24] Ultimately, the ALJ found that *Meeks* did not have a compensable work-related injury.

In the ALJ's initial opinion, he stated, *Meeks'* "demeanor during the hearing failed to create any confidence in the accuracy of his testimony or even his motivation to at least attempt to tell the truth."[25] In support of the ALJ's finding, the court specifically addressed *Meeks'* chronic underreporting of his income to the IRS. Three years of prior returns were amended to include additional income—but only after a third party suit was filed. It was also found out that *Meeks* had claimed his daughter's step-son as a dependent nephew.[26] Surveillance video directly contradicted *Meeks'* claimed activities both in his deposition and trial testimony.[27] In eviscerating *Meeks'* testimony, the ALJ also discredited all of the objective medical findings because they were entirely based on *Meeks'* subjective complaints.[28]

On the day of the event, *Meeks* told the *Bis Salimis* representative that his teeth had been jarred and he later reported that a loose tooth had fallen out. The ALJ denied any claim for the Claimant's alleged dental injuries based upon the trial court's inference that whatever had previously chipped the Claimant's upper teeth also likely knocked out his tooth. Reversing the ALJ, the BRB found that the Claimant did establish a *prima facie* claim for this part of his claim. The ALJ's inference about how the tooth was lost was irrational, not supported by the record, and was "based solely on speculation."[29] The Fifth Circuit affirmed the finding that a *prima facie* claim was established by the report of a loose tooth on the day of the accident and by the later missing tooth. As the Employer did not produce an alternate basis for anything else that could have caused the loose tooth, it did not rebut this issue. Accordingly, the ALJ's "alternate explanation was not supported by substantial evidence in the record." [30] Otherwise, the denial of compensation benefits was upheld.

B. Finding that an Injured Worker with a Low Mental Capacity Gave Inconsistent Testimony Justifies Denying the Claim

Goldsmith sustained a back injury March 1977. He argued that his diagnosed low mental capacity, psychological problems, and the hearing that was held six years after his injury explained any inconsistencies in his testimony.[31] After the BRB's cursory review, it promptly dismissed this argument. The BRB found that *Goldsmith* was not "incoherent or unstable." Thus, the BRB found that substantial evidence supported the ALJ's finding that the injured worker failed to establish that a work-related injury had occurred.[32] Relying on giving ALJ's broad discretion in weighing the evidence and making findings of fact and credibility, the Ninth Circuit affirmed the denial of the LHWCA claim.

C. The Presumption Applies to Determine the Last Responsible Employer/Carrier

Fabre, Jr. offered substantial evidence to support a *prima facie* claim for a work-related asbestosis claim.[33] After discussing how the presumption applies to last responsible employer cases, the Fifth Circuit affirmed the ALJ's finding that *Ramsey Scarlett* was the last responsible employer and therefore liable for injury-related medical benefits.

D. Proving a Physical Injury or that the Injured Worker was Within "The Zone Of Danger" is Not Required to Establish the *Prima Facie* Claim for a Compensable Psychological Injury

The Fourth Circuit explored the issue of whether the causing of and seeing the subsequent aftermath of a deadly accident could establish a compensable psychological work-related injury. *Jackson* operated the forklift that accidently struck and killed his co-worker. After the forklift was removed, the co-worker was found bleeding from the mouth; her leg was wrapped around the forklift's axel; and, her arm "was burned and pretty mangled, hanging off."[34] Before the first responders arrived, the dying co-worker remained in full view of the rapidly growing crowd of onlookers. Throughout this time, *Jackson* stood ten to fifteen feet away from her with clear view of her mortally injured body.[35]

Ceres Marine Terminals (CMT) unsuccessfully argued that the worker must have a physical injury or must be "within a zone of danger" of being placed in immediate risk of physical injury in order to recover for a work-related psychological injury.[36] In stark contrast, the LHWCA has no requirement that there must be any physical injury in order to have a compensable psychological injury.[37] *CMT's* defense medical examiner opined that *Jackson's* PTSD and Major Depression were causally related to the work accident and that *Jackson* required "aggressive psychiatric treatment and psychotherapy" to include psychotropic treatment.[38] The defense medical provider offered the cheery forecast that with his recommended aggressive treatment, the Claimant "might be able to return to work within six to twelve months.[39]

Unhappy with its own defense medical examiner's opinion, *CMT* understandably wanted another medical opinion and asked the OWCP to assign an independent medical examiner (IME) to examine *Jackson*.[40] Happily for *CMT*, the IME psychiatrist ruled out PTSD, opined that there was "significant evidence of malingering," and recommended that *Jackson* was able to return to longshore work.[41] The Fourth Circuit held that the LHWCA did not require an ALJ to give dispositive weight to an independent medical examiner's opinions or find that an IME opinion was binding on the parties.[42] The Fourth Circuit wryly noted that *CMT* had previously argued before the Fifth Circuit that an IME's opinion is not dispositive and thereby it could not be used to resolve any issues.[43] The Fourth Circuit agreed that the ALJ had properly weighed and evaluated all of the medical evidence and that substantial evidence in the record as a whole supported the finding of a compensable, work-related psychological injury.

E. Even Though it Happened at Work, a Cross-dresser's Death By Asphyxiation was Not a Compensable Injury

Truczinskas worked as a military trainer in Saudi Arabia. Given the particular circumstances of his employment, the "zone of danger" *analysis* did not apply to his claim. A co-worker found Truczinskas hanging from a cross beam with a noose around his neck. Pronouncing him dead, a doctor identified cause of death as "asphyxiation by hanging."[44] *Truczinskas'* widow filed a DBA claim for death benefits. The court found that the two "relatively easy" elements of a *prima facie* claim were met as *Truczinskas* sustained a physical harm and conditions existed that could have caused the harm. Accordingly, the presumption attached "[t]hat the injury was not occasioned by the willful intention of the injured employee to injure or kill himself or another.[45] But the ALJ also found that cross-dressing and an alleged affair could have caused an "internal conflict" that could explain the suicide. In the alternative, this evidence could support a finding of misadventure. This was sufficient to meet the substantial evidence standard that requires some evidence that *could* support a finding that the death was due to either of these non-covered causes. The widow offered multiple theories that the death was work-related, including: conservative Muslims were offended by the cross-dressing or alleged affair and killed him; the employer was complicit in a co-worker's cover up of claimed arms trading or selling military intelligence; or, that *Truczinskas* "offended the Saudis" by investigating a threat to Americans. However, there was no evidence to support any of these theories. As the presumption of compensability was rebutted and the widow could not offer convincing evidence of any causal relationship other than where the Claimant worked, the denial of the claim was affirmed.[46]

F. A 400 Pound 60-year-old with a History of Back Injuries Can Prove a *Prima Facie* Claim for Compensability After Being Assigned to Physically Strenuous Work Activity

Fields, weighing about 400 pounds, was sixty years old at the time of injury. He had reported a prior work-related back injury and the occasional passing back pains. *Fields* had been assigned to bending and kneeling down in order to sort, pick up, and move scrap metal. *Fields* related this activity to the increased back pain that escalated to where he had trouble walking even short distances.[47] The First Circuit upheld the BRB's finding that as a matter of law, *Bath Iron Works* did not rebut the presumption of compensability.[48] In denying *Fields'* claim, the ALJ heavily relied upon the defense medical examiner to support the finding that there was no causal relationship between *Fields'* work and his back condition. *Bath Iron Works'* choice of doctor testified that he had visited the Employer's work site several times to observe its workers and that it was his opinion that *Fields'* age-related osteoarthritis and morbid obesity caused his back pain. The employer's doctor did admit that a degenerative condition could become symptomatic with strenuous physical activity.[49] A work-related injury is sustained when the employee's work caused an underlying condition to become symptomatic or otherwise worsened its symptoms. Be that as it may, *Bath Iron Works'* doctor did not address whether the osteoarthritis would have become symptomatic without the work duties of kneeling on a concrete floor and bending over to sort the metal scrap.

G. Testimony of a Recently Demoted Employer that Had Threatened to Have a Work-Related Injury was Not Credible and the Claim Was Denied

Gindville alleged that an unwitnessed right knee injury occurred when he twisted his knee on a gangway. His son testified that he saw his father limping at work and had urged him to report the gangway event. A co-worker testified that he had heard *Gindville* report the injury to the Employer's safety director.[50] In contrast, the safety director's detailed testimony contradicted the *Gindville* and his two co-workers.[51] A week before the alleged gangway accident, the employer's cutbacks resulted in *Gindville's* demotion from his twenty-year long job as a ship boss back down to a regular gang boss. The employer's general manager testified that *Gindville* angrily responded to the demotion and "threatened the company by stating he would purposely get hurt." *Gindville* denied this.[52] *Gindville's* treating physician testified that he had come to him complaining of a recent work-related right knee injury. Unlike the detailed descriptions about his prior work-related injuries, this time *Gindville's* treating physician did not record any history of a work-related injury.[53] Based upon the inconsistencies between the testimony of *Gindville* and his two co-workers, combined with the lack of supporting history in the medical records, the ALJ ruled that the *Gindville's* evidence lacked credibility. The ALJ specifically found that because *Gindville* failed to prove a right knee injury had occurred in the course of employment, so there was no a *prima facie* claim, so no compensation or medical benefits were due.[54] Accordingly, the ALJ denied benefits.[55] The Third Circuit agreed that the ALJ had properly evaluated and discredited credibility of *Gindville's* testimony in finding that because of an absence of credible evidence, the presumption was not invoked.[56]

H. Claimant With a 0.25 BAC that Had Actively Participated in Beer-Thirty from Before Work Until the End of the Day Did Not Prove that the Cement Ledge Whereupon He Landed Caused His Injury

Schwirse worked as an A-registered longshoreman for Marine Terminals Corporation (MTC). Similar to *Wheatley*, *Schwirse* elected to relieve himself outside at work rather than going to the designated facility. This time, however, the weather was not a factor.[57] *Schwirse* drank two beers prior to going to work and three more beers before Noon. After lunch, he drank four to five more beers along with over a half pint of whiskey.[58] At the end of the day, *Schwirse* understandably felt the urge to relieve himself and he availed himself of a nearby bull rail at a dock. Falling over the rail, *Schwirse* landed about six feet below on a concrete and steel ledge.[59] He was taken to a local hospital and treated for a severe right temple laceration. He was also diagnosed with cannabis ingestion and, with a 0.25 blood alcohol level, acute alcohol intoxication.[60] At the hearing, *Schwirse* testified that he had no memory of the event but he asserted that two co-workers had told him that he tripped over an orange warning cone.[61] In an earlier deposition, *Schwirse* testified that neither of the two co-workers saw what happened but that he specifically recalled seeing and tripping over the orange traffic cone located at the edge of the bull rail. The ALJ properly found that *Schwirse* met the first element to invoke the presumption of compensability in that he unquestionably sustained an injury while at work.[62] Then, finding that "there was no direct proof that intoxication (and not something else) caused him to fall," the ALJ awarded benefits.[63]

MTC appealed and the BRB reversed the ALJ's finding that it had rebutted the presumption that the sole cause of the accident was intoxication. Finding that there were no obstructions near the rail and that two doctors testified that the sole cause of the fall was the objectively measured intoxication, the BRB found that MTC had successfully rebutted the § 20 (c) presumption. In affirming the denial of benefits, the Ninth Circuit noted that the sole legal cause of the injury was *Schwirse's* intoxication. "Legal cause" is defined as the factual causal connection and can include active physical forces as well as pre-existing passive conditions.[64] On remand, the ALJ dismissed *Schwirse's* argument that the stationary concrete slab caused the injury.

I. If You Do Not Claim It, the Court Shall Not Award It

The Fifth Circuit's decision in *Amerada Hess* makes the injury allegations in a claim critical to achieving success. *Dover* injured his back and groin in a work-related accident on July 22, 1997. He continued working at light duty until May 1998. After back surgery, *Dover* reached maximum medical improvement in March 2001. In March 2005, *Amerada Hess* reduced the injured worker's compensation benefits and refused to pay for various medical treatments.[65]

Dover attributed his substantial post-injury weight gain to the steroids that were administered as part of the treatment for his compensable back injury. *Dover* further testified that his weight gain was the cause of his four heart attacks. Interestingly, there were no medical records or testimony introduced to support the claimed four heart attacks—including the particular heart attack that *Dover* testified happened in his doctor's office.[66] *Dover's* medical records did confirm treatment depression and an increased blood pressure.[67] Thus, based upon a finding of credible testimony by *Dover* and his wife—and despite the dearth of medical evidence—the ALJ found that *Dover* had presented substantial evidence to invoke the presumption of compensability. The ALJ further ruled that *Amerada Hess* had presented no evidence to rebut *Dover's* self-diagnosed injury-related heart condition and the related four heart attacks. Accordingly, *Dover's* treatment for his heart condition was found as a reasonable and necessary expense related to his compensable back injury.[68]

Dover admitted that he had not looked for any other employment since his injury. In addressing the extent of the injury-related disability, the ALJ determined that even if *Dover* might be able to work part-time, the trial court nevertheless found that Dover was entitled to permanent and total disability benefits. This was based upon the finding that *Amerada Hess* did not demonstrate that it was "more likely than not" that *Dover* "could reasonably perform alternative work."[69] The BRB affirmed the award of permanent and total disability based upon the work-related back injury and the subsequent heart condition.[70] *Amerada Hess* appealed these decisions.

The Fifth Circuit noted that in order to "invoke the presumption, a claimant must make a *prima facie* showing that (1) he suffered a harm and (2) a condition of the workplace "could have caused, aggravated, or accelerated the harm."[71] The undisputed claim for the work-related back and groin injury was sufficient to invoke the presumption of compensability. However, the Fifth Circuit pointedly noted that as the claim only alleged a work-related back and groin injury, the ALJ and the BRB erred in applying the presumption to the subsequently claimed heart condition.[72] Therefore, *Dover's* heart condition is not compensable without a finding that substantial evidence proves that it was the natural or unavoidable result from the back injury treatment.[73] The Fifth Circuit further criticized the total dependence upon lay testimony about *Dover's* alleged heart condition and the self-identified four heart attacks, stating, "[i]t appears to us that such a finding would benefit from, if not require, support of medical experts."[74] Lacking medical testimony or records to support *Dover's* claim about his heart condition, the ALJ had relied on *Dover's* unsupported claims that a doctor told him "steroids will do that to you" and another doctor told him "he might drop dead."[75]

The Fifth Circuit held that the LHWCA does not support the presumption that any and all medical conditions that happen after a work-related injury were caused by the work-related injury. Therefore, there is nothing requiring a finding that all secondary injuries or conditions are covered merely because the injured worker asserts that a subsequent harm *"could have"* been related to the actual compensable injury.[76] To the contrary, the claimant must present substantial evidence that the post-injury secondary condition was the natural or unavoidable result of the initial covered injury.[77]

J. Every Medical Development that Happens After an Injury is Not Automatically Compensable

Vickers worked as a logistics coordinator for SEI in Iraq. On August 14, 2004, a tank fuel adapter explosion severely injured his left arm. Returning to Texas, *Vickers* had orthopedic surgery and was released to full duty in December 2004, and he returned to work in Iraq in January 2005. *Vickers* later had a four or five-day gastrointestinal illness. He returned to Texas in August 2005, for left carpal tunnel release surgery. In November and December 2005, *Vickers* began having numbness, stinging, tingling and pain in his right arm and shoulder, both legs, and in his neck. He was referred to a neurophysiologist and diagnosed with an autoimmune disorder known as chronic inflammatory demyelinating polyneuropathy ("CIDP").[78] On December 21, 2006, he filed a DBA claim seeking permanent and total disability for his left arm injury along with "injuries to other parts of [his] body, [and] other related problems associated with [his] injury and working conditions in Iraq."[79] The ALJ awarded temporary and total disability, finding that *Vickers* met the presumption for injury to his arm and the CIDP based upon medical testimony that the surgeries for his work-related arm injury and the gastritis could have precipitated the CIDP.[80] The ALJ found that the defense medical examiner's opinion—supported by his review of the SEI selected documents—formed the basis of his opinion that the CIDP was not caused by the arm injury. But, the defense doctor did not address whether the CIDP could have been caused by the surgeries and gastritis.[81] After the BRB affirmed the ALJ's finding of compensability, SEI sought a reconsideration, arguing that *Amerada Hess* which had been decided after the BRB's decision now required the BRB to reverse the ALJ's decision.[82] Distinguishing *Vickers* from *Amerada Hess*, the BRB found that *Vickers'* claim included the "sequelae of the arm injury," and denied the rehearing motion.[83]

The Employer appealed to the Fifth Circuit, arguing four issues: 1) it was error to not apply the *Amerada Hess* standard as the CIDP was a secondary condition that was not subject to the presumption; 2) the added catch-all phrase attempting to add other body parts or related problems to the specifically identified injury was insufficient to meet the first element of the presumption of compensability; 3) *Vickers* did not establish a *prima facie* claim as the medical testimony did not pinpoint the cause of the gastritis and CIDP; and, 4) the expert testimony that the CIDP was not related to the Iraq working conditions rebutted the presumption of compensability.[84] The Employer successfully argued that merely including boilerplate that any other body part or related problems that developed could be associated with the injury and working conditions is insufficient to state a compensable claim. Thus, as the claim itself fails, so does the invoking of the presumption.

The Fifth Circuit applied *Amerada Hess*, reversed the BRB, and vacated the ALJ's temporary and total disability award.[85] In order for the presumption to apply, there must be at least an allegation that an injury arose in the scope and course of employment. In short, if a specific claim was not made, then there is nothing that can be the subject of the presumption of compensability.[86] A "vague" claim for a non-specific injury or illness is insufficient to invoke the presumption. Thus, as *Vickers'* claim did not include gastritis or CIDP, neither of these conditions can be presumed to be a work-related harm or related to the course and scope of employment. Demonstrating that a subsequent harm *could* have come from the covered injury does not make it so. Instead, the injured worker must meet the higher substantial evidence standard and prove that the secondary condition naturally or unavoidably resulted from the initial covered injury.[87] Therefore, the Fifth Circuit directed that upon remand, the ALJ must determine whether *Vickers* proved by substantial evidence that the gastritis and CIDP were the natural progression or foreseeable outcome of the left arm injury.[88]

K. Working for Another Employer a Mere Nine Days After an ACL Tear Can Leave it as the Responsible Employer

Amezcua sustained a ACL tear while working for Yusen Terminals on January 9, 2009. He worked for nine more days and was working for SSA on January 22, 2009. The Claimant's treating physician opined that without a second trauma, nine days of continued working did not aggravate the first injury. In contrast, after examining the Claimant several times, the "consulting physician" offered a conflicting opinion that all-post injury weight-bearing activity aggravated the initial injury thereby causing a permanent worsening of the Claimant's disability. Explaining why he gave the non-treating physician's opinions more weight, the ALJ evaluated both doctors examination history, evaluation methods, prior workers' compensation testimony, and professional qualifications. The Ninth Circuit affirmed SSA's liability for the claim under the last responsible employer rule.[89]

L. Working Conditions that Could Cause Asbestosis Supported the Finding that as a Matter of Law the Death Was Work-Related

Wood worked for *Huntington Ingalls* (HII) for seven years and was exposed to airborne asbestos fibers. *HII* stipulated that there were working conditions that could have caused the asbestosis, and the autopsy physician indicated that *Wood* died of bronchopneumonia and that the asbestosis reduced the likelihood of a favorable response to treatment for the bronchopneumonia. The ALJ found that the presumption of compensability was invoked and that *HII* did not rebut it. Therefore, the ALJ found that as a matter of law, *Wood* died from asbestosis.

HII relied on two pathologists and *Wood's* death certificate as rebuttal evidence that he died of sepsis as a consequence of a urinary infection. One pathologist indicated that there was no evidence that asbestosis caused or contributed to *Wood's* death. The other pathologist noted that there was interstitial fibrosis that was "arguably" related to asbestos exposure but that nothing supported an asbestosis diagnosis and *Wood* died of sepsis.[90] The ALJ ruled that no conclusions could be drawn from the death certificate as the doctor that signed it was unaware of the prior asbestosis diagnosis. The two pathologists' opinions were not substantial countervailing evidence because both had failed to diagnose asbestosis. Further, the pathologist that noted the fibrosis failed to address whether it combined with or accelerated the bronchopneumonia that was confirmed with the autopsy.[91]

HII argued that the ALJ misapplied the presumption as the trial court required it to rule out the causal connection between the work exposure and *Wood's* death instead of finding that it offered substantial evidence that the lack of causal connection rebutted the presumption of compensability.[92] Based upon the facts of this case, the BRB affirmed that the ALJ had rationally found that the absence of including asbestosis on the death certification and in medical records was "not evidence of [an] absence of a connection between decedent's asbestosis and death."[93] The BRB found that the ALJ had applied the proper legal standing and properly found that *HII's* burden of proof was to "produce substantial countervailing evidence [to] rebut the presumption that [decedent's] death was caused, at least in part, by his employment."[94]

M. Medical Evidence of a Stroke Occurring After a Legitimate Personnel Change Does Not Meet the Causal Relationship Element

Raiford worked the first shift in *Huntington Ingalls'* paint department's sign shop for nearly thirty years. When *HII* closed that shop, he was reassigned to painting various ships located in the shipyard. On January 30, 2009, *Raiford* left work and went to the hospital thinking that he was having an anxiety attack. Unfortunately, he was diagnosed as already having a stroke and was treated for stroke-related issues of depression and anxiety. Before his death, *Raiford* testified that the shift change caused him problems because he did not drive, the bus was unavailable for the second shift, and he had to hire someone to drive him home after work. He also testified that the shift change affected his sleep and he could not concentrate on his work. *Raiford* believed that the cause of his disability was the change from the first to the second shift at work. The ALJ found that *Raiford* established the first element providing harm from the stroke. However, no matter the result, legitimate personnel actions are not subject to the § 20(a) presumption.

N. Same Employer Expert, Same Opinions, Different Outcomes

Jackson last worked as a longshoreman in April 1980 at the Erato Street Wharf for *New Orleans Stevedoring* (NOS) in New Orleans, Louisiana. Prior to this, he had worked on the river for twenty to thirty years as a longshoreman in a noisy environment.[95] The Claimant explained that due to the loud noise at work, in order to be heard he would have to "holler" to co-workers that were just four or five feet away.[96] *Jackson's* choice of audiologist testified that he had a 20% binaural noise induced hearing loss. Dr. Seidemann was well-known for testifying on the employers' behalf. Over the decades, Dr. Seidemann has performed several noise sampling surveys of longshore work in the New Orleans area. Using his own 1991, 1992, and three 2004 noise studies, Dr. Seidemann did not believe that *Jackson's* occupational noise exposure had anything to do with his documented hearing loss. It was Dr. Seidemann's opinion that *Jackson's* work as a hold-man and derrick-man were some of the quieter jobs in the longshore industry.

The ALJ found that the NOS's expert's testimony was insufficient to rebut the presumption of compensability. Dr. Seidemann's opinions were based on his own noise surveys. None of the surveys were performed where *Jackson* worked and the one survey that was performed in the same city was done twenty-four years after Jackson's last noise exposure. Even Dr. Seidemann had to concede that none of his surveys "would have involved the same type of equipment, configuration of machinery, men and material or atmospheric condition as New Orleans Stevedores."[97] The ALJ awarded compensation benefits.

Now, for a diametrically opposite outcome again based on Dr. Seidemann's testimony. In a hearing loss claim against *Ceres Gulf, Plaisance* made a claim for occupational hearing loss after he had worked more than forty years as a longshoreman.[98] *Plaisance* retired from longshore work in 1987, and it appears that his claim is based upon an April 2005, audiogram.[99] *Plaisance* was a "hook-on man" and worked inside barges, ro-ro ships, containers, and small ships.[100] As fate would have it, the same audiologist from *Jackson* also testified for *Plaisance*. Not surprisingly, Dr. Seidemann again testified for the employer. Here, Dr. Seidemann testified that he "believes with a reasonable degree of audiological certainty that [the] Claimant has no hearing loss due to his work as a longshoreman."[101] The ALJ specifically noted that "Dr. Seidemann has never seen a hearing loss case he believed to be caused by exposure in a longshore workplace."[102] Dr. Seidemann also testified that *Plaisance*, who was eighty years old at the time of testing, had better hearing than what would be expected for an eighty-year old with normal age-based hearing loss.[103] Curiously, the ALJ never questioned the credibility of a defense medical audiologist that dismissed The National Institute for Occupational Safety and Health as "a bunch of ivory-tower scientists" and has never seen a work-related hearing loss because of longshore work.[104]

The ALJ concluded that "the record establishes that it is more likely than not that Claimant was exposed to noise that could have caused hearing loss in some workers ...."[105] The ALJ first found it more probative that *Plaisance's* hearing continued to worsen after he left the work exposure. To the ALJ, the most compelling part of the record was Dr. Seidemann's conclusion that *Plaisance's* hearing was better than other eighty year olds.[106] Thus, *Plaisance's* hearing loss claim was denied. In a curious footnote, the ALJ commended that if he had found that *Plaisance* had established his *prima facie* claim, he would have found that *Ceres Gulf* did not rebut it. Continuing to play 'what if,' the ALJ stated that he would have ordered digital hearing aids as reasonable, necessary, and appropriate medical treatment.[107] The BRB twice overruled the ALJ and held *Ceres Gulf* responsible for the claim.

Ceres Gulf appealed to the Fifth Circuit. In re-weighing the evidence, the Fifth Circuit found that Dr. Seidemann's testimony that relied on his own 1992 noise survey performed for this same employer provided "comprehensive, direct and unequivocal" relevant evidence to negate *Plaisance's* claim that forty-years of work conditions where he was constantly exposed to loud noise could have caused, aggravated, or accelerated his hearing loss.[108] This time, it did not matter that Dr. Seidemann's work for *Ceres Gulf* was years after *Plaisance's* last noise exposure. It did not matter that his noise survey was done in a different location and did not test *Plaisance's* work duties. The ALJ specifically noted that the audiologist did not have the raw data for his own 1992 noise survey thereby he was without the tangible results of his own test. Not to be daunted, Dr. Seidemann still claimed to have tested five unidentified work activities in this 1992 survey. But without his own data, Dr. Seidemann did not know what the 1992 survey really represented. He testified that his survey did not include testing over an eight-hour work day and he did not know how long or what sounds were actually measured.[109] Notably, Dr. Seidemann admitted that each survey of sound levels is limited to its own set of facts and can cannot automatically be accepted as applicable to what might have happened at another time with other equipment.[110] Thus, despite the ALJ's long litany of Dr. Seidemann's testimony's weaknesses at best, and failures at worst, the Fifth Circuit found this testimony "thoroughly grounded in the facts of the case...."[111] Accordingly, it affirmed the initial ALJ order denying compensation benefits.

It is evident that two trial court judges can take strikingly similar testimony from the same defense expert witness and arrive at totally different outcomes. In finding whether an employer offered substantial evidence to rebut the presumption of compensability, there are no hard and fast rules for determining what evidence might meet the substantial evidence standard. It appears that like beauty and pornography, the individual judges know it when they see it.

In the end, the question of whether the injured worker can invoke the presumption of compensability depends on what evidence is found sufficient to persuade a reasonable mind of a coverage and then overcome, by a preponderance of the evidence, all that an employer offers to the contrary.

Endnotes

1. Mar. 4, 1927, ch. 509, § 20, 44 Stat. 1436; The name was changed to the Longshore and Harbor Workers' Compensation Act in 1984 and the name has never been the Longshore Employer's Protection Act.

2. *See, e.g., Wheatley v. Adler*, 407 F.2d 307, 313 (D.C. Cir. 1968).

3. *U. S. Indus. Fed. Sheet Metal Inc., v. Director*, 455 U.S. 608, 615 (1982).

4. *Conoco, Inc. v. Director, OWCP*, 194 F.3d 684, 687 (5th Cir. 1999).

5. *U.S. Indus*. 455 U.S. at 615 (1982) (waking up in bed due to pain is not a work-related injury).

6. *Bath Iron Works Corp. v. Fields*, 599 F.3d 47, 55-56 (1st Cir. 2010).

7. *Director, OWCP v. Greenwich Collieries*, 512 U.S. 267, 208-281 (1994); *Ramsay Scarlett & Co. v, Director, OWCP*, 806 F.3d 327, 331 (5th Cir. 2015).

8. *Amerada Hess Corp. v. Director, OWCP*, 543 F.3d 755, 758-760 (5th Cir. 2008).

9. *Consolidated Edison Co. v. National Labor Relations Board*, 305 U.S. 197, 229 (1938) (citations omitted).

10. *Ramsay Scarlett & Co. v. Director, OWCP*, 806 F.3d 327, 330 (5th Cir. 2015) (citations omitted).

11. *Ramsay Scarlett*, 806 F.3d at 332; *citing, Ceres Gulf, Inc. v. Director, OWCP [Plaisance]*, 683 F. 3d 225, 231 (5th Cir. 2012); *Ortco Contractors, Inc. v. Charpentier*, 332 F.3d 283, 287 (5th Cir.2003).

12. *Truczinskas v. Director, OWCP*, 699 F.3d 672 (1st Cir. 2012).

13. *Greenwich Collieries*, 512 U.S. at 281.

14. *Id.*

15. *Consolidated Edison Co. v. National Labor Relations Board*, 305 U.S. 197, 229 (1938) (citations omitted).

16. *Ramsay Scarlett*, 806 F.3d at 331 (upheld ALJ's finding that the claimant's *prima facie* case was based in part on credibility determinations).

17. *Goldsmith v. Director, OWCP*, 838 F.2d 1079 (9th Cir. 1988).

18. *Greenwich Collieries*, 512 U.S at 281.

19. *Id.*

20. *Southern S. S. Co. v. Norton*, 101 F. 2d 825, 827 (3rd Cir. 1939).

21. *Greenwich Collieries*, 512 U.S. at 277 (citation omitted).

22. *Meeks v. Bis Salimis*, 2010-LHC 01263, slip op. at 3, 5 (ALJ Sept. 19, 2011).

23. *Meeks*, slip op. at 10.

24. *Bis Salimis*, slip op. at 11; *Meeks* slip op. at 5 (Meeks testified that when he was being transferred from the rig to a boat, the basket collided with the boat and flipped).

25. *Meeks*, slip op. at 18.

26. *Id.* at 9.

27. *Id.* at 10.

28. *Id.* at 18-19.

29. *Bis Salimis*, slip op. at 23.

30. *Id.* at 24.

31. *Goldsmith*, 838 F.2d 1079.

32. *Id.* at 1081.

33. *Ramsey Scarlett*, 806 F.3d 327.

34. *Ceres Marine Terminals v. Jackson, OWCP [Jackson]*, No. 15-1041, slip op. at 5, __ F.3d __ (4th Cir. 2017) (amended unpub. Mar. 24, 2016, opinion).

35. *Id.*

36. *Id.* at 9.

37. *Id.* at 15-16.

38. *Id.* at 7.

39. *Id.*

40. § 7(e).

41. *Jackson*, slip op. at 8.

42. *Id.* at 19-20.

43. *Id.* at 20.

44. *Truczinskas*, 699 F.3d at 673.

45. § 20(d).

46. *Truczinskas*, 699 F.3d at 680-682.

47. *Bath Iron*, 599 F.3d 47 at 50-51.

48. *Fields v. Bath Iron Works*, No. 06-0323, slip op. at 4 (BRB Dec. 14, 2006).

49. *Fields*, 559 F.3d at 53-54.

50. *Gindville*, slip at 3.

51. *Id.* at 4.

52. *Id.* at 3.

53. *Id.* at 4.

54. *Gindville v. Director, OWCP*, No. 12-1912, slip at 2 (3rd Cir. April 15, 2013).

55. *Id.* at 5.

56. *Id.* at 7.

57. *Wheatley*, 407 F.2d at 309 (urinating outside in the cold weather could have led to his heart attack).

58. *Schwirse v. Director, OWCP*, 736 F.3d 1165, 1168. (9th Cir. 2013).

59. *Id.* at 1168.

60. www.ghsa.org (all states define driving with a blood alcohol concentration at or above 0.08 percent as a crime).

61. *Schwirse*, 736 F.3d at 1168.

62. *Id.*

63. *Id.*

64. *Id.* at 1167.

65. *Amerada Hess*, 543 F.3d at 758.

66. *Id.*

67. *Id.* at 758-759.

68. *Id.* at 758-760.

69. *Amerada Hess*, 573 F.3d at 759, 764 (as it was not clear whether the ALJ's finding of the compensable heart condition effected the finding of permanent and total disability, this finding was vacated and remanded).

70. *Id.* at 759.

71. *Id.* at 761, *citing, Conoco*, 194 F.3d at 687.

72. *Id.* at 761-762 (the presumption cannot apply to a claim that was not made).

73. *Id.* at 762.

74. *Id.*

75. *Id.* (internal quotes omitted).

76. *Id.* at 763 (emphasis in original).

77. *Id.* at 763-764.

78. *Ins. Co. of Pa.. v. OWCP, [Vickers]*, 713 F. 3d 779, 787, n.1 (5th Cir. 2013) (CIDP is a rare, acquired, immune-mediated inflammatory disorder of the peripheral nervous system.).

79. *Id.* at 781 (internal quotes omitted).

80. *Id.*

81. *Id.* at 781-782.

82. *Amerada Hess*, 543 F.3d 755.

83. *Vickers*, 713 F. 3d at 782.

84. *Id.*

85. *Id.* at 786.

86. *Id.* at 785, citing, *U S. Indus.*, 445 U.S. at 614.

87. *Vickers*, 713 F.3d at 786.

88. An ALJ Order approving $410,000 to fund future periodic payments for Vickers' widow was approved in July 2013. (www.oalj.dol.gov, *Mary E. Vickers, widow v. SEI, Inc.*, 2007-LDC-00080).

89. *SSA Terminals LLC v. Amezuca*, 50 BRBS 1 (CRT) (UPD) (9th Cir. 2016).

90. *Wood v. Huntington Ingalls Industries, Inc.*, 49 BRBS 99, 101 (UPD) (2015).

91. *Wood, Id.* at 101-102.

92. *Wood, Id.* at 102.

93. *Id.*

94. *Id.*

95. *E. J.[Jackson] v. New Orleans Stevedoring Co.*, 42 BRBS 346 (ALJ) (2007).

96. *Id.* at 348, 353-354.

97. *Id.* at 355.

98. *Plaisance v. Ceres Gulf, Inc.*, 2007-LHC-01706 (ALJ 2008) (initial ALJ order); *Ceres Gulf, Inc. v. Director, OWCP [Plaisance]*, 683 F.3d 225 (5th Cir. 2012).

99. *Plaisance*, slip op. at 6-7, 9.

100. *Id.* at 11 (ro-ro refers to a roll on/roll off ship that can easily load wheeled cargo).

101. *Id.* at 14.

102. *Id.* at 14, 22.

103. *Id.* at 10.

104. *Id.* at 22 (The National Institute for Occupational Safety and Health (NOISH) is part of the Centers for Disease Control and Prevention (CDC).

105. *Id.* at 24.

106. *Id.* at 18, 24.

107. *Id.* at 24.

108. *Ceres Gulf*, 683 F.3d at 232.

109. *Plaisance*, slip op. at 15.

110. *Id.*

111. *Ceres Gulf*, 683 F.3d at 232.

Part V
Trial at the OALJ

Chapter 20

Practice before the Office of Administrative Law Judges

Hon. Stephen R. Henley, Chief Administrative Law Judge, U.S. Department of Labor[1]

Synopsis

20.1 Introduction: General Background Information

The Office of Administrative Law Judges ("OALJ") typically adjudicates approximately 2,800 Longshore and Harbor Workers' Compensation Act ("LHWCA") cases annually. These include "extension act" claims which engraft substantive longshore workers' compensation law, namely: the Defense Base Act, 42 U.S.C. § 1651 *et seq.*; the Outer Continental Shelf Lands Act, 43 U.S.C. § 1331 *et seq.*; the Non-Appropriated Fund Instrumentalities Act, 5 U.S.C. § 8171 *et seq.*; the War Hazards Compensation Act, 42 U.S.C. § 1701 *et seq.*; and the District of Columbia Workers' Compensation Act of 1928, 36 D.C. Code § 501 *et seq.* (injuries to employees in the District of Columbia occurring prior to July 26, 1982).

The OALJ has district offices in Boston, Massachusetts; Cherry Hill, New Jersey; Cincinnati, Ohio; Covington, Louisiana; Newport News, Virginia; Pittsburgh, Pennsylvania; and San Francisco, California. The OALJ maintains courtrooms at its national and district offices, and in Long Beach, California; New York, New York; and New London, Connecticut. Judges also conduct hearings in borrowed courtroom space throughout the United States.

20.2 Implementing Authority and Creation of the Office of Administrative Law Judges

As provided in the 1972 amendments to the LHWCA, the legal adjudication of LHWCA claims begins at the OALJ. Section 19(d) of the LHWCA, 33 U.S.C. § 919(d), gives the OALJ this authority and incorporates the formal hearing procedures of the Administrative Procedure Act ("APA"). To protect ALJs' independence, Congress enacted safeguards enumerated in the APA. These include insulating ALJs from direct Congressional influence. While ALJs have focused and limited authority, they are independent. To ensure decisional independence, ALJs can only be removed for "good cause."

Before 1972, Longshore cases commenced at the office of the district director (then called a deputy commissioner) and could be appealed to federal district court, and then to a federal courts of appeals. The amendments replaced the federal district court level of the claims process with the creation of the OALJ as the first level of adjudication, and the Benefits Review Board ("the Board") as the first level of appellate review.

While the OALJ's adjudicatory functions were carved from the district directors' former administrative and adjudicatory functions, as a practical matter, the OALJ hearing process, with some modification, more closely resembles the formal judicial hearing process previously used by the federal district courts. Section 19(d) provides that "hearing[s] shall be conducted by a[n] administrative law judge.... All powers, duties, and responsibilities vested by this chapter, on October 27, 1972, in the deputy commissioners with respect to such hearings shall be vested in such administrative law judges." 33 U.S.C. § 919(d). *See Shell v. Teledyn*

Movible Offshore, Inc., 14 B.R.B.S. 585, 589 (1981), *aff'd* 694 F.2d 720 (5th Cir. 1982) (table).

In *Yates v. Armco Steel Corp.*, 10 B.L.R. 1-132, 1-134 (1987), the Board stated that the deputy commissioner is a nonjudicial officer, and that the bifurcation of administrative and adjudicative functions reflected in Section 19(d) effects a "neatly legislated procedural separation of informal settlement conferences and formal adjudications." *Yates*, 10 B.L.R. 1-132 at 1-135, citing *Shell*, 14 B.R.B.S. at 589. The Board observed that the legislation reflected legislative concerns that the administrative and adjudicative functions had been too closely tied together prior to the 1972 amendments. This legislative concern is reflected in the 1972 House Report which accompanied the 1972 amendments:

> HR. 12006 amends section 19(d) of the [Longshore] Act to make clear that all hearings under this Act are to be conducted in conformity with the Administrative Procedure Act (5 USC 554) by hearing examiners [now called administrative law judges] qualified under the Act. It is the committee's belief that the administration of the Longshoremen's and Harbor Workers' Compensation Act has suffered by virtue of the failure to keep separate the functions of administering the program and sitting in judgment on the hearings.

House Report No. 82-1441, 1972 *U.S. Code Cong. & Adm. News* 4708.

In *Director, OWCP v. Newport News Shipbuilding & Dry Dock Co.*, 514 U.S. 122, 115 S.Ct. 1278 (1995), the Supreme Court spoke in terms of the Director as having a "duty of uniform administration and enforcement" as opposed to the adjudicatory process that initially takes place at the OALJ. In *Ingalls Shipbuilding, Inc. v. Director, OWCP (Yates)*, 519 U.S. 248, 117 S.Ct. 796 (1997), and *Roberts v. Sea-Land Services, Inc.*, __ U.S. __, 132 S.Ct. 1350, 1355 (2012), the Court again referred to the OALJ as the beginning of the adjudicatory process.

20.3 The Claim Process

Longshore and related claims begin at the Director's regional Offices of Workers' Compensation Programs (district directors' offices). The district director provides the setting for an informal conference and informal resolution of a claim. Neither sworn testimony nor stenographic reporting takes place at that level. An aggrieved party may request that the claim be referred to the Office of the Chief Administrative Law Judge for a *de novo* proceeding. 20 C.F.R. §§ 702.331, 702.332.

20.4 Subpoenas

Since all adjudicatory powers were transferred to the OALJ in 1972, only the OALJ has subpoena power, whether the case is before the OALJ or OWCP. *Maine v. Brady-Hamilton Stevedore Co.*, 18 B.R.B.S. 129 (*en banc*) (1986); *see also Armani v. Global Linguist Solutions*, 46 B.R.B.S. 63 (2012).[2] If any party to a claim before the district director needs a subpoena over a person or subpoena *duces tecum*, the request is made for such subpoena to the Chief Administrative Law Judge or his or her designee. Subpoenas originating at the OWCP have no force or authority.

In Maine, the Board noted that when the 1972 amendments transferred to the OALJ duties previously performed by the deputy commissioner, Congress neglected to alter the references to the deputy commissioner's authority which appeared throughout the LHWCA:

> Notwithstanding repeated statutory references to the adjudicatory authority of the deputy commissioner, a fair reading of section 19(d) should dispel any confusion over the present roles of the deputy commissioner and administrative law judge; administrative and prehearing investigative duties are performed by the deputy commissioner.

18 B.R.B.S. at 131. The Board stated that its holding that "deputy commissioners are not empowered to issue subpoenas *duces tecum*, is required by the LHWCA and the clearly expressed legislative intent to maintain a division of responsibilities of the deputy commissioner and the administrative law judge." *Id.* at 131–32. Thus, the Board concluded that:

> The subpoena power, inasmuch as it pertains to claims for compensation under the Act, is solely, an adjunct of the administrative law judges['] authority to conduct formal adjudication. If a party refuses to produce requested evidence at the deputy commissioner level, the other party need only apply to the chief administrative law judge and a subpoena will be issued by that office.

Id. at 132. The regulations under LHWCA also support the Board's holding in *Maine*. The regulations addressing the district director's duties and functions stress the informality of the proceedings at that level. 20 C.F.R. § 702.311–702.319. By contrast, the regulations addressing formal

2. In *Armani*, the Board held that an ALJ may issue a subpoena in a case pending before OWCP only when it is "necessary," *i.e.*, there must be a refusal to produce the evidence requested by the opposing party.

hearings before the OALJ imply a subpoena power. *Id.* §§ 702.340–702.341.

The OALJ Rules of Practice and Procedure ("OALJ Rules" or "Part 18 Rules"), 29 C.F.R. Part 18 (2015), address the OALJ's subpoena process. Rule 18.56, 29 C.F.R. § 18.56, details form and content requirements for subpoenas, service requirements, procedures for producing electronically stored information ("ESI"), duties in responding to a subpoena, and protections for a person subject to a subpoena. It is the responsibility of the parties to prepare and serve subpoenas upon any witness and to tender any required fees and expenses. If the subpoena commands production of documents, ESI, or tangible things or the inspection of premises, then before it is served on the person to whom it is directed, a notice and copy of the subpoena must be served on each party. *Id.* § 18.56(b)(1). Parties desiring subpoenas from an ALJ must make their requests in writing, and specifically state for which case each subpoena is to be issued.[3] The request should be addressed to the judge assigned to hear the case, or if the matter is unassigned or still before the OWCP, the request should be made to the District Chief Judge for the OALJ district office which routinely handles cases in that locale. If there is any question as to which district office is responsible for a case, the party should address inquiries to the Associate Chief Judge for Longshore in the national office. Parties should never use "left over" subpoenas or photocopied subpoena forms.

Enforcement of subpoenas is a two-tiered process. If a person fails to comply with a subpoena, the party adversely affected should by written motion request the ALJ to compel compliance. If the offending party still does not comply, the ALJ may certify the facts to the appropriate federal district court. 33 U.S.C. §927; 29 C.F.R. § 18.56(e).

20.5 The Transfer of Claims to the OALJ

The regulations state that if the district director "is satisfied that any further conference would be unproductive, or if any party has requested a hearing, the district director shall prepare the case for transfer to the Office of the Chief Administrative Law Judge." 20 C.F.R. § 702.316. A claim cannot be stayed at the OWCP level until a disability arises; there are no protective filings under the LHWCA. *Black v. Bethlehem Steel Corp.*, 16 B.R.B.S. 138 (1984). Upon application of an interested party, the district director must order a hearing by referring a claim to the OALJ. *Ingalls Shipbuilding v. Asbestos Health Claimants*, 17 F.3d 130 (5th Cir. 1994) (Director has a "clear, non-discretionary duty" to transfer the case to the OALJ where there are substantive legal or factual disputes); *Employers Liability Assurance Corp. v. Donovan*, 279 F.2d 76 (5th Cir. 1960), *cert. denied*, 364 U.S. 884 (1960); *Atlantic & Gulf Stevedores, Inc. v. Donovan*, 274 F.2d 794, 802 (5th Cir. 1960) (Every agency has a duty to conclude any matter before it with reasonable dispatch and the courts are essentially empowered to review the inaction of an agency and to "compel agency action unlawfully withheld or unreasonably delayed"). In order to compel the district director to transfer claims to the OALJ, a party may seek mandamus through the proper federal district court. *Asbestos Health Claimants*, 17 F.3d 130.

If a claimant moves for a withdrawal while a claim is at OWCP, the district director may grant the request as noted under 20 C.F.R. § 702.225, provided the withdrawal is "for a proper purpose and in the claimant's best interest." However, if there is an outstanding request for hearing filed by the employer, the employer has the right to be heard at the OALJ level and the district director must refer the claim to OALJ. *Ingalls Shipbuilding, Inc. v. Director, OWCP [Boone]*, 102 F.3d 1385 (5th Cir. 1996).

When the OWCP transfers a claim to the OALJ, only a "bare bones" file is physically sent to the OALJ. This file generally consists of LS-18s and a transmittal letter indicating the transfer of the case as well as whether Section 8(f), 33 U.S.C. § 908(f), trust fund relief is being requested by the employer. The transmittal file will indicate whether the OWCP Director has raised "the absolute defense"—untimeliness—and is opposing the Section 8(f) request. This defense must be raised by the Director, as opposed to the district director, directly to the OALJ. *Abbey v. Navy Exchange*, 30 B.R.B.S. 139 (1996).

Since the OWCP's in-house file is not forwarded to the OALJ, any party who intends to offer into evidence anything from the OWCP file, must secure it directly from the district director.

20.6 The OALJ Hearing Process; Authority of the ALJ in General

Section 19(d) of the LHWCA provides that hearings must be conducted in accordance with the APA, 5 U.S.C. § 554 *et seq.* 33 U.S.C. § 919(d); 20 C.F.R. §702.332. Thus, hearings must be conducted in accordance with due process. 5 U.S.C. § 554(b). When new issues arise, adequate and reasonable notice must be provided. *Id.* § 554(b). Discovery must be done systematically and uniformly. *Id.* § 556. Hearsay evidence is generally, but not always, admitted. *Id.* §§ 556, 557. The ALJ determines credibility of witnesses, draws inferences based on evidence and draws adverse inferences. *Id.* A written record and transcript must be made of the devel-

3. Appropriate subpoena forms and information about obtaining subpoenas can be found at: http://www.oalj.dol.gov/SUBPOENAS.HTM.

opment and progression of each case; and the final order must be in writing. *Id.* §§ 552(a)(2)(B), 556(e). The ALJ's decision must be specific and complete, and it must address conflicting evidence. *Id.* §§ 556, 557.

The hearing provisions of the APA are mirrored in Sections 23 and 27 of the Longshore Act and in the regulations governing the adjudication of Longshore claims, 20 C.F.R. §§702.331–702.351. Section 23(a) provides that the hearing officer shall not be bound by common law or statutory rules of evidence, or by technical or formal rules of procedure. *See also* 20 C.F.R. § 702.339. As detailed below, Section 27 provides sanctions where a party disregards an order of an ALJ or misbehaves during a hearing, allowing the ALJ to certify the facts to the district court.

Further, the OALJ Rules of Practice and Procedure, 29 C.F.R. Part 18, Subpart A, apply to the adjudication of Longshore claims unless the LHWCA or its implementing regulations impose a different requirement. 29 C.F.R. § 18.10. The Part 18 regulations incorporate the Federal Rules of Civil Procedure ("FRCP") in situations not covered by any other provision. *Id.*; *see Metropolitan Stevedore Co. v. Brickner*, 11 F.3d 887 (9th Cir. 1993); *Goicochea v. Wards Cove Packing Co.*, 37 B.R.B.S. 4 (2003). Revisions to the 29 C.F.R. Part 18A effective June 18, 2015[4] sought to harmonize the OALJ's procedures with the current FRCP, aid the adjudication of more complex cases, enhance clarity, and promote procedural uniformity while affording judges flexibility.[5] *See* 77 Fed. Reg. 72141, 72142–72148 (Dec. 4, 2012)(29 C.F.R. Part 18, Proposed Rule). Rule 18.12(b) provides that "the judge has all powers necessary to conduct fair and impartial proceedings, including those described in the [APA], 5 U.S.C. 556," and enumerates some of the ALJs' key powers. 29 C.F.R. § 18.12(b). Upon notice to all parties, a judge may waive any rule unless it is prejudicial or unjust to do so. *Id.* § 18.10. ALJs' authority to manage the hearing process is further detailed below.

20.7 Parties and Representatives

Pursuant to § 702.333(a), the necessary parties for a formal hearing are the claimant and the employer or insurance carrier, and the ALJ assigned the case. Section 702.333(b) provides that "[t]he Solicitor of Labor or his designee may appear and participate in any formal hearing held pursuant to these regulations on behalf of the Director as an interested party." In cases where employer seeks Section 8(f) relief, the Director represents the interests of the Special Fund, and the OALJ's Standardized Prehearing Order instructs counsel for the Director to submit a notification indicating whether the Director contests 8(f) relief and intends to participate in the hearing

In OALJ proceedings, most Longshore claimants are represented by an attorney. Alternatively, a claimant may choose a lay representative, or proceed without representation (*pro se*). *See* 20 C.F.R. §702.131(a); 29 C.F.R. §§ 18.21–18.22. The OALJ does not appoint counsel nor can it make attorney referrals. *Id.* § 18.17. Rule 18.22(d) lists "prohibited actions" that representatives may not take, such as misleading a party, witness, or judge; or engaging in "any other action or behavior prejudicial to the fair and orderly conduct of the proceeding." Rule 18.23 elaborates the procedure for disqualification and discipline of representatives.

Pursuant to § 18.21(c), when a party fails to participate in OALJ proceedings without good cause, the judge may, after notice and an opportunity to be heard, dismiss the proceeding or enter a decision. The Board has permitted dismissal of Longshore claims upon abandonment. *See Taylor v. B. Frank Joy Co.*, 22 B.R.B.S. 408 (1989); *cf. Twigg v. Maryland Shipbuilding & Dry Dock Co.*, 23 B.R.B.S. 118 (1989).

20.8 Setting Hearings

Once a case is referred to the OALJ, it is generally forwarded to the district office located in a geographical area where the hearing is likely to occur. The case is then assigned to an ALJ to schedule and conduct a hearing. Cases are generally combined with others in the same geographic location for a docket of hearings. Since the hearing venue for LHWCA cases is national in scope, however, a judge may be assigned a docket outside of his or her geographic area. If there are exigent circumstances, and the case has not yet been assigned to a presiding judge, the parties should contact either the appropriate District Chief Judge or, if necessary, the Associate Chief Judge for the Longshore Program in the national office. Likewise, if an expedited hearing is needed and the case has not yet been assigned to a presiding judge, the parties may file the motion to expedite with the Associate Chief Judge or local District Chief Judge.

Once a case is assigned, the ALJ will issue a docketing or prehearing order. 29 C.F.R. § 18.40. Individual judges' prehearing orders may vary, but most judges use the OALJ's Standardized Notice of Hearing and Prehearing Order. The ALJ has discretionary authority to exclude even relevant and material testimony or evidence for failure to comply with the terms of the prehearing order. *Durham v. Embassy Dairy*, 19 B.R.B.S. 105 (1986). While the regulations require

4. Technical corrections were published on July 1, 2015.

5. These are the first major revisions of Part 18A since 1983. In the preamble to the new Rules, the Department addressed comments regarding the compatibility of the new Rules with Sections 23(a), 26, 27(b), and 31 of the LHWCA. 80 Fed. Reg. at 28769–28770.

the OALJ to give at least 30 days notice of hearing, 20 C.F.R. § 702.335, it is the policy of the OALJ to give considerably more notice, which helps minimize scheduling conflicts and the need to continue hearings.

20.9 Section 8(i)—Settlement of Claims

Rule 18.13 describes the OALJ's settlement judge procedure. The 2015 revisions extended the number of days for the settlement proceeding from 30 to 60 days. 29 C.F.R. § 18.13. Parties may jointly request that a case be assigned to a settlement judge,[6] who receives all information confidentially. If the matter is not resolved, it will proceed to a hearing before the presiding ALJ.

Section 20 C.F.R. § 702.241(c) provides, in part, that "[w]here a case is pending before the ALJ but not set for a hearing, the parties may request the case be remanded to the district director for consideration of the settlement." For efficiency's sake, the parties may, however, choose to have the ALJ rule on the settlement package instead. The regulations provide a checklist of elements needed in the settlement package. *Id.* § 702.242. If the settlement package is deficient, the 30-day time period for ruling on settlement proposals in which both sides are represented by counsel will not commence until the deficiency is corrected. *Id.* § 702.243(b).

The ALJ cannot allow the parties to move for a withdrawal of the claim in lieu of the Section 8(i) settlement process. *Rodman v. Bethlehem Steel Corp.*, 16 B.R.B.S. 123, 127 n.5 (1984); *Matthews v. Mid-States Stevedoring Corp.*, 11 B.R.B.S. 139 (1979); *see also Graham v. Ingalls Shipbuilding/Litton Systems, Inc.*, 9 B.R.B.S. 155 (1978) (claimant's motion for dismissal should be treated as a motion for withdrawal).

When mental incompetence is alleged, the settlement package should contain evidence showing that the claimant has a personal representative, 33 U.S.C. § 911, even if he or she is represented by counsel. In lieu of a personal representative, the package may include evidence that the claimant is able to fully understand the settlement agreement and is able to properly control or administer the settlement proceeds.

20.10 Service, Format, and Timing of Motions and Other Papers

The 2015 Rules detail the procedure for service, format, and timing of motions and other papers. 29 C.F.R. §§ 18.30–18.36. As a general rule, all papers filed with OALJ must be served on every party. *Id.* § 18.30(a)(1). If a party is represented, however, service is made only on the representative, unless the judge also orders service on the party. *Id.* § 18.30(a)(2)(i). Service by electronic means is allowed if the person consented in writing. *Id.* § 18.30(a)(2)(ii)(E).

A judge may allow papers to be filed, signed, or verified by electronic means. *Id.* § 18.30(b)(4). Parties should note the rules for faxing the OALJ limit the situations in which filing by fax is permitted and describe how to file by fax. *Id.* § 18.30(b)(3). To protect privacy, § 18.31 requires the parties to redact personal data identifiers in filings or exhibits, unless ordered otherwise; a person waives the protections as to his or her own information by filing it without redaction and not under seal.

A request for an order must be made by motion. *Id.* § 18.33(a). Motions must be in writing (unless made during a hearing), state with particularity the grounds for seeking the order, state the relief sought, and (unless all parties agree to the relief) be accompanied by affidavits or other evidence. *Id.* For dispositive motions and discovery motions, a memorandum of points and authority must be submitted. *Id.* § 18.33(a) and (c)(4). With few exceptions (e.g., for *pro se* claimants and "joint" motions), a motion must contain a certification that counsel attempted to resolve the issue with opposing counsel. *Id.* § 18.33(c)(3). A party is permitted 14 days of service to respond to a motion. *Id.* § 18.33(d). A representative or unrepresented party who files a motion or other papers with OALJ must sign any such document. By presenting the paper to the ALJ, the person is certifying that the filing is made in good faith, as detailed in § 18.35(b). The sanctions provisions set forth in § 18.35(c) are discussed below.

The 2015 Rules change the method for computing time periods specified in the Part 18 Rules or a judge's order to conform generally to the method used in the FRCP.[7] *Id.* § 18.32. If a party must act within a specified time after service, and service is made by mail, then the period to act is extended for three extra days. *Id.* In the 2015 Rules, most time periods less than 30 days have been set in multiples of seven days.

20.11 Disclosure and Discovery

In Longshore cases, Section 27(a), 33 U.S.C. §927, grants the ALJ broad power to direct and authorize discovery. *See* 5 U.S.C. §556(c); 20 C.F.R. §§702.338–702.341; 29 C.F.R. §§ 18.12, 18.50–18.65. Pursuant to this power, the judge may compel depositions,[8] compel the production of docu-

6. Additional information may be found at: http://www.oalj.dol.gov/SETTLEMENT_JUDGE.HTM

7. E.g., if a period is stated in days or a longer unit of time, intermediate weekends and holidays are no longer excluded.

8. *Percoats v. Marine Terminals Corp.*, 15 B.R.B.S. 151 (1982); *Lopes George Hyman Constr. Co.*, 13 B.R.B.S. 314 (1981).

ments,[9] and compel a claimant to undergo a vocational rehabilitation evaluation.[10]

The OALJ Rules detail disclosure and discovery process in OALJ proceedings. Judges' prehearing orders in Longshore cases generally track these rules. A prehearing order usually directs the parties to arrange an initial conference pursuant to § 18.50(b), similar to FRCP 26(f). The judge may also require the parties to file a discovery plan. Additionally, § 18.44 highlights the judge's authority to order prehearing conference(s), e.g., to facilitate settlement.

The revised OALJ Rules prescribe three sets of disclosures that must be made without awaiting a discovery request, and ALJs' prehearing orders typically track the Part 18 Rules. First, at the commencement of a proceeding before OALJ, each party must automatically provide to the other parties the identity of individuals (including experts) likely to have discoverable information and all documents that the party "may use to support its claims or defenses" (unless the use would be solely for impeachment), as well as a computation of each category of damages. *Id.* § 18.50(c)(1) (*Initial disclosure*).[11] Parties should be mindful of § 18.50(c)(1)(vi) with respect to unacceptable excuses for failing to make the disclosures. Second, within the timeframe specified in the ALJ's prehearing order, parties must disclose to the other parties the identity of any witness who may testify at hearing, either live or by deposition. *Id.* § 18.50(c)(2). With this disclosure, parties must serve written reports of experts they retained to testify, containing information listed in § 18.50(c)(2)(ii); an expert not retained or specially employed to provide expert testimony—a treating physician may fall into this category—need not write a report, but the party must serve an equivalent disclosure about that expert's opinions and their bases. *Id.* § 18.50(c)(2). Rule 18.53 provides for a broad, ongoing duty to supplement prior disclosures and discovery responses. Every required disclosure and discovery request, response, or objection must be signed by the party's representative (or by the unrepresented party) certifying that it is complete and not made for an improper purpose. *Id.* § 18.50(d). Sanctions for improper certification are set forth in § 18.50(d)(3), discussed below. Finally, in addition to required disclosures, at least 21 days before the hearing or as ordered by the judge, a party must provide to the other parties, and file with the ALJ, a prehearing statement described in § 18.80. *Id.* § 18.50(c)(3). Before doing so, the parties must confer in good faith to stipulate to facts to the fullest extent possible, to eliminate duplicative exhibits, and to resolve any objections to exhibits. *Id.* § 18.80.

Rule 18.50(a) provides that discovery may be sought at any time after a judge issues an initial notice or order.[12] The Rules prescribe the procedure for interrogatories[13] (§18.60), production of documents (§ 18.61),[14] physical and mental examinations (§ 18.62), requests for admission (§ 18.63), and depositions (§§ 18.64, 18.65). Rule 18.51(d)(1) provides that a party may depose an expert whose opinions may be presented at the hearing. Rule 18.55 addresses the use of depositions at hearings. Absent an objection, a deposition may be used at a hearing as if the deponent were present and testifying. A party may use for any purpose the deposition of an expert witness, treating physician or examining physician. *Id.* § 18.55(a)(5). The OALJ's subpoena process under § 18.56 is discussed above.

Rule 18.30(b) provides that § 18.50(c) initial disclosures and discovery requests and responses must not be filed with the OALJ until they are used in the proceeding or the judge orders filing. Parties must exchange copies of exhibits by the date prescribed by the ALJ; exhibits are offered in evidence at the hearing. *Id.* § 18.82(c).

Of particular importance in Longshore proceedings is § 18.62, which provides that a party may serve upon another party whose mental or physical condition is in controversy a notice to submit to an examination by a suitably licensed or certified examiner. The rule details the requirements pertaining to notice of examination, objection to the notice, as well as delivery and contents of examiner's report; reports of all earlier examinations of the same condition must also be delivered. The OALJ's Standardized Notice of Hearing and Prehearing Order provides that an examination report must be delivered to the party examined no later than 40 days before the date of the hearing (*i.e.*, the date set in the order for completion of discovery).

The scope of discovery is addressed in § 18.51. A party may obtain discovery of any non-privileged matter that is relevant to a party's claim or defense. Relevant information

9. *Sledge v. Sealand Terminals Inc.*, 14 B.R.B.S. 334 (1981).

10. *Villasenor v. Marine Maint. Indus., Inc.*, 17 B.R.B.S. 99 (1985); *Bonner v. Ryan-Walsh Stevedoring Co.*, 15 B.R.B.S. 321 (1983).

11. In Longshore cases, the representative of the OWCP is exempt from initial disclosures, except when participating in the proceeding under 20 C.F.R. § 702.333(b) or unless an employer has applied for relief under Section 8(f). 29 C.F.R. § 18.50(c)(1)(iii)(B).

12. The Department considered and rejected a public comment suggesting that, to minimize delay, discovery in LHC cases should be available following transfer of the case from the OWCP. It reasoned that the transfer is specific to LHWCA and BLBA claims, and that this concern would be better addressed without creating a special rule or exception. 80 Fed. Reg. at 28776.

13. Objections to interrogatories must be specific. § 18.60(b)(4).

14. Fed. R. Civ. P. 34, as amended in 2015, requires that objections to requests for production be stated with specificity.

need not be admissible at the hearing if the discovery appears reasonably calculated to lead to the discovery of admissible evidence. *Id.* § 18.51(a). However, the scope may be expanded with a judge's order, upon a showing of good cause, to any matter relevant to the subject matter involved in the proceeding. § 18.51(a). Generally, any relevant, nonprivileged document is discoverable unless it was prepared in anticipation of litigation, pertains to expert witnesses, or would be unreasonably burdensome to produce. *See* 77 Fed. Reg. at 72166. Further, discovery is subject to proportionality principle. *See* § 18.51(b)(4) (requiring ALJs to limit discovery in the specified circumstances); *see also* Fed. R. Civ. P. 26(b)(1) (effective Dec. 1, 2015). Unless otherwise stipulated or ordered by the judge, the Rules set limitations on the number of interrogatories (§ 18.60) and the number and length of depositions (§§ 18.64, 18.65). *See also* 18.51(b). The ALJ may also limit the number of § 18.63 requests for admission. § 18.51. Requests for production under § 18.61 are not presumptively limited in number, but are subject to the proportionality principle in § 18.51(b)(4), which applies to all discovery. The Rules also set forth specific limitations on discovery of ESI. § 18.51(b)(2).

The procedures to limit the scope of discovery based on claims of privileged, protected, or sensitive information are addressed by § 18.51 (*Discovery scope and limits*) and § 18.52 (*Protective orders*). Rules 18.51(c) and (d) elaborate the limitations on discovery of hearing preparation materials and experts, respectively. A party may not discover materials prepared in anticipation of litigation or the hearing by or for another party or its representative, unless the information is relevant and the party requesting the information can show that there is a substantial need for the information and the party cannot obtain substantially equivalent information without undue hardship. *Id.* § 18.51(c)(1). Further, § 18.51(c)(2) instructs the judge to protect against disclosure of a party's representative's opinions when ordering the production of hearing preparation material. Rule 18.51(d)(3) provides that work-product protections under § 18.51(c)(1) and (2) do not extend to communications between a party's representative and its retained expert witness to the extent they relate to expert's compensation, or identify facts, data, or assumptions that the party's representative provided and that the expert considered in forming the opinions to be expressed.[15] Further, § 18.51(d)(4) addresses discovery of facts or opinions held by experts employed only for hearing preparation.[16] Notably, to claim a privilege or to protect hearing preparation materials, the party must expressly make the claim and sufficiently describe the nature of withheld documents. *Id.* § 18.51(e).

20.12 Evidence and Witnesses

Pursuant to Section 23(a), the ALJs are not bound by common law or statutory rules of evidence, or by technical or formal rules of procedure except for those provided for in the Act, but may make such investigation or inquiry of conduct such hearing in such manner as to best ascertain the rights of the parties. *See also* 20 C.F.R. § 702.339. The ALJ may receive into evidence the testimony of witnesses and any documents which are "relevant and material." 20 C.F.R. § 702.338. The ALJ has great discretion concerning the admission of evidence, *Hughes v. Bethlehem Steel Corp.*, 17 B.R.B.S. 153, 155 n.1 (1985), and any decisions regarding the admission or exclusion of evidence are reversible only if arbitrary, capricious, or an abuse of discretion. *Champion v. S & M Traylor Bros.*, 14 B.R.B.S. 251 (1981), *rev'd on other grounds*, 690 F.2d 285 (D.C. Cir. 1982); *Smith v. Ceres Terminal*, 9 B.R.B.S. 121 (1978).

As hearings before OALJ follow relaxed standards of admissibility, the admission of evidence depends on whether a reasonable mind might accept it as probative. *Young & Co. v. Shea*, 397 F.2d 185 (5th Cir. 1968), *cert. denied*, 395 U.S. 920 (1969). Hearsay evidence is generally admissible if considered reliable. Hearsay evidence, if it possesses rational probative force, may constitute substantial evidence to support an administrative finding. *Camarillo v. Nat'l Steel & Shipbuilding Co.*, 10 B.R.B.S. 54, 60 (1979). However, agency findings cannot be based solely on hearsay. *Colliton v. Defoe Shipbuilding Co.*, 3 B.R.B.S. 331, 335 (1976). In general, it is proper to admit and consider an *ex parte* medical report where the author is not biased and has no interest in the case, the opposing party has the opportunity to cross-examine or subpoena the witness, and the report is not inconsistent on its face. *See, e.g., Darnell v. Bell Helicopter Int'l*, 16 B.R.B.S. 98 (1984), *aff'd sub. nom. Bell Helicopter Int'l v. Jacobs*, 746 F.2d 1342, 17 B.R.B.S. 13 (CRT) (8th Cir. 1984). The prerequisites to admissibility of expert testimony under Federal Rule of Evidence 702, elaborated in *Daubert v. Merrell Dow Pharmaceuticals, Inc.*, 509 U.S. 579, 113 S.Ct. 2786 (1993) and its progeny, are not applicable to Longshore claims. *Casey v. Georgetown Univ. Medical Ctr.*, 31 B.R.B.S. 147 (1997).

15. § 18.51 (d) is modeled after Fed. R. Civ. P. 26(b)(4). See 77 Fed. Reg. at 72161.

16. Disclosure of non-testifying expert opinions has been addressed in the context of Black Lung claim adjudication. *Fox v. Elk Run Coal Co.*, 739 F.3d 131 (4th Cir. 2014); *see also* Proposed Rule, OWCP, *Black Lung Benefits Act: Disclosure of Medical Information and Payment of Benefits*, 80 Fed. Reg. 23743 (Apr. 29, 2015) (in relevant part, proposed rule would require parties to disclose all medical information developed in connection with a claim for benefits).

Although the ALJ is not obligated to accept all stipulations entered into by the parties, the judge's rejection or modification of a stipulation must be adequately explained. *Grimes v. Exxon Co., U.S.A.*, 14 B.R.B.S. 573 (1981). The ALJ may not reject stipulations without giving the parties prior notice that he or she will not automatically accept the stipulations and without giving them an opportunity to present evidence in support of the stipulations. A stipulation cannot be accepted where it evinces an incorrect application of the law. *McDevitt v. George Hyman Constr. Co.*, 14 B.R.B.S. 677 (1982); *Mitri v. Global Linguist Solutions*, 48 B.R.B.S. 41 (2014). The Board has held that parties may not stipulate to jurisdiction. *Littrell v. Oregon Shipbuilding Co.*, 17 B.R.B.S. 84 (1985); *cf. Perkins v. Marine Terminals Corp.*, 12 B.R.B.S. 219 (1980), *rev'd*, 673 F.2d 1097, 14 B.R.B.S. 771 (9th Cir. 1982). *See also Casey v. Chapman College, Pace Program*, 23 B.R.B.S. 7 (1989). Stipulations of fact are offered in lieu of evidence, and the fact need not be established by record evidence. *Mitri*, 48 B.R.B.S. 41.

Rule 18.84 provides that, official notice may be taken, on motion of a party or on the judge's own, of any adjudicative fact or other matter subject to judicial notice. Advance notice is not required. *See* 77 Fed. Reg. at 72172. Rather, under § 18.84, parties must be given an adequate opportunity to show the contrary of the matter noticed. This is consistent with Board decisions holding that an ALJ must provide the parties with "the opportunity to contradict the noticed facts with evidence to the contrary." *Jordan v. James G. Davis Constr. Corp.*, 9 B.R.B.S. 528.9, 530 (1978).[17]

The treatment of impeachment evidence depends on the particular circuit's previous rulings. Evidence offered "solely for impeachment purposes" does not have to be disclosed pursuant to § 18.50(c)(1).[18] However, in Longshore cases, surveillance evidence is likely to be found, at least in part, substantive and not intended "solely for impeachment." *See Chiasson v. Zapata Gulf Marine Corp.*, 988 F.2d 513, 516–18 (5th Cir. 1993), *cert. denied*, 511 U.S. 1029 (1994) (In a Jones Act case, surveillance videotape of the injured worker's daily activities was, in part, substantive, and thus could not be admitted without proper disclosure pursuant to a discovery request); *see generally* 12-127 Larson's Workers' Compensation Law § 127.10 (2015) (Surveillance Video and Photographic Evidence; Privacy Issues).[19] At the same time, ALJs are mindful of the impeachment value of such evidence. Thus, an ALJ may direct a party who wishes to preserve surveillance evidence for impeachment purposes to schedule a pre-hearing deposition of the person who is the subject of such evidence, in which case the surveillance evidence must be disclosed upon completion of the deposition.

20.13 Conduct of the Hearing

As to the conduct of the actual hearing, the ALJ has discretion. *Wayland v. Moore Dry Dock*, 21 B.R.B.S. 177 (1988). Whenever possible, all issues before the ALJ must be adjudicated in one proceeding in order to avoid piecemeal litigation. *Hudnall v. Jacksonville Shipyards*, 17 B.R.B.S. 174 (1985); 20 C.F.R. §§ 702.338, 702.371. The hearing may be expanded to allow consideration of new issues if the evidence presented warrants their consideration. 20 C.F.R. § 702.336(a). *See Emery v. Bath Iron Works Corp.*, 24 B.R.B.S. 238, 242–43 (1991). However, the ALJ must notify the parties and give them the opportunity to present argument and new evidence on a new issue which arises during the course of a hearing. *Cornell Univ. v. Velez*, 856 F.2d 402, 21 B.R.B.S. 155 (CRT) (1st Cir. 1988); *Klubnikin v. Crescent Wharf & Warehouse Co.*, 16 B.R.B.S. 182 (1984).

OALJ Rules address hearing procedures. *See, e.g.*, 29 C.F.R. 18.80–18.88. If all parties choose to waive the formal hearing, the ALJ may issue a decision and order based on the pleadings, evidence, and briefs. § 18.21(b). Such on-the-record determinations are relatively common in Defense Base Act cases involving claimants who reside outside the U.S. Further, for good cause and with appropriate safeguards, a judge may permit witness testimony or party participation by contemporaneous transmission from a different location. § 18.81. The Rules also address disposition without hearing (§§ 18.70–18.72), including summary decisions (§ 18.72).

17. *See also Maddaleni v. The Pittsburgh & Midway Coal Mining Co.*, 14 B.L.R. 1-135 (1990), *aff'd mem. sub nom. Maddaleni v. Director, OWCP*, No. 90-9583 (10th Cir. 1992). *See generally Shrout v. General Dynamics Corp.*, 27 B.R.B.S. 160 (1993) (Brown, J., dissenting); *see also Lindsay v. Bethlehem Steel Corp.*, 18 B.R.B.S. 20 (1986).

18. *See Hammel v. Eau Galle Cheese Factory*, 407 F.3d 852, 869 (7th Cir. 2005), *cert. denied*, 546 U.S. 1033 (2005) (Under FRCP 26(a)(1)(A) & (3), evidence offered "solely for impeachment purposes" does not have to be disclosed prior to trial); *Denty v. CSX Transp., Inc.*, 168 F.R.D. 549, 1996 U.S. Dist. LEXIS 14928 (E.D. N.C. 1996) (FRCP 26(a)(3) excludes from pretrial discovery material which will be used solely for impeachment; the obvious rationale is that disclosure would substantially impair its impeachment value); *cf. Harrison v. Taiwan Super Young Co. Ltd.*, 1997 U.S. App. LEXIS 274 (9th Cir. 1997) (unpub.) ("The trial court did not abuse its discretion in overruling the FRCP 26(e) objection to admission of the videotape to impeach [plaintiffs]").

19. Discussing different approaches to surveillance evidence in state workers' compensation proceedings. For example, New York requires the employer or carrier to inform the claimant of the existence of the video prior to claimant's testimony about his work activities; else the video is not admissible. *Id., citing Morelli v. Tops Markets*, 107 A.D.3d 1231, 967 N.Y.S.2d 493 (3rd Dept. 2013).

20.14 ALJs' Authority to Regulate Conduct of Adjudication Proceedings; Sanctions

In addition to giving adjudicatory authority to the OALJ, Section 19(d) of the LHWCA incorporates the APA, 5 U.S.C. § 554 *et seq*., into the hearing process. 33 U.S.C. § 919(d); 20 C.F.R. §702.332. The APA grants the ALJs the authority, "[s]ubject to published rules of the agency and within its powers, . . . to regulate the course of a hearing." 5 U.S.C. 556(c)(5). Section 27(a) of the LHWCA provides that ALJs have the power to preserve and enforce order during proceedings, to issue subpoenas, to compel discovery, to examine witnesses, and to take any action under law which is necessary to effectively performing the ALJ's duties. Further, Section 27(b) provides sanctions where a party disregards an order of an ALJ or misbehaves during a hearing, allowing the ALJ to certify the facts to the district court which may punish the party in the same manner as for contempt committed before the court.

The extent of the ALJs' authority to impose sanctions in Longshore cases is discussed in the preamble to the revised Part 18 Rules. *See* 80 Fed. Reg. 28767 (May 19, 2015)(29 C.F.R. Part 18, Final Rule). Provisions for the imposition of sanctions by ALJs, similar to their FRCP counterparts, are found in Rules 18.12, 18.35, 18.50, 18.56, 18.57, 18.64, and 18.87. The Department considered and rejected public comments which asserted that the sanctions provisions had to be deleted or rewritten to exclude proceedings under the LHWCA and BLBA. The Department acknowledged that some of the sanctions may be precluded by Section 27(b), but concluded that the comments overstated the alleged conflicts between the new Rules and the LHWCA, stating:

> The Department agrees with the commenters that section 927(b) provides the district courts with the exclusive power to punish contumacious conduct consisting of a refusal to comply with a judge's order, lawful process or subpoena, or hearing room misbehavior in proceedings under the LHWCA. See Goicochea v. Wards Cove Packing Co., 37 Ben. Rev. Bd. Serv. (MB) 4, 6 (2003) (vacating dismissal of claim as sanction for claimant's refusal to comply with a judge's discovery order). To the extent that any of the new rules conflict with section 927(b), the latter controls. See 29 CFR 18.10(a). However, there are several situations addressed by the new rules involving conduct that likely would fall outside the categories of contumacy requiring certification to a district court for a section 927(b) summary contempt proceeding. See A–Z Intn'l v. Phillips, 323 F.3d 1141, 1146–47 (9th Cir. 2003) (holding that the district court lacked section 927(b) jurisdiction over conduct that did not involve a refusal "to comply with a summons, writ, warrant, or mandate issued by the ALJ"). See, e.g., 29 CFR 18.35(c) (sanctions for violations of §18.35(b) relating to the representations made when presenting a motion or other paper to the judge), 18.50(d)(3) (sanctions for violations of §18.50(d)(1) pertaining to certifications made when signing disclosures and discovery requests, responses and objections), 18.56(d)(1) (sanctions for violations of the duty under §18.56(c)(1) to protect a person subject to a subpoena from undue burden), 18.57(c) (sanctions for failures to disclose information, supplement an earlier response or to admit as required by §§18.50(c), 18.53 and 18.63(a)), 18.57(d) (sanctions for a party's failure to attend its own deposition, serve answers to interrogatories, or respond to a request for inspection), 18.64(d)(2) (sanctions for impeding, delaying or frustrating a deposition), 18.64(g) (sanctions for failing to attend or proceed with a deposition or serve a subpoena on a nonparty deponent when another party, expecting the deposition to be taken, attends), 18.72(h) (sanctions for submitting in bad faith an affidavit or declaration in support of or in opposition to a motion for summary decision). To the extent these provisions address violations of the procedural rules falling outside the scope of section 927(b), there is no conflict with the statute.
>
> The Department also rejects the commenters' argument that section 927(b) provides the exclusive remedy for any misconduct or rules violation occurring in LHWCA and BLBA proceedings. Section 927(b), 44 Stat. 1438 (Mar. 4, 1927) (codified as amended at 33 U.S.C. 927), was originally enacted in 1927, decades before the passage of the APA which also governs adjudications under the LHWCA and the BLBA. 33 U.S.C. 919(d); 30 U.S.C. 932(a); [...]. Notably, the APA's grant of authority to "regulate the course of the hearing," 5 U.S.C. 556(c)(5), provides a judge with an independent basis to take such actions as are necessary to ensure parties a fair and impartial adjudication. Such authority includes the power to compel discovery and impose sanctions for non-compliance pursuant to the OALJ rules of practice and procedure. See Williams v. Consolidation Coal Co., BRB No. 04-0756 BLA, 2005 WL 6748152, at *8 (Ben.

Rev. Bd. Aug. 8, 2005), appeal denied, 453 F.3d 609 (4th Cir. 2006), cert. denied, 549 U.S. 1278 (2007). The bifurcation of general adjudicatory authority and contempt powers between [ALJs] and the district courts under the LHWCA is analogous to adjudication in the federal courts after passage of the Federal Magistrates Act, 28 U.S.C. 604, 631–39, under which magistrate judges have general authority to order non-dispositive discovery sanctions while contempt charges must be referred to a district court judge. See Grimes v. City and County of San Francisco, 951 F. 2d 236, 240–41 (9th Cir. 1991) (discussing the scope and limits of magistrate judges' sanction authority); see also Dodd v. Crown Cent. Petroleum Corp., 36 Ben. Rev. Bd. Serv. (MB) 85, 89 n.6 (2002) (affirming, as not inconsistent with section 927(b), judge's imposition of sanctions pursuant to 29 CFR 18.6(d)(2) for claimant's noncompliance with a discovery order). The Department therefore believes that the commenters' proposal to exempt LHWCA and BLBA proceedings from the judge's authority under the APA to regulate the course of the hearing is neither warranted by the statute nor consistent with the efficient and impartial conduct of administrative hearings."

Id. at 28769–28770 (additional citations omitted); *see also id.* at 28773–28783. The Department disagreed with the proposals to individually identify superseding statutory or regulatory provisions in the Part 18 Rules. It noted that such provisions are subject to change. *Id.* at 28773. It further observed that the Rules apply to all proceedings before OALJ. Additionally, nothing in these Rules would prevent the Department from adopting program-specific procedural rules. *Id.* at 28772–28773.

More generally, the Department rejected comments which asserted that the Part 18 litigation sanctions exceed a judge's authority under the APA, and attempt to arrogate contempt power and claim "inherent judicial authority" that is vested exclusively in the Article III courts. *Id.* at 28770. The Department acknowledged that ALJs have no Article III status or powers, and that neither the APA nor Fed. R. Civ. P. 11 vests contempt powers in ALJs.[20] *Id.* at 28771. The Department further acknowledged that Fed. R. Civ. P. 11 was determined to be unavailable for incorporation in Longshore claims. *Id.* (collecting cases). Nonetheless, it reasoned that the APA empowers ALJs to regulate the course of a hearing. To ensure integrity and efficiency of the adjudicative process, ALJs must be able to impose litigation sanctions for violating procedural rules to the extent such sanctions do not conflict with the substantive statute. *Id.* The preamble notes that ALJs have used "a broad range of sanctions for the nearly 30 years under the prior rules," including evidentiary sanctions. *Id.*

20.15 Decision and Order

The Board has consistently interpreted Section 19(c) of the LHWCA and its implementing regulation, 20 C.F.R. § 702.348, as imposing upon ALJs a duty to issue a compensation order awarding or denying benefits. *See, e.g., Hoodye v. Empire/United Stevedores*, 23 B.R.B.S. 341 (1990).

Further, the APA requires decisions rendered under the APA to include a statement of "findings and conclusions, and the reasons or basis therefor, on all material issues of fact, law, or discretion presented in the record."[21] 5 U.S.C. §557(c)(3)(A). The ALJ must adequately detail the rationale behind his or her decision, and specify which evidence was relied upon and why. *See, e.g., Williams v. Newport News Shipbuilding & Dry Dock Co.*, 17 B.R.B.S. 61 (1985); *see also Gelinas v. Electric Boat Corp.*, 45 B.R.B.S. 69 (2011).

20.16 Motions for Reconsideration

When a decision and order is signed, the ALJ transmits to the district director the signed compensation order and the case file. On receipt thereof, the district director "must formally date and file the transcript, pleadings, and compensation order in his office. Such filing must be accomplished by the close of business on the next succeeding working day, and the district director must, on the same day as the filing was accomplished, serve a copy of the compensation order on the parties and on the representatives of the parties, if any." 20 C.F.R. § 702.349(a). Effective June 10, 2015, a new regulation, 20 C.F.R. 702.349(b), allows parties and their representatives to waive certified mail service and consent to electronic service.

The 20 C.F.R. Part 702 regulations do not specifically provide for the filing of a motion for reconsideration of an ALJ's decision. The Board has held that motions for reconsideration must be filed within 10 days of the filing of the decision and order in the office of the district director. *Kuhn v. Associated Press*, 16 B.R.B.S. 46 (1983); *Bogdis v. Marine Terminals Corp.*, 23 B.R.B.S. 136 (1989); *see*

20. The preamble notes that the Part 18 remedies "do not extend to the full panoply of powers available to Article III judges under their inherent powers or under FRCP 11." *Id.* at 28771, 28776.

21. Citing the APA, the Department rejected a proposal to modify § 18.72 to allow ALJs to enter summary decision in a condensed order (without a complete recitation of all evidence), upon agreement of the parties. 80 Fed. Reg. at 28781.

also Hamilton v. Ingalls Shipbuilding, Inc., 30 B.R.B.S. 84 (1996). The Board has also relied upon its regulation, 20 C.F.R. § 802.206(b)(1), which requires that a motion for reconsideration be filed within 10 days of the filing of the decision in order for an appeal to the Board to be timely. *Galle v. Ingalls Shipbuilding, Inc.*, 33 B.R.B.S. 141 (1999), *aff'd sub nom. Galle v. Director, OWCP*, 246 F.3d 440, 35 B.R.B.S. 17(CRT) (5th Cir. 2001), *cert. denied*, 534 U.S. 1002 (2001). In 2015, the OALJ Rules of Practice and Procedure were amended to state that a motion for reconsideration "must be filed no later than 10 days after service of the decision on the moving party." 29 C.F.R. § 18.93. More generally, post-hearing procedures are detailed in 29 C.F.R. §§ 18.90–18.95.

20.17 Resources

OALJ has made several legal research tools available to the general public on its website: www.oalj.dol.gov. Within the page is a library and within the library is a Longshore section. The Longshore section provides links to pertinent statutory and regulatory materials; the Benefits Review Board's *Longshore Deskbook*;[22] Board decisions; newsletters on recent significant decisions compiled by the OALJ; and law review commentaries. Final ALJ decisions in Longshore cases may be retrieved on the OALJ website. The website's Case Status Lookup feature allows the parties to check the status of a pending case, including whether documents sent by a party have been received by OALJ. The OALJ website also contains a link to various forms to be used in the Longshore claim process before this office (e.g., Prehearing Statement Form, Stipulations Form, subpoena forms, and settlement judge request).

20.18 Closing

OALJ strives to facilitate and optimize the Longshore claim process for the benefit of all who appear before it. Whether one is a claimant, employer, carrier, or representative of any of these, the party is entitled to expect an efficient resolution of the Longshore claim in a professional and fair manner. It is the policy of the OALJ to continue to seek ways to improve on the present system and fine-tune the claims process within the bounds established by the relevant law.

Members of the Longshore bar are welcome to contact the Chief Judge or Associate Chief Judge for Longshore with any comments that they may have concerning the program. The national office telephone number is 202-693-7300. The office is located at 800 K Street, N.W., Suite 400N, Washington, DC 20001-8002.

22. *Available at:* http://www.dol.gov/brb/References/Reference_works/lhca/lsdesk/main.htm.

Chapter 21

Mediating Cases Brought Pursuant to the LHWCA and its Extensions

Roger A. Levy, Esq., Paul M. Doolittle, Esq., and Collins C. Rossi, Esq.

Synopsis

21.1 Introduction

Living with OALJ back-logs large enough to often lead to a several month back log for trial dates has become a way of life for litigants in LHWCA matters. Add to that a year or more from submission to decision. Couple this with mountains of dollars for pre-trial activities, trial time, post-trial briefs, reconsiderations and appeals. Pile on uncertainties in outcomes. Is there an alternative? Settlement of course. However, face-to-face negotiations aren't always fruitful for a variety of reasons. These and other concerns have recently led to a popular option for disposal of LHWCA cases… alternative dispute resolution—or "ADR"—which includes mediation, the topic of this chapter. While this avenue has existed as an alternative for resolving disputes in civil matters for many years, it has only in the past 5–10 years become popular in matters arising under the LHWCA and its extensions. As an example, the author, in a career spanning 40-plus years, was involved as a litigant in no more than half a dozen mediations. Today, many LHWCA attorneys participate in upwards of 20 mediations per year.

The reasons for the backlogs found on OALJ calendars, increased costs to litigate, and uncertainties in outcomes are best left to other discussion forums. Suffice it to say that in the past decade or so, the cause is probably a coalescence of the spike in Defense Base Act cases (the "tail wagging the dog" phenomenon) and budgetary constraints within the Labor Department leading to shortages of examiners at the OWCP as well as judges and staff at OALJ.

To be certain, not all cases are amenable to *ADR* and particularly mediation. For example, in those cases where appellate court review is necessary to clarify, alter, or change the law, lawyers and the parties they represent will want to submit to the judicial process. In others, there may be client control problems or a litigant or his or her lawyer who cannot see the merits or risks in their case resulting in "I want my day in court".

21.2 Ethics for Mediators

by Roger A. Levy, Esq.

Mediation is a quasi-branch of the law. In fact in many states a license to practice law may not be required to serve as a mediator. A few have licensing requirements for mediators. Many jurisdictions have statutes that govern mediation. However, these seem to focus more on the process as opposed to ethics. Few address the ethical responsibilities of the mediator.

Fortunately the legal and mediation professions, through their organizations and societies, have paid attention to the issue. For instance, a "Model Standards of Conduct for Mediators" approved by the American Arbitration Society, the Dispute Resolution Section of the American Bar Association, and the Society of Professionals in Dispute Resolution has emerged as the result of the expansion of this growing field. These rules have been adopted in some jurisdictions; for example, California's Judicial Council under the title

"California's Ethical Standards for Mediators." Much has been written on the Model Standards and some principles, if not cast in concrete, have evolved.

David A. Hoffman, a mediator, arbitrator, and attorney at the Boston Law Collaborative, has authored an excellent article entitled "Ten Principles of Mediation Ethics." In it he discusses the ten most common ethical issues facing mediators. You can find the article in its entirety via a Google search. The high points of each principle along with some examples are discussed below. Some have been consolidated because of their similarity with others.

A. Conflict of Interest (Model Standards of Conduct Sec. III)

A Mediator shall Disclose all Actual and Potential Conflicts of Interest Reasonably Known to the Mediator. After Disclosure, the Mediator shall Decline to Mediate unless all Parties, Choose to retain the Mediator. The Need to Protect Against Conflicts of Interest also Governs Conduct that Occurs During and After the Mediation.

As impartiality and neutrality are essential to a successful mediation, the appearance of a conflict of interest must be avoided. When the conflict is direct such as a financial interest in the outcome, the mediator must obviously decline to serve. Where indirect, the situation is more problematic. An example would be if a mediator is associated with a firm which has as an associate, partner, or someone else who may have a financial interest in the outcome.

Professor Frank Sander of the Harvard Program on Negotiation proposes a "headline test" for determining if a conflict exists. That is "how would you feel about the apparent conflict appearing on the front page of tomorrow's newspaper?"

This writer believes that the safest thing to do in cases of potential conflict is full disclosure and waiver signed by all parties, recognizing such potential conflict and agreement to proceed.

B. Competence (Model Standards of Conduct Sec. IV)

A Mediator shall Mediate Only When the Mediator has the Necessary Qualifications to Satisfy the Reasonable Expectations of the Parties.

Successful mediators may think they can mediate any dispute. Needless to say, this kind of hubris can lead to disasters. It would behoove the mediator to make available, in an honest way, his or her experience in the subject matter at the center of the dispute and his or her experience as a mediator, and if the matter falls outside the bounds of competence the assignment should be declined. Conversely, counsel for a party should not be afraid to ask the mediator for his or her qualifications as typically, especially claimants, may want to know. Fortunately, competency is not really an issue in the LHWCA community, as virtually all mediators and attorneys who practice in this field throughout the country are known to all.

These concepts apply to the fees that will be charged. Regardless of who is paying, everyone involved should know what is being charged for the services. This brings up another point somewhat unique to mediation in LHWCA matters. Generally, the defense agrees to be responsible for the entirety of the mediator's fees and costs. While this is the custom and practice, often dictated by statute, across the board in worker's compensation litigation, claimant's themselves may not be aware of this custom and should be informed to avoid any thoughts of bias due to a lack of "skin in the game" from their side.

C. Impartiality (Model Standards of Conduct Sec. II)

A Mediator Shall Conduct the Mediation in an Impartial Manner.

This point seemingly is covered by the rule governing conflict of interests, but is subtly different as it applies more to the proceedings themselves, as opposed to the matter in dispute. There may be no direct or indirect conflict of interest at the outset, but during the course of proceedings the mediator may come to dislike or unreasonably favor one party over another because of what is said during a caucus (for example a racial or ethnic slur). Such a response might be natural to some degree and easy to overcome. But if it is recognized that moving forward in an impartial manner has become impossible, the mediator must withdraw.

D. Voluntariness or Self Determination (Model Standards of Conduct Sec. I)

A Mediator shall Recognize that Mediation is Based on the Principle of Self Determination by the Parties.

Generally, and virtually always in LHWCA disputes, participation is voluntary. The mediator must be cognizant of this point and be aware that his or her role is to facilitate or help the parties reach their own agreement. If one or the other of the parties wishes to withdraw at any time, that is their prerogative. While sometimes difficult to grasp, the mediator's success rate is not paramount. That the parties reach an agreement of their own free will is all that matters.

E. Confidentiality (Model Standards of Conduct Sec. V)

A Mediator shall Maintain The Reasonable Expectations of the Parties with Regard to Confidentiality.

Confidentiality is a cornerstone to a successful mediation. It ties in to several of the other principles such as Honesty, Self-Determination and Impartiality. The parties need to feel that communication in private caucus sessions are as confidential as conversations between attorney and client. That having been said, parties also need to know that when the mediator goes into caucus with other sides, the information obtained in sessions will be used just as the party's attorney might use it to advocate a client's position in negotiations. It is prudent, however, for the mediator to ask before leaving one caucus for another, if there was anything divulged that the party or counsel does not want to be shared with the opposing side.

There are actually two aspects to confidentiality in mediation. First is the aforementioned confidentiality in presenting one party's position to another when there has been an admonition to withhold specified conversation or documentary material. The other is confidentiality about the proceedings themselves. It is axiomatic that mediators may not be compelled to testify or otherwise divulge what was said or developed during mediation, successful or not. The duty to keep the proceedings confidential applies to the attorneys who participate in the mediation and the mediator as well. In this regard, it is wise to have all parties acknowledge such confidentiality via a written document, executed prior to the proceedings, which sets forth the duty to be confidential, including that of the mediator.

There are some limits or exceptions to the sacred duty of confidentiality. Most, if not all, jurisdictions have codified these limitations. Similar to a psychiatrist's or psychologist's duty to inform if information comes to them concerning a threat to harm another, a mediator may be free to divulge when aware of the same threat, or of child abuse, or planned commission of a crime.

F. Informed Consent and Quality of the Process (Model Standards of Conduct Sec. VI)

A Mediator shall Conduct the Mediation Fairly, Diligently, and in a Manner Consistent with the Principle of Self-Determination by the Parties.

The mediator's goal is to facilitate a resolution. In other ADR roles, the neutral may have a decision-making role. Generally, LHWCA mediators have spent whole careers as litigators or judges in the field. Consequently, it is hard to avoid the temptation to interject their own thoughts on how the case will go at trial and maybe what she or he foresees the settlement positions will be at a later point in the mediation. This is only natural though and that mediator's experience and willingness to voice it may be just what the lawyers were after when selecting him or her to serve. However, the goal of reaching resolution through the parties' self-determination must not be lost. The mediator may assist by making sure that enough data is available for parties to be aware of options and alternatives to enable a meaningful, informed consent. But the guiding principle that any agreement must be the parties' alone should be paramount.

G. Advertising and Solicitation (Model Standards of Conduct Sec. VII) and Fees (Model Standards of Conduct Sec. VIII)

A Mediator shall be Truthful in Advertising and Solicitation for Mediation

A Mediator shall fully Disclose and Explain the Basis of Compensation, Fees and Charges to the Parties

Advertising is permissible but of course, should be honest and truthful in addressing qualifications as a mediator and in the fields of the mediator's expertise. The mediator should not list his "win/loss" record and should be straight forward about fees and costs to be charged.

Fees should be disclosed in advance and reduced to a written agreement. The mediator is impartial and must have no interest in the outcome. Thus, in no event should the fee be contingent on a successful outcome. Likewise, the fee cannot be tied to the amount of the settlement.

H. Obligations to the Mediation Process Mediators have a Duty to Improve the Practice of Mediation (Model Standards of Conduct Sec. 9)

While with us as a means to resolve human disputes for centuries, mediation as a tool in resolving legal disputes, and particularly in LHWCA cases, is a relatively modern development. Accordingly, mediators are duty bound to educate the community about the value of mediation, to make it accessible and to improve their skills individually and those who practice the skill as a whole.

21.3 Being Prepared for Mediation

by Paul M. Doolittle, Esq.

In order for mediation to be productive, the parties need to prepare for same well in advance. Mediation is an expensive endeavor, usually involving travel for the parties and the mediator. For the claimant, the mediation conference is frequently stressful, so appearing without knowing essential facts, such as whether an MSA is required, whether Conditional Payments are an issue, whether an annuity will be proposed, or whether liens exist, is a recipe for failure. The goal of this portion of the chapter is to provide tools for the parties to ensure that they are prepared for mediation.

Will an MSA be necessary? If so, will the mediation take place before or after CMS determines the amount of the MSA? Do the parties wish to settle indemnity and attorney's fees now, and medical later? If so, who will be authorized to treat, and what treatment will be authorized, if any? If the E/C is not willing to bifurcate the settlement, reaching a "number" usually means that the E/C agrees to fund the amount CMS determines is necessary, or leave medical open if CMS determines the proposed MSA is deficient by a significant sum. For more on Medicare Set-Aside Arrangements, see Appendix 20.1.

Claimant lawyers should explain to their client what an MSA is, and how it works, well in advance of mediation. At least one Defense Base Act Carrier now requires that MSAs be professionally administered, so for the Claimant that wants a "complete divorce" from the Employer/Carrier, his MSA funds will be tied up until he passes away, at which time, depending upon the settlement terms, the remaining funds either revert to the Employer/Carrier, or the Claimant's estate.

Have Conditional Payments been made? If so, who takes responsibility for paying same? Well in advance of mediation, the claimant lawyer should go to www.MyMedicare.Gov to create a "Conditional Payment Request Confirmation Page." Upon receipt of the amount of Conditional Payments, the claimant lawyer should review same with the client in order to separate payments made for work, and non-work related treatment. Then, the claimant lawyer should forward to the Employer/Carrier the list of work related treatment that Medicare paid for; the issue of who reimburses Medicare is now up for discussion. For more information on Conditional Payments, see Appendix B.

The parties also need to factor in work-related but non-Medicare covered expenses, such as mileage, deductibles, co-pays, the "gap" (also known as the Doughnut Hole) in prescription coverage pursuant to Medicare Part D, routine hearing exams, hearing aids, exams for fitting hearing aids, long-term custodial care, most dental care, eye examinations related to prescribing glasses, cosmetic surgery, acupuncture, and routine foot care. If you are not sure whether Medicare covers a test, item, or service, visit https://www.medicare.gov/coverage/your-medicare-coverage.html.

Although the MSA may include a recommended surgery, if same requires hospitalization who pays the $1,288 deductible for the hospital inpatient deductible? By the same token, Medicare Part B is not mandatory, unlike Medicare Part A, and if the claimant believes or argues that he would not have a need to purchase Part B but for his work related injury, he will want the Employer/Carrier to pay for same, including his deductibles and co-pays. The Carrier will respond by saying that the Claimant needs or will need Part B for other, non-work related conditions, and then the discussion begins. Medicare Part C, also known as Medicare Advantage, consists of Medicare-approved private health insurance plans for individuals with Part A and Part B coverage. These plans supplement Part A and Part B, and generally offer additional benefits, such as vision, dental, and hearing, or prescription drug coverage. For the Claimant who is concerned with the ability to pay for his treatment post settlement, Part C will provide assurances and allay his fears; the question is who will pay for Part C? If vision, dental, hearing, or prescription drug coverage is necessary as a result of the work related injuries, then it might behoove the Employer/Carrier to pay for Part C, as it will decrease their exposure. Medicare Part D, the prescription drug plan, requires the recipient to pay a premium, a yearly deductible, co-payments or co-insurance, and costs in the coverage gap (Doughnut Hole), which for 2015 were a whopping $4,700 annual out of pocket threshold. Again, you have a worried Claimant at mediation, and an Employer/Carrier that wants a closed file; these issues must be addressed, they need to be addressed *before* mediation, and the Employer/Carrier needs to determine the best route to address Claimant's concerns while also taking into consideration their exposure for future work related medical treatment, regardless of whether same is covered by Medicare.

Another way to reduce Claimant's concern regarding future medical care is to discuss with him, *prior* to mediation, whether he is taking prescriptions—or may change his prescriptions—to those that are covered by Walmart's Retail Prescription Program Drug List; a 30 day supply is only $4 and a 90 day supply is $10. In addition, there are two mail order prescription companies that cater to injured workers, Injured Workers Pharmacy (888) 321-7945, and Summit Pharmacy (877) 678-5400. Both of these vendors will bill per the fee schedule.

Many times a structured annuity will be proposed, and in some cases, they really benefit the Claimant who wants that "mailbox check" or income during retirement, so the Claimant lawyer should discuss this issue, again, well in advance of the mediation, with his client. Providing sample annuities for the Claimant to see, in increments of $50,000, $100,000, etc. is beneficial. If the settlement includes an annuity, the OWCP Procedure Manual recommends the following or similar language be contained in the 8(i) and the Order Approving same:

> Upon payment of the aforesaid monies, the Employer/Carrier shall be forever discharged and released of any further liability for payment of compensation to the employee under the Longshore and Harbor Workers' Compensation Act. Should the carrier or any other party designated to make the continuing payments fail to make the payments, liability to make the payments shall revert to the original Employer/Carrier.

The parties should also attempt, well in advance of mediation, to determine the existence, and amount, of any liens from group health providers, the Veteran's Administration, prior Claimant counsel, etc. It frequently takes time to obtain lien amounts from group health providers, so waiting until the last minute to obtain this information, as well as the name and phone number of the subrogation adjuster, will result in frustrations during the mediation conference. Make sure the adjuster will be *available* during the conference. Counsel for Employer/Carrier should reach out to prior Claimant counsel to ascertain the basis and amount of any lien. Once again, reaching out for the first time, during the mediation conference, is not conducive to a meaningful settlement.

Almost all Employer/Carrier counsel want proof that the Claimant has not applied for Social Security Disability Insurance, so, *prior* to mediation, counsel for Claimant should have his client go to: http://www.ssa.gov/myaccount to create an account, which takes about five minutes. Once the account has been created, click "Get a Benefit Verification Letter" which will show that the Claimant is, or is not, a beneficiary.

If there are other causes of action that will be impacted by settling the underlying claim, those need to be discussed prior to the mediation. Such causes of action include wrongful termination/labor/employment claims, third party claims, etc.

Claimants need to understand "present value," "rated age," and settlement ranges, in addition to the strengths and weaknesses of their case. This discussion should not take place, for the *first time*, at the mediation conference. If the Claimant needs to discuss settlement figures with someone (his wife, his financial expert), then that person should either be present during mediation, or available on quick notice.

Obviously, the more the parties know of and discuss prior to mediation, the smoother the process will be. Claimant will not be as apprehensive as he would otherwise, and the Employer/Carrier will more fully understand Claimant's demand and their potential exposure.

Appendix A

- As part of a workers' compensation settlement, the parties may pursue a CMS-approved Workers' Compensation Medicare Set-Aside Arrangement (WCMSA) to establish certainty, with respect to settlement amount, that must be appropriately exhausted before Medicare begins to pay.
- Those funds are set aside to pay for future medical and prescription drug expenses related to the injury, illness, or disease that would normally be covered by Medicare.
- These funds are deposited into a WCMSA, which is a financial agreement that allocates a portion of the settlement monies to pay specifically for future medical services related to the work-related injury, illness, or disease.
- These funds must be depleted before Medicare will pay for treatment related to the workers' compensation injury, illness, or disease.
- All parties in a workers' compensation case have significant responsibilities under the Medicare Secondary Payer (MSP) laws to protect Medicare's interests when resolving cases that include future medical expenses. The recommended method to protect Medicare's interests is a WCMSA.
- The amount of the WCMSA is determined on a case-by-case basis. Please review the *Determining if a WCMSA is Reasonable* document, provided with the materials herein, to assist you with your WCMSA submission.
- When submitting a WCMSA for review, it may be submitted electronically through the WCMSA Portal (WCMSAP) rather than by paper or CD through the mail. The portal submission is the recommended approach as it is significantly more efficient than sending information through the mail.
- Attorneys, Medicare beneficiaries, insurance carriers, and WCMSA vendors may use the WCMSAP to enter WCMSA case information directly. Registration is required to use the WCMSAP.
- Additional information for attorneys, Medicare beneficiaries, claimants, insurance carriers, representative payees, and WCMSA vendors can be found at:

> https://www.cms.gov/Medicare/Coordination-of-Benefits/Workers-Compensation-Medicare-Set-Aside-Arrangements/WCMSAP/WCMSAP-page.html

Appendix B

- Reporting the case is the first step in the Medicare recovery process. Medicare beneficiaries, through their attorney or otherwise, must notify the BCRC and report the case.
- Attorneys representing beneficiaries must submit proper proof of representation in order for the BCRC to release information, such as a copy of the signed and dated retainer agreement with the beneficiary. Once proof of representation is received, the BCRC may communicate with the attorney or representative and act upon requests such as furnishing the conditional payment information, the recovery demand letter, and addressing questions regarding claims included in the conditional payment information. **Note:** A Consent to Release authorizes an individual or entity to receive *certain information* from the BCRC for a *limited* period of time.
- Once the case is reported, BCRC searches Medicare records for claims paid by Medicare based upon the information reported, identifying claims that Medicare paid that are related to the case that should have been paid by another entity as the primary payer. The BCRC will create an MSP occurrence and post it to Medicare's records. After the MSP occurrence is posted, the BCRC will send a Rights and Responsibilities (RAR) letter explaining what information is needed.
- Within 65 days of issuance of the RAR letter, the BCRC will send a Conditional Payment Letter (CPL) and Payment Summary Form (PSF). The PSF lists all items or services that Medicare has paid conditionally which the BCRC has identified as being related to the pending case.
- On February 27, 2015, CMS issued a rule implementing provisions of the Strengthening Medicare and Repaying Taxpayers Act of 2012 (the SMART ACT). This rule establishes an appeals process for applicable plans in situations where the Secretary seeks MSP recovery directly from an applicable plan. The rule is effective April 28, 2015 and applies to demand letters issued on or after April 28, 2015.
- If a settlement, judgment, award, or other payment has already occurred when you first report the case, a Conditional Payment Notification (CPN) will be issued. A CPN will also be issued when the BCRC is notified of settlement, judgement, award or other payment through an insurer/workers' compensation entity's MMSEA Section 111 report. The CPN provides conditional payment information and advises you on what actions must be taken. You have 30 calendar days to respond.

- Reporting the case is the first step in the Medicare recovery process. Medicare beneficiaries, through their attorney or otherwise, must notify the BCRC and report the case.
- Attorneys representing beneficiaries must submit proper proof of representation in order for the BCRC to release information, such as a copy of the signed and dated retainer agreement with the beneficiary. Once proof of representation is received, the BCRC may communicate with the attorney or representative and act upon requests such as furnishing the conditional payment information, the recovery demand letter, and addressing questions regarding claims included in the conditional payment information. **Note:** A Consent to Release authorizes an individual or entity to receive *certain information* from the BCRC for a *limited* period of time.
- Once the case is reported, BCRC searches Medicare records for claims paid by Medicare based upon the information reported, identifying claims that Medicare paid that are related to the case that should have been paid by another entity as the primary payer. The BCRC will create an MSP occurrence and post it to Medicare's records. After the MSP occurrence is posted, the BCRC will send a Rights and Responsibilities (RAR) letter explaining what information is needed.
- Within 65 days of issuance of the RAR letter, the BCRC will send a Conditional Payment Letter (CPL) and Payment Summary Form (PSF). The PSF lists all items or services that Medicare has paid conditionally which the BCRC has identified as being related to the pending case.
- On February 27, 2015, CMS issued a rule implementing provisions of the Strengthening Medicare and Repaying Taxpayers Act of 2012 (the SMART ACT). This rule establishes an appeals process for applicable plans in situations where the Secretary seeks MSP recovery directly from an applicable plan. The rule is effective April 28, 2015 and applies to demand letters issued on or after April 28, 2015.
- If a settlement, judgment, award, or other payment has already occurred when you first report the case,

a Conditional Payment Notification (CPN) will be issued. A CPN will also be issued when the BCRC is notified of settlement, judgement, award or other payment through an insurer/workers' compensation entity's MMSEA Section 111 report. The CPN provides conditional payment information and advises you on what actions must be taken. You have 30 calendar days to respond.

21.4 Negotiations at Mediation

by Collins C. Rossi, Esq.

Although neither party may realize it, negotiations in a claim under the LHWCA begin right after the injury occurs. The parties begin asserting their positions immediately. The initial issue to be resolved is usually the selection of the physician who has the first opportunity to examine the claimant following the injury. From that point forward the parties continue to go back and forth in an effort to establish the extent of the injuries sustained by the claimant.

While the Code of Federal Regulations has authorized ALJs to act as "settlement judges" for over twenty years, the use of mediation in LHWCA claims (whether through the DOL's settlement judge program or by private mediation) has skyrocketed in the past several years. Here, the discussion with regard to negotiations will be limited, as much as possible, to negotiating at a mediation.

In any negotiation, three elements typically need to be considered. They are *time*, *power*, and *information*. The example above—who will be the first doctor to examine the claimant—contains all three elements. Determining how soon after the injury will the claimant be seen by a physician clearly concerns issues related to time. Determining the identity of the initial examining physician will be arguably give that party greater power over the direction the claim takes. The selection of any physician (claimant's choice, DME, or IME) also controls the information the ALJ considers in determining the amount of benefits the claimant will receive.

A. When to Mediate

Obviously the initial matter to address is when should the parties begin to explore the use of mediation as a method of resolving the claim. There are certain mileposts in the life of a claim that tend to be optimal times to mediate.

Typically, these mileposts arise when there is the development of evidence which could change the direction or status of the claim. Some of these mileposts seem to give the employer/carrier more leverage in suggesting mediation, some give the claimant the edge, and some are mutually beneficial to the parties.

The employer/carrier's receipt of a favorable report from its DME (defense medical examination) or SMO (second medical opinion) is the first example of a milepost where mediation should be considered. Such a report could either break the causal connection between the accident or the injury or determine that the claimant has no disability. If the ALJ accepts the findings in the employer/carrier's DME report, employer/carrier would be able to reduce or terminate compensation payments. Such action definitely changes the status of the claim.

The results of a labor market survey are a second example. If the ALJ accepts the results of the LSM, employer/carrier may be in a position to either reduce of terminate compensation benefits.

The DME or SMO report and labor market survey report seem to give the employer/carrier greater leverage in promoting the use of mediation. The possibility of the termination or reduction of compensation is often sufficient motivation to bring claimant to the bargaining table.

Here, the employer/carrier has essentially two options once receiving a favorable DME or labor market survey. Employer/carrier can advise claimant of its ability to terminate or reduce compensation but will refrain from doing so if claimant agrees to mediation. Alternatively, employer/carrier could make a partial reduction in compensation in accordance with the lower paying jobs in its labor market survey and suggest mediation. Pending an unsuccessful mediation, a further reduction (or termination) could occur. Lastly, employer/carrier could terminate compensation in its entirety and offer mediation at that point.

Claimant's treating physician issuing a report either suggesting surgery, restricting claimant's ability to return to work or rejecting the employment outlined in employer/carrier's labor market survey is an example of evidence which tends to give the claimant more leverage in suggesting mediation. If the ALJ accepts any of the conclusions a report from the claimant's choice of physician, the value of the claim increases. The possibility of the value of the claim increasing may be sufficient motivation to bring employer/carrier to the bargaining table.

Employer/carrier's motivation to mediate may be increase where it obtains the report of a DME which either confirms the conclusions of claimant's choice of physician or finds a claimant has sustained a greater disability than that determined by claimant's choice of physician. A DME's conclusion that claimant needs medical care more extensive than that recommended by claimant's choice of physician is another example.

Due to the fact that claimant has no control over the payment of compensation or medical benefits, the development of medical or vocational evidence favorable to the claimant does not afford the claimant the same ability to apply pressure to mediate as employer/carrier's ability to reduce or terminate compensation. This dynamic may change when the parties learn which ALJ has been assigned to hear the claim or if there is a rapidly approaching trial date.

Examples of mileposts that benefit both parties usually concern scheduling matters regarding the formal hearing of the claim. Discovery deadlines allow the parties to avoid incurring expert fees or other associated costs in preparing for trial. Avoiding the formal hearing and issuance of a compensation order is another example. Where the claimant is not receiving compensation, the delays in the issuance of a decision and order (and hence payment of benefits) is also a factor in a claimant's willingness to mediate.

B. Mediation Preparation

Preparation for mediation should include at least three elements: knowing the factual basis of the claim, knowing the value of the claim (and how the value of the LHWCA claim relates to other existing claims), and determining what benefit the party hopes to obtain from the negotiations.

Knowing the factual basis of the claim is self-explanatory.

From the claimant's standpoint, knowing the value of the claim entails more than being able to determine the value of the claim discounted to present day value. The claimant's financial condition should also be taken into account. Often the claimant's financial situation mandates that a settlement occur sooner rather than later; i.e. awaiting the issuance of a decision and order.

Consideration of a claimant's financial status should not affect the parties' ability to obtain approval of the settlement. Section 8(i) mandates that the criteria for approval of the settlement is that the settlement must be adequate and not obtained under duress. In *Richardson v. Huntington Ingalls*, Inc., 48 BRBS 23 (May 22, 2014), 2014 WL 2649645, BRB No. 13-0476, the Benefits Review Board concluded that the settlement application does not need to contain specific information supporting the adequacy of the settlement. Approval of the settlement as being adequate may be supported by the allegations of the parties. General assertions may be sufficient to justify accepting a significant discount from the judgment value of a claim where the claimant is represented by counsel who is presumed to be competent and ethical. The decision in *Richardson* gives the attorney representing the claimant the necessary latitude to resolve the claim in accordance with what is in the claimant's interests. Therefore, such factors as the delays in obtaining a compensation order, claimant's ability to properly manage the settlement proceeds, and claimant's assessment of his own vocational abilities can be considered when his attorney counsels him regarding acceptance of any settlement offer. The specifics of these issues need not be included in the application for settlement.

Knowledge of the interplay of other benefits with the LHWCA claim should also be evaluated prior to the mediation. A claimant may have a contemporaneous claim for Social Security Disability Insurance (SSDI) or for Social Security Retirement Benefits. If the claimant has a claim for SSDI, the attorney must be aware of claimant's average current earnings (ACE) and how to coordinate both benefit schemes to afford the claimant the maximum recovery.

Longshore claimants' benefits may also need to be coordinated with union benefits or other retirement plans. Often, employers in Defense Base Act claims may provide their employees with long term disability benefits. The provisions of the LTD policy may allow the LTD carrier to file a SSDI claim on behalf of the claimant without specifically obtaining claimant's permission to do so; receipt of LTD benefits may create an implied permission to file the claim on claimant's behalf. When this occurs, both the LTD carrier and Social Security may seek reimbursement of monies paid to or on behalf of the claimant. In this type of situation reimbursement of the LTD carrier or obtaining a Medicare Set Aside Account may be necessary.

Entitlement to medical benefits are often affected by the status of any SSDI or Social Security retirement benefits claim. Here, the need to establish a Medicare Set Aside Account needs to be determined.

Claimants may also have access to additional sources for the payment of future medical benefits. If the claimant is a veteran, VA or TRICARE benefits may be available. Union benefits may also provide a source for the payment of future benefits. These benefits also need to be coordinated with the benefits available to claimant under the LHWCA.

From the employer/carrier's perspective, there is much less to worry about regarding the coordination of benefits. Often the settlement is simply a financial decision. However, issues related to the need for an MSA have to be considered as employer/carrier may find themselves liable to CMS for payments made to or on behalf of the claimant for medical care.

C. Finally—At the Mediation

The non-legal parameters of the mediation should be established at the onset. Parties may have time constraints, travel arrangements or other factors affecting the length of the mediation. Internet access at the mediation site is also a consideration.

If the parties do not have experience from prior mediations, a determination of your opponent's negotiating style must be considered. Some participants see the mediation as no different from any other step in the litigation process; i.e. that there are winners and there are losers. Typically, these participants employ a "win at all costs" mentality at the mediation. Negotiating techniques may often include contingencies which are likely to occur (otherwise known as threats). From the claimant's side, the possibility of the claimant undergoing surgery may be a factor which will increase the amount the employer/carrier may be willing to offer in settlement. From the employer's side, the distinct possibility that a termination of compensation may occur can make claimant more willing to negotiate. Negotiations under these circumstances take place in a "crisis" environment. Participants with this style are typically not open to anything other than trading numbers back and forth and the only acceptable endpoint is a definite dollar amount.

While the constant use of threats is often counterproductive, sometimes they may be necessary to avoid an impasse in negotiations. So called "walk away" power is one example. If one side threatens to abandon the mediation the tone of negotiations may change for the better.

At the opposite end of the spectrum is the participant who cannot make a decision. These participants exist in an environment of fear. Negotiations break down due to the inability of this participant to make a decision.

To effectively deal with either of these mediating styles these participants must be reminded that mediation is a tool in the claims process which is designed to bring about an amicable resolution of the claim. It is not designed to force your opponent into submission.

Probably one of the hardest decisions to make in negotiating a settlement is the starting point; i.e. how much should be offered to be begin the negotiations. This decision is based upon several factors including the negotiating styles of the parties.

Often one side in the mediation will begin negotiating with a "home run" number; i.e. the absolute maximum (or minimum) value of the claim.

Assuming both sides are being reasonable, the range regarding the value of the claim is always the same. The high point of that range, asserted by the claimant is the highest average weekly wage with the lowest residual wage earning capacity. The low end of that range, asserted by employer/carrier, is the lowest average weekly range with the highest residual wage earning capacity.

The discounted present value of the claim can be defined as the current worth of cash to be received in the future with one or more payments, which has been discounted at a specific rate of interest. The present value of future cash flows is always less than the same amount of future cash flows. Stated simply, the present value of a claim is the amount of money which, if invested today, would allow the payment of all future compensation.

The following illustrates the concept of present value. Assume a 42 year old claimant has a life expectancy of 36 years. If that claimant received compensation at the weekly rate of $500.00, that claimant could expect to receive $936,000.00 over the remainder of his life. (36 years equals 1,872 weeks; $500.00 per week for 1,872 weeks equals $936,000.00) If the employer/carrier was able to invest a sum of money and obtain a 5% return on that investment, the employer/carrier could invest approximately $430,000.00 and pay claimant's compensation for the claimant's entire 36 year life expectancy. The $430,000.00 represents the discounted present value of the claim.

Using the above example, the claimant's opening "home run" demand for compensation benefits at the mediation would be $936,000.00, the amount the claimant would be paid if he lives a normal life expectancy and there is no reduction in the weekly compensation rate. Due to the fact that the employer/carrier can invest $430,000.00 and pay claimant compensation for the rest of his life expectancy, that amount typically represents the ultimate the employer/carrier would ever consider paying to resolve the claim. An employer/carrier's settlement authority is typically a fraction of the discounted value.

Since $430,000.00 is the most the employer/carrier would ever pay, their opening offer may be only $10,000.00. The reason this low of an offer may be made could be to establish the midpoint; i.e. the halfway point between the demand and the offer. The midpoint is calculated by adding the most recent demand and most recent offer and dividing by two. The midpoint here is $473,000.00. (The $936,000.00 demand plus the $10,000.00 offer totals $946,000.00 divided by two equals $473,000.00)

Right, wrong or indifferent, the participants in a mediation look to the midpoint as the amount that typically determines each party's subsequent demands and offers. While the midpoint is useful in conveying to the other side the amount you are willing to accept in settlement, it should never be the only factor a participant considers while negotiating. One significant reason to avoid relying only on the midpoint is that the claimant's demands are what lowers the midpoint and the employer/carrier's offers are what raises the midpoint. Each side actually works against itself in establishing the midpoint.

Another problem with concentrating only on the midpoint is that it bogs down the parties' respective abilities to respond to each other's offers. Reliance on the midpoint reduces the negotiations to merely trading numbers. If the emphasis is only on the amount of the settlement, that amount may never be reached. Effective mediations usually develop a rhythm between the participants. When that rhythm establishes momentum, the participants are well on their way to confecting a settlement. Small moves by either side which are made only to affect the midpoint works against any rhythm or momentum in the negotiations.

When the negotiations begin to stall, two techniques can be used to reignite the movement between the parties: the use of brackets, or looking at interests rather than amounts.

Again we use the above example where the claimant initially demanded $936,000.00 and the employer/carrier offered $10,00.00. Assuming each side made four moves each of $10,000.00 the claimant would now be demanding $896,000.00 and the employer/carrier would be offering $50,000.00. Frustration can easily arise. Claimant would contend that employer/carrier has only matched claimant's moves and has only raised their offer $40,000.00. Employer/carrier would respond both that claimant's initial demand was unrealistic and additionally that employer/carrier has increased their opening offer by 400% whereas claimant has only reduced their opening demand by less than 5%.

A bracket is essentially a jump towards the middle by both parties which hopefully jumpstarts renewed movement in the negotiations. Currently the claimant is demanding $896,000.00 and the employer/carrier is offering 50,000.00.

At this time the employer/carrier could propose a bracket where the employer/carrier would increase their offer to $200,000.00 if the claimant would reduce their demand to $500,000.00. In this instance the claimant would have several options. Claimant could accept the bracket and the negotiations would continue from there. Claimant could reject the bracket and ask employer/carrier to make another offer. Lastly, claimant could propose their own bracket; i.e. claimant would reduce their demand to $650.000.00 if employer/carrier would increase their offer to $300,000.00. If the claimant was the one who initially proposed the bracket, employer/carrier would have the same options: accept the bracket, refuse the bracket and request another demand, or propose their own bracket.

Rather than use brackets, determining a party's interests and addressing those interests may be an effective method of reviving stalled negotiations.

Determining interests is seen in the following example. Two people are performing clerical work in the same room. One wants the window open and the other wants it closed. They continue to argue about whether the window should be open and if so how much it should be open. No solution satisfies them both. A third coworker hears the two arguing and asks what they are arguing about. The worker who wants the window open wants to get fresh air. The other worker wants the window shut to avoid the draft. The coworker goes into an adjoining room and opens wide a window in the next room, bringing in fresh air without a draft. Both workers are satisfied. By looking at the coworkers' interests rather than the degree the window was to be opened, a resolution acceptable to both was attained.

The workers arguing over the window only considered options that existed between their respective positions; either the window was open, closed or somewhere in between. When parties only concentrate on the midpoint, the only solution they see is how much money is on the table; i.e. how wide should the window be opened. The third coworker looked to the parties' interests and found a solution which addressed the desires of both. By considering each's interests, the solution was found outside of their respective positions. Opening a window in another room was something neither one considered yet it addressed both of their needs.

Where the negotiations lose traction questions need to be addressed to the opposing side to determine their interests rather than the amount of the settlement. Employer/carrier should initiate communication with the claimant to show the claimant what can be done with the settlement funds; retire debt, obtain retraining. Claimant should impress on employer/carrier that sweetening the pot would prevent a running award, negate the cost of any future medical treatment and eliminate any future costs in defending the claim.

Interests can also be addressed by asking the opposing party what are the consequences if the claim doesn't settle. If the claimant is receiving compensation at the maximum amount for benefits he would be entitled to, going to trial would do little to improve his current condition. He would still receive the same amount in compensation and he would still need to get any medical treatment approved by the employer/carrier. There would be no guarantee for the payment of future benefits; death or re-injury could extinguish his entitlement to benefits.

Conversely, without a settlement, employer/carrier could be faced with a running award. While modification of that award is possible, obtaining modification would take considerable time; additionally, there is no guarantee that modification would be granted. Additionally, costs of defending the claim would continue to accrue.

D. Extras

Sometimes "extras" need to be provided at the end of the mediation where the parties are close to settling yet additional consideration is needed to close the deal.

One typical enticement for the claimant to settle would be for the employer/carrier to continue to pay compensation pending approval of the settlement. Employer/carrier's concern here would be that claimant could indefinitely delay approval of the settlement by not returning a completed 8(i) to the employer/carrier for filing. A possible solution to this situation would be for the employer/carrier to agree to continue payment of weekly benefits with the provision that the claimant return the executed 8(i) to employer/carrier within a certain time limit; e.g. ten days. If claimant fails to return the 8(i) employer/carrier would then terminate compensation.

Rather than continue to pay compensation, employer/carrier could agree to providing the 8(i) to claimant within a certain time limit and then use its best efforts to obtain approval of the 8(i) as soon as possible. (Since claimant has the ability to withdraw from the settlement any time prior to approval, employer/carrier would have the necessary motivation to expedite approval of the settlement.)

Often the parties have to bifurcate the settlement; compensation is settled immediately, medical benefits cannot be settled until an MSA is approved. Often the issue is these instances is the payment of attorney fees to the claimant attorney for services rendered in obtaining approval of the MSA. That attorney may be reluctant to perform services where no payment may be due; i.e. assisting in the approval of an MSA and subsequent 8(i). Here, either a portion of the fees or an additional fee can be paid for whatever services are necessary to obtain the approval of the medical portion of the claim. In the event the employer/carrier chooses not to settle medical benefits because the MSA is too expensive, the parties need to specify what fees, if any, the claimant attorney will be paid for services rendered.

E. Alternate Resolutions

Prior to the mediation, each party should determine what result they hope to obtain from a settlement and work towards that goal. The dollar amount of the settlement, although typically the major consideration of any settlement, is only one element to consider.

From the claimant's perspective, several outcomes should be considered rather than the dollar amount of a final settlement. If the claim cannot be settled in its entirety, the next best option for the claimant may be the employer/carrier reinstituting compensation, agreeing to vocational retraining, or approving medical care. The parties could also enter into stipulations for the entry of a compensation order.

While preparation for the mediation is an absolute necessity, often there is no substitute for experience. No one can script the course the negotiations take in a mediation. It has been said that "no battle plan survives the first contact with the enemy." While a negotiating plan is a necessity going into a mediation, strict adherence to that plan is often fatal. Both sides need to be able to adjust to the course taken by the negotiations. Preparations should include a range within which the claim can be settled. If that range cannot be attained, alternate resolutions, such as those noted above, should be considered.

The failure of the claim to settle at the mediation does not mean the claim will never settle. The vast majority of claims that don't settle at mediation, where the parties are close to totally resolving the claim, seem to settle within a few days of the mediation.

One question participants in a mediation often ask is why is seems like all claims that settle do so in the last twenty minutes of the mediation. This mystery may be answered by Pareto's Law. Vilfredo Pareto, an Italian economist and socialist, set forth the 80/20 rule; i.e. 80% of what you do produces 20% of the results while 20% of what you do produces 80% of the results. Often it's the final minutes of the mediation where most of the work gets done, the 20%, where 80% of the work occurs.

Chapter 22

Trial: Witnesses & Discovery

Alexandra E. Grover, Esq., Jeffrey Winter, Esq., and David Barnett, Esq.

Synopsis

**"By failing to prepare,
you are preparing to fail."**
Benjamin Franklin

The U.S. Department of Labor's Office of Administrative Law Judges ("OALJ") is the "trial court" for many of the Department's programs. The OALJ adjudicates claims involving a variety of labor-related issues, including the Longshore & Harbor Workers' Compensation Act ("LHWCA"), the Defense Base Act ("DBA"), black-lung claims, Fair Labor Standards Act claims, and others. The OALJ has their own set of rules that govern litigation occurring before their office.[1] The focus of this chapter is on the preparation for trials on cases at the OALJ that fall within the purview of the LHWCA and DBA.

Most trial practitioners and litigators are of the belief that "trial" starts the first day you are retained. It is an additional belief that each day of trial builds on the groundwork laid during the previous trial days. The approach of this chapter is to discuss trial preparation embracing these beliefs.

22.1 The First Day of Trial: The Initial Interview

Whether it be the claimant or the adjuster, it is important to determine the real issues[2] rather than the emotional ones.

---

1. The *Rules of Practice and Procedure for Administrative Hearings Before the Office of Administrative Law Judges* (*"Rules of Practice and Procedure"*) were initially adopted in 1983 as an administrative law version of the Federal Rules of Civil Procedure, to provide procedural guidance practicing before the OALJ. Since their enactment in 1983, there have been two minor amendments to the *Rules of Practice and Procedure*: in 1994 regarding service of documents, and in 1999 creating a process for appointing "settlement judges" – administrative law judges appointed to act as mediators in litigated claims, with the agreement of the Parties. Over the past ten years there has been a large increase in the litigation of claims under the LHWCA due to the increased number of claims filed for injuries falling under the DBA—an extension of the LHWCA. As a result of the spike in litigation, the U.S. Department of Labor, the federal agency that administers and supervises all claims under the LHWCA and DBA, among others, determined that the *Rules of Practice and Procedure for Administrative Hearings Before the Office of Administrative Law Judges* needed refinement and modernization. 29 C.F.R. §§18, et al. (2015).

2. Issues that may arise throughout the litigation of a LHWCA or DBA case include:

- Jurisdiction;
- Coverage;
- Average weekly wage and corresponding compensation rate;
- Employer-employee relationship;
- Physical/psychological harm (AOE/COE);
- Timely notice;
- Timely filing;
- Last responsible employer/carrier;
- Disability—nature and extent;
- Suitable alternative employment (including ability to return to usual & customary work, vocational training, job search);

Yes, trial begins the very first time you talk with your client about the case. If you don't think so, then you are failing to prepare.

Claimant's counsel begins the preparation of a claimant for depositions and Carrier's choice examinations. This is also the time to obtain the names and address of all medical providers;[3] obtain wage information from Claimant; and, obtain information on witnesses as needed. What are the real issues and what do you need to prove them?

Similarly, from the defense side of the case, the initial case discussion with the insurance carrier's claims adjuster should be used not only to gather preliminary information about the case, but also to begin obtaining documents that may ultimately be produced. This process can also begin before a defense attorney has been retained—i.e., during the initial case discussion between the claims handler and the employer. While the case may not officially be a "litigated" case when it is first received or filed, the initial case discussion may be used as a tool to get ahead of future discovery issues. There are documents that exist from the outset of a claim that will not only be useful throughout the defense, but will also likely be requested by the opposing party(ies) in future discovery requests. For example, ensuring early receipt of the claimant's personnel and wage records, any transcripts from recorded statements, or incident reports from the employer may help to prevent unnecessary delay in future production or discovery motions.

Reviewing the existing, preliminary documents from the outset may also aid in narrowing the issues to be litigated. The parties will be less likely to spend needless time arguing about issues that could be stipulated upon review of certain documents. For instance, once an incident report has been received with supporting medical records, the employer and their carrier may decide that there are no disputes regarding the fact of injury or the causal relationship between the injury and the claimant's employment. Once the personnel and wage records have been reviewed, the parties may be able to agree on the claimant's average weekly wage. Asking for preliminary documents from the employer and claims adjuster at the beginning stages of a case may not only prevent future discovery issues but may also result in quicker resolution of the disputed issues.

22.2 The Second Day of Trial: What Evidence Is Missing?

What witnesses and documentary evidence are needed to close the gaps of evidentiary proof?

After the preliminary information has been gathered and the initial documents have been reviewed, it is important to determine whether there is a need for fact witnesses, expert witnesses, or additional documentary evidence to support the positions on the disputed issues. Seeking documentary evidence will be covered in the discovery section below.

A. Fact Witnesses

Claimant's counsel, after determining the real issues on the first day of trial, now follows through with the initial impressions. Aside from the claimant, who are the other witnesses needed to clear up and prove the issues? Even though you may not yet be taking depositions, the names, addresses, and contact information of potential witnesses should be obtained as early as possible. Fact witnesses could be the spouse, children, a supervisor, co-employees, employees of other contractors, someone who took pictures, investigators, and medical providers who may not be experts.

It is more common for claimants to use fact witnesses to support their arguments in the LHWCA/DBA arena; however, there are situations in which it is appropriate for the employer and carrier to consider obtaining testimony from fact witnesses. For example, an employee of the employer who receives notice of potential claims, or an employee who is charged with notifying the appropriate insurance carrier of new claims, could have helpful information regarding timely notice (or the lack thereof) under Section 12. Fact witnesses may also be helpful when there are questions regarding whether an injury actually occurred or if there are concerns about a claimant's credibility. In light of the nature of overseas contractor work, many of the supervisors and co-workers who could have helpful information may move employers or jobs long before a claim becomes litigated. In order to avoid the situation in which a potentially helpful fact witness is no longer employed with your client, it is important to consider and obtain contact information for fact witnesses as early as possible.

B. Expert Witnesses

In light of the nature of cases arising under the LHWCA/DBA, expert witnesses are typically limited to medical and vocational witnesses. Among other issues, medical experts may be helpful in determining whether an injury has oc-

- Residual wage earning capacity;
- Medical treatment;
- Borrowed servant;
- Relief from the Special Fund;
- Choice of physician;
- Maximum medical improvement; and
- Atorney's fees.

3. **PRACTICE TIP:** Many DBA claimants may have been treated at Landstühl Regional Medical Center in Germany. The location from which you can obtain these records is: Attn: National Personnel Record Center, Civilian Personnel Records, 1411 Boulder Blvd., Valmeyer, IL 62295; Fax (618) 935-3042.

curred, whether the injury that has occurred was caused by the conditions of the claimant's employment, and/or the extent of a work-related injury. In cases involving unique or complicated medical conditions, a non-testifying medical expert may be necessary to help the parties parse through medical jargon. Vocational experts may be useful when discussing differences in pre- and post-injury earning capacities.

Testifying experts should be carefully vetted, especially as cases arising under the LHWCA/DBA can involve issues that may be unique to even the most experienced physicians. The parties and their legal representatives should keep in mind the preferences of certain physicians as well as the preferences of the judges who preside in the jurisdiction in which the case will land. Many physicians who are used to providing reports in state workers' compensation claims do not like to give deposition or live testimony. Further, while some judges may prefer live expert testimony, there are many judges who would prefer to read the transcript from a pre-trial deposition. Engaging in conferences with experts before they are retained can ensure that the correct expert for the case and jurisdiction is chosen.[4]

22.3 The Third Day of Trial: Piecing Together the Puzzle Through Formal and Informal Discovery

It is only after the parties complete the informal resolution process before the Office of the District Director, OWCP, including filing a claim (form LS-203), publication of the claim to the Employer and Carrier by the District Director (form LS-215a), the completion of an Informal Conference in certain claims with the District Director, submission of a Pre-Hearing Statement (form LS-18), and referral of the claim by the District Director to the OALJ, that a claim is transferred to the Office of Administrative Law Judges. It is only after a claim is transferred to the OALJ, and the OALJ (or the Judge assigned to the case) issues an "initial notice" (i.e., a Docketing Order), or a Notice of Hearing and Pre-Hearing Order (i.e., the Order scheduling trial) that discovery may commence. 20 C.F.R. §18.50(a)(1).

Once issued, the Notice of Hearing and Pre-Hearing Order ("Order") serves as the parties' guide for the remainder of the litigation before the OALJ. As of the writing of this article, the OALJ has a headquarter office as well as seven regional offices, with a total of 40 administrative law judges. Every judge has their own preference when it comes to pre-hearing deadlines and trial specifics.[5] Parties should comply with both the *Rules of Practice and Procedure for Administrative Hearings Before the Office of Administrative Law Judges* and the assigned judge's specific Order. The litigation process can be streamlined, resulting in fewer non-substantive disputes, if all of the parties adhere to the guidelines and deadlines provided in the Order.

A. Initial Disclosures

One of the first opportunities for the parties to exchange information and documents is through initial disclosures. *Rule of Practice and Procedure* §18.50 is the new rule governing disclosures, and incorporates many requirements of the corresponding Federal Rule of Civil Procedure 26.[6] Rule 18.50 outlines disclosure requirements between the parties and mandates the parties "meet and confer" within 14 days from the date of receipt of the Notice of Hearing and Pre-Hearing Order. Rule §18.50 also assists the parties in developing a discovery plan, preserving evidence, and disclosing witnesses and anticipated evidence so that discovery disputes and delays can be avoided.

4. **PRACTICE TIP:** Parties may also use the pre-retention conference as an opportunity to begin obtaining information from each expert that should be disclosed pursuant to 29 C.F.R. § 18.50. The information that must ultimately be disclosed includes but is not limited to the expert's qualifications, publications authored in the previous 10 years, a list of cases in which the expert has testified in the previous 4 years, and a statement of the compensation to be paid to the expert.

5. For example, discovery deadlines may vary depending on the judge assigned to the case; there is no set deadline for any one type of case. Whether the deadline is 45 days, 30 days, or 10 days before trial, making sure the deadline is acknowledged as soon as the Order is received should aid in the litigation process.

6. By mirroring Federal Rule of Civil Procedure 26(a)(1), Rule §18.50(c)(1) requires the parties provide:

> (i) In general. Except as exempted by paragraph (c)(1)(ii) of this section or otherwise ordered by the judge, a party must, without awaiting a discovery request, provide to the other parties:
>
> (A) The name and, if known, the address and telephone number of each individual likely to have discoverable information—along with the subjects of that information—that the disclosing party may use to support its claims or defenses, unless the use would be solely for impeachment;
>
> (B) A copy—or a description by category and location—of all documents, electronically stored information, and tangible things that the disclosing party has in its possession, custody, or control and may use to support its claims or defenses, unless the use would be solely for impeachment; and
>
> (C) A computation of each category of damages claimed by the disclosing party—who must also make available for inspection and copying as under § 18.61 the documents or other evidentiary material, unless privileged or protected from disclosure, on which each computation is based, including materials bearing on the nature and extent of injuries suffered.

The requirement for "Initial Disclosures" is now mandatory across the board, and all parties must comply with Rule §18.50. The failure to make necessary disclosures may result in sanctions by the Court under section Rule §18.57, as the Court deems appropriate. See Federal Rule of Civil Procedure 37. Finally, a party must not avoid the disclosures because it has not investigated a claim, and cannot avoid disclosures based upon objection or failure of the opposing party to comply. The purpose of Rule §18.50 is to provide notice of issues, evidence, and witnesses as early as possible, with the goal of streamlining the litigation process. Like its Federal Rule of Civil Procedure counterpart, it is amazing the procedural issues that can be recognized and corrected at the onset of litigation using this practice.

B. Formal Discovery

29 C.F.R. §	Discovery Method	20 C.F.R. §	F.R.C.P.
18.60	Interrogatories	702.341	Fed. R. Civ. Pro. 33
18.61	Document Production		Fed. R. Civ. Pro. 34
18.62	Physical/Mental Exams		Fed. R. Civ. Pro. 35
18.63	Admissions		Fed. R. Civ. Pro. 36
18.64	Depositions by Oral Exam	702.341	Fed. R. Civ. Pro. 30
18.65	Depositions by Written Exam	702.341	Fed. R. Civ. Pro. 31

Typically, after the initial disclosures, the parties undertake discovery in order to secure necessary evidence for trial. Unlike some state workers' compensation schemes, the LHWCA, and by extension the DBA, give practitioners a variety of discovery methods, including Requests for Production, Interrogatories, Request for Admissions, medical examinations (IMEs), and oral or written depositions. Rules §§18.60–18.65; *see also* Federal Rules of Civil Procedure 22–31, 30, 31, 33–36. It is mandatory that the practitioner become familiar with the various rules impacting discovery, as many limits on discovery in the *Rules of Practice and Procedure* are the same as in the Federal Rules of Civil Procedure, such as limits on the number of interrogatories propounded, time requirements for notices of IME and production of reports, among others.

Regarding the topic of discovery in litigated claims, *Rules of Practice and Procedure*, 20 C.F.R. §§18, *et seq.*, contains specific administrative rules that mirror their counterparts in the Federal Rules of Administrative Procedure. In general, all of these statutes, rules, and regulations govern the practice before the OWCP as well as the OALJ, with the *Rules of Practice and Procedure* specifically dealing with practice and procedure before the OALJ. An intimate familiarity with these statutes, rules, and regulations will assist the practitioner in preparing a claim for trial ("Formal Hearing"), and how to conduct the necessary discovery in their case.

C. Obtaining Documentary Evidence

1. From claimant or client

If not already obtained, the following is a list of documents to obtain from the claimant assuming all issues are to be litigated:

- Job description;
- W-2's, check stubs, or direct deposit[7];
- Photographs[8];
- Video;
- Employment contract;
- Job search records—calendars, logs, internet printouts, and resume;
- Out-of-pocket medical expenses—pharmacy, mileage, co-pays;
- Disability documentation if received benefits from other source other than compensation;
- Last attempt to get medical documentation from overseas through client's contacts;
- Personnel records—termination, medical leave of absence forms, other employment issues that may affect credibility; and,
- Affidavits from co-employees.

2. From employer/carrier

As noted above, it is good practice to begin gathering preliminary documents—such as personnel records, transcripts from recorded statements, and incident reports—from the outset of a claim. Additional documents that may be obtained from the employer include the wage records of "similarly situated" employees (if average weekly wage is being calculated pursuant to 10(b)). It may also be beneficial to obtain payment screens from the insurance carrier as

7. These records are either to prove average weekly wage at the time of injury or claimant's residual earning capacity if she or he has returned to work.

8. May prove jurisdiction, physical or psychological harm.

well as any correspondence that was exchanged between the claims adjuster and the claimant before counsel was retained for either party.

3. From doctors

The backbone of any case arising under the LHWCA/DBA is the claimant's medical treatment. A claimant's treatment records[9] are some of the first records to be reviewed when preparing a party's arguments, and thus, it is important to quickly and efficiently be able to obtain such records. The treatment records may be obtained a number of ways. For an accepted claim in which the employer and carrier are authorizing and paying for medical treatment, it is appropriate for the treating providers to include copies of their reports with their invoices for payment. In such case, the treatment records may be obtained from the claims adjuster. In cases that have not been accepted, counsel may request that the claimant sign a HIPAA-compliant release allowing counsel to informally request the records from each treating provider. If a claimant is not amenable to signing a HIPAA release, then counsel may have to pursue records through a subpoena issued by the Office of Administrative Law Judges.[10]

An additional type of medical evidence that may be utilized in cases arising under the LHWCA/DBA are reports from experts. The more common method of evaluation of an injured worker is under Section 907(d)(4), at the request of the employer/carrier. The terms of art for these examinations will vary among practitioners, parties, and jurisdictions: "expert medical examination" or "IME," "defense medical examination" or "DME," or "compulsory medical examination" or "CME." Regardless of the term of art, the intent is the same: a medical or psychological examination by a physician or expert of the employer/carrier's choice to allow the parties to gain further insight into the injured worker's medical condition. The opinions of these hired experts will often form the basis of the employer/carrier's defenses in a claim—whether to maintain a denial of the claim, confirm the compensability of a claim, or, if benefits were being provided, to suspend provision of further benefits. These examinations are controlled by statute and regulation, and the injured worker must make all reasonable attempts to attend these examinations, or risk suspension of any benefits that may be due.[11]

4. From the DOL

All parties should also consider requesting a complete copy of the DOL's file materials for the claim to ensure that no procedural filings or notices have been ignored. Any party may request the records from any and all of the claimant's previous claims, whether to a similar body part or not, that may have been archived. Not only could the records from previous claims provide further insight into the claimant's past, but the records could ultimately serve as support for pursuit of relief from the Special Fund.

5. From the district director or regional solicitor

The issue of whether an employer and carrier are entitled to relief from the Special Fund pursuant to Section 908(f) is generally included as an issue at the Formal Hearing, regardless of whether a ruling has been made on the foundation issues (such as compensability of a claim, whether permanency has been reached, and whether the claimant is totally or partially disabled). As a result, it is important that an employer and carrier not only preserve their right to pursue 8(f) relief, but also think about the evidence that will be needed to support their claim for such relief. Since the District Director (through the Regional Solicitor) is a party to any litigation proceedings in which Special Fund has been raised as a potential issue, formal discovery requests may be exchanged with the Regional Solicitor in order to narrow the issues for which evidence is needed.

6. From the internet

Research can result in information about the Claimant's job duties as presented by the employer, articles, pictures, or

---

9. Treatment records include but may not be limited to narrative reports from treating providers, work status forms, OWCP-5 forms, Functional Capacity Evaluation reports, diagnostic testing results reports, operative reports, records from hospital admissions, physical therapy records, and psychotherapy notes.

10. Medical records are not subject to the protection of HIPAA where it is necessary for an insurance carrier to comply with workers' compensation laws. The uses and disclosures for which an authorization is not required are set out in 45 C.F.R. § 164.512. Section (l) carves out an exception for workers' compensation programs, entitling insurance carriers to the following:

> (l) Standard: Disclosures for workers' compensation. A covered entity may disclose protected health information as authorized by and to the extent necessary to comply with laws relating to workers' compensation or other similar programs, established by law, that provide benefits for work-related injuries or illness without regard to fault.

11. Under 33 U.S.C. §907(d)(4):

> If at any time the employee unreasonably refuses to submit to medical or surgical treatment, or to an examination by a physician selected by the employer, the Secretary or administrative law judge may, by order, suspend the payment of further compensation during such time as such refusal continues, and no compensation shall be paid at any time during the period of such suspension, unless the circumstances justified the refusal.

videos in regards to war hazards, weather, medical or prescription information, demonstrative evidence—diagrams and charts, information about the relationship between companies for borrowed servant questions, nature of Employer's business for jurisdiction questions, and information about experts, the claimant, and the employer.

Performing social media searches on the claimant and any fact witnesses may also provide valuable information through an informal avenue. Whether a claimant has a website for his self-owned business or is simply active on Facebook, Twitter, etc., the internet can be a source of unlimited types of information.

Remember—all documentary evidence needs to be authenticatable. Which witness is necessary to authenticate the evidence obtained?

D. Enforcing the Discovery Rules

The *Rules of Practice and Procedure* and the Federal Rules of Civil Procedure engage in a balancing act between the right of a Party to obtain broad discovery using any method, and the requirement that the discovery is obtained efficiently. A Party may seek relevant, material information, as long as the request is usable, and the method to respond is efficient and as inexpensive as possible for everyone concerned. *See* ABA Civil Discovery Standard 5; 29 C.F.R. §§18.51–18.52.

There are several tools available that a judge may use to enforce the applicable rules and ensure that the parties are engaging in the discovery process appropriately. For instance, a judge has the authority to compel disclosures and/or discovery, including compelling a discovery answer as well as the production of documents. If the judge has issued an order compelling the production of certain discovery and the compelled party fails to comply with the order, the prevailing party may request sanctions. Sanctions could include prohibiting the compelled party from using certain evidence, striking claims or defenses, staying proceedings until the order is obeyed, dismissing the claim, or deeming admissions. *See generally* 29 C.F.R. § 18.57.

Every party's disclosures, interrogatory answers, request for production responses, and request for admission responses must be supplemented. *See generally* 29 C.F.R. § 18.53. The parties are under a continuing obligation to timely supplement, including producing records that are newly obtained. Sanctions may be ordered by the presiding judge if the supplementation rules are not followed.

The Office of Administrative Law Judges also has extremely useful information and reference materials at http://www.oalj.dol.gov/.

22.4 The Fourth Day of Trial: Making Sense of It All

Until the litigator attempts to tell the story of the client it will be difficult, if not impossible, to determine what evidence is weak or missing, and what issues can or cannot be proven. Can you prove your case—apply the law to the facts as you see them?

Presenting the evidence and the argument as the law applies to that evidence is the sure-fire way to be assured you know your case. Writing the trial brief, outlining the issues, reviewing the evidence, narrowing the issues, and being realistic is the story of the true litigator. It is one thing to think you are ready but, it is another to sit back in an easy chair, brief in hand, absorbing the facts, analyzing the law, critiquing your argument, discussing key issues with someone else, and then going to the office the next day feeling better about what you can and cannot prove.

As evidence is further obtained and issues narrowed, the brief becomes more refined.

Early compilation of trial exhibits, whether in binders or another format, may also aid in finding the gaps in the evidence. Exhibits for trial may include a wide array of documentary evidence, including but not limited to LS forms, personnel records, wage records, Social Security Administration earnings statements, the claimant's tax returns, medical treatment records, expert medical records, vocational reports, curriculum vitae for any experts, deposition transcripts, and investigatory documents (such as social media pages, surveillance, photographs, incident reports). By preparing your exhibits early, it is easier to find which documents need to be obtained, which experts should be deposed, and ultimately, which issues should be stipulated versus litigated.

Many administrative law judges require that the parties meet and confer in order to prepare a set of joint exhibits prior to the Formal Hearing. It should be noted that some practitioners prefer to call the final product "unified" exhibits rather than "joint" exhibits, so as not to mislead the judge if the admissibility of at least some of the exhibits is an issue. The parties do not have to agree to the admissibility, the weight, or the credibility of the exhibits in order to include them as "joint" or "unified" exhibits. For example, if the parties prepare joint exhibits simply to have one set of exhibits instead of three, they may note that the designation of the exhibits as "joint" or "unified" does not mean that the admissibility of the evidence or the weight each document should be given has been agreed to. If the parties have agreed to the admissibility of the exhibits, then such may be noted while reserving arguments regarding the weight each piece of evidence should be given.

22.5 The Fifth Day of Trial: Preparing Your Witnesses

A. Preparing the Claimant

As pointed out in the beginning, trial starts on day one. Explaining to the claimant from the very first interview all the rules about a deposition (without mentioning deposition) is key. The claimant must learn from the beginning to listen to a question and answer just the question—whether it be by a doctor, defense medical examiner, or defense counsel. The claimant is the key fact witness in the case—credibility is crucial. The claimant is not an expert. The claimant does not connect the dots or close the loops. The claimant provides most, if not all, of the foundational facts upon which the experts base their opinions.

The above must be rehearsed with the claimant every time the attorney meets with the claimant and the claimant slips back into bad habits—wandering mind, loose answers, and talking about things other than what was asked. This cannot be done just before the deposition if you expect the claimant to change years of bad habits. Enlist the spouse or friend to help the claimant, at home, to begin answering just the question. The claimant could be reading out loud, twenty minutes each night to improve their reading and comprehension skills.

B. Meeting with Percipient Witnesses

Percipient witnesses play a vital role in establishing many issues, such as:

- Jurisdiction;
- AWW (Section 10(b));
- Employer-employee relationship;
- Physical or psychological harm (AOE/COE);
- Last responsible employer/carrier (facts in regards to exposure);
- Disability—extent;
- Vocational training (OWCP assigned counselor);
- Borrowed servant; and,
- War hazards.

It is important to determine at an early time whether the witness will available for trial, whether the deposition should be taken as soon as possible to get the evidence into the hands of an expert before exhibits are to be exchanged with opposing counsel.

C. Meeting with the Experts

Every judge has their own preference when it comes to whether experts should testify live or via deposition. As a general "rule," administrative law judges on the west coast prefer the parties to have their experts testify live. In those cases, counsel will have usually taken the deposition of each testifying expert prior to the Formal Hearing, but the transcripts from those depositions would not be entered as exhibits. Rather, the previous deposition testimony would be used solely for refreshing the expert's recollection or for impeachment purposes. In other jurisdictions, the judges may prefer that experts testify solely via deposition, allowing for shorter Formal Hearings.

Whether your expert testifies live or via deposition, a pre-testimony meeting is an important part of the process. This time should be used to confer about updated records (whether medical, vocational, etc.) that will be discussed during the deposition and to confirm your understanding of the expert's previous opinions. Time should also be spent discussing and preparing your expert for anticipated cross-examination questions from opposing counsel.

22.6 The Sixth Day of Trial: Putting on Your Case

"We still shall have the proud consolation of saying to our consciences . . . That the cause approved of our judgment, and adored of our hearts, in disaster, in chains, torture, in death, we never faltered in defending."
***A. Lincoln*, 1840.**

After all the preparation, the expense of experts, and the piecing together of your case—prosecution or defense—trial is not the time to falter. If we are true to the end, we will have a clear conscience and know we did our best—win, lose, or draw.

The "trial" for cases falling under the LHWCA and DBA is referred to as the "Formal Hearing." Depending on the jurisdiction and the judge to which the case is assigned, Formal Hearings may last anywhere from a couple of hours to a couple of days. Regardless of the length of the Formal Hearing, the general outline of the proceedings is the same. The attorneys and the judge may engage in an off-the-record conference prior to the Formal Hearing in order to discuss preliminary matters such as the anticipated number of witnesses, the anticipated length of the Formal Hearing, and/or whether there will be any objections to the evidence. Once the judge goes "on the record," counsel will enter an appearance on behalf of their client(s) and present the judge with previously agreed-to stipulations. While the judge reads the stipulations into the record, she or he may request confirmation on or additional information regarding the disputed issues. At this point, the parties will typically request entry of their respective exhibits into the record, and objections by opposing counsel to documentary evidence are noted. The judge will subsequently admit or deny each exhibit, making rulings on the admissibility as necessary. After the entry of exhibits, many judges allow the parties to give opening statements. The claimant will then put on his/her case, calling all fact and expert witnesses who have been chosen to provide live testimony. After the claimant rests, the employer and carrier are given the opportunity to put on their case and call their witnesses. Once both parties have rested, the judge will usually provide a briefing schedule.[12]

The administrative law judges are not bound by common law or statutory rules of evidence, or by technical or formal rules of procedure. 20 C.F.R. §702.339. The ALJ is capable of modifying the type, scope, length, and extent of discovery. Rule §18.51(b)(1).[13]

However, the ALJ is required to receive into evidence the testimony of witnesses and documents which are relevant and material to the matter at issue. 20 C.F.R. §702.338. Whether all the key evidence is admitted and in the record may be vital if the case goes up on appeal.

Many times the order of evidence is determined by the schedule of witnesses, especially experts. With that in mind, be flexible, but try to put on the evidence in a way that makes sense to the outside observer. Administrative law judges like to keep it simple and "fast." Don't make the mistake of making it "loose" as well. It's your case, you represent the client. Sometimes your approach to presenting your case is at odds with the Court's idea of how things should be done or NOT.

There are no hearsay objections. Know what it is to lay a foundation for further questioning on an issue. Remember: it is issues that are being tried, not matters that are stipulated. Also, if the documentary evidence is admitted into evidence at the beginning of trial, then that documentation is in evidence and a foundation may already be laid—the judge just won't be aware of it as he or she has not read it yet.

Some attorneys object to leading questions of experts, but the Federal Rules of Evidence recognize it is okay as they should not be able to be led around. However, some judges discredit the weight of the expert testimony if they feel the expert has been led.

22.7 The Seventh Day of Trial: The Post Trial Brief

In reference to Abraham Lincoln's nomination as the republican nominee for president Judge William D. Kelley is quoted as saying, "Well, we might have done a more brilliant thing, but we could hardly have done a better thing."

As trials vary from circuit to circuit, you must determine what your judge will allow at the time of trial and what may need be addressed in the post-trial brief. For example, trial may not be the place to address all inconsistencies within a witness' testimony or within the medical evidence.

The use of tables and charts or even diagrams may best portray comparisons within the evidentiary record or make it more understandable to the trier of fact who is not so readily acquainted with the facts—even after a trial on the merits.

The following is an example of the outline for a Post-Hearing Brief:

I. Introduction
II. Stipulations
III. Disputed Issues
IV. Statement of Facts
    A. Claimant's Background
    B. Alleged Incident
    C. Medical Evidence
    D. Vocational Evidence
V. Legal Argument
    A. Argument #1
    B. Argument #2
    C. Argument #3
VI. Conclusion

12. Most administrative law judges allow for Post-Hearing Briefs to be filed in lieu of verbal closing arguments being given at the Formal Hearing. The format of the Post-Hearing Brief allows the parties to cite with specificity to testimony in the record as well as point to relevant case law. Depending on judge preference, briefs are often due within 30–45 days after the parties have received the transcript from the Formal Hearing.

13. Partial Trial Objections Checklist:

- Leading;
- Argumentative;
- Confusing;
- Unintelligible;
- Assumes fact not in evidence;
- Asked and answered;
- Beyond scope of director cross exam;
- Insufficient foundation for hypothetical;
- Irrelevant;
- Violation of best evidence rule;
- Question calls for conclusion;
- Self-serving;
- Violates Parol Evidence Rule;
- Document speaks for itself;
- Competency or inadequate qualifications of witness;
- Failure to Lay Proper Foundation; and,
- Exhibit lacks reliability (lack of authentication).

Chapter 23

Ethical Considerations in Longshore Practice

Keith L. Flicker, Esq.[1]

A law practice is not only a competitive business dominated by its economics, influenced by the marketplace, and constrained by relevant commercial and criminal regulations and statutes. It is also a profession marked by extensive formal training and learning, limited to those duly qualified by an impartial licensing authority, with a code of ethics imposing standards qualitatively and significantly beyond those tolerated in business markets.[2] A lawyer's competence, cooperativeness, and efficiency are reflective of his professionalism, that which is expected of the practitioner. The lawyer's ethics, however, daily reflected in his considerations and actions, are required.

Ethical mandates are to be found in numerous sources, including disciplinary rules, court rules, case decisions, advisory opinions and commentaries. A plethora of authorities ranging from the individual licensing states to the American Bar Association have codified the standards by which to assess lawyer behavior. While the codes provide basic principles used by sanctioning bodies to enforce ethical standards, in practice and in fact the lawyer is left to his discretion in his ethical considerations. Almost always exercised in private, that discretion becomes the controlling element of the lawyer's self-administered system of ethical control.

A review of the ethics authorities and practice experience leads to the observation that lawyers are well aware of the ethical guidelines which are a continuous presence in lawyers' actions and deliberations. Short of financial impropriety, blatant undisclosed conflict of interest, and gross misstatement, lawyers generally regard their personal exercise of discretion in addressing ethical issues as reasonable, appropriate, and beyond reproach. However, in circumstances not clearly presenting ethical violations, a lawyer's private ability to fairly assess the ethics issues alongside his personal, financial, and business considerations can yield the improper exercise of that discretion.

This occurs in all areas of law practice and, as well, within the Longshore bar. The Longshore and Harbor Workers' Compensation Act itself, and as extended by the jurisdictional reach of the Defense Base Act and the Non-Appropriated Funds Instrumentalities Act, are by their terms far ranging compensation laws that provide significant financial benefits to extended categories of employees: claimants who have exceedingly slight evidentiary burdens to establish entitlement. Longshore law, as further interpreted and defined by the United States Department of Labor's District Directors, Administrative Law Judges, and Solicitors, enables the prosecution of claims without witness corroboration of an accident event and without the necessity of objective medical proof. Fraudulent claims of trauma-induced injury based solely on a claimant's statement to that effect and continuing medical disability established only by a claimant's subjective complaints of pain abound. Of these, many are made possible by a lawyer's active representation of a claimant with the knowing use of perjured testimony or false evidence.[3] In such matters, the offending lawyer will assert his extensive proper exercise of discretion in assessing the ethical issue presented by denying that one exists. The lawyer, to avoid his independent and non-assignable obligation to present only meritorious claims and contentions,[4] will deny his experience and conveniently defer to the unsupported statements of the claimant, without further reflection. While prosecution of the ethics violation may not be available given the liberality of Longshore law when combined with the exceptional difficulty of establishing the state of the lawyer's knowledge, this in no way denies the seriousness of a lawyer's breach of ethics as an essential factor in the spreading epidemic of fraudulent Longshore claims.

1. The author acknowledges the contributions of his colleagues Lauren C. Hall and Stephanie L. Riemer to the preparation of this chapter.

2. *See, generally, In re: Estate of Freeman*, 34 N.Y.2d 1 (N.Y. 1974).

3. Model Rules of Prof'l Conduct R. 3.3 (2013).

4. Model Rules of Prof'l Conduct R. 3.1 (2013).

A claimant's low burden to establish entitlement to benefits in Longshore law not only presents ethical issues regarding the handling of fraudulent claims with his own representation, but defense counsel is also faced with an ethical challenge when there is suspicion that the claimant has proffered false testimony or concealed evidence of earnings, subsequent employment, or physical ability to perform his prior job duties. The Longshore provision allowing referral to a United States Attorney for criminal prosecution where there has been misrepresentation[5] can be seen from one perspective as in violation of the prohibition against threatening criminal prosecution in a civil matter, if it is improperly sought by a party in a Longshore claim. Threatening to use, or using, the criminal process to coerce adjustment of private civil claims or controversies is a subversion of the legal notion that the civil judicial process is designed for settlement between the parties, whereas the criminal judicial process is designed for protection of society as a whole.[6] When seeking referral to a United States Attorney, counsel must take great care to avoid the impression that he is seeking criminal sanctions to gain leverage in his civil claim.

Apart from outright fraud, Longshore law provisions provide numerous scenarios and opportunities for lawyers to self-administer ethical controls. Among those critical to the administrative and judicial processing of claims are those relating to the roles of the treating physician and medical experts. The statutory right of the claimant to select his treating physician and essentially control his medical care[7] often times leads to the selection of a lawyer-sponsored doctor acutely interested in maintaining his referral status, as well as the development of his health care mill. The lawyer/doctor relationship in such circumstances is often parasitic as the doctor's actions promote the potential financial recovery on the claim, including the referring lawyer's fees. Too often lost in the slanted and overreaching treatment plan, is an impartial medical analysis detailing to the court and the claimant the true state of an alleged disability. While a lawyer-referred treating physician can be appropriate on the basis of qualifications, competence, knowledge of the Longshore law, and even for certain pro-claimant proclivities, there are referrals which serve primarily the interests of the lawyer and thereby exceed his ethical obligations to represent his client within the bounds of the law.[8]

A defense lawyer's quid pro quo referral to a "captive" physician qualified to provide an expert opinion to the court largely because of his reliability to provide pro-employer findings is similarly specious. In making such a referral, the lawyer proffers to the court evidence tainted at its inception. That the practice by claimants' lawyers and defense lawyers is widespread and that the courts accept such practice under the guise that effective cross-examination will lead to the truth is not responsive to the ethical considerations presented. For example, an expert may even go so far as to request the referring attorney's opinion on a claimant's disposition before submitting his or her final report, thus heightening the need for a claimant's attorney or a defense attorney to practice self-discipline and quell his own self-interest in favor of rendering a fair and unbiased report for the factfinder. In the absence of clear ethical rules, an opposing attorney must resort to cross-examination in order to determine whether an expert was aware of the referring attorney's position on the matter in advance of submitting a final report on his or her findings. In cases of excess, such as that presented in occupational hearing loss and pulmonary claims filed on a mass scale for multiple claimants at a single facility, the identity of the findings of a particular examining doctor selected by the claimant's lawyer or defense lawyer establishes the ethical breach. The failure of lawyers, administrators, and the courts to address this issue continues to promote the problem.

Other litigation tactics practiced in Longshore law similarly present circumstances compelling the self-administration of ethics limitations. While not addressed in the federal compensation law, state and federal courts in personal injury matters have disagreed as to whether ex parte communications by a defense lawyer with a claimant's treating physician are allowed or, rather, are per se prejudicial. Such contacts tend to compromise both counsel and the medical witness, as irrelevant and privileged information is likely to be disclosed. The identical situation is presented when a claimant's counsel has ex parte communications with the defense selected medical examiner, and when either counsel so communicates with a Department of Labor independent medical examiner. In order to avoid the ethics query, all communications should be done in the presence of opposing counsel.

In that a claimant's credibility, or lack thereof, in a Longshore matter is generally the most critical element of an employer/carrier's defense, the use of surveillance evidence is ever increasing. As a matter of course defense lawyers retain private investigators to conduct undercover surveillance of a claimant in an effort to obtain electronically recorded evidence of him performing activities wholly at odds with what he asserts are his physical limitations. The capture of

5. 33 U.S.C. § 931.

6. Model Code of Prof'l Responsibility DR 7-105 & EC 7-21 (withdrawn in 1983 and replaced by the ABA Model Rules of Professional Conduct). The concept of the prohibition of threatening criminal prosecution in a civil matter survives generally in Rule 8.4 of the Model Rules of Professional Conduct.

7. 33 U.S.C. § 907.

8. Model Rules of Prof'l Conduct R. 3.3 (2013).

such moments, and their introduction at trial through an investigator is compelling and often determinative of a claim. The courts have uniformly allowed such evidence subject only to certain disclosure and authentication requirements.

However, ethical considerations are presented when the investigator does not simply and passively record a claimant's movements, but rather actively interjects himself into the scenario being recorded. The investigator may approach the claimant under pretense and through bluff obtain statements and actions from the claimant which belie his alleged disabilities. In a manner, the investigator has entrapped the claimant.

In this event the investigator is acting as the defense lawyer's agent. The investigator's direct contacts and discussions with the claimant thereby act as the defense lawyer's communication with the claimant without the claimant's lawyer being present. Such communications have long been prohibited and constitute a breach of the defense attorney's ethical obligations.[9] While the courts continue to address the issue of such surveillance techniques from an evidentiary perspective, as a matter of ethics defense lawyers should instruct their retained investigators not to engage in these practices.

Defense lawyers are further compelled to consider their ethical limits when they direct an employer/carrier to terminate a claimant's Longshore benefits. The ability to take such action unilaterally, when no order is in place, provides to the defense significant negotiating leverage. While in most circumstances the termination of benefits is wholly justified in light of medical and other evidence supportive of the defense, Longshore law does not sanction the employer/carrier for a baseless termination as long as a Form LS-207 Notice of Controversion is timely filed. Defense lawyers, eager to compel a claimant to settlement, may justify a termination without cause as appropriate on the basis that it is not prohibited. Yet, such a self-serving analysis denies that the assertion of an unwarranted defense is an ethical breach.[10]

The Longshore law provision requiring the employer/carrier to pay the approved reasonable attorney fees and costs of the claimant when the prosecution of the claim has been successfully prosecuted,[11] as expanded and liberalized, has led to the addressing of ethics concerns presented by claimants' lawyers' fee petitions. Conceptually, fee recovery is a function of hourly rate, the claimant's lawyer's competency and experience, the difficulty of the case issues, time spent, and the claimant's recovery. There is no contingency fee percentage to be awarded, although in practice a 15% to 20% recovery of a settlement sum is customary.

Recent widespread trends before the Office of Administrative Law Judges in awarding huge fees to claimants' attorneys in matters of small financial recovery to claimants and involving relatively straightforward legal issues are involved has prompted a limited set of claimants' lawyers to submit false and exaggerated fee petitions. In numerous cases in different locales and before different judges, claimants' lawyers have filed petitions claiming entitlement to fees in amounts many times the benefits recovered in the claim, asserting to have spent hundreds of hours on legal research and hundreds more on client interviews and preparation, all for a one or two day trial. While the assertions are patently excessive to an experienced Longshore practitioner, without critical analysis and generally deferring to the veracity of the claimant's lawyer submitting the sworn petition, judges have accepted fee requests subject to what appears to be a developing 25% reduction factor.

The handling of this issue by administrative Law Judges and appellate tribunals has served only to promote the filing of unreal fee petitions. Knowing that a limited reduction factor will be applied, but not an in depth appraisal of the hours claimed, requested amounts are steadily rising. From an ethics standpoint, the improper handling of the matter by the court does not relieve the lawyer of his obligation. Such continued filings only increase the ethics breach.

In a similar vein, fee petitions also present practical ethical problems when they become part of a settlement agreement between the parties.[12] Lawyers are allowed to negotiate their fees as part of a claimant's settlement with defense counsel.[13] Although this practice is legislatively mandated and judicially approved in Longshore practice, it is inapposite with the lawyer's ethical duty of avoiding conflicts with his own client. Specifically, a lawyer shall not acquire a proprietary interest in the cause of action or the subject matter of a litigation the lawyer is conducting for a client.[14] Too often, a claimant loses out on an attractive settlement agreement, which would provide closure and certainty in his obviously disrupted life, because his lawyer refuses to accept the amount of fees offered as part of the settlement.

Finally, an area in which both claimants' lawyers and defense lawyers are faced with issues of ethical import are the global settlement at fixed figures of occupational pulmonary and hearing loss claims filed en masse at a single

9. Model Rules of Prof'l Conduct R. 4.2 (2013).

10. Model Rules of Prof'l Conduct R. 3.3 (2013).

11. 33 U.S.C. § 928.

12. *See*, Patricia A. Krebs & Kourtni R. Mason, *Professional Ethics Across Jurisdictions: The Conundrums That Arise in Litigating Longshore and Harbor Worker's Compensation Act and Defense Base Act Claims*, 12 Loy. Mar. L.J. 57, 68 (2013).

13. 20 C.F.R. § 702.214(e).

14. Model Rules of Prof'l Conduct R. 1.8(I) (2013).

location. While such claim filings have been a predictable event at plant and terminal closings for many years, recently the practice has become even more significant as it has occurred on a larger scale at varied locations. In the New York port, thousands of hearing and pulmonary claims have been filed against all conceivable employers, and in Vieques, Puerto Rico, several hundred heavy metal toxicity claims have been similarly filed. Lawyers for the claimants and the defense are representing numerous claimants and employer/carriers. Given the Longshore law's slight burdens on claims filing and the establishment of a prima facie occupational claim, the costs of defense to the number of employer/carriers affected is staggering. As a consequence, a number of employer/carriers through their defense counsel have settled claims on a pro forma basis, at a single fixed sum, regardless of proof and without the individual analysis of each claim.

Although this solution may appear to present a viable financial resolution to the tremendous burden created by the filings, it does present an ethical issue for the lawyers involved. It is generally agreed that a lawyer representing more than one client may make an aggregate settlement but only if consent is obtained after each client has been advised of the existence and nature of all the claims involved, the total amount of the settlement, and the participation of each person in the settlement.[15] Failing these specific actions, the lawyer confronts an ethics breach. Consequently, in such settlements, a lawyer fulfills his obligations only upon providing full disclosure and obtaining his client's informed consent.

15. Model Rules of Prof'l Conduct R. 1.8(g) (2013).

Chapter 24

Attorney Fees

Revised and updated by Charles Robinowitz, Esq. from the chapter in 2010 by Eric A. Dupree, Esq., Joshua T. Gillelan II, Esq., and Charles Robinowitz, Esq.

Synopsis

When a claimant prevails in a claim under the Longshore and Harbor Workers' Compensation Act, the attorney for the claimant may be entitled to payment of attorney fees and costs from the employer or the workers' compensation carrier. The attorney may also be entitled to fees from the claimant, in which event the fee may be made a lien on the award. Section 28 of the Act, 33 U.S.C. § 928, governs the circumstances where the employer must pay the claimant's attorney fees and costs.

Caution: An attorney may not accept any fee for representing a claimant under the Act that an administrative tribunal or court has not approved. If this does occur, there is a risk of criminal penalties and suspension or disbarment from the practice of law.

24.1 Conditions for Employer Fee Liability

Section 28(a) shifts fee liability to the employer or carrier, when it does not accept a claim within 30 days of receiving notice from the district director, and the claimant prevails. The fact that the employer has paid benefits *before* a claim is filed and before receiving notice of the filing from the district director does not affect the applicability of § 28(a) if no payment is made within the critical 30-day period.[1] If the employer makes payments after the expiration of that period, this does not affect the application of § 28(a).[2]

A carrier may not avoid application of section 28(a) by paying one dollar or a nominal amount. But it may pay one week of benefits and shift liability for fees.[3]

Section 28(b) applies when the employer or carrier initially accepts the claim, but then a dispute develops. In that situation, the Act contemplates an informal conference, a recommendation by the district director, and an opportunity for the employer or carrier to accept the district director's recommendation and avoid fee liability.

If the employer accepts the district director's recommendation within 14 days and the claimant obtains more benefits at hearing or on appeal, or if the district director refers the case for adjudication by an ALJ without making a recommendation for the disposition of the dispute, the Fourth, Fifth, and Sixth Circuits hold that the fees are the responsibility of the claimant, not the employer.[4] The Third and Ninth Circuits hold that the fees in this situation are the responsibility of the employer or carrier because the Act did not contemplate that the fees for successful prosecution of the claim would come out of the claimant's benefits.[5] The Benefits Review Board is following the rule in the Fourth, Fifth, and Sixth Circuits for all claims outside the Ninth Circuit.[6]

If an employer pays the amount the district director recommends, but challenges its liability for this on appeal, it is liable for the claimant's attorney's fees under 28(b), if it loses.[7]

Where the claimant prevails on some issues—for example, establishing statutory coverage and a higher average weekly wage than the employer asserted but failing to establish entitlement to compensation for permanent disability or to medical benefits for some condition, or prevailing on the compensation claim, but not on a § 48a retaliation claim tried along with it—the claimant's lawyer is not entitled to payment from the employer for the services on the issues on which the claimant did not prevail.[8] Where it is difficult to segregate the services on the successful issues from the unsuccessful ones, the law allows an appropriate across-the-board cut if the fees otherwise would not be reasonable for the extent of success "in comparison with the scope of the litigation as a whole."[9] The claimant is entitled to an employer-paid fee for prevailing on coverage, medical expenses, a so-called penalty, or a "nominal" *"de minimis"* award of compensation.[10]

When an employer tenders additional compensation in a written offer, the claimant's lawyer is entitled to an employer-paid fee for services after that date only if the claimant receives more than the offer. Where the award is less than the offer, the employer will be responsible for the fees and costs up to the date of the offer and the time for discussion with the claimant of the offer, and the claimant will be responsible for the fees and costs after that date.

When the claimant is responsible for attorney fees, Section 28(c) governs. In this situation, the administrative tribunals and the courts may consider the claimant's ability to pay in awarding a fee. This will often result in a lower fee, especially in cases where more limited benefits were involved. Any negotiation of a fee with a claimant is void under Section 28(e).[11]

24.2 The Application for Attorney Fees and Costs

When the attorney for the claimant is entitled to an attorney fee, the attorney must file a fee application, with an affidavit or declaration itemizing the services and time spent. The attorney must file a separate claim for fees with each level.[13]

Fees for services before the administrative law judges begin with the referral to that office by the district director. Fees prior to that date are before the district director.[14]

The application must also indicate the professional status of the person who provided the services, such as the lawyer, paralegal or law clerk, and the "normal billing rate" or other evidence of a reasonable hourly rate for that person.[15]

If the attorney fails to properly document his or her fee, a tribunal or court should allow the attorney 30 days to correct this and it should suggest what was missing.[16]

Generally, the attorney may bill in units of 15 minutes, even for brief telephone calls, to compensate for the time to note the file and resume other work.[17] The Fifth Circuit has held that the attorney may not bill in minimum quarter-hour units for the routine review of correspondence.[18]

"Block billing"—the aggregation of all services provided on a given day into a single composite time entry—may be allowed, but it is not a good practice. Attorneys should try to avoid this as much as possible.[19] The regulations require a complete statement of the extent and character of the necessary work done and the hours each staff person devoted to them.[20]

The lawyer should file the fee application with each level within 30 days of prevailing and within 60 days at the Board.[21] In some courts of appeals different deadlines under the local circuit rules apply.[22] The lawyer is not entitled to payment until the dispute is over and all appeals are final.[23] If there are delays between the approval of fees and payment beyond the ordinary payment period for private billing transactions, the claimant's lawyer should file a supplemental fee petition within 30 days of payment.[24]

All fee applications must be served on the other parties. Those seeking fees from the claimant must serve the fee application on him or her as well. The Board's rules allow the parties ten days to respond, with an additional three days if service was by mail, and the courts of appeals generally allow only eight business days, plus three calendar days if service was by mail, by application of the general rule applicable to responses to motions.[25]

ALJs typically provide a slightly longer period by order, often in the orders following their decisions on the merits. Although the Board's rules do not mention replies to objections, and ALJs often make the same omission, they are regularly received and considered, as is certainly the better practice. Among other reasons, this avoids needless motions for reconsideration or appeals presenting belated responses to the objections. Under the general rule for replies to responses to motions in the courts of appeals,[26] only seven business days, plus three days after service by mail, are allowed for a reply.

24.3 Amount of Fees and Expenses Recoverable

The Supreme Court has held that the principles for determination of the amount of a fee under one federal fee-shifting statute apply to all the other federal fee-shifting statutes.[27] Under those principles, the "lodestar," or presumptive, fee is the hours reasonably expended on the litigation times a reasonable market or hourly rate.[28]

It is established, at least in the Ninth Circuit, that administrative law judges may not determine market rates for claimants' attorneys under the Longshore Harbor Workers' Compensation Act based on their own concept of what the market should bear and what they previously allowed under this principle. The Ninth Circuit referred to this as a "tautological self-referential enterprise," a phrase it adopted from a Third Circuit case involving public interest attorney fees. It held this practice is legally incorrect. It perpetuates a court-established rate as a "market," when that rate bears no necessary relationship to the underlying purpose of using the marketplace to create a reasonable attorney fee.[29]

It is also improper for a tribunal to reduce a market rate because the service was simple and not complex. Complexity or simplicity affects the amount of time reasonably necessary for a service, but does not affect the market rate.[30]

While it is theoretically possible to obtain a multiplier or fee enhancer in a very rare case, the Supreme Court disallowed this in what was probably that very rare case, making this impossible as a practical matter.[31] In the *Kenny A.* case, the trial judge allowed the plaintiffs' lawyers a $4.5 million fee enhancer on top of the lodestar. He described the attorneys for the plaintiff as displaying a higher degree of skill, commitment, dedication and professionalism than he had witnessed in 27 years as a federal judge and in 58 years as a lawyer and a federal judge. He felt the results for the plaintiffs were extraordinary, and he was unaware of any other case where the plaintiffs as a class had achieved such a favorable result on such a comprehensive scale. Despite this, the Supreme Court held this did not justify a multiplier or enhancer. It was part of the lawyers' market rate.

24.4 Market Rates

The determination of market rates for claimants' attorneys under the Longshore and Harbor Workers' Compensation Act is still not settled. Generally, claimants' lawyers represent nearly all of their clients on a contingent fee basis, and they do not have a normal "billing rate." In addition, Section 28(e) of the Act specifically prohibits the negotiation of a fee with the claimant and makes it criminal to collect any fee without pre-approval of the tribunal or court.[32] Thus, there are no actual negotiated "market" rates for representation of claimants under the Act.

In determining a prevailing market rate, the Supreme Court has held that for all federal fee-shifting statutes, the standard is the hourly rate in the relevant community that lawyers, whose skills, experience and reputation are comparable to those of the prevailing lawyer, receive from arms-length clients for similar services.[33] This standard applies to claims under the Longshore and Harbor Workers' Compensation Act as well.[34]

Generally, the method to determine market rates is to rely on declarations or affidavits by attorney fee experts familiar with the local community. In vacating the ALJ's market rate in *Christensen v. Stevedoring Services of America*, the Ninth Circuit stated it expected the Benefits Review Board and the other tribunals to rely on current market rates.

One major issue in setting a market rate is determining the applicable community. Generally, this is the forum where the federal district court sits.[35] But the Seventh Circuit held that for Defense Base Act claims, the community may be the country because there is a national market for Defense Base Act cases.[36]

The Ninth Circuit rejected this national market concept in a claim under the Longshore Harbor Workers' Compensation Act. It held that for a claimant's lawyer practicing in Portland, Oregon for a case tried in Portland, Oregon, the ALJ must apply Portland rates, and may not use lower state of Oregon rates or national rates. The reason for this is because there were surveys determining rates in Portland and for the state of Oregon as a whole.[37]

Where there is no survey specific to the area where the claimants' attorney maintains an office, it is proper for an ALJ to base a market rate on a regional survey of rates.[38]

One instructive case for hourly rates is *Ace American Ins. Co. v. Walters*, 2014 WL 523742, 2014 U.S. Dist. Lexis 15883 (S.D. Tex. 2014). In that case, which was an appeal of a Defense Base Act case, the federal district court judge compared the experience and skills of the out-of-town counsel, and equated their rates with senior partners in Texas firms doing intellectual property work. He found the rate was $510 per hour. The insurance carrier had offered no specific evidence that the rate should be any less.

The Benefits Review Board for appeals will apply the rates in the community where the appellate attorney is located; not necessarily where the federal district court sits. For Washington, D.C. attorneys, it will apply the rates the United States Attorney established for its *Laffey* Matrix.[39]

It is also not proper for ALJs to rely on state workers' compensation rates or insurance defense rates, even in part, in determining claimants' attorneys' market rates. These rates are not market rates because they include a discount for referrals of volumes of cases, and they are also lower due in part to long-time relationships between the attorneys and the insurance companies.[40] The Ninth Circuit has vacated an ALJ decision relying in part on state workers' compensation cases, and the Sixth Circuit affirmed an ALJ decision that had rejected state workers' compensation rates as a factor in the market rate.[41] The 2009 Incisive Legal Intelligence Survey, formerly the Altman-Weil Survey, found that the workers' compensation rates and insurance defense rates were typically lower than other legal specialties, but the practitioners earned the same fees as the lawyers in the more expensive legal fields. This is because they have a different method of calculating hours, and they spend long hours on litigation.[42]

The Benefits Review Board had rejected the use of state workers' compensation rates in Longshore and Harbor Workers' Compensation Act in 2010. It has also rejected the use of rates under the Equal Justice Act.[43]

A. Rules in Deciding Fee Awards

In deciding fee awards, the lawyers, the courts and the administrative tribunals must follow certain rules. These are:

1. The party seeking the award has the burden of documenting the number of hours and describing the services;[44]
2. The party seeking the award must submit evidence of the reasonableness of the rates;[45]
3. The requesting party satisfies this burden with his or her own declarations or those of other attorneys, or hourly-rate surveys, addressing prevailing market rates for comparable services in the relevant community, with past fee awards to attorneys of comparable experience in the same region, or with fee awards under other federal fee-shifting statutes involving similar services;[46]
4. The party opposing the fee application has the burden of challenging the accuracy and reasonableness of the rates and hours claimed;[47]
5. The relevant community for the rate determination is usually the forum where the federal court sits or comparable communities, unless qualified local counsel was unavailable;[48]
6. In determining the market rate, the administrative tribunal must determine rates that are in line with those prevailing in the community for similar services by lawyers of comparable skill, experience and reputation;[49]
7. The tribunal must explain clearly and concisely how it determined the fee award;[50]
8. A tribunal may not rely on rates which applied more than two years before the performance of the services;[51]
9. A tribunal errs if it refuses to consider rates in the relevant community outside of the particular practice subject-matter, and a tribunal must determine what the lawyer could have earned by accepting other similar types of cases;[52]
10. There should not be a difference in the market rates depending on whether services are trial time or in the preparation of the case;[53]
11. The tribunals should defer to the professional judgment of the prevailing lawyer in the handling and organization of the workload, and if a tribunal cuts more than 10 percent of a time claimed, it must explain specifically how the services were unnecessary;[54]
12. A tribunal may not apply a de facto office policy or practice in setting a market rate different from that established by evidence of the relevant market;[55] and
13. The burden is on the employer to support reductions with specific reasons or the tribunals should award the hours and rates as requested.[56]

Where there are objections to claimants' attorneys' hours or rates, the tribunals should require the attorneys for the employers and carriers to submit copies of their charges and hours so that the tribunals will have the benefit of the fees necessary to defend the claim. This may reduce fee disputes considerably.[57]

Some ALJs may question or disregard the evidence claimants' attorneys offer of their market rates, and not require expert evidence by the carriers of a reasonable rate. They also do not allow the claimants' attorneys to amend their fee petitions. They then find that since the claimants' attorneys have not satisfied their legal burden, the ALJs must determine the market rates independently. It is doubtful the circuit courts will affirm these types of decisions.[58]

B. Effect of Delay on Market Rates

In cases of delay beyond that which occurs in ordinary private billings between the fee application and payment of a fee award, the attorney is entitled to supplemental fees to compensate for the delay in payment.[59] The Supreme Court has required reasonable compensation for delay in payment of fees, either by the award of interest from the time the services were performed until payment or by application of current, rather than "historical," hourly rates. Because the Fifth and Ninth Circuits have held that the Longshore Harbor Workers' Compensation Act does not allow interest on fee orders,[60] it is necessary to file supplemental declarations of fees to ensure that the fees paid remain "reasonable" by the standard of market-based fees.[61]

At the time of the fee application, the attorney should request a current rate for all services.[62] Despite the United States Supreme Court rule about compensation for delay in payment of attorney fees, the lower courts and tribunals are making this issue more complex in claims under the Longshore Harbor Workers' Compensation Act. The Ninth Circuit stated in *Christensen* that a court does not have to compensate for delays of up to two years because this delay is not egregious under the Longshore and Harbor Workers' Compensation Act.[63] But whether a delay is egregious or not under Longshore and Harbor Workers' Compensation Act is not the legal standard for compensation for delay. The standard is what the Supreme Court stated in *Missouri v. Jenkins*.[64] Did the delay in payment exceed what occurs in private billings?

In an unpublished decision the Ninth Circuit held that a district director may not compensate for eight years of delay in awarding attorney fees by using a market rate four years before as a compromise.[65] The fact that the district director did this and the Benefits Review Board affirmed it in light of the prior Supreme Court rulings was very surprising. The

Fourth Circuit rejected the Board's use of a market rate 10 years old and adjusting it by $50, without an empirical basis. Where the Benefits Review Board does something illegally, there is no presumption on appeal that its actions were correct.[66]

The Benefits Review Board has held that the Consumer Price Index was not a proper measurement of wage increases after an injury compared with the increases in the national average weekly wage.[67] Therefore, the Consumer Price Index should not be a reliable determinant for increases in attorney fee rates. For increases in attorney fees, an attorney probably should consult a survey of attorney fee rates rather than the national average weekly wage.

One district director has been using the Federal Locality Rate increases in salaries for federal employees to increase claimants' attorneys' fees due to delay. This issue is presently on appeal to the Benefits Review Board. The Solicitor, as well as the claimant, is opposing this on the basis that this rate increase is based on political considerations, and does not consider the cost of health care or the job security and retirement benefits of federal employees.[68]

C. Compensable Services

The test for whether services were reasonable and necessary is whether they were reasonable at the time the lawyer performed them, not whether it turned out on hindsight to be fruitful.[69] If the claimant loses on certain preliminary matters but prevails on the ultimate issue, the lawyer is entitled to a fee for all services.[70] The claimant's lawyer is entitled to reasonable fees for preparing the fee application and successfully defending it.[71]

It is not settled whether the employer or the claimant is liable for fees for the services before the employer denied or refused to accept a claim, where the claimant ultimately prevails. The Fifth and Sixth Circuits hold that these services are the claimant's responsibility.[72] The Black Lung Act adopts Section 28 of the Longshore Harbor Workers' Compensation Act, and the Fourth Circuit has held in a Black Lung case that such fees are the employer's responsibility.[73] There is now a regulation under the Black Lung Act expressly adopting the interpretation that the "reasonable fee" for which the employer is liable if the qualifications of § 28(a) are met includes services performed from the beginning.[74] The Benefits Review Board is following the decisions of the Fifth and Sixth Circuits.[75]

The Ninth Circuit, however, has rejected the Fifth and Sixth Circuit views.[76] It held that where the claimant's attorney fees are awardable against the employer under § 28(a), they should include *all* of the attorney's reasonable services, including those performed before the employer's denial of liability within the 30-day grace period after receiving notice of the claim from the district director. It deferred to the longstanding reading of the statute by the Director, that the "thereafter" clause, which reads "shall thereafter have utilized the services of an attorney at law in the successful prosecution of the claim," establishes one of the *conditions for fee liability*, but not a limit on the services for which the employer is liable once all conditions have been satisfied.

The Board has also recognized that limited post-decision "wind-up services"—for example, review of the decision, explaining it to the claimant, and ensuring its proper initial implementation—are compensable services.[77]

The amount of benefits awarded is not a limit on the amount of attorney fees. Otherwise, counsel would be unavailable to claimants to pursue claims with limited benefits. Where the necessary and reasonable services overlap with other related claims, such as third-party tort claims or social security claims, fees are allowed for all services that were necessary for the longshore claim, even if they were performed in the course of the other matters, unless they have already been compensated.[79]

D. Recoverable Expenses

Recoverable out-of-pocket expenses include expert witness fees, photocopies, travel expenses, deposition costs and whatever else may be reasonable and necessary for the claim.[80] A tribunal may not segregate and deny costs where the claimant is partially successful on some issues.[81] In deciding whether costs were reasonable, tribunals and courts should apply the same principle as that for attorney services: were the costs reasonable on foresight—not on hindsight?[82]

24.5 Appellate Review

In appeals of fee awards, the standard of review is whether the fee was arbitrary, capricious, an abuse of discretion or not in accordance with the law. This applies to petitions for review to the Benefits Review Board and to the circuit courts.[83]

One of the issues on appeal of fee awards is whether the lower court or tribunal explained how it determined a market rate. The lower court must give reasons for substantial reductions of time so that the appellate court may determine whether it acted arbitrarily or abused its discretion. This is especially true where the cut in fees is more than 10 percent.[84] A court or tribunal may not determine a market rate for a law office by averaging the rates of the different practitioners in the office.[85] It also must explain its specific reasons for reductions. It may not omit hours without an explanation of the factors for reduction.[86]

Usually, lower courts have a great deal of discretion in determining attorney fees and their fees do not have to be precise. But they must follow the rules regarding attorney fees, and an appellate tribunal or court should vacate the fee if the order violates the rules.[87]

Endnotes

1. *Day v. James Marine, Inc.*, 518 F.3d 411 (6th Cir. 2008); *Richardson v. Continental Grain Co.*, 336 F.3d 1103 (9th Cir. 2003); *Pool Co. v. Cooper*, 274 F.3d 173 (5th Cir. 2001).

2. *Day, supra*, n. 1; *Gordon v. Marine Terminals Corp.*, 41 BRBS 13 (2007).

3. *Green v. Ceres Marine Terminals*, 43 BRBS 173 (2010); *Lincoln v. Director, OWCP*, 744 F.3d 911 (4th Cir. 2014).

4. *Virginia International Terminals v. Edwards*, 398 F.3d 313 (4th Cir.), *cert denied*, 546 U.S. 960 (2005); *Pittsburgh & Conneaut Dock Co. v. Director, OWCP*, 473 F.3d 253 (6th Cir. 2006); *Staftex Staffing v. Director, OWCP*, 237 F.3d 409 (5th Cir. 2000); *Andrepont v. Murphy Exploration & Production Co.*, 566 F.3d 415 (5th Cir. 2009). *But see Savannah Machine & Shipyard Co. v. Director, OWCP*, 642 F.2d 887, 888-89 (5th Cir. 1981); *Hole v. Miami Shipyards Corp.*, 640 F.2d 769, 774 (5th Cir. 1981); *Oilfield Safety & Machine Specialties, Inc. v. Harman Unlimited, Inc.*, 625 F.2d 1248, 1257 (5th Cir. 1980).

5. *Universal Terminal & Stevedoring Co. v. Parker*, 587 F.2d 608 (3d Cir. 1978); *Matulic v. Director, OWCP*, 154 F.3d 1052 (9th Cir. 1998); *National Steel and Shipbuilding Co. v. U.S. Dep't of Labor*, 606 F.2d 875 (9th Cir. 1979).

6. *Davis v. Eller & Co.*, 41 BRBS 58 (2007).

7. *Carey v. Ormet Primary Aluminum Corp.*, 627 F.3d 979 (5th Cir. 2010).

8. *Hensley v. Eckerhart*, 461 U.S. 424 (1983); *George Hyman Construction Co. v. Brooks*, 963 F.2d 1532 (D.C. Cir. 1992); *General Dynamics Corp. v. Horrigan*, 848 F.2d 321 (1st Cir.), *cert. denied*, 488 US. 992 (1988).

9. *Hensley, supra*, n. 8; *Schwarz v. Sec'y of Health & Human Servs.*, 73 F.3d 895, 906 (9th Cir. 1995).

10. *Kinnes v. General Dynamics Corp.*, 25 BRBS 311 (1992) (coverage); *Tahara v. Matson Terminals*, 511 F.3d 950 (9th Cir. 2007) (penalty); *Caudill v. SeaTac Alaska Shipbuilding*, 22 BRBS 10, 16 (1988) (medical expenses); *Keenan v. Director, OWCP*, 392 F.3d 1041 (9th Cir. 2004) (nominal award).

11. *Armor v. Maryland Shipbuilding & Dry Dock Co.*, 19 BRBS 119 (1986), *aff'd on recon.*, 22 BRBS 316 (1989).

12. 20 C.F.R. §§ 702.132(a), 802.203(e).

13. 33 US.C. § 928(c); *Stevedoring Services of Am. v. Price*, 432 F.3d 1112 (9th Cir. 2006).

14. *Owens v. Newport News Shipbuilding & Dry Dock Co.*, 11 BRBS 409 (1979).

15. 20 C.F.R. § 702.132(a); *Newport News Shipbuilding & Dry Dock Co. v. Graham*, 573 F.2d 167 (4th Cir. 1978); *Ayers Steamship Co. v. Bryant*, 544 F.2d 812 (5th Cir. 1977).

16. *Stanhope v. Electric Boat Corp.*, 44 BRBS 107 (2010); *See also Christensen v. Stevedoring Services of America*, 557 F.3d 1049, 1055 (9th Cir. 2009).

17. 20 C.F.R. § 802.203(d)(3); *Neeley v. Newport News Shipbuilding & Dry Dock Co.*, 19 BRBS 138 (1986); *Jarrell v. Newport News Shipbuilding & Dry Dock Co.*, 14 BRBS 883 (1982).

18. *Ross v. Ingalls Shipbuilding, Inc.*, 29 BRBS 42 (1995); *Conoco, Inc. v. Director, OWCP*, 194 F.3d 684, 689 n.2 (5th Cir. 1999), citing unpublished decisions in 1990 and 1995.

19. *Pittsburgh & Conneaut Dock Co., supra*, n. 4; *Trulock v. Hotel Victorville*, 92 Fed. Appx. 433 (9th Cir. 2004); 20 C.F.R. §§ 702. 132(a), 802.203(e).

20. 20 C.F.R. §§ 702.132(a) and 802.203(e).

21. *See* 20 C.F.R. § 802.203(c). Where the Board remands a case, the period for filing the fee application with the Board runs from the decision on remand; where the claimant loses before the Board but successfully challenges its decision before a court of appeals, it runs from entry of the court's judgment. *Id.*

22. *E.g.*, 9TH CIR. RULE 39-1.6 (14 days after expiration of time for petition for rehearing and where the Director, OWCP is a party, 45 days after the court's decision).

23. This includes appeals by the claimant alone, where the employer owes an attorney fee for partial success and that part of the claim is final. *Christensen v. Stevedoring Services of America*, 430 F.3d 1032 (9th Cir. 2005). *But see Vonthronsohnhaus v. Ingalls Shipbuilding, Inc.*, 24 BRBS 154 (1990), which may apply to cases outside the Ninth Circuit. However, to avoid a supplemental fee for delay, the employer may want to pay the fee promptly. *See* text at nn.46-48 *infra*. Where the merits of a claim on which the fee is based are still on appeal, the fee is not payable until the claim is concluded. *Thompson v. Potashnick Construction Co.*, 812 F. 2d 574 (9th Cir. 1987); *Wells v. International Great Lakes Shipping Co.*, 693 F.2d 663 (7th Cir. 1982).

24. *E.g., Johnson v. Director, OWCP*, 183 F.3d 1169 (9th Cir. 1999).

25. FRAP 27(a)(3).

26. FRAP 27(a)(4).

27. *City of Burlington v. Dague*, 505 U.S. 557, 562 (1992); *Anderson v. Director, OWCP*, 91 F.3d 1322, 1324 (9th Cir. 1996).

28. *E.g., Hensley v. Eckerhart, supra*, n. 8.

29. *Christensen v. Stevedoring Services of America*, 557 F.3d at 1054, n. 16.

30. *VanSkike v. Director, OWCP*, 557 F.3d 1041, 1047-48 (9th Cir. 2009).

31. *Perdue v. Kenny A.*, 559 U.S. 542 (2010); *City of Burlington v. Daque, supra*, n. 27.

32. 33 U.S.C. § 928(e).

33. *Missouri v. Jenkins by Agyei*, 491 U.S. 274 (1989); *Blum v. Stenson*, 465 U.S. 886, 895 n. 11 (1984).

34. *City of Burlington v. Dague, supra*, n. 27; *Anderson v. Director, OWCP, supra*, n. 27.

35. *Christensen v. Stevedoring Services of America*, 557 F.3d at 1053; *Beckwith v. Horizon Lines, Inc.*, 43 BRBS 156 (2009); *Holiday v. Newport News Shipbuilding & Dry Dock Co.*, 44 BRBS 67 (2010).

36. *Jeffboat, LLC v. Director, OWCP*, 553 F.3d 487, 490 (7th Cir. 2009).

37. *Shirrod v. Director, OWCP*, 809 F.3d 1082 (9th Cir. 2015).

38. *Obadiaru v. ITT Corp.*, 45 BRBS 17 (2011).

39. *Holiday, supra*, n. 35; *Beckwith, supra*, n. 35.

40. *Norman v. Housing Authority of the City of Montgomery*, 836 F.2d 1292 (11th Cir.1988).

41. *Shirrod, supra*, n. 37; *B & G Mining Co. v. Director, OWCP*, 522 F.3d 657 (6th Cir. 2008).

42. *See* introduction to Incisive Legal Intelligence 2009 Small Law Firm Economic Survey, which stated "In reviewing rates for the various specialties, note that lawyers who litigate for insurers and workers' compensation tend to show lower hourly rates, while those engaged in tax/securities practice, intellectual property (patent, trademark and copyright) or in administrative law will report a much higher amount charged per hour. One might expect the business lawyers to earn more than the insurance defense lawyers; however, their earnings are not as different as their fees would indicate. Different time recording methods and the long hours put in on litigation help to explain this lack of difference."

43. *Christensen v. Stevedoring Services of America*, 44 BRBS 39 (2010); *Beckwith, supra*, n. 35; *Holiday, supra*, n. 35.

44. 20 C.F.R. §§ 702.132 and 802.203.

45. 20 C.F.R. §§ 702.132 and 802.203.

46. *Blum, supra*, n. 33.

47. *Berkstresser v. WMATA*, 16 BRBS 231, 236 (1984).

48. *Bazor v. Boomtown Belle Casino*, 35 BRBS 121, 128 (2001), *rev'd on other grounds*, 313 F.3d 300 (5th Cir. 2002), *cert. denied*, 540 U.S. 814 (2003).

49. *Missouri v. Jenkins, supra*, n. 33; *Blum v. Stenson, supra*, n. 33; *Christensen, supra*, n. 16; *Van Skike, supra*, n. 30.

50. *Cabral v. General Dynamics Corp.*, 13 BRBS 97 (1981).

51. *Bell v. Clackamas County*, 341 F.3d 858, 869 (9th Cir. 2003).

52. *Christensen and Van Skike, supra*, nn. 16, 30. *Cf. Camacho v. Bridgeport Financial, Inc.*, 523 F.3d 973 (9th Cir. 2008).

53. *Kauffman v. Brady-Hamilton Stevedore Co.*, 12 BRBS 544 (1980); *Holmes v. Tampa Ship Repair & Dry Dock Co.*, 8 BRBS 455 (1978).

54. *Moreno v. City of Sacramento*, 534 F.3d 1106 (9th Cir. 2008).

55. *Christensen, supra*, n. 16; *Van Skike, supra*, n. 30: *Camacho, supra*, n. 51.

56. *Monahan v. Portland Stevedoring Co.*, 8 BRBS 653, 657-58 (1978).

57. *See Baker v. Manson Construction Co.*, 39 BRBS 427, 429 (ALJ) (2005).

58. *Van Skike, supra*, n. 30; *Christensen, supra*, n. 16; *Holiday v. Newport News Shipbuilding & Dry Dock Co.*, 591 F.3d 219 (4th Cir. 2009); *Shirrod, supra*, n. 37.

59. *Missouri v. Jenkins, supra*, n. 27; *Bellmer v. Jones Oregon Stevedoring Co.*, 32 BRBS 245 (1998).

60. *Boland Marine & Mfg. Co. v. Rihner*, 41 F.3d 997 (5th Cir. 1995); *Hobbs v. Director, OWCP*, 820 F.2d 1528 (9th Cir. 1987).

61. *Johnson, supra*, n. 24; *Anderson v. Director, OWCP, supra*, n. 27; *Kerns v. Consolidation Coal Co.*, 247 F.3d 143 (4th Cir. 2001).

62. *Missouri v. Jenkins, supra*, n. 33.

63. *Christensen*, 557 F.3d at 1055-56, *supra*, n. 16.

64. *Missouri v. Jenkins, supra*, n. 33.

65. *Modar v. Maritime Services Corp.*, 632 F.Appx 909 (9th Cir. 2015).

66. *Holiday, supra*, n. 58; *Fox v. Vice, infra*, n. 87.

67. *Richardson v. General Dynamics Corp.*, 23 BRBS 327 (1990).

68. *Hardman v. Marine Terminals Corp.*, BRB No. 2016-0132 LHCA.

69. *Snowden v. Ingalls Shipbuilding, Inc.*, 25 BRBS 245, 252 (1991); *Cherry v. Newport News Shipbuilding & Dry Dock Co.*, 8 BRBS 857 (1978).

70. *Cabrales v. County of Los Angeles*, 935 F.2d 1050 (9th Cir. 1991).

71. *Anderson v. Director, OWCP, supra*, n. 27; *Bogden v. Consolidated Coal Co.*, 44 BRBS 121 (2011); *Baumler v. Marinette Marine Corp.*, 40 BRBS 5 (2006); *See Jarrell, supra*, n. 17 for basis for allowing fees for defending fees.

72. *Day v. James Marine, supra*, n. 1; *Watkins v. Ingalls Shipbuilding, Inc.*, No. 93-4367 (5th Cir. 1993) (mem.); *Weaver v. Ingalls Shipbuilding, Inc.*, 282 F.3d 357 (5th Cir. 2002) (following *Watkins*).

73. *Clinchfield Coal Co. v. Harris*, 149 F.3d 307 (4th Cir. 1998).

74. 30 U.S.C. § 932(a); 20 C.F.R. § 725.367.

75. *Childers v. Drummond Co.*, 22 BLR 1-128 (2002).

76. *Dyer v. Cenex Harvest States Coop.*, 563 F.3d 1044 (9th Cir. 2009).

77. *E.g., Everett v. Ingalls Shipbuilding, Inc.*, 32 BRBS 279 (1998), *aff'd on recon. en banc*, 33 BRBS 38 (1999).

78. *Barbera v. Director, OWCP*, 245 F.3d 282 (3rd Cir. 2001); *Battle v. A.J. Ellis Construction Co.*, 16 BRBS 329 (1984); *Jarrell, supra*, n. 17.

79. *Roach v. New York Protective Covering Co.*, 16 BRBS 114 (1984).

80. 33 U.S.C. § 928(d); *Ezell v. Direct Labor, Inc.*, 33 BRBS 19, 31 (1999).

81. *Ezell, supra*, n. 80, 33 BRBS at 29-31.

82. *See Cherry, supra*, n. 66.

83. *Shirrod, supra*, n. 37; *Muscella v. Sun Shipbuilding & Dry Dock Co.*, 12 BRBS 272 (1980).

84. *Moreno, supra*, n. 53.

85. *Carter v. Caleb Brett LLC*, 757 F.3d 866 (9th Cir. 2014).

86. *Carter, id.*

87. *Fox v. Vice*, 563 U.S., 826 (2011).

Part VI

Appellate Practice

Chapter 25

Appellate Procedure Under the Longshore Act

Joshua T. Gillelan II, Esq., Kris R. Marotti, Esq., and Lara D. Merrigan, Esq.

Synopsis

25.1 Basic Appellate Framework

Appeals under the Longshore Act are governed by § 21(b)-(c) of the Act. Since the LHWCA Amendments of 1972 created the Benefits Review Board, appeals from "decisions with respect to claims of employees under this Act" are taken to the Board under § 21(b)(3). (Those who favor strict judicial literalism might assert that decisions on claims by survivors, in death cases, are unappealable, but no one appears to have presented that argument, and the Supreme Court probably has not become quite *that* literalist.) Review at the Board is governed by its rules, codified at 20 C.F.R. §§ 802.101–.407. Any "final order of the Board" is subject to review in the United States court of appeals for "the circuit in which the injury occurred," under § 21(c). Procedures before the courts are governed by the FEDERAL RULES OF APPELLATE PROCEDURE and the LOCAL RULES of the circuit. Those courts' decisions are subject to discretionary review by the Supreme Court on petition for *certiorari*.

In cases under the Act as extended by the Defense Base Act and the Nonappropriated Fund Instrumentalities Act, the course of review is complicated by the fact that many such injuries do not occur within the geographical bounds of any circuit. Each of those statutes was passed before the Board was created, when review of compensation orders was in the United States district courts. Because the pre-1972 judicial-review provision of the Longshore Act vested jurisdiction in the district court for the district in which the injury occurred, each of these extensions of the Act contained a clause specifying that judicial review of compensation orders under them was to be in the district court for the district where "the office of the deputy commissioner" was located.[1] Only one court of appeals has addressed whether the reference to the "deputy commissioner" in these statutes should now be construed to mean the district director (the statutory "deputy commissioner") or, where the underlying compensation order was by an ALJ, him or her; it concluded that the district director's office where the order was filed, and thereby made "effective" under § 21(a), is determinative of the judicial-review forum.[2]

The courts of appeals have split, however, on the question whether the pre-1972 references to the "district court" should continue to govern despite the replacement of those courts, in the Longshore Act itself, by the Board as the forum for initial review of compensation orders.[3] Those references merely echoed the provision of Longshore Act § 21(b) when they were enacted; the only part of those separate judicial-review provisions that was intended to have operative effect was their reference to the deputy commissioners' offices. Should the mention of the district courts continue to be given effect, so as to inject an additional layer of review in DBA and NFIA cases, or should it be read only to produce its intended effect of providing a replacement for the inapplicable phrase "in which the injury occurred" in both the pre-1972 and current judicial-review provisions, and thus only to determine the appropriate court of appeals? The First, Second, Seventh, and Ninth Circuits have adopted the latter reading: the Board's decisions in DBA and NFIA cases are reviewable in the court of appeals for the circuit in which the underlying compensation order was filed.[4] The Fourth, Fifth, Sixth, and Eleventh Circuits have taken the former approach: parties seeking review of Board decisions in such cases must first go to the district court.[5] Fortunately, filing a timely petition for review in the "wrong" federal court is unlikely to result in a loss of appeal rights, as the "transfer" provision of 28 U.S.C. § 1631 allows the case to be transferred to whatever is determined to have been the "right" court, with its timeliness judged by its filing in the original court.

25.2 Reviewable Decisions

A. District Directors' Decisions

Although they rarely exercise it except on attorney-fee, vocational-rehabilitation, and enforcement matters and settlement approvals, district directors have statutory authority to issue binding decisions on a number of subjects and in a variety of situations, in some instances as the statutory "deputy commissioners" and in others by delegation of statutory authority of the Secretary of Labor (particularly under § 7 of the Act, with respect to "medical questions"). When they do—when they act not merely by issuing recommendations but by issuing orders that are in terms compulsory or dispositive, and issued with the formality appropriate to such effect—their decisions are within the Board's review authority.[6] ALJs have no review authority; a district director's *decision* becomes final thirty days after it is filed if an appeal is not filed to the Board (see "Timeliness" below).

The district directors' "supplementary orders" issued under Longshore Act § 18(a), declaring employers in default of payment obligations under existing awards (including additional amounts due for untimely payment under § 14(f)), are subject to review by the district courts to which they may be taken for entry of enforceable judicial judgments, and therefore are not reviewable by appeal to the Board.[7] If, however, the employer pays the amount declared in default, thereby obviating district-court proceedings, the Board has held that the employer is entitled to review of the validity of the supplementary order under § 21(b)(3), and the courts of appeals have agreed.[8] Where the district director's supplementary order *denies* the claimant's application for a declaration of default, that order is subject to appeal by the claimant to the Board.[9]

B. ALJs' Decisions

The statute does not contain the usual "*final* order" requirement for a decision to be subject to immediate appellate review by the Board. Nevertheless, the policies underlying that requirement—avoiding the interruption of the adjudication below with delays attributable to review of interlocutory rulings, avoiding review of matters that turn out not to affect the outcome anyway, and combining review of all challenged rulings (that turn out to have mattered to the outcome) in a single review after the trial-level proceedings have come to a close—are fully applicable. The Board therefore generally follows the contours of that requirement, and usually declines to hear appeals from ALJs' interlocutory decisions. ALJs are not supposed to conclude proceedings before them except by issuance of a dispositive order on the claim,[10] and when they do—for example, hearing and deciding only a coverage issue, and having found the claim to be within the Act's coverage either remanding to the district director or scheduling a further hearing for determination of the amount of liability—review of those decisions is unavailable until they "merge" in a decision making an award or denying the claim.[11] The Board has repeatedly reminded ALJs that they should resolve the entire controversy in matters before them. The appropriate course when the parties and an ALJ agree to present only a coverage or compensability issue for resolution before reaching questions of average weekly wage or extent of disability is for an order finding compensability to conclude with a provision for further proceedings on the extent of the liability. Any challenge to the interlocutory order will be delayed until proceedings have concluded with a "compensation order," making an award or denying the claim.

Under unusual circumstances, where it judges the issue on which a party seeks review of an ALJ's interlocutory ruling to be of sufficient importance and the cost of delaying review to be too great, the Board will exercise its authority to hear an interlocutory appeal.[12] Although the Board is not bound by the technical rules of procedure governing litigation in federal courts, it has relied upon such rules for guidance where the Act and its regulations are silent.[13] It has looked to the collateral order doctrine, as articulated by the United States Supreme Court, in forming a three prong test for when an interlocutory appeal is generally allowable.[14] First, the order must conclusively determine the disputed question. Second, the order must resolve an important issue which is completely separate from the merits of the action. Third, the order must be effectively unreviewable on appeal from a final judgment. If the order at issue fails to satisfy any one of these requirements, it is generally not appealable. However, the Board recognizes an exception: it will hear an appeal of a non-final order if it deems it necessary to properly direct the course of the adjudicatory process.[15]

The fact that an application for an award of fees to the claimant's attorney for successful representation remains pending does not affect the appealability of the decision resolving the compensation claim. The fee proceedings are treated as a separate, collateral matter, and the fee award or denial is reviewable as if it were an entirely separate proceeding. A fee award, like any other dispositive order, becomes final thirty days after it is filed unless an appeal from that order is filed.

C. Benefits Review Board Decisions

Review of the Board's decisions is limited to "final order[s] of the Board." Thus a Board order remanding to a district director or ALJ is not reviewable until after the further proceedings have concluded.[16] The rulings in that order that turn out to affect the eventual outcome are reviewable by the court after the proceedings have run their course to a "final order of the Board."[17]

After the ALJ has acted on remand, if a party still wishes to challenge the Board's earlier decision, it must go back through the Board before proceeding to judicial review. Where no one challenges any ruling in the decision on remand, the party seeking review can file a notice of appeal to the Board and at the same time request a summary decision on the appeal. The Board will generally issue such a decision promptly; the summary affirmance is a "final order of the Board" subject to review—including of the earlier Board decision that is "merged" in it.

The Ninth Circuit has allowed a party to bypass the Board and go straight from the ALJ's decision on remand to the court of appeals if no one has filed a timely appeal to the Board after the ALJ's decision on remand.[18] Other courts of appeals have rejected that rule, resulting in a complete loss of the right to review by the party who relied on it in failing to appeal timely to the Board. In any event, even the Ninth Circuit has urged adherence to the safer course: Always go back to the Board for a "final order" to avoid potential loss of the right to review.

D. Stays of Payment Pending Review

An award is "effective" when filed in the office of the district director, and is enforceable under the procedures of § 18(a) regardless of the filing and pursuit of an appeal (and subject to twenty-percent augmentation of the amount due if not paid within ten days), as well as regardless of the filing of a motion for reconsideration with the ALJ.[19] The only exception is where the liable party secures a "stay" of payments, pending review, from the Board or the court of appeals. Both § 21(b)(3) and § 21(c) restrict the authority to issue stays pending review to cases where "irreparable injury would otherwise ensue to the employer or carrier." The latter provision requires the court issuing a stay to make "a specific finding, based upon evidence submitted to the court and identified by reference thereto," and to "specif[y] the nature of the damage"; and the Board's Rules impose the same requirements on it.[20] It has long been settled that the only "irreparable injury" that will support a stay is, essentially, irretrievable insolvency. Since a couple of decades ago when the courts of appeals corrected the Board's drift toward issuing stays more often where that standard could not be met,[21] stays have been limited to rare situations in which an uninsured employer submits its red-ink balance sheets as exhibits in support of its motion for a stay. Motions for stays are treated as severable and "collateral" to the appeal itself, so orders granting or denying stays are "collateral final orders" subject to immediate review by the court of appeals that would eventually have jurisdiction on the merits.

Attorney-fee awards are not payable so long as timely review is sought of the underlying award of benefits; any award of fees to the claimant's attorney by the district director or ALJ is unenforceable until review has run its course. Where the award is not appealed but the fee award is, the statute is unclear on whether the fee, for securing an award that *has* become final, is payable notwithstanding the appeal. In any event, it is unlikely that the prohibition on any recovery of payments on an award that is later reversed (except by way of credit against any remaining future liability)[22] is applicable to attorney-fee awards. When the award is not promptly paid, however, the claimant's attorney can return to the fee-awarding tribunals once the appeal has run its course and payment is finally made, for supplementation of the fee award to an updated reasonable hourly rate.[23]

25.3 Scope of Review

A. Factual Disputes

Section 21(b)(3) explicitly limits the Board's scope of review of "the findings of fact in the decision under review": they "shall be conclusive if supported by substantial evidence in the record considered as a whole." "Substantial evidence" is "such relevant evidence as a reasonable mind might accept as adequate to support a conclusion," *i.e.*, evidence "having rational probative force,"[24] and the reference to "the record considered as a whole" means that the evidence supporting the decision must retain that force after "tak[ing] into account whatever in the record fairly detracts from its weight."[25] The reviewing tribunal may not redetermine the relative weight of the evidence, or overturn reasonable inferences by the factfinder; it may only weigh the evidence relied upon to determine its substantiality—its capacity to lead a reasonable mind to the contested conclusion—if credited. Questions of witness credibility are particularly within the ALJs' province and reviewable only for the most extreme credulity or skepticism without an apparently reasonable basis.

Although the statute does not similarly specify the scope of review in the courts of appeals, they review the Board's decisions, for errors of law, including failure to apply or to restrict itself to the substantial-evidence scope of its review authority on factual questions. This effectively requires the courts to engage in the same substantial-evidence review as the Board.

B. Questions of Law

Review at both levels also includes challenges on questions of law. Neither ALJs' nor the Board's views on legal questions are entitled to any deference on review; they are not charged with the "administration" of the Act, and their roles are exclusively "quasi-judicial."[26] Review of determinations of applicable law is therefore *de novo*. Where the Director of the OWCP, as administrator, expresses a view on a legal question in litigation, both the Board and most of the courts of appeals grant it at least some level of deference, depending on the indicia of full development and administrative consideration of the statutory construction involved. The Board is, however, entitled to a measure of deference with respect to its constructions of its own rules.

25.4 Petition for Review to the Benefits Review Board

A. Notice of Appeal Form and Contents

The contents of a notice of appeal to the Board (filed directly with the Board's Clerk at P.O. Box 37601, Washington, DC 20013-7601), are set out in 20 C.F.R. § 802.208(a). Any writing that permits identification of the decision being appealed will suffice to protect the right to review, but failure to abide by the rule will slow things down. Most importantly, a copy of the notice of appeal should be sent to the district director, as well as, of course, to the other parties (where they are represented, to their counsel). Note that the Director, OWCP, as the delegate of the Secretary of Labor's authority as administrator of the Act, is a party as a matter of right to all appeals before the Board (although his counsel actually appears to urge a position on his behalf in only a few cases before the Board other than those involving employers' claims for relief from full liability under § 8(f) of the Act). Service of the notice and all filings should be made on the Director's appellate counsel (best directed to the Counsel for Longshore, Division of Black Lung and Longshore Legal Services, N-2117 Frances Perkins Labor Building, Washington, DC 20210). In those cases where the Director has been represented by a regional solicitor's office before the ALJ, a copy should also be sent to the regional attorney. As with all pleadings submitted to the Board, an original and two copies must be submitted for filing.

The notice must also include reference to any motion for reconsideration of the decision that any party has filed and information concerning whether it remains pending or has been ruled upon (see "Timeliness" below).

B. Notice of Appeal Timeliness

The rules governing the timeliness of a notice of appeal to the Board are unusually lenient, but do contain traps for the unwary. First, again, the formal specifications of a proper notice of appeal are not really requirements. Second, a notice is timely if *mailed* to the Board within the statutory thirty days. [**Caution:** This is not true at the court of appeals; see "Petition for Review to the Court of Appeals—Timeliness" below.] Third, even if the notice is misdirected—only to the ALJ, or the district director, or for that matter the Chief Inspector of Eggs of the Minnesota Department of Agriculture (with apologies, if there is such a person, for the flood of notices of appeal to the Board he or she may receive), it may be counted.[27]

When the thirty days *begins* is not so easy. First, it begins with the *filing* of the decision of which review is sought in the district director's office. The date of "issuance" on the headings of ALJs' decisions is of no legal significance. The date the party or counsel *receives* the decision is also irrelevant. Whether the decision is "filed" if the district director's office fails to serve the decision properly is a subject of disagreement among the courts, and a topic of its own. Suffice it to say that if neither the party nor counsel was served, the deadline may be suspended until one of them is.

A common trap arises if any party has filed a motion for reconsideration. If the motion was timely—mailed within ten days of the filing of the decision in the district director's office[28]—it not only stops the thirty-day appeal period, but makes *any notice of appeal filed before it has been disposed of by the ALJ a nullity*.[29] A new notice of appeal must be timely filed after the decision on reconsideration is filed by the district director, or the right to review will be lost. If it is only the original decision of which review is sought, the notice should say so, but it must also recount the timely filing and disposition of the motion for reconsideration, and the date of filing of the most recent decision, that has intervened. A second or third motion for reconsideration may or may not further suspend the time for filing; if it addresses something new in the most recent decision, it probably does, but if not it may not.

The Board's rules provide an extended time limit for cross-appeals, like that applicable on appeal to the courts of appeals from district courts under Fed. R. App. P. 4(a)(3). Where another party files a timely appeal, any other party has fourteen days from that filing (or from service of the other party's notice, if it was not accomplished at the time) to file a notice of a cross-appeal. A party may urge alternative grounds for the result below, even if they were addressed and rejected by the ALJ, without having filed a cross-appeal, but may not ordinarily advance arguments that would expand its rights beyond, or restrict its liabilities below, those recognized by the ALJ without having done so.

C. Briefing

The party appealing is called the "petitioner" in the Board's practice. The petitioner is required to file a "petition for review," "list[ing] the specific issues to be considered on appeal," accompanied by an opening brief in support of the petition. The thirty-day period for filing the petition and supporting brief begins to run upon receipt of the Board's acknowledgement of the filing of the notice of appeal (typically anywhere from a couple of days to a couple of months after the notice is submitted). Any other party then has thirty days from receipt of the petition and opening brief to submit a response brief, and the petitioner then has twenty days from receipt to file a reply brief. Leave to file a surresponse or surreply may be granted by the Board, though a party should not seek leave absent good cause. The Board may also request supplemental briefs on specified issues.

Consistent with its limited scope of review, the Board may not consider any new evidence in connection with an appeal (except, of course, with respect to ancillary matters such as a motion for a stay or an application for an award of attorney fees). New evidence directed to the establishment of either a "mistake in a determination of fact" in the original decision or a "change in [relevant] conditions" since the original hearing may be submitted to the ALJ pursuant to the "modification" procedure of § 22 of the Act. Any party may file an application for modification of the decision, even while an appeal is pending before the Board, but is required to notify the Board when it does so. The Board will then dismiss the appeal, subject to reinstatement at the petitioner's request within thirty days of the disposition of the modification proceedings. If the petitioner also seeks review of the decision in those proceedings, it must file a notice of appeal of that decision as well.[30]

D. Electronic Filing with the Board

The Benefits Review Board has recently launched an electronic filing system. Use of this system is optional. It allows you to file documents with and receive documents from the Board; it does not effectuate service upon other parties. One enormous advantage is that filing a document with the Board electronically is in lieu of paper service to the Board. Although regulations require service of an original and two copies of the document with the Board, electronic filing absolves you of this requirement. Before you may file electronically, you must create an account to do so at https://dol-appeals.entellitrak.com/etk-dol-appeals-prod/login.request.do?service=%2Fhome.do. That website also provides additional direction, including a user guide and answers to frequently asked questions. Once you have created an account, before you are able to file a document in an existing appeal, you must request access to the case via the website. This entails filling out an online form and then waiting for the Benefits Review Board to grant access. Thus, you should ensure you are registered and have access to a case before you rely upon using electronic service to meet a filing deadline. You may also use this portal to file a notice of appeal. You will receive a confirmation email when you have successfully filed. Please be aware that the foregoing describes the current procedure, which may well have changed by the time you are reading this chapter.

E. Oral Argument

Any party may request, by motion, that the Board hold oral argument on an appeal. Such a motion may be filed up to the time for the filing of the petitioner's reply brief. The Board typically holds argument near the location of the claimant's residence. Because of budgetary constraints limiting its travel, however, the Board hears oral argument in very few cases, usually on its own motion rather than that of a party. Where it schedules argument, the Board sometimes directs further briefing in advance of the argument.

F. Decision and Reconsideration

Although the Board is no longer subject to the statutory one-year restriction on its time to decide an appeal that was in effect from 1996 until 2005, it continues to adhere to that time limit in practice. Most appeals are decided ten or eleven months after they are docketed. The Board occasionally grants motions for expedited consideration (or effectively grants them by deciding a case unusually quickly), but has articulated no general standards for when it will "advance the order in which a particular case is to be considered."[31]

Within thirty days of the filing of the Board's dispositive decision, any aggrieved party may seek reconsideration by the panel of three administrative appeals judges who decided the case, and may in addition "suggest the appropriateness" of reconsideration by the Board *en banc* if the panel does not grant the relief requested. Although the Board's rules are silent on the subject, it will consider responses in opposition to a motion for reconsideration that are filed reasonably promptly after the motion.

Even more so than before the ALJ, motions for reconsideration of the Board's decisions on reconsideration are a dangerous business. Unless the decision on the first such motion alters the original decision in some material way and the further motion for reconsideration is directed at that alteration, successive motions for reconsideration do not interrupt the sixty-day period for seeking judicial review.[32]

G. Attorney Fees

A successful claimant's attorney is entitled to an award of fees, generally payable by the employer, for pursuing or defending against the appeal, under § 28 of the Act. The application to the Board for the fee award for services in the proceedings before it must generally be filed within sixty days of issuance of the Board's decision. If the Board has remanded the case to the ALJ, however, the fee application must generally await the outcome of the proceedings on remand (to allow determination of the extent of the claimant's success), and the attorney is permitted sixty days from the decision on remand to file the application. Where the claimant has been unsuccessful before the Board but prevails upon judicial review, his or her attorney has sixty days from "issuance of the court's judgment" to file a fee application with the Board for the work before it.

There is no prohibition on the filing of a fee application *before* the Board has acted on the merits, and where the claimant's attorney has so filed, the Board may make an award of fees in the same decision in which it addresses the merits of the appeal.

25.5 Petition for Review to the Court of Appeals

A. Admission to the Circuit Court Bar

Petitioning attorneys must be admitted to the bar of the appropriate circuit court where the petition for review is filed. Compliance with FED. R. APP. P. 46 is required. The attorney must be of "good moral and professional character" and admitted to the bar of either the United States Supreme Court, a U.S. Circuit Court of Appeals, a U.S. District Court or the highest court of the state.

Each circuit court has specific requirements, forms, and fees for application for admission to its bar. (See examples of Applications in Appendix Forms 1–3). One should review the website for the specific circuit court where the petition will be filed or is pending to obtain the required form for admission and accompanying forms—where applicable—as well as information concerning the applicable filing fee. All of the circuit courts require the movant to attest, under oath, to their good moral and professional character, including responding to questions concerning whether the attorney has been disbarred or suspended from the practice before any court, agency, board, and the like. Certain circuit courts require that the application for admission be filed electronically through the Case Management/Electronic Case Filing System ("CM/ECF"). Other circuits require the application to be filed by mail or that the applicant appear, in person. Additionally, many circuit courts require a sponsoring attorney for the movant, or, in the alternative, a Motion for Admission to be signed by a fellow attorney admitted in the court where the application is being made.[33]

B. Filing Petition

The review jurisdiction of the appropriate court of appeals is invoked by the timely filing of a "petition for review." (See examples in Appendix Forms 4 and 5). The petition is a simple, one-paragraph document, under a heading that names the court, identifies the petitioner as such, and list the other parties before the Board (including the Director, OWCP) as respondents. The body of the petition must specify the caption and date(s) of the Board's order(s) of which review is sought (and, where that it is not the "final order of the Board" within sixty days of which the petition is filed, the caption and date of the final order). It must be accompanied by a certificate of service on counsel for the other parties. The Board is not a respondent, but a copy of the petition should be served on it as well. Upon docketing, the clerk of the court is required to transmit copies to the Board and the other parties, and sufficient copies of the petition should be included for such service, in addition to the original and three copies for the court. Finally, the petition should be accompanied by the filing fee (currently $500), or a motion for leave to proceed *in forma pauperis* pursuant to FED. R. APP. P. 24(b) with an affidavit in the form provided by Form 4 in those RULES' Appendix of Forms. Although the petition for review is the only *jurisdictional* document, the party seeking review should carefully review the local rules of the particular circuit to determine what ancillary filings are required at the time of filing or in short order thereafter (for example, under 5TH CIR. RULE 15.4, the petitioner must file a Statement of Issues to be presented on appeal within 30 days of filing the Petition and serve the Director and counsel for all parties, so appropriate alignment may be determined.)

The courts' local rules, along with the general rules for all courts of appeals, are conveniently available through links on their web sites (www.ca*.uscourts.gov, replacing the asterisk with the number of the circuit).

C. Timeliness

The sixty days for the filing of a petition for review in court begins with the Board's issuance of its final order (see discussion above). If a timely motion for reconsideration is filed by any party, the time begins anew from the Board's order disposing of that motion.[34]

While the originating document for a Board appeal is a notice of appeal, the petition for review begins the proceedings before a circuit court. Two critical points distinguish the timeliness of notices of appeals to the Board from the timeliness of petitions for review. First, a petition for review is timely only if it *reaches the court* by the sixtieth day. Mailing is not good enough, and timely filing the circuit court petition with the Board does not suffice either.[35] And second, unlike the practice either before the Board or with respect to appeals to the courts of appeals from district courts, there is no additional time allowed for a "cross-petition" after another party has filed a timely petition. Technically there is no such thing as a cross-petition. A party desiring to pursue judicial review only if the other side does so can file a timely petition and then withdraw it if the other party does not timely file, but cannot wait beyond the sixtieth day before filing in order to see if the other side files. An attorney who misleads opposing counsel upon inquiry as to his or her intention to file may face disciplinary proceedings (and surely will find a place in the deepest pit of Hell), but the misled attorney's client will be unable to secure judicial review along with the other party.

D. Briefing

Some courts of appeals issue a briefing schedule as soon as a petition for review is docketed; others simply follow Fed. R. App. P. 31(a), under which the petitioner's brief is due thirty days after the Board files the record (or, in some courts, a certified list of the docket entries) with the court; the respondents' briefs are due thirty days after service of the petitioner's brief (thirty-three days from mailing if service was by mail), and the petitioner then may file a reply brief within fourteen days (or seventeen days of mailing). Some courts require the petitioner to file excerpts of the record, defined variously in their local rules, along with the opening brief; others follow the procedures for designation of a joint appendix, either filed along with the opening brief or deferred until after briefing, set out in Fed. R. App. P. 30. Unlike petitions for review, a brief is timely if mailed on the due date. The number of copies required varies widely from circuit to circuit.

Most federal circuit courts have now implemented electronic filing, in which a brief is timely if electronically filed by midnight in the court's time zone. Here, too, reviewing the local rules of the court is not only instrumental but necessary. The electronic procedures are rapidly developing, so even if you have recent experience with a court, verify that nothing has changed before filing. Typically, the clerk will review the electronic brief for completeness, and if complete, will issue an order for paper copies to be submitted. If incomplete, the clerk will order that the electronic brief be corrected and resubmitted to remedy the error, and once remedied, will order the paper copies be served. Where other parties are registered for electronic service, serving them hard copies is usually unnecessary. When serving other parties only electronically, per Fed. R. App. P. 26, a circuit court's local rules may still add three days to the response time as though the triggering document were served by mail. When submitting electronic briefs, do not attempt to first negotiate the process at the literal eleventh hour. Technical issues abound, and when possible, it is best to establish your electronic filing account and explore the court's portal (and your own computer and browser's compatibility) well in advance. If insurmountable problems interfere at the time of filing, document them via screenshots or other methods. Planning ahead is key; the Fifth Circuit, for example, even requires electronic filers to complete electronic learning modules and to provide certification that they have done so.[36]

When filing electronically, consider the added utility that an electronic brief can provide the judges and clerks. Again, local rules and (sometimes 200-plus page) user guides available on individual court websites provide requirements and guidance. Submit briefs in portable document format ("PDF"). Rather than printing the brief to scribble triumphantly with a pen in the signature line, and then scanning it and converting it into PDF format, sign it electronically ("s/ name"[37]), and convert it to that format directly with your word processing software. This allows the text to remain searchable. Not only is this more time-effective, but failure to do so will often result in the court rejecting that draft of your brief. As a convenience, you may include hyperlinks in your brief to authorities you cite, to the record, and to other documents filed in the case. You might choose to do this throughout or only where a particular authority may be difficult to locate or deserves to be highlighted. Your tables of contents and authorities can link to the applicable page numbers within your brief, as can any "infra" or "supra" references. While hyperlinking is not currently a requirement, it is a sufficiently-valued convenience that some courts even include detailed how-to instructions in their user guides.[38] For excerpts of record, it is best (even where not required) to run an optical character recognition ("OCR") program for any scanned documents to ensure that they are also searchable. Some courts, including the Fifth Circuit Court of Appeals, have recently launched their own automated hyperlinking functionality, which only works when counsel adhere to specific citation formats (eg., "USCA*" where the record is paper versus "ROA.*" with the asterisk substituted for the page number to enable the Fifth Circuit's software to automatically link the cited page).[39] As more and more judges approach the bench with only an electronic tablet in hand, briefs with thoughtful additions of electronic dimensions can add power to traditional advocacy. In short, follow the requirements of the court with which you are filing, recognize that these requirements are changing frequently with technological advances, and anticipate how you might aid the judges and their clerks with a well-engineered electronic brief.

1. The petitioner's brief

The cover of the petitioner's brief must be blue and include the circuit court, title of the case, nature of the proceeding and name of the agency or board below (e.g., "Petition for Review of Decision and Order of the Benefits Review Board"), title of brief, and name and contact information for counsel representing the party. FED. R. APP. P. 28(a) 1-10 lists the general contents as follows:

- **Corporate Disclosure Statement**, if required under RULE 26.1
- **Table of Content**, with appropriate page references
- **Table of Cases/Authorities**, with appropriate page references
- **Jurisdictional Statement**, which should include the basis for the agency's subject matter jurisdiction below; the basis for the circuit court's jurisdiction; a statement of timeliness of the petition for review, including relevant dates; and statement as to the finality of the order or judgment appealed from.
- **Statement of Issues** for review on appeal. This should be presented in the form of a question.
- **Statement of the Case**, with appropriate references to the record, appendix and addendum, where applicable.[40] This should consist of a concise summary of the relevant facts, procedural history, and rulings presented for review.
- **Summary of the Argument**, which should consist of a concise summary of the arguments relative to the issues before the court for review. Avoid a mere recitation of the argument headings in the body of the brief.
- **Argument**, which should state the applicable standard of review and include appropriate references to the record, appendix, and addendum where applicable. The Argument should be clear and logical facilitating an ease of comprehension of the relevant facts and the issues for review. Avoid any extraneous or duplicitous information. The circuit courts vary as to where the Standard of Review should appear within the body of the argument. One should review the local rules of the circuit court. Most provide that the applicable Standard of Review may appear within the discussion of each issue or under separate heading placed before the discussion of each issue.
- **Conclusion**, with a statement as to the relief sought.
- **Certification of Compliance** with FED. R. APP. P. 32(a), which details compliance with page limitation, type-volume limitation, and type face requirements.[41] (See examples in Appendix Form 6).
- **Certification of Service** in compliance with FED. R. APP. P. 25.

The above sets out the general briefing order. Each circuit court has specific requirements regarding brief content, sequence, format and appendix requirements. It is imperative that you familiarize yourself with the applicable local rules, as there are various nuances with regard to brief requirements amongst the circuit courts. For example, the Third Circuit Court of Appeals has specific requirements with regard to citations (3RD CIR. R. 28.3), standard of review (RULE 28.1(b)), as well as text size and format[42]; 2ND CIR. R. 28.1 sets forth specific information to be included in the Statement of the Case in the petitioner's brief; 6TH CIR. R. 28(b) sets forth specific briefing requirements for the 6th Circuit; 10TH CIR. R. 28.2 sets forth specific briefing requirement, including a Statement of Prior or Related Appeals to be included in the petitioner's brief; FED. CIR. R. 47.4 requires a Certification of Intention in the petitioner's brief; D.C. CIR. R. 28(a)(3) and the Tenth Circuit require the inclusion of a Glossary regarding abbreviations; and 9TH CIR. R. 28-2.6 and FED. CIR. R. 47.5 require a Statement of Related Cases.

Pursuant to FED. R. APP. P. 30(a), the Petitioner is responsible for preparation of an Appendix. The Appendix should comply with the Federal Rule and the applicable local rules of the circuit court. It should contain materials cited in the brief, including, but not limited to the relevant docket entries in the agency proceedings below, the judgment, order or decision being appealed and any other part of the record, which counsel wishes to bring to the attention of the court.

In determining the contents of the Appendix, if the parties cannot agree, counsel for the petitioner must file a designation of the parts of the records to be included in the Appendix to be circulated to counsel for the respondent within 14 days after the record is filed with the court. Counsel for the respondent may, within 14 days after receiving the designation, serve on the petitioner's counsel a designation of any additional parts, which he or she wishes to be included in the Appendix.[43] The petitioner is responsible for the cost of the Appendix.

2. The respondent's brief

The respondent's brief must have a red cover and comply with format required of circuit court regarding binding, footnotes, paper size, margins, etc. The requirements of the respondent's brief are set forth in FED. R. APP. P. 28(b). Essentially, they are identical to those for the petitioner's brief, with the exception that the Jurisdictional Statement under RULE 28(a)(4), Statement of Issues under RULE 28(a)(5), Statement of the Case under RULE 28(a)(6), or applicable Standard of Review under RULE 28(a)(8)(B) are optional, if respondent is in agreement with the petitioner's statements related thereto in the opening brief. One should review the local rules of the applicable circuit court as to any additional requirements for the content and format of the respondent's brief.

3. Reply brief

The petitioner may file a reply to the respondent's brief, pursuant to FED. R. APP. P. 28(c), which must include a gray cover page, Table of Contents, and Table of Authorities. No further briefing is permitted without court permission.

4. Amicus brief and cross appeals

FED. R. APP. P. 29 deals with the contents and format of a brief of an amicus curiae. FED. R. APP. P. 28.1 addresses the content and format of cross appeals.

5. Supplementing the brief

Precedents that come to a party's attention after briefing may be submitted to the court by letter, in accordance with FED. R. APP. P. 28(i); the other parties may respond in the same form.

6. Request for oral argument

Most circuit court local rules provide for requests for oral argument or waiver. In some circuits, the request is optional (*see* 1ST CIR. R. 34.0(a); 6TH CIR. R. 34(a), while it is mandatory in others (*see* 5TH CIR. R. 28.2.3; 10TH CIR. R. 28.2(C)(4); 11TH CIR. R. 28-1(c)). The request for oral argument by a party on appeal is not a guarantee that the matter will be assigned for argument. Eleventh Circuit Local Rules note that although statements by the petitioner or respondent requesting oral argument or waiver thereof shall be considered, "[t]he Court will accord these statements due, though not controlling, weight in determining whether oral arguments will be heard." *See* FED. R. APP. P. 34(a) and (f) and 11TH CIR. R. 34-3(c).

E. Oral Argument

Most of the circuit courts provide an opportunity for oral argument in most cases. When the court takes a case "under submission" for decision without argument, it is almost invariably an ill omen for the petitioner. Courts will typically send the initial notice of the oral argument date without revealing the assigned panel of judges. At that point, you should notify them without delay (usually within seven days) of any conflicts with the date. Rescheduling after the assigned panel is announced is heavily disfavored for obvious reasons.

In many cases, the time allowed for argument is only five or ten minutes per side. Each member of the three-judge panel will almost always have read the briefs and the decisions below with care. The argument represents the parties' opportunity to learn what problems the judges have with their positions, and to attempt to satisfy their concerns. Cases in which the court is turned around by oral argument are rare, but it happens. Pretty speeches and appeals for sympathy are ineffective; only anticipation of and engagement with the court's questions and doubts can be productive. Counsel must be prepared to point to, rather than substitute their own words for, the precise evidence or ruling below that they contend is critical.

F. Decision, Rehearing, and Mandate

Only the most general statement is possible about the time from briefing to disposition of petitions for review in the courts of appeals. Some courts typically schedule oral argument only a few months after briefing is completed, and issue their decisions within two or three months after argument (or within a week or two if they see no issue worth seriously addressing). Others typically do not set cases for argument until more than a year and a half after briefing, and are more likely to take four to six months, or even longer, after argument to issue an opinion.

Because the Director, OWCP is a party (whether he participates or not), the time allowed for a petition for rehearing by the panel, the full court, or both is forty-five days rather than fourteen. Panel rehearing is appropriate under FED. R. APP. P. 40 if the court has "overlooked or misapprehended" something critical; rehearing *en banc* is reserved by RULE 35 for very few cases—a tiny percentage, and number, of petitions are granted—in which a majority of the judges are convinced by the petition that the panel's decision probably either (a) conflicts with a decision of the Supreme Court or of the same court of appeals, or (b) involves "a question of exceptional importance" as precedent (with the suggestion that it may present such a question if the panel's decision conflicts with established precedent in other circuits). A response to a petition for rehearing is not permitted unless requested by the court, but the court will not ordinarily grant a petition without inviting and considering a response. If the court takes a case *en banc*, it ordinarily provides for briefing anew for the full court.

A decision of the court of appeals is not its final disposition until it issues the "mandate" under RULE 41. The clerk issues the mandate—a copy of the decision, directed back to the Board (with copies to all parties)—a week after the forty-five days for a petition for rehearing expires, or after the court's disposition of any such petition. A party intending to file a petition for *certiorari* in the Supreme Court may move the court of appeals to stay its mandate. *See* RULE 41(d)(2). Until the mandate issues, the court's decision does not take effect. Thus, if a continuing award of compensation is reversed by the court, the employer is not authorized to discontinue payments until the mandate.[44]

Counsel contemplating an attempt to secure Supreme Court review are well advised to associate counsel experienced at representation before the Court to handle all or part of the preparation of the petition for *certiorari* and, if it is one of the eighty or so out of over five thousand per year that is granted, the briefing and argument. At the very least, counsel should consult such a practitioner. It suffices for present purposes to say that review will never be granted simply on the ground that the court of appeals was wrong, or that the client's legitimate rights were violated; the petition must demonstrate that the decision of the court of appeals presents a rather direct and irreconcilable conflict on a question of law with the holding of another circuit (or that of the highest court of a state, particularly if it is within the same circuit), and that even that will not do it without a persuasive showing that the question arises frequently.

G. Fee Applications in Circuit Court Appeals

A successful claimant's attorney is also entitled to fees for work performed before a circuit court of appeals under § 28. A successful claimant is also entitled to an award of costs related to the appeal, pursuant to § 928(d).

The application for fees must generally be filed within 30 days of entry of the final judgment. Review the appropriate local rules for time periods for filing fee applications.

In LHWCA cases, the burden is on the attorney fee applicant to provide satisfactory evidence that the requested hourly rate is reasonable. In determining the reasonableness of the attorney's fee, § 928 has evolved towards the definition of "reasonable" used in other federal fee-shifting statutes.[45] In determining an amount of attorneys' fees to award under a fee-shifting statute, the United States Supreme Court has held that a court must determine the number of hours reasonable expended in preparing and litigating the case and then multiply those hours by a reasonable hourly rate. This sum constitutes the 'lodestar' amount.[46] The fee should take into account the necessary work done, quality of representation, complexity of issues involved and the amount of benefits awarded. The attorney's fee sought should be reasonable commensurate with the legal market rate in the community.[47] In determining the market rate for a prevailing attorney, the court should consider what private attorneys of comparable ability and reputation charge their paying clients for work of similar complexity in the community.[48] The Ninth Circuit Court of Appeals has held that the "relevant community" for hourly rates is broader than that derived from prior fee awards in LHWCA cases.[49]

The application for attorney's fees and costs should be accompanied by an affidavit of counsel in support thereof, wherein counsel should include his or her experience with handling appeals; the attorney's qualifications; attorney's time log related to work performed on the subject appeal, including time spent in preparing the Fee Application;[50] the complexity of the issues involved before the appellate court; the preclusion of other employment by the attorney due to acceptance of the case; and a statement as to the reasonableness of the hourly rate within the relevant legal community, which may include data pertaining to attorneys' fees within the subject market supporting the hourly rate requested.[51]

Endnotes

1. Defense Base Act § 3(b), 42 U.S.C. § 1653(b); Nonappropriated Fund Instrumentalities Act § 2(a) (final paragraph), 5 U.S.C. § 8171(d).

2. *Hice v. Director*, OWCP, 156 F.3d 214, 218 (D.C. Cir. 1998), *followed by McDonald v. Aecom*, 45 BRBS 45 (2011).

3. Note & Comment: Bypassing Redundancy: Resolving the Jurisdictional Dilemma Under the Defense Base Act, 83 Wash. L. Rev. 219 (2008).

4. *Pearce v. Director, OWCP*, 603 F.2d 763, 769–71 (9th Cir. 1979); *Pearce v. Director, OWCP*, 647 F.2d 716, 721 (7th Cir. 1981); *Serv. Emps. Int'l, Inc. v. Director, OWCP*, 595 F.3d 447, 452–5 (2nd Cir. 2010); *Truczinskas v. Director, OWCP*, 699 F.3d 672, 675 (1st Cir. 2012) (circuit courts may directly review Benefits Review Board decisions).

5. *Home Indemnity Co. v. Stillwell*, 597 F.2d 87 (6th Cir.), *cert. denied*, 444 U.S. 869 (1979); *AFIA/CIGNA Worldwide v. Felkner*, 930 F.2d 1111, 1115 n.6, 1121, 1122 (5th Cir.), *cert. denied*, 502 U.S. 906 (1991); *Lee v. Boeing Co.*, 123 F.3d 801, 805 (4th Cir. 1997) (2 to 1 decision); and *ITT Base Services v. Hickson*, 155 F.3d 1272 (11th Cir. 1998).

6. *See generally Healy Tibbitts Builders, Inc. v. Cabral*, 201 F.3d 1090 (9th Cir. 2000).

7. *E.g., Snowden v. Director, OWCP*, 253 F.2d 725, 729–31 (D.C. Cir. 2001), and authorities there cited.

8. *E.g., Sea-Land Service, Inc. v. Barry*, 41 F.3d 903, 906–07 (3d Cir. 1994).

9. *Bray v. Director, OWCP*, 664 F.2d 1045 (5th Cir. 1981).

10. *E.g.*, 20 C.F.R. §§ 702.348–349; *Mitri v. GLS*, 48 BRBS 41 (2014).

11. *E.g., Arjona v. Interport Maintenance*, 24 BRBS 222 (1991).

12. *E.g., Hardgrove v. Coast Guard Exchange System*, 37 BRBS 21 (2003).

13. 33 U.S.C. § 923(a); *see generally Sprague v. Director, OWCP*, 688 F.2d 862 n.16 (1st Cir. 1982).

14. *Tignor v. Newport News Shipbuilding and Dry Dock Co.*, 29 BRBS 135 (1995), *citing Gulfstream Aerospace Corp. v. Mayacamas Corp.*, 485 U.S. 271 (1988).

15. *See Butler v. Ingalls Shipbuilding, Inc.*, 28 BRBS 114 (1994); *Baroumes v. Eagle Marine Services*, 23 BRBS 80 (1989).

16. *E.g., Bish v. Brady-Hamilton Stevedore Co.*, 880 F.2d 1135 (9th Cir. 1989); *Cooper Stevedoring Co. v. Director, OWCP*, 826 F.2d 1011 (11th Cir. 1987); *Newpark Shipbuilding & Repair, Inc. v. Roundtree*, 723 F.2d 399 (5th Cir.) (*en banc*), *cert. denied*, 469 U.S. 818 (1984).

17. *Mijangos v. Avondale Shipyards, Inc.*, 948 F.2d 941, 943–44 (5th Cir. 1991); *Burns v. Director, OWCP*, 41 F.3d 1555, 1561–62 (D.C. Cir. 1994).

18. *Compare National Steel & Shipbuilding Co. v. Director, OWCP (McGregor II)*, 703 F.2d 417, 418–419 (9th Cir. 1983), *with RMK-BRJ v. Brittain*, 832 F.2d 565, 566–567 (11th Cir. 1987); *Aubrey v. Director, OWCP*, 916 F.2d 451, 452 (8th Cir. 1990); *Elliot Coal Mining Co. v. Director, OWCP*, 956 F.2d 448, 449–50 (3d Cir. 1992).

19. *E.g., McCrady v. Stevedoring Services of America*, 23 BRBS 106, 110 (1989).

20. 20 C.F.R. § 802.105.

21. *Rivere v. Offshore Painting Contractors*, 872 F.2d 1187 (5th Cir. 1989); *Edwards v. Director*, OWCP, 932 F.2d 1325 (9th Cir. 1991).

22. *E.g., Stevedoring Services of America, Inc. v. Eggert*, 953 F.2d 552 (9th Cir.), *cert. denied*, 505 U.S. 1230 (1992); *Ceres Gulf v. Cooper*, 957 F.2d 1199 (5th Cir. 1992).

23. *Kerns v. Consolidation Coal Co.*, 176 F.3d 802 (4th Cir. 2001); *Johnson v. Director, OWCP*, 183 F.3d 1169 (9th Cir. 1999); *Anderson v. Director, OWCP*, 91 F.3d 1322 (9th Cir. 1996); *see Missouri v. Jenkins*, 491 U.S. 274, 284 (1989).

24. *E.g., Consolidated Edison Co. v. NLRB*, 305 U.S. 197, 229 (1938).

25. *Universal Camera Corp. v. NLRB*, 340 U.S. 474, 488 (1951).

26. *See generally Potomac Electric Power Co. v. Director, OWCP*, 449 U.S. 268, 279 n.18 (1980); 20 C.F.R. § 801.103.

27. *See* 20 C.F.R. §§ 802.207(a)(2), (b); 802.208(b)–(c).

28. The exact time frame for filing a motion for reconsideration has been disputed from the Benefits Review Board's very first decision published in the Benefits Review Board Service. *See General Dynamics Corporation v. Hines*, 1 BRBS 3 (1974). Unfortunately, it is perhaps less clear now than it was in 1974. See *Galle v. Ingalls Shipbuilding, Inc.*, 33 BRBS 141 (1999), *aff'd sub nom. Galle v. Director, OWCP*, 246 F.3d 440 (5th Cir. 2001), *cert. denied*, 534 U.S. 1002 (2001). The Benefits Review Board's current rule, 20 C.F.R. § 802.206, tolls the time for appeal if a timely motion for reconsideration is filed below. It defines a "timely motion" as that "filed not later than 10 days from the date the decision or order was filed" by the district director. 20 C.F.R. § 802.206(b)(1). It also tolls the appeal if the motion is mailed—but not filed—by that deadline. Under *Galle*, the ten days was calculated per Federal Rules of Civil Procedure 59(e) as only counting *business* days. Though the Benefits Review Board's rules typically count calendar days, instead of business days, the *Galle* court determined it better serves the humanitarian nature of the Longshore Act and the intention of the Benefit's Review Board's rule in tracking Rule 59(e) to apply the more generous business day count in that instance. The Federal Rules, though, have since been liberalized to allow an even more generous 28 days to file a motion for reconsideration, but in counting the expanded deadlines, all *calendar* days are counted. Whether that Federal Rules change which *extended* the time to file, simultaneously and inadvertently *reduced* the time to file in Longshore Act cases via the change from counting business days to calendar days is currently an issue on appeal in *Shah v. Worldwide Language Resources, Inc.*, 50 BRBS 85(UBD) (2016) (Pending Ninth Circuit Court of Appeals Case No. 16-72307). But, since the publication of the new 2015 OALJ rules, the OALJ now has its own competing rule regarding timeliness of a motion for reconsideration. *See* 29 C.F.R. § 18.93 (allowing ten days from service of decision to *file* a motion for reconsideration before the OALJ), 29 C.F.R. § 18.32 (adding three days to time periods triggered by service of a document only when that document is served by mail and the matter is before the OALJ). The application of this OALJ rule and its three-day mailing allowance to tolling appeals before the BRB is being tested now in pending appeal *Zumwalt v. National Steel & Shipbuilding Co.*, BRB No. 2017-0048. It is unclear where the changes in the Federal Rules and the addition of the OALJ rule leave appeals from the OWCP. The safest course is to file such motions for reconsideration within ten days.

29. *E.g., Tideland Welding Service v. Sawyer*, 881 F.2d 157 (5th Cir. 1989), *cert. denied*, 495 U.S. 904 (1990); *Harmar Coal Co. v. Director, OWCP*, 926 F.2d 302, 308 (3d Cir. 1991); *Ætna Casualty & Surety Co. v. Director, OWCP (Jourdan)*, 97 F.3d 815, 819 (5th Cir. 1996). This was formerly the rule with respect to appeals from district courts to the courts of appeals, but was changed by amendment to FED. R. APP. P. 4(a)(4).

30. *See* 20 C.F.R. § 802.301(b)–(c).

31. *See* 20 C.F.R. § 802.303(b)–(c).

32. *Peabody Coal Co. v. Abner*, 118 F.3d 1106 (6th Cir. 1997); *Saban v. United States Dep't of Labor*, 509 F.3d 376 (7th Cir. 2007).

33. Upon review of the circuit court requirements for admissions, the 6th, 9th, 10th, and 11th Circuits either do not require a sponsoring attorney or a Motion for Admission. In the event where the attorney seeking admission has no sponsor or movant within the circuit court, other arrangements can be made for admission.

34. *E.g., Arch Mineral Corp. v. Director, OWCP*, 798 F.2d 215, 217-19 (7th Cir. 1986); *Director, OWCP v. Hileman*, 897 F.2d 1277, 1279 (4th Cir. 1990).

35. A petition that is timely filed in the wrong court of appeals, however, will generally be transferred to the correct court, and treated as timely filed there. *See* text following note 4 above.

36. Fifth Circuit: ECF Standards, available at http://www.ca5.uscourts.gov/docs/default-source/cm-ecf/ecf-filing-standards.pdf (last viewed 4/17/16).

37. Eleventh circuit CM/ECS User Guide, "Signatures," available at http://www.ca11.uscourts.gov/sites/default/files/courtdocs/clk/CMECFGuideToElectronicFiling.pdf (last viewed 4/20/16).

38. Ninth Circuit CM/ECF User Guide, "Creating Cross-Document Hyperlinks," available at http://cdn.ca9.uscourts.gov/datastore/uploads/cmecf/ecf-user-guide.pdf (last viewed 4/16/16).

39. Fifth Circuit, "Citations to Records on Appeal in the Fifth Circuit," available at http://www.ca5.uscourts.gov/docs/default-source/default-document-library/roa-news.pdf (last viewed 4/18/16).

40. Some circuit courts specifically require the inclusion of an addendum with the respondent's brief. See 1ST CIR. R. 28(a)(11); 6TH CIR. R. 30(g)(1); 8TH CIR. R. 28A(g); 9TH CIV. R. 28-2.7; 10TH CIR. R. 28.2, and FED. CIR.

R. 28(a)(11) and D.C. CIR. R. 28(a)(7). Review the applicable local rules regarding the requirements and contents of an addendum to petitioner's brief.

41. Generally, page limitation, word, or line counts begin with the Jurisdictional section and end with the Conclusion section. Review the circuit court's local rule as to RULE 32(a) compliance.

42. *See* http://www.ca3uscourts.gov/cmecf-case-managmentelectronic-case-files.

43. FED. R. CIV. P. 30(b).

44. *Charpentier v. Ortco Contractors*, 480 F.3d 710 (5th Cir. 2007).

45. *City of Burlington v. Dague*, 505 U.S. 557, 562 (1992); *Christensen v. Stevedoring Services of America*, 557 F.3d 1049, 1052 (9th Cir. 2009).

46. *PA v. Del Valley Citizen's Counsel for Clean Air*, 478 U.S. 546 (1986); *Tahara v. Matson Terminals, Inc.*, 511 F.3d 950, 955 (9th Cir. 2007).

47. *Blum v. Stenson*, 465 U.S. 886, 895 (1984); *see also Nasser v. Director, Office Worker's Compensation Programs*, 377 Fed. Appx. 650, 651 (9th Cir. 2010); *Jeffboat, LLC v. Director*, OWCP, 553 F.3d 487 (7th Cir. 2009).

48. Compare *Christensen*, 557 F.3d at 1053 (holding the "relevant legal community" for determining legal market rate in the Ninth Circuit is the litigation forum), with *Jeffboat, LLC*, 553 F.3d at 491 (holding the relevant legal market was based on the community where the Petitioner's attorney practiced, not the litigation forum).

49. *Christensen*, 557 F.3d at 1054.

50. *Anderson v. Director, Office of Worker's Compensation Programs*, 91 F.3d 1322, 1325 (9th Cir. 1996).

51. *Christensen*, 557 F.3d at 1053.

UNITED STATES COURT OF APPEALS
FOR THE FIRST CIRCUIT

APPLICATION AND OATH FOR ADMISSION TO PRACTICE

Pursuant to Fed. R. App. P. 46

(Please type or print all answers and complete all sections)

Applicant's Name ....
First Middle Last Jr.,Sr., III, etc.

Name of Law Firm or Agency...

Business Address...

City..State...Zip.................................

Telephone..Fax..

Professional E-mail ....

Home Address...
(Applicant's Home Address will not be disclosed to the public unless it serves as a professional address.)

City..State...Zip.................................

Have you ever changed your name or been known by any name other than that appearing on the application?

[ ] Yes [ ] No **If yes, please elaborate:** ....

Have you ever been disbarred or suspended from practice before any court, department, bureau, or commission of the United States or of any state, or have you ever received any reprimand from any such court, department, bureau, or commission pertaining to your conduct or fitness as a member of the bar?
[ ] Yes [ ] No **If yes, attach a separate statement describing your complete disciplinary history.**

Name all courts (including state courts) before which you have been admitted to practice and provide the exact admission date for each court (please attach a separate sheet if necessary):

Court Name ....Admission Date.........................Bar No. ....
mm/dd/yyyy

Court Name ....Admission Date.........................Bar No. ....
mm/dd/yyyy

Court Name ....Admission Date.........................Bar No. ....
mm/dd/yyyy

Please provide a certificate of good standing, dated within the past six months for a qualifying state court bar identified above.

APPLICANT'S CERTIFICATION AND OATH

I, ..., do solemnly swear (or affirm) that I will conduct myself as an attorney and counselor of this court, uprightly and according to law; and that I will support the Constitution of the United States. I further swear (or affirm) under the pains and penalties of perjury that all of my responses, including any attachments thereto, are true and correct to the best of my knowledge, information and belief.

....
Signature of Applicant Date

Page 1 of 2

UNITED STATES COURT OF APPEALS
FOR THE FIRST CIRCUIT
APPLICATION AND OATH FOR ADMISSION TO PRACTICE

Pursuant to Fed. R. App. P. 46

Please indicate if you would like to be admitted in person, when the Court is in session. [ ] Yes [ ] No
If yes, you will be notified by the Admissions Clerk via email of the time and place to appear. Sponsors need not appear. Applicants must bring a print-out of their email notification with them when they appear.

SPONSOR'S INFORMATION

Sponsor's Name ....
First Middle Last Jr.,Sr., III, etc.

First Circuit Bar No. ....First Circuit Admission Date..
mm/dd/yyyy

Firm Name...Telephone......................................

Address...

City..State...Zip.................................

SPONSOR'S CERTIFICATION

I, ..., a member attorney, in good standing of the Bar of the United States Court of Appeals for the First Circuit, respectfully recommend that the foregoing application be granted, and certify that the applicant is of good moral and professional character and is eligible for admission pursuant to Fed. R. App. P. 46.

....
Signature of Sponsor Date

Please submit the application and payment through CM/ECF in accordance with the instructions posted on the court's website.

Please verify that the application is complete:

ë Both the applicant's information and sponsor's information sections are complete.

ë Both the applicant and sponsor have signed the application.

ë A certificate of good standing, issued within the past six months, is attached.

ë Any additional court listings and disciplinary histories are attached on separate pages.

Page 2 of 2

United States Court of Appeals for the Ninth Circuit

APPLICATION AND OATH FOR ADMISSION

PERSONAL INFORMATION

Full Name: ______________________ Last 4 digits of SSN: __________ Birth Date: __________

Phone: ______________________ Email: ______________________

MAILING ADDRESS (no P.O. Box addresses)

Firm Name or Agency: ______________________

Street Address, incl. Suite/Apt #: ______________________ City: __________ State: _____ ZIP: _______

BAR INFORMATION

Federal/State Admissions (max. 2)	Status (Active/Inactive)	Admission Date	Bar Number

Answer each question below. If the answer to any of the questions is yes, attach a separate statement providing details.

	YES	NO
1. Have you been known by any name other than that appearing on the application?	○	○
2. Have you ever been disbarred or suspended from practice before any court or government agency?	○	○
3. Are any such actions pending against you?	○	○
4. Are you currently under investigation by, or have you ever received a reprimand from any court or government agency?	○	○

OATH

I, ______________________, certify under penalty of perjury under the laws of the United States of

(TYPE name as you want it to appear on your certificate)

America that the foregoing is true and correct. I do solemnly swear [or affirm] that I will conduct myself as an attorney and counselor of this Court, uprightly and according to law; and that I will support the Constitution of the United States.

Applicant Signature: ______________________ Date: __________

MOTION FOR ADMISSION (to be completed by a sponsor in good standing with the Ninth Circuit Court of Appeals.)

I, ______________________, a member in good standing of the Bar of the United States Court of Appeals for the

(Full name of sponsor)

Ninth Circuit hereby move the admission of ______________________ to the Bar of this Court.

I am satisfied that the applicant possesses the qualifications set forth by Federal Rule of Appellate Procedure 46(a).

Sponsor Signature: ______________________ Date: __________

Phone: __________ Email: ______________________ Admission Date: __________

Firm Name or Agency: ______________________

Street Address, incl. Suite/Apt #: ______________________ City: __________ State: _____ ZIP: _______

See next page for instructions *rev. January 2015*

UNITED STATES COURT OF APPEALS FOR THE ELEVENTH CIRCUIT
Application for Admission to the Bar
(Please Type or Print)

Pursuant to FRAP 46(a), to qualify for admission you must be a member in good standing of the bar of the U.S. Supreme Court, another U.S. Court of Appeals, a U.S. District Court, or the highest court of any state. You must attach to this application (1) a certificate of good standing issued within the previous six months from one of the courts described above, and (2) a list of all state and federal bars of which you are a member, including state bar numbers, and your status with each bar (e.g., active, inactive, retired, etc.). See 11th Cir. R. 46-7. Make check in the non-refundable amount of $196.00 payable to "Clerk, U.S. Court of Appeals, Eleventh Circuit," attach to your application and forward to: Attorney Admissions Clerk, U.S. Court of Appeals, Eleventh Circuit, 56 Forsyth Street, N.W., Atlanta, GA 30303.

PERSONAL INFORMATION

Name: ______________________________
(As you want it to appear on Certificate)

Last 4 digits of Social Security Number: ______________

Phone: ______________________ Fax: ______________

E-Mail: ______________________________

ADDRESS INFORMATION

Office Name: ______________________________

Address 1: ______________________________

Address 2: ______________________________

City: ______________ State: ______________ Zip: ______________

Answer each question. If any answer is yes, attach a statement giving details.

YES	NO		
☐	☐	1.	Have you changed your name or been known by any names or surnames other than the one appearing on this application?
☐	☐	2a.	Have you been disbarred or suspended from practice by any bar or before any court, department, bureau or commission of any State or the United States, or have you received a reprimand from any of them pertaining to your conduct or fitness to practice?
☐	☐	2b.	Are any such proceedings or allegations presently pending against you?
☐	☐	3a.	Have you been a party to criminal proceedings, *or* to civil proceedings in which allegations of fraud, misrepresentation or other dishonesty were made against you?
☐	☐	3b.	Are you presently under investigation for any matter specified in question 3a?

OATH (OR AFFIRMATION)

I, ______________________ do solemnly swear (or affirm) that I will conduct myself as an attorney and counselor of this court, uprightly and according to law; and that I will support the Constitution of the United States. I do further swear (or affirm) that all responses in the foregoing personal statement, including attachments which are incorporated herein by reference, are true and correct to the best of my knowledge, information and belief. I certify that, except as otherwise noted, I am an active member in good standing of each state bar or the bar of the highest court of each state (including the District of Columbia) listed on the attached sheet, and that my license to practice law in the named state is not currently lapsed for any reason, including but not limited to retirement, placement in inactive status, failure to pay bar membership fees or failure to complete continuing education requirements. I understand that I am required to notify the clerk of this court within 14 days of any changes in the status of my state bar memberships. See 11th Cir. R. 46-7.

____
Signature of Applicant

Subscribed and sworn (or affirmed) to before me a Notary Public in and for the County of ______________,

State of ______________, this ______________ day of ______________.

My commission expires: ______________

____
Signature and Seal of Notary

Court Use Only. To be completed by Attorney Admissions Clerk.

Check No: ______________ Money Order No: ______________

EDF: ______________ Receipt No: ______________

Rev.: 4/14

LIST OF BAR MEMBERSHIPS

You must attach a list of all bars of which you are a member, including state bars and state and federal courts to which you are admitted to practice. The list must also include bar numbers (if any), the date of admission, and your status with each bar or court (e.g., active, inactive, retired, etc.). See 11th Cir. R. 46-7. **You may use this page to fulfill this requirement.**

Name of State or Federal Bar or Court	**Bar Number (if any)**	**Date Admitted**	**Status with Bar or Court** (active, inactive, retired, etc.)

Notice to Customers Presenting Checks

When you provide a check as payment, you authorize us either to use information from your check to make a one-time electronic fund transfer from your account or to process the payment as a check transaction. When we use information from your check to make an electronic fund transfer, funds may be withdrawn from your account as soon as the same day you make your payment.

Petition for Review of Order of an Agency, Board, Commission or Officer

United States Court of Appeals for the ____________________ Circuit

A.B., Petitioner)
)
v.) Petition for Review
)
XYZ Commission, Respondent)

(here name all parties bringing the petition)* hereby petition the court for review of the Order of the XYZ Commission (describe the order) entered on

________, 20____.

(s) ____

Attorney for Petitioners ____________________________

Address: ____

* See Rule 15

UNITED STATES COURT OF APPEALS
DISTRICT OF COLUMBIA CIRCUIT

333 Constitution Avenue, NW
Washington, DC 20001-2866
Phone: 202-216-7000 | Facsimile: 202-219-8530

Case Caption: ______________________
Petitioner

v. Case Number: __________

____
Respondent

PETITION FOR REVIEW OF AN AGENCY, BOARD, COMMISSION, OR OFFICER

Notice is hereby given this the _____ day of ______________ 20__ that petitioner(s) ______________________ hereby petitions the United States Court of Appeals for the District of Columbia Circuit for review of the order of the respondent(s) ______________________ entered the _____ day of ______________ 20__.

Attorney for Petitioner(s)/Pro Se Party,

____

____

Address: ______________________

____

____

Telephone: (___) ________

USCA Form 12
AUGUST 2009 (Revised)

Form 6. Certificate of Compliance With Rule 32(a)

Certificate of Compliance With Type-Volume Limitation,
Typeface Requirements, and Type Style Requirements

1. This brief complies with the type-volume limitation of Fed. R. App. P. 32(a)(7)(B) because:

☐ this brief contains [*state the number of*] words, excluding the parts of the brief exempted by Fed. R. App. P. 32(a)(7)(B)(iii), *or*

☐ this brief uses a monospaced typeface and contains [*state the number of*] lines of text, excluding the parts of the brief exempted by Fed. R. App. P. 32(a)(7)(B)(iii).

2. This brief complies with the typeface requirements of Fed. R. App. P. 32(a)(5) and the type style requirements of Fed. R. App. P. 32(a)(6) because:

☐ this brief has been prepared in a proportionally spaced typeface using [*state name and version of word processing program*] in [*state font size and name of type style*], *or*

☐ this brief has been prepared in a monospaced typeface using [*state name and version of word processing program*] with [*state number of characters per inch and name of type style*].

/s/ ______________________

Attorney for ______________

Dated: ____________________

Part VII

Resources

Chapter 26

Online Resources for the Longshore Practitioner

Amie C. Peters, Esq.

Synopsis

There are a number of online resources helpful to the Longshore and DBA practitioner. These online resources are divided into three categories. First are the resources available through the U.S. Department of Labor's website. Second are legal research platforms offered by third party vendors. And the third are online resources helpful in proving one's case.

26.1 U.S. Department of Labor Resources

The Office of Workers' Compensation Program, the Office of Administrative Law Judges and the Benefits Review Board each have a website offering a variety of online resources available. The Office of Workers' Compensation Programs, the Office of Administrative Law Judges and the Benefits Review Board each have online systems useful in communicating with stakeholders. Additionally, the webpages for each of these agencies provide helpful internet links on Longshore specific issues.

A. The Office of Workers' Compensation Program—Division of Longshore & Harbor Workers (DLHWC)

www.dol.gov/owcp/dlhwc/

The OWCP Longshore Division's webpage provides links to basic questions and answers on the four programs currently administered by the DLHWC. The site also has links to a stakeholder portal (SEAPortal), forms, benefits guides, industry notices, and links to other resources.

SEAPortal (www.dol.gov/owcp/SEAPortal)—The SEAPortal is the DLHWC's online access point allowing stakeholders to securely upload documents to the DLSHW on active cases. There is no registry, but a person uploading information needs to enter the OWCP case number, claimant's last name, claimant's date of birth and the date of injury. This basic claim information must exactly match what is on file with the DLHWC. You can upload any document except the original LS-201, LS-202, LS-203 or LS-262, to open the claim. To upload documents, you classify the document into one of the 11 predefined categories, enter the document date, and browse your files to choose the file to be uploaded. Depending on the document classification, you may be limited to either three, 50 or 100 pages and the file must be either a TIF or PDF. Once uploaded, the site provides a document control number (DCN), which can be used to check the status of the document. The OWCP can then access the document through its internal document management system. While it can take up to 30 minutes for the OWCP to access uploaded documents, most claims examiners are saying it has normally taken just a few minutes for them to have access.

Longshore Electronic Access Forms Submission (LEAFS) (https://seaportal.dol-esa.gov/portal/?leaf&program_name=LS)—The LEAFS portal allows carriers to submit annual form LS-513 and the supporting documentation. There is no registration, but carriers must submit the OWCP Sequence Number and the EIN. Once logged in the system will walk the carrier through a five step process that must be completed before any information is submitted to the OWCP. This portal cannot be used to submit case related documents.

OWCP Forms (www.dol.gov/OWCP/DLSHW/forms)—The OWCP forms website includes fillable PDF files for all of its claim forms. The OWCP has recently been updating many of its forms, and publishes those updates on this page.

Procedural Manuel (http://www.dol.gov/owcp/dlhwc/lsproman/proman.htm)—The OWCP publishes its internal procedural manual on its website. This procedural manual gives the OWCP's policies on claims management and can provide basic information on how it will deal with day to day claims management issues.

Longshore Rates Page (http://www.dol.gov/owcp/dlhwc/lsrates.htm)—The OWCP publishes its annual determination of the National Average Weekly Wage and Section 10(f) adjustment. The page also includes a table of the maximum and minimum compensation rates. There are also links to the federal reserve interest rate and the GSA mileage reimbursement rate.

B. Office of Administrative Law Judges (OALJ)

www.oalj.dol.gov

The website provides links to information relevant at the OALJ including recent significant decisions, case status and a library of helpful links. On the right side of the screen, there are two different search options allowing full text and ALJ decision searches.

Rules of Practice & Procedure (www.oalj.gov/LIBRULES.HTM)—The OALJ publishes links to the OALJ's Rules of Practice and Procedure. There is also historical information on the history of the OALJ's rules.

Case Status (www.oalj.dol.gov/OALJ_Case_Status.htm)—By entering a pending OALJ number, you can obtain basic information on cases pending before the OALJ. Once you enter the OALJ or OWCP number, you can find out the status of the case, including dates the case was originally docketed, referred to a regional OALJ office, assigned to an Administrative Law Judge or scheduled for a hearing. The status page does not allow you to provide any information to the OALJ.

Longshore Library Collection (www.oalj.dol.gov/LIBLHC.HTM)—The Longshore Library page provides links to a number of litigation resources helpful for trying cases at the OALJ. The page includes links to the applicable statutes, regulations, research materials, newsletters, agency policy papers and links to other relative Longshore information.

Forms (www.oalj.dol.gov/FORMS.HTM)—The OALJ has four basic forms available on its website. The forms include Subpoenas, Settlement Judge Request Form, LHWCA Prehearing Statement Form, LHWCA Uniform Stipulation Form. While each of the ALJs are granted a great amount of judicial autonomy, these are basic forms that may be usable before most of the judges.

C. Benefits Review Board (BRB)

www.dol.gov/brb/welcome.html

The BRB has a rather sparse website devoted to providing links relevant to the BRB.

Electronic File & Service Request (ERSR) System (http://dol-appeals.entellitrak.com)—A portal allowing users to electronically file documents to the BRB. You must preregister for the system and routinely update your password. E-Filers also have the ability to have BRB documents served electronically to a registered email address rather than by mail. A party is only allowed to see documents it submits and documents from the BRBs. This means documents still need to be served via mail to opposing parties. Additionally, technical issues can make the site tricky for last minute filings. The BRB does have very responsive technical department that answers questions quickly.

BRB Longshore Deskbook (http://www.dol.gov/BRB/???)—A tool helpful in researching Longshore issues. While not an exhaustive summary of BRB holdings, it can be a good place to begin researching a legal issue. The deskbook is generally organized by section of the Longshore Act.

BRB Longshore Decisions (http://www.dol.gov/brb/decisions.htm)—The BRB has consistently published decisions since 1994 on its website. The decisions are published by date issued and whether they were designated as published. You can also do a text search at http://www.dol.gov/appeals/search/search.htm, but the search engine is not as robust as many paid sites.

26.2 Legal Research Sites

In addition to the materials found on the Department of Labor's website, practitioners can find a number of third party applications useful for doing longshore specific research.

Probably the most popular of these legal research sites is **Lexis Advance** (http://advance.lexis.com). This is a paid legal research site with a robust search engine that allows advanced searching abilities. Lexis owns Matthew Bender, the publisher for the Benefits Review Board Service (BRBS). As such, it has the most detailed collection of BRBS decisions dating back to April of 1974. Recently, however, Lexis has broadened the cases published to its site to include unpublished ALJ decisions.

Casemaker (www.casemaker.us) is another legal research site with access to many Longshore decisions. Many bar associations providing free access to Casemaker. If your bar association is not among those who provide free access, you can assess the site by paying a monthly ($60–$95) or annual ($600–$950) fee. Casemaker includes Longshore specific materials in its Federal resources which consistently go back to 1994 and have occasional cases dating back to 1986.

Cornell University **Legal Information Institute** (https://www.law.cornell.edu/) has a free online research service for federal cases, state law resources and statutory materials. Cornell's site is particularly useful for pulling up federal statutes and regulations. It is also useful for searching for Court of Appeal and Supreme Court decisions.

26.3 Online Evidence

Practitioners are increasingly finding evidence supporting their cases online. These resources can be found in a number of internet locations ranging from library websites (university libraries are particularly helpful, as they are increasingly digitizing holdings) to governmental agency websites. While it is not possible to list all such sites here, the following is a list of particularly helpful sites:

- **Board of Medical Specialties** (http://www.abms.org/)—This website allows you to search whether medical providers are board certified.
- **Google Maps** (https://www.google.com/maps)—Google Maps are extremely versatile in proving issues involving locations. The distance calculators are being used to deal with medical mileage and the appropriateness off job locations. The satellite maps are helpful in looking at coverage issues. Also, the satellite maps can be used with witnesses to describe where injuries occur and work environments.
- **Google Scholar** (http://scholar.google.com/)—Google Scholar gives access to many research articles, including medical research articles.
- **NIOSH** (http://www.cdc.gov/niosh/)—National Institute of Occupation Safety and Health has a number of government funded studies on safety and health issues impacting workers. These studies are often used by experts to bolster opinions on causation.
- **OSHA** (https://www.osha.gov/)—Occupational Safety and Health Administration has many helpful resources about worker safety issues.
- **O*Net** (https://www.onetonline.org/)—O*Net collects detailed descriptions of jobs and has helpful resources for helping workers explore new career options. This website is particularly helpful for assessing suitable alternative employment issues.
- **Shipbuilding History** (http://www.shipbuildinghistory.com/)—Shipbuilding History contains a historical database of shipbuilding in the United States. The site includes listings on vessels repaired at various shipyards.

Appendix A

Longshore and Harbor Workers' Compensation Act and its Extensions

US CODE TITLE 33 –NAVIGATION AND NAVIGABLE WATERS

CHAPTER 18—LONGSHORE AND HARBOR WORKERS' COMPENSATION ACT

§ 901. Short title
§ 902. Definitions
§ 903. Coverage
§ 904. Liability for compensation
§ 905. Exclusiveness of liability
§ 906. Compensation
§ 907. Medical services and supplies
§ 908. Compensation for disability
§ 909. Compensation for death
§ 910. Determination of pay
§ 911. Guardian for minor or incompetent
§ 912. Notice of injury or death
§ 913. Filing of claims
§ 914. Payment of compensation
§ 915. Invalid agreements
§ 916. Assignment and exemption from claims of creditors
§ 917. Compensation a lien against assets
§ 918. Collection of defaulted payments; special fund
§ 919. Procedure in respect of claims
§ 920. Presumptions
§ 921. Review of compensation orders
§ 922. Modification of awards
§ 923. Procedure before deputy commissioner or Board
§ 924. Witnesses
§ 925. Witness fees
§ 926. Costs in proceedings brought without reasonable grounds
§ 927. Powers of deputy commissioners or Board
§ 928. Fees for services
§ 929. Record of injury or death
§ 930. Reports to Secretary
§ 931. Penalty for misrepresentation; prosecution of claims
§ 932. Security for compensation
§ 933. Compensation for injuries where third persons are liable
§ 934. Compensation notice
§ 935. Substitution of carrier for employer
§ 936. Insurance policies
§ 937. Certificate of compliance with this Act
§ 938. Penalty for failure to secure payment of compensation
§ 939. Administration by Secretary
§ 940. Deputy commissioners
§ 941. Safety rules and regulations
§ 942. Annual report
§ 943. [Repealed]
§ 944. Special fund
§ 948. Laws inapplicable
§ 948a. Discrimination against employees who bring proceedings; penalties; deposit of payments in special funds; civil actions; entitlement to restoration of employment and compensation, qualifications requirement; liability of employer for penalties and payments; insurance policy exemption from liability
§ 949. Effect of unconstitutionality
§ 950. Separability provision
§§ 951–980. [Reserved]

§ 901. Short title

This Act may be cited as "Longshore and Harbor Workers' Compensation Act."

§ 902. Definitions

When used in this Act –

(1) The term "person" means individual, partnership, corporation, or association.

(2) The term "injury" means accidental injury or death arising out of and in the course of employment, and such occupational disease or infection as arises naturally out of such employment or as naturally or unavoidably results from such accidental injury, and includes an injury caused by the willful act of a third person directed against an employee because of his employment.

(3) The term "employee" means any person engaged in maritime employment, including any longshoreman or other person engaged in longshoring operations, and any harbor-worker including a ship repairman, shipbuilder, and ship-breaker, but such term does not include –

(A) individuals employed exclusively to perform office clerical, secretarial, security, or data processing work;

(B) individuals employed by a club, camp, recreational operation, restaurant, museum, or retail outlet;

(C) individuals employed by a marina and who are not engaged in construction, replacement, or expansion of such marina (except for routine maintenance);

(D) individuals who (i) are employed by suppliers, transporters, or vendors, (ii) are temporarily doing business on the premises of an employer described in paragraph (4), and (iii) are not engaged in work normally performed by employees of that employer under this Act;

(E) aquaculture workers;

(F) individuals employed to build, repair, or dismantle any recreational vessel under sixty-five feet in length;

(G) a master or member of a crew of any vessel; or

(H) any person engaged by a master to load or unload or repair any small vessel under eighteen tons net; if individuals described in clauses (A) through (F) are subject to coverage under a State workers' compensation law.

(4) The term "employer" means an employer any of whose employees are employed in maritime employment, in whole or in part, upon the navigable waters of the United States (including any adjoining pier, wharf, dry dock terminal, building way, marine railway, or other adjoining area customarily used by an employer in loading, unloading, repairing, or building a vessel).

(5) The term "carrier" means any person or fund authorized under section 32 [33 USC § 932] to insure under this Act and includes self-insurers.

(6) The term "Secretary" means the Secretary of Labor.

(7) The term "deputy commissioner" means the deputy commissioner having jurisdiction in respect of an injury or death.

(8) The term "State" includes a Territory and the District of Columbia.

(9) The term "United States" when used in a geographical sense means the several States and Territories and the District of Columbia, including the territorial waters thereof.

(10) "Disability" means incapacity because of injury to earn the wages which the employee was receiving at the time of injury in the same or any other employment; but such term shall mean permanent impairment, determined (to the extent covered thereby) under the guides to the evaluation of permanent impairment promulgated and modified from time to time by the American Medical Association, in the case of an individual whose claim is described in section 10(d)(2) [33 USC § 910(d)(2)];

(11) "Death" as a basis for a right to compensation means only death resulting from an injury.

(12) "Compensation" means the money allowance payable to an employee or to his dependents as provided for in this Act, and includes funeral benefits provided therein.

(13) The term "wages" means the money rate at which the service rendered by an employee is compensated by an employer under the contract of hiring in force at the time of the injury, including the reasonable value of any advantage which is received from the employer and included for purposes of any withholding of tax under subtitle C of the Internal Revenue Code of 1954 [26 USC §§ 3101 et seq.] (relating to employment taxes). The term wages does not include fringe benefits, including (but not limited to) employer payments for or contributions to a retirement, pension, health and welfare, life insurance, training, social security or other employee or dependent benefit plan for the employee's or dependent's benefit, or any other employee's dependent entitlement.

(14) "child" shall include a posthumous child, a child legally adopted prior to the injury of the employee, a child in relation to whom the deceased employee stood in loco parentis for at least one year prior to the time of injury, and a stepchild or acknowledged illegitimate child dependent

upon the deceased, but does not include married children unless wholly dependent on him. "Grandchild" means a child as above defined of a child as above defined. "Brother" and "sister" include stepbrothers and stepsisters, half brothers and half sisters, and brothers and sisters by adoption, but does not include married brothers nor married sisters unless wholly dependent on the employee. "Child", "grandchild", "brother", and "sister" include only a person who is under eighteen years of age, or who, though eighteen years of age or over, is (1) wholly dependent upon the employee and incapable of self-support by reason of mental or physical disability, or (2) a student as defined in paragraph (19) [(18)] of this section.

(15) The term "parent" includes step-parents and parents by adoption, parents-in-law, and any person who for more than three years prior to the death of the deceased employee stood in the place of a parent to him, if dependent on the injured employee.

(16) The terms "widow or widower" includes only the decedent's wife or husband living with or dependent for support upon him or her at the time of his or her death; or living apart for justifiable cause or by reason of his or her desertion at such time.

(17) The terms "adoption" or "adopted" mean legal adoption prior to the time of the injury.

(18) The term "student" means a person regularly pursuing a full-time course of study or training at an institution which is—

(A) a school or college or university operated or directly supported by the United States, or by any State or local government or political subdivision thereof,

(B) a school or college or university which has been accredited by a State or by a State recognized or nationally recognized accrediting agency or body,

(C) a school or college or university not so accredited but whose credits are accepted, on transfer, by not less than three institutions which are so accredited, for credit on the same basis as if transferred from an institution so accredited, or

(D) an additional type of educational or training institution as defined by the Secretary, but not after he reaches the age of twenty-three or has completed four years of education beyond the high school level, except that, where his twenty-third birthday occurs during a semester or other enrollment period, he shall continue to be considered a student until the end of such semester or other enrollment period. A child shall not be deemed to have ceased to be a student during any interim between school years if the interim does not exceed five months and if he shows to the satisfaction of the Secretary that he has a bona fide intention of continuing to pursue a full-time course of education or training during the semester or other enrollment period immediately following the interim or during periods of reasonable duration during which, in the judgment of the Secretary, he is prevented by factors beyond his control from pursuing his education. A child shall not be deemed to be a student under this Act during a period of service in the Armed Forces of the United States.

(19) The term "national average weekly wage" means the national average weekly earnings of production or nonsupervisory workers on private nonagricultural payrolls.

(20) The term "Board" shall mean the Benefits Review Board.

(21) Unless the context requires otherwise, the term "vessel" means any vessel upon which or in connection with which any person entitled to benefits under this Act suffers injury or death arising out of or in the course of his employment, and said vessel's owner, owner pro hac vice, agent, operator, charter or bare boat charterer, master, officer, or crew member.\

(22) The singular includes the plural and the masculine includes the feminine and neuter.

§ 903. Coverage

(a) Except as otherwise provided in this section, compensation shall be payable under this Act in respect of disability or death of an employee, but only if the disability or death results from an injury occurring upon the navigable waters of the United States (including any adjoining pier, wharf, dry dock, terminal, building way, marine railway, or other adjoining area customarily used by an employer in loading, unloading, repairing, dismantling, or building a vessel).

(b) No compensation shall be payable in respect of the disability or death of an officer or employee of the United States, or any agency thereof, or of any State or foreign government, or any subdivision thereof.

(c) No compensation shall be payable if the injury was occasioned solely by the intoxication of the employee or by the willful intention of the employee to injure or kill himself or another.

(d)(1) No compensation shall be payable to an employee employed at a facility of an employer if, as certified by the Secretary, the facility is engaged in the business of building, repairing, or dismantling exclusively small vessels (as defined in paragraph (3) of this subsection), unless the injury occurs while upon the navigable waters of the United States or while upon any adjoining pier, wharf, dock, facility over land for launching vessels, or facility over land for hauling, lifting, or drydocking vessels.

(2) Notwithstanding paragraph (1), compensation shall be payable to an employee –

(A) who is employed at a facility which is used in the business of building, repairing, or dismantling small vessels if such facility receives Federal maritime subsidies; or

(B) if the employee is not subject to coverage under a State workers' compensation law.

(3) For purposes of this subsection, a small vessel means—(A) a commercial barge which is under 900 lightship displacement tons; or

(B) a commercial tugboat, towboat, crew boat, supply boat, fishing vessel, or other work vessel which is under 1,600 tons gross.

(e) Notwithstanding any other provision of law, any amounts paid to an employee for the same injury, disability, or death for which benefits are claimed under this Act pursuant to any other workers' compensation law or section 20 of the Act of March 4, 1915 (38 Stat. 1185, chapter 153; 46 U.S.C. 688) [46 USC Appx § 688] (relating to recovery for injury to or death of seamen) shall be credited against any liability imposed by this Act.

§ 904. Liability for compensation

(a) Every employer shall be liable for and shall secure the payment to his employees of the compensation payable under sections 7, 8, and 9 [33 USC §§ 907, 908, 909]. In the case of an employer who is a subcontractor, only if such subcontractor fails to secure the payment of compensation shall the contractor be liable for and be required to secure the payment of compensation. A subcontractor shall not be deemed to have failed to secure the payment of compensation if the contractor has provided insurance for such compensation for the benefit of the subcontractor.

(b) Compensation shall be payable irrespective of fault as a cause for the injury.

§ 905. Exclusiveness of liability

(a) The liability of an employer prescribed in section 4 [33 USC § 904] shall be exclusive and in place of all other liability of such employer to the employee, his legal representative, husband or wife, parents, dependents, next of kin, and anyone otherwise entitled to recover damages from such employer at law or in admiralty on account of such injury or death, except that if an employer fails to secure payment of compensation as required by this Act, an injured employee, or his legal representative in case death results from the injury, may elect to claim compensation under the Act, or to maintain an action at law or in admiralty for damages on account of such injury or death. In such action the defendant may not plead as a defense that the injury was caused by the negligence of a fellow servant, or that the employee assumed the risk of his employment, or that the injury was due to the contributory negligence of the employee. For purposes of this subsection, a contractor shall be deemed the employer of a subcontractor's employees only if the subcontractor fails to secure the payment of compensation as required by section 4 [33 USC § 904]

(b) In the event of injury to a person covered under this Act caused by the negligence of a vessel, then such person, or anyone otherwise entitled to recover damages by reason thereof, may bring an action against such vessel as a third party in accordance with the provisions of section 33 of this Act [33 USC § 933], and the employer shall not be liable to the vessel for such damages directly or indirectly and any agreements or warranties to the contrary shall be void. If such person was employed by the vessel to provide stevedoring services, no such action shall be permitted if the injury was caused by the negligence of persons engaged in providing stevedoring services to the vessel. If such person was employed to provide shipbuilding, repairing, or breaking services and such person's employer was the owner, owner pro hac vice, agent, operator, or charterer of the vessel, no such action shall be permitted, in whole or in part or directly or indirectly, against the injured person's employer (in any capacity, including as the vessel's owner, owner pro hac vice, agent, operator, or charterer) or against the employees of the employer. The liability of the vessel under this subsection shall not be based upon the warranty of seaworthiness or a breach thereof at the time the injury occurred. The remedy provided in this subsection shall be exclusive of all other remedies against the vessel except remedies available under this Act.

(c) In the event that the negligence of a vessel causes injury to a person entitled to receive benefits under the Act by virtue of section 4 of the Outer Continental Shelf Lands Act (43 U.S.C. 1333) [43 USC § 1333], then such person, or anyone otherwise entitled to recover damages by reason thereof, may bring an action against such vessel in accordance with the provisions of subsection (b) of this section.

Nothing contained in subsection (b) of this section shall preclude the enforcement according to its terms of any reciprocal indemnity provision whereby the employer of a person entitled to receive benefits under this Act by virtue of section 4 of the Outer Continental Shelf Lands Act (43 U.S.C. 1333) [43 USC § 1333] and the vessel agree to defend and indemnify the other for cost of defense and loss or liability for damages arising out of or resulting from death or bodily injury to their employees.

§ 906. Compensation

(a) *Time for commencement.* No compensation shall be allowed for the first three days of the disability, except the benefits provided for in section 7 [33 USC § 907]: Provided, however, That in case the injury results in disability of more than Fourteen days the compensation shall be allowed from the date of the disability.

(b) *Maximum rate of compensation.*

(1) Compensation for disability or death (other than compensation for death required by this Act to be paid in a lump sum) shall not exceed an amount equal to 200 per centum of the applicable national average weekly wage, as determined by the Secretary under paragraph (3).

(2) Compensation for total disability shall not be less than 50 per centum of the applicable national average weekly wage determined by the Secretary under paragraph (3), except that if the employee's average weekly wages as computed under section 10 are less than 50 per centum of such national average weekly wage, he shall receive his average weekly wages as compensation for total disability.

(3) As soon as practicable after June 30 of each year, and in any event prior to October 1 of such year, the Secretary shall determine the national average weekly wage for the three consecutive calendar quarters ending June 30. Such determination shall be the applicable national average weekly wage for the period beginning with October 1 of that year and ending with September 30 of the next year. The initial determination under this paragraph shall be made as soon as practicable after the enactment of this subsection.

(c) *Applicability of determinations.* Determinations under subsection (b)(3) with respect to a period shall apply to employees or survivors currently receiving compensation for permanent total disability or death benefits during such period, as well as those newly awarded compensation during such period.

(d) [Redesignated]

§ 907. Medical services and supplies

(a) *General requirement.* The employer shall furnish such medical, surgical, and other attendance or treatment, nurse and hospital service, medicine, crutches, and apparatus, for such period as the nature of the injury or the process of recovery may require.

(b) *Physician selection; administrative supervision; change of physicians and hospitals.* The employee shall have the right to choose an attending physician authorized by the Secretary to provide medical care under this Act as hereinafter provided. If, due to the nature of the injury, the employee is unable to select his physician and the nature of the injury requires immediate medical treatment and care, the employer shall select a physician for him. The Secretary shall actively supervise the medical care rendered to injured employees, shall require periodic reports as to the medical care being rendered to injured employees, shall have authority to determine the necessity, character, and sufficiency of any medical aid furnished or to be furnished, and may, on his own initiative or at the request of the employer, order a change of physicians or hospitals when in his judgment such change is desirable or necessary in the interest of the employee or where the charges exceed those prevailing within the community for the same or similar services or exceed the provider's customary charges. Change of physicians at the request of employees shall be permitted in accordance with regulations of the Secretary.

(c) *List of unauthorized physicians and health care providers; posting; reasons for inclusion.*

(1) (A) The Secretary shall annually prepare a list of physicians and health care providers in each compensation district who are not authorized to render medical care or provide medical services under this Act. The names of physicians and health care providers contained on the list required under this subparagraph shall be made available to employees and employers in each compensation district through posting and in such other forms as the Secretary may prescribe.

(B) Physicians and health care providers shall be included on the list of those not authorized to provide medical care and medical services pursuant to subparagraph (A) when the Secretary determines under this section, in accordance with the procedures provided in subsection (j), that such physician or health care provider –

(i) has knowingly and willfully made, or caused to be made, any false statement or misrepresentation of a material fact for use in a claim for compensation or claim for reimbursement of medical expenses under this Act;

(ii) has knowingly and willfully submitted, or caused to be submitted, a bill or request for payment under this Act containing a charge which the Secretary finds to be substantially in excess of the charge for the service, appliance, or supply prevailing within the community or in excess of the provider's customary charges, unless the Secretary finds there is good cause for the bill or request containing the charge;

(iii) has knowingly and willfully furnished a service, appliance, or supply which is determined by the Secretary to be substantially in excess of the need of the recipient thereof or to be of a quality which substantially fails to meet professionally recognized standards;

(iv) has been convicted under any criminal statute (without regard to pending appeal thereof) for fraudulent activities in connection with any Federal or State program for which payments are made to physicians or providers of similar services, appliances, or supplies; or

(v) has otherwise been excluded from participation in such program.

(C) Medical services provided by physicians or health care providers who are named on the list published by the Secretary pursuant to subparagraph (A) of this section shall not be reimbursable under this Act; except that the Secretary shall direct the reimbursement of medical claims for services rendered by such physicians or health care providers in cases where the services were rendered in an emergency.

(D) A determination under subparagraph (B) shall remain in effect for a period of not less than three years and until the Secretary finds and gives notice to the public that there is reasonable assurance that the basis for the determination will not reoccur.

(E) A provider of a service, appliance, or supply shall provide to the Secretary such information and certification as the Secretary may require to assure that this subsection is enforced.

(2) Whenever the employer or carrier acquires knowledge of the employee's injury, through written notice or otherwise as prescribed by the Act, the employer or carrier shall forthwith authorize medical treatment and care from a physician selected by an employee pursuant to subsection (b). An employee may not select a physician who is on the list required by paragraph (1) of this subsection. An employee may not change physicians after his initial choice unless the employer, carrier, or deputy commissioner has given prior consent for such change. Such consent shall be given in cases where an employee's initial choice was not of a specialist whose services are necessary for and appropriate to the proper care and treatment of the compensable injury or disease. In all other cases, consent may be given upon a showing of good cause for change.

(d) *Request of treatment or services prerequisite to recovery of expenses; formal report of injury and treatment; suspension of compensation for refusal of treatment or examination; justification.*

(1) An employee shall not be entitled to recover any amount expended by him for medical or other treatment or services unless –

(A) the employer shall have refused or neglected a request to furnish such services and the employee has complied with subsections (b) and (c) and the applicable regulations; or

(B) the nature of the injury required such treatment and services and the employer or his superintendent or foreman having knowledge of such injury shall have neglected to provide or authorize same.

(2) No claim for medical or surgical treatment shall be valid and enforceable against such employer unless, within ten days following the first treatment, the physician giving such treatment furnishes to the employer and the deputy commissioner a report of such injury or treatment, on a form prescribed by the Secretary. The Secretary may excuse the failure to furnish such report within the ten-day period whenever he finds it to be in the interest of justice to do so.

(3) The Secretary may, upon application by a party in interest, make an award for the reasonable value of such medical or surgical treatment so obtained by the employee.

(4) If at any time the employee unreasonably refuses to submit to medical or surgical treatment, or to an examination by a physician selected by the employer, the Secretary or administrative law judge may, by order, suspend the payment of further compensation during such time as such refusal continues, and no compensation shall be paid at any time during the period of such suspension, unless the circumstances justified the refusal.

(e) *Physical examination; medical questions; report of physical impairment; review or reexamination; costs.* In the event that medical questions are raised in any case, the Secretary shall have the power to cause the employee to be examined by a physician employed or selected by the Secretary and to obtain from such physician a report containing his estimate of the employee's physical impairment and such other information as may be appropriate. Any party who is dissatisfied with such report may request a review or reexamination of the employee by one or more different physicians employed or selected by the Secretary. The Secretary shall order such review or reexamination unless he finds that it is clearly unwarranted. Such review or reexamination shall be completed within two weeks from the date ordered unless the Secretary finds that because of extraordinary circumstances a longer period is required. The Secretary shall have the power in his discretion to charge the cost of examination or review under this subsection to the employer, if he is a self-insurer, or to the insurance company which is carrying the risk, in appropriate cases, or to the special fund in section 44 [33 USC § 944].

(f) *Place of examination; exclusion of physicians other than examining physician of Secretary; good cause for conclusions of other physicians respecting impairment; examination by employer's physician; suspension of proceedings and compensation for refusal of examination.* An employee shall submit to a physical examination under subsection (e) at such place as the Secretary may require. The place, or places, shall be designated by the Secretary and shall be reasonably convenient for the employee. No physician selected by the employer, carrier, or employee shall be present at or participate in any manner in such examination, nor shall conclusions of such physicians as to the nature or extent of impairment or the cause of impairment be available to the examining physician unless otherwise ordered, for good cause, by the Secretary. Such employer or carrier shall, upon request, be entitled to have the employee examined immediately thereafter and upon the same premises by a qualified physician or physicians in the presence of such physician as the employee may select, if any. Proceedings shall be suspended and no compensation shall be payable for any period during which the employee may refuse to submit to examination.

(g) *Fees and charges for examinations, treatment, or service; limitation; regulations.* All fees and other charges for medical examinations, treatment, or service shall be limited to such charges as prevail in the community for such treatment, and shall be subject to regulation by the Secretary. The Secretary shall issue regulations limiting the nature and extent of medical expenses chargeable against the employer without authorization by the employer or the Secretary.

(h) *Third party liability.* The liability of an employer for medical treatment as herein provided shall not be affected by the fact that his employee was injured through the fault or negligence of a third party not in the same employ, or that suit has been brought against such third party. The employer shall, however, have a cause of action against such third party to recover any amounts paid by him for such medical treatment in like manner as provided in section 33(b) of this Act [33 USC § 933(b)].

(i) *Physicians' ineligibility for subsection (e) physical examinations and reviews because of workmen's compensation claim employment or fee acceptance or participation.* Unless the parties to the claim agree, the Secretary shall not employ or select any physician for the purpose of making examinations or reviews under subsection (e) of this section who, during such employment, or during the period of two years prior to such employment, has been employed by, or accepted or participated in any fee relating to a workmen's compensation claim from any insurance carrier or any self-insurer.

(j) *Rules and regulations; notice of findings; hearing; judicial review.*

(1) The Secretary shall have the authority to make rules and regulations and to establish procedures, not inconsistent with the provisions of this Act, which are necessary or appropriate to carry out the provisions of subsection (c), including the nature and extent of the proof and evidence necessary for actions under this section and the methods of taking and furnishing such proof and evidence.

(2) Any decision to take action with respect to a physician or health care provider under this section shall be based on specific findings of fact by the Secretary. The Secretary shall provide notice of these findings and an opportunity for a hearing pursuant to section 556 of title 5, United States Code [5 USC § 556], for a provider who would be affected by a decision under this section. A request for a hearing must be filed with the Secretary within thirty days after notice of the findings is received by the provider making such request. If a hearing is held, the Secretary shall, on the basis of evidence adduced at the hearing, affirm, modify, or reverse the findings of fact and proposed action under this section.

(3) For the purpose of any hearing, investigation, or other proceeding authorized or directed under this section, the provisions of section 9 and 10 (relating to the attendance of witnesses and the production of books, papers, and documents) of the Federal Trade Commission Act (15 U.S.C. 49, 50) [15 USC §§ 49, 50] shall apply to the jurisdiction, powers, and duties of the Secretary or any officer designated by him.

(4) Any physician or health care provider, after any final decision of the Secretary made after a hearing to which he was a party, irrespective of the amount in controversy,

may obtain a review of such decision by a civil action commenced within sixty days after the mailing to him of notice of such decision, but the pendency of such review shall not operate as a stay upon the effect of such decision. Such action shall be brought in the court of appeals of the United States for the judicial circuit in which the plaintiff resides or has his principal place of business, or the Court of Appeals for the District of Columbia. As part of his answer, the Secretary shall file a certified copy of the transcript of the record of the hearing, including all evidence submitted in connection therewith. The findings of fact of the Secretary, if based on substantial evidence in the record as a whole, shall be conclusive.

(k) *No loss or diminution of benefits for reliance on prayer or spiritual treatment; physical examination not excepted.*

(1) Nothing in this Act prevents an employee whose injury or disability has been established under this Act from relying in good faith on treatment by prayer or spiritual means alone, in accordance with the tenets and practice of a recognized church or religious denomination, by an accredited practitioner of such recognized church or religious denomination, and on nursing services rendered in accordance with such tenets and practice, without suffering loss or diminution of the compensation or benefits under this Act. Nothing in this subsection shall be construed to except an employee from all physical examinations required by this Act.

(2) If an employee refuses to submit to medical or surgical services solely because, in adherence to the tenets and practice of a recognized church or religious denomination, the employee relies upon prayer or spiritual means alone for healing, such employee shall not be considered to have unreasonably refused medical or surgical treatment under subsection (d).

§ 908. Compensation for disability

Compensation for disability shall be paid to the employee as follows:

(a) *Permanent total disability*: In case of total disability adjudged to be permanent 66 2/3 per centum of the average weekly wages shall be paid to the employee during the continuance of such total disability. Loss of both hands, or both arms, or both feet, or both legs or both eyes, or of any two thereof shall, in the absence of conclusive proof to the contrary, constitute permanent total disability. In all other cases permanent total disability shall be determined in accordance with the facts.

(b) *Temporary total disability*: In case of disability total in character but temporary in quality 66 2/3 per centum of the average weekly wages shall be paid to the employee during the continuance thereof.

(c) *Permanent partial disability*: In case of disability partial in character but permanent in quality the compensation shall be 66 2/3 per centum of the average weekly wages, which shall be in addition to compensation for temporary total disability or temporary partial disability paid in accordance with subdivision (b) or subdivision (e) of this section, respectively, and shall be paid to the employee, as follows:

(1) Arm lost, three hundred and twelve weeks' compensation.

(2) Leg lost, two hundred and eighty-eight weeks' compensation.

(3) Hand lost, two hundred and forty-four weeks' compensation.

(4) Foot lost, two hundred and five weeks' compensation.

(5) Eye lost, one hundred and sixty weeks' compensation.

(6) Thumb lost, seventy-five weeks' compensation.

(7) First finger lost, forty-six weeks' compensation.

(8) Great toe lost, thirty-eight weeks' compensation.

(9) Second finger lost, thirty weeks' compensation.

(10) Third finger lost, twenty-five weeks' compensation.

(11) Toe other than great toe lost, sixteen weeks' compensation.

(12) Fourth finger lost, fifteen weeks' compensation.

(13) Loss of hearing:

(A) Compensation for loss of hearing in one ear, fifty-two weeks.

(B) Compensation for loss of hearing in both ears, two-hundred weeks.

(C) An audiogram shall be presumptive evidence of the amount of hearing loss sustained as of the date thereof, only if (i) such audiogram was administered by a licensed or certified audiologist or a physician who is certified in otolaryngology, (ii) such audiogram, with the report thereon, was provided to the employee at the time it was administered, and (iii) no contrary audiogram made at that time is produced.

(D) The time for filing a notice of injury, under section 12 of this Act [33 USC § 912], or a claim for compensation, under section 13 of this Act [33 USC § 913], shall not begin to run in connection with any claim for loss of hearing under this section, until the employee has received an audiogram, with the accompanying report thereon, which indicates that the employee has suffered a loss of hearing.

(E) Determinations of loss of hearing shall be made in accordance with the guides for the evaluation of permanent impairment as promulgated and modified from time to time by the American Medical Association.

(14) Phalanges: Compensation for loss of more than one phalange of a digit shall be the same as for loss of the entire digit. Compensation for loss of the first phalange shall be one-half of the compensation for loss of the entire digit.

(15) Amputated arm or leg: Compensation for an arm or a leg, if amputated at or above the elbow or the knee, shall be the same as for a loss of the arm or leg; but, if amputated between the elbow and the wrist or the knee and the ankle, shall be the same as for loss of a hand or foot.

(16) Binocular vision or per centum of vision: Compensation for loss of binocular vision or for 80 per centum or more of the vision of an eye shall be the same as for loss of the eye.

(17) Two or more digits: Compensation for loss of two or more digits, or one or more phalanges of two or more digits, of a hand or foot may be proportioned to the loss of use of the hand or foot occasioned thereby, but shall not exceed the compensation for loss of a hand or foot.

(18) Total loss of use: Compensation for permanent total loss of use of a member shall be the same as for loss of the member.

(19) Partial loss or partial loss of use: Compensation for permanent partial loss or loss of use of a member may be for proportionate loss or loss of use of the member.

(20) Disfigurement: Proper and equitable compensation not to exceed $ 7,500 shall be awarded for serious disfigurement of the face, head, or neck or of other normally exposed areas likely to handicap the employee in securing or maintaining employment.

(21) Other cases: In all other cases in the class of disability, the compensation shall be 66 2/3 per centum of the difference between the average weekly wages of the employee and the employee's wage-earning capacity thereafter in the same employment or otherwise, payable during the continuance of partial disability.

(22) In any case in which there shall be a loss of, or loss of use of, more than one member or parts of more than one member set forth in paragraphs (1) to (19) of this subdivision, not amounting to permanent total disability, the award of compensation shall be for the loss of, or loss of use of, each such member or part thereof, which awards shall run consecutively, except that where the injury affects only two or more digits of the same hand or foot, paragraph (17) of this subdivision shall apply.

(23) Notwithstanding paragraphs (1) through (22), with respect to a claim for permanent partial disability for which the average weekly wages are determined under section 10(d)(2) [33 USC § 910(d)(2)], the compensation shall be 66 2/3 per centum of such average weekly wages multiplied by the percentage of permanent impairment, as determined under the guides referred to in section 2(10) [33 USC § 902(10)], payable during the continuance of such impairment.

(d)(1) If an employee who is receiving compensation for permanent partial disability pursuant to section 8(c)(1)—(20) [subsec. (c)(1)—(20) of this section] dies from causes other than the injury, the total amount of the award unpaid at the time of death shall be payable to or for the benefit of his survivors, as follows:

(A) if the employee is survived only by a widow or widower, such unpaid amount of the award shall be payable to such widow or widower,

(B) if the employee is survived only by a child or children, such unpaid amount of the award shall be paid to such child or children in equal shares,

(C) if the employee is survived by a widow or widower and a child or children, such unpaid amount of the award shall be payable to such survivors in equal shares,

(D) if there be no widow or widower and no surviving child or children, such unpaid amount of the award shall be paid to the survivors specified in section 9(d) [33 USC § 909(d)] (other than a wife, husband, or child); and the amount to be paid each such survivor shall be determined by multiplying such unpaid amount of the award by the appropriate percentage specified in section 9(d) [33 USC § 909(d)], but if the aggregate amount to which all such survivors are entitled, as so determined, is less than such unpaid amount of the award, the excess amount shall be divided among such survivors pro rata according to the amount otherwise payable to each under this subparagraph.

(2) Notwithstanding any other limitation in section 9 [33 USC § 909], the total amount of any award for permanent partial disability pursuant to section 8(c)(1)—(20) of [subsec. (c)(1)—(20) of this section] unpaid at time of death shall be payable in full in the appropriate distribution.

(3) An award for disability may be made after the death of the injured employee. Except where compensation is pay-

able under section 8(c)(21) [subsec.(c)(21) of this section], if there be no survivors as prescribed in this section, then the compensation payable under this subsection shall be paid to the special fund established under section 44(a) of this Act [33 USC § 944(a)].

(4) [Redesignated]

(e) *Temporary partial disability*: In case of temporary partial disability resulting in decrease of earning capacity the compensation shall be two-thirds of the difference between the injured employee's average weekly wages before the injury and his wage-earning capacity after the injury in the same or another employment, to be paid during the continuance of such disability, but shall not be paid for a period exceeding five years.

(f) *Injury increasing disability*:

(1) In any case in which an employee having an existing permanent partial disability suffers injury, the employer shall provide compensation for such disability as is found to be attributable to that injury based upon the average weekly wages of the employee at the time of the injury. If following an injury falling within the provisions of section 8(c)(1)-(20) [subsec. (c)(1)-(20) of this section], the employee is totally and permanently disabled, and the disability is found not to be due solely to that injury, the employer shall provide compensation for the applicable prescribed period of weeks provided for in that section for the subsequent injury, or for one hundred and four weeks, whichever is the greater, except that, in the case of an injury falling within the provisions of section 8(c)(13) [subsec. (c)(13) of this section], the employer shall provide compensation for the lesser of such periods. In all other cases of total permanent disability or of death, found not to be due solely to that injury, of an employee having an existing permanent partial disability, the employer shall provide in addition to compensation under paragraphs (b) and (e) of this section, compensation payments or death benefits for one hundred and four weeks only. If following an injury falling within the provisions of 8(c)(1)-(20) [subsec. (c)(1)-(20) of this section], the employee has a permanent partial disability and the disability is found not to be due solely to that injury, and such disability is materially and substantially greater than that which would have resulted from the subsequent injury alone, the employer shall provide compensation for the applicable period of weeks provided for in that section for the subsequent injury, or for one hundred and four weeks, whichever is the greater, except that, in the case of an injury falling within the provisions of section 8(c)(13) [subsec. (c)(13) of this section], the employer shall provide compensation for the lesser of such periods. In all other cases in which the employee has a permanent partial disability, found not to be due solely to that injury, and such disability is materially and substantially greater than that which would have resulted from the subsequent injury alone, the employer shall provide in addition to compensation under paragraphs (b) and (e) of this section, compensation for one hundred and four weeks only.

(2)(A) After cessation of the payments for the period of weeks provided for herein, the employee or his survivor entitled to benefits shall be paid the remainder of the compensation that would be due out of the special fund established in section 44 [33 USC § 944], except that the special fund shall not assume responsibility with respect to such benefits (and such payments shall not be subject to cessation) in the case of any employer who fails to comply with section 32(a) [33 USC § 932(a)].

(B) After cessation of payments for the period of weeks provided for in this subsection, the employer or carrier responsible for payment of compensation shall remain a party to the claim, retain access to all records relating to the claim, and in all other respects retain all rights granted under this Act prior to cessation of such payments.

(3) Any request, filed after the date of enactment of the Longshore and Harbor Workers' Compensation Amendments of 1984 [enacted Sept. 28, 1984], for apportionment of liability to the special fund established under section 44 of this Act [33 USC § 944] for the payment of compensation benefits, and a statement of the grounds therefore, shall be presented to the deputy commissioner prior to the consideration of the claim by the deputy commissioner. Failure to present such request prior to such consideration shall be an absolute defense to the special fund's liability for the payment of any benefits in connection with such claim, unless the employer could not have reasonably anticipated the liability of the special fund prior to the issuance of a compensation order.

(g) *Maintenance for employees undergoing vocational rehabilitation*: An employee who as a result of injury is or may be expected to be totally or partially incapacitated for a remunerative occupation and who, under the direction of the Secretary as provided by section 39(c) of this Act [33 USC § 939(c)], is being rendered fit to engage in a remunerative occupation, shall receive additional compensation necessary for his maintenance, but such additional compensation shall not exceed $ 25 a week. The expense shall be paid out of the special fund established in section 44 [33 USC § 944].

(h) The wage-earning capacity of an injured employee in cases of partial disability under subdivision (c)(21) of this section or under subdivision (e) of this section shall be determined by his actual earnings if such actual earnings fairly and reasonably represent his wage-earning capacity: Provided, however, That if the employee has no actual earnings or his actual earnings do not fairly and reasonably represent his wage-earning capacity, the deputy commissioner may, in the interest of justice, fix such wage-earning capacity as shall be reasonable, having due regard to the nature of his injury, the degree of physical impairment, his usual employment, and any other factors or circumstances in the case which may affect his capacity to earn wages in his disabled condition, including the effect of disability as it may naturally extend into the future.

(i)(1) Whenever the parties to any claim for compensation under this Act, including survivors benefits, agree to a settlement, the deputy commissioner or administrative law judge shall approve the settlement within thirty days unless it is found to be inadequate or procured by duress. Such settlement may include future medical benefits if the parties so agree. No liability of any employer, carrier, or both for medical, disability, or death benefits shall be discharged unless the application for settlement is approved by the deputy commissioner or administrative law judge. If the parties to the settlement are represented by counsel, then agreements shall be deemed approved unless specifically disapproved within thirty days after submission for approval.

(2) If the deputy commissioner disapproves an application for settlement under paragraph (1), the deputy commissioner shall issue a written statement within thirty days containing the reasons for disapproval. Any party to the settlement may request a hearing before an administrative law judge in the manner prescribed by this Act. Following such hearing, the administrative law judge shall enter an order approving or rejecting the settlement.

(3) A settlement approved under this section shall discharge the liability of the employer or carrier, or both. Settlements may be agreed upon at any stage of the proceeding including after entry of a final compensation order.

(4) The special fund shall not be liable for reimbursement of any sums paid or payable to an employee or any beneficiary under such settlement, or otherwise voluntarily paid prior to such settlement by the employer or carrier, or both.

(j)(1) The employer may inform a disabled employee of his obligation to report to the employer not less than semiannually any earnings from employment or self-employment, on such forms as the Secretary shall specify in regulations.

(2) An employee who –

(A) fails to report the employee's earnings under paragraph (1) when requested, or

(B) knowingly and willfully omits or understates any part of such earnings, and who is determined by the deputy commissioner to have violated clause (A) or (B) of this paragraph, forfeits his right to compensation with respect to any period during which the employee was required to file such report.

(3) Compensation forfeited under this subsection, if already paid, shall be recovered by a deduction from the compensation payable to the employee in any amount and on such schedule as determined by the deputy commissioner.

§ 909. Compensation for death

If the injury causes death, the compensation therefore shall be known as a death benefit and shall be payable in the amount and to or for the benefit of the persons following:

(a) Reasonable funeral expenses not exceeding $ 3,000.

(b) If there be a widow or widower and no child of the deceased, to such widow or widower 50 per centum of the average wages of the deceased, during widowhood, or dependent widowerhood, with two years' compensation in one sum upon remarriage; and if there be a surviving child or children of the deceased, the additional amount of 16 2/3 per centum of such wages for each such child; in case of the death or remarriage of such widow or widower, if there be one surviving child of the deceased employee, such child shall have his compensation increased to 50 per centum of such wages, and if there be more than one surviving child of the deceased employee, to such children, in equal parts, 50 per centum of such wages increased by 16 2/3 per centum of such wages for each child in excess of one: Provided, That the total amount payable shall in no case exceed 66 2/3 per centum of such wages. The deputy commissioner having jurisdiction over the claim may, in his discretion, require the appointment of a guardian for the purpose of receiving the compensation of a minor child. In the absence of such a requirement the appointment of a guardian for such purposes shall not be necessary.

(c) If there be one surviving child of the deceased, but no widow or widower, then for the support of such child 50 per centum of the wages of the deceased; and if there be more than one surviving child of the deceased, but no widow or dependent husband, then for the support of such children, in equal parts 50 per centum of such wages increased by 16 2/3 per centum of such wages for each child in excess of one: Provided, That the total amount payable shall in no case exceed 66 2/3 per centum of such wages.

(d) If there be no widow or widower or child, or if the amount payable to a widow or widower and to children shall be less in the aggregate than 66 2/3 per centum of the average wages of the deceased; then for the support of grandchildren or brothers and sisters, if dependent upon the deceased at the time of the injury, and any other persons who satisfy the definition of the term "dependent" in section 152 of title 26 of the United States Code [26 USC § 152], but are not otherwise eligible under this section, 20 per centum of such wages for the support of each such person during such dependency and for the support of each parent, or grandparent, of the deceased if dependent upon him at the time of the injury, 25 per centum of such wages during such dependency. But in no case shall the aggregate amount payable under this subdivision exceed the difference between 66 2/3 per centum of such wages and the amount payable as hereinbefore provided to widow or widower and for the support of surviving child or children.

(e) In computing death benefits, the average weekly wages of the deceased shall not be less than the national average weekly wage as prescribed in section 6(b) [33 USC § 906(b)], but –

(1) the total weekly benefits shall not exceed the lesser of the average weekly wages of the deceased or the benefit which the deceased employee would have been eligible to receive under section 6(b)(1) [33 USC § 906(b)(1)]; and

(2) in the case of a claim based on death due to an occupational disease for which the time of injury (as determined under section 10(i) [33 USC § 910(i)] occurs after the employee has retired, the total weekly benefits shall not exceed one fifty-second part of the employee's average annual earnings during the 52-week period preceding retirement.

(f) All questions of dependency shall be determined as of the time of the injury.

(g) Aliens: Compensation under this chapter [this Act] to aliens not residents (or about to become nonresidents) of the United States or Canada shall be the same in amount as provided for residents, except that dependents in any foreign country shall be limited to surviving wife and child or children, or if there be no surviving wife or child or children, to surviving father or mother whom the employee has supported, either wholly or in part, for the period of one year prior to the date of the injury, and except that the commission [Secretary of Labor] may, at its option or upon the application of the insurance carrier shall, commute all future installments of compensation to be paid to such aliens by paying or causing to be paid to them one-half of the commuted amount of such future installments of compensation as determined by the commission [Secretary of Labor].

§ 910. Determination of pay

Except as otherwise provided in this Act, the average weekly wage of the injured employee at the time of the injury shall be taken as the basis upon which to compute compensation and shall be determined as follows:

(a) If the injured employee shall have worked in the employment in which he was working at the time of the injury, whether for the same or another employer, during substantially the whole of the year immediately preceding his injury, his average annual earnings shall consist of three hundred times the average daily wage or salary for a six-day worker and two hundred and sixty times the average daily wage or salary for a five-day worker, which he shall have earned in such employment during the days when so employed.

(b) If the injured employee shall not have worked in such employment during substantially the whole of such year, his average annual earnings, if a six-day worker, shall consist of three hundred times the average daily wage or salary, and, if a five-day worker, two hundred and sixty times the average daily wage or salary, which an employee of the same class working substantially the whole of such immediately preceding year in the same or in similar employment in the same or a neighboring place shall have earned in such employment during the days when so employed.

(c) If either of the foregoing methods of arriving at the average annual earnings of the injured employee can not reasonably and fairly be applied, such average annual earnings shall be such sum as, having regard to the previous earnings of the injured employee in the employment in which he was working at the time of the injury, and of other employees of the same or most similar class working in the same or most similar employment in the same or neighboring locality, or other employment of such employee, including the reasonable value of the services of the employee if engaged in self-employment, shall reasonably represent the annual earning capacity of the injured employee.

(d)(1) The average weekly wages of an employee shall be one fifty-second part of his average annual earnings.

(2) Notwithstanding paragraph (1), with respect to any claim based on a death or disability due to an occupational disease for which the time of injury (as determined under subsection (i)) occurs –

(A) within the first year after the employee has retired, the average weekly wages shall be one fifty-second part of his average annual earnings during the 52-week period preceding retirement; or

(B) more than one year after the employee has retired, the average weekly wage shall be deemed to be the national average weekly wage (as determined by the Secretary pursuant to section 6(b) [33 USC § 906(b)]) applicable at the time of the injury.

(e) If it be established that the injured employee was a minor when injured, and that under normal conditions his wages should be expected to increase during the period of disability the fact may be considered in arriving at his average weekly wages.

(f) Effective October 1 of each year, the compensation or death benefits payable for permanent total disability or death arising out of injuries subject to this Act shall be increased by the lesser of –

(1) a percentage equal to the percentage (if any) by which the applicable national weekly wage for the period beginning on such October 1, as determined under section 6(b) [33 USC § 906(b)], exceeds the applicable national average weekly wage, as so determined, for the period beginning with the preceding October 1; or

(2) 5 per centum.

(g) The weekly compensation after adjustment under subsection (f) shall be fixed at the nearest dollar. No adjustment of less than $ 1 shall be made, but in no event shall compensation or death benefits be reduced.

(h)(1) Not later than ninety days after the date of enactment of this subsection [Oct. 27, 1972], the compensation to which an employee or his survivor is entitled due to total permanent disability or death which commenced or occurred prior to enactment of this subsection shall be adjusted. The amount of such adjustment shall be determined in accordance with regulations of the Secretary by designating as the employee's average weekly wage the applicable national average weekly wage determined under section 6(b) [33 USC § 906(b)] and (A) computing the compensation to which such employee or survivor would be entitled if the disabling injury or death had occurred on the day following such enactment date and (B) subtracting therefrom the compensation to which such employee or survivor was entitled on such enactment date; except that no such employee or survivor shall receive total compensation amounting to less than that to which he was entitled on such enactment date. Notwithstanding the foregoing sentence, where such an employee or his survivor was awarded compensation as the result of death or permanent total disability at less than the maximum rate that was provided in this Act at the time of the injury which resulted in the death or disability, then his average weekly wage shall be determined by increasing his average weekly wage at the time of such injury by the percentage which the applicable national average weekly wage has increased between the year in which the injury occurred and the first day of the first month following the enactment of this section [enacted Oct. 27, 1972]. Where such injury occurred prior to 1947, the Secretary shall determine, on the basis of such economic data as he deems relevant, the amount by which the employee's average weekly wage shall be increased for the pre-1947 period.

(2) Fifty per centum of any additional compensation or death benefit paid as a result of the adjustment required by paragraphs (1) and (3) of this subsection shall be paid out of the special fund established under section 44 of this Act [33 USC § 944], and 50 per centum shall be paid from appropriations.

(3) For the purposes of subsections (f) and (g) an injury which resulted in permanent total disability or death which occurred prior to the date of enactment of this subsection shall be considered to have occurred on the day following such enactment date.

(i) For purposes of this section with respect to a claim for compensation for death or disability due to an occupational disease which does not immediately result in death or disability, the time of injury shall be deemed to be the date on which the employee or claimant becomes aware, or in the exercise of reasonable diligence or by reason of medical advice should have been aware, of the relationship between the employment, the disease, and the death or disability.

§ 911. Guardian for minor or incompetent

The deputy commissioner may require the appointment by a court of competent jurisdiction, for any person who is mentally incompetent or a minor, of a guardian or other representative to receive compensation payable to such person under this Act and to exercise the powers granted to or to perform the duties required of such person under this Act.

§ 912. Notice of injury or death

(a) *Time limitation; to whom notice given.* Notice of an injury or death in respect of which compensation is payable under this Act shall be given within thirty days after the date of such injury or death, or thirty days after the employee or beneficiary is aware, or in the exercise of reasonable diligence or by reason of medical advice should have been aware, of a relationship between the injury or death and the employment, except that in the case of an occupational disease which does not immediately result in a disability or death, such notice shall be given within one year after the employee or claimant becomes aware, or in the exercise of reasonable diligence or by reason of medical advice should have been aware, of the relationship between the employment, the disease, and the death or disability. Notice shall be given (1) to the deputy commissioner in the compensation district in which the injury or death occurred, and (2) to the employer.

(b) *Form and content.* Such notice shall be in writing, shall contain the name and address of the employee and a statement of the time, place, nature, and cause of the injury or death, and shall be signed by the employee or by some person on his behalf, or in case of death, by any person claiming to be entitled to compensation for such death or by a person on his behalf.

(c) *Delivery requirements; designation of agents.* Notice shall be given to the deputy commissioner by delivering it to him or sending it by mail addressed to his office, and to the employer by delivering it to him or by sending it by mail addressed to him at his last known place of business. If the employer is a partnership, such notice may be given to any partner, or if a corporation, such notice may be given to any agent or officer thereof upon whom legal process may be served or who is in charge of the business in the place where the injury occurred. Each employer shall designate those agents or other responsible officials to receive such notice, except that the employer shall designate as its representatives individuals among first line supervisors, local plant management, and personnel office officials. Such designations shall be made in accordance with regulations prescribed by the Secretary and the employer shall notify his employees and the Secretary of such designation in a manner prescribed by the Secretary in regulations.

(d) *Failure to give notice.* Failure to give such notice shall not bar any claim under this Act (1) if the employer (or his agent or agents or other responsible official or officials designated by the employer pursuant to subsection (c)) or the carrier had knowledge of the injury or death, (2) the deputy commissioner determines that the employer or carrier has not been prejudiced by failure to give such notice, or (3) if the deputy commissioner excuses such failure on the ground that (i) notice, while not given to a responsible official designated by the employer pursuant to subsection (c) of this section, was given to an official of the employer or the employer's insurance carrier, and that the employer or carrier was not prejudiced due to the failure to provide notice to a responsible official designated by the employer pursuant to subsection (c), or (ii) for some satisfactory reason such notice could not be given; nor unless objection to such failure is raised before the deputy commissioner at the first hearing of a claim for compensation in respect of such injury or death.

§ 913. Filing of claims

(a) *Time to file.* Except as otherwise provided in this section, the right to compensation for disability or death under this Act shall be barred unless a claim therefore is filed within one year after the injury or death. If payment of compensation has been made without an award on account of such injury or death, a claim may be filed within one year after the date of the last payment. Such claim shall be filed with the deputy commissioner in the compensation district in which such injury or death occurred. The time for filing a claim shall not begin to run until the employee or beneficiary is aware, or by the exercise of reasonable diligence should have been aware, of the relationship between the injury or death and the employment.

(b) *Failure to file.*

(1) Notwithstanding the provisions of subdivision (a) failure to file a claim within the period prescribed in such subdivision shall not be a bar to such right unless objection to such failure is made at the first hearing of such claim in which all parties in interest are given reasonable notice and opportunity to be heard.

(2) Notwithstanding the provisions of subsection (a), a claim for compensation for death or disability due to an occupational disease which does not immediately result in such death or disability shall be timely if filed within two years after the employee or claimant becomes aware, or in the exercise of reasonable diligence or by reason of medical advice should have been aware, of the relationship between the employment, the disease, and the death or disability, or within one year of the date of the last payment of compensation, whichever is later.

(c) *Effect on incompetents and minors.* If a person who is entitled to compensation under this Act is mentally incompetent or a minor, the provisions of subdivision (a) shall not be applicable so long as such person has no guardian or other authorized representative, but shall be applicable in the case of a person who is mentally incompetent or a minor from the date of appointment of such guardian or other representative, or in the case of a minor, if no guardian is appointed before he becomes of age, from the date he becomes of age.

(d) *Tolling provision.* Where recovery is denied to any person, in a suit brought at law or in admiralty to recover damages in respect of injury or death, on the ground that such person was an employee and that the defendant was an employer within the meaning of this Act and that such employer had secured compensation to such employee under this Act the limitation of time prescribed in subdivision (a) shall begin to run only from the date of termination of such suit.

§ 914. Payment of compensation

(a) *Manner of payment.* Compensation under this Act shall be paid periodically, promptly, and directly to the person entitled thereto, without an award, except where liability to pay compensation is controverted by the employer.

(b) *Period of installment payments.* The first installment of compensation shall become due on the fourteenth day after the employer has been notified pursuant to section 12 [33 USC § 912], or the employer has knowledge of the injury or death, on which date all compensation then due shall be paid. Thereafter compensation shall be paid in installments, semimonthly, except where the deputy commissioner determines that payment in installments should be made monthly or at some other period.

(c) *Notification of commencement or suspension of payment.* Upon making the first payment, and upon suspension of payment for any cause, the employer shall immediately notify the deputy commissioner, in accordance with a form prescribed by the commission, that payment of compensation has begun or has been suspended, as the case may be.

(d) *Right to compensation controverted.* If the employer controverts the right to compensation he shall file with the deputy commissioner on or before the fourteenth day after he has knowledge of the alleged injury or death, a notice, in accordance with a form prescribed by the commission, stating that the right to compensation is controverted, the name of the claimant, the name of the employer, the date of the alleged injury or death, and the grounds upon which the right to compensation is controverted.

(e) *Additional compensation for overdue installment payments payable without award.* If any installment of compensation payable without an award is not paid within fourteen days after it becomes due, as provided in subdivision (b) of this section, there shall be added to such unpaid installment an amount equal to 10 per centum thereof, which shall be paid at the same time as, but in addition to, such installment, unless notice is filed under subdivision (d) of this section, or unless such nonpayment is excused by the deputy commissioner after a showing by the employer that owing to conditions over which he had no control such installment could not be paid within the period prescribed for the payment.

(f) *Additional compensation for overdue installment payments payable under terms of award.* If any compensation, payable under the terms of an award, is not paid within ten days after it becomes due, there shall be added to such unpaid compensation an amount equal to 20 per centum thereof, which shall be paid at the same time as, but in addition to, such compensation, unless review of the compensation order making such award is had as provided in section 21 [33 USC § 921] and an order staying payment has been issued by the Board or court.

(g) *Notice of payment; penalty.* Within sixteen days after final payment of compensation has been made, the employer shall send to the deputy commissioner a notice, in accordance with a form prescribed by the commission [Secretary of Labor], stating that such final payment has been made, the total amount of compensation paid, the name of the employee and of any other person to whom compensation has been paid, the date of the injury or death, and the date to which compensation has been paid. If the employer fails to so notify the deputy commissioner within such time the commission [Secretary of Labor] shall assess against such employer a civil penalty in the amount of $ 100.

(h) *Investigations, examinations, and hearings for controverted, stopped or suspended payments.* The deputy commissioner (1) may upon his own initiative at any time in a case in which payments are being made without an award, and (2) shall in any case where right to compensation is controverted, or where payments of compensation have been stopped or suspended, upon receipt of notice from any person entitled to compensation, or from the employer, that the right to compensation is controverted, or that payments of compensation have been stopped or suspended, make such investigations, cause such medical examinations to be made, or hold such hearings, and take such further action as he considers will properly protect the rights of all parties.

(i) *Deposit by employer*. Whenever the deputy commissioner deems it advisable he may require any employer to make a deposit with the Treasury of the United States to secure the prompt and convenient payment of such compensation, and payments therefrom upon any awards shall be made upon order of the deputy commissioner.

(j) *Reimbursement for advance payments*. If the employer has made advance payments of compensation, he shall be entitled to be reimbursed out of any unpaid installment or installments of compensation due.

(k) *Receipt for payment*. An injured employee, or in case of death his dependents or personal representative, shall give receipts for payment of compensation to the employer paying the same and such employer shall produce the same for inspection by the deputy commissioner, whenever required.

(l) [Redesignated]

§ 915. Invalid agreements

(a) No agreement by an employee to pay any portion of premium paid by his employer to a carrier or to contribute to a benefit fund or department maintained by such employer for the purpose of providing compensation or medical services and supplies as required by this Act shall be valid, and any employer who makes a deduction for such purpose from the pay of any employee entitled to the benefits of this act shall be guilty of a misdemeanor and upon conviction thereof shall be punished by a fine of not more than $ 1,000.

(b) No agreement by an employee to waive his right to compensation under this Act shall be valid.

§ 916. Assignment and exemption from claims of creditors

No assignment, release, or commutation of compensation or benefits due or payable under this Act, except as provided by this Act, shall be valid, and such compensation and benefits shall be exempt from all claims of creditors and from levy, execution, and attachment or other remedy for recovery or collection of a debt, which exemption may not be waived.

§ 917. Compensation a lien against assets

Where a trust fund which complies with section 302(c) of the Labor-Management Relations Act of 1947 (29 U.S.C. 186(c) [29 USC § 186(c)]) established pursuant to a collective-bargaining agreement in effect between an employer and an employee covered under this Act has paid disability benefits to an employee which the employee is legally obligated to repay by reason of his entitlement to compensation under this Act or under a settlement, the Secretary shall authorize a lien on such compensation in favor of the trust fund for the amount of such payments.

§ 918. Collection of defaulted payments; special fund

(a) In case of default by the employer in the payment of compensation due under any award of compensation for a period of thirty days after the compensation is due and payable, the person to whom such compensation is payable may, within one year after such default, make application to the deputy commissioner making the compensation order or [for] a supplementary order declaring the amount of the default. After investigation, notice, and hearing, as provided in section 19 [33 USC § 919], the deputy commissioner shall make a supplementary order, declaring the amount of the default, which shall be filed in the same manner as the compensation order. In case the payment in default is an installment of the award, the deputy commissioner may, in his discretion, declare the whole of the award as the amount in default. The applicant may file a certified copy of such supplementary order with the clerk of the Federal district court for the judicial district in which the employer has his principal place of business or maintains an office, or for the judicial district in which the injury occurred. In case such principal place of business or office or place where the injury occurred is in the District of Columbia, a copy of such supplementary order may be filed with the clerk of the Supreme Court of the District of Columbia [United States District Court for the District of Columbia]. Such supplementary order of the deputy commissioner shall be final, and the court shall upon the filing of the copy enter judgment for the amount declared in default by the supplementary order if such supplementary order is in accordance with law. Review of the judgment so entered may be had as in civil suits for damages at common law. Final proceedings to execute the judgment may be had by writ of execution in the form used by the court in suits at common law in actions of assumpsit. No fee shall be required for filing the supplementary order nor for entry of judgment thereon, and the applicant shall not be liable for costs in a proceeding for review of the judgment unless the court shall otherwise direct. The court shall modify such judgment to conform to any later compensation order upon presentation of a certified copy thereof to the court.

(b) In cases where judgment cannot be satisfied by reason of the employer's insolvency or other circumstances precluding payment, the Secretary of Labor may, in his discretion and to the extent he shall determine advisable after consideration of current commitments payable from the special fund established in section 44 [33 USC § 944], make payment from such fund upon any award made under this Act and in addition, provide any necessary medical, surgical, and other treatment required by section 7 of the Act [33 USC § 907] in any case of disability where there has been a default in furnishing medical treatment by reason of the insolvency of the employer. Such an employer shall be liable for payment into such fund of the amounts paid therefrom by the Secretary of Labor under this subsection; and for the purpose of enforcing his liability, the Secretary of Labor for the benefit of the fund shall be subrogated to all the rights of the person receiving such payment or benefits as against the employer and may by a proceeding in the name of the Secretary of Labor under section 18 [33 USC § 918] or under subsection (c) of section 21 of this Act [33 USC § 921(c)], or both, seek to recover the amount of the default or so much thereof as in the judgment of the Secretary is possible, or the Secretary may settle and compromise any such claim.

§ 919. Procedure in respect of claims

(a) *Filing of claim.* Subject to the provisions of section 13 [33 USC § 913] a claim for compensation may be filed with the deputy commissioner in accordance with regulations prescribed by the commission [Secretary of Labor] at any time after the first seven days of disability following any injury, or at any time after death, and the deputy commissioner shall have full power and authority to hear and determine all questions in respect of such claim.

(b) *Notice of claim.* Within ten days after such claim is filed the deputy commissioner, in accordance with regulations prescribed by the commission [Secretary of Labor], shall notify the employer and any other person (other than the claimant), whom the deputy commissioner considers an interested party, that a claim has been filed. Such notice may be served personally upon the employer or other person, or sent to such employer or person by registered mail.

(c) *Investigations; order for hearing; notice; rejection or award.* The deputy commissioner shall make or cause to be made such investigations as he considers necessary in respect of the claim, and upon application of any interested party shall order a hearing thereon. If a hearing on such claim is ordered the deputy commissioner shall give the claimant and other interested parties at least ten days' notice of such hearing, served personally upon the claimant and other interested parties or sent to such claimant and other interested parties by registered mail or by certified mail, and shall within twenty days after such hearing is had, by order, reject the claim or make an award in respect of the claim. If no hearing is ordered within twenty days after notice if given as provided in subdivision (b), the deputy commissioner shall, by order, reject the claim or make an award in respect of the claim.

(d) *Provisions governing conduct of hearing; hearing examiners.* Notwithstanding any other provisions of this Act, any hearing held under this Act shall be conducted in accordance with the provisions of section 554 of title 5 of the United States Code [5 USC §§ 554]. Any such hearing shall be conducted by a [an] administrative law judge qualified under section 3105 of that title [5 USC § 3105]. All powers, duties, and responsibilities vested by this Act, on the date of enactment of the Longshoremen's and Harbor Workers' Compensation Act Amendments of 1972 [enacted Oct. 27, 1972], in the deputy commissioners with respect to such hearings shall be vested in such administrative law judges.

(e) *Filing and mailing of order rejecting claim or making award.* The order rejecting the claim or making the award (referred to in this Act as a compensation order) shall be filed in the office of the deputy commissioner, and a copy thereof shall be sent by registered mail or by certified mail to the claimant and to the employer at the last known address of each.

(f) *Awards after death of employee.* An award of compensation for disability may be made after the death of an injured employee.

(g) *Transfer of case.* At any time after a claim has been filed with him, the deputy commissioner may, with the approval of the Commission [Secretary of Labor], transfer such case to any other deputy commissioner for the purpose of making investigation, taking testimony, making physical examinations or taking such other necessary action therein as may be directed.

(h) *Physical examination of injured employee.* An injured employee claiming or entitled to compensation shall submit to such physical examination by a medical officer of the United States or by a duly qualified physician designated or approved by the commission [Secretary of Labor] as the deputy commissioner may require. The place or places shall be reasonably convenient for the employee. Such physician or physicians as the employee, employer, or carrier may select and pay for may participate in an examination if the employee, employer, or carrier so requests. Proceedings shall be suspended and no compensation be payable for any period during which the employee may refuse to submit to examination.

§ 920. Presumptions

In any proceeding for the enforcement of a claim for compensation under this Act it shall be presumed, in the absence of substantial evidence to the contrary –

(a) That the claim comes within the provisions of this Act.

(b) That sufficient notice of such claim has been given.

(c) That the injury was not occasioned solely by the intoxication of the injured employee.

(d) That the injury was not occasioned by the willful intention of the injured employee to injure or kill himself or another.

§ 921. Review of compensation orders

(a) *Effectiveness and finality of order.* A compensation order shall become effective when filed in the office of the deputy commissioner as provided in section 19 [33 USC § 919], and, unless proceedings for the suspension or setting aside of such order are instituted as provided in subdivision (b) of this section, shall become final at the expiration of the thirtieth day thereafter.

(b) *Benefits Review Board; establishment; members; chairman; quorum; voting; questions reviewable; record; conclusiveness of findings; stay of payments; remand.*

(1) There is hereby established a Benefits Review Board which shall be composed of five members appointed by the Secretary from among individuals who are especially qualified to serve on such Board. The Secretary shall designate one of the members of the Board to serve as chairman. The Chairman shall have the authority, as delegated by the Secretary, to exercise all administrative functions necessary to operate the Board.

(2) For the purpose of carrying out its functions under this Act, three members of the Board shall constitute a quorum and official action can be taken only on the affirmative vote of at least three members.

(3) The Board shall be authorized to hear and determine appeals raising a substantial question of law or fact taken by any party in interest from decisions with respect to claims of employees under this Act and the extensions thereof. The Board's orders shall be based upon the hearing record. The findings of fact in the decision under review by the Board shall be conclusive if supported by substantial evidence in the record considered as a whole. The payment of the amounts required by an award shall not be stayed pending final decision in any such proceeding unless ordered by the Board. No stay shall be issued unless irreparable injury would otherwise ensue to the employer or carrier.

(4) The Board may, on its own motion or at the request of the Secretary, remand a case to the administrative law judge for further appropriate action. The consent of the parties in interest shall not be a prerequisite to a remand by the Board.

(5) Notwithstanding paragraphs (1) through (4), upon application of the Chairman of the Board, the Secretary may designate up to four Department of Labor administrative law judges to serve on the Board temporarily, for not more than one year. The Board is authorized to delegate to panels of three members any or all of the powers which the Board may exercise. Each such panel shall have no more than one temporary member. Two members shall constitute a quorum of a panel. Official adjudicative action may be taken only on the affirmative vote of at least two members of a panel. Any party aggrieved by a decision of a panel of the Board may, within thirty days after the date of entry of the decision, petition the entire permanent Board for review of the panel's decision. Upon affirmative vote of the majority of the permanent members of the Board, the petition shall be granted. The Board shall amend its Rules of Practice to conform with this paragraph. Temporary members, while serving as members of the Board, shall be compensated at the same rate of compensation as regular members.

(c) *Court of appeals; jurisdiction; persons entitled to review; petition; record; determination and enforcement; service of process; stay of payments.* Any person adversely affected or aggrieved by a final order of the Board may obtain a review of that order in the United States court of appeals for the circuit in which the injury occurred, by filing in such court within sixty days following the issuance of such Board order a written petition praying that the order be modified or set aside. A copy of such petition shall be forthwith transmitted by the clerk of the court, to the Board, and to the other parties, and thereupon the Board shall file in the court the record in the proceedings as provided in section 2112 of title 28, United States Code [28 USC § 2112]. Upon such filing, the court shall have jurisdiction of the proceeding and shall have the power to give a decree affirming, modifying, or setting aside, in whole or in part, the order of the Board and enforcing same to the extent that such order is affirmed or modified. The orders, writs, and processes of the court in such proceedings may run, be served, and be returnable anywhere in the United States. The payment of the amounts required by an award shall not be stayed pending final decision in any such proceeding unless ordered by the court. No stay shall be issued unless irreparable injury would otherwise ensue to the employer or carrier. The order of the court allowing any stay shall contain a specific finding, based upon evidence submitted to the court and identified by reference thereto, that irreparable damage would result to the employer, and specifying the nature of the damage.

(d) *District Court; jurisdiction; enforcement of orders; application of beneficiaries of awards or deputy commissioner; process for compliance with orders.* If any employer or his officers or agents fails to comply with a compensation order making an award, that has become final, any beneficiary of such award or the deputy commissioner making the order, may apply for the enforcement of the order to the Federal district court for the judicial district in which the injury occurred (or to the United States District Court for the District of Columbia if the injury occurred in the District). If the court determines that the order was made and served in accordance with law, and that such employer or his officers or agents have failed to comply therewith, the court shall enforce obedience to the order by writ of injunction or by other proper process, mandatory or otherwise, to enjoin upon such person and his officers and agents compliance with the order.

(e) *Institution of proceedings for suspension, setting aside, or enforcement of compensation orders.* Proceedings for suspending, setting aside, or enforcing a compensation order, whether rejecting a claim or making an award, shall not be instituted otherwise than as provided in this section and section 18 [33 USC § 918].

§ 922. Modification of awards

Upon his own initiative, or upon the application of any party in interest (including an employer or carrier which has been granted relief under section 8(f) [33 USC § 908(f)]), on the ground of a change in conditions or because of a mistake in a determination of fact by the deputy commissioner, the deputy commissioner may, at any time prior to one year after the date of the last payment of compensation, whether or not a compensation order has been issued, or at any time prior to one year after the rejection of a claim, review a compensation case (including a case under which payments are made pursuant to section 44(i) [33 USC § 944(i)]) in accordance with the procedure prescribed in respect of claims in section 19 [33 USC § 919], and in accordance with such section issue a new compensation order which may terminate, continue, reinstate, increase, or decrease such compensation, or award compensation. Such new order shall not affect any compensation previously paid, except that an award increasing the compensation rate may be made effective from the date of the injury, and if any part of the compensation due or to become due is unpaid, an award decreasing the compensation rate may be made effective from the date of the injury, and any payment made prior thereto in excess of such decreased rate shall be deducted from any unpaid compensation, in such manner and by such method as may be determined by the deputy commissioner with the approval of the Secretary. This section does not authorize the modification of settlements.

§ 923. Procedure before deputy commissioner or Board

(a) In making an investigation or inquiry or conducting a hearing the deputy commissioner or Board shall not be bound by common law or statutory rules of evidence or by technical or formal rules of procedure, except as provided by this Act [33 USC §§ 901 et seq.]; but may make such investigation or inquiry or conduct such hearing in such manner as to best ascertain the rights of the parties. Declarations of a deceased employee concerning the injury in respect of which the investigation or inquiry is being made or the hearing conducted shall be received in evidence and shall, if corroborated by other evidence, be sufficient to establish the injury.

(b) Hearings before a deputy commissioner or Board shall be open to the public and shall be stenographically reported, and the deputy commissioners or Board, subject to the approval of the Secretary, are authorized to contract for the reporting of such hearings. The Secretary shall by regulation provide for the preparation of a record of the hearings and other proceedings before the deputy commissioners or Board.

§ 924. Witnesses

No person shall be required to attend as a witness in any proceeding before a deputy commissioner at a place outside of the State of his residence and more than one hundred miles from his place of residence unless his lawful mileage and fee for one day's attendance shall be first paid or tendered to him; but the testimony of any witness may be taken by deposition or interrogatories according to the rules of practice of the Federal district court for the judicial district in which the case is pending (or of the Supreme Court of the District of Columbia [United States District Court for the District of Columbia] if the case is pending in the District).

§ 925. Witness fees

Witnesses summoned in a proceeding before a deputy commissioner or whose depositions are taken shall receive the same fees and mileage as witnesses in courts of the United States.

§ 926. Costs in proceedings brought without reasonable grounds

If the court having jurisdiction of proceedings in respect of any claim or compensation order determines that the proceedings in respect of such claim or order have been instituted or continued without reasonable ground, the costs of such proceedings shall be assessed against the party who has so instituted or continued such proceedings.

§ 927. Powers of deputy commissioners or Board

(a) The deputy commissioner or Board shall have power to preserve and enforce order during any such proceedings; to issue subpoenas for, to administer oaths to, and to compel the attendance and testimony of witnesses, or the production of books, papers, documents, and other evidence, or the taking of depositions before any designated individual competent to administer oaths; to examine witnesses; and to do all things conformable to law which may be necessary to enable him effectively to discharge the duties of his office.

(b) If any person in proceedings before a deputy commissioner or Board disobeys or resists any lawful order or process, or misbehaves during a hearing or so near the place thereof as to obstruct the same, or neglects to produce, after having been ordered to do so, any pertinent book, paper, or document, or refuses to appear after having been subpoenaed, or upon appearing refuses to take the oath as a witness, or after having taken the oath refuses to be examined according to law, the deputy commissioner or Board shall certify the facts to the district court having jurisdiction in the place in which he is sitting (or to the Supreme Court of the District of Columbia [United States District Court for the District of Columbia] if he is sitting in such District) which shall thereupon in a summary manner hear the evidence as to the acts complained of, and, if the evidence so warrants, punish such person in the same manner and to the same extent as for a contempt committed before the court, or commit such person upon the same conditions as if the doing of the forbidden act had occurred with reference to the process of or in the presence of the court.

§ 928. Fees for services

(a) *Attorney's fee; successful prosecution of case.* If the employer or carrier declines to pay any compensation on or before the thirtieth day after receiving written notice of a claim for compensation having been filed from the deputy commissioner, on the ground that there is no liability for compensation within the provisions of this Act, and the person seeking benefits shall thereafter have utilized the services of an attorney at law in the successful prosecution of his claim, there shall be awarded, in addition to the award of compensation, in a compensation order, a reasonable attorney's fee against the employer or carrier in an amount approved by the deputy commissioner, Board, or court, as the case may be, which shall be paid directly by the employer or carrier to the attorney for the claimant in a lump sum after the compensation order becomes final.

(b) *Attorney's fee; successful prosecution for additional compensation; independent medical evaluation of disability controversy; restriction of other assessments.* If the employer or carrier pays or tenders payment of compensation without an award pursuant to section 14(a) and (b) of this Act [33 USC § 914(a), (b)], and thereafter a controversy develops over the amount of additional compensation, if any, to which the employee may be entitled, the deputy commissioner or Board shall set the matter for an informal conference and following such conference the deputy commissioner or Board shall recommend in writing a disposition of the controversy. If the employer or carrier refuse to accept such written recommendation, within fourteen days after its receipt by them, they shall pay or tender to the employee in writing the additional compensation, if any, to which they believe the employee is entitled. If the employee refuses to accept such payment or tender of compensation, and thereafter utilizes the services of an attorney at law, and if the compensation thereafter awarded is greater than the amount paid or tendered by the employer or carrier, a reasonable attorney's fee based solely upon the difference between the amount awarded and the amount tendered or paid shall be awarded in addition to the amount of compensation. The foregoing sentence shall not apply if the controversy relates to degree or length of disability, and if the employer or carrier offers to submit the case for evaluation by physicians employed or selected by the Secretary, as authorized in section 7(e) [33 USC § 907(e)] and offers to tender an amount of compensation based upon the degree or length of disability found by the independent medical report at such time as an evaluation of disability can be made. If the claimant is successful in review proceedings before the Board or court in any such case an award may be made in favor of the claimant and against the employer or carrier for a reasonable attorney's fee for claimant's counsel in accord with the above provisions. In all other cases any claim for legal services shall not be assessed against the employer or carrier.

(c) *Approval; payment; lien.* In all cases fees for attorneys representing the claimant shall be approved in the manner herein provided. If any proceedings are had before the Board or any court for review of any action, award, order, or decision, the Board or court may approve an attorney's fee for the work done before it by the attorney for the claimant. An approved attorney's fee, in cases in which the obligation to pay the fee is upon the claimant, may be made a lien upon the compensation due under an award; and the deputy commissioner, Board, or court shall fix in the award approving the fee, such lien and manner of payment.

(d) *Costs; witnesses' fees and mileage; prohibition against diminution of compensation to claimant.* In cases where an attorney's fee is awarded against an employer or carrier there may be further assessed against such employer or carrier as costs, fees and mileage for necessary witnesses attending the hearing at the instance of claimant. Both the necessity for the witness and the reasonableness of the fees of expert witnesses must be approved by the hearing officer, the Board, or the court, as the case may be. The amounts awarded against an employer or carrier as attorney's fees, costs, fees and mileage for witnesses shall not in any respect affect or diminish the compensation payable under this Act.

(e) *Unapproved fees; solicitation; penalty.* A person who receives a fee, gratuity, or other consideration on account of services rendered as a representative of a claimant, unless the consideration is approved by the deputy commissioner, administrative law judge, Board, or court, or who makes it a business to solicit employment for a lawyer, or for himself, with respect to a claim or award for compensation under this Act, shall, upon conviction thereof, for each offense be punished by a fine of not more than $ 1,000 or be imprisoned for not more than one year, or both.

§ 929. Record of injury or death

Every employer shall keep a record in respect of any injury to an employee. Such record shall contain such information of disease, other disability, or death in respect of such injury as the Secretary may be regulation require, and shall be available to inspection by the Secretary or by any State authority at such times and under such conditions as the Secretary may by regulation prescribe.

§ 930. Reports to Secretary

(a) *Time for sending; contents; copy to deputy commissioner.* Within ten days from the date of any injury, which causes loss of one or more shifts of work, or death or from the date that the employer has knowledge of a disease or infection in respect of such injury, the employer shall send to the Secretary a report setting forth (1) the name, address, and business of the employer; (2) the name, address, and occupation of the employee; (3) the cause and nature of the injury or death; (4) the year, month, day, and hour when and the particular locality where the injury or death occurred; and (5) such other information as the Secretary may require. A copy of such report shall be sent at the same time to the deputy commissioner in the compensation district in which the injury occurred. Notwithstanding the requirements of this subsection, each employer shall keep a record of each and every injury regardless of whether such injury results in the loss of one or more shifts of work.

(b) *Additional reports.* Additional reports in respect of such injury and of the condition of such employee shall be sent by the employer to the Secretary and to such deputy commissioner at such times and in such manner as the Secretary may prescribe.

(c) *Use as evidence.* Any report provided for in subdivision (a) or (b) shall not be evidence of any fact stated in such report in any proceeding in respect of such injury or death on account of which the report is made.

(d) *Compliance by mailing.* The mailing of any such report and copy in a stamped envelope, within the time prescribed in subdivisions (a) or (b), to the Secretary and deputy commissioner, respectively, shall be a compliance with this section.

(e) *Penalty for failure or refusal to send report.* Any employer, insurance carrier, or self-insured employer who knowingly and willfully fails or refuses to send any report required by this section or knowingly or willfully makes a false statement or misrepresentation in any such report shall be subject to a civil penalty not to exceed $ 10,000 for each such failure, refusal, false statement, or misrepresentation.

(f) *Tolling provision.* Where the employer or the carrier has been given notice, or the employer (or his agent in charge of the business in the place where the injury occurred) or the carrier has knowledge, of any injury or death of an employee and fails, neglects, or refuses to file report thereof as required by the provisions of subdivision (a) of this section, the limitations in subdivision (a) of section 13 of this Act [33 USC § 913(a)] shall not begin to run against the claim of the injured employee or his dependents entitled to compensation, or in favor of either the employer or the carrier, until such report shall have been furnished as required by the provisions of subdivision (a) of this section.

§ 931. Penalty for misrepresentation; prosecution of claims

(a)(1) Any claimant or representative of a claimant who knowingly and willfully makes a false statement or representation for the purpose of obtaining a benefit or payment under this Act shall be guilty of a felony, and on conviction thereof shall be punished by a fine not to exceed $10,000, by imprisonment not to exceed five years, or by both.

(2) The United States attorney for the district in which the injury is alleged to have occurred shall make every reasonable effort to promptly investigate each complaint made under this subsection.

(b)(1) No representation fee of a claimant's representative shall be approved by the deputy commissioner, an administrative law judge, the Board, or a court pursuant to section 28 of this Act [33 USC § 928], if the claimant's representative is on the list of individuals who are disqualified from representing claimants under this Act maintained by the Secretary pursuant to paragraph (2) of this subsection.

(2)(A) The Secretary shall annually prepare a list of those individuals in each compensation district who have represented claimants for a fee in cases under this Act and who are not authorized to represent claimants. The names of individuals contained on the list required under this subparagraph shall be made available to employees and employers in each compensation district through posting and in such other forms as the Secretary may prescribe.

(B) Individuals shall be included on the list of those not authorized to represent claimants under this Act if the Secretary determines under this section, in accordance with the procedure provided in subsection (j) of section 7 of this Act [33 USC § 907(j)], that such individual –

(i) has been convicted (without regard to pending appeal) of any crime in connection with the representation of a claimant under this Act or any workers' compensation statute;

(ii) has engaged in fraud in connection with the presentation of a claim under this or any workers' compensation statute, including, but not limited to, knowingly making false representations, concealing or attempting to conceal material facts with respect to a claim, or soliciting or otherwise procuring false testimony;

(iii) has been prohibited from representing claimants before any other workers' compensation agency for reasons of professional misconduct which are similar in nature to those which would be grounds for disqualification under this paragraph; or

(iv) has accepted fees for representing claimants under this Act which were not approved, or which were in excess of the amount approved pursuant to section 28 [33 USC § 928].

(C) Notwithstanding subparagraph (B), no individual who is on the list required to be maintained by the Secretary pursuant to this section shall be prohibited from presenting his or her own claim or from representing without fee, a claimant who is a spouse, mother, father, sister, brother, or child of such individual.

(D) A determination under subparagraph (A) shall remain in effect for a period of not less than three years and until the Secretary finds and gives notice to the public that there is reasonable assurance that the basis for the determination will not reoccur.

(3) No employee shall be liable to pay a representation fee to any representative whose fee has been disallowed by reason of the operation of this paragraph.

(4) The Secretary shall issue such rules and regulations as are necessary to carry out this section.

(c) A person including, but not limited to, an employer, his duly authorized agent, or an employee of an insurance carrier who knowingly and willfully makes a false statement or representation for the purpose of reducing, denying, or terminating benefits to an injured employee, or his dependents pursuant to section 9 [33 USC § 909]if the injury results in death, shall be punished by a fine not to exceed $ 10,000, by imprisonment not to exceed five years, or by both.

§ 932. Security for compensation

(a) Every employer shall secure the payment of compensation under this Act –

(1) By insuring and keeping insured the payment of such compensation with any stock company or mutual company or association, or with any other person or fund, while such person or fund is authorized (A) under the laws of the United States or of any State, to insure workmen's compensation, and (B) by the Secretary, to insure payment of compensation under this Act; or

(2) By furnishing satisfactory proof to the Secretary of his financial ability to pay such compensation and receiving an authorization from the Secretary to pay such compensation directly. The Secretary may, as a condition to such authorization, require such employer to deposit in a depository designated by the Secretary either an indemnity bond or securities (at the option of the employer) of a kind and in an amount determined by the Secretary, based on the em-

ployer's financial condition, the employer's previous record of payments, and other relevant factors, and subject to such conditions as the Secretary may prescribe, which shall include authorization to the Secretary in case of default to sell any such securities sufficient to pay compensation awards or to bring suit upon such bonds, to procure prompt payment of compensation under this Act. Any employer securing compensation in accordance with the provisions of this paragraph shall be known as a self-insurer.

(b) In granting authorization to any carrier to insure payment of compensation under this Act, the Secretary may take into consideration the recommendation of any State authority having supervision over carriers or over workmen's compensation, and may authorize any carrier to insure the payment of compensation under this Act in a limited territory. Any marine protection and indemnity mutual insurance corporation or association, authorized to write insurance against liability for loss or damage from personal injury and death, and for other losses and damages, incidental to or in respect of the ownership, operation, or chartering of vessels on a mutual assessment plan, shall be deemed a qualified carrier to insure compensation under this Act. The Secretary may suspend or revoke any such authorization for good cause shown after a hearing at which the carrier shall be entitled to be heard in person or by counsel and to present evidence. No suspension or revocation shall affect the liability of any carrier already incurred.

§ 933. Compensation for injuries where third persons are liable

(a) *Election of remedies.* If on account of a disability or death for which compensation is payable under this Act, the person entitled to such compensation determines that some person other than the employer or a person or persons in his employ is liable in damages, he need not elect whether to receive such compensation or to recover damages against such third person.

(b) *Acceptance of compensation acting as assignment.* Acceptance of compensation under an award in a compensation order filed by the deputy commissioner, an administrative law judge, or the Board shall operate as an assignment to the employer of all rights of the person entitled to compensation to recover damages against such third person unless such person shall commence an action against such third person within six months after such acceptance. If the employer fails to commence an action against such third person within ninety days after the cause of action is assigned under this section, the right to bring such action shall revert to the person entitled to compensation. For the purpose of this subsection, the term "award" with respect to a compensation order means a formal order issued by the deputy commissioner, an administrative law judge, or Board.

(c) *Payment into section 944 fund operating as assignment.* The payment of such compensation into the fund established in section 44 [33 USC § 944] shall operate as an assignment to the employer of all right of the legal representative of the deceased (hereinafter referred to as "representative") to recover damages against such third person.

(d) *Institution of proceedings or compromise by assignee.* Such employer on account of such assignment may either institute proceedings for the recovery of such damages or may compromise with such third person either without or after instituting such proceeding.

(e) *Recoveries by assignee.* Any amount recovered by such employer on account of such assignment, whether or not as the result of a compromise, shall be distributed as follows:

(1) The employer shall retain an amount equal to –

(A) the expenses incurred by him in respect to such proceedings or compromise (including a reasonable attorney's fee as determined by the deputy commissioner or Board);

(B) the cost of all benefits actually furnished by him to the employee under section 7 [33 USC § 907];

(C) all amounts paid as compensation;

(D) the present value of all amounts thereafter payable as compensation, such present value to be computed in accordance with a schedule prepared by the Secretary, and the present value of the cost of all benefits thereafter to be furnished under section 7 [33 USC § 907], to be estimated by the deputy commissioner, and the amounts so computed and estimated to be retained by the employer as a trust fund to pay such compensation and the cost of such benefits as they become due, and to pay any sum finally remaining in excess thereof to the person entitled to compensation or to the representative; and

(2) The employer shall pay any excess to the person entitled to compensation or to the representative.

(f) *Institution of proceedings by person entitled to compensation.* If the person entitled to compensation institutes proceedings within the period prescribed in section 33(b) [subsec. (b) of this section] the employer shall be required to pay as compensation under this Act, a sum equal to the excess of the amount which the Secretary determines is payable on account of such injury or death over the net amount recovered against such third person. Such net amount shall be equal to the actual amount recovered less the expenses reasonably incurred by such person in respect to such proceedings (including reasonable attorneys' fees).

(g) *Settlement with third person.*

(1) If the person entitled to compensation (or the person's representative) enters into a settlement with a third person referred to in subsection (a) for an amount less than the compensation to which the person (or the person's representative) would be entitled under this Act, the employer shall be liable for compensation as determined under subsection (f) only if written approval of the settlement is obtained from the employer and the employer's carrier, before the settlement is executed, and by the person entitled to compensation (or the person's representative). The approval shall be made on a form provided by the Secretary and shall be filed in the office of the deputy commissioner within thirty days after the settlement is entered into.

(2) If no written approval of the settlement is obtained and filed as required by paragraph (1), or if the employee fails to notify the employer of any settlement obtained from or judgment rendered against a third person, all rights to compensation and medical benefits under this Act shall be terminated, regardless of whether the employer or the employer's insurer has made payments or acknowledged entitlement to benefits under this Act.

(3) Any payments by the special fund established under section 44 [33 USC § 944] shall be a lien upon the proceeds of any settlement obtained from or judgment rendered against a third person referred to under subsection (a). Notwithstanding any other provision of law, such lien shall be enforceable against such proceeds, regardless of whether the Secretary on behalf of the special fund has agreed to or has received actual notice of the settlement or judgment.

(4) Any payments by a trust fund described in section 17 [33 USC § 917] shall be a lien upon the proceeds of any settlement obtained from or judgment recorded against a third person referred to under subsection (a). Such lien shall have priority over a lien under paragraph (3) of this subsection.

(h) *Subrogation.* Where the employer is insured and the insurance carrier has assumed the payment of the compensation, the insurance carrier shall be subrogated to all the rights of the employer under this section.

(i) *Right to compensation as exclusive remedy.* The right to compensation or benefits under this Act shall be the exclusive remedy to an employee when he is injured, or to his eligible survivors or legal representatives if he is killed, by the negligence or wrong of any other person or persons in the same employ: Provided, That this provision shall not affect the liability of a person other than an officer or employee of the employer.

§ 934. Compensation notice

Every employer who has secured compensation under the provisions of this Act shall keep posted in a conspicuous place or places in and about his place or places of business typewritten or printed notices, in accordance with a form prescribed by the Secretary, stating that such employer has secured the payment of compensation in accordance with the provisions of this Act. Such notices shall contain the name and address of the carrier, if any, with whom the employer has secured payment of compensation and the date of the expiration of the policy.

§ 935. Substitution of carrier for employer

In any case where the employer is not a self-insurer, in order that the liability for compensation imposed by this Act may be most effectively discharged by the employer, and in order that the administration of this Act in respect of such liability may be facilitated, the Secretary shall by regulation provide for the discharge, by the carrier for such employer, of such obligations and duties of the employer in respect of such liability, imposed by this Act upon the employer, as it considers proper in order to effectuate the provisions of this Act. For such purposes (1) notice to or knowledge of an employer of the occurrence of the injury shall be notice to or knowledge of the carrier, (2) jurisdiction of the employer by a deputy commissioner, the Board, or the Secretary, or any court under this Act shall be jurisdiction of the carrier, and (3) any requirement by a deputy commissioner, the Board, or the Secretary, or any court under any compensation order, finding, or decision shall be binding upon the carrier in the same manner and to the same extent as upon the employer.

§ 936. Insurance policies

(a) Every policy or contract of insurance issued under authority of this Act shall contain (1) a provision to carry out the provisions of section 35 [33 USC § 935], and (2) a provision that insolvency or bankruptcy of the employer and/or discharge therein shall not relieve the carrier from payment of compensation for disability or death sustained by an employee during the life of such policy or contract.

(b) No contract or policy of insurance issued by a carrier under this Act shall be canceled prior to the date specified in such contract or policy for its expiration until at least thirty days have elapsed after a notice of cancellation has been sent to the deputy commissioner and to the employer in accordance with the provisions of subdivision (c) of section 12 [33 USC § 912(c).]

§ 937. Certificate of compliance with this Act

No stevedoring firm shall be employed in any compensation district by a vessel or by hull owners until it presents to such vessel or hull owners a certificate issued by a deputy commissioner assigned to such district that it has complied with the provisions of this Act [33 USC §§ 901 et seq.] requiring the securing of compensation to its employees. Any person violating the provisions of this section shall be punished by a fine of not more than $ 1,000, or by imprisonment for not more than one year, or by both such fine and imprisonment.

§ 938. Penalty for failure to secure payment of compensation

(a) *Failure to secure payment of compensation.* Any employer required to secure the payment of compensation under this Act who fails to secure such compensation shall be guilty of a misdemeanor and, upon conviction thereof, shall be punished by a fine of not more than $ 10,000, or by imprisonment for not more than one year, or by both such fine and imprisonment; and in any case where such employer is a corporation, the president, secretary, and treasurer thereof shall be also severally liable to such fine or imprisonment as herein provided for the failure of such corporation to secure the payment of compensation; and such president, secretary, and treasurer shall be severally personally liable, jointly with such corporation, for any compensation or other benefit which may accrue under the said Act in respect to any injury which may occur to any employee of such corporation while it shall so fail to secure the payment of compensation as required by section 32 of this Act [33 USC § 932].

(b) *Avoiding payment of compensation.* Any employer who knowingly transfers, sells, encumbers, assigns, or in any manner disposes of, conceals, secretes, or destroys any property belonging to such employer, after one of his employees has been injured within the purview of this Act, and with intent to avoid the payment of compensation under this Act to such employee or his dependents, shall be guilty of a misdemeanor and, upon conviction thereof, shall be punished by a fine of not more than $ 10,000, or by imprisonment for not more than one year, or by both such fine and imprisonment; and in any case where such employer is a corporation, the president, secretary, and treasurer thereof shall be also severally liable to such penalty of imprisonment as well as jointly liable with such corporation for such fine.

(c) *Effect on other liability of employer.* This section shall not affect any other liability of the employer under this Act.

§ 939. Administration by Secretary

(a) *Prescribing rules and regulations; appointing and fixing compensation of employees; making expenditures.* Except as otherwise specifically provided, the Secretary shall administer the provisions of this Act, and for such purpose the Secretary is authorized (1) to make such rules and regulations; (2) to appoint and fix the compensation of such temporary technical assistants and medical advisers, and, subject to the provisions of the civil service laws, to appoint, and, in accordance with the Classification Act of 1923, to fix the compensation of such deputy commissioners (except deputy commissioners appointed under subdivision (a) of section 40 [33 USC § 940(a)]) and other officers and employees; and (3) to make such expenditures (including expenditures for personal services and rent at the seat of government and elsewhere, for law books, books of reference, periodicals, and for printing and binding) as may be necessary in the administration of this Act. All expenditures of the Secretary in the administration of this Act shall be allowed and paid as provided in section 45 [33 USC § 945] upon the presentation of itemized vouchers therefor approved by the Secretary.

(b) *Establishing compensation districts.* The Secretary shall establish compensation districts, to include the high seas and the areas within the United States to which this Act applies, and shall assign to each such district one or more deputy commissioners, as the Secretary deems advisable. Judicial proceedings under sections 18 and 21 of this Act [33 USC §§ 918, 921] in respect of any injury or death occurring on the high seas shall be instituted in the district court within whose territorial jurisdiction is located the office of the deputy commissioner having jurisdiction in respect of such injury or death (or in the Supreme Court of the District of Columbia [United States District Court for the District of Columbia] if such office is located in such District).

(c) *Furnishing information and assistance; directing vocational rehabilitation.*

(1) The Secretary shall, upon request, provide persons covered by this Act with information and assistance relating to the Act's coverage and compensation and the procedures for obtaining such compensation and including assistance in

processing a claim. The Secretary may, upon request, provide persons covered by this Act with legal assistance in processing a claim. The Secretary shall also provide employees receiving compensation information on medical, manpower, and vocational rehabilitation services and assist such employees in obtaining the best such services available.

(2) The Secretary shall direct the vocational rehabilitation of permanently disabled employees and shall arrange with the appropriate public or private agencies in State or Territories, possessions, or the District of Columbia for such rehabilitation. The Federal Board for Vocational Education shall cooperate with the Secretary in such educational work. The Secretary may in its discretion furnish such prosthetic appliances or other apparatus made necessary by an injury upon which an award has been made under this Act to render a disabled employee fit to engage in a remunerative occupation. Where necessary rehabilitation services are not available otherwise, the Secretary of Labor may, in his discretion, use the fund provided for in section 44 [44 USC § 944] in such amounts as may be necessary to procure such services, including necessary prosthetic appliances or other apparatus. This fund shall also be available in such amounts as may be authorized in annual appropriations for the Department of Labor for the costs of administering this subsection.

§ 940. Deputy commissioners

(a) *Appointment; use of personnel and facilities of boards, commissions, or other agencies; expenses and salaries.* The Secretary may appoint as deputy commissioners any member of any board, commission [Secretary], or other agency of a State to act as deputy commissioner for any compensation district or part thereof in such State, and may make arrangements with such board, commission [Secretary], or other agency for the use of the personnel and facilities thereof in the administration of this Act. The Secretary may make such arrangements as may be deemed advisable by it for the payment of expenses of such board, commission [Secretary], or other agency, incurred in the administration of this Act pursuant to this section, and for the payment of salaries to such board, commission [Secretary], or other agency, or the members thereof, and may pay any amounts agreed upon to the proper officers of the State, upon vouchers approved by the Secretary.

(b) *Appointment in Territories and District of Columbia; compensation.* In any Territory of the United States or in the District of Columbia a person holding an office under the United States may be appointed deputy commissioner and for services rendered as deputy commissioner may be paid compensation, in addition to that he is receiving from the United States, in an amount fixed by the Secretary in accordance with the Classification Act of 1923.

(c) *Transfers to other districts; temporary details.* Deputy commissioners (except deputy commissioners appointed under subdivision (a) of this section) may be transferred from one compensation district to another and may be temporarily detailed from one compensation district for service in another in the discretion of the Secretary.

(d) *Maintaining offices.* Each deputy commissioner shall maintain and keep open during reasonable business hours an office, at a place designated by the Secretary, for the transaction of business under this Act, at which office he shall keep his official records and papers. Such office shall be furnished and equipped by the Secretary, who shall also furnish the deputy commissioner with all necessary clerical and, other assistants, records, books, blanks, and supplies. Wherever practicable such office shall be located in a building owned or leased by the United States; otherwise the Secretary shall rent suitable quarters.

(e) *Records and papers.* If any deputy commissioner is removed from office, or for any reason ceases to act as such deputy commissioner, all of his official records and papers and office equipment shall be transferred to his successor in office or, if there be no successor, then to the Secretary or to a deputy commissioner designated by the Secretary.

(f) *Conflict of interest.* Neither a deputy commissioner or Board member nor any business associate of a deputy commissioner shall appear as attorney in any proceeding under this Act, and no deputy commissioner or Board member shall act in any such case in which he is interested, or when he is employed by any party in interest or related to any party in interest by consanguinity or affinity within the third degree, as determined by the common law.

§ 941. Safety rules and regulations

(a) *Safe place of employment; installation of safety devices and safeguards.* Every employer shall furnish and maintain employment and places of employment which shall be reasonably safe for his employees in all employments covered by this Act and shall install, furnish, maintain, and use such devices and safeguards with particular reference to equipment used by and working conditions established by such employers as the Secretary may determine by regulation or order to be reasonably necessary to protect the life, health, and safety of such employees, and to render safe such employment and places of employment, and to prevent injury to his employees. However, the Secretary may not make determinations by regulation or order under this section as to matters within the scope of title 52 of the Revised Statutes and Acts supplementary or amendatory thereto, the Act of June 15, 1917 (ch. 30, 40 Stat. 220), as amended or section 4(e) of the Act of August 7, 1953 (ch. 345, 67 Stat. 462), as amended [43 USC § 1333(e)].

(b) *Studies and investigations by the Secretary.* The Secretary, in enforcing and administering the provisions of this section, is authorized in addition to such other powers and duties as are conferred upon him –

(1) to make studies and investigations with respect to safety provisions and the causes and prevention of injuries in employments covered by this Act, and in making such studies and investigations to cooperate with any agency of the United States or with any State agency engaged in similar work;

(2) to utilize the services of any agency of the United States or any State agency engaged in similar work (with the consent of such agency) in connection with the administration of this section;

(3) to promote uniformity in safety standards in employments covered by this Act through cooperative action with any agency of the United States or with any State agency engaged in similar work;

(4) to provide for the establishment and supervision of programs for the education and training of employers and employees in the recognition, avoidance, and prevention of unsafe working conditions in employments covered by this Act, and to consult with and advise employers as to the best means of preventing injuries;

(5) to hold such hearings, issue such orders, and make such decisions, based upon findings of fact, as are deemed to be necessary to enforce the provisions of this section, and for such purposes the Secretary and the district courts shall have the authority and jurisdiction provided by section 5 of the Act of June 30, 1936 (ch. 881, 49 Stat. 2036), as amended [41 USC § 39], and the Secretary shall be represented in any court proceedings as provided in the Act of May 4, 1928 (ch. 502, 45 Stat. 490), as amended [33 USC § 921a].

(c) *Inspection of places and practices of employment.* The Secretary or his authorized representative may inspect such places of employment, question such employees, and investigate such conditions, practices, or matters in connection with employment subject to this Act, as he may deem appropriate to determine whether any person has violated any provision of this section, or any rule or regulation issued thereunder, or which may aid in the enforcement of the provisions of this section. No employer or other person shall refuse to admit the Secretary or his authorized representatives to any such place or shall refuse to permit any such inspection.

(d) *Requests for advice; variations from safety rules and regulations.* Any employer may request the advice of the Secretary or his authorized representative, in complying with the requirements of any rule or regulation adopted to carry out the provisions of this section. In case of practical difficulties or unnecessary hardships, the Secretary in his discretion may grant variations from any such rule or regulation, or particular provisions thereof, and permit the use of other or different devices if he finds that the purpose of the rule or regulation will be observed by the variation and the safety of employees will be equally secured thereby. Any person affected by such rule or regulation, or his agent, may request the Secretary to grant such variation, stating in writing the grounds on which his request is based. Any authorization by the Secretary of a variation shall be in writing, shall describe the conditions under which the variation shall be permitted, and shall be published as provided in section 3 of the Administrative Procedure Act (ch. 324, 60 Stat. 237), as amended. A properly indexed record of all variations shall be kept in the office of the Secretary and open to public inspection.

(e) *Jurisdiction to restrain violations.* The United States district courts, together with the District Court for the Territory of Alaska, shall have jurisdiction for cause shown, in any action brought by the Secretary, represented as provided in the Act of May 4, 1928 (ch. 502, 45 Stat. 490), as amended [33 USC § 921a], to restrain violations of this section or of any rule, regulation, or order of the Secretary adopted to carry out the provisions of this section.

(f) *Violations and penalties.* Any employer who, willfully, violates or fails or refuses to comply with the provisions of subsection (a) of this section, or with any lawful rule, regulation, or order adopted to carry out the provisions of this section, and any employer or other person who willfully interferes with, hinders, or delays the Secretary or his authorized representative in carrying out his duties under subsection (c) of this section by refusing to admit the Secretary or his authorized representative to any place, or to permit the inspection or examination of any employment or place of employment, or who willfully hinders or delays the Secretary or his authorized representative in the performance of his duties in the enforcement of this section, shall be guilty of an offense, and, upon conviction thereof, shall be punished for each offense by a fine of not less than $ 100 nor more than $ 3,000; and in any case where such employer is a corporation, the officer who willfully permits any such violation to occur shall be guilty of an offense, and, upon conviction thereof, shall be punished also for each offense by a fine of not less than $ 100 nor more than $ 3,000. The liability hereunder shall not affect any other liability of the employer under this Act.

(g) *Inapplicability to certain employments.*

(1) The provisions of this section shall not apply in the case of any employment relating to the operations for the exploration, production, or transportation by pipeline of mineral resources upon the navigable waters of the United States, nor under the authority of the Act of August 7, 1953 (ch. 345, 67 Stat. 462) [43 USC §§ 1331 et seq.], nor in the case of any employment in connection with lands (except filled in, made or reclaimed lands) beneath the navigable waters as defined in the Act of May 22, 1953 (ch. 65, 67 Stat. 29) [43 USC §§ 1301 et seq.] nor in the case of any employment for which compensation in case of disability or death is provided for employees under the authority of the Act of May 17, 1928 (ch. 612, 45 Stat. 600), as amended, nor under the authority of the Act of August 16, 1941 (ch. 357, 55 Stat. 622), as amended [42 USC §§ 1651 et seq.].

(2) The provisions of this section, with the exception of paragraph (1) of subsection (b), shall not be applied under the authority of the Act of September 7, 1916 (ch. 458, 39 Stat. 742), as amended.

§ 942. Annual report

The Secretary shall make to Congress at the beginning of each regular session, commencing at the beginning of the second regular session after the enactment of the Longshore and Harbor Workers' Compensation Act Amendments of 1984 [enacted Sept. 28, 1984], a report of the administration of this Act for the preceding fiscal year, including a detailed statement of receipts of and expenditures from the fund established in section 44 [33 USC § 944], together with such recommendations as the Secretary deems advisable.

§ 943. [Repealed]

§ 944. Special fund

(a) *Establishment; administration; custody, trust.* There is hereby established in the Treasury of the United States a special fund. Such fund shall be administered by the Secretary. The Treasurer of the United States shall be the custodian of such fund, and all moneys and securities in such fund shall be held in trust by such Treasurer and shall not be money or property of the United States.

(b) *Disbursements; bond of custodian.* The Treasurer is authorized to disburse moneys from such fund only upon order of the Secretary. He shall be required to give bond in an amount to be fixed and with securities to be approved by the Secretary of the Treasury and the Comptroller General of the United States conditioned upon the faithful performance of his duty as custodian of such fund.

(c) *Payments into fund.* Payments into such fund shall be made as follows:

(1) Whenever the Secretary determines that there is no person entitled under this Act to compensation for the death of an employee which would otherwise be compensable under this Act, the appropriate employer shall pay $ 5,000 as compensation for the death of such an employee.

(2) At the beginning of each calendar year the Secretary shall estimate the probable expenses of the fund during that calendar year and the amount of payments required (and the schedule therefor) to maintain adequate reserves in the fund. Each carrier and self-insurer shall make payments into the fund on a prorated assessment by the Secretary determined by –

(A) computing the ratio (expressed as a percent) of (i) the carrier's or self-insured's workers' compensation payments under this Act during the preceding calendar year, to (ii) the total of such payments by all carriers and self-insureds under this Act during such year;

(B) computing the ratio (expressed as a percent) of (i) the payments under section 8(f) of this Act [33 USC § 908(f)] during the preceding calendar year which are attributable to the carrier or self-insured, to (ii) the total of such payments during such year attributable to all carriers and self-insureds;

(C) dividing the sum of the percentages computed under subparagraphs (A) and (B) for the carrier or self-insured by two; and

(D) multiplying the percent computed under subparagraph (C) by such probable expenses of the fund (as determined under the first sentence of this paragraph).

(3) All amounts collected as finds and penalties under the provisions of this Act shall be paid into such fund.

(d) *Investigations; records, availability; recordkeeping; provisions of sections 49 and 50 of title 15 applicable to Secretary.*

(1) For the purpose of making rules, regulations, and determinations under this section under and for providing enforcement thereof, the Secretary may investigate and gather appropriate data from each carrier and self-insurer. For that purpose, the Secretary may enter and inspect such places and records (and make such transcriptions thereof), question such employees, and investigate such facts, conditions, practices, or matters as he may deem necessary or appropriate.

(2) Each carrier and self-insurer shall make, keep, and preserve such records, and make such reports and provide such additional information, as prescribed by regulation or order of the Secretary, as the Secretary deems necessary or appropriate to carry out his responsibilities under this section.

(3) For the purpose of any hearing or investigation related to determinations or the enforcement of the provisions of this section, the provisions of sections 9 and 10 (relating to the attendance of witnesses and the production of books, papers, and documents) of the Federal Trade Commission Act of September 16, 1914, as amended (U.S.C., title 15, secs. 49 and 50) [15 USC §§ 49, 50], are hereby made applicable to the jurisdiction, powers, and duties of the Secretary of Labor.

(e) *Depositories; investments.* The Treasurer of the United States shall deposit any moneys paid into such fund into such depository banks as the Secretary may designate and may invest any portion of the funds which, in the opinion of the Secretary, is not needed for current requirements, in bonds or notes of the United States or of any Federal land bank.

(f) *Limitation of liability.* Neither the United States nor the Secretary shall be liable in respect of payments authorized under section 8 [33 USC § 908] in an amount greater than the money or property deposited in or belonging to such fund.

(g) *Audit by Comptroller General; finality of payment determinations; credits of disbursing officers.* The Comptroller General of the United States shall audit the account for such fund, but the action of the Secretary in making payments from such fund shall be final and not subject to review, and the Comptroller General is authorized and directed to allow credit in the accounts of any disbursing officer of the Secretary for payments made from such fund authorized by the Secretary.

(h) *Civil actions for civil penalties.* All civil penalties and unpaid assessments provided for in this Act shall be collected by civil suit brought by the Secretary.

(i) Proceeds available for certain payments. The proceeds of this fund shall be available for payments:

(1) Pursuant to section 10 [33 USC § 910] with respect to certain initial and subsequent annual adjustments in compensation for total permanent disability or death.

(2) Under section 8(f) and (g), under section 18(b), and under section 39(c) [33 USC §§ 908(f) and (g), 918(b), and 939(c)].

(3) To repay the sums deposited in the fund pursuant to subsection (d).

(4) To defray the expense of making examinations as provided in section 7(e) [33 USC § 907(e)].

(j) *Audit to be included in report.* The fund shall be audited annually and the results of such audit shall be included in the annual report required by section 42 [33 USC § 942].

(k) [Redesignated]

§§ 945—947. [Repealed]

§ 948. Laws inapplicable

Nothing in sections 4283, 4284, 4285, 4286, or 4289 of the Revised Statutes, as amended [46 USC §§ 183, 184—186, 188], nor in section 18 of the Act entitled "An act to remove certain burdens on the American merchant marine and encourage the American foreign carrying trade, and for other purposes," approved June 26, 1884, as amended [46 USC § 189], shall be held to limit the amount for which recovery may be had (1) in any suit at law or in admiralty where an employer has failed to secure compensation as required by this Act [33 USC §§ 901 et seq.], or (2) in any proceeding for compensation, any addition to compensation, or any civil penalty.

§ 948a. Discrimination against employees who bring proceedings; penalties; deposit of payments in special funds; civil actions; entitlement to restoration of employment and compensation, qualifications requirement; liability of employer for penalties and payments; insurance policy exemption from liability

It shall be unlawful for any employer or his duly authorized agent to discharge or in any other manner discriminate against an employee as to his employment because such employee has claimed or attempted to claim compensation from such employer, or because he has testified or is about to testify in a proceeding under this chapter. The discharge or refusal to employ a person who has been adjudicated to have filed a fraudulent claim for compensation is not a violation of this section. Any employer who violates this section shall be liable to a penalty of not less than $1,000 or more than $5,000, as may be determined by the deputy commissioner. All such penalties shall be paid to the deputy commissioner for deposit in the special fund as described in section 944 of this title, and if not paid may be recovered in a civil action brought in the appropriate United States district court. Any employee so discriminated against shall be restored to his employment and shall be compensated by his employer for any loss of wages arising out of such discrimination: Provided, That if such employee shall cease to be qualified to perform the duties of his employment, he shall not be entitled to such restoration and compensation. The employer alone and not his carrier shall be liable for such penalties and payments. Any provision in an insurance policy undertaking to relieve the employer from the liability for such penalties and payments shall be void.

§ 949. Effect of unconstitutionality

If any part of this Act is adjudged unconstitutional by the courts, and such adjudication has the effect of invalidating any payment of compensation under this Act, the period intervening between the time the injury was sustained and the time of such adjudication shall not be computed as a part of the time prescribed by law for the commencement of any action against the employer in respect of such injury; but the amount of any compensation paid under this Act on account of such injury shall be deducted from the amount of damages awarded in such action in respect of such injury.

§ 950. Separability provision

If any provision of this Act is declared unconstitutional or the applicability thereof to any person or circumstances is held invalid, the validity of the remainder of the Act and the applicability of such provision to other persons and circumstances shall not be affected thereby.

§§ 951—980. [Reserved]

Appendix B

Code of Federal Regulations

SUBCHAPTER A—LONGSHOREMEN'S AND HARBOR WORKERS' COMPENSATION ACT AND RELATED STATUTES

PART 701—GENERAL; ADMINISTERING AGENCY; DEFINITIONS AND USE OF TERMS

AUTHORITY: 5 U.S.C. 301; Reorg. Plan No. 6 of 1950, 15 FR 3174, 64 Stat. 1263; 33 U.S.C. 939; 36 D.C.Code 501 et seq.; 42 U.S.C. 1651 et seq.; 43 U.S.C. 1331; 5 U.S.C. 6171 et seq.; Secretary's Order 1-89; Employment Standards Order No. 90-02.

SOURCE: 38 FR 26860, Sept. 26, 1973, unless otherwise noted.

RULES IN THIS SUBCHAPTER

§ 701.101 Scope of this subchapter and subchapter B.

(a) This subchapter contains the regulations governing the administration of the Longshore and Harbor Workers' Compensation Act (LHWCA) and its direct extensions, the Defense Base Act (DBA), the Outer Continental Shelf Lands Act (OCSLA), and the Nonappropriated Fund Instrumentalities Act (NFLA), and such other amendments and extensions as may hereinafter be enacted.

(b) The regulations also apply to claims filed under the District of Columbia Workmen's Compensation Act (DCCA). That law applies to all claims for injuries or deaths based on employment events that occurred prior to July 26, 1982, the effective date of the District of Columbia Workers' Compensation Act.

(c) The regulations governing administration of the Black Lung Benefits Program are in subchapter B of this chapter.

[50 FR 391, Jan. 3, 1985, as amended at 51 FR 4281, Feb. 3, 1986]

§ 701.102 Organization of this subchapter.

This part 701 is intended to provide a general description of the regulations in this subchapter, information as to the persons and agencies within the Department of Labor authorized by the Secretary of Labor to administer the Longshoremen's and Harbor Workers' Compensation Act and its extensions and the regulations in this subchapter, and guidance as to the meaning and use of specific terms in the several parts of this subchapter. Part 702 of this subchapter contains the general administrative regulations governing claims filed under the LHWCA, and part 703 of this subchapter contains the regulations governing authorization of insurance carriers, authorization of self-insurers, and issuance of certificates of compliance with said insurance regulations, as required by sections 32 and 37 of the LHWCA, 33 U.S.C. 932, 937. Inasmuch as the extensions of the LHWCA (see 701.101) incorporate by reference nearly all of the provisions of the LHWCA, such that the regulations governing the latter apply to the extensions with very few exceptions, it has been determined that no useful purpose would be served by repeating the same provisions for each of the extensions. Accordingly, the regulations in parts 702 and 703 shall apply to the administration of the extensions (DBA, DCCA, OCSLA and NFIA), unless otherwise noted. The exceptions to the general applicability of parts 702 and 703 of this subchapter are set forth in succeeding parts in this subchapter. Part 704 of this subchapter contains the exceptions for the DBA, the DCCA, the OCSLA, and the NFIA.

OFFICE OF WORKERS' COMPENSATION PROGRAMS

§ 701.201 Establishment of Office of Workers' Compensation Programs.

The Assistant Secretary of Labor for Employment Standards, by authority vested in him or her by the Secretary of Labor in Secretary's Order No. 7-87 (52 FR 48466), established in the Employment Standards Administration (ESA) an Office of Workers' Compensation Programs (OWCP). The Assistant Secretary further designated as the head thereof a Director, who shall administer the programs assigned to that office by the Assistant Secretary.

[55 FR 28606, July 12, 1990]

§ 701.202 Transfer of functions.

Pursuant to the authority vested in him or her by the Secretary of Labor, the Assistant Secretary for Employment Standards transferred from the Bureau of Employees' Compensation to the Office of Workers' Compensation Programs all functions of the Department of Labor with respect to the administration of benefits programs under the following statutes:

(a) The Longshore and Harbor Workers' Compensation Act, as amended and extended, 33 U.S.C. 901 et seq.;

(b) Defense Base Act, 42 U.S.C. 1651 et seq.;

(c) District of Columbia Workmen's Compensation Act, 36 D.C. Code 501 et seq.;

(d) Outer Continental Shelf Lands Act, 43 U.S.C. 1331;

(e) Nonappropriated Fund Instrumentalities Act, 5 U.S.C. 8171 et seq.;

(f) Title IV of the Federal Mine Safety and Health Act of 1977, as amended, 30 U.S.C. 901 et seq.

[55 FR 28606, July 12, 1990]

§ 701.203 Historical background.

Administration of the Longshoremen's and Harbor Workers' Compensation Act (and the Federal Employees' Compensation Act, formerly known as the U.S. Employees' Compensation Act), was initially vested in an independent establishment known as the U.S. Employees' Compensation Commission. By Reorganization Plan No. 2 of 1946 (3 CFR 1943-1949 Comp., p. 1064; 60 Stat. 1095, effective July 16, 1946), the Commission was abolished and its functions were transferred to the Federal Security Agency to be performed by a newly created Bureau of Employees' Compensation within such Agency. By Reorganization Plan No. 19 of 1950 (15 FR 3178, 64 Stat. 1263) said Bureau was transferred to the Department of Labor, and the authority formerly vested in the Administrator, Federal Security Agency, was vested in the Secretary of Labor. By Reorganization Plan No. 6 of 1950 (15 FR 3174, 64 Stat. 1263), the Secretary of Labor was authorized to make from time to time such provisions as he shall deem appropriate, authorizing the performance of any of his functions by any other officer, agency or employee of the Department of Labor.

Terms Used in This Subchapter

§ 701.301 Definitions and use of terms.

(a) As used in this subchapter, except where the context clearly indicates otherwise:

(1) Act means the Longshoremen's and Harbor Workers' Compensation Act, as amended (33 U.S.C. 901 et seq.), also referred to in this subchapter as LHWCA, and includes the provisions of any statutory extension of such Act (see 701.101) pursuant to which compensation on account of an injury is sought.

(2) Secretary means the Secretary of Labor, United States Department of Labor, or his authorized representative.

(3) Employment Standards Administration means the Employment Standards Administration in the United States Department of Labor, headed by the Assistant Secretary of Labor for Employment Standards.

(4) [Reserved]

(5) Office of Workers' Compensation Programs or OWCP or the Office means the Office of Workers' Compensation Programs in the Department of Labor, described in 701.201 of this part. Whenever the term Office of Workmen's Compensation Programs appears in this part or in part 702, it shall have the same meaning as Office of Worker's Compensation Programs.

(6) Director means the Director, OWCP, or his authorized representative.

(7) District Director means a person appointed as provided in sections 39 and 40 of the LHWCA or his or her designee, authorized by the Director to perform functions with respect to the processing and determination of claims for compensation under such Act and its extensions as provided therein and under this subchapter. These regulations substitute this term for the term "Deputy Commissioner" which is used in the statute. This substitution is for administrative purposes only and in no way affects the power or authority of the position as established in the statute.

(8) Administrative Law Judge means an administrative law judge appointed as provided in 5 U.S.C. 3105 and subpart B of 5 CFR part 930 (see 37 FR 16737), who is qualified to preside at hearings under 5 U.S.C. 557 and is empowered by the Secretary to conduct formal hearings whenever necessary in respect of any claim for compensation arising under the LHWCA and its extensions.

(9) Chief Administrative Law Judge means the Chief Judge of the Office of Administrative Law Judges, United States Department of Labor.

(10) Board or Benefits Review Board means the Benefits Review Board established by section 21 of the LHWCA (33 U.S.C. 921) as amended and constituted and functioning pursuant to the provisions of chapter VII of this Title 20 and Secretary of Labor's Order No. 38-72 (38 FR 90).

(11) Department means the United States Department of Labor.

(12)(i) Employee means any person engaged in maritime employment, including:

(A) Any longshore worker or other person engaged in longshoring operations;

(B) Any harbor worker, including a ship repairer, shipbuilder and shipbreaker;

(C) Any other individual to whom an injury may be the basis for a compensation claim under the LHWCA as amended, or any of its extensions;

(ii) The term does not include:

(A) A master or member of a crew of any vessel;

(B) Any person engaged by a master to load or unload or repair any small vessel under eighteen tons net.

(iii) Nor does this term include the following individuals (whether or not the injury occurs over the navigable waters of the United States) where it is first determined that they are covered by a state workers' compensation act:

(A) Individuals employed exclusively to perform office clerical, secretarial, security, or data processing work (but not longshore cargo checkers and cargo clerks);

(B) Individuals employed by a club (meaning a social or fraternal organization whether profit or nonprofit), camp, recreational operation (meaning any recreational activity, including but not limited to scuba diving, commercial rafting, canoeing or boating activities operated for pleasure of owners, members of a club or organization, or renting, leasing or chartering equipment to another for the latter's pleasure), restaurant, museum or retail outlet;

(C) Individuals employed by a marina, provided they are not engaged in its construction, replacement or expansion, except for routine maintenance such as cleaning, painting, trash removal, housekeeping and small repairs;

(D) Employees of suppliers, vendors and transporters temporarily doing business on the premises of a covered employer, provided they are not performing work normally performed by employees of the covered employer;

(E) Aquaculture workers, meaning those employed by commercial enterprises involved in the controlled cultivation and harvest of aquatic plants and animals, including the cleaning, processing or canning of fish and fish products, the cultivation and harvesting of shellfish, and the controlled growing and harvesting of other aquatic species;

(F) Individuals engaged in the building, repairing or dismantling of recreational vessels under 65 feet in length. For purposes of this subparagraph recreational vessel means a vessel manufactured or operated primarily for pleasure, or rented, leased or chartered by another for the latter's pleasure, and length means a straight line measurement of the overall length from the foremost part of the vessel to the aftmost part of the vessel, measured parallel to the center line. The measurement shall be from end to end over the deck, excluding sheer.

(13) Employer includes any employer who may be obligated as an employer under the provisions of the LHWCA as amended or any of its extensions to pay and secure compensation as provided therein.

(14) Carrier means an insurance carrier or self-insurer meeting the requirements of section 32 of the LHWCA as amended and of this subchapter with respect to authorization to provide insurance fulfilling the obligation of an employer to secure the payment of compensation due his employees under the LHWCA as amended or a statutory extension thereof.

(15) The terms wages, national average weekly wage, injury, disability, death, and compensation shall have the meanings set forth in section 2 of the LHWCA.

(16) Claimant includes any person claiming compensation or benefits under the provisions of the LHWCA as amended or a statutory extension thereof on account of the injury or death of an employee.

(b) The definitions contained in paragraph (a) of this section shall not be considered to derogate from any definitions or delimitations of terms in the LHWCA as amended or any of its statutory extensions in any case where such statutory definitions or delimitations would be applicable.

(c) As used in this subchapter, the singular includes plural and the masculine includes the feminine.

[38 FR 26860, Sept. 26, 1973, as amended at 42 FR 3848, Jan. 21, 1977; 50 FR 391, Jan. 3, 1985; 51 FR 4281, Feb. 3, 1986; 55 FR 28606, July 12, 1990]

COVERAGE UNDER STATE COMPENSATION PROGRAMS

§ 701.401 Coverage under state compensation programs.

(a) Exclusions from the definition of "employee" under 701.301(a)(12), and the employees of small vessel facilities otherwise covered which are exempted from coverage under 702.171, are dependent upon coverage under a state workers' compensation program. For these purposes, a worker or dependent must first claim compensation under the appropriate state program and receive a final decision on the merits of the claim, denying coverage, before any claim may be filed under this Act.

(b) The intent of the Act is that state law will apply to those categories of employees if it otherwise would. Accordingly, not withstanding any contrary state law, claims by any of the categories of workers excluded under 701.301 or 702.171 must be made to and processed by the state and a merit decision denying coverage on jurisdictional grounds must be made before coverage or benefits under the Act may be sought.

(c) The time for filing notice and claim under the Act (see subpart B of part 702) does not begin to run for purposes of claims by those workers or dependents described in 701.301 (a)(12) and 702.171, until a final adverse decision denying coverage under a state compensation act is received.

[50 FR 392, Jan. 3, 1985]

PART 702—ADMINISTRATION AND PROCEDURE

Subpart A—General Provisions

ADMINISTRATION

702.101 Establishment of compensation districts.
702.102 Establishment of suboffices and jurisdictional areas.
702.103 Effect of establishment of suboffices and jurisdictional areas.
702.104 Transfer of individual case file.
702.105 Use of the title District Director in place of Deputy Commissioner.

RECORDS

702.111 Employer's records.
702.112 Records of the OWCP.
702.113 Inspection of records of the OWCP.
702.114 Copying of records of OWCP.

FORMS

702.121 Forms.

REPRESENTATION

702.131 Representation of parties in interest.
702.132 Fees for services.
702.133 Unapproved fees; solicitation of claimants; penalties.
702.134 Payment of claimant's attorney's fees in disputed claims.
702.135 Payment of claimant's witness fees and mileage in disputed claims.

INFORMATION AND ASSISTANCE FOR CLAIMANTS

702.136 Requests for information and assistance.

COMMUTATION OF PAYMENTS AND SPECIAL FUND

702.142 Commutation of payments; aliens not residents or about to become nonresidents.
702.143 Establishment of special fund.
702.144 Purpose of the special fund.
702.145 Use of the special fund.
702.146 Source of the special fund.
702.147 Enforcement of special fund provisions.
702.148 Insurance carriers' and self-insured employers' responsibility.

LIENS ON COMPENSATION

702.161 Liens against assets of insurance carriers and employers.
702.162 Liens on compensation authorized under special circumstances.

CERTIFICATION OF EXEMPTION

702.171 Certification of exemption, general.
702.172 Certification; definitions.
702.173 Exemptions; requirements, limitations.
702.174 Exemptions; necessary information.
702.175 Effect of work on excluded vessels; reinstatement of certification.

Subpart B—Claims Procedures

EMPLOYER'S REPORTS

702.201 Reports from employers of employee's injury or death.
702.202 Employer's report; form and contents.
702.203 Employer's report; how given.
702.204 Employer's report; penalty for failure to furnish and/or falsifying
702.205 Employer's report; effect of failure to report upon time limitations.

NOTICE

702.211 Notice of employee's injury or death; designation of responsible official.
702.212 Notice; when given; when given for certain occupational diseases.
702.213 Notice; by whom given.
702.214 Notice; form and contents.
702.215 Notice; how given.
702.216 Effect of failure to give notice.
702.217 Penalty for false statement, misrepresentation.

CLAIMS

702.221 Claims for compensation; time limitations.
702.222 Claims; exceptions to time limitations.
702.223 Claims; time limitations; time to object.
702.224 Claims, notification of employer of filing by employee.
702.225 Withdrawal of claim.

NONCONTROVERTED CLAIMS

702.231 Noncontroverted claims; payment of compensation without an award.
702.232 Payments without an award; when; how paid.
702.233 Penalty for failure to pay without an award.
702.234 Report by employer of commencement and suspension of payments.
702.235 Report by employer of final payment of compensation.
702.236 Penalty for failure to report termination of payments.

AGREED SETTLEMENTS

702.241 Definitions and supplementary information.
702.242 Information necessary for a complete settlement application.
702.243 Settlement application; how submitted, how approved, how disapproved, criteria.

CONTROVERTED CLAIMS

702.251 Employer's controversion of the right to compensation.
702.252 Action by district director upon receipt of notice of controversion.

CONTESTED CLAIMS

702.261 Claimant's contest of actions taken by employer or carrier with respect to the claim.
702.262 Action by district director upon receipt of notice of contest.

DISCRIMINATION

702.271 Discrimination; against employees who bring proceedings, prohibition and penalty.
702.272 Informal recommendation by district director.
702.273 Adjudication by Office of the Chief Administrative Law Judge.
702.274 Employer's refusal to pay penalty.

THIRD PARTY

702.281 Third party action.

AUTHORITY: 5 U.S.C. 301, 8171 et seq.; Reorganization Plan No. 6 of 1950, 15 FR 3174, 3 CFR, 1949-1953, Comp. p. 1004, 64 Stat. 1263; 33 U.S.C. 939; 36 D.C. Code 501 et seq.; 42 U.S.C. 1651 et seq.; 43 U.S.C. 1331; Secretary's Order 1-93, 58 FR 21190.

SOURCE: 38 FR 26861, Sept. 26, 1973, unless otherwise noted.

EDITORIAL NOTE: Nomenclature changes to part 702 appear at 55 FR 28606, July 12, 1990.

Subpart A—General Provisions

ADMINISTRATION

§ 702.101 Establishment of compensation districts.

Pursuant to section 39(b) of the Longshoremen's and Harbor Workers' Compensation Act, 33 U.S.C. 939(b), the following compensation districts have been established:

District No. 1. Comprises the States of Massachusetts, Maine, New Hampshire, Vermont, Rhode Island, and Connecticut; with headquarters at Boston, Mass.
District No. 2. Comprises the States of New York and New Jersey; with headquarters at New York, N.Y.
District No. 3. Comprises the States of Pennsylvania, Delaware, and West Virginia; with headquarters at Philadelphia, Pa.

District No. 4. Comprises the State of Maryland and the District of Columbia; with headquarters at Baltimore, Md.
District No. 5. Comprises the State of Virginia; with headquarters at Norfolk, Va.
District No. 6. Comprises the States of Florida, North Carolina, Kentucky, Tennessee, South Carolina, Georgia, Alabama, and Mississippi; with headquarters at Jacksonville, Fla.
District No. 7. Comprises the States of Louisiana and Arkansas; with headquarters at New Orleans, La.
District No. 8. Comprises the States of Texas, Oklahoma, and New Mexico, with headquarters at Houston, Texas.
District No. 9. [Reserved]
District No. 10. Comprises the States of Illinois, Indiana, Iowa, Kansas, Michigan, Minnesota, Missouri, Nebraska, Ohio and Wisconsin; with headquarters in Chicago, Illinois. District No. 11. [Reserved]
District No. 12. [Reserved]
District No. 13. Comprises the States of Arizona, Nevada, and that part of the State of California north of the northern boundaries of the counties of San Luis Obispo, Kern, and San Bernardino; with headquarters at San Francisco, Calif.
District No. 14. Comprises the States of Alaska, Colorado, Idaho, Montana, North Dakota, South Dakota, Oregon, Utah, Washington and Wyoming; with headquarters in Seattle, Washington.
District No. 15. Comprises the State of Hawaii; with headquarters at Honolulu, Hawaii.
District No. 16. [Reserved]
District No. 17. [Reserved]
District No. 18. Comprises that part of the State of California south of the northern boundaries of the counties of San Luis Obispo, Kern, and San Bernardino; with headquarters in Long Beach, Calif.

[42 FR 3848, Jan. 21, 1977, as amended at 43 FR 50171, Oct. 27, 1978; 44 FR 17657, Mar. 23, 1979; 51 FR 4282, Feb. 3, 1986]

§ 702.102 Establishment of suboffices and jurisdictional areas.

(a) As administrative exigencies from time to time may require, the Director may, by administrative order, establish special areas outside the continental United States, Alaska, and Hawaii, or change or modify any areas so established, notwithstanding their inclusion within an established compensation district. Such areas shall be designated "jurisdictional areas." The Director shall also designate which of his district directors shall be in charge thereof.

(b) To further aid in the efficient administration of the OWCP, the Director may from time to time establish suboffices within compensation districts or jurisdictional areas, and shall designate a person to be in charge thereof.

§ 702.103 Effect of establishment of suboffices and jurisdictional areas.

Whenever the Director establishes a suboffice or jurisdictional area, those reports, records, or other documents with respect to processing of claims that are required to be filed with the district director of the compensation district in which the injury or death occurred, may instead be required to be filed at the suboffice, or office established for the jurisdictional area.

§ 702.104 Transfer of individual case file.

(a) At any time after a claim is filed, the district director having jurisdiction thereof may, with the prior or subsequent approval of the Director, transfer such case to the district director in another compensation district for the purpose of making an investigation, ordering medical examinations, or taking such other action as may be necessary or appropriate to further develop the claim. If, after filing a claim, the claimant moves to another compensation district, the district director may, upon request by the claimant or the employer and with the approval of the Director, transfer the case to such other compensation district.

(b) The district director making the transfer may by letter or memorandum to the district director to whom the case is transferred give advice, comments, suggestions, or directions if appropriate to the particular case. The transfer of cases shall be by registered or certified mail. All interested parties shall be advised of the transfer.

[42 FR 45301, Sept. 9, 1977]

§ 702.105 Use of the title District Director in place of Deputy Commissioner.

Wherever the statute refers to Deputy Commissioner, these regulations have substituted the term District Director. The substitution is purely an administrative one, and in no way effects the authority of or the powers granted and responsibilities imposed by the statute on that position.

[55 FR 28606, July 12, 1990]

RECORDS

§ 702.111 Employer's records.

Every employer shall maintain adequate records of injury sustained by employees while in his employ, and which shall also contain information of disease, other impairments or disabilities, or death relating to said injury. Such records shall be available for inspection by the OWCP or by any State authority. Records required by this section shall be retained by the employer for three years following the date of injury; this applies to records for lost-time and no-lost-time injuries.

(Approved by the Office of Management and Budget under control number 1215-0160)

(Pub. L. No. 96-511, 94 Stat. 2812 (44 U.S.C. 3501 et seq.))

[38 FR 26861, Sept. 26, 1973, as amended at 47 FR 145, Jan. 5, 1982; 50 FR 393, Jan. 3, 1985]

§ 702.112 Records of the OWCP.

All reports, records, or other documents filed with the OWCP with respect to claims are the records of the OWCP. The Director shall be the official custodian of those records maintained by the OWCP at its national office, and the district director shall be the official custodian of those records maintained at the headquarters office in each compensation district.

§ 702.113 Inspection of records of the OWCP.

Any party in interest may be permitted to examine the record of the case in which he is interested. The official custodian of the record sought to be inspected shall permit or deny inspection in accordance with the Department of Labor's regulations pertaining thereto (see 29 CFR part 70). The original record in any such case shall not be removed from the office of the custodian for such inspection. The custodian may, in his discretion, deny inspection of any record or part thereof which is of a character specified in 5 U.S.C. 552(b) if in his opinion such inspection may result in damage, harm, or harassment to the beneficiary or to any other person. For special provisions concerning release of information regarding injured employees undergoing vocational rehabilitation, see 702.508.

§ 702.114 Copying of records of OWCP.

Any party in interest may request copies of records he has been permitted to inspect. Such requests shall be addressed to the official custodian of the records sought to be copied. The official custodian shall provide the requested copies under the terms and conditions specified in the Department of Labor's regulations relating thereto (see 29 CFR part 70).

FORMS

§ 702.121 Forms.

The Director may from time to time prescribe, and require the use of, forms for the reporting of any information required to be reported by the regulations in this subchapter, or by the Act or any of its extensions.

REPRESENTATION

§ 702.131 Representation of parties in interest.

(a) Claimants, employers and insurance carriers may be represented in any proceeding under the Act by an attorney or other person previously authorized in writing by such claimant, employer or carrier to so act.

(b) The Secretary shall annually publish a list of individuals who are disqualified from representing claimants under the Act. Individuals on this list are not authorized to represent claimants under the Act subject to the provision of section 31(b)(2)(C) of the Act, 33 U.S.C. 931(b)(2)(C), and they shall not have their representation fee approved as provided in section 28(e), 33 U.S.C. 928(e).

(c) Individuals shall be included on the list mentioned in (b) if the Secretary determines, after proceedings under 702.432(b) through 702.434, that such individual:

(1) Has been convicted (without regard to pending appeal) of any crime in connection with the representation of a claimant under this Act or any workers' compensation statute;

(2) Has engaged in fraud in connection with the presentation of a claim under this or any workers' compensation statute, including, but not limited to, knowingly making false representations, concealing or attempting to conceal material facts with respect to a claim, or soliciting or otherwise procuring false testimony;

(3) Has been prohibited from representing claimants before any other workers' compensation agency for reasons of professional misconduct which are similar in nature to those which would be grounds for disqualification under this section; or

(4) Has accepted fees for representing claimants under the Act which were not approved, or which were in excess of the amount approved pursuant to section 28 of the Act, 33 U.S.C. 928.

[38 FR 26861, Sept. 26, 1973, as amended at 50 FR 394, Jan. 3, 1985]

§ 702.132 Fees for services.

(a) Any person seeking a fee for services performed on behalf of a claimant with respect to claims filed under the Act shall make application therefor to the district director, administrative law judge, Board, or court, as the case may be, before whom the services were performed (See 33 U.S.C. 928(c)). The application shall be filed and serviced upon the other parties within the time limits specified by such district director, administrative law judge, Board, or court. The application shall be supported by a complete statement of the extent and character of the necessary work done, described with particularity as to the professional status (e.g., attorney, paralegal, law clerk, or other person assisting an attorney) of each person performing such work, the normal billing rate for each such person, and the hours devoted by each such person to each category of work. Any fee approved shall be reasonably commensurate with the necessary work done and shall take into account the quality of the representation, the complexity of the legal issues involved, and the amount of benefits awarded, and when the fee is to be assessed against the claimant, shall also take into account the financial circumstances of the claimant. No contract pertaining to the amount of a fee shall be recognized. (b) No fee shall be approved for a representative whose name appears on the Secretary's list of disqualified representatives under 702.131(b).

(c) Where fees are included in a settlement agreement submitted under 702.241, et seq. approval of that agreement shall be deemed approval of attorney fees for purposes of this subsection for work performed before the Administrative Law Judge or district director approving the settlement.

[50 FR 394, Jan. 3, 1985]

§ 702.133 Unapproved fees; solicitation of claimants; penalties.

Under the provisions of section 28(e) of the Act, 33 U.S.C. 928(e), any person who receives any fees, other consideration, or any gratuity on account of services rendered as a representative of a claimant, unless such consideration or gratuity is approved under 702.132, or who makes it a business to solicit employment for an attorney, or for himself in respect of any claim under the Act, shall upon conviction thereof, for each offense be punished by a fine of not more than $1,000 or by imprisonment for not more than 1 year, or by both fine and imprisonment.

§ 702.134 Payment of claimant's attorney's fees in disputed claims.

(a) If the employer or carrier declines to pay any compensation on or before the 30th day after receiving written notice from the district director of a claim for compensation having been filed, on the ground that there is no liability for compensation within the provisions of this Act, and the person seeking benefits shall thereafter have utilized the services of an attorney at law in the successful prosecution of his claim, there shall be awarded, in addition to the award of compensation, in a compensation order, a reasonable attorney's fee against the employer or carrier in an amount approved by the person, administrative body or court before whom the service was performed, which shall be paid directly by the employer or carrier to the attorney for the claimant in a lump sum after the compensation order becomes final (Act, section 28(a)).

(b) If the employer or carrier pays or tenders payment of compensation without an award pursuant to 702.231 and section 14 (a) and (b) of this Act, and thereafter a controversy develops over the amount of additional compensation, if any, to which the employee may be entitled, the district director, administrative law judge, or Board shall set the matter for an informal conference and following such conference the district director, administrative law judge, or Board shall recommend in writing a disposition of the controversy. If the employer or carrier refuses to accept such written recommendation, within 14 days after its receipt by them, they shall pay or tender to the employee in writing the additional compensation, if any, to which they believe the employee is entitled. If the employee refuses to accept such payment or tender of compensation, and thereafter utilizes the services of an attorney at law, and if the compensation thereafter awarded is greater than the amount paid or tendered by the employer or carrier, a reasonable attorney's fee based solely upon the difference between the amount awarded and the amount tendered or paid shall be awarded in addition to the amount of compensation. The foregoing sentence shall not apply if the controversy relates to degree or length of disability, and if the employer or carrier offers to submit the case for evaluation by physicians employed or selected by the district director, as authorized by section 7(e) of the Act and 702.408, and offers to tender an amount of compensation based upon the degree or length of disability found by the independent medical report at such time as an evaluation of disability can be made. If the claimant is successful in review proceedings before the Board or court in any such case an award may be made in favor of the claimant and against the employer or carrier for a reasonable attorney's fee for claimant's counsel in accord with the above provisions. In all other cases any claim for legal services shall not be assessed against the employer or carrier (see Act, section 28(b)).

§ 702.135 Payment of claimant's witness fees and mileage in disputed claims.

In cases where an attorney's fee is awarded against an employer or carrier there may be further assessed against such employer or carrier as costs, fees and mileage for necessary witnesses attending the hearing at the instance of claimant. Both the necessity for the witness and the reasonableness of the fees of expert witnesses must be approved by the hearing officer, the Board, or the court, as the case may be. The amounts awarded against an employer or carrier as attorney's fees, costs, fees and mileage for witnesses shall not in any respect affect or diminish the compensation payable under this Act (see Act, section 28 (d)).

INFORMATION AND ASSISTANCE FOR CLAIMANTS

§ 702.136 Requests for information and assistance.

(a) General assistance. The Director shall, upon request, provide persons covered by the Act with information and assistance relating to the Act's coverage and compensation and the procedures for obtaining such compensation including assistance in processing a claim.

(b) Legal assistance to claimants. The Secretary may, upon request, provide a claimant with legal assistance in processing a claim under the Act. Such assistance may be made available to a claimant in the discretion of the Solicitor of Labor or his designee at any time prior to or during which the claim is being processed and shall be furnished without charge to the claimant. Legal representation of the claimant in adjudicatory proceedings may be furnished in cases in which the Secretary's interest in the case is not adverse to that of the claimant.

(c) Other assistance. The district directors and their staff, as designees of the Director, shall promptly and fully comply with the request of a claimant receiving compensation for information about, and assistance in obtaining, medical, manpower, and vocational rehabilitation services (see also subparts D and E of this part).

Commutation of Payments and Special Fund

§ 702.142 Commutation of payments; aliens not residents or about to become nonresidents.

(a) Pursuant to section 9(g) of the Act, 33 U.S.C. 909(g), compensation paid to aliens not residents, or about to become nonresidents, of the United States or Canada shall be in the same amount as provided for residents except that dependents in any foreign country shall be limited to surviving spouse and child or children, or if there be no surviving spouse or child or children, to surviving father or mother whom the employee has supported, either wholly or in part, for the period of 1 year prior to the date of injury, and except that the Director, OWCP, may, at his option, or upon the application of the insurance carrier he shall, commute all future installments of compensation to be paid to such aliens by paying or causing to be paid to them one-half of the commuted amount of such future installments of compensation as determined by the Director.

(b) Applications for commutation under this section shall be made in writing to the district director having jurisdiction, and forwarded by the district director to the Director, for final action.

(c) Applications for commutations shall be made effective, if approved by the Director, on the date received by the district director, or on a later date if shown to be appropriate on the application.

(d) Commutations shall not be made with respect to a person journeying abroad for a visit who has previously declared an intention to return and has stated a time for returning, nor shall any commutation be made except upon the basis of a compensation order fixing the right of the beneficiary to compensation.

[50 FR 394, Jan. 3, 1985]

§ 702.143 Establishment of special fund.

Congress, by section 44 of the Act, 33 U.S.C. 944, established in the U.S. Treasury a special fund, to be administered by the Secretary. The Treasurer of the United States is the custodian of such fund, and all monies and securities in such fund shall be held in trust by the Treasurer and shall not be money or property of the United States. The Treasurer shall make disbursements from such funds only upon the order of the Director, OWCP, as delegatee of the Secretary. The Act requires that the Treasurer give bond, in an amount to be fixed and with securities to be approved by the Secretary of the Treasury and the Comptroller General of the United States, conditioned upon the faithful performance of his duty as custodian of such fund.

§ 702.144 Purpose of the special fund.

This special fund was established to give effect to a congressional policy determination that, under certain circumstances, the employer of a particular employee should not be required to bear the entire burden of paying for the compensation benefits due that employee under the Act. Instead, a substantial portion of such burden should be borne by the industry generally. Section 702.145 describes this special circumstance under which the particular employer is relieved of some of his burden. Section 702.146 describes the manner and circumstances of the input into the fund.

§ 702.145 Use of the special fund.

(a) Under section 10 of the Act. This section provides for initial and subsequent annual adjustments in compensation and continuing payments to beneficiaries in cases of permanent total disability or death which commenced or occurred prior to enactment of the 1972 Amendments to this Act (Pub. L. 92-576, approved Oct. 27, 1972). At the discretion of the Director, such payments may be paid directly by him to eligible beneficiaries as the obligation accrues, one-half from the special fund and one-half from appropriations, or he may require insurance carriers or self-insured employers already making payments to such beneficiaries to pay such additional compensation as the amended Act requires. In the latter case such carriers and self-insurers shall be reimbursed by the Director for such additional amounts paid, in the proportion of one-half the amount from the special fund and one-half the amount from appropriations. To obtain reimbursement, the carriers and self-insurers shall submit claims for payments made by them during previous periods at intervals of not less than 6 months. A form has been prescribed for such purpose and shall be used. No administrative claims service expense incurred by the carrier or self-insurer shall be included in the claim and no such expense shall be allowed. The amounts reimbursed to such carrier or self-insurer shall be limited to amounts actually due and previously paid to beneficiaries.

(b) Under section 8(f) of the Act (Second Injuries). In any case in which an employee having an existing permanent partial disability suffers injury, the employer shall provide compensation for such disability as is found to be attributable to that injury based upon the average weekly wages of the employee at the time of injury. If, following an injury falling within the provisions of section 8(c)(1)-(20), the employee with the pre-existing permanent partial disability becomes permanently and totally disabled after the second injury, but such total disability is found not to be due solely to his second injury, the employer (or carrier) shall be liable for compensation as provided by the provisions of section 8(c)(1)-(20) of the Act, 33 U.S.C. 908(c)(1)-(20) or for 104 weeks, whichever is greater. However, if the injury is a loss of hearing covered by section 8(c)(13), 33 U.S.C. 908(c)(13), the liability shall be the lesser of these periods. In all other cases of a second injury causing permanent total disability (or death), wherein it is found that such disability (or death) is not due solely to the second injury, and wherein the employee had a pre-existing permanent partial disability, the employer (or carrier) shall first pay compensation under section 8(b) or (e) of the Act, 33 U.S.C. 908(b) or (e), if any is payable thereunder, and shall then pay 104 weeks compensation for such total disability or death, and none otherwise. If the second injury results in permanent partial disability, and if such disability is compensable under section 8(c)(1)-(20) of the Act, 33 U.S.C. 908(c)(1)-(20), but the disability so compensable did not result solely from such second injury, and the disability so compensable is materially and substantially greater than that which would have resulted from the second injury alone, then the employer (or carrier) shall only be liable for the amount of compensation provided for in section 8(c)(1)-(20) that is attributable to such second injury, or for 104 weeks, whichever is greater. However, if the injury is a loss of hearing covered by section 8(c)(13), 33 U.S.C. 908(c)(13), the liability shall be the lesser of these periods. In all other cases wherein the employee is permanently and partially disabled following a second injury, and wherein such disability is not attributable solely to that second injury, and wherein such disability is materially and substantially greater than that which would have resulted from the second injury alone, and wherein such disability following the second injury is not compensable under section 8(c)(1)-(20) of the Act, then the employer (or carrier) shall be liable for such compensation as may be appropriate under section 8(b) or (e) of the Act, 33 U.S.C. 908(b) or (e), if any, to be followed by a payment of compensation for 104 weeks, and none other. The term "compensation" herein means money benefits only, and does not include medical benefits. The procedure for determining the extent of the employer's (or carrier's) liability under this paragraph shall be as provided for in the adjudication of claims in subpart C of this part 702. Thereafter, upon cessation of payments which the employer is required to make under this paragraph, if any additional compensation is payable in the case, the district director shall forward such case to the Director for consideration of an award to the person or persons entitled thereto out of the special fund.

Any such award from the special fund shall be by order of the Director or Acting Director.

(c) Under sections 8(g) and 39(c)(2) of the Act. These sections, 33 U.S.C. 908(g) and 939(c)(2), respectively, provide for vocational rehabilitation of disabled employees, and authorize, under appropriate circumstances, a maintenance allowance for the employee (not to exceed $25 a week) in additional to other compensation benefits otherwise payable for his injury-related disability. Awards under these sections are made from the special fund upon order of the Director or his designee. The district directors may be required to make investigations with respect to any case and forward to the Director their recommendations as to the propriety and need for such maintenance.

(d) Under section 39(c)(2) of the Act. In addition to the maintenance allowance for the employee discussed in paragraph (c) of this section, the Director is further authorized to use the fund in such amounts as may be necessary to procure the vocational training services.

(e) Under section 7(e) of the Act. This provision, 33 U.S.C. 907(e), authorizes payment by the Director from the special fund for special medical examinations, i.e., those obtained from impartial specialists to resolve disputes, when such special examinations are deemed necessary under that statutory provision. The Director has the discretionary power, however, to charge the cost of such examination to the insurance carrier or self-insured employer.

(f) Under section 18(b) of the Act. This section, 33 U.S.C. 918(b), provides a source for payment of compensation benefits in cases where the employer is insolvent, or other circumstances preclude the payment of benefits due in any case. In such situations, the district director shall forward the case to the Director for consideration of an award from the special fund, together with evidence with respect to the employer's insolvency or other reasons for nonpayment of benefits due. Benefits, as herein used, means medical care or supplies within the meaning of section 7 of the Act, 33 U.S.C. 907, and subpart D of this part 702, as well as monetary benefits. Upon receipt of the case, the Director shall promptly determine whether an award from the special fund is appropriate and advisable in the case, having due regard for all other current commitments from the special fund. If such an award is made, the employer shall be liable for the repayment into the fund of the amounts paid therefrom, as provided in 33 U.S.C. 918(b).

(The information collection requirements contained in paragraph (a) were approved by the Office of Management and Budget under control number 1215-0065. The information collection requirements contained in paragraph (b) were approved by the Office of Management and Budget under control number 1215-0073)

(Pub. L. No. 96-511)

[38 FR 26861, Sept. 26, 1973, as amended at 49 FR 18294, Apr. 30, 1984; 51 FR 4282, Feb. 3, 1986]

§ 702.146 Source of the special fund.

(a) All amounts collected as fines and penalties under the several provisions of the Act shall be paid into the special fund (33 U.S.C. 44(c)(3)).

(b) Whenever an employee dies under circumstances creating a liability on an employer to pay death benefits to the employee's beneficiaries, and whenever there are no such beneficiaries entitled to such payments, the employer shall pay $5,000 into the special fund (Act, section 44(c)(1)). In such cases, the compensation order entered in the case shall specifically find that there is such liability and that there are no beneficiaries entitled to death benefits, and shall order payment by the employer into the fund. Compensation orders shall be made and filed in accordance with the regulations in subpart C of this part 702, except that for this purpose the district director settling the case under 702.315 shall formalize the memorandum of conference in a compensation order, and shall file such order as provided for in 702.349.

(c) The Director annually shall assess an amount against insurance carriers and self-insured employers authorized under the Act and part 703 of this subchapter to replenish the fund. That total amount to be charged all carriers and self-insurers to be assessed shall be based upon an estimate of the probable expenses of the fund during the calendar year. The assessment against each carrier and self-insurer shall be based upon (1) the ratio of the amount each paid during the prior calendar year for compensation in relation to the amount all such carriers of self-insurers paid during that period for compensation, and (2) the ratio of the amount of payments made by the special fund for all cases being paid under section 8(f) of the Act, 33 U.S.C. 908(f), during the preceding calendar year which are attributable to the carrier or self-insurer in relation to the total of such payments during such year attributable to all carriers and self-insurers. The resulting sum of the percentages from paragraphs (c) (1) and (2) of this section will be divided by two, and the resulting percentage multiplied by the probable expenses of the fund. The Director may, in his or her discretion, condition continuance or renewal of authorization under part 703 upon prompt payment of the assessment. However, no action suspending or revoking such authorization shall be taken without affording such carrier or self-insurer a hearing before the Director or his/her designee.

[38 FR 26861, Sept. 26, 1973, as amended at 50 FR 395, Jan. 3, 1985; 51 FR 4282, Feb. 3, 1986]

702.147 - Enforcement of special fund provisions.

(a) As provided in section 44(d)(1) of the Act, 33 U.S.C. 944(d)(1), for the purpose of making rules, regulations, and determinations under the special fund provisions in section 44 and for providing enforcement thereof, the Director may investigate and gather appropriate data from each carrier and self-insured employer, and may enter and inspect such places and records (and make such transcriptions of records), question such employees, and investigate such facts, conditions, practices, or other matters as he may deem necessary or appropriate. The Director may require the employer to have audits performed of claims activity relating to this Act. The Director may also require detailed reports of payments made under the Act, and of estimated future liabilities under the Act, from any or all carriers of self-insurers. The Director may require that such reports be certified and verified in whatever manner is considered appropriate.

(b) Pursuant to section 44(d)(3) of the Act, 33 U.S.C. 944(d)(3), for the purpose of any hearing or investigation related to determinations or the enforcement of the provisions of section 44 with respect to the special fund, the provisions of 15 U.S.C. 49 and 50 as amended (the Federal Trade Commission Act provisions relating to attendance of witnesses and the production of books, papers, and documents) are made applicable to the jurisdiction, powers, and duties of the Director, OWCP, as the Secretary's delegatee.

(c) Civil penalties and unpaid assessments shall be collected by civil suits brought by and in the name of the Secretary.

(Approved by the Office of Management and Budget under control number 1215-0160)

[38 FR 26861, Sept. 26, 1973, as amended at 50 FR 395, Jan. 3, 1985]

§ 702.148 Insurance carriers' and self-insured employers' responsibilities.

(a) Each carrier and self-insured employer shall make, keep, and preserve such records, and make such reports and provide such additional information as the Director prescribes or orders, which he considers necessary or appropriate to effectively carry out his responsibilities.

(b) Consistent with their greater direct liability stemming from the amended assessment formula, employers and insurance carriers are given the authority to monitor their claims in the special fund as outlined in paragraph (c) of this section. For purposes of monitoring these claims, employers and insurance carriers remain parties in interest to the claim and are allowed access to all records relating to the claim. Similarly, employers and insurance carriers can initiate proceeding to modify an award of compensation after the special fund has assumed the liability to pay benefits. It is intended that employers and insurance carriers have neither a greater nor a lesser responsibility in this new role that they not have with regard to cases that remain their sole liability. (See 702.373(d).)

(c) An employer or insurance carrier may conduct any reasonable investigation regarding cases placed into the special fund by the employer or insurance carrier. Such investigation may include, but shall not be limited to, a semi-annual request for earnings information pursuant to section 8(j) of the Act, 33 U.S.C. 908(j) (See 702.285) periodic medical examinations, vocational rehabilitation evaluations, and requests for any additional information needed to effectively monitor such a case.

(Approved by the Office of Management and Budget under control number 1215-0118)

(Pub. L. No. 96-511, 94 Stat. 2812 (44 U.S.C. 3501 et seq.))

[38 FR 26861, Sept. 26, 1973, as amended at 47 FR 145, Jan. 5, 1982; 50 FR 395, Jan. 3, 1985]

LIENS ON COMPENSATION

§ 702.161 Liens against assets of insurance carriers and employers.

Where payments have been made from the special fund pursuant to section 18(b) of the Act, 33 U.S.C. 918(b) and 704.145(f) the Secretary of Labor shall, for the benefit of the fund, be subrogated to all the rights of the person receiving such payments. The Secretary may institute proceedings under either section 18 or 21(d) of the Act, 33 U.S.C. 918 or 921(d), or both, to recover the amount expended by the fund or so much as in the judgement of the Secretary is possible, or the Secretary may settle or compromise any such claim.

[50 FR 395, Jan. 3, 1985]

§ 702.162 Liens on compensation authorized under special circumstances.

(a) Pursuant to section 17 of the Act, 33 U.S.C. 917, when a trust fund which complies with section 302(c) of the Labor-Management Relations Act of 1947, 29 U.S.C. 186(c) [LMRA], established pursuant to a collective bargaining agreement in effect between an employer and an employee entitled to compensation under this Act, has paid disability benefits to an employee which the employee is legally obligated to repay by reason of his entitlement to compensation under this Act, a lien shall be authorized on such compensation in favor of the trust fund for the amount of such payments.

(b) (1) An application for such a lien shall be filed on behalf of the trust fund with the district director for the compensation district where the claim for compensation has been filed, 20 CFR 702.101. Such application shall include a certified statement by an authorized official of the trust fund that:

(i) The trust fund is entitled to a lien in its favor by reason of its payment of disability payments to a claimant-employee (including his name therein);

(ii) The trust fund was created pursuant to a collective bargaining agreement covering
the claimant-employee;

(iii) The trust fund complies with section 302(c) of the Labor-Management Relations Act of 1947, 29 U.S.C. 186(c);

(iv) The trust agreement contains a subrogation provision entitling the fund to reimbursement for disability benefits paid to the claimant-employee who is entitled to compensation under the Longshoremen's Act;

(2) The statement shall also state the amount paid to the named claimant-employee and whether such disability benefit payments are continuing to be paid.

(3) If the claimant has signed a statement acknowledging receipt of disability benefits from the trust fund and/or a statement recognizing the trust fund's entitlement to a lien against compensation payments which may be received under the Longshoremen's and Harbor Worker's Compensation Act as a result of his present claim and for which the fund is providing disability payments, such statement(s) shall also be included with or attached to the application.

(c) Upon receipt of this application, the district director shall, within a reasonable time, notify the claimant, the employer and/or its compensation insurance carrier that the request for a lien has been filed and each shall be provided with a copy of the application. If the claimant disputes the right of the trust fund to the lien or the amount stated, if any, he shall, within 30 days after receipt of the application or such other longer period as the district director may set, notify the district director and he shall be given an opportunity to challenge the right of the trust fund to, or the amount of, the asserted lien; notice to either the employer or its compensation insurance carrier shall constitute notice to both of them.

(d) If the claim for compensation benefits is resolved without a formal hearing and if there is no dispute over the amount of the lien or the right of the trust fund to the lien, the district director may order and impose the lien and he shall notify all parties of the amount of the lien and manner in which it is to be paid.

(e) If the claimant's claim for compensation cannot be resolved informally, the district director shall transfer the case to the Office of the Chief Administrative Law Judge for a formal hearing, pursuant to section 19(d) of the Act, 33 U.S.C. 919(d), and 20 CFR 702.317. The district director shall also submit therewith the application for the lien and all documents relating thereto. (f) If the administrative law judge issues a compensation order in favor of the claimant, such order shall establish a lien in favor of the trust fund if it is determined that the trust fund has satisfied all of the requirements of the Act and regulations.

(g) If the claim for compensation is not in dispute, but there is a dispute as to the right of the trust fund to a lien, or the amount of the lien, the district director shall transfer the matter together with all documents relating thereto to the Office of the Chief Administrative Law Judge for a formal hearing pursuant to section 19(d) of the Act, 33 U.S.C. 919(d), and 20 CFR 702.317.

(h) In the event that either the district director or the administrative law judge is not satisfied that the trust fund qualifies for a lien under section 17, the district director or administrative law judge may require further evidence including but not limited to the production of the collective bargaining agreement, trust agreement or portions thereof.

(i) Before any such lien is approved, if the trust fund has provided continued disability payments after the application for a lien has been filed, the trust fund shall submit a further certified statement showing the total amount paid to the claimant as disability payments. The claimant shall likewise be given an opportunity to contest the amount alleged in this subsequent statement.

(j) In approving a lien on compensation, the district director or administrative law judge shall not order an initial payment to the trust fund in excess of the amount of the past due compensation. The remaining amount to which the trust fund is entitled shall thereafter be deducted from the affected employee's subsequent compensation payments and paid to the trust fund, but any such payment to the trust fund shall not exceed 10 percent of the claimantemployee's bi-weekly compensation payments.

(Approved by the Office of Management and Budget under control number 1215-0160)

[42 FR 45301, Sept. 9, 1977, as amended at 50 FR 395, Jan. 3, 1985; 51 FR 4282, Feb. 3, 1986]

CERTIFICATION OF EXEMPTION

§ 702.171 Certification of exemption, general.

An employer may apply to the Director or his/her designee to certify a particular facility as one engaged in the building, repairing or dismantling of exclusively small vessels, as defined. Once certified, injuries sustained at that facility would not be covered under the Act except for injuries which occur over the navigable waters of the United States including any adjoining pier, wharf, dock, facility over land for launching vessels or for hauling, lifting or drydocking vessels. A facility otherwise covered under the Act remains covered until certification of exemption is issued; a certification will be granted only upon submission of a complete application (described in 702.174), and only for as long as a facility meets the requirements detailed in section 3(d) of the Act, 33 U.S.C. 903(d). This exemption from coverage is not intended to be used by employers whose facilities from time to time may temporarily meet the criteria for qualification but only for facilities which work on exclusively small vessels, as defined.

[50 FR 396, Jan. 3, 1985]

§ 702.172 Certification; definitions.

For purposes of 702.171 through 702.175 dealing with certification of small vessel facilities, the following definitions are applicable.

(a)(1) "Small vessel" means only those vessels described in section 3(d)(3) of the Act, 33 U.S.C. 903(d)(3), that is:

(i) A commercial barge which is under 900 lightship displacement tons (long); or

(ii) A commercial tugboat, towboat, crewboat, supply boat, fishing vessel or other work vessel which is under 1,600 tons gross.

(2) For these purposes: (i) One gross ton equals 100 cubic feet, as measured by the current formula contained in the Act of May 6, 1894 as amended through 1974 (46 U.S.C. 77); (ii) one long ton equals 2,240 lbs; and (iii) "Commercial" as it applies to "vessel" means any vessel engaged in commerce but does not include military vessels or Coast Guard vessels.

(b) "Federal Maritime Subsidy" means the construction differential subsidy (CDS) or operating differential subsidy under the Merchant Marine Act of 1936 (46 U.S.C. 1101 et seq.).

(c) "facility" means an operation of an employer at a particular contiguous geographic location.

[51 FR 4283, Feb. 3, 1986]

§ 702.173 Exemptions; requirements, limitations.

(a) Injuries at a facility otherwise covered by the Act are exempted only upon certification that the facility is: (1) Engaged in the building, repairing or dismantling of exclusively small commercial vessels; and (2) does not receive a Federal maritime subsidy.

(b) The exemption does not apply to: (1) Injuries at any facility which occur over the navigable waters of the United States or upon any adjoining pier, wharf, dock, facility over land for launching vessels or for hauling, lifting or drydocking vessels; or (2) where the employee at such facility is not subject to a State workers' compensation law.

[50 FR 396, Jan. 3, 1985]

§ 702.174 Exemptions; necessary information.

(a) Application. Before any facility is exempt from coverage under the Act, the facility must apply for and receive a certificate of exemption from the Director or his/her designee. The application must be made by the owner of the facility; where the owner is a partnership it shall be made by a partner and where a corporation by an officer of the corporation or the manager in charge of the facility for which an exemption is sought. The information submitted shall include the following:

(1) Name, location, physical description and a site plan or aerial photograph of the facility for which an exemption is sought.

(2) Description of the nature of the business.

(3) An affidavit (signed by a partner if the facility is owned by a partnership or an officer if owned by a corporation) vertifying and/or acknowledging that:

(i) the facility is, as of the date of the application, engaged in the business of building, repairing or dismantling exclusively small commercial vessels and that it does not then nor foreseeably will it engage in the building, repairing or dismantling of other than small vessels.

(ii) The facility does not receive any Federal maritime subsidy.

(iii) The signator has the duty to immediately inform the district director of any change in these or other conditions likely to result in a termination of an exemption.

(iv) the employer has secured appropriate compensation liability under a State workers' compensation law.

(v) Any false, relevant statements relating to the application or the failure to notify the district director of any changes in circumstances likely to result in termination of the exemption will be grounds for revocation of the exemption certificate and will subject the employer to all provisions of the Act, including all duties, responsibilities and penalties, retroactive to the date of application or date of change in circumstances, as appropriate.

(b) Action by the Director. The Director or his/her designee shall review the application within thirty (30) days of its receipt.

(1) Where the application is complete and shows that all requirements under 702.173 are met, the Director shall promptly notify the employer by certified mail, return receipt requested, that certification has been approved and will be effective on the date specified. The employer is required to post notice of the exemption at a conspicuous location.

(2) Where the application is incomplete or does not substantiate that all requirements of section 3(d) of the Act, 33 U.S.C. 903(d), have been met, or evidence shows the facility is not eligible for exemption, the Director shall issue a letter which details the reasons for the deficiency or the rejection. The employer/applicant may reapply for certification, correcting deficiencies and/or responding to the reasons for the Director's denial. The Director or his/her designee shall issue a new decision within a reasonable time of reapplication following denial. Such action will be the final administrative review and is not appealable to the Administrative Law Judge or the Benefits Review Board.

(c) The Director or another designated individual at any time has the right to enter on and inspect any facility seeking exemption for purposes of verifying information provided on the application form.

(d) Action by the employer. Immediately upon receipt of the certificate of exemption from coverage under the Act the employer shall post:

(1) A general notice in a conspicuous place that the Act does not cover injuries sustained at the facility in question, the basis of the exemption, the effective date of the exemption and grounds for termination of the exemption.

(2) A notice, where applicable, at the entrances to all areas to which the exemption does not apply.

(Approved by the Office of Management and Budget under control number 1215-0160)

[50 FR 396, Jan. 3, 1985, as amended at 51 FR 4283, Feb. 3, 1986]

§ 702.175 Effect of work on excluded vessels; reinstatement of certification.

(a) When a vessel other than a small commercial vessel, as defined in 702.172, enters a facility which has been certified as exempt from coverage, the exemption shall automatically terminate as of the date such a vessel enters the facility. The exemption shall also terminate on the date a contract for a Federal maritime subsidy is entered into, and, in the situation where the facility undertakes to build a vessel other than a small vessel, when the construction first takes on the characteristics of a vessel, i.e., when the keel is laid. All duties, obligations and requirements imposed by the Act, including the duty to secure compensation liability as required by sections 4 and 32 of the Act, 33 U.S.C. 904 and 932, and to keep records and forward reports, are effective immediately. The employer shall notify the Director or his/her designee immediately where this occurs.

(b) Where an exemption certification is terminated because of circumstances described in (a), the employer may apply for reinstatement of the exemption once the event resulting in termination of the exemption ends. The reapplication shall consist of a reaffirmation of the nature of the business, an explanation of the circumstances leading to the termination of exemption, and an affidavit by the appropriate person affirming that the circumstances prompting the termination no longer exists nor will they reoccur in the forseeable future and that the facility is engaged in building, repairing or dismantling exclusively small vessels. The Director or the Director's designee shall respond to the complete reapplication within ten working days of receipt.

[50 FR 397, Jan. 3, 1985, as amended at 51 FR 4283, Feb. 3, 1986]

Subpart B—Claims Procedures

EMPLOYER'S REPORTS

§ 702.201 Reports from employers of employee's injury or death.

(a) Within 10 days from the date of an employee's injury or death, or 10 days from the date an employer has knowledge of an employee's injury or death, including any disease or death proximately caused by the employment, the employer shall furnish a report thereof to the district director for the compensation district in which the injury or death occurred, and shall thereafter furnish such additional or supplemental reports as the district director may request.

(b) No report shall be filed unless the injury causes the employee to lose one or more shifts from work. However, the employer shall keep a record containing the information specified in 702.202. Compliance with the current OSHA injury record keeping requirements at 29 CFR part 1904 will satisfy the record keeping requirements of this section for no lost time injuries.

(Approved by the Office of Management and Budget under control number 1215-0160)

[38 FR 26861, Sept. 26, 1973, as amended at 50 FR 397, Jan. 3, 1985; 51 FR 4283, Feb. 3, 1986]

§ 702.202 Employer's report; form and contents.

The employer's report of an employee's injury or death shall be in writing and on a form prescribed by the Director for this purpose, and shall contain:

(a) The name, address and business of the employer;

(b) The name, address, occupation and Social Security Number (SSN) of the employee;

(c) The cause, nature, and other relevant circumstances of the injury or death;

(d) The year, month, day, and hour when, and the particular locality where, the injury or death occurred;

(e) Such other information as the Director may require.

(Approved by the Office of Management and Budget under control numbers 1215-0031 and 1215-0063)

[58 FR 68032, Dec. 23, 1993]

§ 702.203 Employer's report; how given.

The employer's report, an original and one copy, may be furnished by delivering it to the appropriate office of the district director, or by mailing it to said office.

§ 702.204 Employer's report; penalty for failure to furnish and/or falsifying.

Any employer, insurance carrier, or self-insured employer who knowingly and willingly fails or refuses to send any report required by 702.201, or who knowingly and willfully makes a false statement or misrepresentation in any report, shall be subject to a civil penalty not to exceed $10,000 for each such failure, refusal, false statement or misrepresentation.

[50 FR 397, Jan. 3, 1985]

§ 702.205 Employer's report; effect of failure to report upon time limitations.

Where the employer, or agent in charge of the business, or carrier has been given notice or has knowledge of an employee's injury or death, and fails, neglects, or refuses to file a report thereof as required by 702.201, the time limitations provisions with respect to the filing of claims for compensation for disability or death (33 U.S.C. 913(a), and see 702.221) shall not begin to run until such report shall have been furnished as required herein.

[38 FR 26861, Sept. 26, 1973, as amended at 50 FR 397, Jan. 3, 1985]

Notice

§ 702.211 Notice of employee's injury or death; designation of responsible official.

(a) In order to claim compensation under the Act, an employee or claimant must first give notice of the fact of an injury or death to the employer and also may give notice to the district director for the compensation district in which the injury or death occurred. Notice to the employer must be given to that individual whom the employer has designated to receive such notices. If no individual has been so designated notice may be given to: (1) The first line supervisor (including foreman, hatchboss or timekeeper), local plant manager or personnel office official; (2) to any partner if the employer is a partnership; or (3) if the employer is a corporation, to any authorized agent, to an officer or to the person in charge of the business at the place where the injury occurred. In the case of a retired employee, the employee/claimant may submit the notice to any of the above persons, whether or not the employer has designated an official to receive such notice.

(b) In order to facilitate the filing of notices, each employer shall designate at least one individual responsible for receiving notices of injury or death; this requirement applies to all employers. The designation shall be by position and the employer shall provide the name and/or position, exact location and telephone number of the individual to all employees by the appropriate method described below.

(1) Type of individual. Designees must be a first line supervisor (including a foreman, hatchboss or timekeeper), local plant manager, personnel office official, company nurse or other individual traditionally entrusted with this duty, who is located full-time on the premises of the covered facility. The employer must designate at least one individual at each place of employment or one individual for each work crew where there is no fixed place of employment (in that case, the designation should always be the same position for all work crews).

(2) How designated. The name and/or title, the location and telephone number of the individual who is selected by the employer to receive all notices shall be given to the district director for the compensation district in which the facility is located; posting on the worksite in a conspicuous place shall fulfill this requirement. A redesignation shall be effected by a change in posting.

(3) Publication. Every employer shall post the name and/or position, the exact location and telephone number of the designated official. The posting shall be part of the general posting requirement, done on a form prescribed by the Director, and placed in a conspicuous location. Posting must be done at each worksite.

(4) Effect of failure to designate. Where an employer fails to properly designate and to properly publish the name and/or position of the individual authorized to receive notices of injury or death, such failure shall constitute satisfactory reasons for excusing the employee/claimant's failure to give notice as authorized by section 12(d)(3)(ii) of the Act, 33 U.S.C. 912(d)(3)(ii).

(Approved by the Office of Management and Budget under control number 1215-0160)

[50 FR 397, Jan. 3, 1985, as amended at 51 FR 4283, Feb. 3, 1986]

§ 702.212 Notice; when given; when given for certain occupational diseases.

(a) For other than occupational diseases described in (b), the employee must give notice within thirty (30) days of the date of the injury or death. For this purpose the date of injury or death is:

(1) The day on which a traumatic injury occurs,

(2) The date on which the employee or claimant is or by the exercise of reasonable diligence or by reason of medical advice, should have been aware of a relationship between the injury or death and the employment; or

(3) In the case of claims for loss of hearing, the date the employee receives an audiogram, with the accompanying report which indicates the employee has suffered a loss of hearing that is related to his or her employment. (See 702.441).

(b) In the case of an occupational disease which does not immediately result in disability or death, notice must be given within one year after the employee or claimant becomes aware, or in the exercise of reasonable diligence or by reason of medical advice, should have been aware, of the relationship between the employment, the disease and the death or disability. For purposes of these occupational diseases, therefore, the notice period does not begin to run until the employee is disabled, or in the case of a retired employee, until a permanent impairment exists.

(c) For purposes of workers whose coverage under this Act is dependent on denial of coverage under a State compensation program, as described in 701.401, the time limitations set forth above do not begin to run until a final decision denying State coverage is issued under the State compensation act.

(Approved by the Office of Management and Budget under control number 1215-0160)

[50 FR 397, Jan. 3, 1985, as amended at 51 FR 4283, Feb. 3, 1986]

§ 702.213 Notice; by whom given

Notice shall be given by the injured employee or someone on his behalf, or in the case of death, by the deceased employee's beneficiary or someone on his behalf.

[38 FR 26861, Sept. 26, 1973. Redesignated at 50 FR 397, Jan. 3, 1985]

§ 702.214 Notice; form and content

Notice shall be in writing on a form prescribed by the Director for this purpose; such form shall be made available to the employee or beneficiary by the employer. The notice shall be signed by the person authorized to give notice, and shall contain the name, address and Social Security Number (SSN) of the employee and, in death cases, also the SSN of the person seeking survivor benefits, and a statement of the time, place, nature and cause of the injury or death.

[58 FR 68032, Dec. 23, 1993]

§ 702.215 Notice; how given

Notice shall be effected by delivering it_by hand or by mail at the address posted by the employer_to the individual designated to receive such notices. Notice when given to the district director, may be by hand or by mail on a form supplied by the Secretary, or orally in person or by telephone.

(Approved by the Office of Management and Budget under control number 1215-0160)

[50 FR 398, Jan. 3, 1985]

§ 702.216 Effect of failure to give notice

Failure to give timely notice to the employer's designated official shall not bar any claim for compensation if: (a) The employer, carrier, or designated official had actual knowledge of the injury or death; or (b) the district director or ALJ determines the employer or carrier has not been prejudiced: or (c) the district director excuses failure to file notice. For purposes of this subsection, actual knowledge shall be deemed to exist if the employee's immediate supervisor was aware of the injury and/or in the case of a hearing loss, where the employer has furnished to the employee an audiogram and report which indicates a loss of hearing. Failure to give notice shall be excused by the district director if: a) Notice, while not given to the designated official, was given to an official of the employer or carrier, and no prejudice resulted; or b) for some other satisfactory reason, notice could not be given. Failure to properly designate and post the individual so designated shall be considered a satisfactory reason. In any event, such defense to a claim must be raised by the employer/carrier at the first hearing on the claim.

[51 FR 4283, Feb. 3, 1986]

§ 702.217 Penalty for false statement, misrepresentation.

(a) Any claimant or representative of a claimant who knowingly and willfully makes a false statement or representation for the purpose of obtaining a benefit or payment under this Act shall be guilty of a felony, and on conviction thereof shall be punished by a fine not to exceed $10,000, by imprisonment not to exceed five years, or by both.

(b) Any person including, but not limited to, an employer, its duly authorized agent or an employee of an insurance carrier, who knowingly and willingly makes a false statement or representation for the purpose of reducing, denying or terminating benefits to an injured employee, or his dependents pursuant to section 9, 33 U.S.C. 909, if the injury results in death, shall be punished by a fine not to exceed $10,000, by imprisonment not to exceed five years, or both.

[50 FR 398, Jan. 3, 1985]

Claims

§ 702.221 Claims for compensation; time limitations.

(a) Claims for compensation for disability or death shall be in writing and filed with the district director for the compensation district in which the injury or death occurred. The Social Security Number (SSN) of the injured employee and, in cases of death, the SSN of the person seeking survivor benefits shall also be set forth on each claim. Claims may be filed anytime after the seventh day of disability or anytime following the death of the employee. Except as provided below, the right to compensation is barred unless a claim is filed within one year of the injury or death, or (where payment is made without an award) within one year of the date on which the last compensation payment was made.

(b) In the case of a hearing loss claim, the time for filing a claim does not begin to run until the employee receives an audiogram with the accompanying report which indicates the employee has sustained a hearing loss that is related to his or her employment. (See 702.441).

(Approved by the Office of Management and Budget under control number 1215-0160)

[50 FR 398, Jan. 3, 1985, as amended at 51 FR 4284, Feb. 3, 1986; 58 FR 68032, Dec. 23, 1993]

§ 702.222 Claims; exceptions to time limitations.

(a) Where a person entitled to compensation under the Act is mentally incompetent or a minor, the time limitation provision of 702.221 shall not apply to a mentally incompetent person so long as such person has no guardian or other authorized representative, but 702.221 shall be applicable from the date of appointment of such guardian or other representative. In the case of minor who has no guardian before he or she becomes of age, time begins to run from the date he or she becomes of age.

(b) Where a person brings a suit at law or in admiralty to recover damages in respect of an injury or death, or files a claim under a State workers' compensation act because such person is excluded from this Act's coverage by reason of section 2(3) or 3(d) of the Act (33 U.S.C. 902(3) or 903(d)), and recovery is denied because the person was an employee and defendant was an employer within the meaning of the Act, and such employer had secured compensation to such employee under the Act, the time limitation in 702.221 shall not begin to run until the date of termination of such suit or proceeding.

(c) Notwithstanding the provisions in paragraph (a) of this section, where the claim is one based on disability or death due to an occupational disease which does not immediately result in death or disability, it must be filed within two years after the employee or claimant becomes aware, or in the exercise of reasonable diligence or by reason of medical advice, should have been aware of the relationship between the employment, the disease and the death or disability, or within one year of the date of last payment of compensation, whichever is later. For purposes of occupational disease, therefore, the time limitation for filing a claim does not begin to run until the employee is disabled, or in the case of a retired employee, where a permanent impairment exists.

(d) The time limitations set forth above do not apply to claims filed under section 49 of the Act, 33 U.S.C.
949.

(Approved by the Office of Management and Budget under control number 1215-0160)

[50 FR 398, Jan. 3, 1985]

§ 702.223 Claims; time limitations; time to object

Notwithstanding the requirements of 702.221, failure to file a claim within the period prescribed in such section shall not be a bar to such right unless objection to such failure is made at the first hearing of such claim in which all parties in interest are given reasonable notice and opportunity to be heard.

[38 FR 26861, Sept. 26, 1973. Redesignated and amended at 50 FR 397, Jan. 3, 1985]

§ 702.224 Claims; notification of employer of filing by employee

Within 10 days after the filing of a claim for compensation for injury or death under the Act, the district director shall give written notice thereof to the employer or carrier, served personally or by certified mail.

[38 FR 26861, Sept. 26, 1973. Redesignated at 50 FR 397, Jan. 3, 1985]

§ 702.225 Withdrawal of a claim.

(a) Before adjudication of claim. A claimant (or an individual who is authorized to execute a claim on his behalf) may withdraw his previously filed claim: Provided, That:

(1) He files with the district director with whom the claim was filed a written request stating the reasons for withdrawal;

(2) The claimant is alive at the time his request for withdrawal is filed;

(3) The district director approves the request for withdrawal as being for a proper purpose and in the claimant's best interest; and

(4) The request for withdrawal is filed, on or before the date the OWCP makes a determination on the claim.

(b) After adjudication of claim. A claim for benefits may be withdrawn by a written request filed after the date the OWCP makes a determination on the claim: Provided, That:

(1) The conditions enumerated in paragraphs (a) (1) through (3) of this section are met; and

(2) There is repayment of the amount of benefits previously paid because of the claim that is being withdrawn or it can be established to the satisfaction of the Office that repayment of any such amount is assured.

(c) Effect of withdrawal of claim. Where a request for withdrawal of a claim is filed and such request for withdrawal is approved, such withdrawal shall be without prejudice to the filing of another claim, subject to the time limitation provisions of section 13 of the Act and of the regulations in this part.

[38 FR 26861, Sept. 26, 1973. Redesignated at 50 FR 397, Jan. 3, 1985]

NONCONTROVERTED CLAIMS

§ 702.231 Noncontroverted claims; payment of compensation without an award

Unless the employer controverts its liability to pay compensation under this Act, the employer or insurance carrier shall pay periodically, promptly and directly to the person entitled thereto benefits prescribed by the Act. For this purpose, where the employer furnishes to an employee a copy of an audiogram with a report thereon, which indicates the employee has sustained a hearing loss causally related to factors of that employment, the employer or insurance carrier shall pay appropriate compensation or at that time controvert the liability to pay compensation under this Act.

[50 FR 399, Jan. 3, 1985]

§ 702.232 Payments without an award; when; how paid

The first installment of compensation shall become due by the fourteenth (14th) day after the employer has been notified, through the designated official or by any other means described in 702.211 et seq., or has actual knowledge of the injury or death. All compensation due on that fourteenth (14th) day shall be paid then and appropriate compensation due thereafter must be paid in semi-monthly installments, unless the district director determines otherwise.

[50 FR 399, Jan. 3, 1985]

702.233 Penalty for failure to pay without an award

If any installment of compensation payable without an award is not paid within 14 days after it becomes due, there shall be added to such unpaid installment an amount equal to 10 per centum thereof which shall be paid at the same time as, but in addition to, such installment unless the employer files notice of controversion in accordance with 702.261, or unless such nonpayment is excused by the district director after a showing by the employer that owing to conditions over which he had no control such installment could not be paid within the period prescribed for the payment.

§ 702.234 Report by employer of commencement and suspension of payments

Immediately upon making the first payment of compensation, and upon the suspension of payments once begun, the employer shall notify the district director having jurisdiction over the place where the injury or death occurred of the commencement or suspension of payments, as the case may be.

702.235 Report by employer of final payment of compensation.

(a) Within 16 days after the final payment of compensation has been made, the employer, the insurance carrier, or where the employer is self-insured, the employer shall notify the district director on a form prescribed by the Secretary, stating that such final payment has been made, the total amount of compensation paid, the name and address of the person(s) to whom payments were made, the date of the injury or death and the name of the injured or deceased employee, and the inclusive dates during which compensation was paid.

(b) A "final payment of compensation" for the purpose of applying the penalty provision of 702.236 shall be deemed any one of the following:

(1) The last payment of compensation made in accordance with a compensation order awarding disability or death benefits, issued by either a district director or an administrative law judge;

(2) The payment of an agreed settlement approved under section 8(i) (A) or (B), of the Act, 33 U.S.C. 908(i);

(3) The last payment made pursuant to an agreement reached by the parties through informal proceedings;

(4) Any other payment of compensation which anticipates no further payments under the Act.

(Approved by the Office of Management and Budget under control number 1215-0024)

(Pub. L. No. 96-511)

[42 FR 45302, Sept. 9, 1977, as amended at 49 FR 18294, Apr. 30, 1984; 50 FR 399, Jan. 3, 1985]

§ 702.236 Penalty for failure to report termination of payments

Any employer failing to notify the district director of termination of payments in accordance with 702.235 shall be assessed a civil penalty in the amount of $100.

AGREED SETTLEMENTS

§ 702.241 Definitions and supplementary information.

(a) As used hereinafter, the term adjudicator shall mean district director or administrative law judge (ALJ).

(b) If a settlement application is submitted to an adjudicator and the case is pending at the Office of Administrative Law Judges, the Benefits Review Board, or any Federal circuit court of appeals, the parties may request that the case be remanded to the adjudicator for consideration of the application. The thirty day period as described in paragraph (f) of this section begins when the remanded case is received by the adjudicator.

(c) If a settlement application is first submitted to an ALJ, the thirty day period mentioned in paragraph (f) of this section does not begin until five days before the date the formal hearing is set. This rule does not preclude the parties from submitting the application at any other time such as (1) after the case is referred for hearing, (2) at the hearing, or (3) after the hearing but before the ALJ issues a decision and order. Where a case is pending before the ALJ but not set for a hearing, the parties may request the case be remanded to the district director for consideration of the settlement.

(d) A settlement agreement between parties represented by counsel, which is deemed approved when not disapproved within thirty days, as described in paragraph (f) of this section, shall be considered to have been filed in the office of the district director on the thirtieth day for purposes of sections 14 and 21 of the Act, 33 U.S.C. 914 and 921.

(e) A fee for representation which is included in an agreement that is approved in the manner described in paragraph (d) of this section, shall also be considered approved within the meaning of section 28(e) of the Act, 33 U.S.C. 928(e).

(f) The thirty day period for consideration of a settlement agreement shall be calculated from the day after receipt unless the parties are advised otherwise by the adjudicator. (See 702.243(b)). If the last day of this period is a holiday or occurs during a weekend, the next business day shall be considered the thirtieth day.

(g) An agreement among the parties to settle a claim is limited to the rights of the parties and to claims then in existence; settlement of disability compensation or medical benefits shall not be a settlement of survivor benefits nor shall the settlement affect, in any way, the right of survivors to file a claim for survivor's benefits.

(h) For purposes of this section and 702.243 the term counsel means any attorney admitted to the bar of any State, territory or the District of Columbia.

[50 FR 399, Jan. 3, 1985, as amended at 51 FR 4284, Feb. 3, 1986]

§ 702.242 Information necessary for a complete settlement application.

(a) The settlement application shall be a self-sufficient document which can be evaluated without further reference to the administrative file. The application shall be in the form of a stipulation signed by all parties and shall contain a brief summary of the facts of the case to include: a description of the incident, a description of the nature of the injury to include the degree of impairment and/or disability, a description of the medical care rendered to date of settlement, and a summary of compensation paid and the compensation rate or, where benefits have not been paid, the claimant's average weekly wage.

(b) The settlement application shall contain the following:

(1) A full description of the terms of the settlement which clearly indicates, where appropriate, the amounts to be paid for compensation, medical benefits, survivor benefits and representative's fees which shall be itemized as required by 702.132.

(2) The reason for the settlement, and the issues which are in dispute, if any.

(3) The claimant's date of birth and, in death claims, the names and birth dates of all dependents.

(4) Information on whether or not the claimant is working or is capable of working. This should include, but not be limited to, a description of the claimant's educational background and work history, as well as other factors which could impact, either favorably or unfavorably, on future employability.

(5) A current medical report which fully describes any injury related impairment as well as any unrelated conditions. This report shall indicate whether maximum medical improvement has been reached and whether further disability or medical treatment is anticipated. If the claimant has already reached maximum medical improvement, a medical report prepared at the time the employee's condition stabilized will satisfy the requirement for a current medical report. A medical report need not be submitted with agreements to settle survivor benefits unless the circumstances warrant it.

(6) A statement explaining how the settlement amount is considered adequate.

(7) If the settlement application covers medical benefits an itemization of the amount paid for medical expenses by year for the three years prior to the date of the application. An estimate of the claimant's need for future medical treatment as well as an estimate of the cost of such medical treatment shall also be submitted which indicates the inflation factor and/or the discount rate used, if any. The adjudicator may waive these requirements for good cause.

(8) Information on any collateral source available for the payment of medical expenses.

(Approved by the Office of Management and Budget under control number 1215-0160)

[50 FR 399, Jan. 3, 1985, as amended at 51 FR 4284, Feb. 3, 1986]

§ 702.243 Settlement application; how submitted, how approved, how disapproved, criteria.

(a) When the parties to a claim for compensation, including survivor benefits and medical benefits, agree to a settlement they shall submit a complete application to the adjudicator. The application shall contain all the information outlined in 702.242 and shall be sent by certified mail, return receipt requested or submitted in person, or by any other delivery service with proof of delivery to the adjudicator. Failure to submit a complete application shall toll the thirty day period mentioned in section 8(i) of the Act, 33 U.S.C. 908(i), until a complete application is received.

(b) The adjudicator shall consider the settlement application within thirty days and either approve or disapprove the application. The liability of an employer/insurance carrier is not discharged until the settlement is specifically approved by a compensation order issued by the adjudicator. However, if the parties are represented by counsel, the settlement shall be deemed approved unless specifically disapproved within thirty days after receipt of a complete application. This thirty day period does not begin until all the information described in 702.242 has been submitted. The adjudicator shall examine the settlement application within thirty days and shall immediately serve by certified mail on all parties notice of any deficiency. This notice shall also indicate that the thirty day period will not commence until the deficiency is corrected.

(c) If the adjudicator disapproves a settlement application, the adjudicator shall serve on all parties a written statement or order containing the reasons for disapproval. This statement shall be served by certified mail within thirty days of receipt of a complete application (as described in 702.242.) if the parties are represented by counsel. If the disapproval was made by a district director, any party to the settlement may request a hearing before an ALJ as provided in sections 8 and 19 of the Act, 33 U.S.C. 908 and 919, or an amended application may be submitted to the district director. If, following the hearing, the ALJ disapproves the settlement, the parties may: (1) Submit a new application, (2) file an appeal with the Benefits Review Board as provided in section 21 of the Act, 33 U.S.C. 921, or (3) proceed with a hearing on the merits of the claim. If the application is initially disapproved by an ALJ, the parties may (1) submit a new application or (2) proceed with a hearing on the merits of the claim.

(d) The parties may submit a settlement application solely for compensation, or solely for medical benefits or for compensation and medical benefits combined.

(e) If either portion of a combined compensation and medical benefits settlement application is disapproved the entire application is disapproved unless the parties indicate on the face of the application that they agree to settle either portion independently.

(f) When presented with a settlement, the adjudicator shall review the application and determine whether, considering all of the circumstances, including, where appropriate, the probability of success if the case were formally litigated, the amount is adequate. The criteria for determining the adequacy of the settlement application shall include, but not be limited to:

(1) The claimant's age, education and work history;

(2) The degree of the claimant's disability or impairment;

(3) The availability of the type of work the claimant can do;

(4) The cost and necessity of future medical treatment (where the settlement includes medical benefits).

(g) In cases being paid pursuant to a final compensation order, where no substantive issues are in dispute, a settlement amount which does not equal the present value of future compensation payments commuted, computed at the discount rate specified below, shall be considered inadequate unless the parties to the settlement show that the amount is adequate. The probability of the death of the beneficiary before the expiration of the period during which he or she is entitled to compensation shall be determined according to the most current United States Life Table, as developed by the United States Department of Health and Human Services, which shall be updated from time to time. The discount rate shall be equal to the coupon issue yield equivalent (as determined by the Secretary of the Treasury) of the average accepted auction price for the last auction of 52 weeks U.S. Treasury Bills settled immediately prior to the date of the submission of the settlement application.

[50 FR 399, Jan. 3, 1985, as amended at 51 FR 4284, Feb. 3, 1986]

CONTROVERTED CLAIMS

§ 702.251 Employer's controversion of the right to compensation

Where the employer controverts the right to compensation after notice or knowledge of the injury or death, or after receipt of a written claim, he shall give notice thereof, stating the reasons for controverting the right to compensation, using the form prescribed by the Director. Such notice, or answer to the claim, shall be filed with the district director within 14 days from the date the employer receives notice or has knowledge of the injury or death. The original notice shall be sent to the district director having jurisdiction, and a copy thereof shall be given or mailed to the claimant.

(Approved by the Office of Management and Budget under control number 1215-0023)

(Pub. L. No. 96-511)

[38 FR 26861, Sept. 26, 1973, as amended at 49 FR 18294, Apr. 30, 1984]

§ 702.252 Action by district director upon receipt of notice of controversion

Upon receiving the employer's notice of controversion, the district director shall forthwith commence proceedings for the adjudication of the claim in accordance with the procedures set forth in subpart C of this part.

CONTESTED CLAIMS

§ 702.261 Claimant's contest of actions taken by employer or carrier with respect to the claim

Where the claimant contests an action by the employer or carrier reducing, suspending, or terminating benefits, including medical care, he should immediately notify the office of the district director having jurisdiction, in person or in writing, and set forth the facts pertinent to his complaint.

§ 702.262 Action by district director upon receipt of notice of contest

Upon receipt of the claimant's notice of contest, the district director shall forthwith commence proceedings for adjudication of the claim in accordance with the procedures set forth in subpart C of this part.

DISCRIMINATION

§ 702.271 Discrimination; against employees who bring proceedings, prohibition and penalty.

(a) No employer or its duly authorized agent may discharge or in any manner discriminate against an employee as to his/her employment because that employee: (1) has claimed or attempted to claim compensation under this Act; or (2) has testified or is about to testify in a proceeding under this Act; except that to discharge or refuse to employ a person who has been adjudicated to have filed a fraudulent claim for compensation or otherwise made a false statement or misrepresentation under section 31(a)(1) of the Act, 33 U.S.C. 931(a)(1) is not a violation of this section. Any employer who violates this section shall be liable to a penalty of not less than $1,000 or more than $5,000 to be paid (by the employer alone, and not by a carrier) to the district director for deposit in the special fund described in section 44 of the Act, 33 U.S.C. 944; and shall restore that employee to his or her employment along with all wages lost due to the discrimination unless that employee has ceased to be qualified to perform the duties of the employment.

(b) When a district director receives a complaint from an employee alleging discrimination as defined under section 49, he or she shall notify the employer, and within five working days, initiate specific inquiry to determine all the facts and circumstances pertaining thereto. This may be accomplished by interviewing the employee, employer representatives and other parties who may have information about the matter. Interviews may be conducted by written correspondence, telephone or personal interview.

(c) If circumstances warrant, the district director may also conduct an informal conference on the issue as described in 702.312 through 702.314.

(d) Any employee discriminated against is entitled to be restored to his employment and to be compensated by the employer for any loss of wages arising out of such discrimination provided that the employee is qualified to perform the duties of the employment. If it is determined that the employee has been discriminated against, the district director shall also determine whether the employee is qualified to perform the duties of the employment. The district director may use medical evidence submitted by the parties or he may arrange to have the employee examined by a physician selected by the district director. The cost of the medical examination arranged for by the district director may be charged to the special fund established by section 44, 33 U.S.C. 944.

[42 FR 45302, Sept. 9, 1977, as amended at 50 FR 400, Jan. 3, 1985]

§ 702.272 Informal recommendation by district director.

(a) If the district director determines that the employee has been discharged or suffered discrimination and is able to resume his or her duties, the district director will recommend that the employer reinstate the employee and/or make such restitution as is indicated by the circumstances of the case, including compensation for any wage loss suffered as the result of the discharge or discrimination. The district director may also assess the employer an appropriate penalty, as determined under authority vested in the district director by the Act. If the district director determines that no violation occurred he shall notify the partries of his findings and the reasons for recommending that the complaint be denied. If the employer and employee accept the district director's recommendation, it will be incorporated in an order and mailed to each party within 10 days.

(b) If the parties do not agree to the recommendation, the district director shall, within 10 days after receipt of the rejection, prepare a memorandum summarizing the disagreement, mail a copy to all interested parties, and shall within 14 days thereafter refer the case to the Office of the Chief Administrative Law Judge for hearing pursuant to 702.317.

[42 FR 45302, Sept. 9, 1977]

§ 702.273 Adjudication by Office of the Chief Administrative Law Judge

The Office of Administrative Law Judges is responsible for final determinations of all disputed issues connected with the discrimination complaint, including the amount of penalty to be assessed, and shall proceed with a formal hearing as described in 702.331 to 702.394.

[42 FR 45302, Sept. 9, 1977]

§ 702.274 Employer's refusal to pay penalty

In the event the employer refuses to pay the penalty assessed, the district director shall refer the complete administrative file to the Associate Director, Division of Longshore and Harbor Workers' Compensation, for subsequent transmittal to the Associate Solicitor for Employee Benefits, with the request that appropriate legal action be taken to recover the penalty.

[42 FR 45302, Sept. 9, 1977]

Third Party

§ 702.281 Third party action.

(a) Every person claiming benefits under this Act (or the representative) shall promptly notify the employer and the district director when:

(1) A claim is made that someone other than the employer or person or persons in its employ, is liable in damages to the claimant because of the injury or death and identify such party by name and address.

(2) Legal action is instituted by the claimant or the representative against some person or party other than the employer or a person or persons in his employ, on the ground that such other person is liable in damages to the claimant on account of the compensable injury and/or death; specify the amount of damages claimed and identify the person or party by name and address.

(3) Any settlement, compromise or any adjudication of such claim has been effected and report the terms, conditions and amounts of such resolution of claim.

(b) Where the claim or legal action instituted against a third party results in a settlement agreement which is for an amount less than the compensation to which a person would be entitled under this Act, the person (or the person's representative) must obtain the prior, written approval of the settlement from the employer and the employer's carrier before the settlement is executed. Failure to do so relieves the employer and/or carrier of liability for compensation described in section 33(f) of Act, 33 U.S.C. 933(f) and for medical benefits otherwise due under section 7 of the Act, 33 U.S.C. 907, regardless of whether the employer or carrier has made payments of acknowledged entitlement to benefits under the Act. The approval shall be on a form provided by the Director and filed, within thirty days after the settlement is entered into, with the district director who has jurisdiction in the district where the injury occurred.

[42 FR 45303, Sept. 9, 1977, as amended at 50 FR 400, Jan. 3, 1985; 51 FR 4284, Feb. 3, 1986]

Report of Earnings

§ 702.285 Report of earnings.

(a) An employer, carrier or the Director (for those cases being paid from the Special Fund) may require an employee to whom it is paying compensation to submit a report on earnings from employment or self-employment. This report may not be required any more frequently than semiannually. The report shall be made on a form prescribed by the Director and shall include all earnings from employment and self-employment and the periods for which the earnings apply. The employee must return the complete report on earnings even where he or she has no earnings to report.

(b) For these purposes the term "earnings" is defined as all monies received from any employment and includes but is not limited to wages, salaries, tips, sales commissions, fees for services provided, piecework and all revenue received from self-employment even if the business or enterprise operated at a loss of if the profits were reinvested.

(Approved by the Office of Management and Budget under control number 1215-0160)

[50 FR 400, Jan. 3, 1985]

§ 702.286 Report of earnings; forfeiture of compensation.

(a) Any employee who fails to submit the report on earnings from employment or selfemployment under 702.285 or, who knowingly and willingly omits or understates any part of such earnings, shall upon a determination by the district director forfeit all right to compensation with respect to any period during which the employee was required to file such a report. The employee must return the completed report on earnings (even where he or she reports no earnings) within thirty (30) days of the date of receipt; this period may be extended for good cause, by the district director, in determining whether a violation of this requirement has occurred.

(b) Any employer or carrier who believes that a violation of paragraph (a) of this section has occurred may file a charge with the district director. The allegation shall be accompanied by evidence which includes a copy of the report, with proof of service requesting the information from the employee and clearly stating the dates for which the employee was required to report income. Where the employer/carrier is alleging an omission or understatement of earnings, it shall, in addition, present evidence of earnings by the employee during that period, including copies of checks, affidavits from employers who paid the employee earnings, receipts of income from self-employment or any other evidence showing earnings not reported or under-reported for the period in question. Where the district director finds the evidence sufficient to support the charge he or she shall convene an informal conference as described in subpart C and shall issue a compensation order affiming or denying the charge and setting forth the amount of compensation for the specified period. If there is a conflict over any issue relating to this matter any party may request a formal hearing before an Administrative Law Judge as described in subpart C.

(c) Compensation forfeited under paragraph (b) of this section, if already paid, shall be recovered by a deduction from the compensation payable to the employee if any, on such schedule as determined by the district director. The district director's discretion in such cases extends only to rescheduling repayment by crediting future compensation and not to whether and in what amounts compensation is forfeited. For this purpose, the district director shall consider the employee's essential expenses for living, income from whatever source, and assets, including cash, savings and checking accounts, stocks, bonds, and other securities.

[50 FR 400, Jan. 3, 1985]

Subpart C—Adjudication Procedures

General

702.301 Scope of this subpart.

The regulations in this subpart govern the adjudication of claims in which the employer has filed a notice of controversion under 702.251, or the employee has filed notice of contest under 702.261. In the vast majority of cases, the problem giving rise to the controversy results from misunderstandings, clerical or mechanical errors, or mistakes of fact or law. Such problems seldom require resolution through formal hearings, with the attendant production of expert witnesses. Accordingly, by 702.311 et seq., the district directors are empowered to amicably and promptly resolve such problems by informal procedures. Where there is a genuine dispute of fact or law which cannot be so disposed of informally, resort must be had to the formal hearing procedures as set forth beginning at 702.331. Supplementary compensation orders, modifications, and interlocutory matters are governed by regulations beginning with 702.371. Thereafter, appeals from compensation orders are discussed beginning with 702.391 (the regulations of the Benefits Review Board are set forth in full in part 802 of this title).

Action by District Directors

§ 702.311 Handling of claims matters by district directors; informal conferences.

The district director is empowered to resolve disputes with respect to claims in a manner designed to protect the rights of the parties and also to resolve such disputes at the earliest practicable date. This will generally be accomplished by informal discussions by telephone or by conferences at the district director's office. Some cases will be handled by written correspondence. The regulations governing informal conferences at the district director's office with all parties present are set forth below. When handling claims by telephone, or at the office with only one of the parties, the district director and his staff shall make certain that a full written record be made of the matters discussed and that such record be placed in the administrative file. When claims are handled by correspondence, copies of all communications shall constitute the administrative file.

§ 702.312 Informal conferences; called by and held before whom.

Informal conferences shall be called by the district director or his designee assigned or reassigned the case and held before that same person, unless such person is absent or unavailable. When so assigned, the designee shall perform the duties set forth below assigned to the district director, except that a compenstion order following an agreement shall be issued only by a person so designated by the Director to perform such duty.

[42 FR 45303, Sept. 9, 1977]

§ 702.313 Informal conferences; how called; when called.

Informal conferences may be called upon not less than 10 days' notice to the parties, unless the parties agree to meet at an earlier date. The notice may be given by telephone, but shall be confirmed by use of a written notice on a form prescribed by the Director. The notice shall indicate the date, time and place of the conference, and shall also specify the matters to be discussed. For good cause shown conferences may be rescheduled. A copy of such notice shall be placed in the administrative file.

§ 702.314 Informal conferences; how conducted; where held.

(a) No stenographic report shall be taken at informal conferences and no witnesses shall be called. The district director shall guide the discussion toward the achievement of the purpose of such conference, recommending courses of action where there are disputed issues, and giving the parties the benefit of his experience and specialized knowledge in the field of workmen's compensation.

(b) Conferences generally shall be held at the district director's office. However, such conferences may be held at any place which, in the opinion of the district director, will be of greater convenience to the parties or to their representatives.

§ 702.315 Conclusion of conference; agreement on all matters with respect to the claim.

(a) Following an informal conference at which agreement is reached on all issues, the district director shall (within 10 days after conclusion of the conference), embody the agreement in a memorandum or within 30 days issue a formal compensation order, to be filed and mailed in accordance with 702.349. If either party requests that a formal compensation order be issued the district director shall, within 30 days of such request, prepare, file, and serve such order in accordance with 702.349. Where the problem was of such nature that it was resolved by telephone discussion or by exchange of written correspondence, the parties shall be notified by the same means that agreement was reached and the district director shall prepare a memorandum or order setting forth the terms agreed upon. In either instance, when the employer or carrier has agreed to pay, reinstate or increase monetary compensation benefits, or to restore or appropriately change medical care benefits, such action shall be commenced immediately upon becoming aware of the agreement, and without awaiting receipt of the memorandum or the formal compensation order.

(b) Where there are several conferences or discussions, the provisions of paragraph (a) of this section do not apply until the last conference. The district director shall, however, prepare and place in his administrative file a short, succinct memorandum of each preceding conference or discussion.

[38 FR 26861, Sept. 26, 1973, as amended at 42 FR 45303, Sept. 9, 1977]

§ 702.316 Conclusion of conference; no agreement on all matters with respect to the claim.

When it becomes apparent during the course of the informal conference that agreement on all issues cannot be reached, the district director shall bring the conference to a close, shall evaluate all evidence available to him or her, and after such evaluation shall prepare a memorandum of conference setting forth all outstanding issues, such facts or allegations as appear material and his or her recommendations and rationale for resolution of such issues. Copies of this memorandum shall then be sent by certified mail to each of the parties or their representatives, who shall then have 14 days within which to signify in writing to the district director whether they agree or disagree with his or her recommendations. If they agree, the district director shall proceed as in 702.315(a). If they disagree (Caution: See 702.134), then the district director may schedule such further conference or conferences as, in his or her opinion, may bring about agreement; if he or she is satisfied that any further conference would be unproductive, or if any party has requested a hearing, the district director shall prepare the case for transfer to the Office of the Chief Administrative Law Judge (See 702.317, 702.331-702.351).

[42 FR 42551, Aug. 23, 1977]

§ 702.317 Preparation and transfer of the case for hearing.

A case is prepared for transfer in the following manner:

(a) The district director shall furnish each of the parties or their representatives with a copy of a prehearing statement form.

(b) Each party shall, within 21 days after receipt of such form, complete it and return it to the district director and serve copies on all other parties. Extensions of time for good cause may be granted by the district director.

(c) Upon receipt of the completed forms, the district director, after checking them for completeness and after any further conferences that, in his or her opinion, are warranted, shall transmit them to the Office of the Chief Administrative Law Judge by letter of transmittal together with all available evidence which the parties intend to submit at the hearing (exclusive of X-rays, slides and other materials not suitable for mailing which may be offered into evidence at the time of hearing); the materials transmitted shall not include any recommendations expressed or memoranda prepared by the district director pursuant to 702.316.

(d) If the completed pre-hearing statement forms raise new or additional issues not previously considered by the district director or indicate that material evidence will be submitted that could reasonably have been made available to the district director before he or she prepared the last memorandum of conference, the district director shall transfer the case to the Office of the Chief Administrative Law Judge only after having considered such issues or evaluated such evidence or both and having issued an additional memorandum of conference in conformance with 702.316.

(e) If a party fails to complete or return his or her pre-hearing statement form within the time allowed, the district director may, at his or her discretion, transmit the case without that party's form. However, such transmittal shall include a statement from the district director setting forth the circumstanes causing the failure to include the form, and such party's failure to submit a pre-hearing statement form may, subject to rebuttal at the formal hearing, be considered by the administrative law judge, to the extent intransigence is relevant, in subsequent rulings on motions which may be made in the course of the formal hearing.

(Approved by the Office of Management and Budget under control number 1215-0085)

(Pub. L. No. 96-511)

[42 FR 42551, Aug. 23, 1977, as amended at 49 FR 18295, Apr. 30, 1984]

§ 702.318 The record; what constitutes; nontransferability of the administrative file.

For the purpose of any further proceedings under the Act, the formal record of proceedings shall consist of the hearing record made before the administrative law judge (see 702.344). When transferring the case for hearing pursuant to 702.317, the district director shall not transfer the administrative file under any circumstances.

§ 702.319 Obtaining documents from the administrative file for reintroduction at formal hearings.

Whenever any party considers any document in the administrative file essential to any further proceedings under the Act, it is the responsibility of such party to obtain such document from the district director and reintroduce it for the record before the administrative law judge. The type of document that may be obtained shall be limited to documents previously submitted to the district director, including documents or forms with respect to notices, claims, controversions, contests, progress reports, medical services or supplies, etc. The work products of the district director or his staff shall not be subject to retrieval. The procedure for obtaining documents shall be for the requesting party to inform the district director in writing of the documents he wishes to obtain, specifying them with particularity. Upon receipt, the district director shall cause copies of the requested documents to be made and then:

(a) Place the copies in the file together with the letter of request, and (b) promptly forward the originals to the requesting party. The handling of multiple requests for the same document shall be within the discretion of the district director and with the cooperation of the requesting parties.

Special Fund

§ 702.321 Procedures for determining applicability of section 8(f) of the Act.

(a) Application: filing, service, contents. (1) An employer or insurance carrier which seeks to invoke the provisions of section 8(f) of the Act must request limitation of its liability and file, in duplicate, with the district director a fully documented application. A fully documented application shall contain the following information: (i) A specific description of the pre-existing condition relied upon as constituting an existing permanent partial disability; (ii) the reasons for believing that the claimant's permanent disability after the injury would be less were it not for the pre-existing permanent partial disability or that the death would not have ensued but for that disability. These reasons must be supported by medical evidence as specified in paragraph (a)(1)(iv) of this section; (iii) the basis for the assertion that the pre-existing condition relied upon was manifest in the employer; and (iv) documentary medical evidence relied upon in support of the request for section 8(f) relief. This medical evidence shall include, but not be limited to, a current medical report establishing the extent of all impairments and the date of maximum medical improvement. If the claimant has already reached maximum medical improvement, a report prepared at that time will satisfy the requirement for a current medical report. If the current disability is total, the medical report must explain why the disability is not due solely to the second injury. If the current disability is partial, the medical report must explain why the disability is not due solely to the second injury and why the resulting disability is materially and substantially greater than that which would have resulted from the subsequent injury alone. If the injury is loss of hearing, the pre-existing hearing loss must be documented by an audiogram which complies with the requirements of 702.441. If the claim is for survivor's benefits, the medical report must establish that the death was not due solely to the second injury. Any other evidence considered necessary for consideration of the request for section 8(f) relief must be submitted when requested by the district director or Director.

(2) If claim is being paid by the special fund and the claimant dies, an employer need not reapply for section 8(f) relief. However, survivor benefits will not be paid until it has been established that the death was due to the accepted injury and the eligible survivors have been identified. The district director will issue a compensation order after a claim has been filed and entitlement of the survivors has been verified. Since the employer remains a party in interest to the claim, a compensation order will not be issued without the agreement of the employer.

(b) Application: Time for filing. (1) A request for section 8(f) relief should be made as soon as the permanency of the claimant's condition becomes known or is an issue in dispute. This could be when benefits are first paid for permanent disability, or at an informal conference held to discuss the permanency of the claimant's condition. Where the claim is for death benefits, the request should be made as soon as possible after the date of death. Along with the request for section 8(f) relief, the applicant must also submit all the supporting documentation required by this section, described in paragraph (a), of this section. Where possible, this documentation should accompany the request, but may be submitted separately, in which case the district director shall, at the time of the request, fix a date for submission of the fully documented application. The date shall be fixed as follows:

(i) Where notice is given to all parties that permanency shall be an issue at an informal conference, the fully documented application must be submitted at or before the conference. For these purposes, notice shall mean when the issues of permanency is noted on the form LS-141, Notice of Informal Conference. All parties are required to list issue reasonably anticipated to be discussed at the conference when the initial request for a conference is made and to notify all parties of additional issues which arise during the period before the conference is actually held.

(ii) Where the issue of permanency is first raised at the informal conference and could not have reasonably been anticipated by the parties prior to the conference, the district director shall adjourn the conference and establish the date by which the fully documented application must be submitted and so notify the employer/carrier. The date shall be set by the district director after reviewing the circumstances of the case.

(2) At the request of the employer or insurance carrier, and for good cause, the district director, at his/her discretion, may grant an extension of the date for submission of the fully documented application. In fixing the date for submission of the application under circumstances other than described above or in considering any request for an extension of the date for submitting the application, the district director shall consider all the circumstances of the case, including but not limited to: Whether the claimant is being paid compensation and the hardship to the claimant of delaying referral of the case to the Office of Administrative Law Judges (OALJ); the complexity of the issues and the availability of medical and other evidence to the employer; the length of time the employer was or should have been aware that permanency is an issue; and, the reasons listed in support of the request. If the employer/carrier requested a specific date, the reasons for selection of that date will also be considered. Neither the date selected for submission of the fully documented application nor any extension therefrom can go beyond the date the case is referred to the OALJ for formal hearing.

(3) Where the claimant's condition has not reached maximum medical improvement and no claim for permanency is raised by the date the case is referred to the OALJ, an application need not be submitted to the district director to preserve the employer's right to later seek relief under section 8(f) of the Act. In all other cases, failure to submit a fully documented application by the date established by the district director shall be an absolute defense to the liability of the special fund. This defense is an affirmative defense which must be raised and pleaded by the Director. The absolute defense will not be raised where permanency was not an issue before the district director. In all other cases, where permanency has been raised, the failure of an employer to submit a timely and fully documented application for section 8(f) relief shall not prevent the district director, at his/her discretion, from considering the claim for compensation and transmitting the case for formal hearing. The failure of an employer to present a timely and fully documented application for section 8(f) relief may be excused only where the employer could not have reasonably anticipated the liability of the special fund prior to the consideration of the claim by the district director. Relief under section 8(f) is not available to an employer who fails to comply with section 32(a) of the Act, 33 U.S.C. 932(a).

(c) Application: Approval, disapproval. If all the evidence required by paragraph (a) was submitted with the application for section 8(f) relief and the facts warrant relief under this section, the district director shall award such relief after concurrence by the Associate Director, DLHWC, or his or her designee. If the district director or the Associate Director or his or her designee finds that the facts do not warrant relief under section 8(f) the district director shall advise the employer of the grounds for the denial. The application for section 8(f) relief may then be considered by an administrative law judge. When a case is transmitted to the Office of Administrative Law Judges the district director shall also attach a copy of the application for section 8(f) relief submitted by the employer, and notwithstanding 702.317(c), the district director's denial of the application.

(Approved by the Office of Management and Budget under control number 1215-0160)

[51 FR 4285, Feb. 3, 1986]

FORMAL HEARINGS

§ 702.331 Formal hearings; procedure initiating.

Formal hearings are initiated by transmitting to the Office of the Chief Administrative Law Judge the pre-hearing statement forms, the available evidence which the parties intend to submit at the formal hearing, and the letter of transmittal from the district director as provided in 702.316 and 702.317.

[42 FR 42552, Aug. 23, 1977]

§ 702.332 Formal hearings; how conducted.

Formal hearings shall be conducted by the administrative law judge assigned the case by the Office of the Chief Administrative Law Judge in accordance with the provisions of the Administrative Procedure Act, 5 U.S.C. 554 et seq. All hearings shall be transcribed.

§ 702.333 Formal hearings; parties.

(a) The necessary parties for a formal hearing are the claimant and the employer or insurance carrier, and the administrative law judge assigned the case.

(b) The Solicitor of Labor or his designee may appear and participate in any formal hearing held pursuant to these regulations on behalf of the Director as an interested party.

§ 702.334 Formal hearings; representatives of parties.

The claimant and the employer or carrier may be represented by persons of their choice.

§ 702.335 Formal hearings; notice.

On a form prescribed for this purpose, the Office of the Chief Administrative Law Judge shall notify the parties (See 702.333) of the place and time of the formal hearing not less than 30 days in advance thereof.

[42 FR 42552, Aug. 23, 1977]

§ 702.336 Formal hearings; new issues.

(a) If, during the course of the formal hearing, the evidence presented warrants consideration of an issue or issues not previously considered, the hearing may be expanded to include the new issue. If in the opinion of the administrative law judge the new issue requires additional time for preparation, the parties shall be given a reasonable time within which to prepare for it. If the new issue arises from evidence that has not been considered by the district director, and such evidence is likely to resolve the case without the need for a formal hearing, the administrative law judge may remand the case to the district director for his or her evaluation and recommendation pursuant to, 702.316.

(b) At any time prior to the filing of the compensation order in the case, the administrative law judge may in his discretion, upon the application of a party or upon his own motion, give notice that he will consider any new issue. The parties shall be given not less than 10 days' notice of the hearing on such new issue. The parties may stipulate that the issue may be heard at an earlier time and shall proceed to a hearing on the new issue in the same manner as on an issue initially considered.

[38 FR 26861, Sept. 26, 1973, as amended at 42 FR 42552, Aug. 23, 1977]

§ 702.337 Formal hearings; change of time or place for hearings; postponements.

(a) Except for good cause shown, hearings shall be held at convenient locations not more than 75 miles from the claimant's residence.

(b) Once a formal hearing has been scheduled, continuances shall not be granted except in cases of extreme hardship or where attendance of a party or his or her representative is mandated at a previously scheduled judicial proceeding. Unless the ground for the request arises thereafter, requests for continuances must be received by the Chief Administrative Law Judge at least 10 days before the scheduled hearing date, must be served upon the other parties and must specify the extreme hardship or previously scheduled judicial proceeding claimed.

(c) The Chief Administrative Law Judge or the administrative law judge assigned to the case may change the time and place of the hearing, or temporarily adjourn a hearing, on his own motion or for good cause shown by a party. The parties shall be given not less than 10 days' notice of the new time and place of the hearing, unless they agree to such change without notice.

[42 FR 42552, Aug. 23, 1977]

§ 702.338 Formal hearings; general procedures.

All hearings shall be attended by the parties or their representatives and such other persons as the administrative law judge deems necessary and proper. The administrative law judge shall inquire fully into the matters at issue and shall receive in evidence the testimony of witnesses and any documents which are relevant and material to such matters. If the administrative law judge believes that there is relevant and material evidence available which has not been presented at the hearing, he may adjourn the hearing or, at any time, prior to the filing of the compensation order, reopen the hearing for the receipt of such evidence. The order in which evidence and allegations shall be presented and the procedures at the hearings generally, except as these regulations otherwise expressly provide, shall be in the discretion of the administrative law judge and of such nature as to afford the parties a reasonable opportunity for a fair hearing.

§ 702.339 Formal hearings; evidence.

In making an investigation or inquiry or conducting a hearing, the administrative law judge shall not be bound by common law or statutory rules of evidence or by technical or formal rules of procedure, except as provided by 5 U.S.C. 554 and these regulations; but may make such investigation or inquiry or conduct such hearing in such a manner as to best ascertain the rights of the parties.

§ 702.340 Formal hearings; witnesses.

(a) Witnesses at the hearing shall testify under oath or affirmation. The administrative law judge may examine the witnesses and shall allow the parties or their representatives to do so.

(b) No person shall be required to attend as a witness in any proceeding before an administrative law judge at a place more than 100 miles from his place of residence, unless his lawful mileage and fees for one day's attendance shall be paid or tendered to him in advance of the hearing date.

§ 702.341 Formal hearings; depositions; interrogatories.

The testimony of any witness, including any party represented by counsel, may be taken by deposition or interrogatory according to the Federal Rules of Civil Procedure as supplemented by local rules of practice for the Federal district court for the judicial district in which the case is pending. However, such depositions or interrogatories must be completed within reasonable times to be fixed by the Chief Administrative Law Judge or the administrative law judge assigned to the case.

[42 FR 42552, Aug. 23, 1977]

§ 702.342 Formal hearings; witness fees.

Witnesses summoned in a formal hearing before an administrative law judge or whose depositions are taken shall receive the same fees and mileage as witnesses in courts of the United States (33 U.S.C. 925).

§ 702.343 Formal hearings; oral argument and written allegations.

Any party upon request shall be allowed a reasonable time for presentation of oral argument and shall be permitted to file a pre-hearing brief or other written statement of fact or law. A copy of any such pre-hearing brief or other written statement shall be filed with the Chief Administrative Law Judge or the administrative law judge assigned to the case before or during the proceeding at which evidence is submitted to the administrative law judge and shall be served upon each other party. Posthearing briefs will not be permitted except at the request of the administrative law judge or upon averment on the record of a party that the case presents a specific novel or difficult legal or factual issue (or issues) that cannot be adequately addressed in oral summation. When permitted, any such brief shall be limited to the issue or issues specified by the administrative law judge or by the party in his or her averment and shall be due from any party desiring to address such issue or issues within 15 days of the conclusion of the proceeding at which evidence is submitted to the administrative law judge. Enlargement of the time for filing such briefs shall be granted only if the administrative law judge is persuaded that the brief will be helpful to him or her and that the enlargement granted will not delay decision of the case.

[42 FR 42552, Aug. 23, 1977]

§ 702.344 Formal hearings; record of hearing.

ll formal hearings shall be open to the public and shall be stenographically reported. All evidence upon which the administrative law judge relies for his final decision shall be contained in the transcript of testimony either directly or by appropriate reference. All medical reports, exhibits, and any other pertinent document or record, in whole or in material part, shall be incorporated into the record either by reference or as an appendix.

§ 702.345 Formal hearings; consolidated issues; consolidated cases.

(a) When one or more additional issues are raised by the administrative law judge pursuant to 702.336, such issues may, in the discretion of the administrative law judge, be consolidated for hearing and decision with other issues pending before him.

(b) When two or more cases are transferred for formal hearings and have common questions of law or which arose out of a common accident, the Chief Administrative Law Judge may consolidate such cases for hearing.

§ 702.346 Formal hearings; waiver of right to appear.

If all parties waive their right to appear before the administrative law judge or to present evidence or argument personally or by representative, it shall not be necessary for the administrative law judge to give notice of and conduct an oral hearing. A waiver of the right to appear and present evidence and allegations as to facts and law shall be made in writing and filed with the Chief Administrative Law Judge or the administrative law judge. Where such a waiver has been filed by all parties, and they do not appear before the administrative law judge personally or by representative, the administrative law judge shall make a record of the relevant written evidence submitted by the parties, together with any pleadings they may submit with respect to the issues in the case. Such documents shall be considered as all of the evidence in the case and the decision shall be based on them.

§ 702.347 Formal hearings; termination.

(a) Formal hearings are normally terminated upon the conclusion of the proceeding at which evidence is submitted to the administrative law judge.

(b) In exceptional cases the Chief Administrative Law Judge or the administrative law judge assigned to the case may, in his or her discretion, extend the time for official termination of the hearing.

[42 FR 42552, Aug. 23, 1977]

§ 702.348 Formal hearings; preparation of final decision and order; content.

Within 20 days after the official termination of the hearing as defined by 702.347, the administrative law judge shall have prepared a final decision and order, in the form of a compensation order, with respect to the claim, making an award to the claimant or rejecting the claim. The compensation order shall contain appropriate findings of facts and conclusions of law with respect thereto, and shall be concluded with one or more paragraphs containing the order of the administrative law judge, his signature, and the date of issuance.

§ 702.349 Formal hearings; filing and mailing of compensation orders; disposition of transcripts.

The administrative law judge shall, within 20 days after the official termination of the hearing, deliver by mail, or otherwise, to the office of the district director having original jurisdiction, the transcript of the hearing, other documents or pleadings filed with him with respect to the claim, together with his signed compensation order. Upon receipt thereof, the district director, being the official custodian of all records with respect to such claims within his jurisdiction, shall formally date and file the transcript, pleadings, and compensation order (original) in his office. Such filing shall be accomplished by the close of business on the next succeeding working day, and the district director shall, on the same day as the filing was accomplished, send by certified mail a copy of the compensation order to the parties and to representatives of the parties, if any. Appended to each such copy shall be a paragraph entitled "proof of service" containing the certification of the district director that the copies were mailed on the date stated, to each of the parties and their representatives, as shown in such paragraph.

§ 702.350 Finality of compensation orders.

Compensation orders shall become effective when filed in the office of the district director, and unless proceedings for suspension or setting aside of such orders are instituted within 30 days of such filing, shall become final at the expiration of the 30th day after such filing, as provided in section 21 of the Act 33 U.S.C. 921. If any compensation payable under the terms of such order is not paid within 10 days after it becomes due, section 14(f) of the Act requires that there be added to such unpaid compensation an amount equal to 20 percent thereof which shall be paid at the same time as, but in addition to, such compensation unless review of the compensation order is had as provided in such section 21 and an order staying payment has been issued by the Benefits Review Board or the reviewing court.

§ 702.351 Withdrawal of controversion of issues set for formal hearing; effect.

Whenever a party withdraws his controversion of the issues set for a formal hearing, the administrative law judge shall halt the proceedings upon receipt from said party of a signed statement to that effect and forthwith notify the district director who shall then proceed to dispose of the case as provided for in 702.315.

INTERLOCUTORY MATTERS, SUPPLEMENTARY ORDERS, AND MODIFICATIONS

§ 702.371 Interlocutory matters.

Compensation orders shall not be made or filed with respect to interlocutory matters of a procedural nature arising during the pendency of a compensation case.

§ 702.372 Supplementary compensation orders.

(a) In any case in which the employer or insurance carrier is in default in the payment of compensation due under any award of compensation, for a period of 30 days after the compensation is due and payable, the person to whom such compensation is payable may, within 1 year after such default, apply in writing to the district director for a supplementary compensation order declaring the amount of the default. Upon receipt of such application, the district director shall institute proceedings with respect to such application as if such application were an original claim for compensation, and the matter shall be disposed of as provided for in 702.315, or if agreement on the issue is not reached, then as in 702.316 et seq. (b) If, after disposition of the application as provided for in paragraph (a) of this section, a supplementary compensation order is entered declaring the amount of the default, which amount may be the whole of the award notwithstanding that only one or more installments is in default, a copy of such supplementary order shall be forthwith sent by certified mail to each of the parties and their representatives. Thereafter, the applicant may obtain and file with the clerk of the Federal district court for the judicial district where the injury occurred or the district in which the employed has his principal place of business or maintains an office, a certified copy of said order and may seek enforcement thereof as provided for by section 18 of the Act, 33 U.S.C. 918.

§ 702.373 Modification of awards.

(a) Upon his/her own initiative, or upon application of any party in interest (including an employer or carrier which has been granted relief under section 8(f) of the Act, 33 U.S.C. 908(f)), the district director may review any compensation case (including a case under which payments are made pursuant to section 44(i) of the Act, 33 U.S.C. 944(i)) in accordance with the procedure in subpart C of this part, and after such review of the case under 702.315, or review at formal hearings under the regulations governing formal hearings in subpart C of this part, file a new compensation order terminating, continuing reinstating, increasing or decreasing such compensation, or awarding compensation. Such new order shall not affect any compensation previously paid, except that an award increasing the compensation rate may be made retroactive from the date of injury, and if any part of the compensation due or to become due is unpaid, an award decreasing the compensation rate may be made effective from the date of the injury, and any payment made prior thereto in excess of such decreased rate shall be deducted from any unpaid compensation, in such manner and by such method as may be determined by the district director or the administrative law judge. Settlements cannot be modified.

(b) Review of a compensation case under this section may be made at any time prior to 1 year after the date of the last payment of compensation, whether or not a compensation order has been issued, or at any time prior to 1 year after the rejection of a claim.

(c) Review of a compensation case may be had only for the reason that there is a change in conditions or that there was a mistake in the determination of facts.

(d) If the investigation, described in 702.148(c), discloses a change in conditions and the employer or insurance carrier intends to pursue modification of the award of compensation the district director and claimant shall be notified through an informal conference. At the conclusion of the informal conference the district director shall issue a recommendation either for or against the modification. This recommendation shall also be sent to the Associate Director, Division of Longshoremen's and Harbor Workers' Compensation (DLHWC) for a determination on whether or not to participate in the modification proceeding on behalf of the special fund. Lack of concurrence of the Associate Director, DLHWC or lack of participation by a representative of the special fund shall not be a bar to the modification proceeding.

[38 FR 26861, Sept. 26, 1973, as amended at 50 FR 401, Jan. 3, 1985]

Appeals

§ 702.391 Appeals; where.

Appeals may be taken to the Benefits Review Board, U.S. Department of Labor, Washington, D.C. 20210, by filing a notice of appeals with the office of the district director for the compensation district in which the decision or order appealed from was filed and by submitting to the Board a petition for review of such decision or order, in accordance with the provisions of part 802 of this title 20.

§ 702.392 Appeals; what may be appealed.

An appeal raising a substantial question of law or fact may be taken from a decision with respect to a claim under the Act. Such appeals may be taken from compensation orders when they have been filed as provided for in 702.349.

§ 702.393 Appeals; time limitations.

The notice of appeal (see 702.391) shall be filed with the district director within 30 days of the filing of the decision or order complained of, as defined and described in 802.205 and 802.206 of this title. A petition for review of the decision or order is required to be filed within 30 days after receipt of the Board's acknowledgment of the notice of appeal, as provided in 802.210 of this title.

§ 702.394 Appeals; procedure.

The procedure for appeals to the Benefits Review Board shall be as provided by the Board in its Rules of Practice and Procedure, set forth in part 802 of this title.

Subpart D—Medical Care and Supervision

§ 702.401 Medical care defined.

(a) Medical care shall include medical, surgical, and other attendance or treatment, nursing and hospital services, laboratory, X-ray and other technical services, medicines, crutches, or other apparatus and prosthetic devices, and any other medical service or supply, including the reasonable and necessary cost of travel incident thereto, which is recognized as appropriate by the medical profession for the care and treatment of the injury or disease.

(b) An employee may rely on treatment by prayer or spiritual means alone, in accordance with the tenets and practice of a recognized church or religious denomination, by an accredited practitioner of such recognized church or religious denomination, and nursing services rendered in accordance with such tenets and practice without loss or diminution of compensation or benefits under the Act. For purposes of this section, a recognized church or religious denomination shall be any religious organization: (1) That is recognized by the Social Security Administration for purposes of reimbursements for treatment under Medicare and Medicaid or (2) that is recognized by the Internal Revenue Service for purposes of tax exempt status.

[38 FR 26861, Sept. 26, 1973, as amended at 50 FR 402, Jan. 3, 1985]

§ 702.402 Employer's duty to furnish; duration.

It is the duty of the employer to furnish appropriate medical care (as defined in 702.401(a)) for the employee's injury, and for such period as the nature of the injury or the process of recovery may require.

[50 FR 402, Jan. 3, 1985]

§ 702.403 Employee's right to choose physician; limitations.

The employee shall have the right to choose his/her attending physician from among those authorized by the Director, OWCP, to furnish such care and treatment, except those physicians included on the Secretary's list of debarred physicians. In determining the choice of a physician, consideration must be given to availability, the employee's condition and the method and means of transportation. Generally 25 miles from the place of injury, or the employee's home is a reasonable distance to travel, but other pertinent factors must also be taken into consideration.

[50 FR 402, Jan. 3, 1985]

§ 702.404 Physician defined.

The term physician includes doctors of medicine (MD), surgeons, podiatrists, dentists, clinical psychologists, optometrists, chiropractors, and osteopathic practitioners within the scope of their practice as defined by State law. The term includes chiropractors only to the extent that their reimbursable services are limited to treatment consisting of manual manipulation of the spine to correct a subluxation shown by X-ray or clinical findings. Physicians defined in this part may interpret their own X-rays. All physicians in these categories are authorized by the Director to render medical care under the Act. Naturopaths, faith healers, and other practitioners of the healing arts which are not listed herein are not included within the term "physician" as used in this part.

[42 FR 45303, Sept. 9, 1977]

§702.405 Selection of physician; emergencies.

Whenever the nature of the injury is such that immediate medical care is required and the injured employee is unable to select a physician, the employer shall select a physician. Thereafter the employee may change physicians when he is able to make a selection. Such changes shall be made upon obtaining written authorization from the employer or, if consent is withheld, from the district director. The Director will direct reimbursement of medical claims for services rendered by physicians or health care providers who are on the list of those excluded from providing care under the Act, if such services were rendered in an emergency. (See 702.417 and 702.435(b)).

[38 FR 26861, Sept. 26, 1973, as amended at 50 FR 402, Jan. 3, 1985]

§ 702.406 Change of physicians; non-emergencies.

(a) Whenever the employee has made his initial, free choice of an attending physician, he may not thereafter change physicians without the prior written consent of the employer (or carrier) or the district director. Such consent shall be given in cases where an employee's initial choice was not of a specialist whose services are necessary for, and appropriate to, the proper care and treatment of the compensable injury or disease. In all other cases, consent may be given upon a showing of good cause for change.

(b) The district director for the appropriate compensation district may order a change of physicians or hospitals when such a change is found to be necessary or desirable or where the fees charged exceed those prevailing within the community for the same or similar services or exceed the provider's customary charges.

[38 FR 26861, Sept. 26, 1973, as amended at 50 FR 402, Jan. 3, 1985]

§ 702.407 Supervision of medical care.

The Director, OWCP, through the district directors and their designees, shall actively supervise the medical care of an injured employee covered by the Act. Such supervision shall include:

(a) The requirement that periodic reports on the medical care being rendered be filed in the office of the district director, the frequency thereof being determined by order of the district director or sound judgment of the attending physician as the nature of the injury may dictate;

(b) The determination of the necessity, character and sufficiency of any medical care furnished or to be furnished the employee, including whether the charges made by any medical care provider exceed those permitted under the Act;

(c) The determination of whether a change of physicians, hospitals or other persons or locales providing treatment should be made or is necessary;

(d) The further evaluation of medical questions arising in any case under the Act, with respect to the nature and extent of the covered injury, and the medical care required therefor.

[38 FR 26861, Sept. 26, 1973, as amended at 50 FR 402, Jan. 3, 1985]

§ 702.408 Evaluation of medical questions; impartial specialists.

In any case in which medical questions arise with respect to the appropriate diagnosis, extent, effect of, appropriate treatment, and the duration of any such care or treatment, for an injury covered by the Act, the Director, OWCP, through the district directors having jurisdiction, shall have the power to evaluate such questions by appointing one or more especially qualified physicians to examine the employee, or in the case of death to make such inquiry as may be appropriate to the facts and circumstances of the case. The physician or physicians, including appropriate consultants, should report their findings with respect to the questions raised as expeditiously as possible. Upon receipt of such report, action appropriate therewith shall be taken.

§ 702.409 Evaluation of medical questions; results disputed.

Any party who is dissatisfied with such report may request a review or reexamination of the employee by one or more different physicians employed by or selected by the Director, and such review or reexamination shall be granted unless it is found that it is clearly unwarranted. Such review shall be completed within 2 weeks from the date ordered unless it is impossible to complete the review and render a report thereon within such time period. Upon receipt of the report of this additional review and reexamination, such action as may be appropriate shall forthwith be taken.

§ 702.410 Duties of employees with respect to special examinations.

(a) For any special examination required of an employee by 702.408 and 702.409, the employee shall submit to such examination at such place as is designated in the order to report, but the place so selected shall be reasonably convenient for the employee.

(b) Where an employee fails to submit to an examination required by 702.408 and 702.409, the district director or administrative law judge may order that no compensation otherwise payable shall be paid for any period during which the employee refuses to submit to such examination unless circumstances justified the refusal.

(c) Where an employee unreasonably refuses to submit to medical or surgical treatment, or to an examination by a physician selected by the employer, the district director or administrative law judge may by order suspend the payment of further compensation during such time as the refusal continues. Except that refusal to submit to medical treatment because of adherence to the tenets of a recognized church or religious denomination as described in 702.401(b) shall not cause the suspension of compensation.

[42 FR 45303, Sept. 9, 1977, as amended at 50 FR 402, Jan. 3, 1985; 51 FR 4286, Feb. 3, 1986]

§ 702.411 Special examinations; nature of impartiality of specialists.

(a) The special examinations required by 702.408 shall be accomplished in a manner designed to preclude prejudgment by the impartial examiner. No physician previously connected with the case shall be present, nor may any other physician selected by the employer, carrier, or employee be present. The impartial examiner may be made aware, by any party or by the OWCP, of the opinions, reports, or conclusions of any prior examining physician with respect to the nature and extent of the impairment, its cause, or its effect upon the wage-earning capacity of the injured employee, if the district director determines that, for good cause, such opinions, reports, or conclusions shall be made available. Upon request, any party shall be given a copy of all materials made available to the impartial examiner.

(b) The impartiality of the specialists shall not be considered to have been compromised if the district director deems it advisable to, and does, apprise the specialist by memorandum of those undisputed facts pertaining to the nature of the employee's employment, of the nature of the injury, of the postinjury employment activity, if any, and of any other facts which are not disputed and are deemed pertinent to the type of injury and/or the type of examination being conducted.

(c) No physician selected to perform impartial examinations shall be, or shall have been for a period of 2 years prior to the examination, an employee of an insurance carrier or self-insured employer, or who has accepted or participated in any fee from an insurance carrier or self-insured employer, unless the parties in interest agree thereto.

[38 FR 26861, Sept. 26, 1973, as amended at 42 FR 45303, Sept. 9, 1977]

§ 702.412 Special examinations; costs chargeable to employer or carrier.

(a) The Director or his designee ordering the special examination shall have the power, in the exercise of his discretion, to charge the cost of the examination or review to the employer, to the insurance carrier, or to the special fund established by section 44 of the Act, 33 U.S.C. 944.

(b) The Director or his designee may also order the employer or the insurance carrier to provide the employee with the services of an attendant, where the district director considers such services necessary, because the employee is totally blind, has lost the use of both hands, or both feet or is paralyzed and unable to walk, or because of other disability making the employee so helpless as to require constant attendance in the discretion of the district director. Fees payable for such services shall be in accord with the provisions of 702.413.

[42 FR 45303, Sept. 9, 1977]

§ 702.413 Fees for medical services; prevailing community charges.

All fees charged by medical care providers for persons covered by this Act shall be limited to such charges for the same or similar care (including supplies) as prevails in the community in which the medical care provider is located and shall not exceed the customary charges of the medical care provider for the same or similar services. Official state medical fee schedules for workers' compensation charges may be used as guidelines in determining the prevailing community rate where available and to the extent appropriate. The opinion of the OWCP district medical director that a charge by a medical care provider disputed under the provisions of 702.414 exceeds the charge which prevails in the community in which said medical care provider is located shall constitute sufficient evidence to warrant further proceedings pursuant to 702.414 and to permit the Director to direct the claimant to select another medical provider for care to the claimant.

[51 FR 4286, Feb. 3, 1986]

§ 702.414 Fees for medical services; unresolved disputes on prevailing charges.

(a) The Director may, upon written complaint of an interested party, or upon the Director's own initiative, investigate any medical care provider or any fee for medical treatment, services, or supplies that appears to exceed prevailing community charges for similar treatment, services or supplies or the provider's customary charges. Such investigation may initially be conducted informally through contact of the medical care provider by the district medical director. If this informal investigation is unsuccessful further proceedings may be undertaken. These proceedings may include, but not be limited to: An informal conference involving all interested parties; agency interrogatories to the pertinent medical care provider; and issuance of subpoenas duces tecum for documents having a bearing on the dispute.

(b) The failure of any medical care provider to present any evidence required by the Director pursuant to this section without good cause shall not prevent the Director from making findings of fact.

(c) After any proceeding under this section the Director shall make specific findings on whether the fee exceeded the prevailing community charges or the provider's customary charges and provide notice of these findings to the affected parties.

(d) The Director may suspend any such proceedings if after receipt of the written complaint the affected parties agree to withdraw the controversy from agency consideration on the basis that such controversy has been resolved by the affected parties. Such suspension, however, shall be at the discretion of the Director.

[51 FR 4286, Feb. 3, 1986]

§ 702.415 Fees for medical services; unresolved disputes on charges; procedure.

After issuance of specific findings of fact and proposed action by the Director as provided in 702.414 any affected provider employer or other interested party has the right to seek a hearing pursuant to section 556 of title 5, United States Code. Upon written request for such a hearing, the matter shall be referred by the District Director to the OALJ for formal hearing in accordance with the procedures in subpart C of this part. If no such request for a hearing is filed with the district director within thirty (30) days the findings issued pursuant to 702.414 shall be final.

[51 FR 4286, Feb. 3, 1986]

§ 702.416 Fees for medical services; disputes; hearings; necessary parties.

At formal hearings held pursuant to 702.415, the necessary parties shall be the person whose fee or cost charge is in question and the Director, or their representatives. The employer or carrier may also be represented, and other parties, or associations having an interest in the proceedings, may be heard, in the discretion of the administrative law judge.

§ 702.417 Fees for medical services; disputes; effect of adverse decision.

If the final decision and order upholds the finding of the Director that the fee or charge in dispute was not in accordance with prevailing community charges or the provider's customary charges, the person claiming such fee or cost charge shall be given thirty (30) days after filing of such decision and order to make the necessary adjustment. If such person still refuses to make the required readjustment, such person shall not be authorized to conduct any further treatments or examinations (if a physician) or to provide any other services or supplies (if by other than a physician). Any fee or cost charge subsequently incurred for services performed or supplies furnished shall not be a reimbursable medical expense under this subpart. This prohibition shall apply notwithstanding the fact that the services performed or supplies furnished were in all other respects necessary and appropriate within the provision of these regulations. However, the Director may direct reimbursement of medical claims for services rendered if such services were rendered in an emergency (see 702.435(b)). At the termination of the proceedings provided for in this section the district director shall determine whether further proceedings under 702.432 should be initiated.

[50 FR 403, Jan. 3, 1985]

MEDICAL PROCEDURES

§ 702.418 Procedure for requesting medical care; employee's duty to notify employer.

(a) As soon as practicable, but within 30 days after occurrence of an injury covered by the Act, or within 30 days after an employee becomes aware, or in the exercise of reasonable diligence should be aware, of the relationship between an injury or disease and his employment, the injured employee or someone on his behalf shall give written notice thereof to the district director having jurisdiction over the place where the injury occurred and to the employer. If a form has been prescribed for such purpose it shall be used, if available and practicable under the circumstances. Notices filed under subpart B of this part, if on the form prescribed by the Director for such purpose, satisfy the written notice requirements of this subpart.

(b) In the case of an occupational disease which does not immediately result in a disability or death, such notice shall be given within one year after the employee becomes aware, or in the exercise of reasonable diligence or by reason of medical advice should have been aware, of the relationship between the employment, the disease, and the death or disability. Notice shall be given: (1) To the district director in the compensation district in which the injury or death occurred, and (2) to the employer.

(Approved by the Office of Management and Budget under control number 1215-0160)

[50 FR 403, Jan. 3, 1985]

§ 702.419 Action by employer upon acquiring knowledge or being given notice of injury.

Whenever an employer acquires knowledge of an employee's injury, through receipt of a written notice or otherwise, said employer shall forthwith authorize, in writing, appropriate medical care. If a form is prescribed for this purpose it shall be used whenever practicable. Authorization shall also be given in cases where an employee's initial choice was not of a specialist whose services are necessary for and appropriate to the proper care and treatment of the compensable injury or disease. In all other cases, consent may be given upon a showing of good cause for change.

[50 FR 403, Jan. 3, 1985]

§ 702.420 Issuance of authorization; binding effect upon insurance carrier.

The issuance of an authorization for treatment by the employer shall bind his insurance carrier to furnish and pay for such care and services.

§ 702.421 Effect of failure to obtain initial authorization.

An employee shall not be entitled to recover for medical services and supplies unless:

(a) The employer shall have refused or neglected a request to furnish such services and the employee has complied with sections 7 (b) and (c) of the Act, 33 U.S.C. 907 (b) and (c) and these regulations; or

(b) The nature of the injury required such treatment and services and the employer or his superintendent or foreman having knowledge of such injury shall have neglected to provide or authorize same.

[50 FR 403, Jan. 3, 1985]

§ 702.422 Effect of failure to report on medical care after initial authorization.

(a) Notwithstanding that medical care is properly obtained in accordance with these regulations, a finding by the Director that a medical care provider has failed to comply with the reporting requirements of the Act shall operate as a mandatory revocation of authorization of such medical care provider. The effect of a final finding to this effect operates to release the employer/carrier from liability of the expenses of such care. In addition to this, when such a finding is made by the Director, the claimant receiving treatment will be directed by the district director to seek authorization for medical care from another source.

(b) For good cause shown, the Director may excuse the failure to comply with the reporting requirements of the Act and further, may make an award for the reasonable value of such medical care.

[50 FR 403, Jan. 3, 1985]

Debarment of Physicians and Other Providers of Medical Services and Suppliers and Claims Representatives

§ 702.431 Grounds for debarment.

A physician or health care provider shall be debarred if it is found, after appropriate investigation as described in 702.414 and proceedings under 702.432 and 702.433, that such physician or health care provider has:

(a) Knowingly and willfully made, or caused to be made, any false statement or misrepresentation of a material fact for use in a claim for compensation or claim for reimbursement of medical expenses under this Act;

(b) Knowingly and willfully submitted, or caused to be submitted, a bill or request for payment under this Act containing a charge which the Director finds to be substantially in excess of the charge for the service, appliance, or supply prevailing within the community or in excess of the provider's customary charges, unless the Director finds there is good cause for the bill or request containing the charge;

(c) Knowingly and willfully furnished a service, appliance, or supply which is determined by the Director to be substantially in excess of the need of the recipient thereof or to be of a quality which substantially fails to meet professionally recognized standards;

(d) Been convicted under any criminal statute, without regard to pending appeal thereof, for fraudulent activities in connection with federal or state program for which payments are made to physicians or providers of similar services, appliances, or supplies; or has otherwise been excluded from participation in such program.

(e) The fact that a physician or health care provider has been convicted of a crime previously described in

(d), or excluded or suspended, or has resigned in lieu of exclusion or suspension, from participation in any program as described in (d), shall be a prima facie finding of fact for purposes of section 7(j)(2) of the Act, 33 U.S.C. 907(j)(2).

[50 FR 404, Jan. 3, 1985]

§ 702.432 Debarment process.

(a) Pertaining to health care providers. Upon receipt of information indicating that a physician or health care provider has engaged in activities enumerated in subparagraphs (a) through (c) of 702.431, the Director, through the Director's designees, may evaluate the information (as described in 702.414) to ascertain whether proceedings should be initiated against the physician or health care provider to remove authorization to render medical care or service under the Longshore and Harbor Workers' Compensation Act.

(b) Pertaining to health care providers and claims representatives. If after appropriate investigation the Director determines that proceedings should be initiated, written notice thereof sent certified mail, return receipt requested, shall be provided to the physician, health care provider or claims representative containing the following:

(1) A concise statement of the grounds upon which debarment will be based;

(2) A summary of the information upon which the director has relied in reaching an initial decision that debarment proceedings should be initiated;

(3) An invitation to the physician, health care provider or claims representative to: (i) Resign voluntarily from participation in the program without admitting or denying the allegations presented in the written notice; or (ii) request a decision on debarment to be based upon the existing agency record and any other information the physician, health care provider or claims representative may wish to provide;

(4) A notice of the physician's, health care provider's or claims representative's right, in the event of an adverse ruling by the Director, to request a formal hearing before an administrative law judge;

(5) A notice that should the physician, health care provider or claims representative fail to provide written answer to the written notice described in this section within thirty (30) days of receipt, the Director may deem the allegations made therein to be true and may order exclusion of the physician, health care provider or claims representative without conducting any further proceedings; and

(6) The name and address of the district director who shall be responsible for receiving the answer from the physician, health care provider or claims representative.

(c) Should the physician, health care provider or claims representative fail to file a written answer to the notice described in this section within thirty (30) days of receipt thereof, the Director may deem the allegations made therein to be true and may order debarment of the physician, health care provider or claims representative.

(d) The physician, health care provider or claims representative may inspect or request copies of information in the agency records at any time prior to the Director's decision.

(e) The Director shall issue a decision in writing, and shall send a copy of the decision to the physician, health care provider or claims representative by certified mail, return receipt requested. The decision shall advise the physician, health care provider or claims representative of the right to request, within thirty (30) days of the date of an adverse decision, a formal hearing before an administrative law judge under the procedures set forth herein. The filing of such a request for hearing within the time specified shall operate to stay the effectiveness of the decision to debar.

[50 FR 404, Jan. 3, 1985]

§ 702.433 Requests for hearing.

(a) A request for hearing shall be sent to the district director and contain a concise notice of the issues on which the physician, health care provider or claims representative desires to give evidence at the hearing with identification of witnesses and documents to be submitted at the hearing.

(b) If a request for hearing is timely received by the district director, the matter shall be referred to the Chief Administrative Law Judge who shall assign it for hearing with the assigned administrative law judge issuing a notice of hearing for the conduct of the hearing. A copy of the hearing notice shall be served on the physician, health care provider or claims representative by certified mail, return receipt requested.

(c) If a request for hearing contains identification of witnesses or documents not previously considered by the Director, the Director may make application to the assigned administrative law judge for an offer of proof from the physician, health care provider or claims representative for the purpose of discovery prior to hearing. If the offer of proof indicates injection of new issues or new material evidence not previously considered by the Director, the Director may request a remand order for purposes of reconsideration of the decision made pursuant to 702.432 of these regulations.

(d) The parties may make application for the issuance of subpoenas upon a showing of good cause therefore to the administrative law judge.

(e) The administrative law judge shall issue a recommended decision after the termination of the hearing. The recommended decision shall contain appropriate findings, conclusions and a recommended order and be forwarded, together with the record of the hearing, to the Assistant Secretary for Employment Standards for a final decision. The recommended decision shall be served upon all parties to the proceeding.

(f) Based upon a review of the record and the recommended decision of the administrative law judge, the Assistant Secretary for Employment Standards shall issue a final decision.

[50 FR 404, Jan. 3, 1985, as amended at 55 FR 28606, July 12, 1990]

§ 702.434 Judicial review.

(a) Any physician, health care provider or claims representative, after any final decision of the Assistant Secretary for Employment Standards made after a hearing to which such person was a party, irrespective of the amount of controversy, may obtain a review of such decision by a civil action commenced within sixty (60) days after the mailing to him or her of notice of such decision, but the pendency of such review shall not operate as a stay upon the effect of such decision. Such action shall be brought in the Court of Appeals of the United States for the judicial circuit in which the plaintiff resides or has his or her principal place of business, or the Court of Appeals for the District of Columbia pursuant to section 7(j)(4) of the Act, 33 U.S.C. 907(j)(4).

(b) As part of the Assistant Secretary for Employment Standards' answer, he or she shall file a certified copy of the transcript of the record of the hearing, including all evidence submitted in connection therewith.

(c) The findings of fact of the Assistant Secretary for Employment Standards, if based on substantial evidence in the record as a whole, shall be conclusive.

[50 FR 405, Jan. 3, 1985, as amended at 55 FR 28606, July 12, 1990]

§ 702.435 Effects of debarment.

(a) The Director shall give notice of the debarment of a physician, hospital, or provider of medical support services or supplies to:

(1) All OWCP district offices;

(2) The Health Care Financing Administration;

(3) The State or Local authority responsible for licensing or certifying the debarred party;

(4) The employers and authorized insurers under the Act by means of an annual bulletin sent to them by the Director; and

(5) The general public by posting in the district office in the jurisdiction where the debarred party maintains a place of business.

If a claims representative is debarred, the Director shall give notice to those groups listed in paragraphs (a) (1), (3), (4), and (5) of this section.

(b) Notwithstanding any debarment under this subpart, the Director shall not refuse a claimant reimbursement for any otherwise reimbursable medical expense if the treatment, service or supply was rendered by debarred provider in an emergency situation. However, such claimant will be directed by the Director to select a duly qualified provider upon the earliest opportunity.

[50 FR 405, Jan. 3, 1985]

§ 702.436 Reinstatement.

(a) If a physician or health care provider has been debarred or pursuant to 702.431(d) or if a claims representative has been debarred pursuant to 702.131(c) (1) or (3) the person debarred will be automatically reinstated upon notice to the Director that the conviction or exclusion has been reversed or withdrawn. However, such reinstatement will not preclude the Director from instituting debarment proceedings based upon the subject matter involved.

(b) A physician, health care provider or claims representative otherwise debarred by the Director may apply for reinstatement to participate in the program by application to the Director after three years from the date of entry of the order of exclusion. Such application for reinstatement shall be addressed to the Associate Director for the Longshore program, and shall contain a statement of the basis of the application along with any supporting documentation.

(c) The Director may further investigate the merits of the reinstatement application by requiring special reporting procedures from the applicant for a probationary period not to exceed six months to be monitored by the district office where the provider maintains a place of business.

(d) At the end of aforesaid probationary period, the Director may order full reinstatement of the physician, health care provider or claims representative if such reinstatement is clearly consistent with the program goal to protect itself against fraud and abuse and, further, if the physician, health care provider or claims representative has given reasonable assurances that the basis for the debarment will not be repeated.

[50 FR 405, Jan. 3, 1985]

HEARING LOSS CLAIMS

§ 702.441 Claims for loss of hearing.

(a) Claims for hearing loss pending on or filed after September 28, 1984 (the date of enactment of Pub. L. 98-426) shall be adjudicated with respect to the determination of the degree of hearing impairment in accordance with these regulations.

(b) An audiogram shall be presumptive evidence of the amount of hearing loss on the date administered if the following requirements are met:

(1) The audiogram was administered by a licensed or certified audiologist, by a physician certified by the American Board of Otolaryngology, or by a technician, under an audiologist's or physician's supervision, certified by the Council of Accreditation on Occupational Hearing Conservation, or by any other person considered qualified by a hearing conservation program authorized pursuant to 29 CFR 1910.95(g)(3) promulgated under the Occupational Safety and Health Act of 1970 (29 U.S.C. 667). Thus, either a professional or trained technician may conduct audiometric testing. However, to be acceptable under this subsection, a licensed or certified audiologist or otolaryngologist, as defined, must ultimately interpret and certify the results of the audiogram. The accompanying report must set forth the testing standards used and describe the method of evaluating the hearing loss as well as providing an evaluation of the reliability of the test results.

(2) The employee was provided the audiogram and a report thereon at the time it was administered or within thirty (30) days thereafter.

(3) No one produces a contrary audiogram of equal probative value (meaning one performed using the standards described herein) made at the same time. "Same time" means within thirty (30) days thereof where noise exposure continues or within six (6) months where exposure to excessive noise levels does not continue. Audiometric tests performed prior to the enactment of Public Law 98-426 will be considered presumptively valid if the employer complied with the procedures in this section for administering audiograms.

(c) In determining the amount of pre-employment hearing loss, an audiogram must be submitted which was performed prior to employment or within thirty (30) days of the date of the first employmentrelated noise exposure. Audiograms performed after December 27, 1984 must comply with the standards described in paragraph (d) of this section.

(d) In determining the loss of hearing under the Act, the evaluators shall use the criteria for measuring and calculating hearing impairment as published and modified from time-to-time by the American Medical Association in the Guides to the Evaluation of Permanent Impairment, using the most currently revised edition of this publication. In addition, the audiometer used for testing the individual's threshold of hearing must be calibrated according to current American National Standard Specifications for Audiometers. Audiometer testing procedures required by hearing conservation programs pursuant to the Occupational Safety and Health Act of 1970 should be followed (as described at 29 CFR 1910.95 and appendices).

(Approved by the Office of Management and Budget under control number 1215-0160)

[50 FR 405, Jan. 3, 1985]

Subpart E—Vocational Rehabilitation

§ 702.501 Vocational rehabilitation; objective.

The objective of vocational rehabilitation is the return of permanently disabled persons to gainful employment commensurate with their physical or mental impairments, or both, through a program of reevaluation or redirection of their abilities, or retraining in another occupation, or selective job placement assistance.

§ 702.502 Vocational rehabilitation; action by district directors.

All injury cases which are likely to result in, or have resulted in, permanent disability, and which are of a character likely to require review by a vocational rehabilitation adviser on the staff of the Director, shall promptly be referred to such adviser by the district director or his designee having charge of the case. A form has been prescribed for such purpose and shall be used. Medical data and other pertinent information shall accompany the referral.

(Approved by the Office of Management and Budget under control number 1215-0051)

(Pub. L. No. 96-511)

[38 FR 26861, Sept. 26, 1973, as amended at 49 FR 18294, Apr. 30, 1984]

§ 702.503 Vocational rehabilitation; action by adviser.

The vocational rehabilitation adviser, upon receipt of the referral, shall promptly consider the feasibility of a vocational referral or request for cooperative services from available resources or facilities, to include counseling, vocational survey, selective job placement assistance, and retraining. Public or private agencies may be utilized in arranging necessary vocational rehabilitation services under the Federal Vocational Rehabilitation Act, 29 U.S.C. 31 et seq.

§ 702.504 Vocational rehabilitation; referrals to State Employment Agencies.

Vocational rehabilitation advisers will arrange referral procedures with State Employment Service units within their assigned geographical districts for the purpose of securing employment counseling, job classification, and selective placement assistance. Referrals shall be made to State Employment Offices based upon the following:

(a) Vocational rehabilitation advisers will screen cases so as to refer only those disabled employees who are considered to have employment potential;

(b) Only employees will be referred who have permanent, compensable disabilities resulting in a significant vocational handicap and loss of wage earning capacity;

(c) Disabled employees, whose initial referral to former private employers did not result in a job reassignment or in a job retention, shall be referred for employment counseling and/or selective placement unless retraining services consideration is requested;

(d) The vocational rehabilitation advisers shall arrange for employees' referrals if it is ascertained that they may benefit from registering with the State Employment Service;

(e) Referrals will be made to appropriate State Employment Offices by letter, including all necessary information and a request for a report on the services provided the employee when he registers;

(f) The injured employee shall be advised of available job counseling services and informed that he is being referred for employment and selective placement;

(g) A followup shall be made within 60 days on all referrals to assure uniform reporting by State agencies on cases referred for a vocational survey.

§ 702.505 Vocational rehabilitation; referrals to other public and private agencies.

Referrals to such other public and private agencies providing assistance to disabled persons such as public welfare agencies, Public Health Services facilities, social services units of the Veterans Administration, the Social Security Administration, and other such agencies, shall be made by the vocational rehabilitation adviser, where appropriate, on an individual basis when requested by disabled employees. Such referrals do not provide for a service cost reimbursement by the Department of Labor.

§ 702.506 Vocational rehabilitation; training.

Vocational rehabilitation training shall be planned in anticipation of a short, realistic, attainable vocational objective terminating in remunerable employment, and in restoring wage-earning capacity or increasing it materially. The following procedures shall apply in arranging for or providing training:

(a) The vocational rehabilitation adviser shall arrange for and develop all vocational training programs.

(b) Training programs shall be developed to meet the varying needs of eligible beneficiaries, and may include courses at colleges, technical schools, training at rehabilitation centers, on-the-job training, or tutorial courses. The courses shall be pertinent to the occupation for which the employee is being trained.

(c) Training may be terminated if the injured employee fails to cooperate with the Department of Labor or with the agency supervising his course of training. The employee shall be counseled before training is terminated.

(d) Reports shall be required at periodic intervals on all persons in approved training programs.

§ 702.507 Vocational rehabilitation; maintenance allowance.

(a) An injured employee who, as a result of injury, is or may be expected to be totally or partially incapacitated for a remunerative occupation and who, under the direction of the Director is being rendered fit to engage in a remunerative occupation, shall be paid additional compensation necessary for this maintenance, not exceeding $25 a week. The expense shall be paid out of the special fund established in section 44 of the Act, 33 U.S.C. 944.

The maximum maintenance allowance shall not be provided on an automatic basis, but shall be based on the recommendation of a State agency that a claimant is unable to meet additional costs by reason of being in training.

(b) When required by reason of personal illness or hardship, limited periods of absence from training may be allowed without terminating the maintenance allowance. A maintenance allowance shall be terminated when it is shown to the satisfaction of the Director that a trainee is not complying reasonably with the terms of the training plan or is absenting himself without good cause from training so as to materially interfere with the accomplishment of the training objective.

§ 702.508 Vocational rehabilitation; confidentiality of information.

The following safeguards will be observed to protect the confidential character of information released regarding an individual undergoing rehabilitation:

(a) Information will be released to other agencies from which an injured employee has requested services only if such agencies have established regulations assuring that such information will be considered confidential and will be used only for the purpose for which it is provided;

(b) Interested persons and agencies have been advised that any information concerning rehabilitation program employees is to be held confidential;

(c) A rehabilitation employee's written consent is secured for release of information regarding disability to a person, agency, or establishment seeking the information for purposes other than the approved rehabilitation planning with such employee.

Subpart F—Occupational Disease Which Does Not Immediately Result in Death or Disability

Source: 50 FR 406, Jan. 3, 1985, unless otherwise noted.

§ 702.601 Definitions.

(a) Time of injury. For purposes of this subpart and with respect to an occupational disease which does not immediately result in death or disability, the time of injury shall be deemed to be the date on which the employee or claimant becomes aware, or in the exercise of reasonable diligence or by reason of medical advice should have been aware, of the relationship between the employment, the disease, and the death or disability.

(b) Disability. With regard to an occupational disease for which the time of injury, as defined in 702.601(a), occurs after the employee was retired, disability shall mean permanent impairment as determined according to the Guides to the Evaluation of Permanent Impairment which is prepared and modified from timeto-time by the American Medical Association, using the most currently revised edition of this publication. If this guide does not evaluate the impairment, other professionally recognized standards may be utilized. The disability described in this paragraph shall be limited to permanent partial disability. For that reason they are not subject to adjustments under section 10(f) of the Act, 33 U.S.C. 910(f).

(c) Retirement. For purposes of this subpart, retirement shall mean that the claimant, or decedent in cases involving survivor's benefits, has voluntarily withdrawn from the workforce and that there is no realistic expectation that such person will return to the workforce.

[50 FR 406, Jan. 3, 1985, as amended at 51 FR 4286, Feb. 3, 1986]

§ 702.602 Notice and claims.

(a) Time for giving notice of injury or death. Refer to 702.207.

(b) Time for filing of claims. Refer to 702.212.

§ 702.603 Determining the payrate for compensating occupational disease claims which become manifest after retirement.

(a) If the time of injury occurs within the first year after the employee has retired, the payrate for compensation purposes shall be one fifty-second part of the employee's average annual earnings during the fifty-two week period preceding retirement.

(b) If the time of injury occurs more than one year after the employee has retired the payrate for compensation purposes shall be the national average weekly wage, determined according to section 6(b)(3) of the Act, 33 U.S.C. 906(b)(3), at the time of injury.

§ 702.604 Determining the amount of compensation for occupational disease claims which become manifest after retirement.

(a) If the claim is for disability benefits and the time of injury occurs after the employee has retired, compensation shall be 66\2/3\ percent of the payrate, as determined under 702.603, times the disability, as determined according to 702.601(b).

(b) If the claim is for death benefits and the time of injury occurs after the decedent has retired, compensation shall be the percent specified in section 9 of the Act, 33 U.S.C. 909, times the payrate determined according to 702.603. Total weekly death benefits shall not exceed one fifty-second part of the decedent's average annual earnings during the fifty-two week period preceding retirement, such benefits shall be subject to the limitation provided for in section 6(b)(1) of the Act, 33 U.S.C. 906(b)(1).

[50 FR 406, Jan. 3, 1985, as amended at 51 FR 4286, Feb. 3, 1986]

PART 703—INSURANCE REGULATIONS

Issuance of Certificates of Compliance

703.501 Issuance of certificates of compliance.
703.502 Same; employer operating temporarily in another compensation district.
703.503 Return of certificates of compliance.

Authority: 5 U.S.C. 301; Reorg. Plan No. 6 of 1950, 15 FR 3174, 64 Stat. 1263; 33 U.S.C. 939; 36 D.C. Code 501 et seq.; 42 U.S.C. 1651 et seq.; 43 U.S.C. 1331; 5 U.S.C. 6171 et seq.; Secretary's Order 1-89; Employment Standards Order No. 90-02.

Source: 38 FR 26873, Sept. 26, 1973, unless otherwise noted.

Editorial Note: Nomenclature changes to part 703 appear at 55 FR 28606, July 12, 1990.

§ 703.001 Scope of part.

This part 703 contains the regulations of the OWCP governing the authorization of insurance carriers, the authorization of self-insurers, and the issuance of certificates of compliance. Such provisions are required by the LHWCA, but in almost every instance apply, and hereby are applied, to the extensions of the LHWCA. In those few instances where a separate provision is required, tailored to meet the specific requirements of one of the extended acts, such separate provisions are placed in the succeeding parts of this subchapter.

§ 703.002 Forms.

Any information required by the regulations in this part to be submitted to the OWCP shall be submitted on such forms as the Director may deem appropriate and may authorize from time to time for such purpose.

§ 703.003 Failure to secure coverage; penalties.

(a) Each employer is required to secure coverage under this Act either through an authorized insurance carrier or by becoming an authoried self-insurer. An employer who fails to secure coverage by either manner described in section 32(a), (1) or (2) of the Act, 33 U.S.C. 932(a), is subject, upon conviction, to a fine of not more than $10,000, or by imprisonment for not more than one year, or both.

(1) Where the employer is a corporation: the president, secretary and treasurer each will also be subject to this fine and/or imprisonment, in addition to the fine against the corporation and each is personally liable, jointly with the corporation, for all compensation or other benefits payable under the Act during the time failure to secure coverage continues.

(b) Any employer who willingly and knowingly transfers, sells, encumbers, assigns or in any manner disposes of, conceals, secretes, or destroys any property belonging to the employer after an employee sustains an injury covered by this Act, with the intention to avoid payment to that employee or his/her dependents of compensation under this Act shall be guilty of a misdemeanor and punished upon conviction by a fine of not more than $10,000 and/or imprisonment for one year.

(1) Where the employer is a corporation: the president, secretary and treasurer are also each liable to imprisonment and, along with the corporation, jointly liable for the fine.

[50 FR 406, Jan. 3, 1985]

Authorization of Insurance Carriers

§ 703.101 Types of companies which may be authorized by the OWCP.

The OWCP will consider for the granting of authority to write insurance under the Longshoremen's and Harbor Workers' Compensation Act and its extensions the application of any stock company, mutual company or association, or any other person or fund, while authorized under the laws of the United States or for any State to insure workmen's compensation. The term "carrier" as used in this part means any person or fund duly authorized to insure workmen's compensation benefits under said Act, or its extensions.

§ 703.102 Applications for authority to write insurance; how filed; evidence to be submitted; other requirements.

An application for authority to write insurance under this Act shall be made in writing, signed by an officer of the applicant duly authorized to make such application, and transmitted to the Office of Workmen's Compensation Programs, U.S. Department of Labor, Washington, DC 20210. Such application shall be accompanied by full and complete information regarding the history and experience of such applicant in the writing of workmen's compensation insurance, together with evidence that it has authority in its charter or form of organization to write such insurance, and evidence that the applicant is currently authorized to insure workmen's compensation liability under the laws of the United States or of any State. The statements of fact in each application and in the supporting evidence shall be verified by the oath of the officer of the applicant who signs such application. Each applicant shall state in its application the area or areas, in which it intends to do business. In connection with any such application the following shall be submitted, the Office reserving the right to call for such additional information as it may deem necessary in any particular case:

(a) A copy of the last annual report made by the applicant to the insurance department or other authority of the State in which it is incorporated, or the State in which its principal business is done.

(b) A certified copy from the proper State authorities of the paper purporting to show the action taken upon such report, or such other evidence as the applicant desires to submit in respect of such report, which may obviate delay caused by an inquiry of the OWCP of the State authorities relative to the standing and responsibility of the applicant.

(c) A full and complete statement of its financial condition, if not otherwise shown, and, if a stock company, shall show specifically its capital stock and surplus.

(d) A copy of its charter or other formal outline of its organization, its rules, its bylaws, and other documents, writings, or agreements by and under which it does business, and such other evidence as it may deem proper to make a full exposition of its affairs and financial condition.

[38 FR 26873, Sept. 26, 1973; 50 FR 406, Jan. 3, 1985]

§ 703.103 Stock companies holding Treasury certificates of authority.

A stock company furnishing evidence that it is authorized to write workmen's compensation insurance under the laws of the United States or of any State, which holds a certificate of authority from the Secretary of the Treasury as an acceptable surety on Federal bonds, unless requested to do so, need not transmit to the Office with its application copies of such financial reports as are on file in the Department of the Treasury. The acceptance by that Department of such a company will be considered by the Office in conjunction with the application of such company, provided there has been compliance with the other requirements of the regulations in this part.

§ 703.104 Applicants currently authorized to write insurance under the extensions of the LHWCA.

Any applicant currently authorized by the Office to write insurance under any extension of the LHWCA need not support its application under the LHWCA or any other LHWCA extension with the evidence required by the regulations in this part, except the form of policy and endorsement which it proposes to use, unless specifically requested by the Office, but instead its application may refer to the fact that it has been so authorized.

§ 703.105 Copies of forms of policies to be submitted with application.

With each application for authority to write insurance there shall be submitted for the approval of the Office copies of the forms of policies which the applicant proposes to issue in writing insurance under the LHWCA, or its extensions, to which shall be attached the appropriate endorsement to be used in connection therewith.

§ 703.106 Certificate of authority to write insurance.

No corporation, company, association, person, or fund shall write insurance under this Act without first having received from the OWCP a certificate of authority to write such insurance. Any such certificate issued by the Office, after application therefor in accordance with these regulations, may authorize the applicant to write such insurance in a limited territory as determined by the Office. Any such certificate may be suspended or revoked by the Office prior to its expiration for good cause shown, but no suspension or revocation shall affect the liability of any carrier already incurred. Good cause shall include, without limitation, the failure to maintain in such limited territory a regular business office with full authority to act on all matters falling within the Act, and the failure to promptly and properly perform the carrier's responsibilities under the Act and these regulations, with special emphasis upon lack of promptness in making payments when due, upon failure to furnish appropriate medical care, and upon attempts to offer to, or urge upon, claimants inequitable settlements. A hearing may be requested by the aggrieved party and shall be held before the Director or his representative prior to the taking of any adverse action under this section.

§ 703.108 Period of authority to write insurance.

Effective with the end of the authorization period July 1, 1983, through June 30, 1984, annual reauthorization of authority to write insurance coverage under the Act is no longer necessary. Beginning July 1, 1984, and thereafter, newly issued Certificates of Authority will show no expiration date. Certificates of Authority will remain in force for so long as the carrier complies with the requirements of the OWCP.

[50 FR 406, Jan. 3, 1985]

§ 703.109 Longshoremen's endorsement; see succeeding parts for endorsements for extensions.

(a) The following form of endorsement application to the standard workmen's compensation and employer's liability policy, shall be used, if required by the OWCP, with the form of policy approved by the Office for use by an authorized carrier:

For attachment to Policy No. ___,

The obligations of the policy include the Longshoremen's and Harbor Workers' Compensation Act, 33 U.S.C. 901 et seq., and all laws amendatory thereof or supplementary thereto which may be or become effective while this policy is in force.

The company will be subject to the provisions of 33 U.S.C. 935. Insolvency or bankruptcy of the employer and/or discharge therein shall not relieve the company from payment of compensation and other benefits lawfully due for disability or death sustained by an employe during the life of the policy.

The company agrees to abide by all the provisions of this Act, and all lawful rules, regulations, orders, and decisions of the Office of Workmen's Compensation Programs, U.S. Department of Labor, unless and until set aside, modified, or reversed by appropriate appellate authority as provided for by said Act.

This endorsement shall not be cancelled prior to the date specified in this policy for its expiration until at least 30 days have elapsed after a notice of cancellation has been sent to the District Director and to this employer.

All terms, conditions, requirements, and obligations, expressed in this policy or in any other endorsement attached thereto which are not inconsistent with or inapplicable to the provisions of this endorsement are hereby made a part of this endorsement as fully and completely as if wholly written herein.

§ 703.110 Other forms of endorsements and policies.

Where the form of endorsement prescribed by 703.109 is not appropriate when used in conjunction with a form of policy approved for use by the Office no modification thereof shall be used unless specifically approved by the Office. Where the form of policy is designed to include therein the obligations of the insurer under said Act without the use of the appropriate endorsements, the policy shall contain the provisions required to be included in any of the endorsements. Such a policy, however, shall not be used until expressly approved by the Office.

§ 703.111 Submission of new forms of policies for approval; other endorsements.

No new forms of policies or modification of existing forms of policies shall be used by an insurer authorized by the Office under the regulations in this part to write insurance under said Act except after submission to and approval by the Office. No endorsement altering any provisions of a policy approved by the Office shall be used except after submission to and approval by the Office.

§ 703.112 Terms of policies.

A policy or contract of insurance shall be issued for the term of not less than 1 year from the date that it becomes effective, but if such insurance be not needed except for a particular contract or operation, the term of the policy may be limited to the period of such contract or operation.

§ 703.113 Marine insurance contracts.

A longshoremen's policy, or the longshoremen's endorsement provided for by 703.109 for attachment to a marine policy, may specify the particular vessel or vessels in respect of which the policy applies and the address of the employer at the home port thereof. The report of the issuance of a policy or endorsement required by 703.116 to be made by the carrier shall be made to the district director for the compensation district in which the home port of such vessel or vessels is located, and such report shall show the name and address of the owner as well as the name or names of such vessel or vessels.

§ 703.114 Notice of cancellation.

Cancellation of a contract or policy of insurance issued under authority of said Act shall not become effective otherwise than as provided by 33 U.S.C. 936(b); and notice of a proposed cancellation shall be given to the district director and to the employer in accordance with the provisions of 33 U.S.C. 912(c), 30 days before such cancellation is intended to be effective.

§ 703.115 Discharge by the carrier of obligations and duties of employer.

Every obligation and duty in respect of payment of compensation, the providing of medical and other treatment and care, the payment or furnishing of any other benefit required by said Act and in respect of the carrying out of the administrative procedure required or imposed by said Act or the regulations in this part upon an employer shall be discharged and carried out by the carrier except that the prescribed report of injury or death shall be sent by the employer to the district director and to the insurance carrier as required by 33 U.S.C. 930. Such carrier shall be jointly responsible with the employer for the submission of all reports, notices, forms, and other administrative papers required by the district director or the Office in the administration of said Act to be submitted by the employer, but any form or paper so submitted where required therein shall contain in addition to the name and address of the carrier, the full name and address of the employer on whose behalf it is submitted. Notice to or knowledge of an employer of the occurrence of the injury or death shall be notice to or knowledge of such carrier. Jurisdiction of the employer by a district director, the Office, or appropriate appellate authority under said Act shall be jurisdiction of such carrier. Any requirement under any compensation order, finding, or decision shall be binding upon such carrier in the same manner and to the same extent as upon the employer.

§ 703.116 Report by carrier of issuance of policy or endorsement.

Each carrier shall report to the district director assigned to a compensation district each policy and endorsement issued by it to an employer who carries on operations in such compensation district. The report shall be made in such manner and on such form as the district or the Office may require.

§ 703.117 Report; by whom sent.

The report of issuance of a policy and endorsement provided for in 703.116 shall be sent by the home office of the carrier, except that any carrier may authorize its agency or agencies in any compensation district to make such reports to the district director, provided the carrier shall notify the district director in such district of the agencies so duly authorized.

§ 703.118 Agreement to be bound by report.

Every applicant for authority to write insurance under the provisions of this Act, shall be deemed to have included in its application an agreement that the acceptance by the district director of a report of the issuance of a policy of insurance, as provided for by 703.116, shall bind the carrier to full liability for the obligations under this Act of the employer named in said report, and every certificate of authority to write insurance under this Act shall be deemed to have been issued by the Office upon consideration of the carrier's agreement to become so bound. It shall be no defense to this agreement that the carrier failed or delayed to issue the policy to the employer covered by this report.

[50 FR 406, Jan. 3, 1985]

§ 703.119 Report by employer operating temporarily in another compensation district.

Where an employer having operations in one compensation district contemplates engaging in work subject to the Act in another compensation district, his carrier may submit to the district director of such latter district a report pursuant to 703.116 containing the address of the employer in the first mentioned district with the additional notation "No present address in ____ compensation district. Certificate requested when address given."

§ 703.120 Name of one employer only shall be given in each report.

A separate report of the issuance of a policy and endorsement, provided for by 703.116, shall be made for each employer covered by a policy. If a policy is issued insuring more than one employer, a separate report for each employer so covered shall be sent to the district director concerned, with the name of only one employer on each such report.

§ 703.121 Multiple policies covering the same employer in the same compensation district prohibited; action upon receipt of a second report.

An employer operating within any compensation district shall have such operations in that district insured by not more than one insurance carrier. Accordingly, where a report provided for by 703.116 is received, and where reports on file show that a named employer is insured by another insurance carrier under a policy with an unexpired term, the district director shall inform the employer of the pre-existing coverage and of the OWCP's prohibition against multiple policies.

[39 FR 14942, Apr. 29, 1974]

AUTHORIZATION OF SELF-INSURERS

§ 703.301 Employers who may be authorized as self-insurers.

The Office will consider for the granting of authority to secure by self-insurance the payment of compensation under the Longshoremen's and Harbor Workers' Compensation Act, or its extensions, any employer who, pursuant to the regulations in this part, furnishes to the Office satisfactory proof of such employer's ability to pay compensation directly, and who agrees to immediately cancel any existing policy as of the time of the OWCP's approval of the employer to be self-insured, or who does not become otherwise insured under this Act. The succeeding regulations relating to self-insurers require the deposit of security in the form either of an indemnity bond or negotiable securities (at the option of the employer) of a kind and in an amount determined by the Office, and prescribe the conditions under which such deposit shall be made. The term "self-insurer" as used in these regulations means any employer securing compensation in accordance with the provisions of 33 U.S.C. 932(a)(2) and with these regulations.

[39 FR 14922, Apr. 29, 1974]

§ 703.302 Application for authority to become a self-insurer; how filed; information to be submitted; other requirements.

Application for authority to become a self-insurer may be made by any employer desiring such privilege and shall be addressed to the OWCP and be made on a form provided by the Office. Such application shall contain:

(a) A statement of the employer's payroll report for the preceding 12 months; (b) a statement of the average number of employees engaged in employment within the purview of the LHWCA or any of its extensions for the preceding 12 months; (c) a statement of the number of injuries to such employees resulting in disability of more than 7 days' duration, or in death, during each of 3 years next preceding the date of the application; (d) a certified financial report for each of the three years preceding the application; (e) a description of the facilities maintained or the arrangements made for the medical and hospital care of injured employees; and (f) a statement describing the provisions and maximum amount of any excess or catastrophic insurance. The Office may in its discretion require the applicant to submit such further information or such evidence as the Office may deem necessary to have in order to enable it to give adequate consideration to such application. Such application shall be signed by the applicant over his typewritten name and if the applicant is not an individual, by an officer of the applicant duly authorized to make such application over his typewritten name and official designation and shall be sworn to by him. If the applicant is a corporation, the corporate seal shall be affixed. The application shall be filed with the OWCP national office in Washington, DC. The regulations in this part shall be binding upon each applicant hereunder and the applicant's consent to be bound by all requirements of the said regulations shall be deemed to be included in and a part of the application, as fully as though written therein.

(Approved by the Office of Management and Budget under control number 1215-0160)

(Pub. L. No. 96-511)
[38 FR 26873, Sept. 26, 1973, as amended at 50 FR 406, Jan. 3, 1985]

§ 703.303 Decision upon application of employer; deposit of negotiable securities or indemnity bond.

The decision of the Office to grant an application of an employer for authority to pay compensation under said Act as a self-insurer will be transmitted to the applicant on a form prescribed by the Office. Such grant shall be conditioned upon a deposit of security in the form of an indemnity bond or of negotiable securities in an amount fixed by the Office, and the execution and filing of an agreement and undertaking in the form prescribed by the Office, as required by 703.304.

§ 703.304 Filing of agreement and undertaking.

The applicant for the privilege of self-insurance shall as a condition subsequent to receiving authorization to act as a self-insurer, execute and file with the Office and agreement and undertaking in a form prescribed and provided by the Office in whch the applicant shall agree: (a) To pay when due, as required by the provisions of said Act, all compensation payable on account of injury or death of any of its employees injured within the purview of said Act; (b) in such cases to furnish medical, surgical, hospital, and other attendence, treatment and care as required by the provisions of said Act; (c) to deposit with the Office an indemnity bond in the amount which the Office shall fix, or to deposit negotiable securities as provided for by the regulations in this part in the amount which the Office shall fix, accordingly as elected in the application; (d) to authorize the Office to sell such negotiable securities so deposited or any part thereof and from the proceeds thereof to pay such compensation, medical, and other expenses and any accrued penalties imposed by law as it may find to be due and payable; and (e) to obtain and maintain, if required by the Office, excess or catastrophic insurance, in amounts to be determined by the Office.

[50 FR 407, Jan. 3, 1985]

§ 703.305 Decision upon application of employer; furnishing of indemnity bond or deposit of negotiable securities required.

The applicant for the privilege of self-insurance, as a condition subsequent to receiving authorization to act as self-insurer, shall give security for the payment of compensation and the discharge of all other obligations under the said Act, in the amount fixed by the Office, which may be in the form of an indemnity bond with sureties satisfactory to the Office, or of a deposit of negotiable securities as provided in the regulations in this part. The amount of such security so to be fixed and required by the Office shall be such as the Office shall deem to be necessary and sufficient to secure the performance by the applicant of all obligations imposed upon him as an employer by the Act. In fixing the amount of such security the Office will take into account the financial standing of the employer, the nature of the work in which he is engaged, the hazard of the work in which the employees are employed, the payroll exposure, and the accident experience as shown in the application and the Office's records, and any other facts which the Office may deem pertinent. Additional security may be required at any time in the discretion of the Office. The indemnity bond which is required by these regulations shall be in such form, and shall contain such provisions, as the Office may prescribe: Provided, That only surety companies approved by the United States Treasury Department under the laws of the United States and the rules and regulations governing bonding companies may act as sureties on such indemnity bonds.

[50 FR 407, Jan. 3, 1985]

§ 703.306 Kinds of negotiable securities which may be deposited; conditions of deposit; acceptance of deposits.

An applicant for the privilege of self-insurance electing to deposit negotiable securities to secure his obligations under said Act in the amount fixed by the Office under the regulations in this part shall deposit any negotiable securities acceptable as security for the deposit of public monies of the United States under regulations issued by the Secretary of the Treasury. The approval, valuation, acceptance, and custody of such securities is hereby committed to the several Federal Reserve Banks and the Treasurer of the United States when authorized under the regulations in this part to receive deposits of such securities.

[50 FR 407, Jan. 3, 1985]

§ 703.307 Deposits of negotiable securities with Federal Reserve banks or the Treasurer of the United States; authority to sell such securities; interest thereon.

Deposits of securities provided for by the regulations in this part shall be made with any Federal Reserve bank or any branch of a Federal Reserve bank designated by the Office, or the Treasurer of the United States, and shall be held subject to the order of the Office with power in the Office, in its discretion in the event of default by the said self-insurer, to collect the interest and the principal as they may become due, to sell the securities or any of them as may be required to discharge the obligations of the selfinsurer under said Act and to apply the proceeds to the payment of any compensation or medical expense for which the self-insurer may be liable. The Office may, however, whenever it deems it unnecessary to resort to such securities for the payment of compensation, authorize the self-insurer to collect interest on the securities deposited by him.

§ 703.308 Substitution and withdrawal of negotiable securities.

No substitution or withdrawal of negotiable securities deposited by a self-insurer shall be made except upon authorization by the Office. A self-insurer discontinuing business, or discontinuing operations within the purview of said Act, or providing security for the payment of compensation by insurance under the provisions of said Act may apply to the Office for the withdrawal of securities deposited under the regulations in this part. With such application shall be filed a sworn statement setting forth:

(a) A list of all outstanding cases in each compensation district in which compensation is being paid, with the names of the employees and other beneficiaries, giving a description of causes of injury or death, and a statement of the amount of compensation paid; (b) a similar list of all pending cases in which no compensation has as yet been paid; and (c) a similar list of all cases in which injury or death has occurred within 1 year prior to such application or in which the last payment of compensation was made within 1 year prior to such application. In such cases withdrawals may be authorized by the Office of such securities as in the opinion of the Office may not be necessary to provide adequate security for the payment of outstanding and potential liabilities of such self-insurer under said Act.

§ 703.309 Increase or reduction in the amount of indemnity bond or negotiable securities.

Whenever in the opinion of the Office the principal sum of the indemnity bond filed or the amount of negotiable securities deposited by a self-insurer is insufficient to afford adequate security for the payment of compensation and medical expenses under said Act, the self-insurer shall, upon demand by the Office, file such additional indemnity bond or deposit under the regulations in this part such additional amount of negotiable securities as the Office may require. At any time upon application of a self-insurer, or on the initiative of the Office, when in its opinion the facts warrant, the principal sum of an indemnity bond required to be given or the amount of negotiable securities required to be deposited may be reduced. A self-insurer seeking such reduction shall furnish such information as the Office may request relative to his current affairs, the nature and hazard of the work of his employees, the amount of the payroll of his employees engaged in maritime employment within the purview of the said Act, his financial condition, his accident experience, and such other evidence as may be deemed material, including a record of payments of compensation made by him.

§ 703.310 Reports required of self-insurers; examination of accounts of self-insurer.

At such times as the Office may require or prescribe, each self-insurer shall submit such of the following reports as may be requested:

(a) A certified financial statement of the self-insurer's assets and liabilities, or a balance sheet.

(b) A sworn statement showing by classifications the payroll of employees of the self-insurer who are engaged in employment within the purview of the LHWCA or any of its extensions.

(c) A sworn statement covering the 6 months' period preceding the date of such report, listing by compensation districts all death and injury cases which have occurred during such period, together with a report of the status of all outstanding claims, showing the particulars of each case.

Whenever it deems it to be necessary, the Office may inspect or examine the books of account, records, and other papers of a self-insurer for the purpose of verifying any financial statement submitted to the Office by self-insurer or verifying any information furnished to the Office in any report required by this section, or any other section of the regulations in this part, and such self-insurer shall permit the Office or its duly authorized representative to make such an inspection or examination as the Office shall require. In lieu of this requirement the Office may in its discretion accept an adequate report of a certified public accountant.

(Approved by the Office of Management and Budget under control number 1215-0033)

(Pub. L. No. 96-511)
[38 FR 26873, Sept. 26, 1973, as amended at 49 FR 18294, Apr. 30, 1984; 50 FR 407, Jan. 3, 1985]

§ 703.311 Period of authorization as self-insurer.

(a) Effective with the end of the authorization period July 1, 1983, through June 30, 1984, annual reauthorization of the self-insurance privilege is no longer necessary. Beginning July 1, 1984, and thereafter, newly approved and renewed self-insurance authorizations will remain in effect for so long as the self-insurer complies with the requirements of the OWCP.

(b) A self-insurer who currently has on file an indemnity bond, will receive from the office, on or about May 10 of each year, a bond form for execution in contemplation of the continuance of the selfinsurance authorization, and the submission of such bond duly executed in the amount indicated by the office will be deemed and treated as a condition of the continuing authorization.

[50 FR 407, Jan. 3, 1985]

§ 703.312 Revocation of privilege of self-insurance.

The Office may for good cause shown suspend or revoke the authorization of any self-insurer. Failure by a self-insurer to comply with any provision or requirement of law or of the regulations in this part, or with any lawful order or communication of the Office, or the failure or insolvency of the surety on his indemnity bond, or impairment of financial responsibility of such self-insurer, shall be deemed good cause for such suspension or revocation.

Issuance of Certificates of Compliance

§ 703.501 Issuance of certificates of compliance.

Every employer who has secured the payment of compensation as required by 33 U.S.C. 932 and by the regulations in this part may request a certificate from the district director in the compensation district in which he has operations, and for which a certificate is required by 33 U.S.C. 937, showing that such employer has secured the payment of compensation. Only one such certificate will be issued to an employer in a compensation district, and it will be valid only during the period for which such employer has secured such payment. An employer so desiring may have photocopies of such a certificate made for use in different places within the compensation district. Two forms of such certificates have been provided by the Office, one form for use where the employer has obtained insurance generally under these regulations, and one for use where the employer has been authorized as a self-insurer.

§ 703.502 Same; employer operating temporarily in another compensation district.

A district director receiving a report of the issuance of a policy of insurance with the notation authorized by 703.119, will file such report until he receives from the insured employer named therein a request for certificate of compliance, giving the address of the employer within the compensation district of such district director. Upon receipt of such a request the district director will send the proper certificate of compliance to such employer at such address.

§ 703.503 Return of certificates of compliance.

Upon the termination by expiration, cancellation or otherwise, of a policy of insurance issued under the provisions of law and these regulations, or the revocation or termination of the privilege of selfinsurance granted by the Office, all certificates of compliance issued on the basis of such insurance or selfinsurance shall be void and shall be returned by the employer to the district director issuing them with a statement of the reason for such return. An employer holding certificate of compliance under an insurance policy which has expired, pending renewal of such insurance need not return such certificate of compliance if such expired insurance is promptly replaced. An employer who has secured renewal of insurance upon the expiration of policy under said Act or whose self-insurance thereunder is reauthorized without a break in the continuity thereof need not return an expired certificate of compliance.

PART 704—SPECIAL PROVISIONS FOR LHWCA EXTENSIONS

Authority: 5 U.S.C. 301; Reorg. Plan No. 6 of 1950, 15 FR 3174, 64 Stat. 1263; 33 U.S.C. 939; 36 D.C. Code 501 et seq.; 42 U.S.C. 1651 et seq.; 43 U.S.C. 1331; 5 U.S.C. 6171 et seq.; Secretary's Order 1-89; Employment Standards Order No. 90-02.

Source: 38 FR 26877, Sept. 26, 1973, unless otherwise noted.

Editorial Note: Nomenclature changes to part 704 appear at 55 FR 28606, July 12, 1990.

§ 704.001 Extensions covered by this part.

(a) Defense Base Act (DBA).
(b) District of Columbia Workmen's Compensation Act (DCCA).
(c) Outer Continental Shelf Lands Act (OCSLA).
(d) Nonappropriated Fund Instrumentalities Act (NFIA).

§ 704.002 Scope of part.

The regulations governing the administration of the LHWCA as set forth in parts 702 and 703 of this subchapter govern the administration of the LHWCA extensions (see 704.001) in nearly every respect, and are not repeated in this part 704. Such special provisions as are necessary to the proper administration of each of the extensions are set forth in this part. To the extent of any inconsistency between regulations in parts 702 and 703 of this subchapter and those in this part, the latter supersedes those in parts 702 and 703 of this subchapter.

Defense Base Act

§ 704.101 Administration; compensation districts.

For the purpose of administration of this Act areas assigned to the compensation districts established for administration of the Longshoremen's and Harbor Workers' Compensation Act as set forth in part 702 of this subchapter shall be extended in the following manner to include:

(a) Canada, east of the 75th degree west longitude, Newfoundland, and Greenland are assigned to District No. 1.

(b) Canada, west of the 75th degree and east of the 110th degree west longitude, is assigned to District No. 10.

(c) Canada, west of the 110th degree west longitude, and all areas in the Pacific Ocean north of the 45th degree north latitude are assigned to District No. 14.

(d) All areas west of the continents of North and South America (except coastal islands) to the 60th degree east longitude, except for Iran, are assigned to District No. 15.

(e) Mexico, Central and South America (including coastal islands); areas east of the continents of North and South America to the 60th degree east longitude, including Iran, and any other areas or locations not covered under any other district office, are assigned to District No. 2.

§ 704.102 Commutation of payments to aliens and nonresidents.

Authority to commute payments to aliens and nonnationals who are not residents of the United States and Canada, section 2(b) of the Defense Base Act, 42 U.S.C. 1652(b), though separately stated in this Act, is identical in language to section 9(g) of the Longshoremen's Act. Thus, except for the different statutory citation, the LHWCA regulation at 702.142 of this subchapter shall apply.

§ 704.103 Removal of certain minimums when computing or paying compensation.

The minimum limitation on weekly compensation for disability established by section 6 of the LHWCA, 33 U.S.C. 906, and the minimum limit on the average weekly wages on which death benefits are to be computed under section 9 of the LHWCA, 33 U.S.C. 909, shall not apply in computing compensation and death benefits under this Act; section 2(a), 42 U.S.C. 1652(a).

§ 704.151 DBA endorsement.

The following form of endorsement applicable to the standard workmen's compensation and employers' liability policy shall be used, if required by the OWCP, with the form of policy approved by the Office for use by an authorized carrier:

For attachment to Policy No. __,

The obligations of the policy include the Longshoremen's and Harbor Workers' Compensation Act, as extended by the provisions of the Defense Base Act, and all laws amendatory thereof or supplementary thereto which may be or become effective while this policy is in force.

The Company will be subject to the provisions of 33 U.S.C. 935. Insolvency or bankruptcy of the employer and/or discharge therein shall not relieve the Company from payment of compensation and other benefits lawfully due for disability or death sustained by an employee during the life of the policy.

The Company agrees to abide by all the provisions of said Acts and all lawful rules, regulations, orders, and decisions of the Office of Workmen's Compensation Programs, Department of Labor, unless and until set aside, modified, or reversed by appropriate appellate authority as provided for by said Acts.

This endorsement shall not be canceled prior to the date specified in this policy for its expiration until at least 30 days have elapsed after a notice of cancellation has been sent to the District Director and to this employer.

All terms, conditions, requirements, and obligations expressed in this policy or in any other endorsement attached thereto which are not inconsistent with or inapplicable to the provisions of this endorsement are hereby made a part of this endorsement as fully and completely as if wholly written herein.

DISTRICT OF COLUMBIA WORKMEN'S COMPENSATION ACT

§ 704.201 Administration; compensation districts.

For the purpose of administration of this Act, the District of Columbia shall be the compensation district and is designated as District No. 40.

§ 704.251 DCCA endorsement.

The following form of endorsement applicable to the standard workmen's compensation and employer's liability policy shall be used, if required by the OWCP, with the form of policy approved by the Office for use by an authorized carrier:

For attachment to Policy No. __,

The obligations of the policy include the District of Columbia Workmen's Compensation Act, and the applicable provisions of the Longshoremen's and Harbor Workers' Compensation Act, and all laws amendatory of either of said Acts or supplementary thereto which may be or become effective while this policy is in force.

The company will be subject to the provisions of 33 U.S.C. 935. Insolvency or bankruptcy of the employer and/or discharge therein shall not relieve the company from payment of compensation and other benefits lawfully due for disability or death sustained by an employee during the life of the policy.

The company agrees to abide by all the provisions of said District of Columbia Workmen's Compensation Act and all lawful rules, regulations, orders, and decisions of the Office of Workmen's Compensation Programs, Department of Labor, unless and until set aside, modified, or reversed by appropriate appellate authority as provided for by said Act.

This endorsement shall not be canceled prior to the date specified in this policy for its expiration until at least 30 days have elapsed after a notice of cancellation has been sent to the District Director for the District of Columbia and to this employer.

All terms, conditions, requirements, and obligations expressed in this policy or in any other endorsement attached thereto which are not inconsistent with or inapplicable to the provisions of this endorsement are hereby made a part of this endorsement as fully and completely as if wholly written herein.

OUTER CONTINENTAL SHELF LANDS ACT

§ 704.301 Administration; compensation districts.

For the purpose of administration of this Act, the compensation districts established under the Longshoremen's and Harbor Workers' Compensation Act as set forth in part 702 of this subchapter shall administer this Act, and their jurisdiction for this purpose is extended, where appropriate, to include those parts of the Outer Continental Shelf adjacent to the State or States in such districts having adjacent shelf areas.

§ 704.351 OCSLA endorsement.

The following form of endorsement applicable to the standard workmen's compensation and employer's liability policy shall be used, if required by the OWCP, with the form of policy approved by the Office for use by an authorized carrier:

For attachment to Policy No. ___,

The obligations of the policy include the Longshoremen's and Harbor Workers' Compensation Act, as extended by the Outer Continental Shelf Lands Act, and all the laws amendatory thereof or supplementary thereto which may be or become effective while this policy is in force.

The company will be subject to the provisions of 33 U.S.C. 935. Insolvency or bankruptcy of the employer and/or discharge therein shall not relieve the company from payment of compensation and other benefits lawfully due for disability or death sustained by an employee during the life of the policy.

The company agrees to abide by all the provisions of said laws and all the lawful rules, regulations, orders and decisions of the Office of Workmen's Compensation Programs, Department of Labor, until set aside, modified, or reversed by appropriate appellate authority as provided for by said Acts.

This endorsement shall not be canceled prior to the date specified in this policy for its expiration until at least 30 days have elapsed after a notice of cancellation has been sent to the District Director and to his employer.

All terms, conditions, requirements, and obligations expressed in this policy or in any other endorsement attached thereto which are not inconsistent with or inapplicable to the provisions of this endorsement are hereby made a part of this endorsement as fully and completely as if wholly written herein.

NONAPPROPRIATED FUND INSTRUMENTALITIES ACT

§ 704.401 Administration; compensation districts.

For the purpose of administration of this Act within the continental United States, Hawaii, and Alaska, the compensation districts established for administration of the Longshoremen's and Harbor Workers' Compensation Act as set forth in part 702 of this subchapter are established as the administrative districts under this Act. For the purpose of administration of this Act outside the continental United States, Alaska, and Hawaii, the compensation districts established for such overseas administration of the Defense Base Act as set forth in 704.101 are established as the administrative districts under this Act.

§ 704.451 NFIA endorsement.

The following form of endorsement applicable to the standard workmen's compensation and employer's liability policy shall be used, if required by the OWCP, with the form of policy approved by the Office for use by an authorized carrier:

For attachment to Policy No. ___,

The obligations of the policy include the Longshoremen's and Harbor Workers' Compensation Act, as extended by the Nonappropriated Fund Instrumentalities Act, and all of the laws amendatory thereof or supplementary thereto which may be or become effective while this policy is in force.

The company will be subject to the provisions of 33 U.S.C 935. Insolvency or bankruptcy of the employer and/or discharge therein shall not relieve the company from payment of compensation and other benefits lawfully due for disability or death sustained by an employee during the life of the policy.

The company agrees to abide by all the provisions of said Acts and all the lawful rules, regulations, orders, and decisions of the Office of Workmen's Compensation Programs, Department of Labor, unless and until set aside, modified, or reversed by appropriate appellate authority as provided for by said Acts.

This endorsement shall not be canceled prior to the date specified in this policy for its expiration until at least 30 days have elapsed after a notice of cancellation has been sent to the District Director and to the within named employer.

All terms, conditions, requirements, and obligations expressed in this policy or in any other endorsement attached thereto which are not inconsistent with or inapplicable to the provisions of this endorsement are hereby made a part of this endorsement as fully and completely as if wholly written herein.

PART 801—ESTABLISHMENT AND OPERATION OF THE BOARD

INTRODUCTORY

AUTHORITY: 5 U.S.C. 301; Reorganization Plan No. 6 of 1950, 15 FR 3174; 33 U.S.C. 901 et seq.; 30 U.S.C. 901 et seq.; Secretary of Labor's Order 38-72, 38 FR 90, January 3, 1973.

SOURCE: 52 FR 27290, July 20, 1987, unless otherwise noted.

§ 801.1 Purpose and scope of this part.

This part 801 describes the establishment and the organizational structure of the Benefits Review Board of the Department of Labor, sets forth the general rules applicable to operation of the Board, and defines terms used in this chapter.

§ 801.2 Definitions and use of terms.

(a) For purposes of this chapter, except where the content clearly indicates otherwise, the following definitions apply:

(1) Acts means the several Acts listed in 801.102 and 802.101 of this chapter, as amended and extended, unless otherwise specified.

(2) Board means the Benefits Review Board established by section 21 of the LHWCA (33 U.S.C. 921) as described in 801.101, and as provided in this part and Secretary of Labor's Order No. 38-72 (38 FR 90). Mention in these regulations of the "permanent Board" refers to the five permanent Board members only.

(3) Chairman or Chairman of the Board means Chairman of the Benefits Review Board. The Chairman of the Board is officially entitled Chief Administrative Appeals Judge.

(4) Secretary means the Secretary of Labor.

(5) Department means the Department of Labor.

(6) Judge means an administrative law judge appointed as provided in 5 U.S.C. 3105 and subpart B of 5 CFR part 930, who is qualified to preside at hearings under 5 U.S.C. 557 and is empowered by the Secretary to conduct formal hearings whenever necessary in respect of any claim for benefits or compensation arising under the Acts.

(7) Chief Administrative Law Judge means the Chief Administrative Law Judge of the Department of Labor.

(8) Director means the Director of the Office of Workers' Compensation Programs of the Department of Labor (hereinafter OWCP).

(9) Deputy commissioner means a person appointed as provided in sections 39 and 40 of the LHWCA or his designee, authorized by the Director to make decisions and orders in respect to claims arising under the Acts.

(10) Party or Party in Interest means the Secretary or his designee and any person or business entity directly affected by the decision or order from which an appeal to the Board is taken.

(11) Day means calendar day.

(12) Member means a member of the Benefits Review Board. Unless specifically stated otherwise, the word "member" shall apply to permanent, temporary and interim members. Permanent Board members are officially entitled Administrative Appeals Judges. Temporary and interim Board members are designated as Acting Administrative Appeals Judges.

(b) The definitions contained in this part shall not be considered to derogate from the definitions of terms in the respective Acts.

(c) The definitions pertaining to the Acts contained in the several parts of chapter VI of this title 20 shall be applicable to this chapter as is appropriate.

[52 FR 27290, July 20, 1987, as amended at 52 FR 28640, July 31, 1987]

§ 801.3 Applicability of this part to 20 CFR part 802.

Part 802 of title 20, Code of Federal Regulations, contains the rules of practice and procedure of the Board. This part 801, including the definitions and usages contained in 801.2, is applicable to part 802 of this chapter as appropriate.

ESTABLISHMENT AND AUTHORITY OF THE BOARD

§ 801.101 Establishment.

By Pub. L. 92-576, 82 Stat. 1251, in an amendment made to section 21 of the Longshore and Harbor Workers' Compensation Act (33 U.S.C. 921), there was established effective November 26, 1972, a Benefits Review Board, which is composed of members appointed by the Secretary of Labor.

§ 801.102 Review authority.

(a) The Board is authorized, as provided in 33 U.S.C. 921(b), as amended, to hear and determine appeals raising a substantial question of law or fact taken by any party in interest from decisions or orders with respect to claims for compensation or benefits arising under the following Acts, as amended and extended:

(1) The Longshore and Harbor Workers' Compensation Act (LHWCA), 33 U.S.C. 901 et seq.;

(2) The Defense Base Act (DBA), 42 U.S.C. 1651 et seq.;

(3) The District of Columbia Workmen's Compensation Act (DCWCA), 36 D.C. Code 501 et seq. (1973);

(4) The Outer Continental Shelf Lands Act (OCSLA), 43 U.S.C. 1331 et seq.;

(5) The Nonappropriated Fund Instrumentalities Act (NFIA), 5 U.S.C. 8171 et seq.;

(6) Title IV, section 415 and part C of the Federal Mine Safety and Health Act of 1977, Public Law

95-164, 91 Stat. 1290 (formerly the Federal Coal Mine Health and Safety Act, hereinafter, FCMHSA, of 1969) as amended by the Black Lung Benefits Reform Act of 1977, Public Law 92-239, 92 Stat. 95, the Black Lung Benefits Revenue Act of 1977, Public Law 95-227, 92 Stat. 11, and the Black Lung Benefits Amendments of 1981, Public Law 97-119, 95 Stat. 1643 (30 U.S.C. 901 et seq.).

§ 801.103 Organizational placement.

As prescribed by the statute, the functions of the Benefits Review Board are quasijudicial in nature and involve review of decisions made in the course of the administration of the above statutes by the Employment Standards Administration in the Department of Labor. It is accordingly found appropriate for organizational purposes to place the Board in the Office of the Deputy Secretary and it is hereby established in that Office, which shall be responsible for providing necessary funds, personnel, supplies, equipment, and records services for the Board.

§ 801.104 Operational rules.

The Deputy Secretary of Labor may promulgate such rules and regulations as may be necessary or appropriate for effective operation of the Benefits Review Board as an independent quasi-judicial body in accordance with the provisions of the statute.

Members of the Board

§ 801.201 Composition of the Board.

(a) The Board shall be composed of five permanent members appointed by the Secretary from among individuals who are especially qualified to serve thereon. Each permanent member shall serve an indefinite term subject to the discretion of the Secretary.

(b) The member designated by the Secretary as Chairman of the Board shall serve as chief administrative officer of the Board and shall have the authority, as delegated by the Secretary, to exercise all administrative functions necessary to operate the Board.

(c) The four remaining members shall be the associate members of the Board.

(d) Upon application of the Chairman of the Board, the Secretary may designate up to four Department of Labor administrative law judges to serve as temporary Board members in addition to the five permanent Board members. Up to four such temporary members may serve at any one time. The term of any temporary Board member shall not exceed 1 year from date of appointment.

§ 801.202 Interim appointments.

(a) Acting Chairman. In the event that the Chairman of the Board is temporarily disabled or unavailable to perform his or her duties as prescribed in this chapter VII, he or she shall designate a permanent member to serve as Acting Chairman until such time as the Secretary designates an Acting Chairman. In the event that the Chairman is physically unable to make such designation, the next senior permanent member shall serve as Acting Chairman until such time as the Secretary of Labor designates an Acting Chairman.

(b) Interim members. In the event that a permanent member of the Board is temporarily unable to carry out his or her responsibilities because of disqualification, illness, or for any other reason, the Secretary of Labor may, in his or her discretion, appoint a qualified individual to serve in the place of such permanent member for the duration of that permanent member's inability to serve.

§ 801.203 Disqualification of Board Members.

(a) During the period in which the Chairman or the other members serve on the Board, they shall be subject to the Department's regulations governing ethics and conduct set forth at 20 CFR part 0.

(b) Notice of any objection which a party may have to any Board member who will participate in the proceeding shall be made by such party at the earliest opportunity. The Board member shall consider such objection and shall, in his or her discretion, either proceed with the case or withdraw.

§ 801.301 Quorum and votes of the permanent Board; panels within the Board.

(a) For the purpose of carrying out its functions under the Acts, whenever action is taken by the entire permanent Board sitting en banc, three permanent members of the Board shall constitute a quorum, and official action of the permanent Board can be taken only on the concurring vote of at least three permanent members.

(b) The Board may delegate any or all of its powers except en banc review to panels of three members. Each panel shall consist of at least two permanent members. Two members of the panel shall constitute a quorum and official panel action can be taken only on the concurring vote of two members of the panel.

(c) A panel decision shall stand unless vacated or modified by the concurring vote of at least three permanent members sitting en banc.

(d) En banc action is not available in cases arising under the District of Columbia Workmen's Compensation Act.

§ 801.302 Procedural rules.

Procedural rules for performance by the Board of its review functions and for insuring an adequate record for any judicial review of its orders, and such amendments to the rules as may be necessary from time to time, shall be promulgated by the Deputy Secretary. Such rules shall incorporate and implement the procedural requirements of section 21(b) of the Longshore and Harbor Workers' Compensation Act.

§ 801.303 Location of Board's proceedings.

The Board shall hold its proceedings at 800 K Street, NW., suite 500, Washington, DC 20001-8001, unless for good cause the Board orders that proceedings in a particular matter be held in another location.

[56 FR 54538, Oct. 22, 1991]

§ 801.304 Business hours.

The office of the Clerk of the Board at Washington, DC shall be open from 8:30 a.m._5:00 p.m. on all days, except Saturdays, Sundays, and legal holidays, for the purpose of receiving notices of appeal, petitions for review, other pleadings, motions, and other papers.

Representation

§ 801.401 Representation before the Board.

On any issues requiring representation of the Secretary, the Director, Office of Workers' Compensation Programs, a deputy commissioner, or an administrative law judge before the Board, such representation shall be provided by attorneys designated by the Solicitor of Labor. Representation of all other persons before the Board shall be as provided by the rules of practice and procedure promulgated under 801.302 (see part 802 of this chapter).

§ 801.402 Representation of Board in court proceedings.

Except in proceedings in the Supreme Court of the United States, any representation of the Benefits Review Board in court proceedings shall be by attorneys designated by the Solicitor of Labor.

PART 802—RULES OF PRACTICE AND PROCEDURE

Subpart A—General Provisions

INTRODUCTORY

Subpart B—Prereview Procedures

COMMENCING APPEAL: PARTIES

NOTICE OF APPEAL

INITIAL PROCESSING

Subpart C—Procedure for Review

ACTION BY THE BOARD

ORAL ARGUMENT BEFORE THE BOARD

Subpart D—Completion of Board Review

DISMISSALS

DECISION OF THE BOARD

RECONSIDERATION

JUDICIAL REVIEW

AUTHORITY: 5 U.S.C. 301; Reorganization Plan No. 6 of 1950, 15 FR 3174; 33 U.S.C. 901 et seq.; 30 U.S.C. 901 et seq.; Secretary of Labor's Order 38-72, 38 FR 90, January 3, 1973.

SOURCE: 52 FR 27292, July 20, 1987, unless otherwise noted.

Subpart A—General Provisions

INTRODUCTORY

§ 802.101 Purpose and scope of this part.

(a) The purpose of part 802 is to establish the rules of practice and procedure governing the operation of the Benefits Review Board.

(b) Except as otherwise provided, the rules promulgated in this part apply to all appeals taken by any party from decisions or orders with respect to claims for compensation or benefits under the following Acts:

(1) The Longshore and Harbor Workers' Compensation Act (LHWCA), 33 U.S.C. 901 et seq.;

(2) The Defense Base Act (DBA), 42 U.S.C. 1651 et seq.;

(3) The District of Columbia Workmen's Compensation Act (DCWCA), 36 D.C. Code 501 et seq. (1973);

(4) The Outer Continental Shelf Lands Act (OCSLA), 43 U.S.C. 1331 et seq.;

(5) The Nonappropriated Fund Instrumentalities Act (NFIA), 5 U.S.C. 8171 et seq.;

(6) Title IV, section 415 and part C of the Federal Mine Safety and Health Act of 1977, Public Law 95-164, 91 Stat. 1290 (formerly the FCMHSA of 1969), as amended by the Black Lung Benefits Reform Act of 1977, Public Law 95-239, 92 Stat. 95, the Black Lung Benefits Revenue Act of 1977, Public Law 95229, 92 Stat. 11, and the Black Lung Benefits Amendments of 1981, Public Law 97-119, 95 Stat. 1643 (30 U.S.C. 901 et seq.).

§ 802.102 Applicability of part 801 of this chapter.

Part 801 of this chapter VII sets forth rules of general applicability covering the composition, authority, and operation of the Benefits Review Board and definitions applicable to this chapter. The provisions of part 801 of this chapter are fully applicable to this part 802.

§ 802.103 Powers of the Board.

(a) Conduct of proceedings. Pursuant to section 27(a) of the LHWCA, the Board shall have power to preserve and enforce order during any proceedings for determination or adjudication of entitlement to compensation or benefits or for liability for payment thereof, and to do all things in accordance with law which may be necessary to enable the Board to effectively discharge its duties.

(b) Contumacy. Pursuant to section 27(b) of the LHWCA, if any person in proceedings before the Board disobeys or resists any lawful order or process, or misbehaves during a hearing or so near the place thereof as to obstruct the same, the Board shall certify the facts to the Federal district court having jurisdiction in the place in which it is sitting (or to the U.S. District Court for the District of Columbia if it is sitting in the District) which shall thereupon in a summary manner hear the evidence as to the acts complained of, and if the evidence so warrants, punish such person in the same manner and to the same extent as for a contempt committed before the court, or commit such person upon the same conditions as if the doing of the forbidden act had occurred with reference to the process or in the presence of the court.

§ 802.104 Consolidation; severance.

(a) Cases may, in the sole discretion of the Board, be consolidated for purposes of an appeal upon the motion of any party or upon the Board's own motion where there exist common parties, common questions of law or fact or both, or in such other circumstances as justice and the administration of the Acts require.

(b) Upon its own motion, or upon motion of any party, the Board may, for good cause, order any proceeding severed with respect to some or all issues or parties.

§ 802.105 Stay of payment pending appeal.

(a) As provided in section 14(f) of the LHWCA and sections 415 and 422 of the Black Lung Benefits Act, the payment of the amounts required by an award of compensation or benefits shall not be stayed or in any way delayed beyond ten days after it becomes due pending final decision in any proceeding before the Board unless so ordered by the Board. No stay shall be issued unless irreparable injury would otherwise ensue to the employer, coal mine operator or insurance carrier. Any order of the Board permitting any stay shall contain a specific finding, based upon evidence submitted to the Board and identified by reference thereto, that irreparable injury would result to such employer, operator or insurance carrier, and specify the nature and extent of the injury.

(b) When circumstances require, the Board, in its discretion, may issue a temporary order not to exceed 30 days granting a motion for stay of payment prior to the expiration of the ten-day period allowed for filing responses to motions pursuant to § 802.219(e). Following receipt of a response to the motion or expiration of the response time provided in § 802.219(e), the Board will issue a subsequent order ruling on the motion for stay of payment.

[52 FR 27292, July 20, 1987, as amended at 53 FR 16519, May 9, 1988]

Subpart B—Prereview Procedures

Commencing Appeal: Parties

§ 802.201 Who may file an appeal.

(a) A party. (1) Any party or party-in-interest adversely affected or aggrieved by a decision or order issued pursuant to one of the Acts over which the Board has appellate jurisdiction may appeal a decision or order of an administrative law judge or deputy commissioner to the Board by filing a notice of appeal pursuant to this subpart. (See 802.205(b) and (c) for exceptions to this general rule.) A party who files a notice of appeal shall be deemed the petitioner. The Director, OWCP, when acting as a representative of the Special Fund established under the Longshore and Harbor Workers' Compensation Act or the Black Lung Disability Trust Fund established by the Black Lung Benefits Act, or, when appealing a decision or order which affects the administration of one of the Acts, shall be considered a party adversely affected.

(2) When a decision or order is favorable to a party (i.e., the prevailing party), the prevailing party may file a cross-appeal pursuant to 802.205(b) to challenge any adverse findings of fact or conclusions of law in the same proceeding.

(b) Representative parties. In the event that a party has not attained the age of 18, is not mentally competent, or is physically unable to file and pursue or defend an appeal, the Board may permit any legally appointed guardian, committee, or other appropriate representative to file and pursue or defend the appeal, or it may in its discretion appoint such representative for purposes of the appeal. The Board may require any legally appointed representative to submit evidence of that person's authority.

§ 802.202 Appearances by attorneys and other authorized persons; denial or authority to appear.

(a) Appearances. Any party or intervenor or any representative duly authorized pursuant to 802.201(b) may appear before and/or submit written argument to the Board by attorney or any other person, including any representative of an employee organization, duly authorized pursuant to paragraph (d)(2) of this section. (b) Any individual petitioner or respondent or his duly authorized representative pursuant to 802.201(b) or an officer of any corporate party or a member of any partnership or joint venture which is a party may participate in the appeal on his or her own behalf, or on behalf of such business entity.

(c) For each instance in which appearance before the Board is made by an attorney or duly authorized person other than the party or his legal guardian, committee, or representative, there shall be filed with the Board a notice of appearance. Any attorney or other duly authorized person of record who intends to withdraw from representation shall file prior written notice of intent to withdraw from representation of a party or of substitution of counsel or other representative.

(d) Qualifications—(1) Attorneys. An attorney at law who is admitted to practice before the Federal courts or before the highest court of any State, the District of Columbia, or any territory or commonwealth of the United States, may practice before the Board unless he or she has been disqualified from representing claimants under the Act pursuant to 33 U.S.C. 931(b)(2)(C), or unless authority to appear has been denied pursuant to 802.202(e)(1) and (3). An attorney's own representation that he or she is in good standing before any of such courts shall be sufficient proof thereof, unless otherwise ordered by the Board.

(2) Persons not attorneys. Any person who is not an attorney at law may be admitted to appear in a representative capacity unless he or she has been disqualified from representing claimants under the Act pursuant to 33 U.S.C. 931(b)(2)(C). An application by a person not an attorney at law for admission to appear in a proceeding shall be submitted in writing to the Board at the time such person's appearance is entered. The application shall state such person's name, address, telephone number, general education, any special training or experience in claims representation, and such person's relationship, if any, to the party being represented. The Board may, at any time, make further inquiry as to the qualification or ability of such person to render assistance. In the event of a failure to make application for admission to appear, the Board shall issue an order to show cause why admission to appear should not be denied. Admission to appear in a particular case shall not be deemed a blanket authorization to appear in other cases.

(e) Denial of authority to appear—(1) Attorneys. The Board may deny the privilege of appearing to any attorney, within applicable statutory constraints, e.g., 5 U.S.C. 555, who has been disbarred or suspended from the practice of law; who has surrendered his or her license while under investigation or under threat of disciplinary action; or who, after notice of an opportunity for hearing in the matter is found by the Board to have engaged in any conduct which would result in the loss of his or her license. No provision hereof shall apply to any attorney who appears on his or her own behalf.

(2) Persons not attorneys. The Board may deny the privilege of appearing to any person who, in the Board's judgment, lacks sufficient qualification or ability to render assistance. No provision hereof shall apply to any person who appears on his or her own behalf.

(3) Denial of authority to appear may be considered, after notice of and opportunity for a hearing, by the panel (constituted pursuant to 801.301) which is assigned to decide the appeal in which the attorney or other person has entered an appearance. If such proceeding reveals facts suggesting that one of the circumstances described in 33 U.S.C. 931(b)(2)(C) exists, the Board shall refer that information to the Director, OWCP, for further proceedings pursuant to 33 U.S.C. 931(b)(2)(C) and 907(j). An attorney or other person may appeal a panel's decision to deny authority to appear to the entire permanent Board sitting en banc.

[52 FR 27292, July 20, 1987, as amended at 53 FR 16519, May 9, 1988]

§ 802.203 Fees for services.

(a) No fee for services rendered on behalf of a claimant in the successful pursuit or successful defense of an appeal shall be valid unless approved pursuant to 33 U.S.C. 928, as amended.

(b) All fees for services rendered in the successful pursuit or successful defense of an appeal on behalf of a claimant shall be subject to the provisions and prohibitions contained in 33 U.S.C. 928, as amended.

(c) Within 60 days of the issuance of a decision or non-interlocutory order by the Board, counsel or, where appropriate, representative for any claimant who has prevailed on appeal before the Board may file an application with the Board for a fee. Where the Board remands the case and the administrative law judge on remand issues an award, a fee petition may be filed within 60 days of the decision on remand. In the event that a claimant who was unsuccessful before the Board prevails on appeal to the court of appeals, his or her representative may within 60 days of issuance of the court's judgment file a fee application with the Board for services performed before the Board.

(d) A fee application shall include only time spent on services performed while the appeal was pending before the Board and shall be complete in all respects, containing all of the following specific information:

(1) A complete statement of the extent and character of the necessary work done;

(2) The professional status of each person for whom a fee is claimed who performed services on behalf of the claimant (if such professional status is other than attorney, a definition of the professional status of such individual must be included in the fee petition, including a statment of that individual's professional training, education and experience) and a statement that the attorney was a member in good standing of a state bar at the time the services were performed;

(3) The number of hours, in quarter hour increments, devoted by each person who performed services on behalf of the claimant and the dates on which such services were performed in each category of work;

(4) The normal billing rate for each person who performed services on behalf of the claimant. The rate awarded by the Board shall be based on what is reasonable and customary in the area where the services were rendered for a person of that particular professional status.

(e) Any fee approved shall be reasonably commensurate with the necessary work done and shall take into account the quality of the representation, the complexity of the legal issues involved, the amount of benefits awarded, and, when the fee is to be assessed against the claimant, shall also take into account the financial circumstances of the claimant. A fee shall not necessarily be computed by multiplying time devoted to work by an hourly rate.

(f) No contract pertaining to the amount of a fee shall be recognized.

(g) A fee application shall be served on all other parties and accompanied by a certificate of service. The Board will not take action on the fee application until such service is effected. Any party may respond to the application within 10 days of receipt of the application. The response shall be filed with the Board and served on all other parties.

NOTICE OF APPEAL

§ 802.204 Place for filing notice of appeal.

Any notice of appeal shall be sent by mail to the U.S. Department of Labor, Benefits Review Board, P.O. Box 37601, Washington, DC 20013-7601, or otherwise presented to the Clerk of the Board at 200 Constitution Avenue, NW., Room S-5220, Washington, DC 20210. A copy shall be served on the deputy commissioner who filed the decision or order being appealed and on all other parties by the party who files a notice of appeal. Proof of service of the notice of appeal on the deputy commissioner and other parties shall be included with the notice of appeal.

[52 FR 27292, July 20, 1987, as amended at 56 FR 54538, Oct. 22, 1991; 62 FR 10666, Mar. 7, 1997]

§ 802.205 Time for filing.

(a) A notice of appeal, other than a cross-appeal, must be filed within 30 days from the date upon which a decision or order has been filed in the Office of the Deputy Commissioner pursuant to section 19(e) of the LHWCA or in such other office as may be established in the future (see Secs. 702.349 and 725.478 of this title). (b) If a timely notice of appeal is filed by a party, any other party may initiate a cross-appeal by filing a notice of appeal within 14 days of the date on which the first notice of appeal was filed, or within the time prescribed by paragraph (a) of this section, whichever period last expires. In the event that such other party was not properly served with the first notice of appeal, such party may initiate a cross-appeal by filing a notice of appeal within 14 days of the date that service is effected.

(c) Failure to file within the period specified in paragraph (a) or (b) of this section (whichever is applicable) shall foreclose all rights to review by the Board with respect to the case or matter in question. Any untimely appeal will be summarily dismissed by the Board for lack of jurisdiction.

§ 802.206 Effect of motion for reconsideration on time for appeal.

(a) A timely motion for reconsideration of a decision or order of an administrative law judge or deputy commissioner shall suspend the running of the time for filing a notice of appeal.

(b)(1) In a case involving a claim filed under the Longshore and Harbor Workers' Compensation Act or its extensions (see 802.101(b)(1)–(5)), a timely motion for reconsideration for purposes of paragraph (a) of this section is one which is filed not later than 10 days from the date the decision or order was filed in the Office of the Deputy Commissioner.

(2) In a case involving a claim filed under title IV of the Federal Mine Safety and Health Act, as amended (see 802.101(b)(6)), a timely motion for reconsideration for purposes of paragraph (a) of this section is one which is filed not later than 30 days from the date the decision or order was served on all parties by the administrative law judge and considered filed in the Office of the Deputy Commissioner (see Secs. 725.478 and 725.479(b), (c) of this title).

(c) If the motion for reconsideration is sent by mail and the fixing of the date of delivery as the date of filing would result in a loss or impairment of reconsideration rights, it will be considered to have been filed as of the date of mailing. The date appearing on the U.S. Postal Service postmark (when available and legible) shall be prima facie evidence of the date of mailing. If there is no such postmark or it is not legible, other evidence such as, but not limited to, certified mail receipts, certificates of service and affidavits may also be used to establish the mailing date.

(d) If a motion for reconsideration is granted, the full time for filing an appeal commences on the date the subsequent decision or order on reconsideration is filed as provided in 802.205.

(e) If a motion for reconsideration is denied, the full time for filing an appeal commences on the date the order denying reconsideration is filed as provided in 802.205. (f) If a timely motion for reconsideration of a decision or order of an administrative law judge or deputy commissioner is filed, any appeal to the Board, whether filed prior to or subsequent to the filing of the timely motion for reconsideration, shall be dismissed without prejudice as premature. Following decision by the administrative law judge or deputy commissioner pursuant to either paragraph (d) or (e) of this section, a new notice of appeal shall be filed with the Clerk of the Board by any party who wishes to appeal. During the pendency of an appeal to the Board, any party having knowledge that a motion for reconsideration of a decision or order of an administrative law judge or deputy commissioner has been filed shall notify the Board of such filing.

§ 802.207 When a notice of appeal is considered to have been filed in the office of the Clerk of the Board.

(a) Date of receipt. (1) Except as otherwise provided in this section, a notice of appeal is considered to have been filed only as of the date it is received in the office of the Clerk of the Board. (2) Notices of appeal submitted to any other agency or subdivision of the Department of Labor or of the U.S. Government or any State government shall be promptly forwarded to the office of the Clerk of the Board. The notice shall be considered filed with the Clerk of the Board as of the date it was received by the other governmental unit if the Board finds that it is in the interest of justice to do so.

(b) Date of mailing. If the notice of appeal is sent by mail and the fixing of the date of delivery as the date of filing would result in a loss or impairment of appeal rights, it will be considered to have been filed as of the date of mailing. The date appearing on the U.S. Postal Service postmark (when available and legible) shall be prima facie evidence of the date of mailing. If there is no such postmark or it is not legible, other evidence, such as, but not limited to, certified mail receipts, certificate of service and affidavits, may be used to establish the mailing date.

§ 802.208 Contents of notice of appeal.

(a) A notice of appeal shall contain the following information:

(1) The full name and address of the pettioner;

(2) The full name of the injured, disabled, or deceased employee;

(3) The full names and addresses of all other parties, including, among others, beneficiaries, employers, coal mine operators, and insurance carriers where appropriate;

(4) The case file number which appears on the decision or order of the administrative law judge;

(5) The claimant's OWCP file number;

(6) The date of filing of the decision or order being appealed;

(7) Whether a motion for reconsideration of the decision or order of the administrative law judge has been filed by any party, the date such motion was filed, and whether the administrative law judge has acted on such motion for reconsideration (see 802.206);

(8) The name and address of the attorney or other person, if any, who is representing the petitioner.

(b) Paragraph (a) of this section notwithstanding, any written communication which reasonably permits identification of the decision from which an appeal is sought and the parties affected or aggrieved thereby, shall be sufficient notice for purposes of 802.205.

(c) In the event that identification of the case is not possible from the information submitted, the Clerk of the Board shall so notify the petitioner and shall give the petitioner a reasonable time to produce sufficient information to permit identification of the case. For purposes of 802.205, the notice shall be deemed to have been filed as of the date the insufficient information was received.

§ 802.209 Transmittal of record to the Board.

Upon receipt of a copy of the notice of appeal or upon request of the Board, the deputy commissioner or other office having custody of such record shall immediately forward to the Clerk of the Board the official record of the case, which record includes the transcript or transcripts of all formal proceedings with exhibits, all decisions and orders rendered in the case.

Initial Processing

§ 802.210 Acknowledgment of notice of appeal.

Upon receipt by the Board of a notice of appeal, the Clerk of the Board shall as expeditiously as possible notify the petitioner and all other parties and the Solicitor of Labor, in writing, that a notice of appeal has been filed.

§ 802.211 Petition for review.

(a) Within 30 days after the receipt of an acknowledgment of a notice of appeal issued pursuant to 802.210, the petitioner shall submit a petition for review to the Board which petition lists the specific issues to be considered on appeal.

(b) Each petition for review shall be accompanied by a supporting brief, memorandum of law or other statement which: Specifically states the issues to be considered by the Board; presents, with appropriate headings, an argument with respect to each issue presented with references to transcripts, pieces of evidence and other parts of the record to which the petitioner wishes the Board to refer; a short conclusion stating the precise result the petitioner seeks on each issue and any authorities upon which the petition relies to support such proposed result. The Longshore Desk Book and Black Lung Desk Book are not intended as final legal authorities and should not be cited or relied upon as such.

(c) Copies of the petition for review and accompanying documents must be served upon all parties and the Solicitor of Labor.

(d) Failure to submit a petition for review and brief within the 30-day period or to comply with any part of this section may, in the discretion of the Board, cause the appeal to be deemed abandoned (see 802.402).

(e) When a party appears pro se the Board may, in its discretion, waive formal compliance with the requirements of this section and may, depending upon the particular circumstances, prescribe an alternate method of furnishing such information as may be necessary for the Board to decide the merits of any such appeal.

§ 802.212 Response to petition for review.

(a) Within 30 days after the receipt of a petition for review, each party upon whom it was served may submit to the Board a brief, memorandum, or other statement in response to it.

(b) Arguments in response briefs shall be limited to those which respond to arguments raised in petitioner's brief and to those in support of the decision below. Other arguments will not be considered by the Board (see 802.205(b)).

§ 802.213 Reply briefs.

(a) Within 20 days after the receipt of a brief, memorandum, or statement submitted in response to the petition for review pursuant to 802.212, any party upon whom it was served may file a brief, memorandum, or other statement in reply to it.

(b) Arguments in reply briefs shall be limited to those which reply to arguments made in the response brief. Any other arguments in a reply brief will not be considered by the Board.

§ 802.214 Intervention.

(a) If a person or legal entity shows in a written petition to intervene that his, her, or its rights are affected by any proceeding before the Board, the Board may permit that person or legal entity to intervene in the proceeding and to participate within limits prescribed by the Board.

(b) The petition to intervene shall state precisely:

(1) The rights affected, and

(2) The nature of any argument the person or legal entity intends to make.

§ 802.215 Additional briefs.

Additional briefs may be filed or ordered in the discretion of the Board and shall be submitted within time limits specified by the Board.

§ 802.216 Service and form of papers.

(a) All papers filed with the Board, including notices of appeal, petitions for review, briefs and motions, shall be secured at the top and shall have a caption, title, signature of the party (or his attorney or other representative), date of signature, and certificate of service.

(b) For each paper filed with the Board, the original and two legible copies shall be submitted.

(c) A copy of any paper filed with the Board shall be served on each party and the Solicitor of Labor, by the party submitting the paper.

(d) Any paper required to be given or served to or by the Board or any party shall be served by mail or otherwise presented. All such papers served shall be accompanied by a certificate of service.

(e) All papers (exclusive of documentary evidence) submitted to the Benefits Review Board shall conform to standard letter dimensions (8.5x11 inches).

§ 802.217 Waiver of time limitations for filing.

(a) The time periods specified for submitting papers described in this part, except that for submitting a notice of appeal, may be enlarged for a reasonable period when in the judgment of the Board an enlargement is warranted.

(b) Any request for an enlargement of time pursuant to this section shall be directed to the Clerk of the Board and must be received by the Clerk on or prior to the date on which the paper is due. (c) Any request for an enlargement of time pursuant to this section shall be submitted in writing in the form of a motion, shall specify the reasons for the request, and shall specify the date to which an enlargement of time is requested.

(d) Absent exceptional circumstances, no more than one enlargement of time shall be granted to each party. (e) Absent a timely request for an enlargement of time pursuant to this section and the Board's granting that request, any paper submitted to the Board outside the applicable time period specified in this part shall be accompanied by a separate motion stating the reasons therefor and requesting that the Board accept the paper although filed out of time.

(f) When a paper filed out of time is accepted by the Board, the time for filing a response shall begin to run from the date of a party's receipt of the Board's order disposing of the motion referred to in paragraph (e) of this section.

§ 802.218 Failure to file papers; order to show cause.

(a) Failure to file any paper when due pursuant to this part, may, in the discretion of the Board, constitute a waiver of the right to further participation in the proceedings.

(b) When a petition for review and brief has not been submitted to the Board within the time limitation prescribed by 802.211, or within an enlarged time limitation granted pursuant to 802.217, the petitioner shall be ordered to show cause to the Board why his or her appeal should not be dismissed pursuant to 802.402.

§ 802.219 Motions to the Board; orders.

(a) An application to the Board for an order shall be by motion in writing. A motion shall state with particularity the grounds therefor and shall set forth the relief or order sought.

(b) A motion shall be a separate document and shall not be incorporated in the text of any other paper filed with the Board, except for a statement in support of the motion. If this paragraph is not complied with, the Board will not consider and dispose of the motion.

(c) If there is no objection to a motion in whole or in part by another party to the case, the absence of an objection shall be stated on the motion.

(d) The rules applicable to service and form of papers, 802.216, shall apply to all motions.

(e) Within 10 days of the receipt of a copy of a motion, a party may file a written response with the Board.

(f) As expeditiously as possible following receipt of a response to a motion or expiration of the response time provided in paragraph (e) of this section, the Board shall issue a dispositive order.

(g) Orders granted by Clerk. The Clerk of the Board may enter orders on behalf of the Board in procedural matters, including but not limited to:

(1) First motions for extensions of time for filing briefs and any papers other than notices of appeal or cross-appeal;

(2) Motions for voluntary dismissals of appeals;

(3) Orders to show cause why appeals should not be dismissed for failure to timely file a petition for review and brief (see 802.218(b)); and

(4) Unopposed motions which are ordinarily granted as of course, except that the Clerk may, in his or her discretion, refer such motions for disposition to a motions panel as provided by paragraph (h) of this section.

(h) All other motions. All other motions will be referred for disposition to a panel of three members constituted pursuant to 801.301. Any member may request that any motion be considered by the entire permanent Board en banc except as provided in 801.301(d).

(i) Reconsideration of orders. Any party adversely effected by any interlocutory order issued under paragraph (g) or (h) may file a motion to reconsider, vacate or modify the order within 10 days from its filing, stating the grounds for such request. Any motion for reconsideration, vacation or modification of an interlocutory order shall be referred to a three-member panel that may include any member who previously acted on the matter. Suggestions for en banc reconsideration of interlocutory orders shall not be accepted. Reconsideration of all other orders will be treated under 802.407 of this part.

§ 802.220 Party not represented by an attorney; informal procedure.

A party to an appeal who is not represented by an attorney shall comply with the procedural requirements contained in this part, except as otherwise specifically provided in 802.211(e). In its discretion, the Board may prescribe additional informal procedures to be followed by such party.

§ 802.221 Computation of time.

(a) In computing any period of time prescribed or allowed by these rules, by direction of the Board, or by any applicable statute which does not provide otherwise, the day from which the designated period of time begins to run shall not be included. The last day of the period so computed shall be included, unless it is a Saturday, Sunday, or legal holiday, in which event the period runs until the end of the next day which is not a Saturday, Sunday, or legal holiday.

(b) Whenever a paper is served on the Board or on any party by mail, paragraph (a) of this section will be deemed complied with if the envelope containing the paper is postmarked by the U.S. Postal Service within the time period allowed, computed as in paragraph (a) of this section. If there is no such postmark, or it is not legible, other evidence, such as, but not limited to, certified mail receipts, certificate of service and affidavits, may be used to establish the mailing date.

(c) A waiver of the time limitations for filing a paper, other than a notice of appeal, may be requested by proper motion filed in accordance with Secs. 802.217 and 802.219.

Subpart C—Procedure for Review

§ 802.301 Scope of review.

(a) The Benefits Review Board is not empowered to engage in a de novo proceeding or unrestricted review of a case brought before it. The Board is authorized to review the findings of fact and conclusions of law on which the decision or order appealed from was based. Such findings of fact and conclusions of law may be set aside only if they are not, in the judgment of the Board, supported by substantial evidence in the record considered as a whole or in accordance with law.

(b) Parties shall not submit new evidence to the Board. Any evidence submitted by a party which is not part of the record developed at the hearing before the administrative law judge will be returned without being considered by the Board.

(c) Any party who considers new evidence necessary to the adjudication of the claim may apply for modification pursuant to section 22 of the Longshore and Harbor Workers' Compensation Act, 33 U.S.C. 922. A party who files a petition for modification shall promptly notify the Board of such filing. Upon receipt of such notification, the Board shall dismiss the case without prejudice. Should the petition for modification be declined, the petitioner may file a request for reinstatement of his or her appeal with the Board within 30 days of the date the petition is declined. Should the petition for modification be accepted, any party adversely affected by the decision or order granting or denying modification may file a new appeal with the Board within 30 days of the date the decision or order on modification is filed.

[52 FR 27292, July 20, 1987, as amended at 53 FR 16519, May 9, 1988]

§ 802.302 Docketing of appeals.

(a) Maintenance of dockets. A docket of all proceedings shall be maintained by the Board. Each proceeding shall be assigned a number in chronological order upon the date on which a notice of appeal is received. Correspondence or further applications in connection with any pending case shall refer to the docket number of that case.

(b) Inspection of docket; publication of decision. The docket of the Board shall be open to public inspection. The Board shall publish its decisions in a form which is readily available for inspection, and shall allow the public to inspect its decisions at the permanent location of the Board.

Oral Argument Before the Board

§ 802.303 Decision; no oral argument.

(a) In the event that no oral argument is ordered pursuant to 802.306, the Board shall proceed to review the record of the case as expeditiously as possible after all briefs, supporting statements, and other pertinent documents have been received.

(b) Each case shall be considered in the order in which it becomes ready for decision, regardless of docket number, although for good cause shown, upon the filing of a motion to expedite by a party, the Board may advance the order in which a particular case is to be considered.

(c) The Board may advance an appeal on the docket on its own motion if the interests of justice would be served by so doing.

§ 802.304 Purpose of oral argument.

Oral argument may be held by the Board in any case:

(a) When there is a novel issue not previously considered by the Board; or

(b) When in the interests of justice oral argument will serve to assist the Board in carrying out the intent of any of the Acts; or

(c) To resolve conflicting decisions by administrative law judges on a substantial question of law.

§ 802.305 Request for oral argument.

(a) During the pendency of an appeal, but not later than the expiration of 20 days from the date of receipt of the response brief provided by 802.212, any party may request oral argument. The Board on its own motion may order oral argument at any time.

(b) A request for oral argument shall be submitted in the form of a motion, specifying the issues to be argued and justifying the need for oral argument (see 802.219).

(c) The party requesting oral argument shall set forth in the motion suggested dates and alternate cities convenient to the parties when and where they would be available for oral argument.

§ 802.306 Action on request for oral argument.

As expeditiously as possible after the date upon which a request for oral argument is received, the Board shall determine whether the request shall be granted or denied.

§ 802.307 Notice of oral argument.

(a) In cases where a request for oral argument has been approved or where oral argument has been ordered, the Board shall give all parties a minimum of 30 days' notice, in writing, by mail, of the scope of argument and of the time when, and place where, oral argument will be held.

(b) Once oral argument has been scheduled by the Board, continuances shall not be granted except for good cause shown by a party, such as in cases of extreme hardship or where attendance of a party or his or her representative is mandated at a previously scheduled judicial proceeding. Unless the ground for the request arises thereafter, requests for continuances must be received by the Board at least 15 days before the scheduled date of oral argument, must be served upon the other parties and must specify good cause why the requesting party cannot be available for oral argument.

(c) The Board may cancel or reschedule oral argument on its own motion at any time.

§ 802.308 Conduct of oral argument.

(a) Oral argument shall be held in Washington, DC, unless the Board orders otherwise, and shall be conducted at a time reasonably convenient to the parties. For good cause shown, the presiding judge of the panel may, in his or her discretion, postpone an oral argument to a more convenient time.

(b) The proceedings shall be conducted under the supervision of the Chairman or, if the Chairman is not on the panel, the senior judge, who shall regulate all procedural matters arising during the course of the argument.

(c) Within the discretion of the Board, oral argument shall be open to the public and may be presented by any party, representative, or duly authorized attorney. Presentation of oral argument may be denied by the Board to a party who has not significantly participated in the appeal prior to oral argument.

(d) The Board shall determine the scope of any oral argument presented and shall so inform the parties in its notice scheduling oral argument pursuant to 802.307.

(e) The Board in its discretion shall determine the amount of time allotted to each party for argument and rebuttal.

§ 802.309 Absence of parties.

The unexcused absence of a party or his or her authorized representative at the time and place set for argument shall not be the occasion for delay of the proceeding. In such event, argument on behalf of other parties may be heard and the case shall be regarded as submitted on the record by the absent party. The presiding judge may, with the consent of the parties present, cancel the oral argument and treat the appeal as submitted on the written record.

Subpart D—Completion of Board Review

DISMISSALS

§ 802.401 Dismissal by application of party.

(a) At any time prior to the issuance of a decision by the Board, the petitioner may move that the appeal be dismissed. If granted, such motion for dismissal shall be granted with prejudice to the petitioner.

(b) At any time prior to the issuance of a decision by the Board, any party or representative may move that the appeal be dismissed.

§ 802.402 Dismissal by abandonment.

(a) Upon motion by any party or representative or upon the Board's own motion, an appeal may be dismissed upon its abandonment by the party or parties who filed the appeal. Within the discretion of the Board, a party may be deemed to have abandoned an appeal if neither the party nor his representative participates significantly in the review proceedings.

(b) An appeal may be dismissed on the death of a party only if the record affirmatively shows that there is no person who wishes to continue the action and whose rights may be prejudiced by dismissal.

DECISION OF THE BOARD

§ 802.403 Issuance of decisions; service.

(a) The Board shall issue written decisions as expeditiously as possible after the completion of review proceedings before the Board. The transmittal of the decision of the Board shall indicate the availability of judicial review of the decision under section 21(c) of the LHWCA when appropriate.

(b) The original of the decision shall be filed with the Clerk of the Board. A copy of the Board's decision shall be sent by certified mail or otherwise presented to all parties to the appeal and the Director. The record on appeal, together with a transcript of any oral proceedings, any briefs or other papers filed with the Board, and a copy of the decision shall be returned to the appropriate deputy commissioner for filing.

(c) Proof of service of Board decisions shall be certified by the Clerk of the Board or by another employee in the office of the Clerk of the Board who is authorized to certify proof of service.

§ 802.404 Scope and content of Board decisions.

(a) In its decision the Board shall affirm, modify, vacate or reverse the decision or order appealed from, and may remand the case for action or proceedings consistent with the decision of the Board. The consent of the parties shall not be a prerequisite to a remand ordered by the Board.

(b) In appropriate cases, such as where the issues raised on appeal have been thoroughly discussed and disposed of in prior cases by the Board or the courts, or where the findings of fact and conclusions of law are both correct and adequately discussed, the Board in its discretion may issue a brief, summary decision in writing, disposing of the appeal.

(c) In cases which cannot be disposed of as in paragraph (b) of this section, a full, written decision discussing the issues and applicable law shall be issued.

§ 802.405 Remand.

(a) By the Board. Where a case is remanded, such additional proceedings shall be initiated and such other action shall be taken as is directed by the Board.

(b) By a court. Where a case has been remanded by a court, the Board may proceed in accordance with the court's mandate to issue a decision or it may in turn remand the case to an administrative law judge or deputy commissioner with instructions to take such action as is ordered by the court and any additional necessary action.

§ 802.406 Finality of Board decisions.

A decision rendered by the Board pursuant to this subpart shall become final 60 days after the issuance of such decision unless a written petition for review praying that the order be modified or set aside, pursuant to section 21(c) of the LHWCA, is filed in the appropriate U.S. court of appeals prior to the expiration of the 60-day period herein described, or unless a timely request for reconsideration by the Board has been filed as provided in 802.407. If a timely request for reconsideration has been filed, the 60-day period for filing such petition for review will run from the issuance of the Board's decision on reconsideration.

RECONSIDERATION

§ 802.407 Reconsideration of Board decisions.

(a) Any party-in-interest may, within 30 days from the filing of a decision or non-interlocutory order by a panel or the Board pursuant to 802.403(b), request reconsideration of such decision by those members who rendered the decision. The panel of members who heard and decided the appeal will rule on the motion for reconsideration. If any member of the original panel is unavailable, the Chariman shall designate a new panel member.

(b) Except as provided in 801.301(d), a party may, within 30 days from the filing of a decision or non-interlocutory order by a panel of the Board pursuant to 802.403(b), suggest the appropriateness of reconsideration by the permanent members sitting en banc. Such suggestion, however, must accompany a motion for reconsideration directed to the panel which rendered the decision. The suggestion for reconsideration en banc must be clearly marked as such.

(c) Except as provided in 801.301(d), even where no party has suggested reconsideration en banc, any permanent member may petition the permanent Board for reconsideration en banc of a panel decision.

(d) Reconsideration en banc shall be granted upon the affirmative vote of the majority of permanent members of the Board. A panel decision shall stand unless vacated or modified by the concurring vote of at least three permanent members.

§ 802.408 Notice of request for reconsideration.

(a) In the event that a party requests reconsideration of a decision or order, he or she shall do so in writing, in the form of a motion, stating the supporting rationale for the request, and include any material pertinent to the request.

(b) The request shall be sent by mail, or otherwise presented, to the Clerk of the Board. Copies shall be served on all other parties.

§ 802.409 Grant or denial of request.

All requests for reconsideration shall be reviewed by the Board and shall be granted or denied in the discretion of the Board.

JUDICIAL REVIEW

§ 802.410 Judicial review of Board decisions.

(a) Within 60 days after a decision by the Board has been filed pursuant to 802.403(b), any party adversely affected or aggrieved by such decision may file a petition for review with the appropriate U.S. Court of Appeals pursuant to section 21(c) of the LHWCA.

(b) The Director, OWCP, as designee of the Secretary of Labor responsible for the administration and enforcement of the statutes listed in 802.101, shall be deemed to be the proper party on behalf of the Secretary of Labor in all review proceedings conducted pursuant to section 21(c) of the LHWCA.

§ 802.411 Certification of record for judicial review.

The record of a case including the record of proceedings before the Board shall be transmitted to the appropriate court pursuant to the rules of such court.

PART 18—RULES OF PRACTICE AND PROCEDURE FOR ADMINISTRATIVE HEARINGS BEFORE THE OFFICE OF ADMINISTRATIVE LAW JUDGES

Subpart A—General

AUTHORITY: 5 U.S.C. 301; 5 U.S.C. 551-553; 5 U.S.C. 571 note; E.O. 12778; 57 Fed. Reg. 7292.

SOURCE: 48 FR 32538, July 15, 1983, unless otherwise noted.

Subpart A—General

§ 18.1 Scope of rules.

(a) General application. These rules of practice are generally applicable to adjudicatory proceedings before the Office of Administrative Law Judges, United States Department of Labor. Such proceedings shall be conducted expeditiously and the parties shall make every effort at each stage of a proceeding to avoid delay. To the extent that these rules may be inconsistent with a rule of special application as provided by statute, executive order, or regulation, the latter is controlling. The Rules of Civil Procedure for the District Courts of the United States shall be applied in any situation not provided for or controlled by these rules, or by any statute, executive order or regulation.

(b) Waiver, modification, or suspension. Upon notice to all parties, the administrative law judge may, with respect to matters pending before him or her, modify or waive any rule herein upon a determination that no party will be prejudiced and that the ends of justice will be served thereby. These rules may, from time to time, be suspended, modified or revoked in whole or part.

§ 18.2 Definitions.

For purposes of these rules:

(a) Adjudicatory proceeding means a judicial-type proceeding leading to the formulation of a final order;

(b) Administrative law judge means an administrative law judge appointed pursuant to the provisions of 5 U.S.C. 3105 (provisions of the rules in this part which refer to administrative law judges may be applicable to other Presiding Officers as well);

(c) Administrative Procedure Act means those provisions of the Administrative Procedure Act, as codified, which are contained in 5 U.S.C. 551 through 559;

(d) Complaint means any document initiating an adjudicatory proceeding, whether designated a complaint, appeal or an order for proceeding or otherwise;

(e) Hearing means that part of a proceeding which involves the submission of evidence, either by oral presentation or written submission;

(f) Order means the whole or any part of a final procedural or substantive disposition of a matter by the administrative law judge in a matter other than rulemaking;

(g) Party includes a person or agency named or admitted as a party to a proceeding;

(h) Person includes an individual, partnership, corporation, association, exchange or other entity or organization;

(i) Pleading means the complaint, the answer to the complaint, any supplement or amendment thereto, and any reply that may be permitted to any answer, supplement or amendment;

(j) Respondent means a party to an adjudicatory proceeding against whom findings may be made or who may be required to provide relief or take remedial action;

(k) Secretary means the Secretary of Labor and includes any administrator, commissioner, appellate body, board, or other official thereunder for purposes of appeal of recommended or final decisions of administrative law judges;

(l) Complainant means a person who is seeking relief from any act or omission in violation of a statute, executive order or regulation;

(m) The term petition means a written request, made by a person or party, for some affirmative action;

(n) The term Consent Agreement means any written document containing a specified proposed remedy or other relief acceptable to all parties;

(o) Commencement of Proceeding is the filing of a request for hearing, order of reference, or referral of a claim for hearing.

§ 18.3 Service and filing of documents.

(a) Generally. Copies of all documents shall be served on all parties of record. All documents should clearly designate the docket number, if any, and short title of the matter. If the matter involves a program administered by the Office of Workers' Compensation Programs (OWCP), the document should contain the OWCP number in addition to the docket number. All documents to be filed shall be delivered or mailed to the Chief Docket Clerk, Office of Administrative Law Judges, 800 K Street, NW., Suite 400, Washington DC 20001-8002, or to the OALJ Regional Office to which the proceeding may have been transferred for hearing. Each document filed shall be clear and legible. (b) By parties. All motions, petitions, pleadings, briefs, or other documents shall be filed with the Office of Administrative Law Judges with a copy, including any attachments, to all other parties of record. When a party is represented by an attorney, service shall be made upon the attorney. Service of any document upon any party may be made by personal delivery or by mailing a copy to the last known address. The person serving the document shall certify to the manner and date of service.

(c) By the Office of Administrative Law Judges. Service of notices, orders, decisions and all other documents, except complaints, shall be made by regular mail to the last known address.

(d) Service of complaints. Service of complaints or charges in enforcement proceedings shall be made either:

(1) By delivering a copy to the individual, partner, officer of a corporation, or attorney of record; (2) by leaving a copy at the principal office, place of business, or residence; (3) by mailing to the last known address of such individual, partner, officer or attorney. If done by certified mail, service is complete upon mailing. If done by regular mail, service is complete upon receipt by addressee.

(e) Form of pleadings. (1) Every pleading shall contain a caption setting forth the name of the agency under which the proceeding is instituted, the title of the proceeding, the docket number assigned by the Office of Administrative Law Judges, and a designation of the type of pleading or paper (e.g., complaint, motion to dismiss, etc.). The pleading or papers shall be signed and shall contain the address and telephone number of the party or person representing the party. Although there are no formal specifications for documents, they should be typewritten when possible on standards size (8.5 x 11) paper legal size (8.5 x 14) paper will not be accepted after July 31, 1983.

(2) Illegible documents, whether handwritten, typewritten, photocopied, or otherwise will not be accepted. Papers may be reproduced by any duplicating process, provided all copies are clear and legible.

[48 FR 32538, July 15, 1983, as amended at 56 FR 54708, Oct. 22, 1991]

§ 18.4 Time computations.

(a) Generally. In computing any period of time under these rules or in an order issued hereunder the time begins with the day following the act, event, or default, and includes the last day of the period, unless it is a Saturday, Sunday or legal holiday observed by the Federal Government in which case the time period includes the next business day. When the period of time prescribed is seven (7) days or less, intermediate Saturdays, Sundays, and holidays shall be excluded in the computation.

(b) Date of entry of orders. In computing any period of time involving the date of the entry of an order, the date of entry shall be the date the order is served by the Chief Docket Clerk.

(c) Computation of time for delivery by mail. (1) Documents are not deemed filed until received by the Chief Clerk at the Office of Administrative Law Judges. However, when documents are filed by mail, five (5) days shall be added to the prescribed period.

(2) Service of all documents other than complaints is deemed effected at the time of mailing.

(3) Whenever a party has the right or is required to take some action within a prescribed period after the service of a pleading, notice, or other document upon said party, and the pleading, notice or document is served upon said party by mail, five (5) days shall be added to the prescribed period.

§ 18.5 Responsive pleadings_answer and request for hearing.

(a) Time for answer. Within thirty (30) days after the service of a complaint, each respondent shall file an answer.

(b) Default. Failure of the respondent to file an answer within the time provided shall be deemed to constitute a waiver of his right to appear and contest the allegations of the complaint and to authorize the administrative law judge to find the facts as alleged in the complaint and to enter an initial or final decision containing such findings, appropriate conclusions, and order.

(c) Signature required. Every answer filed pursuant to these rules shall be signed by the party filing it or by at least one attorney, in his or her individual name, representing such party. The signature constitutes a certificate by the signer that he or she has read the answer; that to the best of his or her knowledge, information and belief there is good ground to support it; and that it is not interposed for delay.

(d) Content of answer—(1) Orders to show cause. Any person to whom an order to show cause has been directed and served shall respond to the same by filing an answer in writing. Arguments opposing the proposed sanction should be supported by reference to specific circumstances or facts surrounding the basis for the order to show cause.

(2) Complaints. Any respondent contesting any material fact alleged in a complaint, or contending that the amount of a proposed penalty or award is excessive or inappropriate or contending that he or she is entitled to judgment as a matter of law, shall file an answer in writing. An answer shall include:

(i) A statement that the respondent admits, denies, or does not have and is unable to obtain sufficient information to admit or deny each allegation; a statement of lack of information shall have the effect of a denial; any allegation not expressly denied shall be deemed to be admitted;

(ii) A statement of the facts supporting each affirmative defense.

(e) Amendments and supplemental pleadings. If and whenever determination of a controversy on the merits will be facilitated thereby, the administrative law judge may, upon such conditions as are necessary to avoid prejudicing the public interest and the rights of the parties, allow appropriate amendments to complaints, answers, or other pleadings; provided, however, that a complaint may be amended once as a matter of right prior to the answer, and thereafter if the administrative law judge determines that the amendment is reasonably within the scope of the original complaint. When issues not raised by the pleadings are reasonably within the scope of the original complaint and are tried by express or implied consent of the parties, they shall be treated in all respects as if they had been raised in the pleadings, and such amendments may be made as necessary to make them conform to the evidence. The administrative law judge may, upon reasonable notice and such terms as are just, permit supplemental pleadings setting forth transactions, occurrences or events which have happened since the date of the pleadings and which are relevant to any of the issues involved.

§ 18.6 Motions and requests.

(a) Generally. Any application for an order or any other request shall be made by motion which, unless made during a hearing or trial, shall be made in writing unless good cause is established to preclude such submission, shall state with particularity the grounds therefor, and shall set forth the relief or order sought. Motions or requests made during the course of any hearing or appearance before an administrative law judge shall be stated orally and made part of the transcript. Whether made orally or in writing, all parties shall be given reasonable opportunity to state an objection to the motion or request.

(b) Answers to motions. Within ten (10) days after a motion is served, or within such other period as the administrative law judge may fix, any party to the proceeding may file an answer in support or in opposition to the motion, accompanied by such affidavits or other evidence as he or she desires to rely upon. Unless the administrative law judge provides otherwise, no reply to an answer, response to a reply, or any further responsive document shall be filed.

(c) Oral arguments or briefs. No oral argument will be heard on motions unless the administrative law judge otherwise directs. Written memoranda or briefs may be filed with motions or answers to motions, stating the points and authorities relied upon in support of the position taken.

(d) Motion for order compelling answer: sanctions. (1) A party who has requested admissions or who has served interrogatories may move to determine the sufficiency of the answers or objections thereto. Unless the objecting party sustains his or her burden of showing that the objection is justified, the administrative law judge shall order that an answer be served. If the administrative law judge determines that an answer does not comply with the requirements of these rules, he or she may order either that the matter is admitted or that an amended answer be served.

(2) If a party or an officer or agent of a party fails to comply with a subpoena or with an order, including, but not limited to, an order for the taking of a deposition, the production of documents, or the answering of interrogatories, or requests for admissions, or any other order of the administrative law judge, the administrative law judge, for the purpose of permitting resolution of the relevant issues and disposition of the proceeding without unnecessary delay despite such failure, may take such action in regard thereto as is just, including but not limited to the following:

(i) Infer that the admission, testimony, documents or other evidence would have been adverse to the non-complying party;

(ii) Rule that for the purposes of the proceeding the matter or matters concerning which the order or subpoena was issued be taken as established adversely to the non-complying party;

(iii) Rule that the non-complying party may not introduce into evidence or otherwise rely upon testimony by such party, officer or agent, or the documents or other evidence, in support of or in opposition to any claim or defense;

(iv) Rule that the non-complying party may not be heard to object to introduction and use of secondary evidence to show what the withheld admission, testimony, documents, or other evidence should have shown.

(v) Rule that a pleading, or part of a pleading, or a motion or other submission by the noncomplying party, concerning which the order or subpoena was issued, be stricken, or that a decision of the proceeding be rendered against the non-complying party, or both.

§ 18.7 Prehearing statements.

(a) At any time prior to the commencement of the hearing, the administrative law judge may order any party to file a prehearing statement of position.

(b) A prehearing statement shall state the name of the party or parties on whose behalf it is presented and shall briefly set forth the following matters, unless otherwise ordered by the administrative law judge:

(1) Issues involved in the proceeding;

(2) Facts stipulated pursuant to the procedures together with a statement that the party or parties have communicated or conferred in a good faith effort to reach stipulation to the fullest extent possible;

(3) Facts in dispute;

(4) Witnesses, except to the extent that disclosure would be privileged, and exhibits by which disputed facts will be litigated;

(5) A brief statement of applicable law;

(6) The conclusion to be drawn;

(7) Suggested time and location of hearing and estimated time required for presentation of the party's or parties' case;

(8) Any appropriate comments, suggestions or information which might assist the parties in preparing for the hearing or otherwise aid in the disposition of the proceeding.

§ 18.8 Prehearing conferences.

(a) Purpose and scope. (1) Upon motion of a party or upon the administrative law judge's own motion, the judge may direct the parties or their counsel to participate in a conference at any reasonable time, prior to or during the course of the hearing, when the administrative law judge finds that the proceeding would be expedited by a prehearing conference. Such conferences normally shall be conducted by conference telephonic communication unless, in the opinion of the administrative law judge, such method would be impractical, or when such conferences can be conducted in a more expeditious or effective manner by correspondence or personal appearance. Reasonable notice of the time, place and manner of the conference shall be given.

(2) At the conference, the following matters shall be considered:

(i) The simplification of issues;

(ii) The necessity of amendments to pleadings;

(iii) The possibility of obtaining stipulations of facts and of the authenticity, accuracy, and admissibility of documents, which will avoid unnecessary proof;

(iv) The limitation of the number of expert or other witnesses;

(v) Negotiation, compromise, or settlement of issues;

(vi) The exchange of copies of proposed exhibits;

(vii) The identification of documents or matters of which official notice may be requested;

(viii) A schedule to be followed by the parties for completion of the actions decided at the conference; and

(ix) Such other matters as may expedite and aid in the disposition of the proceeding.

(b) Reporting. A prehearing conference will be stenographically reported, unless otherwise directed by the administrative law judge.

(c) Order. Actions taken as a result of a conference shall be reduced to a written order, unless the administrative law judge concludes that a stenographic report shall suffice, or, if the conference takes place within 7 days of the beginning of the hearing, the administrative law judge elects to make a statement on the record at the hearing summarizing the actions taken.

§ 18.9 Consent order or settlement; settlement judge procedure.

(a) Generally. At any time after the commencement of a proceeding, the parties jointly may move to defer the hearing for a reasonable time to permit negotiation of a settlement or an agreement containing findings and an order disposing of the whole or any part of the proceeding. The allowance of such deferment and the duration thereof shall be in the discretion of the administrative law judge, after consideration of such factors as the nature of the proceeding, the requirements of the public interest, the representations of the parties and the probability of reaching an agreement which will result in a just disposition of the issues involved.

(b) Content. Any agreement containing consent findings and an order disposing of a proceeding or any part thereof shall also provide:

(1) That the order shall have the same force and effect as an order made after full hearing;

(2) That the entire record on which any order may be based shall consist solely of the complaint, order of reference or notice of administrative determination (or amended notice, if one is filed), as appropriate, and the agreement;

(3) A waiver of any further procedural steps before the administrative law judge; and

(4) A waiver of any right to challenge or contest the validity of the order entered into in accordance with the agreement.

(c) Submission. On or before the expiration of the time granted for negotiations, the parties or their authorized representative or their counsel may:

(1) Submit the proposed agreement containing consent findings and an order for consideration by the administrative law judge, or

(2) Notify the administrative law judge that the parties have reached a full settlement and have agreed to dismissal of the action, or

(3) Inform the administrative law judge that agreement cannot be reached.

(d) Disposition. In the event an agreement containing consent findings and an order is submitted within the time allowed therefor, the administrative law judge, within thirty (30) days thereafter, shall, if satisfied with its form and substance, accept such agreement by issuing a decision based upon the agreed findings.

(e)(1) Settlement judge procedure; purpose. This paragraph establishes a voluntary process whereby the parties may use a settlement judge to mediate settlement negotiations. A settlement judge is an active or retired administrative law judge who convenes and presides over settlement conferences and negotiations, confers with the parties jointly and/or individually, and seeks voluntary resolution of issues. Unlike a presiding judge, a settlement judge does not render a formal judgment or decision in the case; his or her role is solely to facilitate fair and equitable solutions and to provide an assessment of the relative merits of the respective positions of the parties.

(2) How initiated. A settlement judge may be appointed by the Chief Administrative Law Judge upon a request by a party or the presiding administrative law judge. The Chief Administrative Law Judge has sole discretion to decide whether to appoint a settlement judge, except that a settlement judge shall not be appointed when_

(i) A party objects to referral of the matter to a settlement judge;

(ii) Such appointment is inconsistent with a statute, executive order, or regulation;

(iii) The proceeding arises pursuant to the Longshore and Harbor Workers' Compensation Act, 33 U.S.C. 901 et seq., and associated acts such as the District of Columbia Workmen's Compensation Act, 36 DC Code 501 et seq.; or

(iv) The proceeding arises pursuant to Title IV of the Federal Mine Safety and Health Act, 30 U.S.C. 901 et seq., also known as the Black Lung Benefits Act.

(3) Selection of settlement judge. (i) The selection of a settlement judge is at the sole discretion of the Chief Administrative Law Judge, provided that the individual selected_

(A) is an active or retired administrative law judge, and

(B) is not the administrative law judge assigned to hear and decide the case.

(ii) The settlement judge shall not be appointed to hear and decide the case.

(4) Duration of proceeding. Unless the Chief Administrative Law Judge directs otherwise, settlement negotiations under this section shall not exceed thirty days from the date of appointment of the settlement judge, except that with the consent of the parties, the settlement judge may request an extension from the Chief Administrative Law Judge. The negotiations will be terminated immediately if a party unambiguously indicates that it no longer wishes to participate, or if in the judgment of the settlement judge, further negotiations would be fruitless or otherwise inappropriate.

(5) General powers of the settlement judge. The settlement judge has the power to convene settlement conferences; to require that parties, or representatives of the parties having the authority to settle, participate in conferences; and to impose other reasonable requirements on the parties to expedite an amicable resolution of the case, provided that all such powers shall terminate immediately if negotiations are terminated pursuant to paragraph (e)(4).

(6) Suspension of discovery. Requests for suspension of discovery during the settlement negotiations shall be directed to the presiding administrative law judge who shall have sole discretion in granting or denying such requests.

(7) Settlement conference. In general the settlement judge should communicate with the parties by telephone conference call. The settlement judge may, however, schedule a personal conference with the parties when:

(i) The settlement judge is scheduled to preside in other proceedings in a place convenient to all parties and representatives involved;

(ii) The offices of the attorneys or other representatives of the parties, and the settlement judge, are in the same metropolitan area; or

(iii) The settlement judge, with the concurrence of the Chief Administrative Law Judge, determines that a personal meeting is necessary for a resolution of substantial issues, and represents a prudent use of resources.

(8) Confidentiality of settlement discussions. All discussions between the parties and the settlement judge shall be off-the-record. No evidence regarding statements or conduct in the proceedings under this section is admissible in the instant proceeding or any subsequent administrative proceeding before the Department, except by stipulation of the parties. Documents disclosed in the settlement process may not be used in litigation unless obtained through appropriate discovery or subpoena. The settlement judge shall not discuss any aspect of the case with any administrative law judge or other person, nor be subpoenaed or called as a witness in any hear-

ing of the case or any subsequent administrative proceedings before the Department with respect to any statement or conduct during the settlement discussions.

(9) Contents of consent order or settlement agreement. Any agreement disposing of all or part of the proceeding shall be written and signed by a parties. Such agreement shall conform to the requirements of paragraph (b) of this section.

(10) Report of the settlement. If a settlement is reached, the parties shall report to the presiding judge in writing within seven working days of the termination of negotiations. The report shall include a copy of the settlement agreement and/or proposed consent order. If a settlement is not reached, the parties shall report this to the presiding judge without further elaboration.

(11) Review of agreement by presiding judge. A settlement agreement arrived at with the help of a settlement judge shall be treated by the presiding judge as would be any other settlement agreement.

(12) Non-reviewable decisions. Decisions concerning whether a settlement judge should be appointed, the selection of a particular settlement judge, or the termination of proceedings under this section, are not subject to review by Department officials.

[48 FR 32538, July 15, 1983, as amended at 58 FR 38500, July 16, 1993]

§ 18.10 Parties, how designated.

(a) The term party whenever used in these rules shall include any natural person, corporation, association, firm, partnership, trustee, receiver, agency, public or private organization, or governmental agency. A party who seeks relief or other affirmative action shall be designated as plaintiff, complainant or claimant, as appropriate. A party against whom relief or other affirmative action is sought in any proceeding shall be designated as a defendant or respondent, as appropriate. When a party to the proceeding, the Department of Labor shall be either a party or party-in-interest.

(b) Other persons or organizations shall have the right to participate as parties if the administrative law judge determines that the final decision could directly and adversely affect them or the class they represent, and if they may contribute materially to the disposition of the proceedings and their interest is not adequately represented by existing parties.

(c) A person or organization wishing to participate as a party under this section shall submit a petition to the administrative law judge within fifteen (15) days after the person or organization has knowledge of or should have known about the proceeding. The petition shall be filed with the administrative law judge and served on each person or organization who has been made a party at the time of filing. Such petition shall concisely state:

(1) Petitioner's interest in the proceeding, (2) how his or her participation as a party will contribute materially to the disposition of the proceeding, (3) who will appear for petitioner, (4) the issues on which petitioner wishes to participate, and (5) whether petitioner intends to present witnesses.

(d) If objections to the petition are filed, the administrative law judge shall then determine whether petitioners have the requisite interest to be a party in the proceedings, as defined in paragraphs (a) and (b) of this section, and shall permit or deny participation accordingly. Where petitions to participate as parties are made by individuals or groups with common interests, the administrative law judge may request all such petitioners to designate a single representative, or he or she may recognize one or more of such petitioners. The administrative law judge shall give each such petitioner written notice of the decision on his or her petition. If the petition is denied, he or she shall briefly state the grounds for denial and shall then treat the petition as a request for participation as amicus curiae. The administrative law judge shall give written notice to each party of each petition granted.

§ 18.11 Consolidation of hearings.

When two or more hearings are to be held, and the same or substantially similar evidence is relevant and material to the matters at issue at each such hearing, the Chief Administrative Law Judge or the administrative law judge assigned may, upon motion by any party or on his or her own motion, order that a consolidated hearing be conducted. Where consolidated hearings are held, a single record of the proceedings may be made and the evidence introduced in one matter may be considered as introduced in the others, and a separate or joint decision shall be made, at the discretion of the administrative law judge as appropriate.

§ 18.12 Amicus curiae.

A brief of an amicus curiae may be filed only with the written consent of all parties, or by leave of the administrative law judge granted upon motion, or on the request of the administrative law judge, except that consent or leave shall not be required when the brief is presented by an officer of an agency of the United States, or by a state, territory or commonwealth. The amicus curiae shall not participate in any way in the conduct of the hearing, including the presentation of evidence and the examination of witnesses.

§ 18.13 Discovery methods.

Parties may obtain discovery by one or more of the following methods: Depositions upon oral examination or written questions; written interrogatories; production of documents or other evidence for inspection and other purposes; and requests for admission. Unless the administrative law judge orders otherwise, the frequency or sequence of these methods is not limited.

§ 18.14 Scope of discovery.

(a) Unless otherwise limited by order of the administrative law judge in accordance with these rules, the parties may obtain discovery regarding any matter, not privileged, which is relevant to the subject matter involved in the proceeding, including the existence, description, nature, custody, condition, and location of any books, documents, or other tangible things and the identity and location of persons having knowledge of any discoverable matter.

(b) It is not ground for objection that information sought will not be admissible at the hearing if the information sought appears reasonably calculated to lead to the discovery of admissible evidence.

(c) A party may obtain discovery of documents and tangible things otherwise discoverable under paragraph

(a) of this section and prepared in anticipation of or for the hearing by or for another party's representative (including his or her attorney, consultant, surety, indemnitor, insurer, or agent) only upon a showing that the party seeking discovery has substantial need of the materials in the preparation of his or her case and that he or she is unable without undue hardship to obtain the substantial equivalent of the materials by other means. In ordering discovery of such materials when the required showing has been made, the administrative law judge shall protect against disclosure of the mental impressions, conclusions, opinions, or legal theories of an attorney or other representative of a party concerning the proceeding.

§ 18.15 Protective orders.

(a) Upon motion by a party or the person from whom discovery is sought, and for good cause shown, the administrative law judge may make any order which justice requires to protect a party or person from annoyance, embarrassment, oppression, or undue burden or expense, including one or more of the following:

(1) The discovery not be had;

(2) The discovery may be had only on specified terms and conditions, including a designation of the time or place;

(3) The discovery may be had only by a method of discovery other than that selected by the party seeking discovery;

(4) Certain matters not relevant may not be inquired into, or that the scope of discovery be limited to certain matters;

(5) Discovery be conducted with no one present except persons designated by the administrative law judge; or

(6) A trade secret or other confidential research, development or commercial information may not be disclosed or be disclosed only in a designated way.

§ 18.16 Supplementation of responses.

A party who has responded to a request for discovery with a response that was complete when made is under no duty to supplement his response to include information thereafter acquired, except as follows:

(a) A party is under a duty to supplement timely his response with respect to any question directly addressed to:

(1) The identity and location of persons having knowledge of discoverable matters; and

(2) The identity of each person expected to be called as an expert witness at the hearing, the subject matter on which he or she is expected to testify and the substance of his or her testimony.

(b) A party is under a duty to amend timely a prior response if he or she later obtains information upon the basis of which:

(1) He or she knows the response was incorrect when made; or

(2) He or she knows that the response though correct when made is no longer true and the circumstances are such that a failure to amend the response is in substance a knowing concealment.

(c) A duty to supplement responses may be imposed by order of the administrative law judge or agreement of the parties.

§ 18.17 Stipulations regarding discovery.

Unless otherwise ordered, a written stipulation entered into by all the parties and filed with the Chief Administrative Law Judge or the administrative law judge assigned may: (a) Provide that depositions be taken before any person, at any time or place, upon sufficient notice, and in any manner and when so taken may be used like other depositions, and (b) modify the procedures provided by these rules for other methods of discovery.

§ 18.18 Written interrogatories to parties.

(a) Any party may serve upon any other party written interrogatories to be answered in writing by the partyserved, or if the party served is a public or private corporation or a partnership or association or governmental agency, by any authorized officer or agent, who shall furnish such information as is available to the party. A copy of the interrogatories, answers, and all related pleadings shall be served on the administrative law judge and upon all parties to the proceeding.

(b) Each interrogatory shall be answered separately and fully in writing under oath or affirmation, unless it is objected to, in which event the reasons for objection shall be stated in lieu of an answer. The answers and objections shall be signed by the person making them. The party upon whom the interrogatories were served shall serve a copy of the answer and objections upon all parties to the proceeding within thirty (30) days after service of the interrogatories, or within such shorter or longer period as the administrative law judge may allow.

(c) An interrogatory otherwise proper is not necessarily objectionable merely because an answer to the interrogatory involves an opinion or contention that relates to fact or the application of law to fact, but the administrative law judge may order that such an interrogatory need not be answered until after designated discovery has been completed or until a prehearing conference or other later time.

§ 18.19 Production of documents and other evidence; entry upon land for inspection and other purposes; and physical and mental examination.

(a) Any party may serve on any other party a request to:

(1) Produce and permit the party making the request, or a person acting on his or her behalf, to inspect and copy any designated documents, or to inspect and copy, test, or sample any tangible things which are in the possession, custody, or control of the party upon whom the request is served; or

(2) Permit entry upon designated land or other property in the possession or control of the party upon whom the request is served for the purpose of inspection and measuring, photographing, testing, or for other purposes as stated in paragraph (a)(1) of this section.

(3) Submit to a physical or mental examination by a physician.

(b) The request may be served on any party without leave of the administrative law judge.

(c) The request shall:

(1) Set forth the items to be inspected either by individual item or by category;

(2) Describe each item or category with reasonable particularity;

(3) Specify a reasonable time, place, and manner of making the inspection and performing the related acts;

(4) Specify the time, place, manner, conditions, and scope of the physical or mental examination and the person or persons by whom it is to be made. A report of examining physician shall be made in accordance with Rule 35(b) of the Federal Rules of Civil Procedure, title 28 U.S.C., as amended.

(d) The party upon whom the request is served shall serve on the party submitting the request a written response within thirty (30) days after service of the request.

(e) The response shall state, with respect to each item or category:

(1) That inspection and related activities will be permitted as requested; or

(2) That objection is made in whole or in part, in which case the reasons for objection shall be stated.

(f) A copy of each request for production and each written response shall be served on all parties and filed with the Office of Administrative Law Judges.

§ 18.20 Admissions.

(a) A party may serve upon any other party a written request for the admission, for purposes of the pending action only, of the genuineness and authenticity of any relevant document described in or attached to the request, or for the admission of the truth of any specified relevant matter of fact.

(b) Each matter of which an admission is requested is admitted unless, within thirty (30) days after service of the request or such shorter or longer time as the administrative law judge may allow, the party to whom the request is directed serves on the requesting party:

(1) A written statement denying specifically the relevant matters of which an admission is requested;

(2) A written statement setting forth in detail the reasons why he or she can neither truthfully admit nor deny them; or

(3) Written objections on the ground that some or all of the matters involved are privileged or irrelevant or that the request is otherwise improper in whole or in part.

(c) An answering party may not give lack of information or knowledge as a reason for failure to admit or deny unless the party states that he or she has made reasonable inquiry and that the information known or readily obtainable by him or her is insufficient to enable the party to admit or deny.

(d) The party who has requested the admissions may move to determine the sufficiency of the answers or objections. Unless the administrative law judge determines that an objection is justified, he or she shall order that an answer be served. If the administrative law judge determines that an answer does not comply with the requirements of this section, he or she may order either that the matter is admitted or that an amended answer be served. The administrative law judge may, in lieu of these orders, determine that final disposition of the request be made at a prehearing conference or at a designated time prior to hearing.

(e) Any matter admitted under this section is conclusively established unless the administrative law judge on motion permits withdrawal or amendment of the admission.

(f) Any admission made by a party under this section is for the purpose of the pending action only and is not an admission by him or her for any other purpose nor may it be used against him or her in any other proceeding.

(g) A copy of each request for admission and each written response shall be served on all parties and filed with the Office of Administrative Law Judges.

§ 18.21 Motion to compel discovery.

(a) If a deponent fails to answer a question propounded or a party upon whom a request is made pursuant to 18.18 through 18.20, or a party upon whom interrogatories are served fails to respond adequately or objects to the request, or any part thereof, or fails to permit inspection as requested, the discovering party may move the administrative law judge for an order compelling a response or inspection in accordance with the request.

(b) The motion shall set forth:

(1) The nature of the questions or request;

(2) The response or objections of the party upon whom the request was served; and

(3) Arguments in support of the motion.

(c) For purposes of this section, an evasive answer or incomplete answer or response shall be treated as a failure to answer or respond.

(d) In ruling on a motion made pursuant to this section, the administrative law judge may make and enter a protective order such as he or she is authorized to enter on a motion made pursuant to 18.15(a).

§ 18.22 Depositions.

(a) When, how, and by whom taken. The deposition of any witness may be taken at any stage of the proceeding at reasonable times. Depositions may be taken by oral examination or upon written interrogatories before any person having power to administer oaths.

(b) Application. Any party desiring to take the deposition of a witness shall indicate to the witness and all other parties the time when, the place where, and the name and post office address of the person before whom the deposition is to be taken; the name and address of each witness; and the subject matter concerning which each such witness is expected to testify.

(c) Notice. Notice shall be given for the taking of a deposition, which shall be not less than five (5) days written notice when the deposition is to be taken within the continental United States and not less than twenty (20) days written notice when the deposition is to be taken elsewhere.

(d) Taking and receiving in evidence. Each witness testifying upon deposition shall be sworn, and any other party shall have the right to cross-examine. The questions propounded and the answers thereto, together with all objections made, shall be reduced to writing; read by or to, and subscribed by the witness; and certified by the person administering the oath. Subject to such objections to the questions and answers as were noted at the time of taking the deposition and which would have been valid if the witness were personally present and testifying, such deposition may be read and offered in evidence by the party taking it as against any party who was present or represented at the taking of the deposition or who had due notice thereof.

(e) Motion to terminate or limit examination. During the taking of a deposition, a party or deponent may request suspension of the deposition on grounds of bad faith in the conduct of the examination, oppression of a deponent or party or improper questions propounded. The deposition will then be adjourned. However, the objecting party or deponent must immediately move the administrative law judge for a ruling on his or her objections to the deposition conduct or proceedings. The administrative law judge may then limit the scope or manner of the taking of the deposition.

[48 FR 32538, July 15, 1983; 49 FR 2739, Jan. 20, 1984]

§ 18.23 Use of depositions at hearings.

(a) Generally. At the hearing, any part or all of a deposition, so far as admissible under the rules of evidence, may be used against any party who was present or represented at the taking of the deposition or who had due notice thereof in accordance with any one of the following provisions:

(1) Any deposition may be used by any party for the purpose of contradicting or impeaching the testimony of the deponent as a witness.

(2) The deposition of expert witnesses, particularly the deposition of physicians, may be used by any party for any purpose, unless the administrative law judge rules that such use would be unfair or a violation of due process.

(3) The deposition of a party or of anyone who at the time of taking the deposition was an officer, director, or duly authorized agent of a public or private corporation, partnership, or association which is a party, may be used by any other party for any purpose.

(4) The deposition of a witness, whether or not a party, may be used by any party for any purpose if the presiding officer finds:

(i) That the witness is dead; or

(ii) That the witness is out of the United States or more than 100 miles from the place of hearing unless it appears that the absence of the witness was procured by the party offering the deposition; or

(iii) That the witness is unable to attend to testify because of age, sickness, infirmity, or imprisonment; or

(iv) That the party offering the deposition has been unable to procure the attendance of the witness by subpoena; or

(v) Upon application and notice, that such exceptional circumstances exist at to make it desirable, in the interest of justice and with due regard to the importance of presenting the testimony of witnesses orally in open hearing, to allow the deposition to be used.

(5) If only part of a deposition is offered in evidence by a party, any other party may require him or her to introduce all of it which is relevant to the part introduced, and any party may introduce any other parts.

(6) Substitution of parties does not affect the right to use depositions previously taken; and, when a proceeding in any hearing has been dismissed and another proceeding involving the same subject matter is afterward brought between the same parties or their representatives or successors in interest, all depositions lawfully taken and duly filed in the former proceeding may be used in the latter as if originally taken therefor.

(b) Objections to admissibility. Except as provided in this paragraph, objection may be made at the hearing to receiving in evidence any deposition or part thereof for any reason which would require the exclusion of the evidence if the witness were then present and testifying.

(1) Objections to the competency of a witness or to the competency, relevancy, or materiality of testimony are not waived by failure to make them before or during the taking of the deposition, unless the ground of the objection is one which might have been obviated or removed if presented at that time.

(2) Errors and irregularities occurring at the oral examination in the manner of taking the deposition, in the form of the questions or answers, in the oath or affirmation, or in the conduct of parties and errors of any kind which might be obviated, removed, or cured if promptly presented, are waived unless reasonable objection thereto is made at the taking of the deposition.

(3) Objections to the form or written interrogatories are waived unless served in writing upon the party propounding them.

(c) Effect of taking or using depositions. A party shall not be deemed to make a person his or her own witness for any purpose by taking his or her deposition. The introduction in evidence of the deposition or any part thereof for any purpose other than that of contradicting or impeaching the deponent makes the deponent the witness of the party introducing the deposition, but this shall not apply to the use by any other party of a deposition as described in paragraph (a)(2) of this section. At the hearing, any party may rebut any relevant evidence contained in a deposition whether introduced by him or her or by any other party.

§ 18.24 Subpoenas.

(a) Except as provided in paragraph (b) of this section, the Chief Administrative Law Judge or the presiding administrative law judge, as appropriate, may issue subpoenas as authorized by statute or law upon written application of a party requiring attendance of witnesses and production of relevant papers, books, documents, or tangible things in their possession and under their control. A subpoena may be served by certified mail or by any person who is not less than 18 years of age. A witness, other than a witness for the Federal Government, may not be required to attend a deposition or hearing unless the mileage and witness fee applicable to witnesses in courts of the United States for each date of attendance is paid in advance of the date of the proceeding.

(b) If a party's written application for subpoena is submitted three (3) working days or less before the hearing to which it relates, a subpoena shall issue at the discretion of the Chief Administrative Law Judge or presiding administrative law judge, as appropriate.

(c) Motion to quash or limit subpoena. Within ten (10) days of receipt of a subpoena but no later than the date of the hearing, the person against whom it is directed may file a motion to quash or limit the subpoena, setting forth the reasons why the subpoena should be withdrawn or why it should by limited in scope. Any such motion shall be answered within ten (10) days of service, and shall be ruled on immediately thereafter. The order shall specify the date, if any, for compliance with the specifications of the subpoena.

(d) Failure to comply. Upon the failure of any person to comply with an order to testify or a subpoena, the party adversely affected by such failure to comply may, where authorized by statute or by law, apply to the appropriate district court for enforcement of the order or subpoena.

§ 18.25 Designation of administrative law judge.

Hearings shall be held before an administrative law judge appointed under 5 U.S.C. 3105 and assigned to the Department of Labor. The presiding judge shall be designated by the Chief Administrative Law Judge.

§ 18.26 Conduct of hearings.

Unless otherwise required by statute or regulations, hearings shall be conducted in conformance with the Administrative Procedure Act, 5 U.S.C. 554.

§ 18.27 Notice of hearing.

(a) Generally. Except when hearings are scheduled by calendar call, the administrative law judge to whom the matter is referred shall notify the parties by mail of a day, time, and place set for hearing thereon or for a prehearing conference, or both. No date earlier than fifteen (15) days after the date of such notice shall be set for such hearing or conference, except by agreement of the parties. Service of such notice shall be made by regular, first-class mail, unless under the circumstances it appears to the administrative law judge that certified mail, mailgram, telephone, or any combination of these methods should be used instead.

(b) Change of date, time and place. The Chief Administrative Law Judge or the administrative law judge assigned to the case may change the time, date and place of the hearing, or temporarily adjourn a hearing, on his or her own motion or for good cause shown by a party. The parties shall be given not less than ten (10) days notice of the new hearing date, unless they agree to such change without such notice.

(c) Place of hearing. Unless otherwise required by statute or regulation, due regard shall be given to the convenience of the parties and the witnesses in selecting a place for the hearing.

§ 18.28 Continuances.

(a) When granted. Continuances will only by granted in cases of prior judicial commitments or undue hardship, or a showing of other good cause.

(b) Time limit for requesting. Except for good cause arising thereafter, requests for continuances must be filed within fourteen (14) days prior to the date set for hearing.

(c) How filed. Motions for continuances shall be in writing. At least 3--x3\1/2\-- of blank space shall be provided on the last page of the motion to permit space for the entry of an order by the administrative law judge. Copies shall be served on all parties. Any motions for continuances made within ten (10) days of the date of the scheduled proceeding shall, in addition to the written request, be telephonically conveyed to the administrative law judge or a member of his or her staff and to all other parties. Motions for continuances, based on reasons not reasonably ascertainable prior thereto, may also be made on the record at calendar calls, prehearing conferences or hearings.

(d) Ruling. Time permitting, the administrative law judge shall issue a written order in advance of the scheduled proceeding date which either allows or denies the request. Otherwise the ruling may be made orally by telephonic communication to the party requesting same who shall be responsible for telephonically notifying all other parties. Oral orders shall be confirmed in writing.

[48 FR 32538, July 15, 1983; 49 FR 2739, Jan. 20, 1984]

§ 18.29 Authority of administrative law judge.

(a) General powers. In any proceeding under this part, the administrative law judge shall have all powers necessary to the conduct of fair and impartial hearings, including, but not limited to, the following:

(1) Conduct formal hearings in accordance with the provisions of this part;

(2) Administer oaths and examine witnesses;

(3) Compel the production of documents and appearance of witnesses in control of the parties;

(4) Compel the appearance of witnesses by the issuance of subpoenas as authorized by statute or law;

(5) Issue decisions and orders;

(6) Take any action authorized by the Administrative Procedure Act;

(7) Exercise, for the purpose of the hearing and in regulating the conduct of the proceeding, such powers vested in the Secretary of Labor as are necessary and appropriate therefor;

(8) Where applicable, take any appropriate action authorized by the Rules of Civil Procedure for the United States District Courts, issued from time to time and amended pursuant to 28 U.S.C. 2072; and

(9) Do all other things necessary to enable him or her to discharge the duties of the office.

(b) Enforcement. If any person in proceedings before an adjudication officer disobeys or resists any lawful order or process, or misbehaves during a hearing or so near the place thereof as to obstruct the same, or neglects to produce, after having been ordered to do so, any pertinent book, paper or document, or refuses to appear after having been subpoenaed, or upon appearing refuses to take the oath as a witness, or after having taken the oath refuses to be examined according to law, the administrative law judge responsible for the adjudication, where authorized by statute or law, may certify the facts to the Federal District Court having jurisdiction in the place in which he or she is sitting to request appropriate remedies.

§ 18.30 Unavailability of administrative law judge.

In the event the administrative law judge designated to conduct the hearing becomes unavailable, the Chief Administrative Law Judge may designate another administrative law judge for the purpose of further hearing or other appropriate action.

§ 18.31 Disqualification.

(a) When an administrative law judge deems himself or herself disqualified to preside in a particular proceeding, such judge shall withdraw therefrom by notice on the record directed to the Chief Administrative Law Judge.

(b) Whenever any party shall deem the administrative law judge for any reason to be disqualified to preside, or to continue to preside, in a particular proceeding, that party shall file with the administrative law judge a motion to recuse. The motion shall be supported by an affidavit setting forth the alleged grounds for disqualification. The administrative law judge shall rule upon the motion.

(c) In the event of disqualification or recusal of an administrative law judge as provided in paragraph (a) or

(b) of this section, the Chief Administrative Law Judge shall refer the matter to another administrative law judge for further proceedings.

§ 18.32 Separation of functions.

No officer, employee, or agent of the Federal Government engaged in the performance of investigative or prosecutorial functions in connection with any proceeding shall, in that proceeding or a factually related proceeding, participate or advise in the decision of the administrative law judge, except as a witness or counsel in the proceedings.

§ 18.33 Expedition.

Hearings shall proceed with all reasonable speed, insofar as practicable and with due regard to the convenience of the parties.

§ 18.34 Representation.

(a) Appearances. Any party shall have the right to appear at a hearing in person, by counsel, or by other representative, to examine and cross-examine witnesses, and to introduce into the record documentary or other relevant evidence, except that the participation of any intervenor shall be limited to the extent prescribed by the administrative law judge.

(b) Each attorney or other representative shall file a notice of appearance. Such notice shall indicate the name of the case or controversy, the docket number if assigned, and the party on whose behalf the appearance is made.

(c) Rights of parties. Every party shall have the right of timely notice and all other rights essential to a fair hearing, including, but not limited to, the rights to present evidence, to conduct such crossexamination as may be necessary for a full and complete disclosure of the facts, and to be heard by objection, motion, and argument.

(d) Rights of participants. Every participant shall have the right to make a written or oral statement of position. At the discretion of the administrative law judge, participants may file proposed findings of fact, conclusions of law and a post hearing brief.

(e) Rights of witnesses. Any person compelled to testify in a proceeding in response to a subpoena may be accompanied, represented, and advised by counsel or other representative, and may purchase a transcript of his or her testimony.

(f) Office of the Solicitor. The Department of Labor shall be represented by the Solicitor of Labor or his or her designee and shall participate to the degree deemed appropriate by the Solicitor.

(g) Qualifications—(1) Attorneys. An attorney at law who is admitted to practice before the Federal courts or before the highest court of any State, the District of Columbia, or any territory or commonwealth of the United States, may practice before the Office of Administrative Law Judges. An attorney's own representation that he or she is in good standing before any of such courts shall be sufficient proof thereof, unless otherwise ordered by the administrative law judge. Any attorney of record must file prior notice in writing of intent to withdraw as counsel.

(2) Persons not attorneys. Any citizen of the United States who is not an attorney at law shall be admitted to appear in a representative capacity in an adjudicative proceeding. An application by a person not an attorney at law for admission to appear in a proceeding shall be submitted in writing to the Chief Administrative Law Judge prior to the hearing in the proceedings or to the administrative law judge assigned at the commencement of the hearing. The application shall state generally the applicant's qualifications to appear in the proceedings. The administrative law judge may, at any time, inquire as to the qualification or ability of such person to render legal assistance.

(3) Denial of authority to appear. The administrative law judge may deny the privilege of appearing to any person, within applicable statutory constraints, e.g. 5 U.S.C. 555, who he or she finds after notice of and opportunity for hearing in the matter does not possess the requisite qualifications to represent others; or is lacking in character or integrity; has engaged in unethical or improper professional conduct; or has engaged in an act involving moral turpitude. No provision hereof shall apply to any person who appears on his or her own behalf or on behalf of any corporation, partnership, or association of which the person is a partner, officer, or regular employee.

(h) Authority for representation. Any individual acting in a representative capacity in any adjudicative proceeding may be required by the administrative law judge to show his or her authority to act in such capacity. A regular employee of a party who appears on behalf of the party may be required by the administrative law judge to show his or her authority to so appear.

[48 FR 32538, July 15, 1983; 49 FR 2739, Jan. 20, 1984]

§ 18.35 Legal assistance.

The Office of Administrative Law Judges does not have authority to appoint counsel, nor does it refer parties to attorneys.

§ 18.36 Standards of conduct.

(a) All persons appearing in proceedings before an administrative law judge are expected to act with integrity, and in an ethical manner.

(b) The administrative law judge may exclude parties, participants, and their representatives for refusal to comply with directions, continued use of dilatory tactics, refusal to adhere to reasonable standards of orderly and ethical conduct, failure to act in good faith, or violation of the prohibition against ex parte communications. The administrative law judge shall state in the record the cause for suspending or barring an attorney or other representative from participation in a particular proceeding. Any attorney or other representative so suspended or barred may appeal to the Chief Judge but no proceeding shall be delayed or suspended pending disposition of the appeal; provided, however, that the administrative law judge shall suspend the proceeding for a reasonable time for the purpose of enabling the party to obtain another attorney or representative.

§ 18.37 Hearing room conduct.

Proceedings shall be conducted in an orderly manner. The consumption of food or beverage, smoking, or rearranging of courtroom furniture, unless specifically authorized by the administrative law judge, are prohibited.

[48 FR 32538, July 15, 1983; 49 FR 2739, Jan. 20, 1984]

§ 18.38 Ex parte communications.

(a) The administrative law judge shall not consult any person, or party, on any fact in issue unless upon notice and opportunity for all parties to participate. Communications by the Office of Administrative Law Judges, the assigned judge, or any party for the sole purpose of scheduling hearings or requesting extensions of time are not considered ex-parte communications, except that all other parties shall be notified of such request by the requesting party and be given an opportunity to respond thereto.

(b) Sanctions. A party or participant who makes a prohibited ex parte communication, or who encourages or solicits another to make any such communication, may be subject to any appropriate sanction or sanctions, including, but not limited to, exclusion from the proceedings and adverse ruling on the issue which is the subject of the prohibited communication.

§ 18.39 Waiver of right to appear and failure to participate or to appear.

(a) Waiver of right to appear. If all parties waive their right to appear before the administrative law judge or to present evidence or argument personally or by representative, it shall not be necessary for the administrative law judge to give notice of and conduct an oral hearing. A waiver of the right to appear and present evidence and allegations as to facts and law shall be made in writing and filed with the Chief Administrative Law Judge or the administrative law judge. Where such a waiver has been filed by all parties and they do not appear before the administrative law judge personally or by representative, the administrative law judge shall make a record of the relevant written evidence submitted by the parties, together with any pleadings they may submit with respect to the issues in the case. Such documents shall be considered as all of the evidence in the case, and the decision shall be based on them.

(b) —Abandonment by Party. A request for hearing may be dismissed upon its abandonment or settlement by the party or parties who filed it. A party shall be deemed to have abandoned a request for hearing if neither the party nor his or her representative appears at the time and place fixed for the hearing and either (a) prior to the time for hearing such party does not show good cause as to why neither he or she nor his or her representative can appear or (b) within ten (10) days after the mailing of a notice to him or her by the administrative law judge to show cause, such party does not show good cause for such failure to appear and fails to notify the administrative law judge prior to the time fixed for hearing that he or she cannot appear. A default decision, under 18.5(b), may be entered against any party failing, without good cause, to appear at a hearing.

§ 18.40 Motion for summary decision.

(a) Any party may, at least twenty (20) days before the date fixed for any hearing, move with or without supporting affidavits for a summary decision on all or any part of the proceeding. Any other party may, within ten (10) days after service of the motion, serve opposing affidavits or countermove for summary decision. The administrative law judge may set the matter for argument and/or call for submission of briefs.

(b) Filing of any documents under paragraph (a) of this section shall be with the administrative law judge, and copies of such documents shall be served on all parties.

(c) Any affidavits submitted with the motion shall set forth such facts as would be admissible in evidence in a proceeding subject to 5 U.S.C. 556 and 557 and shall show affirmatively that the affiant is competent to testify to the matters stated therein. When a motion for summary decision is made and supported as provided in this section, a party opposing the motion may not rest upon the mere allegations or denials of such pleading. Such response must set forth specific facts showing that there is a genuine issue of fact for the hearing.

(d) The administrative law judge may enter summary judgment for either party if the pleadings, affidavits, material obtained by discovery or otherwise, or matters officially noticed show that there is no genuine issue as to any material fact and that a party is entitled to summary decision. The administrative law judge may deny the motion whenever the moving party denies access to information by means of discovery to a party opposing the motion.

§ 18.41 Summary decision.

(a) No genuine issue of material fact. (1) Where no genuine issue of a material fact is found to have been raised, the administrative law judge may issue a decision to become final as provided by the statute or regulations under which the matter is to be heard. Any final decision issued as a summary decision shall conform to the requirements for all final decisions.

(2) An initial decision and a final decision made under this paragraph shall include a statement of:

(i) Findings of fact and conclusions of law, and the reasons therefor, on all issues presented; and

(ii) Any terms and conditions of the rule or order.

(3) A copy of any initial decision and final decision under this paragraph shall be served on each party.

(b) Hearings on issue of fact. Where a genuine question of material fact is raised, the administrative law judge shall, and in any other case may, set the case for an evidentiary hearing.

§ 18.42 Expedited proceedings.

(a) When expedited proceedings are required by statute or regulation, or at any time after commencement of a proceeding, any party may move to advance the scheduling of a proceeding.

(b) Except when such proceedings are required or as otherwise directed by the Chief Administrative Law Judge or the administrative law judge assigned, any party filing a motion under this section shall:

(1) Make the motion in writing;

(2) Describe the circumstances justifying advancement;

(3) Describe the irreparable harm that would result if the motion is not granted; and

(4) Incorporate in the motion affidavits to support any representations of fact.

(c) Service of a motion under this section shall be accomplished by personal delivery or by telephonic or telegraphic communication followed by mail. Service is complete upon personal delivery or mailing.

(d) Except when such proceedings are required, or unless otherwise directed by the Chief Administrative Law Judge or the administrative law judge assigned, all parties to the proceeding in which the motion is filed shall have ten (10) days from the date of service of the motion to file an opposition in response to the motion.

(e) Following the timely receipt by the administrative law judge of statements in response to the motion, the administrative law judge may advance pleading schedules, prehearing conferences, and the hearing, as deemed appropriate: provided, however, that a hearing on the merits shall not be scheduled with less than five (5) working days notice to the parties, unless all parties consent to an earlier hearing.

(f) When expedited hearings are required by statute or regulation, such hearing shall be scheduled within sixty (60) days from the receipt of request for hearing or order of reference. The decision of the administrative law judge shall be issued within twenty (20) days after receipt of the transcript of any oral hearing or within twenty (20) days after the filing of all documentary evidence if no oral hearing is conducted.

§ 18.43 Formal hearings.

(a) Public. Hearings shall be open to the public. However, in unusual circumstances, the administrative law judge may order a hearing or any part thereof closed, where to do so would be in the best interests of the parties, a witness, the public or other affected persons. Any order closing the hearing shall set forth the reasons for the decision. Any objections thereto shall be made a part of the record.

(b) Jurisdiction. The administrative law judge shall have jurisdiction to decide all issues of fact and related issues of law.

(c) Amendments to conform to the evidence. When issues not raised by the request for hearing, prehearing stipulation, or prehearing order are tried by express or implied consent of the parties, they shall be treated in all respects as if they had been raised in the pleadings. Such amendment of the pleadings as may be necessary to cause them to conform to the evidence may be made on motion of any party at any time; but failure to so amend does not affect the result of the hearing of these issues. The administrative law judge may grant a continuance to enable the objecting party to meet such evidence.

§ 18.44 [Reserved]

§ 18.45 Official notice.

Official notice may be taken of any material fact, not appearing in evidence in the record, which is among the traditional matters of judicial notice: Provided, however, that the parties shall be given adequate notice, at the hearing or by reference in the administrative law judge's decision, of the matters so noticed, and shall be given adequate opportunity to show the contrary.

§ 18.46 In camera and protective orders.

(a) Privileges. Upon application of any person the administrative law judge may limit discovery or introduction of evidence or issue such protective or other orders as in his or her judgment may be consistent with the objective of protecting privileged communications.

(b) Classified or sensitive matter. (1) Without limiting the discretion of the administrative law judge to give effect to any other applicable privilege, it shall be proper for the administrative law judge to limit discovery or introduction of evidence or to issue such protective or other orders as in his or her judgment may be consistent with the objective of preventing undue disclosure of classified or sensitive matter. Where the administrative law judge determines that information in documents containing sensitive matter should be made available to a respondent, he or she may direct the party to prepare an unclassified or nonsensitive summary or extract of the original. The summary or extract may be admitted as evidence in the record.

(2) If the administrative law judge determines that this procedure is inadequate and that classified or otherwise sensitive matter must form part of the record in order to avoid prejudice to a party, he or she may advise the parties and provide opportunity for arrangements to permit a party or a representative to have access to such matter. Such arrangements may include obtaining security clearances or giving counsel for a party access to sensitive information and documents subject to assurances against further disclosure.

§ 18.47 Exhibits.

(a) Identification. All exhibits offered in evidence shall be numbered and marked with a designation identifying the party or intervenor by whom the exhibit is offered.

(b) Exchange of exhibits. When written exhibits are offered in evidence, one copy must be furnished to each of the parties at the hearing, and one copy to the administrative law judge, unless the parties previously have been furnished with copies or the administrative law judge directs otherwise. If the administrative law judge has not fixed a time for the exchange of exhibits the parties shall exchange copies of exhibits at the earliest practicable time, preferably before the hearing, or at the latest at the commencement of the hearing.

(c) Substitution of copies for original exhibits. The administrative law judge may permit a party to withdraw original documents offered in evidence and substitute true copies in lieu thereof.

§ 18.48 Records in other proceedings.

In case any portion of the record in any other proceeding or civil or criminal action is offered in evidence, a true copy of such portion shall be presented for the record in the form of an exhibit unless the administrative law judge directs otherwise.

§ 18.49 Designation of parts of documents.

Where relevant and material matter offered in evidence is embraced in a document containing other matter not material or relevant and not intended to be put in evidence, the participant offering the same shall plainly designate the matter so offered, segregating and excluding insofar as practicable the immaterial or irrelevant parts. If other matter in such document is in such bulk or extent as would necessarily encumber the record, such document will not be received in evidence, but may be marked for identification, and if properly authenticated, the relevant and material parts thereof may be read into the record, or if the administrative law judge so directs, a true copy of such matter in proper form shall be received in evidence as an exhibit, and copies shall be delivered by the participant offering the same to the other parties or their attorneys appearing at the hearing, who shall be afforded an opportunity to examine the entire document and to offer in evidence in like manner other material and relevant portions thereof.

§ 18.50 Authenticity.

The authenticity of all documents submitted as proposed exhibits in advance of the hearing shall be deemed admitted unless written objection thereto is filed prior to the hearing, except that a party will be permitted to challenge such autheiticity at a later time upon a clear showing of good cause for failure to have filed such written objection.

§ 18.51 Stipulations.

The parties may by stipulation in writing at any stage of the proceeding, or orally made at hearing, agree upon any pertinent facts in the proceeding. It is desirable that the facts be thus agreed upon so far as and whenever practicable. Stipulations may be received in evidence at a hearing or prior thereto, and when received in evidence, shall be binding on the parties thereto.

§ 18.52 Record of hearings.

(a) All hearings shall be mechanically or stenographically reported. All evidence upon which the administrative law judge relies for decision shall be contained in the transcript of testimony, either directly or by appropriate reference. All exhibits introduced as evidence shall be marked for identification and incorporated into the record. Transcripts may be obtained by the parties and the public from the official reporter at rates not to exceed the applicable rates fixed by the contract with the reporter.

(b) Corrections. Corrections to the official transcript will be permitted upon motion. Motions for correction must be submitted within ten (10) days of the receipt of the transcript unless additional time is permitted by the administrative law judge. Corrections of the official transcript will be permitted only when errors of substance are involved and only upon approval of the administrative law judge.

§ 18.53 Closing of hearings.

The administrative law judge may hear arguments of counsel and may limit the time of such arguments at his or her discretion, and may allow briefs to be filed on behalf of either party but shall closely limit the time within which the briefs for both parties shall be filed, so as to avoid unreasonable delay.

§ 18.54 Closing the record.

(a) When there is a hearing, the record shall be closed at the conclusion of the hearing unless the administrative law judge directs otherwise.

(b) If any party waives a hearing, the record shall be closed on the date set by the administrative law judge as the final date for the receipt of submissions of the parties to the matter.

(c) Once the record is closed, no additional evidence shall be accepted into the record except upon a showing that new and material evidence has become available which was not readily available prior to the closing of the record. However, the administrative law judge shall make part of the record, any motions for attorney fees authorized by statutes, and any supporting documentation, any determinations thereon, and any approved correction to the transcript.

§ 18.55 Receipt of documents after hearing.

Documents submitted for the record after the close of the hearing will not be received in evidence except upon ruling of the administrative law judge. Such documents when submitted shall be accompanied by proof that copies have been served upon all parties, who shall have an opportunity to comment thereon. Copies shall be received not later than twenty (20) days after the close of the hearing except for good cause shown, and not less than ten (10) days prior to the date set for filing briefs. Exhibit numbers should be assigned by counsel or the party.

§ 18.56 Restricted access.

On his or her own motion, or on the motion of any party, the administrative law judge may direct that there be a restricted access portion of the record to contain any material in the record to which public access is restricted by law or by the terms of a protective order entered in the proceedings. This portion of the record shall be place in a separate file and clearly marked to avoid improper disclosure and to identify it as a portion of the official record in the proceedings.

§ 18.57 Decision of the administrative law judge.

(a) Proposed findings of fact, conclusions, and order. Within twenty (20) days of filing of the transcript of the testimony or such additional time as the administrative law judge may allow, each party may file with the administrative law judge, subject to the judge's discretion under 18.55, proposed findings of fact, conclusions of law, and order together with a supporting brief expressing the reasons for such proposals. Such proposals and brief shall be served on all parties, and shall refer to all portions of the record and to all authorities relied upon in support of each proposal.

(b) Decision of the administrative law judge. Within a reasonable time after the time allowed for the filing of the proposed findings of fact, conclusions of law, and order, or within thirty (30) days after receipt of an agreement containing consent findings and order disposing of the disputed matter in whole, the administrative law judge shall make his or her decision. The decision of the administrative law judge shall include findings of fact and conclusions of law, with reasons therefor, upon each material issue of fact or law presented on the record. The decision of the administrative law judge shall be based upon the whole record.

It shall be supported by reliable and probative evidence. Such decision shall be in accordance with the regulations and rulings of the statute or regulation conferring jurisdiction.

§ 18.58 Appeals.

The procedures for appeals shall be as provided by the statute or regulation under which hearing jurisdiction is conferred. If no provision is made therefor, the decision of the administrative law judge shall become the final administrative decision of the Secretary.

§ 18.59 Certification of official record.

Upon timely receipt of either a notice or a petition, the Chief Administrative Law Judge shall promptly certify and file with the reviewing authority, appellate body, or appropriate United States District Court, a full, true, and correct copy of the entire record, including the transcript of proceedings.

Source: 55 FR 13219, Apr. 9, 1990, unless otherwise noted.

Index to the Code of Federal Regulations

About the Editors

Steven M. Birnbaum, Esq., attended New York University and studied law at New College of California School of Law in San Francisco. From 1978 through 1982 he served as staff attorney for Legal Assistance to the Elderly. In 1983 he began his private practice, specializing in worker's compensation under the Longshore and Harbor Workers' Compensation Act and the California Labor Code. Mr. Birnbaum is a certified specialist in workers' compensation (State Bar of California). He is also the only California State Bar member to be additionally certified in Maritime and Admiralty Law. He is a special vice president of the Workplace Injury Law and Advocacy group and was president in 2009. He frequently lectures for Loyola University (New Orleans). He is a member of the Advisory Board for the LexisNexis's Benefits Review Board Reports. He is an Advisory Board member for Loyola University, New Orleans Annual Longshore Conference. He was distinguished in being awarded WILG's Lifetime Achievement Award in 2014.

Ralph R. Lorberbaum, Esq., received his B.B.A. from the University of Georgia in 1970 and his doctorate juris from Emory University in 1973. He has been in private practice with a sub-specialty in Longshore work since 1978. He serves on the Benefits Review Board Service Advisory Board and is an officer in the Workers' Compensation Section of the Association of Trial Lawyers of America and the Georgia Trial Lawyers Association. He practice focuses primarily on representation of claimant's under Georgia Workers' Compensation and the Longshore and Harbor's Compensation Act.

About the Contributors

David C. Barnett, Esq. is the founding and managing partner of Barnett, Lerner, Karsen, & Frankel, P.A. Mr. Barnett has successfully litigated many of the seminal cases relied upon by claimant attorneys under the Defense Base Act. Some examples include *Mechler v. Dyncorp*, where the Second Circuit Court of Appeals agreed with Mr. Barnett that the time for filing a claim seeking wage and medical benefits is when the injured worker is aware they are unable to earn wages because of an accident. In *Rice v. SEII*, the Court ruled that, even though the treating doctors released the claimant back to work without any restrictions, since the doctors advised against returning to work in Iraq, the claimant was entitled to get paid ⅔ of the difference between the Iraq wages and what the claimant could earn near her home. In *Fraser v. KBR*, the Court awarded wage and medical benefits after Mr. Barnett was able to discredit the insurance company's psychiatrist. In *Obadiaru v. ITT*, the claimant returned to work on a light duty status, but his continued work caused additional problems. The Court ruled that the light work caused a worsening of the claimant's condition, resulting in a second claim entitling the claimant to medical and wage benefits.

In 2009 Mr. Barnett founded and created a National Joint Bar Association comprised of attorneys throughout the United States working to streamline the litigation process and the ensure the bar, as a whole, was recognized nationally as a stakeholder in any legislation or rules changes. Mr. Barnett served as President of the DOL-Joint Bar Association from 2009 through 2012, and he currently remains on the Board of Directors and serves as Treasurer. In 2009-10, Mr. Barnett served as Chairman of the Longshore Section of the Workers Injury Law Group. Mr. Barnett previously served on the Board of Directors for Florida Workers Advocates while also being a member of the Florida Admiralty Lawyer's Association, Broward County Bar Association and American Bar Association.

Mr. Barnett has lectured and taught continuing education classes throughout the United States over the past twenty years and has had many articles published. In the Spring of 2014, Mr. Barnett co-authored a law review article for the *Loyola University New Orleans Maritime Law Journal* titled Discovery Issues and Ethical Considerations Under the Rules of Practice and Procedure for Administrative Hearings Before the Office of Administrative Law Judges while in the Fall of 2012 he published an article titled Psychiatric Claims Under the Longshore and Harbor Workers' Compensation Act in the *Loyola Maritime Law Journal.* In 2008 he was a contributing author in the *Defense Base Act and War Hazards Compensation Handbook, 2008, Edition*, LexisNexis. Mr. Barnett also wrote part of the State of Florida Board Certification Course and Examination for Insurance Adjusters.

In addition to his professional experience, Mr. Barnett is also involved in many charitable organizations throughout South Florida. He previously served on the Board of Directors for Easter Seals of South Florida and he currently serves on the Board of Directors for The Victory Center, a nonprofit school focused on educating children with autism.

D. A. Bass-Frazier, Esq. has represented injured workers in LHWCA claims since 1989. She received her BM from the University of South Alabama, her MLS, *summa cum laude*, from Louisiana State University, and her JD, with honors, from Florida State University. She has used online search engines since 1980 and has extensive experience as a reference librarian in public, university, law, and aerospace libraries. She is a member of MENSA, Beta Phi Mu, and Phi Delta Phi. In addition to publishing articles on Southern American history, Ms. Bass-Frazier maintains a web page devoted to Alabama's early settlers and mid-19th century military history.

Alan G. Brackett, Esq. is a founding member of Mouledoux, Bland, Legrand & Brackett, LLC in New Orleans, Louisiana. He obtained a B.A. in history in 1982 from Tulane University and his J.D. from Tulane Law School in 1984. His practice focuses on personal injury litigation, particularly in the fields of Longshore compensation and Jones Act defense. He leads the firm's workers' compensation practice group, which handles claims arising under the Longshore and Harbor Workers' Compensation Act, Defense Base Act, War Hazards Compensation Act, Non-Appropriated Funds

Instrumentalities Act, and Louisiana Workers' Compensation Act. He is admitted to practice in all Louisiana State and federal courts, the Supreme Court of the United States, and the United States Courts of Appeals for the Fifth, Ninth and Eleventh Circuits.

Alan is recognized in Best Lawyers in America, has been recognized by New Orleans CityBusiness as one of the city's Top 50 Lawyers and has been named a Louisiana SuperLawyer since 2008. He is a member of the Louisiana State, American, Federal and New Orleans Bar Associations, the Louisiana and New Orleans Associations of Defense Counsel, the Defense Research Institute, the Southeastern Admiralty Law Institute and the Maritime Law Association of the United States. Alan is a fellow in the Louisiana Bar Foundation, where he serves on the Board of Directors, is a fellow in the American Bar Foundation, and is an Assistant Bar Examiner for the State of Louisiana. He is a fellow in the College of Workers' Compensation Lawyers, and is a past president of the DOL – Joint Bar Association, Inc. He has served as Chairman of the Advisory Committee and Seminar Moderator for Loyola Law School's Annual Longshore Conference since 1998.

Norman Cole, Esq. joined Sather, Byerly & Holloway, LLP in 2005, and became a partner in 2012. He defends claims under the Oregon Workers' Compensation Act and the Longshore & Harbor Workers' Compensation Act. Norman was admitted to the Oregon State Bar in 1974. He was a Deputy District Attorney and then Chief Deputy District Attorney for Clatsop County before joining SAIF Corporation in 1979 as a Trial Counsel and Special Assistant Attorney General. In 1983, Norman also began defending claims under the Longshore & Harbor Workers' Compensation Act. He later became SAIF's legal division pulmonary and asbestos disease claim specialist.

Norm has been a featured speaker on workers' compensation topics at seminars sponsored by the National Business Institute and Northwest Longshore Administrators' Association, among other organizations. He writes a quarterly Longshore & Harbor Workers' Compensation Act case law review for the Northwest Longshore Administrators' Association.

Paul M. Doolittle, Esq. graduated from the Oklahoma City University College of Law in 1987, where he served as an editor on the Law Review. Paul has served on the Board of Directors of Florida Workers' Advocates for over fifteen years, is a Past Chair of the Workers' Compensation Section of the Florida Justice Association (a.k.a. the Academy of Florida Trial Lawyers), is "AV" rated by Martindale-Hubble, and, for the last twenty five years, has practiced workers' compensation, Longshore, and Defense Base Act litigation in Jacksonville, Florida.

Paul has mediated well over 1,500 cases arising under the Longshore and Harbor Workers' Compensation Act, and its extensions, specifically, the Defense Base Act; for the past seven years, Paul has mediated such disputes several times a week throughout the United States.

Paul frequently lectures on Longshore and Defense Base Act matters, and his latest article, Death Benefits Under the Longshore and Defense Base Acts, was published in the Fall 2012 edition of the *Loyola Maritime Law Journal*, Vol. II, No. 1.

Eric A. Dupree, Esq.'s legal career commenced at 0830 hrs July 5, 1971. After reading the office procedure manual, he passed an oral exam administered by the firm's office manager, a retired chief petty officer, who then introduced him to what he believes was the firm's fist photocopy machine. Though fresh from the ranches of Wyoming, Dupree quickly learned urban survival skills, making extra money serving difficult legal process. He cut a deal with the office manager: if the filing and photocopy work was completed, he could shadow the firm's lawyers to the courthouse. By 1975 he was preparing cases for trial, and is the subject "paralegal" of the oft-cited seminal attorney fee decision in *Morris v. California Stevedore and Ballast.*

Dupree attended the University of Wyoming for two years on a partial academic scholarship, followed by a year and a half at the University of San Francisco, graduating early with honors and a B.A. in economics. He then attended law school at UC Hastings, graduating in June 1979. That summer he took the California bar exam, and to the amazement of some but not all, passed. He managed to work his way through school and finished debt-fee with a $230.00 cash reserve.

In the intervening years he has been accepted for admission to practice before all of the California State and Federal District Courts and the Court of Appeals for the Fifth and Ninth Circuits. He has been an active member in many legal organizations on both sides of the litigation bar. At present he serves as a committee member on the Governmental Affairs Committee of the Longshore subsection of the Workers Injury Law and Advocacy Group (WILG). He is a regular presenter at WILG's CLE seminars and conventions.

He currently practices out of San Diego, California, representing injured maritime employees on the West Coast, frequently on referral or in association with other attorneys.

Dupree has lectured frequently to bar and industry associations nationwide, with a special emphasis on maritime litigation, in particular the Longshore Act. He taught Admiralty Law for four years at Thomas Jefferson School of Law in San Diego, and would like to return to teaching when his children become independent. He has published law journal articles and authored and co-authored chapters in The Longshore Textbook.

In addition to his law license, Dupree holds a California real estate broker license, a 100-ton near coastal motor vessel master's license, and a California commercial driver's license. He was the founder and principle of Round Rock Inc., a wholesale building and landscape stone distributor, from 1996 through 2003.

His passions are raising his children, making difficult cases seem easy, cooking, bringing old vessels back to functional life, and story-telling.

Kenneth G. Engerrand, Esq. practices law as President of Brown Sims, P.C. in its Houston, Texas office. For nearly 40 years he has lectured on legal subjects in courses and seminars presented by The University of Texas, Tulane University, The University of Houston, Louisiana State University, Loyola University, South Texas College of Law, and The University of St. Thomas, as well as to meetings and seminars presented for The United States Department of Labor, The State Bar of Texas, The State Bar of Louisiana, The International Association of Drilling Contractors, The Workers' Compensation Educational Conference, The National Association of Marine Surveyors, The International Transportation Management Association, the Houston Claims Association, and a host of other groups. Mr. Engerrand earned his B.A., magna cum laude, from Florida State University and his J.D., with honors, from the University of Texas School of Law, and he is a member of many professional organizations, including the Maritime Law Association, American and Houston Bar Associations, Defense Research Institute, Texas Association of Defense Counsel, Order of the Coif, Phi Beta Kappa, Phi Kappa Phi, Phi Delta Phi, Mariners Club, Propeller Club, State Bar of Texas and the Texas Bar Foundation. Mr. Engerrand supports a number of civic, industry, and charitable groups and serves as a trustee of the Judge John R. Brown Scholarship Foundation. He has written extensively, and his publications include: *Admiralty Jury Trials Reconsidered*, 12 Loy. Mar. L.J. 73 (2013); *The Relationship Among General Maritime Law, OPA, and OCSLA*, 25 U. San. Fran. Mar. L.J. 253 (2013); *Vessel Status Reconsidered*, 11 Loy. Mar. L.J. 213 (2013); *Forum Selection and Arbitration Clauses in Seamen's Injury Claims*, 11 Loy. Mar. L.J. 109 (2012); *Indemnity for Gross Negligence in Maritime Oilfield Contracts*, 10 Loy. Mar. L.J. 319 (2012); *A Tedious Balance: Third-Party Claims under the Longshore and Harbor Workers' Compensation Act*, 10 Loy. Mar. L.J. 1 (2011); *Jones Act Issues after Norfolk Southern Railway v. Sorrell*, 6 Loy. Mar. L. J. 1 (2008); *Primer on Maintenance and Cure*, 18 U. San. Fran. Mar. L.J. 41 (2005-06); *Primer of Remedies on the Outer Continental Shelf*, 4 Loy. Mar. L. J. 19 (2005); *Medicare Set-Asides and Protecting the Parties' Interests in Longshore Claims*, 3 Loy. Mar. L.J. 11 (2004); *The Fleet Rule for Seaman Status: The Peril of Perils*, 2 Loy. Mar. L.J. 92 (2003); *DOHSA's Reach: What Are The High Seas Beyond A Marine League From Shore?* 1 Loy. Mar. L.J. 1 (2002); *Changes in Pursuing and Defending Attorney's Fees Claims in The Fifth and Ninth Circuits*, 14 U. San Fran. Mar. L.J. 155 (2001-02); *Recent Developments in Admiralty Law in the United States Supreme Court, The Fifth Circuit, and the Eleventh Circuit*, 24 Tulane Mar. L. J. 741 (2000); *Recent Developments in Admiralty Law in the United States Supreme Court, The Fifth Circuit, and the Eleventh Circuit*, 20 Hous. J. Int'l L. 265 (1998); *Removal and Remand of Admiralty Suits*, 21 Tulane Mar. L. J. 383 (1997); *Recent Developments in Admiralty Law in the United States Supreme Court, The Fifth Circuit, and the Eleventh Circuit*, 18 Hou. J. Int'l L. 709 (1996); *Seaman Status Reconstructed*, 32 S. Tex. L. Rev. 169 (1991); *Admiralty Law*, 23 Tort & Ins. L.J. 251 (1988); *Seaman Status Reconsidered*, 24 S. Tex. L.J. 431 (1983); *The Continuing Conflict Between Congress & The Supreme Court Over The Standard of Care in Longshore Third Party Actions*, 22 S. Tex. L.J. 423 (1981); *Troubled Waters for Seaman's Wrongful Death Actions*, 12 J. Mar. Law & Com. 327 (1980), reprinted in 21 S. Tex. L.J. 191 (1980). His articles have been cited and quoted by the United States Supreme Court as well as appellate and district courts from California to Massachusetts.

Thomas C. Fitzhugh III, Esq. earned a B.S. in Geophysics from Texas A&M University and a J.D. (with honors) from the University of Texas. Since 1976 he has been in private practice in Houston, specializing in admiralty and maritime litigation, and also serving as a Special Master and Mediator for federal courts. As President of the Longshore Institute, Mr. Fitzhugh edits The Longshore Newsletter and The Longshore Procedure Manual, publications interpreting the Longshore and Harbor Workers' Compensation Act (and its extension), and presents seminars on the LHWCA to the bar and insurance industry. These include a quarterly Webinar and an annual Ultimate Jones Act program. A frequent lecturer and author on maritime law topics and the Longshore Act, Mr. Fitzhugh is a Fellow of the Texas Bar Foundation, the Houston Bar Foundation, and a member of the College of the State Bar of Texas. As an adjunct professor at Texas A&M University in maritime law, Mr. Fitzhugh serves as Executive Vice President and General Counsel to the Maritime Security Council and has represented the United States on the Maritime Security Committee of the Baltic & International Maritime Council (BIMCO), based in Copenhagen, Denmark.

Lewis S. Fleishman, Esq. is the sole practitioner of the law firm Lewis S. Fleishman, PLLC. For the past thirty years he has concentrated on Maritime Law including the Defense Base Act, and the Longshore Harbor Workers' Compensation Act. Prior to commencing practice in Texas, Mr. Fleishman was employed as an Assistant Attorney Genera by the State of New Mexico. He prosecuted cases under the Uniform Licensing Act. Additionally, Mr. Fleishman has extensive criminal appellate and state post-conviction experience. Mr. Fleishman graduated from Rutgers School of Law, Camden. He conducted his undergraduate work at the University of California, Los Angeles, where he graduated cum laude. Mr. Fleishman is admitted to practice law in Texas, New Mexico (inactive), California (inactive), the Navajo Nation (inactive), and numerous federal courts. Mr. Fleishman clerked for the Honorable John Devine, U.S. Magistrate, Trenton, New Jersey.

Keith L. Flicker, Esq. is a graduate of the Columbia University School of Law (J.D., 1978) and received a degree in Economics from New York University, where he graduated summa cum laude and was the recipient of the N.Y.U. Founder's Day Award (B.A., 1974). He is a member of the New York and New Jersey bars, and is admitted to practice before the state and federal courts of those jurisdictions. He is also admitted to practice before the United States Courts of Appeals for the First, Second Third, Fourth, Sixth, Ninth and Federal Circuits and the United States Supreme Court. In 1985, he founded the firm of Flicker, Garelick & Associates, LLP, focusing on the insurance, marine and intermodal transportation industries with a concentration on the defense of carriers and employers with exposures under the Defense Base Act ("DBA"), Longshore & Harbor Workers' Compensation Act ("LHWCA"), Jones Act and related statutes.

As a senior trial counsel and advisor to many of the federal compensation industry's leading corporations, Mr. Flicker has tried hundreds of cases before the administrative bodies and courts that are charged with the judicial resolution of DBA and longshore claims. He has also tried dozens of maritime and commercial cases, jury and non-jury alike, before federal and state courts throughout the country. He regularly speaks at and presents seminars to employers, adjusters, attorneys, underwriters, brokers and managers involved in federal compensation and maritime litigation matters.

Mr. Flicker is the author of the "Defense Base Act Exclusivity" and "Zone of Special Danger" chapters in the *Defense Base Act and War Hazards Compensation Act Handbook* (LexisNexis, 2008 and 2010) and is a contributor to the *Longshore Textbook* (Lawyers & Judges Publishing Co., Inc. 6th Edition 2010). Mr. Flicker is also a recent contributor to the Journal of International Peace Operations, a journal published by the International Stability Operations Association and is frequently interviewed by national media outlets concerning issues involving the DBA. Mr. Flicker is a member of the Board of Directors of the DOL - Joint Bar Association, an organization that works to promote and improve the efficient handling of claims and cases administered by the United States Department of Labor.

Dr. Jess Ghannam, Ph.D. is Clinical Professor of Psychiatry and Global Health Sciences in the School of Medicine at UCSF. His research areas include evaluating the long-term health consequences of war on displaced communities and the psychological and psychiatric effects of armed conflict on children.

He is also a consultant with the Center for Constitutional Rights, Reprieve and other international NGOs that work with torture survivors. Locally he works to promote and enhance the health and wellness of refugee, displaced, and immigrant populations from the Middle East, North Africa and South Asia and has established a community-based Mental Health Treatment Programs to support these communities.

At UCSF Dr. Ghannam develops culturally competency training programs for staff, students and faculty working with patients from the Middle East. Dr. Ghannam specializes in working with chronic illness, including chronic pain and cancer. He also works and does research in the area of Global Health and Post Traumatic Stress Disorder. Dr. Ghannam is also a Qualified Medical Examiner (QME) for the State of California and serves as an IME.

Joshua T. Gillelan II, Esq. received his B.A. from St. John's College in Annapolis, and his J.D. from the University of Maryland in 1973. As a member of the Longshore staff of the Office of the Solicitor of Labor in Washington, DC, from 1973 until 2004, he represented the Director, OWCP, in more than 300 cases before the United States courts of appeals, including many of the most important precedent-setting cases decided since the 1972 Amendments to the Act, and hundreds of cases before the Benefits Review Board. He established the LCNLC in July 2004 for the co-representation of LHWCA claimants and Jones Act plaintiffs, particularly on appeal.

Howard S. Grossman, Esq. is one of the leading personal injury attorneys in South Florida, known for his accessibility, compassion and tenacious trial preparation. For over 25 years, Howard has litigated complex personal injury, medical malpractice, maritime injury, long shore workers' compensation, and Defense Base Act cases. He takes pride not only in advocating for victims of personal injury, but in providing them with the resources and information they need to return to everyday life. His dedication to clients extends beyond a settlement as he keeps in touch with clients for years after their case has closed.

In addition to the Florida Bar, Howard is admitted to the U.S. District Courts for the Middle and Southern Districts of Florida, U.S. District Court of Colorado, U.S. District Court of the Southern District of Texas, U.S. Court of Appeals, 11th Circuit. Worker's Compensation Emeritus Specialist from 2007 -2015. He is AV-rated by Martindale Hubell and has been elected a "Super Lawyer" by his peers in the State of Florida. He is a past President of the South Palm Beach County Bar Association.

Born in Brooklyn New York, Howard has lived most of his adult life in South Florida. Howard is a past-president of the South Palm Beach County Bar Association and an active member of the American Justice Association, Palm Beach County Bar Association, and Florida Justice Association (Eagle Member).

Alexandra E. Grover, Esq. is a shareholder in the Houston office of Brown Sims. She specializes in the defense of claims arising under the Longshore and Harbor Workers' Compensation Act and its statutory extensions, including the Defense Base Act. Ms. Grover also maintains a general civil litigation practice. Ms. Grover graduated magna cum laude with a Bachelor of Arts in Political Science from the University of St. Thomas (2006), and she graduated cum laude with a Doctor of Jurisprudence from South Texas College of Law (2009). Ms. Grover was admitted to the State Bar of Texas in 2009. While attending law school, Ms. Grover interned with both Magistrate Judge Calvin Botley and District Judge David Hittner at the United States District Court for the Southern District of Texas.

Joseph B. Guilbeau, Esq. is a member of the Metairie, LA law firm of Juge, Napolitano, Guilbeau, Ruli & Frieman, PLC. He earned his B.S. degree in Mathematics from the University of Southwestern Louisiana in 1976 and graduated from Loyola Law School with a J.D. in 1984. Joe is a member of the Louisiana Association of Defense Counsel and Defense Research Institute. His primary area of practice is the representation of employers and insurers under the Louisiana Workers' Compensation and Longshore and Harbor Workers' Compensation Acts. He has been a speaker at the Annual Longshore Conference and other Seminars sponsored by Louisiana Association of Business and Industry, Louisiana Association of Self-Insured Employers, Lorman Educational Services, and the National Business Institute.

Chief Judge Stephen R. Henley is the Chief Administrative Law Judge for the United States Department of Labor in Washington, D.C. Before assuming his current position on October 18, 2015, he was the Associate Chief Administrative Law Judge for Longshore and a line Administrative Law Judge in the Office of Administrative Law Judges, U.S. Department of Labor. Before joining the Department of Labor in May 2012, he was an Administrative Law Judge with the Social Security Administration in Fayetteville, North Carolina. Prior to his appointment as an Administrative Law Judge in August 2011, Judge Henley served nearly 30 years in the United States Army, from which he retired in 2011 after 5 ½ years as Chief Trial Judge of the Trial Judiciary, the longest serving Army Chief Trial Judge. Judge Henley served more than thirteen years as a military trial judge presiding over criminal cases around the globe, ranging from capital murder, rape and robbery to drug distribution, desertion and fraud, including courts-martial in Afghanistan, Iraq, Kuwait, and Kosovo and military commissions convened in Guantanamo Bay, Cuba. Judge Henley is a graduate of Providence College, Duke University, The George Washington University and The Judge Advocate General's School. He formerly served as an Adjunct Professor at The George Washington University Law School and was the recipient of the 2011 Judge Advocates Foundation MG William K. Suter Distinguished Judicial Service Award. Judge Henley currently serves as a member of the D.C. Bar Committee on Admissions.

Paul B. Howell, Esq. was born in Jackson, Mississippi in 1957. He attended undergraduate school at the University of Mississippi where he served as editor of the Daily Mississippian. Paul graduated with a Bachelor of Arts degree in journalism and political science in 1979. Subsequently, he attended the University of Mississippi Law School where he served as a member of the Moot Court Board. He graduated in 1981. Paul moved to Gulfport, Mississippi and joined Franke & Salloum in 1982. He is a partner in the firm and practices mainly in the areas of workers' compensation defense under the Longshore and Harbor Workers' Compensation Act and the Mississippi Workers' Compensation Act. He is a member of the Harrison County Bar Association, the American Bar Association, the Fifth Circuit Bar Association, the Mississippi State Bar, the United States Supreme Court Bar, the Mississippi Defense Lawyers Association and the

Defense Research Institute. He is on the Benefits Review Board Service Advisory Board and lectures on Federal and State Workers' Compensation issues.

Frank B. Hugg, Esq., received his A.B. from Dartmouth and his juris doctorate from Florida State University at Tallahassee in 1973. He moved to California in 1975, and joined the defense firm of Hanna, Brophy, MacLean, MacAleer and Jensen, later serving with the firm of Mullen and Filippi. In 1981 he began his private practice, specializing in Longshore and Harbor Workers' Compensation, State of California Workers' Compensation, California Labor Code and O.S.H.A. matters. Frank was lead counsel before the California Supreme Court in *Sea-Land vs. Lopez*, associate counsel before the United States Supreme Court in *Rasmussen v. Director, OWCP*, and has participated in numerous cases before the Ninth Circuit Court of Appeals and the California District Courts of Appeal. He is a frequent speaker on maritime matters at applicant, defense and educational meetings. He is married with two children. In his little spare time, he is active in the Asian Art Museum of San Francisco, an avid squash player, and a golf nut.

John F. Karpousis, Esq. is a Partner at Freehill Hogan and Mahar, having received his Juris Doctor from Fordham University School of Law in 1993. Mr. Karpousis has tried over 50 cases before the United States Department of Labor, Office of Administrative Law Judges and Benefits Review Board and is a published author and frequent lecturer on matters involving the Longshore Harbor Workers' Compensation Act, and has taught several Continuing Legal Education seminars on Longshore Act matters to other attorneys. The author wishes to acknowledge the efforts of David Bury, 3L at Tulane Law School for his research contributions to this article.

Robert Kessner, Esq., received his B.A. from the University of Colgate and his J.D. from Boston University School of Law. Mr. Kessner is a founding member of the firm, Kessner, Umebayashi, Bain & Matsunaga. He is a member of the American Bar Association, Hawaii State Bar Association, Association of Trial Lawyers, Industrial Claims Association and Maritime Claims Associations. He has practiced in the area of the defense of workers' compensations claims for insurance carriers and self-insured employers since 1977. He also authors and lectures in the area of state and federal workers' compensation law.

Roger A. Levy, Esq., received his B.S. from California State University at Chico, and his juris doctorate from Golden Gate University in 1969. Mr. Levy was a founding partner of Laughlin, Falbo, Levy & Moresi LLP in 1985 and became *Of Counsel* in 1999 and retired from the firm in 2016. His practice has focused on the defense of workers' compensation matters before both state and federal administrative agencies. His primary concentration and specialization has been the defense of cases brought under the United States Longshore and Harbor Workers' Compensation Act, including its extensions, the Defense Base Act, the Non-Appropriated Fund Instrumentalities Act, and the Outer Continental Shelf Lands Act, as well as related maritime civil caves such as those brought under the Jones Act and Suits in Admiralty Act.

Since 2004, he has served as a Mediator throughout the U.S. in cases related to these areas of practice, especially the Defense Base Act and presently is the principal in Levy Mediations.

He has presented at numerous conferences, seminars, and conventions locally and nationally for agency, industry, and professional groups including the American Bar Association. He has authored many articles pertaining to his practice area, and served as Editor-in-Chief of both the 1st and 2nd editions of the *Defense Base Act and War Hazards Compensaton Act Handbook*, a LexisNexis publication.

His memberships include: California State Bar Association, American Bar Association, Industrial Claims Association, Longshore Claims Association, Northwest Claims Association.

Monica Fekete Markovich, Esq. practices law as a Shareholder and Director of Brown Sims, P.C. in its Houston, Texas location. Brown Sims, P.C. was established in 1968 as an admiralty firm with the purpose of serving its clients in the Gulf Coast area and abroad. Since that time, the firm's practice has expanded to include a broad range of legal services throughout the general scope of civil litigation. Ms. Markovich's current practice focuses on the defense of claims brought under the Longshore and Harbor Workers' Compensation Act (and its extensions including the Defense Base Act) and the Texas Workers' Compensation Act, "non-subscriber" litigation, and other death and personal injury defense. Ms. Markovich is a member of the State Bar of Texas, and has been Board Certified in Workers' Compensation Law by the Texas Board of Legal Specialization since 2004. Ms. Markovich served on the Board of Directors and as a President (2014) of the DOL-Joint Bar Association, Inc. She has been serving on the Benefits Review Board Service Advisory Board since 2008. Ms. Markovich has lectured on legal subjects including at seminars presented by The University of Texas, Louisiana State University, Loyola Law School, URIMA, The State Bar of Texas and the U.S. Chamber of Commerce. Ms. Markovich received her Bachelor of Arts (1990) and Doctor of Jurisprudence (1993) from the University of Texas in Austin.

Kris R. Marotti, Esq. of Tarro & Marotti Law Firm, LLC has been practicing law for over 25 years, having been admitted to the Rhode Island bar in September 1991. She is a member of the United States Court of Appeals for the First Circuit. She has handled many appeals involving extensive brief writing and oral argument before the Rhode Island Supreme Court and the United States Court of Appeals for the First Circuit. She has extended her appellate practice to the fields of Defense Base Act and Longshore and Harbor Workers' Act claims in the United States District Court of Appeals for the First Circuit and the United States Department of Labor Benefits Review Board.

Brian P. McElreath, Esq. is a partner at Lueder, Larkin & Hunter in Charleston, South Carolina. He received his B.A. in Monetary Economics and Finance in a joint degree program from the University of North Carolina at Asheville and North Carolina State University and his J.D. from the Charleston School of Law where he was a member of the Maritime Law Bulletin. He practices extensively in the areas of workers' compensation defense, defense of claims arising under the Longshore and Harbor Workers' Compensation Act and its extensions, 905(b) claims, and subrogation. Brian is a member of the South Carolina, Georgia, and Virginia Bar Associations, the Maritime Law Association of the United States, the Southeastern Admiralty Law Institute, the Claims & Litigation Management Alliance, and the DOL – Joint Bar Association.

Robert A. McLaughlin, Esq. is a 1984 graduate of Boston University, where he majored in economics. He went on to earn a Master's Degree in Economics at Claremont Graduate School in 1986. He graduated from the University of San Diego School of Law in 1990. That same year he was admitted to the California State Bar. He is also a member of the San Diego County Bar Association.

Mr. McLaughlin is currently on the executive board in the role as Treasurer of the California Applicant's Attorneys Association and is a board member of the Workers' Injury Law and Advocacy Group. Mr. McLaughlin is a past President of the San Diego County Chapter of CAAA. Mr. McLaughlin is also a board member of the Workers' Injury Law and Advocacy Group.

Mr. McLaughlin is a frequent speaker on workers' compensation issues and has been a panelist and speaker at several conventions and seminars hosted by defense, applicant and third-party organizations. He is a frequent speaker at CAAA conventions and seminars. His paper on HIPAA (Health Insurance Portability and Accountability Act), the Privacy Rule and the Longshore Act was published in the Loyola Maritime Law Journal in November 2013.

Michael P. McQuinn, Esq. is an associate attorney with the law firm of Thomas, Quinn & Krieger LLP in San Francisco, California. Mr. McQuinn represents maritime and defense-related employers and insurance carriers in claims under the Longshore and Harbor Workers' Compensation Act and its extensions.

Prior to joining Thomas, Quinn & Krieger LLP, Mr. McQuinn served in the Administration of California Governor Edmund G. (Jerry) Brown Jr. as Assistant General Counsel of the Department of Business Oversight, California's banking, securities, and financial services regulator, from 2013 to 2015.

Mr. McQuinn received his Juris Doctorate degree from the University of San Francisco School of Law. During law school, Mr. McQuinn served as a legal extern in the Office of the Governor where he advised the Governor on judicial appointments and education policy matters. Mr. McQuinn also held an externship in the Legal Division of the California Department of Fair Employment and Housing, California's civil rights enforcement agency, where he assisted in the successful prosecution of the Law School Admissions Council for violation of the Unruh Civil Rights Act and the Americans with Disabilities Act in its administration of the Law School Admissions Test. While externing for the Department of Fair Employment and Housing, Mr. McQuinn authored amendments to the California Education Code (Assembly Bill 2122, Stats. of 2012, ch. 583) that prohibited the Law School Admissions Council from unlawfully flagging test scores earned under accommodated testing conditions by examinees with disabilities.

Lara Duerig Merrigan, Esq. received her Bachelor of Arts from California State University Fresno in 2003 and her Juris Doctorate degree magna cum laude from the University of San Francisco in 2007. During law school, she was a member of the McAuliffe Honor Society and was awarded the Arthur C. Zief, Jr., scholarship. She served as a Senior Literary Editor of the University of San Francisco Maritime Law Journal. She competed in the national Judge John R. Brown Admiralty Moot Court Competition in 2006 and 2007, where she won the award for second best oral argument overall in 2007. In 2006, she served as a judicial extern to Justice Joyce Kennard of the California Supreme Court.

Ms. Merrigan began her legal career representing employers and carriers, primarily in claims brought under the Longshore and Harbor Workers' Compensation Act and its extensions. She has also handled various other legal issues in admiralty and maritime law, including both injury and cargo loss claims. Ms. Merrigan launched her solo career in 2015, and her practice now focuses on appellate and other post-hearing work on behalf of plaintiffs and claimants.

Amie C. Peters, Esq. is a maritime attorney dedicated to helping workers understand and litigate workplace injury cases. Amie leads a dedicated legal staff at her firm, Blue Water Legal PLLC, in beautiful Edmonds, Washington. She received her B.A. in Government and History from Eastern Washington University (with honors) and her J.D. from University of Washington School of Law. Amie is also very active in the legal community, holding leadership positions in the Washington State Association for Justice and Workers Injury Law & Advocacy Group. She is also past president of the DOL-Joint Bar Association. Amie routinely speaks nationwide at legal education seminars and publishes on various workers' compensation, maritime and practice management topics.

Charles Robinowitz, Esq. has his undergraduate degree in government from Cornell University and his law degree from the University of Virginia. Before attending law school, he was a graduate student in Swedish government for one year at Stockholm University. Following law school he was a law clerk for one year for Judge Richard H. Levet, a senior judge in the United States District Court for the Southern District of New York. He is a member of the New York and Oregon Bars, and is also admitted to practice in the federal district court in Oregon, the Fourth and Ninth Circuit Courts of Appeal and the United States Supreme Court. He is a member of the Multnomah Bar Association, the Oregon Trial Lawyers' Association, where he has served on its Amicus Curiae committee for nearly 10 years, and the American Association for Justice. He has been in private practice in Portland, Oregon, since 1969, and has represented the claimants in many of the leading cases involving maritime workers in the Ninth Circuit including its recent decisions in *Christensen*, *Van Skike* and *Dyer* as well as *Johnson v. Director, OWCP* and *Anderson v. Director, OWCP* involving attorney fees under the Longshore and Harbor Workers' Compensation Act.

Bobbi N. Roquemore, Esq. is an associate attorney in the Schouest, Bamdas, Soshea & BenMaier P.L.L.C.'s Houston office. Bobbi focuses her practice on the defense of claims arising under the Longshore and Harbor Workers' Compensation Act (LHWCA) and the Defense Base Act (DBA).

Prior to joining the firm, Bobbi served a two-year federal clerkship with the Hon. Clement J. Kennington at the United States Department of Labor, Office of Administrative Law Judges. Here, she wrote Decisions and Orders and discovery orders for federal workers' compensation cases arising under the LHWCA, DBA, Non-Appropriated Funds Instrumentalities Act (NFIA), and Outer Continental Shelf Lands Act (OCSLA); Black Lung Benefits Act (BLBA); whistleblower cases arising under the Federal Rail Safety Act (FRSA), Sarbanes-Oxley Act (SOX), Consumer Product Safety Improvement Act (CPSIA), and several other acts; and immigration labor appeals. Bobbi's experience as a clerk provides her with specific insight regarding the handling of these matters at the OALJ level.

Bobbi earned her Juris Doctorate, cum laude, from Loyola University New Orleans College of Law, where she was the Articles/Symposium Editor of the Loyola Law Review. She also earned a Certificate in International Legal Studies from Loyola. Bobbi served as a judicial intern for the Hon. Elizabeth C. Lanier at the Louisiana Workers' Compensation Court – District 9. Shortly after completing law school, Bobbi was awarded First Place in the College of Workers' Compensation Lawyers' national writing competition.

Bobbi earned a Bachelor of Arts in Journalism from Marquette University. She was a journalist at the Dallas Morning News and Milwaukee Journal Sentinel prior to pursuing her law degree.

Bobbi took a special interest in the area of professional athletes and workers' compensation following an internship with the New Orleans Saints. Her publications include "Creating a Level Playing Field: The Case for Bringing Workers' Compensation for Professional Athletes into a Single Federal System by Extending the Longshore Act" (57 Loy. L. Rev. 793 (2011)) and "Comparing Workers' Compensation Coverage of Professional Athletes in Social Insurance Systems Worldwide – and Why a National System for Athletes Could Work in America." (Workers' First Watch, Spring 2013).

Bobbi is admitted to the practice in the State of Louisiana, the United States District Court for the Eastern District of Louisiana, and the United States Court of Appeals for the Fifth Circuit.

Collins C. Rossi, Esq, a native of New York, graduated from the Loyola University School of Law in New Orleans in 1982 after which he served a two year judicial clerkship with the Office of Administrative Law Judges in New Orleans. He has been in private practice since that time and a sole practitioner since 1998. While the majority of his practice consists of representing employers, carriers and self-insureds in both the federal and Louisiana workers' compensation schemes as well as defending personal injury and general liability claims. A significant portion of his practice consists of litigating casualty and maritime claims as well as other employment related matters, In addition to his legal practice Mr. Rossi established Pre-Trial Solutions of Louisiana, a mediation and arbitration firm which concentrates on the expeditious resolution of both personal injury and workers compensation claims. Mr. Rossi is also a certified mediator and a member of the Louisiana Mediation Registry. His nationwide practice assists parties in the resolution of matters under the Longshore and Harbor Workers' Compensation Act, OSCLA and DBA. He mediates disputes for Louisiana workers' compensation (including third-party actions) and personal injury claims. His mediation practice is suited to any type of industrial accident involving compensation, liability and indemnity claims. He is familiar with coverage matters under both personal and commercial policies. He is a member of the Advisory Board for the Loyola University Law School Annual Longshore Conference.

John L. Schouest, Esq. is the Managing Partner of Schouest, Bamdas, Soshea & BenMaier P.L.L.C.. In his more than 25 years of practicing law, John has represented and counseled clients in the defense of personal injury and property damage claims arising under GL, EL, MEL, Foreign Voluntary, and other coverage or self insured situations.

John grew up with a family business of inland and coastwise towing, which led to an interest in General Maritime and Admiralty law. His practice regularly includes matters involving the Jones Act, LHWCA (Longshore), OCSLA, Offshore Service Industries, and Transportation. His Longshore experience has translated to an active and international Defense Base Act (DBA) practice.

John is rated AV Preeminent by Martindale-Hubbell, which indicates a demonstration of the highest professional and ethical standards and is the highest rating a lawyer can receive. He has also been selected as a Texas Super Lawyer and included in The Best Lawyers in America ® – (Peer Review)

Scott L. Thaler, Esq., is an associate at Grossman Attorneys at Law. His practice includes Defense Base Act claims as well as Longshore and Harbor Workers' Compensation Act claims. Mr. Thaler's civil practice also includes personal injury and wrongful death claims, automobile, products liability, and medical malpractice.

Prior to joining Grossman Attorneys at Law, Mr. Thaler worked as a prosecutor in the Miami-Dade State Attorney's Office where he gained invaluable litigation skills as he tried in excess of forty cases to jury verdict.

Michael W. Thomas, Esq. received his Bachelor of Arts from the University of Buffalo in 1987, and his Juris Doctorate from the University of Houston in 1993. Until 1997, he represented plaintiffs in personal injury claims, but has since defended employers and insurance carriers in claims arising under the Longshore and Harbor Workers' Compensation Act, Defense Base Act, Outer Continental Shelf Lands Act, Non-Appropriated Funds Instrumentalities Act, War Hazards Compensation Act, California Workers' Compensation Act and Jones Act. Mr. Thomas has been admitted to practice before all courts in the State of California, several Federal District Courts nationally, the 2nd, 4th, 5th and 9th Federal Circuit Courts of Appeal, and the Supreme Court of the United States. Mr. Thomas is a contributing author for The Longshore Textbook and the Defense Base Act Handbook, has written a variety of articles, and lectured on numerous occasions on topics related to his practice.

Ruth Bennett Whitfield, Esq. joined the Army & Air Force Exchange Service (The Exchange) in 1995 and is a Senior Associate General Counsel in the Employment and Labor Law Division of the General Counsel's Office. Her primary duties involve defending NAFI workers' compensation claims in both administrative and federal courts and OSHA matters. Ms. Whitfield received her undergraduate degree in Business Management from Southeastern Louisiana University and her Juris Doctorate from Louisiana State University. Prior to joining the Exchange, she held a judicial clerkship with the United States Department of Labor, Office of Administrative Law Judges and worked with a defense firm, where she defended insurance companies, self-insured employers, and state guaranty funds, in workers' compensation cases along the Gulf Coast and Eastern United States from Texas through Virginia. Ms. Bennett Whitfield is a prior contributor to *The Longshore Textbook* and has lectured at various continuing legal education seminars and legal conferences.

Jeffrey Winter, Esq. is licensed to practice law in the State of California. He has tried to conclusion 40+ jury trials; argued before the Ninth Circuit Court of Appeals and the Fourth Appellate District for the State of California; and tried many Longshore/DBA cases over the last 29 years. Mr. Winter has spoken and presented at seminars and conferences regionally and nationally many times addressing Longshore, workers' compensation trial practice, and maritime issues. He has been recognized both locally and nationally as a Top Lawyer handling workers' compensation cases. He was also invited to serve as commissioner by the State Bar of California to assist in establishing the requirements for certification as a specialist in maritime/longshore matters.

Index

B

C